244

Psychology and Law
The State of the Discipline

Perspectives in
Law & Psychology

Sponsored by the American Psychology-Law Society/Division 41 of the American Psychological Association

Series Editor: RONALD ROESCH, *Simon Fraser University*
Burnaby, British Columbia, Canada

Editorial Board: MARY DURHAM, JANE GOODMAN-DELAHUNTY, THOMAS GRISSO, STEPHEN D. HART, MARSHA LISS, EDWARD P. MULVEY, JAMES R. P. OGLOFF, NORMAN G. POYTHRESS, JR., DON READ, AND REGINA SCHULLER

Psychology and Law
The State of the Discipline

Edited by

Ronald Roesch
Stephen D. Hart

and

James R. P. Ogloff

Simon Fraser University
Burnaby, British Columbia, Canada

KLUWER ACADEMIC / PLENUM PUBLISHERS
NEW YORK, BOSTON, DORDRECHT, LONDON, MOSCOW

Library of Congress Cataloging-in-Publication Data

Psychology and law : the state of the discipline / edited by Ronald
   Roesch, Stephen D. Hart and James R.P. Ogloff.
        p.   cm. -- (Perspectives in law & psychology ; v. 10)
     Includes bibliographical references and index.
     ISBN 0-306-45949-3 (hardcover). -- ISBN 0-306-45950-7 (pbk.)
     1. Law--Psychological aspects. 2. Psychology, Forensic.
   I. Roesch, Ronald, 1947-   . II. Hart, Stephen D. (Stephen David),
   1962-   . III. Ogloff, James R. P. IV. Series: Perspectives in law
   and psychology ; v. 10.
   K346.P79 1998
   340'.19--dc21   98-45167
                                                                        CIP

ISBN 0-306-45949-3 (Hardbound)
ISBN 0-306-45950-7 (Paperback)

© 1999 Kluwer Academic / Plenum Publishers, New York
233 Spring Street, New York, N.Y. 10013

10 9 8 7 6 5 4 3 2 1

A C.I.P. record for this book is available from the Library of Congress.

Printed in the United States of America

Contributors

DONALD N. BERSOFF • School of Law, Villanova University, Villanova, Pennsylvania 19085; Department of Clinical and Health Psychology, Medical College of Pennsylvania–Hahnemann University of the Health Sciences, Philadelphia, Pennsylvania 19102

AMY L. BRADFIELD • Department of Psychology, Iowa State University, Ames, Iowa 50011

BRIAN L. CUTLER • College of Arts and Sciences, Florida International University, Miami, Florida 33199

JANE GOODMAN-DELAHUNTY • Administrative Judge, U.S. Equal Employment Opportunity Commission, Los Angeles District Office, Roybal Federal Building, Fourth Floor, 255 East Temple Street, Los Angeles, California 90012

KEVIN S. DOUGLAS • Department of Psychology and the Mental Health, Law, and Policy Institute, Simon Fraser University, Burnaby, British Columbia, V5A 1S6, Canada

DAVID FINKELMAN • Division of Human Development, St. Mary's College, St. Mary's City, Maryland 20686

PATRICIA GRIFFIN • 8503 Flourtown Avenue, Wyndmoor, Pennsylvania 19038

STEPHEN D. HART • Department of Psychology and the Mental Health, Law, and Policy Institute, Simon Fraser University, Burnaby, British Columbia, V5A 1S6, Canada

KIRK HEILBRUN • Department of Clinical and Health Psychology, Law-Psychology Program, Allegheny University of the Health Sciences and School of Law, Villanova University, Philadelphia, Pennsylvania 19102-1192

MONICA J. KERR • Department of Psychology, University of Kentucky, Lexington, Kentucky 40506-0044

MARSHA B. LISS • Child Exploitation and Obscenity Section, U.S. Department of Justice, 1331 F Street, N.W., Sixth Floor, Washington, DC 20530-0001

DENIS M. MCCARTHY • Department of Psychology, University of Kentucky, Lexington, Kentucky 40506-0044

MARCIA J. MCKINLEY-PACE • Department of Psychology, George Mason University, Fairfax, Virginia 22030

ROBERT A. NICHOLSON • Department of Psychology, University of Tulsa, Tulsa, Oklahoma 74104

MICHAEL T. NIETZEL • Department of Psychology, University of Kentucky, Lexington, Kentucky 40506-0044

JAMES R. P. OGLOFF •Department of Psychology and the Mental Health, Law, and Policy Institute, Simon Fraser University, Burnaby, British Columbia, V5A 1S6, Canada

STEVEN D. PENROD • Law–Psychology Program, University of Nebraska, Lincoln, Nebraska 68588-0308

RONALD ROESCH • Department of Psychology and the Mental Health, Law, and Policy Institute, Simon Fraser University, Burnaby, British Columbia, V5A 1S6, Canada

CHRISTOPHER D. WEBSTER • University of Toronto, Toronto, Ontario, M5T 1R8, Canada

GARY WELLS • Department of Psychology, Iowa State University, Ames, Iowa 50011

EDWARD F. WRIGHT • Department of Psychology, St. Francis Xavier University, Antigonish, Nova Scotia, B2G 2W5, Canada

Preface

This book grew out of American Psychology–Law Society (APLS)-sponsored "State of the Discipline" symposia presented at Annual Meetings of the American Psychological Association. The first, presented in Los Angeles in 1994, was organized by the Divisional Conference Program Chairs, Margaret Coggins and Stephen Hart, and chaired by then APLS President Ronald Roesch. The featured speakers were Robert Nicholson, Michael Nietzel, Christopher D. Webster, and Gary Wells. The second symposium was presented in New York in 1995, chaired by Roesch and Hart, and featured presentations by Patricia Griffin, Jane Goodman-Delahunty, Marsha Liss, and Donald Bersoff. In these symposia, leading scholars were selected to review and critique the literature in eight topic areas, which were chosen to represent the diversity of topics in the field of psychology and law. Despite diversity of subject matter and methods, the reviews were uniformly excellent. We decided that they could form the basis of an interesting edited volume, a snapshot of our field at the end of the 20th century. We asked the symposia presenters to expand the material covered in the symposia and prepare chapters that would provide up-to-date and definitive reviews of the state of the discipline for each topic. In order to present a broader overview of the field beyond those covered in the two symposia, we also invited Steven Penrod to review the literature on juror perceptions of eyewitness testimony. James Ogloff and David Finkelman agreed to provide a broad overview of the history and development of the field, and Ogloff also contributed a chapter on ethics and professional issues.

Psychology and law involves psychologists from virtually all of the specialty areas of psychology. Clinically trained psychologists probably constitute the majority, but it is also evident that developmental, social, community, industrial/organizational, and other experimental psychologists have much to add to our understanding of the relevance of psychology to legal issues. We have endeavored to reflect this range of activity in the chapters in this volume.

Following the introductory overview by Ogloff and Finkelman, the book is organized into four broad sections that we believe reflect the breadth of the field. Part I, "Human Behavior in the Trial Process," comprises a review of research on juries (Michael T. Nietzel, Denis M. McCarthy, and Monica J. Kerr), and two reviews focusing on eyewitness evidence and testimony (Gary L. Wells, Edward F. Wright, and Amy L. Bradfield; Steven D. Penrod and Brian Cutler). Part II, "Forensic Assessment and Treatment," has chapters on forensic assessment (Robert A. Nicholson), the evaluation of risk for violence (Kevin S. Douglas and Christopher D. Webster), and the clinical management of forensic patients (Kirk Heilbrun and Patricia Griffin). Part III, "Issues in Civil Law," includes chapters on employment law (Jane Goodman-Delahunty) and family law (Marsha B. Liss and Marcia J. McKinley-Pace). Part IV, "Professional Issues," has chapters on training in psychology and law (Donald N. Bersoff) and forensic ethics and professional issues (James R. P. Ogloff). Finally, the Specialty Guidelines for Forensic Psychologists are reprinted in their entirety in the Appendix. These guidelines, developed by APLS and the American Academy of Forensic Psychology, provide a comprehensive delineation and overview of the ethical and professional issues forensic psychologists encounter in both research and practice.

We hope this volume will serve as an interesting introduction and overview for people who are unfamiliar with the field of psychology and law, especially graduate students and advanced undergraduate students. Given that the chapters provide a critical review of the literature, we also believe that the book will provide a topical update for researchers and practitioners already working in this rapidly developing field. As the chapters so aptly illustrate, the field has blossomed in the past two decades. This book is the tenth in the series, Perspectives in Law and Psychology, which published its first volume in 1977. There are seven other volumes currently in various stages of production. The primary collegial organization, the American Psychology–Law Society (Division 41 of the American Psychological Association), has more than doubled its membership in the past 10 years; its scholarly journal, *Law and Human Behavior*, is generally recognized as the leading journal in this field. During this period, research has produced findings that are advancing the field in a number of ways. It is already possible to discern the effect of recent research on the delivery of clinical assessment and intervention services in forensic settings, the manner in which lineups are conducted and eyewitness testimony is presented in court, and the way in which forensic psychologists are being trained. Graduate programs in psychology and law are now producing psychologists who are well trained in both disciplines, which will further enhance both the research and practice in this discipline. We believe that the field will continue to grow, and the research and clinical contributions of psychologists will continue to have a positive impact on the civil and criminal justice systems.

We express our gratitude to the authors for their effort and patience in preparing the chapters. Thanks also to Thomas Grisso, past editor of the Division 41 Book Series, and to Eliott Werner, senior editor at Plenum Press, for shepherding the project to completion.

Contents

I. HUMAN BEHAVIOR IN THE TRIAL PROCESS

CHAPTER 3. WITNESSES TO CRIME: SOCIAL AND COGNITIVE FACTORS
GOVERNING THE VALIDITY OF PEOPLE'S REPORTS

Gary L. Wells, Edward F. Wright, and Amy L. Bradfield

CHAPTER 4. PREVENTING MISTAKEN CONVICTIONS IN EYEWITNESS
IDENTIFICATION TRIALS: THE CASE AGAINST TRADITIONAL
SAFEGUARDS

Steven D. Penrod and Brian Cutler

II. FORENSIC ASSESSMENT AND TREATMENT

CHAPTER 5. FORENSIC ASSESSMENT

Robert A. Nicholson

CHAPTER 6. PREDICTING VIOLENCE IN MENTALLY AND PERSONALITY
DISORDERED INDIVIDUALS

Kevin S. Douglas and Christopher D. Webster

CHAPTER 7. FORENSIC TREATMENT: A REVIEW OF PROGRAMS AND
RESEARCH

Kirk Heilbrun and Patricia Griffin

III. ISSUES IN CIVIL LAW

CHAPTER 8. CIVIL LAW: EMPLOYMENT AND DISCRIMINATION

Jane Goodman-Delahunty

CHAPTER 9. BEST INTERESTS OF THE CHILD: NEW TWISTS
ON AN OLD THEME

Marsha B. Liss and Marcia J. McKinley-Pace

IV. ETHICS AND PROFESSIONAL ISSUES

CHAPTER 10. PREPARING FOR TWO CULTURES: EDUCATION AND TRAINING IN LAW AND PSYCHOLOGY

Donald N. Bersoff

CHAPTER 11. ETHICAL AND LEGAL CONTOURS OF FORENSIC PSYCHOLOGY

James R. P. Ogloff

1

Psychology and Law

An Overview

JAMES R. P. OGLOFF AND DAVID FINKELMAN

As this chapter—and this book—make clear, the field of law and psychology has experienced considerable growth in the past two decades. Indeed, during that period concepts such as the insanity defense, risk prediction, scientific jury selection, "repressed" memories, and, we say reluctantly, criminal profiling have been the topics of considerable media attention and public debate. Along with the hype that has accompanied these and other topics within law and psychology, there has been a concomitant profusion of empirical research. The subsequent chapters in this book show that although progress has been made during this the field's "developmental phase," there is still much room for the field to grow and develop.

In this opening chapter, we introduce unfamiliar readers to the field of law and psychology. For those who already have some familiarity with the field, we provide a historical overview of the development of the field. We then offer a discussion of the conceptualization of the relationship between psychology and law. We end with a brief mention of the role that psychology has played, and can continue to play, in public policy. We turn now to a discussion of the meaning of *law, psychology,* and the field of *law and psychology.*

JAMES R. P. OGLOFF • Graduate Program in Law and Psychology, Simon Fraser University, Burnaby, British Columbia, V5A 1S6, Canada. DAVID FINKELMAN • Division of Human Development, St. Mary's College, St. Mary's City, Maryland 20686.

Psychology and Law: The State of the Discipline, edited by Ronald Roesch, Stephen D. Hart, and James R. P. Ogloff. Kluwer Academic/Plenum Publishers, New York, 1999.

1

WHAT IS LAW?

Law is commonly defined as a body of rules for the guidance of human conduct that is imposed on and enforced among the members of a given state (see *United States Fidelity and Guaranty Co. v. Guenther*, 1930). In this sense, the law is a set of rules that forms the pattern of behavior of the members in society. The law is characterized by three elements. First, the law is extensive and covers virtually every aspect of life. If you think about it for a moment, you will realize that your behavior today has already been controlled by the law. If you drove in your car, your car presumably was licensed, and you also must have a driver's license. You stopped at red lights and stop signs (hopefully). If you bought coffee or a snack, you had to pay for it. Indeed, the law regulates everything from how our births our registered to how our property (and we) will be disposed of on death.

Second, not only is the law extensive, but because laws attempt to set down rules by which we govern ourselves, laws must be dynamic. That is, the law must constantly undergo changes to cope with the evolving needs of the society. For example, recent medical research suggests that the brain tissue of unborn fetuses may be useful in prohibiting the development of certain neurological impairments, such as Parkinson's disease. Therefore, laws must be developed to determine whether this is an acceptable practice in our society, and, if so, the law must then regulate the acquisition and use of the brain tissue.

Third, while the previous two elements of the law focus on its rule-making nature, the law also serves as a means of resolving conflicts that arise in society. For example, if you agree with your neighbor to build a fence between your properties, and you go ahead and have the fence built and pay for it only to learn that your neighbor does not wish to pay his or her portion of the bill, you have a dispute that could be settled in court. Likewise, anytime that a person is charged with breaking one of the rules of society, the law has developed careful procedures for determining if that person is guilty. Now that we have some understanding of what the law is and the nature of law, we turn to the question of what psychology is.

WHAT IS PSYCHOLOGY?

Psychology is currently defined as the scientific study of behavior and mental processes. Three elements of this definition should be emphasized. First, because psychology is a social science, it is empirical in nature. This means that rather than relying strictly on intuitive theories, psychologists develop and test hypotheses that emerge from their theories. By designing objective and measurable tests of their theories, psychologists attempt to obtain a better understanding of behavior and mental processes. Second, because it is impossible to "read a person's mind" or otherwise know what a person is thinking, psychologists often rely on observing an individual's behavior across situations. Third, by studying behavior across situations, psychologists can obtain information about a person's thought processes, or cognitions.

WHAT IS PSYCHOLOGY AND LAW?

Now that we have reviewed the definition of law and the definition of psychology, let us turn to a discussion of the definition of *psychology and law*. It is impossible that every person who works in this area has a different notion of what law and psychology is. The reason is simple: There is no definition of the field that is generally acceptable. Indeed, the field of law and psychology can be as broad as the law itself. Therefore, it is necessary to adopt a definition that is broad enough to include all potential realms of work done within the law and psychology interface. Furthermore, the work done in law and psychology focuses on the law and its effects on individuals and society. Beyond that, of course, the law also is influenced by people and society. Thus, a suitably broad definition is that law and psychology is the scientific study of the effect the law has on people, and the effect people have on the law (see Small, 1993).

All laws are designed with an ultimate purpose in mind: to regulate human behavior. As the definition of psychology shows, psychologists are interested in studying behavior and mental processes. Therefore, psychologists who work in the area of law and psychology are interested in evaluating the assumptions that the law must make about human behavior, and the ways in which the law responds to the changes in society that require changes in law.

THE ROOTS OF PSYCHOLOGY AND LAW

The seeds that formed the roots of the present-day psychology and law movement were planted when, at the turn of the century, legal education evolved from an apprenticeship model to a university-based system (Ogloff, Tomkins, & Bersoff, 1996; Stevens, 1983).[1] It was at that time that legal scholars began to insist that to fully understand the law, we must

---

[1]Many of the thoughts in this section of the chapter are taken from Ogloff, Tomkins, and Bersoff (1996). We are indebted to Alan Tomkins and Donald Bersoff for their insight into the development of legal psychology.

examine and understand the social contexts from which the law was derived, which ultimately are influenced by the law (Friedman, 1985; Purcell, 1973). This perspective came to be known as "sociological jurisprudence" (White, 1976). It was no longer enough to "know the law" by studying judicial opinions, the method that had become the cornerstone of legal systems in North America that were based on English common law. Indeed, Oliver Wendell Holmes (1897) wrote that "for the rational study of law ... the black-letter may be the man of the present, but the man of the future is the man of statistics and the master of economics" (p. 469).

Following sociological jurisprudence, other movements evolved that also challenged the law to be aware of social and legal "realities" (Purcell, 1973; Schlegel, 1979; Tomkins & Oursland, 1991; Twining, 1973; White, 1972). These movements, such as legal realism, advocated drawing on the social sciences for methodologies and perspectives from which to examine law, legal process, and legal decision making (Kalman, 1986; Schlegel, 1979; Twining, 1973).

The first director of Harvard's Psychological Laboratory, Hugo Munsterberg, a student of Wilhelm Wundt at the University of Leipzig, is considered to be the "founder" of applied psychology (Boring, 1950; Hale, 1980; Moskowitz, 1977). Among other things, Munsterberg advocated applying psychology to the law and criticized lawyers and judges for not embracing the research of psychologists that could be applied to law (Loh, 1981). Munsterberg published *On the Witness Stand* (1908), a book in which he reviewed a number of psychology and law topics. He ended his introduction by writing that "my only purpose is to turn the attention of serious men to an absurdly neglected field which demands the full attention of the social community" (p. 12).

Unfortunately, rather than embracing psychology and psychological research, lawyers and scholars, including such luminaries as the renowned legal evidence scholar, John H. Wigmore, chastised Munsterberg (see Moore, 1907). Their criticism was that Munsterberg's claims were exaggerated, and that psychology had not ascertained the data necessary to support Munsterberg's criticisms of the law. In a satire published in the *Illinois Law Review* (1909), Wigmore subjected Munsterberg's work to the scrutiny of cross-examination in a mock libel trial in which Munsterberg was accused of claiming more than his science could support or offer. Not surprisingly, Munsterberg was found guilty of exaggerating his claims (Ogloff et al., 1996).

Despite Munsterberg's "trial," movements such as sociological jurisprudence and legal realism led to the integration of social science, including psychology, into the law school curriculum. From the 1920s until the 1940s, several eminent law schools included social science material in their law courses. Even more surprising, perhaps, is that psychologists and other social scientists were hired as part of law faculties beginning in the late 1920s (Kalman, 1986; Loh, 1981; Schlegel, 1979; Stevens, 1983). With such a promising start, one might wonder what happened to the law and social science movement.

Without getting into too much detail here, suffice it to say that the early movement simply did not generate enough momentum to sustain itself. Other movements in law developed that overcame the initial force of the law and social science movement.[2] Although the law and social science movement waned, it did not die—law and psychology is "bigger and better" now than ever. Indeed, the movement began to regain its momentum in the 1960s and has gained considerable speed since that time (Ogloff et al., 1996). A significant milestone occurred along the way in 1976 when, for the first time, "psychology and the law" was reviewed in the *Annual Review of Psychology* (Tapp, 1976). In fact, in some ways, the law and psychology movement appears to be approximately where it was in the 1920s with the sociological jurisprudence movement. As was the case then, psychology has once again made its way into casebooks and the law school curriculum. Some law schools even have opened up more doors to social scientists, bringing them once again into law schools as faculty (Grisso, Sales, & Bayless, 1982; Melton, 1990; Melton, Monahan, & Saks, 1987; Ogloff et al., 1996; Tapp, 1976; Wexler, 1990).

THE HISTORICAL STRANDS OF PSYCHOLOGY AND LAW

As we have noted, psychology and the law interact in many different arenas. A look at the history of legal psychology shows a number of separate "strands." Many of these are discussed in more detail in later chapters, but we will provide a brief overview here.

Chronologically, the longest strand is almost certainly the one involving the insanity defense (Ogloff, Roberts, & Roesch, 1993). The defense itself goes back many centuries, and the use of expert testimony in such cases can be traced at least as far back as the famous case of Daniel M'Naghten in 1843, who shot and killed Edward Drummond, the secretary of the prime minister of England. The insanity defense remains the object of considerable controversy even today. Until relatively recently, most of the expert testimony in insanity defense cases was provided by psychia-

[2]Among the current movements is that of "law and economics." Although economics is a social science, its methods and fields of inquiry differ sufficiently from psychology so as not to warrant discussion here.

trists; psychologists and other mental health professionals (e.g., social workers) did not play a substantial role until the 1960s or later.

Psychologists and psychiatrists have also long been involved with the treatment and disposition of children and adolescents—especially juvenile offenders—in the legal system. In 1909, psychiatrist William Healy and psychologist Grace Fernald "established the first clinic specifically designed for youthful offenders—the Juvenile Psychopathic Institute" (Bartol & Bartol, 1987, p. 7), to serve the newly created juvenile court.

Another important strand is the psychological study of eyewitness testimony (see Chapters 3 and 4). This was an area that was explored almost exclusively by psychologists rather than psychiatrists. Some of the earliest pioneers in psychology studied this topic; probably the best-known of this early group was Hugo Munsterberg, who published a number of books and articles on this topic in the early years of this century (e.g., Munsterberg, 1908).

A few psychologists also worked in prisons and police departments during this period (Bartol & Bartol, 1987), primarily administering psychological tests, especially intelligence tests, to either prisoners or police officers. Another psychologist, William Marston, contributed to the development of the polygraph. Marston, who also held a law degree, "discovered a significant positive correlation between systolic blood pressure and lying, which became the basis of the modern polygraph" (Bartol & Bartol, 1987, p. 12). Marston was also one of the first to conduct systematic research on the jury, and he testified as an expert witness in the case of *Frye v. U.S.* (1923; Faigman, Porter, & Saks, 1994).

However, for most of the period through the early decades of this century, the actual impact of psychology on the legal system was quite limited. There were narrow areas in which psychologists and psychiatrists had some influence, such as the insanity defense and in the juvenile justice system. But the early work on eyewitness testimony by Munsterberg and others had little real impact on the legal system (Loftus & Monahan, 1981). Indeed, as noted earlier, Munsterberg's attempts to introduce psychology into the legal system were met with scathing criticism by one of the most important legal figures of his day, J. H. Wigmore (1909).

An important reason for this lack of influence lay in an attitude about the nature of law that was widely held within the legal community. For most of the 19th century and into the 20th, legal thinking in this country was dominated by a view that has variously been called "formalistic," "logical," and "mechanical." According to this view, the law—and, in particular, the judicial task—was simply a matter of applying legal rules and principles (in a "logical" and "mechanical" way) to the facts of a particular case. Whether the social effects of doing so were beneficial or harmful was irrelevant. Moreover, the law was seen as a self-contained, autonomous discipline, needing no help from outside sources to guide it. From this point of view, the law needed little help from psychology or any other field.

This view was challenged by a number of legal scholars. One of the early challengers was Oliver Wendell Holmes, a towering figure in American jurisprudence. (Holmes sat on the Massachusetts Supreme Judicial Court and eventually on the U.S. Supreme Court.) One of his most famous quotations, written late in the 19th century, shows his dissatisfaction with the prevailing mechanical view, and his own view that the law needed to broaden its purview:

> The life of the law has not been logic: it has been experience. The felt necessities of the time, the prevalent moral and political theories, intuitions of public policy, avowed or unconscious, even the prejudices which judges share with their fellow-men, have had a good deal more to do than the syllogism in determining the rules by which men should be governed. (Holmes, 1881/1963, p. 1)

One of the early important cases that led to the demise of the mechanical view was *Muller v. Oregon* (1908). Curt Muller was a laundry owner who had been convicted of violating an Oregon statute that limited the workday of women who worked in factories or laundries to 10 hours. Muller argued that the statute was unconstitutional—a violation of the right to contract—and appealed his conviction to the U.S. Supreme Court. Arguing on behalf of the state of Oregon was Louis D. Brandeis, one of the nation's best-known lawyers, who was himself later to sit on the Court. As part of the case, Brandeis submitted an extensive brief. Only a small part of the brief was devoted to legal arguments; the great majority of it contained nonlegal materials relating the injurious effects of long workdays on women's health. It concluded with empirical studies bearing on the topic of the effects of excessive work, especially on women, and reports of various commissions and conferences, both in the United States and Europe. The Supreme Court upheld the constitutionality of the statute, and in his majority opinion, Justice Brewer made reference to the "very copious collection" of material that Brandeis had submitted. The term *Brandeis brief* soon was used to describe any collection of nonlegal materials submitted in a court case, and the term remains in use today.

The original Brandeis brief remains the source of some controversy. For one thing, it is ironic that the liberal Brandeis compiled a brief that made reference to "the periodical semi-pathological state of women" and the existence of "general 'female weakness'" (quoted in Monahan & Loftus, 1982, p. 463); "this argument infringed on efforts, already underway, to secure equal treatment for women in other areas" (Monahan &

Walker, 1994, p. 8). Brandeis believed this was necessary, however, because the Supreme Court had recently upheld a similar statute that applied to men in *Lochner v. N.Y.* (1905). The brief has also been criticized because of the low quality of the empirical evidence presented; it consisted primarily of "broad value-laden statements supported largely by casual observation and opinion" (Monahan & Walker, 1994, p. 8). But it must also be remembered that social science research was in a primitive state at this time.

Over the next few decades, criticisms of the formalist view and suggestions to broaden the scope of legal thinking culminated in what became known as the legal realist movement, which emerged in clear form in about 1930 (White, 1972). The movement had a deep and lasting impact on legal thinking, scholarship, and practice. Melton (1990) has pointed to three important tenets of legal realism:

1. Law is the behavior of judges, whose decisions are necessarily affected by their personal experiences and biases.
2. Law is intended to promote social welfare.
3. To accomplish the ultimate goal of promotion of the commonweal, the legal system profits from systematic examination of social reality.

If these tenets are accepted, it is clear that psychology can provide assistance to the law in reaching its goals. It can help in examining the "personal experiences and biases" of judges, and, perhaps more important, can aid in the "systematic examination of social reality."

Although legal realism as an identifiable movement had lost its force and vitality by the 1950s, many of its ideas have been incorporated into the fabric of contemporary legal thinking. It has become a cliche to say, "we are all realists now" (Finkelman & Grisso, 1994; Monahan & Walker, 1994).

The effects of the realist revolution can be seen in the famous Supreme Court school desegregation case, *Brown v. Board of Education* (1954). Over four decades later, the case is still "the best-known use of social science in any area of law" (Monahan & Walker, 1994, p. 148). Thirty-two social scientists—sociologists, anthropologists, psychologists, and psychiatrists—signed a Brandeis brief that was submitted on behalf of the plaintiffs. It described the damaging effects of segregated schools on the children who attended them. The Court ruled unanimously that segregated schools were unconstitutional. In its decision, the Court cited a number of the sources mentioned in the brief in its famous footnote 11, "the most controversial footnote in American constitutional law" (Rosen, 1980, p. 9).

The Court's decision was greeted by many as a sign that social science research had "come of age"; it had been taken seriously by the Supreme Court and had a visible impact on its decision. But the social science contribution was also the object of criticism. Some of the criticism came from those who opposed the decision. But even some of those who favored it expressed doubts. Cahn (1955), for example, worried about grounding constitutional rights in contemporary thinking in the social sciences. His concern was that although social psychologists of the day were liberal and egalitarian, the possibility existed that in the future it would be possible for racist or otherwise unpalatable notions to be presented as science. With such notions shrouded in science, peoples' constitutional rights would be jeopardized.

In any case, the years since the Brown decision have seen a growing influence of psychology on the law. The remaining chapters of this book provide many examples of this influence, but we can give a few examples here:

1. The great increase in number and diversity of psychologists giving expert testimony on a wide variety of topics, ranging from validity of eyewitness testimony to sex discrimination to the use of hypnosis
2. An increase in the number and diversity of court-ordered evaluations (e.g., for competence to stand trial, child custody determinations, assessments of risk for future violence)
3. An increased use of psychologists as consultants in the law (e.g., jury and trial consultants)
4. An increase in the number of amicus briefs filed with the Supreme Court of the United States and other courts on behalf of psychologists or of psychology as a profession, especially by the American Psychological Association
5. The increased citation of psychological and other social science materials by the courts
6. An increase in testimony by psychologists before Congressional committees and other attempts to shape or influence legislation

In addition, a number of professional organizations dealing with various aspects of the relationship between psychology (and related disciplines) and the law have been founded. These include the American Psychology-Law Society (APLS; Division 41 of the American Psychological Association), the Law and Society Association (LASA), the American Academy of Psychiatry and the Law (AAPL), and the American Board of Forensic Psychology (ABFP). Several journals have also been introduced in the area including *Law and Human Behavior, Behavioral Sciences and the Law, Law and Society Review,* and *Psychology, Public Policy, and Law;* law-related articles also appear more frequently in traditional psychology journals, and psychology-related articles in law reviews; and numerous books on all aspects of the relationship between psychology and law have been published. Two organizations founded by the courts also deserve mention. The Federal Judicial Center and the National Center for State Courts conduct research on the judicial system and employ psychologists and other social scientists to do so. There has also been a great increase in activity on the educational front, such as joint J.D./Ph.D. programs and interdisciplinary programs and courses in both graduate schools and law schools, as well as courses on psychology and law at the undergraduate level (Ogloff et al., 1996; Roesch, Grisso, & Poythress, 1986).

CONCEPTUALIZING THE RELATIONSHIP BETWEEN PSYCHOLOGY AND LAW

Just as there are many ways in which psychology and law interact, there are many ways of conceptualizing the relationship. One can use the ready-made categories of the law (e.g., criminal law, family law, property, torts) or the categories of psychology (e.g., clinical psychology, developmental psychology, social psychology). But there have also been attempts to think about the relationship more abstractly. We will discuss two of them here.

HANEY'S TAXONOMY

Craig Haney (1980) proposed a threefold taxonomy of ways in which psychology and the law can be related to each other: psychology *in* the law, psychology *and* law, and psychology *of* law.

Psychology in the Law

Here, "psychology ... is used *by* the law in the ordinary conduct of legal business" (p. 153). Examples include testimony by psychologists in cases involving the insanity defense and the use of psychological techniques in jury selection. In these interactions between the two disciplines, "the legal system dominates and completely dictates the form and application of psychology in law" (p. 170; italics in original).

Psychology and Law

This interaction involves "the co-equal and conjoint use of psychological principles to analyze and examine the legal system" (p. 154). Examples include studying how a court decides whether a confession has been coerced, "what police lineup procedures unduly bias identification by witnesses," "whether the process of death qualification prejudices the jury that results" (p. 154), the study of what [psychological] factors affect "the decisions to arrest, charge, prosecute, and take a defendant to trial" (p. 155). This relationship "represents an attempt by psychologists to assert power and compel legal change" (p. 170).

Psychology of Law

Here, the law becomes "an object of psychological study in itself" (p. 156). Examples would include attempts "to help explain the very *origins* and existence of law" (p. 156), "why people 'need' law (or feel that they do)" (p. 156), and "why, how, and under what circumstances people obey the law" (p. 156; italics in original). Here, "psychology is used to explore the nature and sources of legal power" (p. 170). It shows us "the outer limits of legal reform" (p. 157). Not much work has yet been done in psychology in this area—"much of the basic work in this area has been done by anthropologists" (p. 156).

MONAHAN AND WALKER'S PROPOSAL

The other attempt to characterize more abstractly the relationship between psychology is that of John Monahan and Laurens Walker (1988; Walker & Monahan, 1987, 1988). Monahan and Walker's scheme is both broader and narrower than Haney's; it is broader in that it is concerned with all the social sciences, not only psychology; but narrower in that it deals primarily with the use of social science research in litigation. Thus, it is not concerned with the assessment of particular persons for specific purposes, such as criminal responsibility or competency to strand trial; or with the area that Haney calls "psychology *of* law."

To understand the Monahan and Walker scheme, it is helpful first to discuss an earlier distinction, first made by Davis (1942), between adjudicative facts and legislative facts. *Adjudicative facts* are facts particular to the case at hand (e.g., in a case involving a traffic accident, whether the light was red or green). *Legislative facts* are broader and not confined to the case at hand. To take examples from cases we have already discussed, they would include the facts that excessive work harms women's health, and that segregated schools have harmful effects on the children who attend them. Based on this distinction, Monahan and Walker have created three categories. They propose that social science research can be used as *social fact* (corresponding roughly to Davis's adjudicative fact), as *social authority* (corresponding to legislative fact), or to provide a *social framework* (a new, hybrid category that combines aspects of both adjudicative and legislative fact).

Social fact research concerns the immediate parties to a case and addresses issues specific to that case. It is generally commissioned by one of the parties to the case just for that purpose. Examples include statistical analyses to support claims of sex discrimination, surveys conducted to see if a product is confused with another one in trademark infringement cases, and surveys of community standards in obscenity cases (Walker & Monahan, 1988).

Social frameworks involve using "general conclusions from social science research in determining factual issues in a specific case" (Walker & Monahan, 1987, p. 570). Unlike the social fact category just discussed, the studies that are used are not designed and conducted specifically for the case, but rather they are "off the rack"; that is, they are usually "published before the events of the cases took place" (Walker & Monahan, 1987, p. 568). Examples include studies of eyewitness accuracy, statistics showing murderers have low recidivism rates, and research on battered woman syndrome and abused child syndrome.

Social authority involves using social science research to choose, create, or change a legal rule. This is the most far-reaching use of such research. We have already noted what are perhaps the two most famous historical examples: *Muller v. Oregon* (1908), in which social science research was used to support the argument that laws prohibiting excessive workdays should be constitutional, and *Brown v. Board of Education* (1954), in which research was used to argue that segregated public schools should be unconstitutional.

Two other important aspects of the Monahan and Walker scheme should be noted. The first concerns how social science evidence should be presented to the judge or jury. Monahan and Walker proposed that in social framework and social authority cases, the social science evidence be presented in briefs or jury instructions rather than by expert testimony. In social fact cases, information pertaining to the methodology used should likewise be presented in briefs or jury instructions; only information regarding the application of the research should be presented through expert testimony. Augmenting their proposal would involve a marked change from current practice in which most social science evidence of all forms is presented via expert testimony.

The other important part of the Monahan and Walker plan concerns the issue of precedential effect: How should courts treat the findings of other courts in regard to social science evidence? Monahan and Walker believed that in most cases social science research should be treated the way that law is treated; that is, lower courts should be bound by the findings of higher courts, while higher courts should be free to reevaluate the findings of lower courts, as is the case with regard to legal precedent.

Only in the application of social fact research should higher courts be bound by the findings of lower courts.

CONFLICT BETWEEN PSYCHOLOGY AND THE LAW

Although the disciplines of psychology and law have had much (and increasing) interaction, the relationship has not been conflict free, as we have already seen in Wigmore's criticism of Munsterberg and the controversy over the psychological (and other social science) contribution to the *Brown* desegregation case. Bersoff (1986) has suggested that if "the relationship between experimental psychologists and the courts ... were to be examined by a Freudian, the analyst would no doubt conclude that it is a highly neurotic, conflict-ridden, ambivalent affair" (p. 155). This description could be extended to most other areas of psychology as well. Indeed, numerous writers have commented on the problem and on occasion have offered solutions. Haney (1980) has provided an extensive discussion of issues that serve as sources of conflict between the two disciplines (see the list that follows). Each issue is described as a dichotomy, which, as Haney points out, is an oversimplification: "They represent bright lines drawn through relative shades of gray" (p. 159). Also, they are not entirely independent of each other; there is overlap between and among them.

1. *Psychology emphasizes creativity; the law emphasizes conservatism.* Psychologists are encouraged to be creative in their research and theorizing; they are rewarded for novel ideas, if they are fruitful. In the law, by contrast, the concept of *stare decisis* (legal precedent) prevails. A number of commentators have called attention to the conservative nature of the law. Holmes (1954) called the law "the government of the living by the dead" (p. 34). Freund (1967) observed that "no Nobel prize is awarded for the most revolutionary decision of the year" (p. 394).

2. *The law is authoritative; psychology is empirical.* In the legal system, lower courts are bound by the decisions of higher courts; there is a hierarchy of power that must be observed. In psychology, the appeal is not to authority but to empirical test: "Psychology and other social sciences are largely *empirical* enterprises whose principles and propositions depend for their confirmation upon the collection of consistent and supporting data" (Haney, 1980, p. 160; italics in original). Moreover, as Haney points out, "law cannot be 'disproven,' but only 'overruled'" (p. 160).

3. *Psychology relies on experimentation; the law relies on adversarial process.* In psychology, the goal is the enlargement of understanding and knowledge through the use of experimentation or other forms of unbiased, objective investigation. Although no psychologist is ever completely un-

biased this is the goal, and it serves as the motive for the use of experimentation and other objective methods.

The legal system, on the other hand, is governed by the adversarial process, where the goal is not knowledge or understanding but victory. "Under our adversary system the role of counsel is not to make sure the truth is ascertained but to advance his client's cause by any ethical means" (Friendly, 1975, p. 1288). Distortion, bias, selective reporting of facts, and so on, are, in many cases, not only acceptable but desirable.

This conflict between the two fields can put particular stress on psychologists who testify as expert witnesses (as we will discuss in more detail shortly).

4. *The law is prescriptive; psychology is descriptive.* "The pronouncements of the law are primarily *prescriptive*—they tell people how they should behave (and provide for certain consequences if they do not). In contrast, psychology is essentially a *descriptive* discipline, seeking to describe behavior as it actually occurs" (Haney, 1980, p. 163; italics in original).

5. *The law is idiographic; psychology is nomothetic.* In each legal case, the law's focus is on the fact pattern that is specific to that case. In psychology, the emphasis is on developing broader principles and theories that have greater generality. Psychologists who testify on the basis of research that was not conducted with a specific case in mind (e.g., general research on the topic of eyewitness testimony) have frequently been looked on skeptically; sometimes they have not been allowed to testify at all. Clinical psychologists and psychiatrists—who share the law's idiographic focus—are more likely to be welcomed by the legal system. Indeed, testimony by clinicians has been accepted and, in some cases, welcomed or even invited into courts for many years now (Melton, Petrila, Poythress, & Slobogin, 1997).

6. *The law emphasizes certainty; psychology is probabilistic.* The law emphasizes certainty, and the related concepts of predictability and finality. In a criminal case, for example, a defendant is either guilty or not guilty. In a civil case, either the plaintiff is victorious or the defendant is (though doctrines like "contributory negligence" may reduce the amount of damages awarded). In both kinds of cases, evidence is either admissible or it is not. Once a decision has been rendered by the highest court in a jurisdiction, there is great reluctance to overturn it. Psychologists, by contrast, are much more comfortable with probabilities. Perhaps the simple fact that a course in statistics (which is based on probability) is a requirement in most psychology programs has a good deal to do with this. Moreover, psychologist' "most unequivocal statement—that a relationship is 'statistically significant'—is in terms of explicit probabilities" (Haney, 1980, p. 166). (The law's difficulty in handling probabilistic evidence is discussed in more depth later in this chapter.)

7. *Psychology is proactive; law is reactive.* Psychologists study issues that they themselves choose to study, while the law deals with issues brought to it by persons outside the system, namely clients.

8. *Psychology is academic; law is operational.* Psychologists tend to operate in academic settings, and so their activities are often removed from "real-world" economic and social concerns. The law, however, is an applied discipline, strongly influenced by such concerns. "Academic psychologists are trained to observe, lawyers to intervene"; "academic psychologists are attracted to things that are new and 'interesting,' lawyers to things that work" (Haney, 1980, p. 168).

HOW MUCH INFLUENCE HAS PSYCHOLOGY EXERTED ON COURTS?

As we have seen, psychology has been involved in diverse and sometimes controversial ways in the judicial system. But what about the "bottom-line" question: How much impact has psychology actually had? In some domains, the impact has been substantial. In determinations of competency to stand trial, for example, courts almost always follow the recommendation of the clinician (Roesch, Ogloff, & Golding, 1993). In other domains, the impact varies widely as a function of a number of factors, including subject matter (in certain areas where psychologists have traditionally been seen as having expertise, such as the insanity defense, or in child custody cases, their impact has been greater) and the particular judge (some are much more receptive to psychologists than others).

The broader impact of psychology and social science evidence on the courts has been the subject of considerable commentary. Some have suggested that the courts use social science evidence and arguments to do what they would have done anyway: "Judges use social science findings when they reaffirm the judge's position" (Wasby, 1980, p. 16). Even if this were true, however, there do appear to be some cases in which psychology has been influential. Tremper (1987) discussed several Supreme Court cases in which the Court's opinion followed the reasoning, sources, or language of the amicus brief submitted by the American Psychological Association.[3]

---

[3]Amicus curiae of "friend of the court" briefs to the courts are typically submitted by professional organizations or groups and summarize research relevant to a particular legal case, describing implications for legal issues before a court (Roesch, Golding, Hans, & Reppucci, 1991).

On the other hand, there are other cases where the courts seem to have seriously misrepresented or distorted social science findings. Saks (1974), for example, in reviewing Supreme Court decisions on jury size and decision rule (unanimity of jury decisions) (see Chapter 2,) opined that "the quality of social science scholarship displayed in these decisions would not win a passing grade in a high school psychology class" (p. 18). Supreme Court decisions on the prediction of dangerousness have likewise drawn highly critical commentary from the social science community (e.g., Risinger, Denbeaux, & Saks, 1989). Even where the Court has not misrepresented the contributions of psychologists, it has sometimes dismissed them as "irrelevant" or "insufficient." However, this tactic on the part of the Court has drawn differing responses from psychologists and others. Some have criticized the Court for ignoring or minimizing the social science evidence presented to it (e.g., Bersoff, 1986; Ewing, 1991; Haney, 1993). But others have argued that even in such cases, psychology has played an important role (Faigman, 1989; Grisso & Saks, 1991). They point out that the Court must deal with this evidence in some manner, so when it rules in a direction opposite to what the evidence suggests, it is forced to articulate more clearly and accurately the actual basis for its decision. "Psychology's input may compel judges to act like judges, stating clearly the fundamental values and normative premises on which their decisions are grounded, rather than hiding behind empirical errors or uncertainties. In this sense, we can regard psychology's recent efforts as successes" (Grisso & Saks, 1991, p. 208).

PSYCHOLOGY AND PUBLIC POLICY

Almost every topic in this book—and in psychology and law generally—has some public policy implications (see, generally, Reppucci, 1985). Here, we will simply discuss some of the best-known topics—explicit attempts to analyze and (sometimes) influence public policy. Two preliminary points are worth making: (a) Unlike many of the other topics in this book, these often involve legislation rather than litigation; and (b) these topics are often the focus of organized effort on the part of psychology— for example, lobbying efforts on the part of the American Psychological Association.

MENTAL HEALTH POLICY

This is one of the largest and most active areas having public policy implications. Important issues include the following: What policies should governments (federal, state, local) implement with regard to the supply and distribution of mental health services? How much money should be spent on these services? How should it be spent (for example, how much on hospital-based vs. community-based services)? What specific types of services and programs should be supported? To what degree, and in what ways, should participation of the private sector, nongovernmental organizations and private citizens be encouraged? There are also mental health policy issues having to do with the professional practice of psychology. What should the criteria for licensing and certification be? What criteria (education, training, experience, etc.) should be required? What should the relationship be between psychology and the other mental health professions? A topic of intense current interest is *managed care*. Rising health care costs have led insurance companies to use aggressive measures in an attempt to control these costs. Because of attempts at national health care policy, the legal aspects of managed care have become more prominent.

OTHER EXAMPLES

Here are a few other public policy issues with implications for psychology: (a) funding for psychological research. A substantial amount of psychological research is supported by government (especially federal) money. Psychologists obviously have a stake in how much money is made available for this purpose, and how it is spent. (b) Youth violence. An APA representative testified before a Senate committee on the relationship between youth violence and welfare, asserting that the relationship was spurious (Burnette, 1995). (c) Violence against women. The APA created a Task Force on Male Violence Against Women, which, among other things, published a book entitled *No Safe Haven* (Koss et al., 1994), which contains some policy recommendations. (d) Children's television. An APA representative told a hearing held by the Federal Communications Commission that "an unregulated commercial television marketplace leads to virtually no educational programming for children" (Wiggins, 1994, p.6). (e) Welfare reform. Psychologists have worked to "ensure that any legislation that's enacted does not harm women and children" and that "policy initiatives be based on scientific research" (DeAngelis, 1995, p. 38).

CONCLUSION

Although the roots of law and psychology were planted at the turn of the century, the "tree" has been slow to grow and only has begun to bear fruit recently. As this chapter shows, despite the common purpose of the

field of psychology and of the law—to understand and control behavior—
there are many areas of conflict between the fields. Notwithstanding these
differences, though, as the law becomes more open to the empirical realities introduced by the social sciences, it is probable that psychology will
become even more welcome in the legal system. It is incumbent upon
those who work in the field of law and psychology to ensure that our work
is carefully conducted and scientifically valid. Caution also must be taken
to educate courts and legislatures to ensure that social science findings are
not distorted or otherwise misrepresented. Once the labors of legal psychologists produce valid results, though, we are obligated to ensure that
such findings make their way into the legal system to ensure—as much as
possible—that the assumptions the law makes about people are accurate
and that justice is served.

REFERENCES

Bartol, C. R., & Bartol, A. M. (1987). History of forensic psychology. In I. B. Wiener & A. K.
    Hess (Eds.), *Handbook of forensic psychology* (pp. 3–21). New York: Wiley.
Bersoff, D. N. (1986). Psychologists and the judicial system: Broader perspectives. *Law and
    Human Behavior, 10*, 151–165.
Boring, E. G. (1950). *A history of experimental psychology* (2nd ed.). New York: Appleton-
    Century-Crofts.
Brown v. Board of Education, 375 U.S. 483 (1954).
Burnette, J. (1995, August). Bersoff testifies on youth violence. *APA Monitor*, p. 1.
Cahn, E. (1955). Jurisprudence. *New York University Law Review, 30*, 150–169.
Davis, K. C. (1942). An approach to problems of evidence in the administrative process.
    Harvard Law Review, 55, 364–386.
DeAngelis, T. (1995, February). Calling for all data to inform welfare-reform debate. *APA
    Monitor*, p. 3.
Ewing, C. P. (1991). Preventive detention and execution: The constitutionality of punishing
    future crimes. *Law and Human Behavior, 15*, 139–163.
Faigman, D. L. (1989). To have and have not: Assessing the value of social science to the law
    as science and policy. *Emory Law Journal, 38*, 1005–1095.
Faigman, D. L., Porter, E., & Saks, M. J. (1994). Check your crystal ball at the courthouse door,
    please: Exploring the past, understanding the present, and worrying about the future
    of scientific evidence. *Cardozo Law Review, 15*, 1799–1835.
Finkelman, D., & Grisso, T. (1994). Therapeutic jurisprudence: From idea to application. *New
    England Journal on Criminal and Civil Confinement, 20*, 243–257.
Freund, P. (1967). Is the law ready for human experimentation? *American Psychologist, 22*, 393–399.
Friedman, L. M. (1985). *A history of American law* (2nd ed.). New York: Simon & Schuster.
Friendly, H. (1975). Some kind of hearing. *University of Pennsylvania Law Review, 123*, 1267–
    1317.
Frye v. United States, 293 F. 1013, 34 A. L. R. 145 (D.C. Cir. 1923).
Grisso, T., & Saks, M. J. (1991). Psychology's influence on constitutional interpretation: A
    comment on how to succeed. *Law and Human Behavior, 15*, 371–398.

Grisso, T., Sales, B. D., & Bayless, S. (1982). Law-related courses and programs in graduate psychology departments. *American Psychologist, 37,* 267–278.

Hale, M. (1980). *Human science and social order: Hugo Munsterberg and origins of applied psychology.* Philadelphia, PA: Temple University Press.

Haney, C. (1980). Psychology and legal change: On the limits of factual jurisprudence. *Law and Human Behavior, 4,* 147–200.

Haney, C. (1993). Psychology and legal change: The impact of a decade. *Law and Human Behavior, 17,* 371–398.

Holmes, O. W. (1897). The path of the law. *Harvard Law Review, 10,* 457–478.

Holmes, O. W. (1954). Learning and science (a speech given to the Harvard Law School Association, June 25, 1895). In M. Lerner (Ed.), *The mind and faith of Justice Holmes.* New York: Modern Library, 1954.

Holmes, O. W. (1963). *The common law.* Cambridge, MA: Harvard University Press. (Original work published 1881)

Kalman, L. (1986). *Legal realism at Yale, 1927–1960.* Chapel Hill: University of North Carolina Press.

Koss, M. P., Goodman, L. A., Browne, A., Fitzgerald, L. F., Keita, G. P., & Russo, N. F. (1994). *No safe haven: Male violence against women.* Washington, DC: American Psychological Association.

Lochner v. N.Y., 198 U.S. 45 (1905).

Loftus, E., & Monahan, J. (1981). "The psychologist as expert witness." Reply to Sokal. *American Psychologist, 36,* 316–317.

Loh, W. (1981). Psycholegal research: Past and present. *Michigan Law Review, 79,* 659–707.

Melton, G. B. (1990). Realism in psychology and humanism in law: Psycholegal studies at Nebraska. *Nebraska Law Review, 69,* 251–277.

Melton, G. B., Monahan, J., & Saks, M. J. (1987). Psychologists as law professors. *American Psychologist, 42,* 502–509.

Melton, G. B., Petrola, Poytherers, N., & Slobogin, C. (1997). *Psychological evaluations for the courts: A handbook for mental health professionals and lawyers* (2nd ed.). New York: Guilford.

Monahan, J., & Loftus, E. (1982). The psychology of law. *Annual review of psychology* (Vol. 33, pp. 441–475). Palo Alto, CA: Annual Reviews.

Monahan, J., & Walker, L. (1988). Social science in law: A new paradigm. *American Psychologist, 43,* 465–472.

Monahan, J., & Walker, L. (1994). *Social science in law: Cases and materials* (3rd ed.). Westbury, NY: Foundation Press.

Moore, C. (1907). Yellow psychology. *Law Notes, 11,* 125–127.

Moskowitz, M. J. (1977). Hugo Munsterberg: A study in the history of applied psychology. *American Psychologist, 32,* 824–842.

Muller v. Oregon, 208 U.S. 412 (1907).

Munsterberg, H. (1908). *On the witness stand: Essays on psychology and crime.* New York: Doubleday.

Ogloff, J. R. P. (1990). Law and psychology in Canada: The need for training and research. *Canadian Psychology, 31,* 61–73.

Ogloff, J. R. P., Roberts, C. F., & Roesch, R. (1993). The insanity defense: Legal standards and clinical assessment. *Applied and Preventive Psychology, 2,* 163–178.

Ogloff, J. R. P., Tomkins, A. J., & Bersoff, D. N. (1996). Education and training in psychology and law/criminal justice. *Criminal Justice and Behavior, 23,* 200–235.

Purcell, E. A., Jr. (1973). *The crisis of democratic theory: Scientific naturalism and the problem of value.* Louisville: University Press of Kentucky.

Reppucci, N. D. (1985). Psychology in the public interest. In A. M. Rogers & C. J. Scheirer

(Eds.), *The G. Stanley Hall lecture series* (Vol. 5, pp. 125–156). Washington, DC: American Psychological Association.

Risinger, D. M., Denbeaux, M. P., & Saks, M. J. (1989). Exorcism of ignorance as a proxy for rational knowledge: The lessons of handwriting identification "expertise." *University of Pennsylvania Law Review, 137,* 731–792.

Roesch, R., Grisso, T., & Poythress, N. G., Jr. (1986). Training programs, courses, and workshops in psychology and law. In M. F. Kaplan (Ed.), *The impact of social psychology on procedural justice* (pp. 83–108). Springfield, IL: Thomas.

Tremper, C. R. (1987). Sanguinity and disillusionment: Where law meets social science. *Law and Human Behavior, 11,* 267–276.

Roesch, R., Ogloff, J. R. P., & Golding, S. L. (1993). Competency to stand trial: Legal and clinical issues. *Applied and Preventive Psychology, 2,* 43–51.

Rosen, P. L. (1980). History and state of the art of applied social research in the courts. In M. J. Sasks & C. H. Baron (Eds.), *The use/nonuse/misuse of applied social research in the courts* (pp. 9–15). Cambridge, MA: Abt.

Saks, M. J. (1974). Ignorance of science is no excuse. *Trial, 10,* 18–20.

Schlegel, J. (1979). American legal realism and empirical social science: From the Yale experience. *Buffalo Law Review, 28,* 459–586.

Small, M. A. (1993). Legal psychology and therapeutic jurisprudence. *Saint Louis University Law Journal, 37,* 675–700.

Stevens, R. (1983). *Law school: Legal education in America from the 1850s to the 1890s.* Chapel Hill: University of North Carolina Press.

Tapp, J. L. (1976). Psychology and law. An overture. *Annual review of psychology* (Vol. 27, pp. 359–404). Palo Alto, CA: Annual Reviews.

Tomkins, A. J., & Oursland, K. (1991). Social and social scientific perspectives in judicial interpretations of the Constitution: A historical view and an overview. *Law and Human Behavior, 15,* 101–120.

Twining, W. (1973). *Karl Llewellyn and the realist movement.* London: Weidenfeld & Nicolson.

United States Fidelity and Guaranty Co. v. Guenther, 281 U.S. 34 (1930).

Walker, L., & Monahan, J. (1987). Social frameworks: A new use of social science in law. *Virginia Law Review, 73,* 559–598.

Walker, L., & Monahan, J. (1988). Social facts: Scientific methodology as legal precedent. *California Law Review, 76,* 877–896.

Wasby, S. L. (1980). History and state of the art of applied social research in the courts. In M. J. Saks & C. H. Baron (Eds.), *The use/nonuse/misuse of applied social research in the courts* (pp. 15–18). Cambridge, MA: Abt.

Wexler, D. B. (1990). Training in law and behavioral sciences: Issues from a legal educator's perspective. *Behavioral Sciences and the Law, 8,* 197–204.

White, G. E. (1972). From sociological jurisprudence to realism: Jurisprudence and social change in early twentieth-century America. *Virginia Law Review, 58,* 999–1028.

White, G. E. (1976). *The American judicial tradition: Profiles of leading American judges.* New York: Oxford University Press.

Wiggins, G. (1994, February). Children's TV needs fine-tuning, says APA. *APA Monitor,* p. 6.

Wigmore, J. (1909). Professor Munsterberg and the psychology of testimony: Being a report of the case of Cokestone v. Munsterberg. *Illinois Law Review, 3,* 399–445.

I

Human Behavior
in the Trial Process

2

Juries

The Current State of the Empirical Literature

MICHAEL T. NIETZEL, DENIS M. McCARTHY, AND MONICA J. KERN

In 1908, when Hugo Munsterberg, then director of the Harvard Psychological Laboratory, published *On the Witness Stand*, he claimed that experimental psychology surpassed existing legal processes as a method for assessing a host of forensic claims. Showing the exuberance with which he repeatedly managed to annoy his contemporaries, Munsterberg charged "The psychological inspirations of the bench are often directly the opposite of demonstrable facts" (p. 19). Claims like these did little to forge a good working alliance between litigators and psychologists during the first half of the 20th century (Loh, 1984) despite occasional calls from both quarters for a rapprochement.

An important turning point in this history was the Chicago Jury Project of the 1950s, which represented a methodological high-water mark in jury studies, but which was cut short by the outcry following the discovery that the investigators had taped several jury deliberations. The influence of the Chicago Jury Project was also constrained by its limited "small groups" theoretical viewpoint, but as Davis (1989) observed, the Chicago Jury Project did stimulate renewed interest in the study of trial procedures and jury performance. In the 1960s and 1970s jury research

MICHAEL T. NIETZEL, DENIS M. McCARTHY, AND MONICA J. KERN • Department of Psychology, University of Kentucky, Lexington, Kentucky 40506-0027.

Psychology and Law: The State of the Discipline, edited by Ronald Roesch, Stephen D. Hart, and James R. P. Ogloff. Kluwer Academic/Plenum Publishers, New York, 1999.

proliferated, typically in laboratory experiments that attempted to simulate relevant courtroom/jury phenomena. Among the topics capturing the greatest attention in this era were procedural justice, trial procedures, juror and litigant characteristics, and jury performance. This period of research has been reviewed in several chapters, books, review articles, and proceedings (Davis, Bray, & Holt, 1977; Gerbasi, Zuckerman, & Reis, 1977; Penrod & Hastie, 1979; Saks & Hastie, 1978; Wrightsman, 1978), including two *Annual Review of Psychology* chapters (Monahan & Loftus, 1982; Tapp, 1976). Numerous recommendations also were offered during this period for improving the quality of jury research with respect to the questions it asked and how it asked them.

Our current concern is with reviewing the past decade and a half of jury research, describing its scope, and summarizing some of the discoveries of this literature, using meta-analytic methods. We concentrate both on the methodology of this generation of jury research as well as some of its substantive findings.

A word about the context of this review: The functioning and even the continued existence of the American jury are under a barrage of criticism and second-guessing. For several years, politicians and many judges, including late Supreme Court Chief Justice Warren Burger, have questioned whether jurors have the ability to understand and decide complex cases. Lay jurors are under frequent attack in the popular media for, as an example, succumbing

> all too easily to emotional appeals. Some are stymied by the least bit of complexity. Many filter facts through such a thick mesh of prejudice that the facts become unrecognizable. Common sense mutates into mutual decision. And the unfortunate reality is that this isn't always an accident. Through the deceptive, frequently cynical process of jury selection, lawyers can and often do steer some of the least capable and least fair-minded people on to some of the most important cases. (Adler, 1994)

Many cite the O. J. Simpson criminal trial as a leading example of all that is wrong with the jury system; one of the many fallouts of this trial is a renewed call for jury "reforms," including the end of jury sequestration, greater limits on peremptory challenges, and elimination of the requirement for unanimous verdicts in felony cases.

How well informed are these critiques? Are juries as incapable of intelligent decisions and fair process as the pundits would have us believe, or, conversely, does the supposed expertise of judges immunize members of the bench against the information-processing limitations that have so often been attributed to lay jurors? Does our jury system work so badly that its curtailment or even elimination is now warranted? The present review describes what we know about juror behavior and jury performance based on empirical research rather than on the politicized agendas that drive some of the most-repeated commentaries and conjectures.

THE SCOPE OF JURY RESEARCH

First, in order to gauge the scope of scholarship on jury and juror behavior, we surveyed 10 of the leading journals in social psychology, forensic psychology, and criminal justice/legal studies. We began our search in 1977, the year in which *Law and Human Behavior*, probably the leading journal for publication of empirical jury research, was inaugurated. Among applied and social psychology outlets, we reviewed each volume of the following journals, all of which are known to publish research pertaining to juries from 1977 through 1994: *Journal of Applied Psychology, Journal of Personality and Social Psychology, Journal of Applied Social Psychology,* and *Personality and Social Psychology Bulletin.* In the area of psychology and the law, we reviewed each volume of *Law and Human Behavior* and *Behavioral Sciences and the Law* for the same time period. Finally, we surveyed the following four journals in the broad discipline of legal studies: *Criminal Justice and Behavior, Crime and Delinquency, Law and Society Review,* and *Journal of Legal Studies.*

We searched these volumes to locate original empirical studies in which investigators described, predicted, manipulated, or measured juror behavior, jury decision making, or jury process. We located 265 studies. Obviously, we have not catalogued every empirical study of jurors or jury behavior during this period because such studies occasionally appear in a myriad of diverse sources, including law reviews and specialty journals. We focused only on journals published in the United States. We did not count unpublished theses, dissertations, and technical reports, and we excluded books or chapters in books reporting original juror/jury data. Table 2.1 summarizes the frequency with which the various journals contributed to this literature.

Our initial search was aimed at answering three basic questions about the 1977–1994 jury literature: (a) What is the overall magnitude of this literature, and what trends are evident in the frequency with which jury phenomena are being studied? (b) What are the major variables and questions that investigators have been studying? (c) What are the primary methodological characteristics of this literature?

We believe our search strategy allowed trustworthy answers to each of these questions. Although it is possible that the exclusion of unpublished manuscripts, books, non-English publications, or other scholarly products might introduce some biases to our answers, we question whether such distortions would be anything but small and rather unimportant. Other reviews could test this assumption, however, by contrasting their reviews of alternative data bases with the one reported here.

Briefly, here are the answers to the initial questions about the overall contours of recent jury research literature. Figure 2.1 shows the publication

TABLE 2.1. FREQUENCY OF EMPIRICAL JURY
ARTICLES IN 10 SELECTED JOURNALS

Journal	Percentage
Law and Human Behavior	40.0
Behavior Sciences and the Law	8.0
Journal of Applied Social Psychology	25.0
Journal of Personality and Social Psychology	9.0
Journal of Applied Psychology	5.0
Personality and Social Psychology Bulletin	5.0
Law and Society Review	5.0
Criminal Justice and Behavior	2.0
Crime and Delinquency	1.0
Journal of Legal Studies	.4

trends in empirical jury studies over this 18-year period. The frequency of jury studies has obviously fluctuated over this period; the 1987–1991 interval saw sustained, robust activity, but the greatest single-year volume was in 1994.

Table 2.2 summarizes the major topics that jury investigators have concentrated on recently. We classified the published research into the following nine basic categories: (a) evaluation of criminal defense strate-

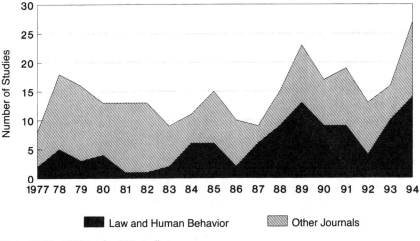

■ Law and Human Behavior   ▨ Other Journals

Note: 1977 - 1994 total = 265 studies.

FIGURE 2.1. Empirical jury studies by journal and year.

TABLE 2.2. PERCENTAGE OF JURY STUDIES BY TOPIC
IN 10 SELECTED JOURNALS, 1977–1994

Topic	Percentage
Criminal defense strategies	
(nullification, insanity/GBMI, self-defense, battered spouse)	9
Capital punishment, death qualification, other sentencing	11
Juror characteristics	10
Judicial instructions	8
Litigation strategies	
(stealing thunder, empty chair inference, joinder, openings, voir dire, jury methods)	18
Witness performance	
(expert or child witness, eyewitnesses, witness behavior)	20
Evaluation of evidence	
(influence of extraneous factors or statistical evidence)	11
Offender/plaintiff or offense characteristics	10
Miscellaneous	
(cameras in the Court, jury vs. judicial decisions, verdict trends, pretrial publicity)	3

gies; (b) examination of capital punishment, death qualification, and other sentencing issues; (c) influence of juror characteristics; (d) effects of judicial instructions; (e) evaluation of general litigation strategies; (f) study of witness performance; (g) evaluation of evidence by jurors; (h) effects of offender/plaintiff or offense characteristics on jurors/juries; and (i) review of a miscellaneous group. Among these groupings, the impact of various litigation strategies, the influence of different types of witnesses, and the effects of juror or litigant characteristics were the most frequently studied.

Of course, many studies addressed more than one topic and therefore could have been classified in more than one of our categories. However, we assigned each study to only one category, based on our collective judgment of its primary focus. The overwhelming majority (89%) of jury studies in this era investigated criminal rather than civil trials, a concentration that many commentators have observed as perhaps a misplaced emphasis in this literature.

Figure 2.2 shows that the majority of this literature is based on jury simulation methods, using undergraduates as subjects. In fact, an empirical study of real juries or jurors was rare (11%) in these sources. Despite this pattern, research on real juries is being conducted. Witness, for example, Jury Verdict Research's recent survey of 3,300 product liability trials, showing a 13% decline (54% to 41%) in plaintiff verdicts between 1987 and

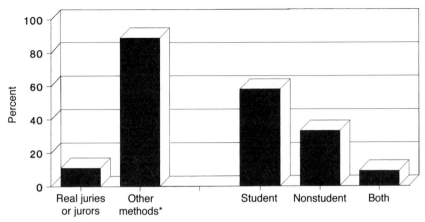

*Includes mock trials as well as interview and questionnaire studies.

FIGURE 2.2. Comparison of methodological features of 265 jury studies from 1977 to 1994.

1993 (Geyelin, 1994; see also Vidmar, 1994 for a discussion of other jury verdict studies). Generally, however, real-jury studies are not of the analytic type preferred by research psychologists (for a notable exception see Heuer & Penrod, 1994), and they often are plagued by sampling problems, independent variable confounds, definitional and criterion variability, and missing data that limit their validity (Vidmar, 1994). However, studies of jury verdict statistics can provide useful information about jury performance, particularly when investigators are mindful of methodological problems, focus their inquiries with the help of theoretical guidance, and are appropriately cautious about the conclusions these data allow.

Many commentators (e.g., Dillehay & Nietzel, 1980; Konecni & Ebbesen, 1979) have pointed out conceptual and practical limitations of the mock-jury methodology. We will not repeat these criticism here, nor will we take the nihilistic position that such methods cannot teach us anything about jury phenomena because it is clear that well-conducted experimental simulations can illuminate real-trial phenomena. However, it does seem appropriate to suggest that investigators who claim to study jury phenomena, who offer conclusions about what variables affect jury outcomes, and who wish to offer prescriptions for jury reforms be expected to study real juries and jurors once in a while.

In order to assess whether the use of more realistic methodologies were gaining frequency in contemporary research, we correlated year of publication with the percentage of studies employing real juries/jurors and found that more recent research was more likely to involve the study of real juries ($r = .32$); it was also more likely to be based on samples that were not restricted exclusively to college subjects ($r = .23$).

MAJOR JURY RESEARCH CONTROVERSIES

So much for the easy questions. How about the more difficult issues? What has the last nearly two decades of jury research taught us? Are there any lessons to be learned from this literature about jury process and performance? What areas of agreement have been established? Are jurors as inept and as biased as some critics (Adler, 1994) allege?

In order to answer these questions, we selected four major jury/juror controversies that were believed to be among the most interesting and that have been addressed frequently by recent investigators. These four controversies share several characteristics. First, a sizable published literature exists for each one. Second, in each case, mixed results have been reported, leading to different conclusions and recommendations by reviewers. Third, each controversy has important practical implications and potential social policy ramifications for how juries perform in the legal system or how trial procedures might be changed to facilitate better jury performance. In fact, these four controversies have attained sufficient visibility in the justice system that they attract attention not only from psycholegal scholars but from the general public as well. Because we also were aware, at the time we began our review, that meta-analyses of different portions of the jury research literature were also being conducted by other investigators (e.g., Steven Penrod, personal communication, July 1994), we focused on the following four topics:

1. The relationship between jurors' attitudes about the death penalty and their verdicts or their evaluations of evidence in capital trials.
2. The effects of judicial instructions on juror comprehension and jury behavior.
3. The influence of expert testimony by psychologists (or other mental health professionals) on jury verdicts and decision making.
4. The influence of joinder of criminal charges on jury verdicts and decision making. (Joinder is but one example of various litigation strategies or procedural variations that have been explored in the literature. Rather than attempting to meta-analyze many different litigation/procedural variations in the limited space available to us, we selected joinder because a fairly well-focused experimental literature exists on the question.)

For each of these topics, we conducted meta-analytic reviews of the published literature in order to summarize the magnitude of basic relationships and discover what variables might moderate these relationships. These meta-analyses provided quantitative literature reviews in which the results of a study were treated as units of analysis and subjected to statistical analyses themselves. We meta-analyzed studies published in both journals and books between 1960 and 1994. Studies were located through a PsychLit research, using several key words and examination of the reference lists of studies identified through this search. Note, then, that our review was not confined to the 10 journals that we initially surveyed in order to describe the general magnitude of jury research and empirical topics.

1.   *What is the relationship between individuals' death penalty attitudes and aspects of juror behavior, such as verdicts for capital defendants or attitudes toward criminal justice?*

This question has often been posed in a more narrow form: Are juries that have been pruned of staunch death penalty opponents through a process known as death qualification, under either the Supreme Court standards of *Witherspoon v. Illinois* (1968) or *Wainwright v. Witt* (1985), more prone to convict defendants or to construe evidence differently than juries retaining jurors who are strongly scrupled about, or opposed to, the death penalty? An extensive empirical literature now interpreted by several commentators (Elliott, 1991; Ellsworth, 1991; Finch & Ferraro, 1986; Mauro, 1991) has addressed these questions. A portion of this literature also served as the empirical foundation for the APA amicus brief in the case of *Lockhart v. McCree* (1986), in which the Supreme Court held that it was not unconstitutional to exclude from the guilt phase of capital trials those jurors who resolutely opposed the death penalty.

In order to examine the empirical literature's answer to the question of whether there is a link between death penalty attitudes and juror decisions, we conducted a meta-analysis of 20 studies that we identified as pertinent to this question (see Appendix A). These studies yielded 42 effect sizes concerned with the relationship between death penalty attitudes and one of three types of outcomes: (a) guilt-innocence verdicts, (b) sentencing tendencies, and (c) more general attitudes about crime or the criminal justice system.

In addition, we coded 11 effect sizes from three additional studies (also in Appendix A) that examined relationships between a death qualification process (rather than an individual juror belief) and a measure of verdict, sentencing, or related attitudes. The first process study was Haney's (1984) investigation of the effects of death qualification itself on juror attitudes and decisions. The second study in this category was Cox and Tanford's

(1989) multiple experiments about the effects of using a death qualification questionnaire. The final study was Nietzel, Dillehay, and Himelein's (1987) investigation of the effects of different methods for conducting capital voir dire and the use of voir dire consultants on capital jury verdicts.

In order to reduce the problem of statistical nonindependence involved when one derives multiple effect sizes from the same study, we computed and analyzed only the median value of multiple dependent measures that tapped a specific type of effect size. We did code each instance of a different type of effect size (e.g., verdicts, recommended sentences, other criminal justice attitudes) per study so our analysis did not eliminate totally the problem of effect size nonindependence. For example, if there were two conceptually similar measures of verdict and three similar measures of attitudes toward the criminal justice system in a given study, we coded one median effect size for verdict and one for attitudes. Given the exploratory nature of this review, we decided it was preferable to learn as much as possible from multiple effect size studies, while trying to shrink the threat of nonindependence to some degree. In order to gauge how much of a problem nonindependence of multiple effect sizes might be, we also report summary effect sizes based on only one effect size—the median—per study. We followed these same procedures in all the meta-analyses reported here. Effect sizes were computed for each study, using procedures outlined by Rosenthal (1994) and reported as the Pearson correlation coefficient r.

The average effect size for the relationship of individual juror beliefs about the death penalty to the three types of jury outcome was .16. Weighted by the size of samples, a procedure recommended by Hunter and Schmidt (1990) so that larger studies with smaller sampling error variance are given greater weight in the meta-analysis, the effect size was .14. The 95% confidence interval for this effect was .11–.21. Using each study as the unit for metanalysis, the average effect size was .17, with a confidence interval of .11–.23.

We next determined whether these effect sizes were homogeneous by calculating a chi-square with $k-1$ degrees of freedom, where k = the number of effect sizes (Snedecor & Cochran, 1989). A nonsignificant test can be interpreted as meaning that the effect sizes do not vary beyond what is expected from sampling error. A significant test suggests that the effect sizes are not homogenous, and that certain moderator variables may account for the beyond-chance variability. For effect sizes, computed with the study as the unit of analysis, we obtained a chi-square (19) = 65.00, $p < .001$, indicating significant heterogeneity of effect sizes.

Table 2.3 contrasts the effect sizes for various kinds of study characteristics and for the three kinds of dependent measures: verdicts, sentenc-

TABLE 2.3. EFFECT SIZES FOR RESEARCH
ON THE RELATIONSHIP BETWEEN DEATH PENALTY
ATTITUDES AND JURY DECISION MAKING

Category	Effect Sizes	
Juror outcomes	r	n
Verdicts	.11	19
Sentencing	.24	9
Other criminal justice attitudes	.18	14
Subjects		
College students	.10	11
Other	.19	31
Deliberations		
Yes	.15	9
No	.17	33
Stimulus format		
Real trials	.10	6
Written transcripts	.10	11
Videotapted	.17	9
Audiotapted	.34	5
Questionnaires	.16	11
Effect size parameters		
Continuous dependent measures	.20	21
Dichotomous dependent measures	.12	21
Death penalty attitudes—dichotomous	.14	28
Death penalty attitudes—continuous	.21	14
Voir dire process studies	.26	11

ing, and related attitudes. Not surprisingly, the relationship between death penalty attitudes and other measures of sentencing severity ($r = .24$) was stronger than the effect size for verdicts (.11) or other attitudes (.18). The more strongly one believes in the death penalty, the greater one's endorsement of other indices of sentence severity. Effects were nearly twice as large for non college samples ($r = .19$) compared with college subjects ($r = .10$). Effect sizes also varied as a function of mode of stimulus presentation; audiotaped simulations yielded effect sizes twice as large as for any other format. Deliberation versus no deliberation did not moderate effect sizes to any appreciable extent. Continuous measures of effect sizes yielded larger effect sizes than dichotomous measures. Likewise, continuous measures of death penalty attitudes produced larger effects than dichotomized attitudes. This last difference is particularly significant, given that *Witt* suggests a dimensional rather than a categorical approach (as was implied by *Witherspoon*) to assessing death-qualification (Neises & Dillehay, 1987).

The mean effect size derived from the 11 death qualification process effect sizes was .26, considerably larger but not significantly different from the average individual attitude-outcome effect. The average effect size for the Haney (1984) study was .31, indicating that exposure to death qualification procedures was related to higher levels of conviction and pro-prosecution sentiments. The effect size in the Cox and Tanford (1989) study of a special questionnaire was .32. Finally, in the Nietzel et al. (1987) study, the effect size of individualized voir dire on sentencing verdicts was .20, while the effect of using voir dire consultants was .26.

How should one interpret these effects, particularly the average .11 relationship between death penalty beliefs and verdicts, which is the effect size of most relevance to the death-qualification debate? Skeptics are likely to dismiss a variable that accounts for only 1% to 2% of verdict variance as too trivial to warrant much concern. Reformers, on the other hand, could observe that this magnitude of effect exceeds that associated with certain medical treatments, such as aortacoronary bypass surgery, chemotherapy for breast cancer, and drug therapy for patients with hypertension, that are regarded as highly successful interventions (Lipsey & Wilson, 1993; Rosenthal, 1992).

A helpful method for portraying the practical importance of an effect size is the binomial effect size display (Rosenthal & Rubin, 1982). Portrayed as a binomial effect—and all other factors remaining equal—replacing death penalty advocates with death penalty opponents would reduce the rate of individual jurors' guilty verdicts for capital defendants from 55% to 44%. Should any reader be unfortunate enough to be a capital defendant some day, this is an effect you probably would not regard as trivial or tell your attorney to forget about. At the same time, it clearly indicates that guilty verdicts are not heavily biased, and certainly not dictated, by jurors' general endorsement of capital punishment. The overwhelming amount of variance in verdicts for defendants charged with capital crimes does not appear to be associated with jurors' beliefs about the death penalty.

2. *How effective are judicial instructions in controlling juror behavior? Do instructions from the judge insure that jurors understand important legal principles, consider evidence for the limited purposes that they are permitted to consider, disregard evidence they are told to ignore, apply appropriate standards to the evaluation of evidence, and generally behave in ways that the instructions are intended to promote?*

Opinions about the efficacy of judicial instructions are typically sharply divided between psycholegal researchers on the one hand and trial judges and appellate courts on the other. Researchers usually question whether judicial instructions, especially in their common form where formal, legal language abounds, are adequately comprehended, accurately recalled, reasonably considered, or reliably applied by jurors. Trial and reviewing judges, on the other hand, have generally assumed, with a confidence bordering on "of course the sun rises in the east," that judicial admonitions have their intended effects and/or that most deficiencies in judicial instructions do not have constitutional implications (*Gacy v. Welborn*, 1993). The courts routinely rely on judicial instructions to be the cure for all sorts of potential evidentiary problems and/or the guide that leads jurors through a thicket of confusing or ambiguous legal standards. On this matter, at least, jurors appear to agree with the researchers. In their superb field study of jury performance, Heuer and Penrod (1994) discovered that jurors generally regarded judges' pattern instructions as liabilities for their performance, particularly in those cases concerned with more complex legal issues.

We searched the literature for empirical studies that compared the effects of a judicial instruction with a no-instruction condition on at least one measure of juror/jury decision making. We identified 48 published studies reporting such effect sizes, representing one of the larger literatures in the legal psychology arena (see appendix B).

In addition to coding methodological variations in these studies, we coded seven different types of content/goals of judicial instructions. The seven different kinds of instructional content/goals were as follows: (a) definitions of legal principles, (b) instructions for jurors to ignore pretrial publicity, (c) instructions about jury nullification, (d) instructions to disregard evidence or to use it for limited purposes, (e) instructions about jurors' evaluation of eyewitness testimony, (f) instructions regarding the joinder of criminal charges, and (g) instructions about jurors' evaluation of confessions. A miscellaneous category was also coded.

Across 150 instructional effect sizes, once again using only the median value for multiple-measure effect sizes, the average effect size was $r = .10$. The 95% confidence interval for this effect size was .08–.12. Weighted by the size of samples, the average r was .07. Using each study as the unit for meta-analysis, we obtained an average $r = .13$, with a confidence interval of .08–.17.

For this literature, using a study as the unit of analysis, we computed chi-square $(42) = 70.36$, $p < .001$, indicating significant heterogeneity of instructional effect sizes. Table 2.4 summarizes the effect sizes for several methodological contrasts as well as for the seven different types of judicial instructions. Among the more interesting differences is that the average verdict effect size $(r = .13)$ was larger than any other measure of instructional effects (e.g., attitudes toward the criminal justice system, impressions of a litigating party, and even memory for the instructions themselves). Instructions about a jury's prerogatives regarding nullification

TABLE 2.4. EFFECT SIZES FOR RESEARCH ON THE RELATIONSHIP
BETWEEN JUDICIAL INSTRUCTIONS AND JURY DECEISION MAKING

Category	Regular	Enhanced	Enhanced vs. None	Enhanced vs. Regular
	r (n)	r (n)	r (n)	r (n)
Sample				
1 = college students	.12 (104)	.12 (35)	.13 (17)	.11 (18)
2 = other	.06 (44)	.12 (32)	.20 (9)	.09 (23)
3 = both	.01 (2)	—	—	—
Deliberation				
1 = following	.13 (48)	.13 (30)	.20 (10)	.09 (20)
2 = without	.08 (102)	.12 (37)	.12 (16)	.11 (21)
Nature of effect size				
1 = verdict	.13 (101)	.13 (29)	.16 (15)	.10 (14)
2 = sentence	.01 (6)	—	—	—
3 = attitudes/impressions	.04 (24)	.09 (11)	.11 (4)	.09 (7)
4 = memory for trial facts	.02 (12)	.01 (11)	.00 (3)	.02 (8)
5 = memory for instruction	.09 (7)	.20 (16)	.28 (4)	.17 (12)
Trial or evidence format				
1 = real trial	—	−.02 (4)	—	−.02 (4)
2 = transcripts	.16 (62)	.04 (16)	.07 (7)	.02 (9)
3 = videotape	.06 (75)	.15 (41)	.16 (18)	.15 (23)
4 = audiotape	.12 (5)	.27 (4)	.50 (1)	.18 (3)
5 = live reenactment	.00 (5)	—	—	—
6 = questionnaire	.15 (3)	.00 (2)	—	.00 (2)
Effect size parameter				
1 = dichotomous	.13 (59)	.15 (23)	.17 (13)	.12 (10)
2 = other	.08 (91)	.11 (44)	.13 (13)	.09 (31)
Type of instructions				
1 = definitional	.08 (42)	.11 (43)	.14 (16)	.09 (27)
2 = pretrial publicity	.02 (9)	—	—	—
3 = nullification	.22 (5)	.31 (4)	.33 (2)	.29 (2)
4 = disregard or limit	.16 (37)	—	—	—
5 = eyewitness	.11 (19)	.17 (10)	.21 (4)	.15 (6)
6 = joinder	.05 (16)	—	—	—
7 = confession	.04 (8)	.07 (6)	.06 (4)	.10 (2)
8 = miscellaneous	.10 (14)	.00 (4)	—	.00 (4)

Note. There were 150 effect sizes total for the regular instructions studies and 67 effect sizes total for studies with enhanced instructions (26 effect sizes testing enhanced vs. no instrucitons and 41 effect sizes testing enhanced vs. regular instructions).

yielded the largest average effect ($r = .22$), but this estimate is based on only five effect sizes so its reliability is suspect. The next largest effect was for instructions to disregard certain information as evidence or interpret it in limited ways ($r = .16$). Smaller effects were found for live reenactments of trials versus other kinds of simulations, for simulations that did not

include some group deliberation, and for continuous as opposed to dichotomous dependent variables (a difference that is confounded with the
tendency for verdicts to show larger effect sizes).

We also coded a second general category of judicial instructions that
we termed *enhanced instructions*. These instructions represented attempts
by researchers to increase the comprehensibility or impact of judicial
instructions through a deliberate change in their form or delivery. Some
instructions were enhanced by translating overly technical legal language
into plain English designed to be more understandable by jurors. Others
were enhanced through multiple deliveries before the presentation of
evidence, both before and after the presentation of evidence, or in concurrent, multiple modes (e.g., written and oral presentations of instructions
rather than only an oral presentation). Other instructions were enhanced
by adding extra content or a fuller explanation of content than that found
in standard pattern instructions. In each case, enhanced instructions represented investigators' attempts to boost the impact of the instructions based
on theoretical predictions or prior empirical research.

The average effect size for 41 comparisons of enhanced instructions
with standard instructions was $r = .10$ (with a 95% confidence interval of
.05–.15). It is important to note that this contrast involves the difference
between enhanced and standard instructions. We also computed the average effect for enhanced instructions versus no instructions. Based on 26
effect sizes, the average effect for this contrast was $r = .15$ (with a 95%
confidence interval of .08–.22). These results suggest that enhanced instructions can exert a small, additional impact over and above standard
judicial instructions.

For the enhanced versus standard instruction comparisons, using
study as the unit for meta-analysis, we computed a chi-square $(11) = 18.90$,
$p < .10$, indicating nonsignificant (but note the small n) heterogeneity of
these effects. However, the effects of instructional enhancement versus
standard instructions appeared particularly strong for instructions governing jurors' nullification behavior $(r = .29)$ and their evaluations of
eyewitnesses $(r = .15)$. In both cases, however, these effect sizes were based
on very small samples.

A comparison of our first two meta-analyses reveals an obvious irony.
The magnitude of conviction proneness associated with attitudes toward
the death penalty is about the same as, or even a little larger than, the
effectiveness of standard judicial instructions in controlling jurors' behavior. This pattern appears to present a dilemma, but whose dilemma is it?
Can judges reconcile their tendency to minimize any death qualification
conviction bias as a Constitutional problem with their confidence that
routine judicial instructions provide effective trial controls, given that both

have essentially the same effect? Conversely, can social scientists argue that standard judges' instructions are hopelessly ineffective influences on jurors at the same time they decry the essentially equal impact (or lack of impact) of jurors' death penalty attitudes on their decision making?

One could try to resolve the inconsistency by arguing that the presence of a biasing factor is a greater ill in the system than the absence of a debiasing control or safeguard. However, if bias is the ultimate product, whether it arises from an active process versus a failed attempt to cure it may not be an important distinction. In addition, the caution that "death is different" could heighten our concern over any bias that intrudes into capital trials; however, judicial instructions are often applied in capital litigation so they can have life-and-death consequences also (*Gacy v. Welborn*, 1993).

Two methodological factors may have contributed to this dilemma. The first factor is the differential power of the two literatures and the tendency of reviewers to pay too much homage to statistical significance levels. The average sample size in the death penalty–conviction-proneness literature was 362. The average sample size in studies evaluating judicial instructions was 138. Obviously, smaller effect sizes were more likely to be reported as statistically significant in the former literature. In fact, given an average effect size of $r = .10$ for the instructions literature and $r = .16$ for the death qualification literature, the approximate power of the conviction-proneness literature was .68, three times the power of .22 for judicial instruction research. A second factor is that many studies measure the effect of judicial instructions only indirectly (e.g., through verdicts or sentences rather than reports of how the instructions were understood and processed) and may therefore be failing to capture their full impact. Nonetheless, verdicts and sentences are the measures that matter the most if one is primarily interested in jury outcomes.

Finally, it is important to consider the existing literature on enhanced judicial instructions. The effects of these enhanced or "boosted" judicial instructions indicate that well-crafted instructions can produce some additional benefit. This remains an important area for further study, particularly given recent data by Tanford (1991) that legislatures and special legal commissions have at times modified judicial instructions in ways suggested by the empirical research on enhanced instructions. Yet, Tanford's review also indicated that appellate courts have not responded positively to this literature, if anything revising their standards for judicial instructions in ways that would lessen their impact on jurors.

3. *What effect does expert testimony by psychologists have on juror opinion and jury verdicts?*

Psychologists increasingly find themselves in demand as expert witnesses for all kinds of civil and criminal litigation. As the criterion for allowing expert testimony has shifted from the conservative *Frye* (1923) test to the more open Federal Rule 702, which permits expert testimony to be given if it is relevant to the dispute and will help fact finders reach appropriate decisions, expert testimony by psychologists has become something of a growth industry. Whether judges' applications of the standards for admitting expert testimony set forth in the *Daubert* (1993) decision will retard or promote this growth remains to be seen.

Mental status defenses, psychological and neuropsychological damages, limits on the accuracy of eyewitnesses, trademark infringement, human factors and product liability, predictions of future dangerousness, validity of employee selection tests, assessments of hostile work environments, and descriptions of psychological syndromes are some of the primary topics for which psychological expertise has been provided to juries.

Expert testimony on these topics has been criticized, often by psychologists themselves (e.g., McCloskey & Egeth, 1983; Morse, 1978). Four challenges are common: (a) the adversarial system corrupts experts' objectivity and ultimately leads to public skepticism about the integrity of professional witnesses and their scholarly disciplines; (b) experts are asked to give absolute, ultimate opinions about matters for which their expertise allows only probabilistic, descriptive answers; (c) in response to adversarial pressures, experts often exaggerate the level of scientific evidence and consensus concerning the technical topics about which they testify; and (d) the impact of expert testimony is problematic either because it dominates jurors opinions and is therefore too influential, or because it does not exceed the average layperson's knowledge and is therefore gratuitous.

These concerns are debated with a vigor that exceeds what we know about the influence of expert psychological testimony on jurors. Some data exist about juror attitudes toward different kinds of experts (Saks & Wissler, 1984) and the contrasting opinions of expert testimony held by judges, lawyers jurors, and experts themselves (Shuman, Whitaker, & Champagne, 1994), but little is known about how much weight jurors place on expert testimony or how jury verdicts may be affected by expert testimony. (Incidentally, the lack of empirical data on the effects of expert testimony on jury decision making is not confined to psychology. In order to locate research that examined the effects of nonpsychological testimony on jurors, we conducted computer searches of Applied Science and Technology, F and S Index International, F and S Index U.S., Inspec, NTIS Psychlit, Medline, Grateful MED, and Bioethics, using the following key words in various combinations: *ballistics, civil, DNA, fingerprint, voiceprint, polygraph, crime scene, profile, forensic, engineer, chemist, blood typing, jury, expert testi-*

mony, and *court*. No citations on effects of expert testimony were located.) We therefore wanted to answer the question of how much juror decision making was influenced by psychological expert testimony.

Our search identified 22 published studies that compared the effects of some type of psychological expert testimony with a no-expert control on a juror/jury decision (see appendix C). We categorized six different topics of testimony: (a) testimony about parameters of eyewitness accuracy, (b) testimony about insanity defenses, (c) testimony about child witnesses, (d) testimony in criminal litigation involving battered-spouse or rape-trauma syndrome, (e) testimony about the effects of hypnosis on memory, and (f) testimony on other topics (e.g., polygraph evidence, extent of civil damages).

Based on a total of 149 effect sizes, the average effect of expert psychological testimony on jury/juror decisions was $r = .15$ (with a 95% confidence interval of .13–.18). Weighted by the size of the samples, the average effect was $r = .11$. Using each study as the unit for meta-analysis, the average effects was $r = .17$, with a 95% confidence interval of .11–.24. Chi-square tests indicated significant heterogeneity of effects sizes, whether calculated for individual effect sizes, chi-square $(148)=460.7, p < .001$, or for the study as the unit of analysis, chi-square $(21) = 69.3, p < .001$.

As indicated in Table 2.5, the range of average effect sizes across different types of expert testimony was fairly tight; the smallest effect was for insanity testimony ($r = .08$, but only two effect sizes were coded), and the largest was for testimony about battered spouse and rape trauma syndromes and about the evaluation of eyewitness testimony (both $rs = .18$).

What does this meta-analysis say about the influence of psychological expert testimony? First, these results provide little justification for critics who fret that experts will dominate jurors' opinions. Neither do they support the view that psychological experts make no difference and are therefore only an expensive waste of court time.

In order to explore the effects of experts a bit more fully, we coded one additional aspect of their testimony that has been discussed in the literature, using various descriptions—namely, how specific or conclusionary is the expert's assertions about the case at trial. Testimony in which an expert offers an opinion on the ultimate legal issue before the fact finder (e.g., does the defendant's mental state at the time of the offense meet the test of insanity) is sometimes called *ultimate opinion* testimony. What we termed *specific/conclusionary* testimony is exemplified by the expert who, as in Brekke and Borgida (1988), debunks a set of myths about sexual assault and then connects these debunked myths to the actual case under consideration; by contrast, the *general* testimony in Brekke and Borgida (1988) consisted only of the nonspecific myth debunking. Another illustration is

TABLE 2.5. EFFECT SIZE FOR RESEARCH
ON THE RELATIONSHIP BETWEEN EXPERT PSYCHOLOGICAL
TESTIMONY AND JURY DECISION MAKING

Category	Effect size	
Type of subject	*r*	*n*
undergraduate	.17	96
other	.14	44
both	.08	9
Deliberation		
following	.15	79
without	.16	70
Type of dependent variable		
verdict	.15	100
understanding content	.16	39
recall content	.18	1
sentence	.50	1
usefulness	.12	5
award	.15	3
Trial format		
witten	.21	22
videotape	.13	101
audiotape	.21	24
live simulation	.17	2
Type of effect size		
continuous	.16	85
dichotomous	.15	64
Type of expert testimony		
eyewitness	.18	41
insanity	.08	2
child witness	.12	5
battered spouse/rape-trauma testimony	.18	33
other information	.13	53
hypnosis	.15	15
Kind of comparison*		
general vs. no expert	.16	16
specific vs. no expert	.22	16
general vs. specific	.13	24
expert vs. no expert	.15	75
expert vs. expert	.14	18

*When the expert condition was clearly identified as involving general or
nonconclusionary testimony, effect sizes were categorized as "general vs. no
expert." When the expert condition was not clearly identified as to its general
versus specific qualities, effect sizes were categorized as "expert vs. no expert." The expert vs. expert category refers to a collection of effect sizes
involving adversarial vs. nonadversarial expert testimony, testimony followed or not followed by cross-examination, and comparisons of prosecution
(plaintiff) vs. defense experts.

provided by Schuller's (1992) study of battered woman syndrome in which the general expert testified about published research on battered woman syndrome in contrast with the specific/conclusionary expert who added an opinion that the defendant on trial fit the syndrome described by the research. As indicated in Table 2.5, we coded 24 effect sizes for specific/ conclusionary versus general testimony contrasts within the same study. The mean effect size for this contrast was $r = .13$, with stronger effects associated with specific expert testimony. The average of 16 effect sizes for a specific versus no expert contrast was $r = .22$. These results suggest a substantial increase in the impact of expert testimony on juror opinions when that testimony is more specific and/or conclusive about the case at hand. Still, the effect is modest and leaves opportunity for both foes and fans of ultimate opinion testimony to find support for their positions.

4. *To what extent does joinder of criminal charges (as an example of one litigation strategy or procedural variation) affect juror/jury decisions?*

Courts permit criminal defendants to be tried for multiple charges within the same trial when the charged offenses are of the same or similar character, are part of the same transaction, or are connected together as part of scheme or plan (Rule 8, Federal Rules of Criminal Procedure). This procedure is known as joinder. Balanced against joinder's presumed advantages, such as efficiency and protecting defendants against having to prepare for a series of trials, is its biggest disadvantage: possible bias against the multiply charged defendant. Rule 14 of the FRCP provides that if either the prosecution or the defense is prejudiced by joinder, it may move to sever the charges to separate trials.

Bias against defendants facing joined charges may arise from three psychological processes that are typical of active information processors and discussed by Tanford, Penrod, and Collins (1985). (a) a misremembering and/or confusing evidence about the multiple charges, (b) perceiving accumulating evidence against the defendant across the charges, and (c) concluding that a defendant has a criminal disposition because of the multiplicity of the charges.

Our meta-analysis of the joinder literature was designed to answer two questions. First, to what degree does joinder of charges (versus single charge conditions) bias jury verdicts? Second, what are the effects of joinder on two of the primary mechanisms by which bias might be mediated: memory intrusions and more negative evaluations of defendants.

To answer the question about verdicts, we added 2 effect sizes from two studies (Bordens & Horowitz, 1986; Tanford, 1985) to the 10 joinder effect sizes previously reported in Tanford et al.'s (1985) meta-analysis of this same question (see appendix D). As indicated in Table 2.6, the mean effect size for these 12 joinder effects on verdicts was $r = .25$. Because 90%

TABLE 2.6. EFFECT SIZES FOR RESEARCH
ON THE RELATIONSHIP BETWEEN JOINDER
AND JURY DECISION MAKING

Category	Effect Sizes	
	r	n
Type of subject		
Undergraduate	.26	30
other	.26	3
Deliberation		
following	.33	2
without	.25	31
Type of dependent variable		
verdict	.25	12
memory for trial facts	.27	10
ratings of defendant	.25	11
Trail format		
written	.30	9
videotape	.22	11
audiotape	.26	13
Effect size parameter		
continuous	.27	26
dichotomous	.20	7

of these effect sizes involved nondeliberating undergraduates, it was not possible to analyze differential effects of subject and deliberation status.

We also conducted a meta-analysis for the effects of joinder on memory intrusions and attitudes toward the defendant, two possible mediators of bias against defendants facing joined charges. We coded 10 memory intrusion effect sizes, for which the average $r = .27$; we located 11 attitude-toward-defendant effect sizes, for which the average $r = .25$. Small cell sizes within these two categories again precluded further analysis of the moderating influence of methodological features.

Considering all joinder effect sizes ($n = 33$), the average r was .26, with a 95% confidence interval of $r = .18–.34$. Using the individual study as the unit for meta-analysis, the average effect size was $r = .28$. The chi-square test for heterogeneity of joinder effect sizes was nonsignificant, an outcome that appears to be a joint function of a fairly small number of effect sizes that were also very similar in magnitude.

These results clearly indicate that joinder of charges can disadvantage criminal defendants. The narrow variations of jury simulation research on this topic precludes an assessment of how robust the effect might be to different methodologies.

CONCLUSION

Based on the published empirical studies of juries/jurors conducted during the last two decades, what conclusions can we draw about the psychology of the jury? We offer three preliminary observations based on our methodological review and the four substantive areas we meta-analyzed.

1. *The methodology of contemporary jury research is unnecessarily constrained.* The published literature has relied largely on a simulation methodology applied to criminal litigation. This approach has several merits especially from the perspective of jury researchers. It permits replicable, internally valid, factorially designed investigations of theory-driven psycholegal questions. However, if researchers remain too wedded to simulation methods, they are likely to continue to pay one price that has been a continuing disappointment to them over the past 15 years—being judged irrelevant by important legal policy makers, including legislators and appellate courts. It simply remains too easy to dismiss, on the basis of external invalidity, mock jury results that do not fit with judicial preferences.

We encourage the continuation of the trend toward greater method realism in jury research that our review revealed. If psycholegal researchers want to put an end to an ecological invalidity objection constantly trumping their research's implications, they have at least two options. First, they can heed Kurt Lewin's advice about the power of a good theory and show how fundamental psychological processes, well established by basic research that makes no pretense of simulating courtroom conditions, can be applied to juries. Second, they can replace the single methodological pillar of mock jury research with a foundation laid on four coordinated research corners: archival records, observations of and interviews with jurors, ecologically valid experimental simulations, and experimental or quasi-experimental designs employing real juries. A researcher's claims that rest on this base will not be as easily toppled as those perched on a single column.

The psycholegal researchers' preoccupation with criminal litigation has exacted an additional cost. it has prevented them from mining the richer materials that civil trials can routinely yield—attributions about differential responsibility among multiple actors; judgments about the nature of causation from multiple sources; more differentiated dependent measures in terms of fault-finding, compensatory awards and punitive damages; and more elaborate tests of information-processing abilities required in complex civil trials.

2. *The view of jurors that emerges from the recent empirical literature is that not only do they strive to be conscientious decision makers, they can succeed*

in being competent ones despite the mistaken assumptions often made about them by the courts. We find support for this view in prior integrative summaries (e.g., Hans & Vidmar, 1986) and in our present meta-analyses, as shown by these findings:

- The death qualification literature suggests that jurors are reasonably successful in not letting their beliefs about the highly emotional topic of capital punishment dictate their decisions about the guilt of capital defendants. Whether *any* amount of spillover from death penalty attitude to guilt and innocence verdict is acceptable is a more difficult social policy question.
- Research on judicial instructions indicates that when instructions are not psychologically well crafted, they are minimally effective. When admonitions or directives from a judge are worded and delivered in ways designed to increase their effects, jurors are, to some degree, better informed, guided, and even constrained by these instructions.
- Jurors appear to give a balanced consideration to expert testimony. Their decisions are not dictated by experts, neither are they immune to experts' opinions, especially when these opinions are expressed in case-specific language or include clear conclusionary statements.

3. *As Diamond and Caspar (1992) observed, recent jury research has revealed that jurors are active interpreters of trial information rather than passive recipients of evidence.* This evidence comes from many sources, including Pennington and Hastie's (1986, 1988) private story model of decision making, Wrightsman and colleagues' (e.g., Pyszczynski & Wrightsman, 1981) research on the power of opening statements, and even our own meta-analysis of joinder, which can be interpreted as revealing that jurors' nearly irresistible tendency to fit evidence into a coherent overall narrative can bias verdicts against defendants in trials joined to facilitate summation of evidence.

To the extent that the law assumes or encourages a passive participant role for jurors, it will also find fault with their performance, question whether the lay jury is able to decide complex litigation matters, and advocate using alternative fact finders in such litigation (for a review, see Johnson & Wiggins, 1994). The law's mistrust of juries may largely result from the law not taking jurors seriously enough, not giving them sufficient help to overcome some well-known limits on human information-processing abilities, and not realizing that most of these limits apply to experts (i.e., judges) just as strongly as to lay fact finders. When the law operates with naive assumptions or incorrect understanding of juror psychology and then insists on litigation conditions that institutionalize these assumptions, jurors will be handicapped in their performance, just as Munsterberg warned almost a century ago.

REFERENCES

Adler, S. J. (1994). *The jury: Trial and error in the American courtroom.* New York: Times Books.

Bordens, K. S., & Horowitz, I. A. (1986). Prejudicial joinder of multiple offenses: Relative effects of cognitive processing and criminal schema. *Basic and Applied Social Psychology, 7,* 243–258.

Brekke, N., & Borgida, E. (1988). Expert psychological testimony in rape trials: A social-cognitive analysis. *Journal of Personality and Social Psychology, 55,* 372–386.

Cox, M., & Tanford, S. (1989). An alternative method of capital jury selection. *Law and Human Behavior, 13,* 167–184.

Daubert v. Merrell Dow Pharmaceuticals, 113 S. Ct. 2786 (1993).

Davis, J. (1989). Psychology and law: The last 15 years. *Journal of Applied Social Psychology, 19,* 199–230.

Davis, J., Bray, R., & Holt, R. (1977). The empirical study of decision process in juries: A critical review. In J. Tapp & F. Levine (Eds.), *Law, justice and the individual in society* (pp. 326–362). New York: Holt, Rinehart, & Winston.

Diamond, S. S., & Caspar, J. D. (1992). Blindfolding the jury to verdict consequences: Damages, experts, and the civil jury. *Law and Society Review, 26,* 513–563.

Dillehay, R. C., & Nietzel, M. T. (1980). Conceptualizing mock jury/juror research: Critique and illustrations. In K. S. Larsen (Ed.), *Social psychology: Crisis or failure.* Monmouth, OR: Institute for Theoretical History.

Elliot, R. (1991). Social science data and the APA: The *Lockhart* brief as a case in point. *Law and Human Behavior, 15,* 59–76.

Ellsworth, P. C. (1991). To tell what we know or wait for Godot? *Law and Human Behavior, 15,* 77–90.

Finch, M., & Ferraro, M. (1986). The empirical challenge to death qualified juries: On further examination. *Nebraska Law Review, 65,* 21–74.

Frye v. United States, 293 F. 1013, 34 A.L.R. 145 (C.D. Cir. 1923).

Gacy v. Welborn, 994 F. 2d 305 (7th Cir. 1993).

Gerbasi, K. C., Zuckerman, M., & Reis, H. T. (1977). Justice needs a new blindfold: A review of mock jury research. *Psychological Bulletin, 84,* 323–345.

Geyelin, M. (1994, July 12). Legal beat. *The Wall Street Journal,* p. B2.

Haney, C. (1984). On the selection of capital juries: The biasing effects of the death qualification process. *Law and Human Behavior, 8,* 121–132.

Hans, V. P., & Vidmar, N. (1986). *Judging the jury.* New York: Plenum Press.

Heuer, L., & Penrod, S. (1994). Juror notetaking and question asking during trials: A national field experiment. *Law and Human Behavior, 18,* 121–150.

Hunter, J. E., & Schmidt, F. L. (1990). Dichotomization of continuous variables: The implications for meta-analysis. *Journal of Applied Psychology, 75,* 334–349.

Johnson, M., & Wiggins, E. C. (1994). Drawing on the experiences of alternative decision makers: Can we preserve the jury in complex civil litigation? *Behavioral Sciences and the Law, 12,* 161–179.

Konecni, V. J., & Ebbesen, E. B. (1979). External validity of research in legal psychology. *Law and Human Behavior, 3,* 39–70.

Lipsey, M. W., & Wilson, D. B. (1993). The efficacy of psychological, educational, and behavioral treatment: Confirmation from meta-analysis. *American Psychologist, 48,* 1181–1209.

Lockhart v. McCree, 106 S. Ct. 1758 (1986).

Loh, W. D. (1984). *Social research in the judicial process.* New York: Russell Sage Foundation.

Mauro, R. (1991). Tipping the scales toward death: The biasing effects of death qualification. In P. Suedfeld & P. Tetlock (Eds.), *Psychology and social policy* (pp. 243–254). New York: Hemisphere Press.

McCloskey, M., & Egeth, H. E. (1983). Eyewitness identification: What can a psychologist tell a jury? *American Psychologist, 38,* 550–563.

Monahan, J., & Loftus, E. (1982). The psychology of law. *Annual Review of Psychology, 33,* 441–475.

Morse, S. J. (1978). Law and mental health professionals: The limits of expertise. *Professional Psychology, 9,* 389–399.

Munsterberg, H. (1908). *On the witness stand: Essays on psychology and crime.* New York: Clark Boardman.

Neises, M. L., & Dillehay, R. C. (1987). Death qualification and conviction proneness: *Witt* and *Witherspoon* compared. *Behavioral Sciences and the Law, 5,* 479–494.

Nietzel, M. T., Dillehay, R. C., & Himelein, M. J. (1987). Effects of voir dire variations in capital trials: A replication and extension. *Behavioral Sciences and the Law, 5,* 467–477.

Pennington, N., & Hastie, R. (1986). Evidence evaluation in complex decision making. *Journal of Personality and Social Psychology, 51,* 242–258.

Pennington, N., & Hastie, R. (1988). Explanation-based decision making: Effects of memory structure on judgment. *Journal of Experimental Psychology: Learning Memory and Cognition, 14,* 521–533.

Penrod, S., & Hastie, R. (1979). Models of jury decision making: A critical review. *Psychological Bulletin, 86,* 462–492.

Pyszczynski, T., & Wrightsman, L. (1981). The effects of opening statements on mock jurors' verdicts in a simulated criminal trial. *Journal of Applied Social Psychology, 11,* 301–313.

Rosenthal, R. (1992). Effect size estimation, significance testing, and the file-drawer problem. *Journal of Parapsychology, 56,* 57–58.

Rosenthal, R. (1994). *Meta-analytic procedures for social research.* Newbury Park, CA: Sage.

Rosenthal, R., & Rubin, D. B. (1982). A simple, general purpose display of magnitude of experimental effect. *Journal of Educational Psychology, 74,* 166–169.

Saks, M. J., & Hastie, R. (1978). *Social psychology in court.* New York: Van Nostrand Reinhold.

Saks, M. J., & Wissler, R. L. (1984). Legal and psychological bases of expert testimony: Surveys of the law and of jurors. *Behavioral Sciences and the Law, 449.*

Schuller, R. A. (1992). The impact of battered woman syndrome on jury decision processes. *Law and Human Behavior, 16,* 597–620.

Shuman, D. W., Whitaker, E., & Champagne, A. (1994). An empirical examination of the use of expert witnesses in the courts: Part II. A three city study. *Jurimetrics Journal,* 193–208.

Snedecor, G. W., & Cochran, W. G. (1989). *Statistical methods* (8th ed.). Ames: Iowa State University Press.

Tanford, J. A. (1991). Law reforms by courts, legislatures, and commissions following empirical research on jury instructions. *Law and Society Review, 25,* 155–176.

Tanford, S. (1985). Decision-making processes in joined criminal trials. *Criminal Justice and Behavior, 12,* 367–385.

Tanford, S., Penrod, S., & Collins, R. (1985). Decision making in joined criminal trials: The influence of charge similarity, evidence similarity, and limiting instructions. *Law and Human Behavior, 9,* 319–337.

Tapp, J. L. (1976). Psychology and the law: An overture. *Annual Review of Psychology, 27,* 359–404.

Vidmar, N. (1994). Making inferences about jury behavior from jury verdict statistics: Cautions about the Lorelei's Lied. *Law and Human Behavior, 18*, 599–617.
Wainwright v. Witt, 105 S. Ct. 884 (1985).
Witherspoon v. Illinois, 391 U.S. 510, 88 S. Ct. 1770, 20 L. Ed. 2d 776 (1968).
Wrightsman, L. S. (1978). The American trial jury on trial: Empirical evidence and procedural modifications. *Journal of Social Issues, 34*, 137–164.

APPENDIX A: DEATH QUALIFICATION REFERENCES

Bernard, J. L., & Dwyer, W. O. (1984). Witherspoon v. Illinois: The court was right. *Law and Psychology Review, 8*, 105–114.
Bronson, L. (1970). On the conviction proneness and the representativeness of the death qualified jury: An empirical study of Colorado veniremen. *Colorado Law Review, 42*, 1–32.
Cowan, C. L., Thompson, W. C., & Ellsworth, P. C. (1984). The effects of death qualification on jurors' predisposition to convict and on the quality of deliberation. *Law and Human Behavior, 8*, 53–79.
Cox, M., & Tanford, S. (1989). An alternative method of jury selection. *Law and Human Behavior, 13*, 167–183.
Cullen, F. T., Clark, G. A., Cullen, J. B., & Mathers, R. A. (1985). Attribution, salience and attitudes towards criminal sanctioning. *Criminal Justice and Behavior, 12*, 305–331.
Elliot, R., & Robinson, R. J. (1991). Death penalty attitudes and the tendency to acquit or convict: Some data. *Law and Human Behavior, 15*, 389–404.
Ellsworth, P. C., Bukaty, R. M., Cowan, C. L., & Thompson, W. C. (1984). The death qualified jury and the defense of insanity. *Law and Human Behavior, 8*, 81–93.
Ellsworth, P. C., & Ross, L. (1983). Public opinion and capital punishment: A close examination of the views of abolitionists and retentionists. *Crime and Delinquency, 29*, 116–169.
Fitzgerald, R., & Ellsworth, P. C. (1984). Due process versus crime control: Death qualification and jury attitudes. *Law and Human Behavior, 8*, 31–51.
Goldberg, F. (1970). Towards expansion of Witherspoon: Capital scruples, jury bias and the use of psychological presumptions in the law. *Harvard Civil Rights Law Journal, 5*, 53.
Haney, C. (1984). On the selection of capital juries: The biasing effects of the death qualification process. *Law and Human Behavior, 8*, 121–132.
Haney, C., Hurtado, A., & Vega, L. (1994). "Modern" death qualification: New data on its biasing effects. *Law and Human Behavior, 18*, 619–634.
Harris, L., & Associates. (1971). Study number 2016. In W. White, The constitutional invalidity of convictions imposed by death qualified juries. *Cornell Law Review, 58*, 1176–1220.
Horowitz, I. A., & Seguin, D. G. (1986). The effects of bifurcation and death qualification on assignment of penalty in capital crimes. *Journal of Applied Social Psychology, 16*, 165–185.
Jurow, G. (1971). New data on the effect of a death qualified jury on the guilt determination process. *Harvard Law Review, 84*, 567–611.
Luginbuhl, J., & Middendorf, K. (1988). Death penalty beliefs and juror's responses to aggravating and mitigating circumstances in capital trials. *Law and Human Behavior, 12*, 263–281.
Moran, G., & Comfort, J. C. (1986). Neither "tentative" nor "fragmentary": Verdict preference of impaneled felony jurors as a function of attitude towards capital punishment. *Journal of Applied Psychology, 71*, 146–155.
Neapolitan, J. (1983). Support for and opposition to capital punishment: Some associated social psychological factors. *Criminal Justice and Behavior, 10*, 195–208.

Neises, M. L., & Dillehay, R. C. (1987). Death qualification and conviction proneness: Witt and Witherspoon compared. *Behavioral Sciences and the Law, 5,* 479–494.

Nietzel, M. T., Dillehay, R. C., & Himelein, M. J. (1987). Effects of voir dire variations in capital trials: A replication and extension. *Behavioral Sciences and the Law, 5,* 467–477.

Rokeach, M., & McClellan, D. D. (1969). Dogmatism and the death penalty: A reinterpretation of the Duquesne Poll data. *Duquesne Law Review, 8,* 125–135.

Thompson, W. C., Cowan, C. L., Ellsworth, P. C., & Harrington, J. D. (1984). Death penalty attitudes and conviction proneness. *Law and Human Behavior, 8,* 95–113.

Zeisel, H. (1968). *Some data on juror attitudes towards capital punishment.* Monograph. Center for Studies in Criminal Justice, University of Chicago Law School.

APPENDIX B: INSTRUCTIONS REFERENCES

DEFINITIONAL INSTRUCTIONS

Cornish, W. R., & Sealy, A. P. (1973). Juries and the rules of evidence. *Criminal Law Review, 29,* 209–223.

Cruse, D., & Browne, B. A. (1987). Reasoning in a jury trial: The influence of instructions. *The Journal of General Psychology, 114,* 129–133.

Elwork, A., Sales, B. D., & Alfini, J. J. (1977). Juridic decisions: In ignorance of the law or in light of it? *Law and Human Behavior, 1,* 163–189.

Hegelson, V. S., & Shaver, K. G. (1990). Presumption of innocence: Congruence bias induced and overcome. *Journal of Applied Social Psychology, 20,* 276–302.

Heuer, L., & Penrod, S. D. (1989). Instructing jurors: A field experiment with written and preliminary instructions. *Law and Human Behavior, 13,* 409–430.

Kassin, S. M., & Wrightsman, L. S. (1979). On the requirements of proof: The timing of judicial instruction and mock juror verdicts. *Journal of Personality and Social Psychology, 37,* 1877–1887.

Luginbuhl, J. (1992). Comprehension of judges' instructions in the penalty phase of a capital trial. *Law and Human Behavior, 16,* 203–218.

Pfeifer, J. E., & Ogloff, J. R. (1991). Ambiguity and guilt determinations: A modern racism perspective. *Journal of Applied Social Psychology, 21,* 1713–1725.

Prager, I. G., Deckelbaum, G., & Cutler, B. L. (1989). Improving juror understanding from intervening causation instructions. *Forensic Reports, 3,* 187–193.

Reed, R. (1980). Jury simulation: The impact of judge's instructions and attorney tactics on decision making. *Journal of Criminal Law and Criminology, 71,* 68–72.

Reifman, A., Gusick, S. M., & Ellsworth, P. C. (1992). Real jurors' understanding of the law in real cases. *Law and Human Behavior, 16,* 539–554.

Severance, L. J., Greene, E., & Loftus, E. F. (1984). Toward criminal jury instructions that jurors can understand. *Journal of Criminal Law and Criminology, 75,* 198–233.

Severance, L. J., & Loftus, E. F. (1982). Improving the ability of jurors to comprehend and apply criminal jury instructions. *Law and Society Review, 17,* 172–196.

Smith, V. L. (1993). When prior knowledge and the law collide. *Law and Human Behavior, 17,* 507–536.

Smith, V. L. (1991). Impact of pretrial instruction on jurors' information processing and decision making. *Journal of Applied Psychology, 76,* 220–228.

Smith, V. L. (1991). Prototypes in the courtroom: Lay representations of legal concepts. *Journal of Personality and Social Psychology, 61,* 857–872.

Weiten, W. (1980). The attraction-leniency effect in jury research: An examination of external validity. *Journal of Applied Social Psychology, 10,* 340–347.

PRETRIAL PUBLICITY INSTRUCTIONS

Kramer, G. P., Kerr, N. L., & Carroll, J. S. (1990). Pretrial publicity, judicial remedies, and jury bias. *Law and Human Behavior, 14,* 409–438.
Sue, S., Smith, R. E., & Gilbert, R. (1974). Biasing effects of pretrial publicity on judicial decisions. *Journal of Criminal Justice, 2,* 163–171.

NULLIFICATION INSTRUCTIONS

Hill, E. L., & Pfeifer, J. E. (1992). Nullification instructions and juror guilt ratings: An examination of modern racism. *Contemporary Social Psychology, 16,* 6–10.
Horowitz, I. A. (1985). The effect of jury nullification instruction on verdicts and jury functioning in criminal trials. *Law and Human Behavior, 9,* 25-36.
Horowitz, I. A. (1988). Jury nullification: The impact of judicial instructions, arguments, and challenges on jury decision making. *Law and Human Behavior, 12,* 403–438.
Kerwin, J., & Shaffer, D. (1991). The effects of jury dogmatism on reactions to jury nullification instructions. *Personality and Social Psychology Bulletin, 17,* 140–146.

DISREGARD OR LIMITED USE OF EVIDENCE INSTRUCTIONS

Carretta, T. R., & Moreland, R. L. (1983). The direct and indirect effects of inadmissible evidence. *Journal of Applied Social Psychology, 13,* 291–309.
Cavoukian, A., & Heslegrave, R. J. (1980). The admissibility of polygraph evidence in court: Some empirical findings. *Law and Human Behavior, 4,* 117–132.
Doob, A. N., & Kirshenbaum, H. M. (1972). Some empirical evidence on the effects of s.12 of the Canada Evidence Act upon the accused. *Criminal Law Quarterly, 14,* 88–96.
Harris, R. J. (1978). The effect of jury size and judge's instructions on memory for pragmatic implications from courtroom testimony. *Bulletin of the Psychonomic Society, 11,* 129–132.
Kerwin, J., & Shaffer, D. R. (1994). Mock jurors versus mock juries: The role of deliberations in reactions to inadmissible testimony. *Personality and Social Psychology Bulletin, 20,* 153–162.
Lenehan, G. E., & O'Neill, P. (1981). Reactance and conflict as determinants of judgment in a mock jury experiment. *Journal of Applied Social Psychology, 11,* 231–239.
Sue, S., Smith, R. E., & Caldwell, C. (1973). Effects of inadmissible evidence on the decisions of simulated jurors: A moral dilemma. *Journal of Applied Social Psychology, 3,* 345–353.
Tanford, S., & Cox, M. (1987). Decision processes in civil cases: The impact of impeachment evidence on liability and credibility judgments. *Social Behavior, 2,* 165–182.
Tanford, S., & Cox, M. (1988). The effects of impeachment evidence and limiting instructions on individual and group decision making. *Law and Human Behavior, 12,* 477–498.
Thompson, W. C., Fong, G. T., & Rosenhan, D. L. (1981). Inadmissible evidence and juror verdicts. *Journal of Personality and Social Psychology, 40,* 453–463.
Werner, C. M., Kagehiro, D. K., & Strube, M. J. (1982). Conviction proneness and the authoritarian juror: Inability to disregard information or attitudinal bias? *Journal of Applied Psychology, 67,* 629–636.

Wolf, S., & Montgomery, D. A. (1977). Effects of inadmissible evidence and level of judicial admonishment to disregard on the judgments of mock jurors. *Journal of Applied Social Psychology, 7,* 205–219.

EYEWITNESS TESTIMONY INSTRUCTIONS

Cutler, E. L., Dexter, H. R., & Penrod, S. D. (1990). Nonadversarial methods for sensitizing jurors to eyewitness evidence. *Journal of Applied Social Psychology, 20,* 1197–1207.
Greene, E. (1988). Judge's instruction on eyewitness testimony: Evaluation and revision. *Journal of Applied Social Psychology, 18,* 252–276.
Hoffheimer, M. H. (1982). Effect of particularized instructions on evaluation of eyewitness identification evidence. *Law and Psychology Review, 13,* 43–58.
Katzev, R. D., & Wishart, S. S. (1985). The impact of judicial commentary concerning eyewitness identifications on jury decision making. *Journal of Criminal Law and Criminology, 76,* 733–745.
Kennedy, T. D., & Haygood, R. C. (1992). The discrediting effect in eyewitness testimony. *Journal of Applied Social Psychology, 22,* 70–82.

JOINDER OF OFFENSES INSTRUCTIONS

Greene, E., & Loftus, E. F. (1985). When crimes are joined at trial. *Law and Human Behavior, 9,* 193–207.
Tanford, S. (1985). Decision-making processes in joined criminal trials. *Criminal Justice and Behavior, 12,* 367–385. (Data also found in Tanford and Penrod, 1984, *Journal of Personality and Social Psychology.*)
Tanford, S., Penrod, S., & Collins, R. (1985). Decision making in joined criminal trials: The influence of charge similarity, evidence similarity, and limiting instructions. *Law and Human Behavior, 9,* 319–337.

CONFESSION EVIDENCE

Kassin, S. M., & Wrightsman, L. S. (1981). Coerced confessions, judicial instructions and mock juror verdicts. *Journal of Applied Social Psychology, 11,* 489–506.

MISCELLANEOUS

Archer, R. L., Foushee, H. C., & Davis, M. H. (1979). Emotional empathy in a courtroom simulation: A person-situation interaction. *Journal of Applied Social Psychology, 9,* 275–291.
Greenwald, J. P., Tomkins, A. J., Kenning, M., & Zavodny, D. (1990). Psychological self-defense jury instructions: Influence on verdicts for battered women defendants. *Behavioral Sciences and the Law, 8,* 171–180.
Kassin, S. M., Smith, V. L., & Tulloch, W. F. (1990). The dynamite charge: Effects on the perceptions and deliberation behavior of mock jurors. *Law and Human Behavior, 14,* 523–536.
Smith, V. L., & Kassin, S. M. (1993). The effects of the dynamite charge on the deliberations of deadlocked mock juries. *Law and Human Behavior, 17,* 625–644.

APPENDIX C: EXPERT TESTIMONY REFERENCES

EYEWITNESS RELIABILITY

Blonstein, R., & Geiselman, E. (1990). Effects of witnessing conditions and expert witness testimony on creditability of an expert witness. *American Journal of Forensic Psychology, 8,* 11–19.

Cutler, B. L., Dexter, H. R., & Penrod, S. D. (1989). Expert testimony and jury decision making: An empirical analysis. *Behavioral Sciences and the Law, 7,* 215–225.

Cutler, B. L., Dexter, H. R., & Penrod, S. D. (1990). Nonadversarial methods for sensitizing jurors to eyewitness evidence. *Journal of Applied Social Psychology, 20,* 1197–1207.

Cutler, B. L., Penrod, S. D., & Dexter, H. R. (1989). The eyewitness, the expert psychologist and the jury. *Law and Human Behavior, 13,* 311–332.

Fox, S. G., & Walters, H. A. (1986). The impact of general versus specific expert testimony and eyewitness confidence upon mock juror judgment. *Law and Human Behavior, 10,* 215–228.

Hosch, H. M., Beck, E. L., & McIntyre, P. (1980). Influence of expert testimony regarding eyewitness accuracy on jury decisions. *Law and Human Behavior, 4,* 287–296.

Loftus, E. F. (1980). Impact of expert psychological testimony on the unreliability of eyewitness identification. *Journal of Applied Psychology, 65,* 9–15.

Maas, A., Brigham, J. C., & West, S. G. (1985). Testifying on eyewitness reliability: Expert advice is not always persuasive. *Journal of Applied Social Psychology, 15,* 207–229.

McCloskey, M., & Egeth, H. E. (1983). Eyewitness identification: What can a psychologist tell a jury? *American Psychologist, 38,* 550–563.

Wells, G. L., Lindsay, R. C. L., & Tousignant, J. P. (1980). Effect of expert psychological advice on human performance in judging the validity of eyewitness testimony. *Law and Human Behavior, 4,* 275–286.

CHILD TESTIMONY

Crowley, M. J., O'Callaghan, M. G., & Ball, P. J. (1994). The juridical impact of psychological expert testimony in a simulated child sexual abuse trial. *Law and Human Behavior, 18,* 89–104.

Gabora, N. J., Spanos, N. P., & Joab, A. (1993). The effects of complainant age and expert psychological testimony in a simulated child sexual abuse trial. *Law and Human Behavior, 17,* 103–120.

INSANITY DEFENSE

Fulero, S. M., & Finkel, N. J. (1991). Barring ultimate issue testimony: An "insane" rule? *Law and Human Behavior, 15,* 495–507.

OTHER CRIMINAL TOPICS

Brekke, N., & Borgida, E. (1988). Expert psychological testimony in rape trials: A social-cognitive analysis. *Journal of Personality and Social Psychology, 55,* 372–386.

Kasian, M., Spanos, N. P., Terrance, C. A., & Peebles, S. (1993). Battered women who kill: Jury simulation and legal defenses. *Law and Human Behavior, 17,* 289–312.

Kovera, M. B., Levy, R. J., Borgida, E., & Penrod, S. (1994). Expert testimony in child sexual abuse cases: Effects of expert evidence type and cross-examination. *Law and Human Behavior, 18,* 653–674.

Schuller, R. A. (1992). The impact of battered woman syndrome evidence on jury decision processes. *Law and Human Behavior, 16,* 597–620.

Spanos, N. P., Dubreuil, S. C., & Gwynn, M. I. (1991–92). The effects of expert testimony concerning rape on the verdicts and beliefs of mock jurors. *Imagination, Cognition, and Personality, 11,* 37–51.

OTHER INFORMATION

Brekke, N. J., Enko, P. J., Clavet, G., & Seelau, E. (1991). Of juries and court appointed experts: The impact of nonadversarial versus adversarial expert testimony. *Law and Human Behavior, 15,* 451–476.

Raitz, A., Greene, E., Goodman, J., & Loftus, E. F. (1990). Determining damages: The influence of expert testimony on jurors' decision making. *Law and Human Behavior, 14,* 385–396.

HYPNOSIS

Diamond, S. S., & Caspar, J. D. (1992). Blindfolding the jury to verdict consequences: Damages, experts and the civil jury. *Law and Society Review, 26,* 513–563.

Spanos, N. P., Gwynn, M. I., & Terrade, K. (1989). Effects on mock jurors of experts favorable and unfavorable toward hypnotically elicited eyewitness testimony. *Journal of Applied Psychology, 74,* 922–926.

APPENDIX D: JOINDER REFERENCES

Bordens, K. S., & Horowitz, I. A. (1983). Information processing in joined and severed trials. *Journal of Applied Social Psychology, 13,* 351–370.

Bordens, K. S., & Horowitz, I. A. (1986). Prejudicial joinder of multiple offenses: Relative effects of cognitive processing and criminal schema. *Basic and Applied Social Psychology, 7,* 243–258.

Greene, E., & Loftus, E. F. (1985). When crimes are joined at trial. *Law and Human Behavior, 9,* 193–208.

Horowitz, I. A., Bordens, K. S., & Feldman, M. S. (1980). A comparison of verdicts obtained in severed and joined criminal trials. *Journal of Applied Social Psychology, 10,* 444–456.

Tanford, S. (1985). Decision-making processes in joined criminal trials. *Criminal Justice and Behavior, 12,* 367–385.

Tanford, S., & Penrod, S. (1982). Biases in trials involving defendants charged with multiple offenses. *Journal of Applied Social Psychology, 12,* 453–480.

Tanford, S., Penrod, S., & Collins, R. (1985). Decision making in joined criminal trials: The influence of charge similarity, evidence similarity, and limiting instructions. *Law and Human Behavior, 9,* 319–337.

3

Witnesses to Crime

Social and Cognitive Factors Governing the Validity
of People's Reports

GARY L. WELLS, EDWARD F. WRIGHT,
AND AMY L. BRADFIELD

A criminal trial involves people who take the stand and recount events that they witnessed firsthand. The purpose of their testimony is to aid the triers of fact in making determinations about a critical past event, which in turn, allows the judge and/or jury to render a verdict based on these facts. Almost all witness testimony takes the form of a recounting or retelling of some prior event as observed by the witness.[1] A police officer who describes when and where she found a bloody glove, a bystander who says he heard three shots, an eyewitness who describes the assailant, or a friend of the accused who recalls a conversation are all recounting prior events that they witnessed.

The accuracy of people's recountings of witnessed events is essential to criminal justice. Inaccurate tellings can lead to incorrect verdicts; accurate tellings are usually needed to reach correct verdicts. The relation

---

[1]Exceptions include expert witnesses who might be giving opinion testimony regarding, for example, some aspect of the evidence or the accused's state of mind.

GARY L. WELLS AND AMY L. BRADFIELD • Department of Psychology, Iowa State University, Ames, Iowa 50011.   EDWARD F. WRIGHT • Department of Psychology, St. Francis Xavier University, Antigonish, Nova Scotia, B2G 2W5, Canada.

Psychology and Law: The State of the Discipline, edited by Ronald Roesch, Stephen D. Hart, and James R. P. Ogloff. Kluwer Academic/Plenum Publishers, New York, 1999.

between witness accuracy and verdict correctness is not a one-to-one relation, of course, because incorrect verdicts can be reached even when testimony is accurate and correct verdicts can occur in spite of inaccurate testimony. Nevertheless, a system of justice that is not sensitive to maximizing the accuracy of witnesses' testimony is a system that risks false verdicts and undermines a cornerstone of the justice system, the public's faith in it.

There are two broad categories that can be said to affect the accuracy of witness testimony. There is prevaricating or "lying" on the one hand, and an honest mistake or "unintentional error" on the other. The justice system is constantly on guard against lying, as evidenced by the truth oath that witnesses give prior to taking the witness stand and the severe penalties for perjury. This chapter is concerned only with the second broad category, namely, unintentional errors. It reviews the current state of our knowledge of the social and cognitive factors governing unintentional errors in witness testimony. Although the scientific study of human memory has been going on for more than 100 years and some researchers directed their work at eyewitness reliability issues early in this century (see Wells & Loftus, 1984a), the empirical work and theory described in this chapter have been generated primarily within the last 15–20 years.

ORGANIZING THEMES

Much of the empirical literature relating to the accuracy of witness testimony tends to have a specific focus on a narrowly defined question or hypothesis rather than a broad view of factors relating to the accuracy issue. A given study, for example, might focus specifically on the question of whether a person's ability to identify a face is impaired by later viewing of other faces, or whether repeated questioning of witnesses leads them to have inflated confidence in their answers. It is not our intent to list all of these hypotheses and describe the results of a large number of seemingly unrelated variables from what is now a voluminous literature. Space does not permit this approach, and we do not think that it would be useful at this time. In some ways, our task in this chapter is somewhat more daunting: to single out what we think are key findings, critical issues, and overarching conclusions based on our understanding of the empirical and theoretical literature on witnesses to crime.

As a way of organizing this chapter, we have divided the literature into two general domains of inquiry. First, we discuss the traditional experimental literature on eyewitness testimony, which primarily uses experimentally manufactured events and draws on social and cognitive levels of explanation to identify causes of accurate and inaccurate testimony. Then, we discuss the emerging literature on adult recovery of repressed memories from childhood.

This chapter complements the chapter by Penrod and Cutler (Chapter 4, this volume) in which they review evidence regarding safeguards against mistaken convictions in eyewitness identification trials. These safeguards include cross examination, motions to suppress the identification evidence, juror's common knowledge about memory processes, and expert testimony on eyewitness identification issues.[2] Our emphasis, however, is somewhat different. While Penrod and Cutler focus primarily on the issue of whether current legal safeguards are effective against mistaken convictions based on faulty eyewitness accounts, our emphasis is on the issue of how these faulty eyewitness accounts come about in the first place and how to prevent their occurrence.

Our discussion of the literature is guided in large part by a distinction between system variables and estimator variables (Wells, 1978). *System variables* are those that affect the accuracy of witness testimony over which the justice system has (or could have) some control. *Estimator variables* are also related to witness accuracy, but the justice system has no control over estimator variables. The amount of attention that a witness paid to the witnessed event, for instance, might be important for estimating the likely accuracy of the witness, but the justice system cannot exert control over such a variable and, hence, it is not a system variable. How a question is asked by a police investigator, on the other hand, might have considerable impact on the accuracy of the answer, and because the form of the question is (or could be) controlled by the justice system, this would be a system variable. Our treatment of the empirical and theoretical literature is admittedly biased toward an emphasis on system variables. Our bias stems from a belief that much of the problem with the accuracy of witness testimony owes to the methods that the system uses to obtain the information from these witnesses. This emphasis on system variables facilitates our ability to articulate concrete recommendations for improving the accuracy of witness testimony. We end the chapter with what we think are useful, general conclusions about how to improve and assess the accuracy of witness testimony.

---

[2] It is noteworthy, we think, that current legal safeguards are restricted to the *detection* of mistaken identification rather than the *prevention* of mistaken identification. Most of the practical advances in eyewitness identification research, on the other hand, have been in the area of prevention of false eyewitness identifications rather than its detection (Wells, 1993).

MEMORY AS ONE COMPONENT OF TESTIMONY

Some readers might notice that we have avoided using the word *memory* as one that can be interchanged with *testimony*. We prefer to use terms such as *accounts* or *reports* rather than *memories* or *recall*. This is because we think it is useful to maintain a clear distinction between memory, as traditionally construed, and what witnesses report. We define memory as the mental trace of a previously experienced event. As such, we do not think that memory processes per se encompass all of what governs witnesses' reports of some prior event. In part, this distinction between memory and testimony depends on what theory of memory one chooses to endorse. Consider, for instance, the way in which misleading questions influence subsequent reports of a prior event. Some theorists contend that the misleading question serves to alter the person's original memory trace (e.g., a blue briefcase is transformed in memory to a black briefcase, or a stop sign is replaced in memory with a yield sign; see Loftus & Palmer, 1974). Other theorists contend that a misleading question does not affect the original memory trace but instead operates through one of several other processes (such as demand characteristics or creation of a second memory) to bias the report toward the misleading information (e.g., McCloskey & Zaragoza, 1985). We take no particular position on questions of this type. We do contend, however, that variables can affect the accuracy of witnesses' accounts of prior events regardless of whether or not the original memory trace is altered. Hence, for our purposes, we construe memory as a component of testimony or an element that places some constraints on a witness's testimony, but we do not believe that testimony and memory are the same thing.

By way of example, consider the eyewitnesses who says that he or she is absolutely certain that the accused is the person he or she saw robbing a store clerk. Contrast this with an eyewitness who says that he or she thinks that the accused might be the person who robbed the store clerk, but can't be sure. The testimony given by these two witnesses is quite different in a qualitative way and in a way that has consequences for the accused. The differences in the testimony of the two witnesses, however, might have little or nothing to do with their memories. The memory traces for both witnesses might be identical (equally clear or fuzzy), but the confident witness might have learned that the accused has a prior record for offenses of this type or might have been told of fingerprints traced to the accused, while the unconfident witness might not know these things. One could argue, of course, that the prior record or fingerprint information changed the witness's memory trace, but we don't think that changes in memory are required to produce this type of change in testimony.

EYEWITNESS ACCOUNTS

The bulk of the scientific eyewitness literature has used events created by the researchers, which allows them to control the precise details of the event and gives them the ability to score eyewitnesses' reports for accuracy and completeness. A smaller but growing part of the literature has used eyewitnesses to actual crimes and conducted various analyses of the eyewitnesses' reports. Particularly growing in importance and number are the cases in the U.S. (in the 1990s) in which people who were convicted of crimes prior to 1990 (prior to forensic DNA testing) have had their evidence analyzed using forensic DNA techniques. As of March, 1994, 40 people who had been convicted by juries of serious crimes (some of whom were sentenced to death) had been freed based on DNA analyses showing that they were not the perpetrators of the crimes for which they had been convicted (Wells et al., 1998). Importantly, in 36 of these 40 cases eyewitness identification testimony from confident but mistaken eyewitnesses was the primary evidence that led to their convictions.

The DNA cases are useful in showing that mistaken identification by eyewitnesses is probably the largest single cause of the conviction of innocent persons. Nevertheless, it is the controlled experiments that have been the backbone of eyewitness scientists' knowledge about the factors governing eyewitness identification evidence. The literature that has emerged from this type of work is voluminous and spread throughout a wide variety of scientific psychology journals. Readers are referred to several scholarly books that have reported original research and have summarized portions of the literature that have appeared in the scientific journals (Ceci, Toglia, & Ross, 1987; Clifford & Bull, 1978; Cutler & Penrod, 1995; Dent & Flin, 1992; Doris, 1991; Lloyd-Bostock & Clifford, 1983; Loftus, 1979; Ross, Read, & Toglia, 1994; Shepherd, Ellis, & Davies, 1982; Wells, 1988; Wells & Loftus, 1984b; Yarmey, 1979).

There are various ways to describe the nature of this work. In general, it can be noted that the research falls into two broad categories. First, there is research directed at the question of what variables influence the accuracy of eyewitness reports and how these variables exert their influence. This is the category of research that most people think about when they make reference to eyewitness research. In the second research category, however, many researchers have examined the question of how people, such as jurors, naturally go about the process of evaluating eyewitness accuracy. These two categories of research complement each other in important ways. When researchers find some set of variables that affect eyewitness accuracy, the question arises as to whether or not jurors are likely to take those variables into account when they assess the credibility of an eyewitness. Conversely, when researchers find that jurors seem to be paying attention to certain variables in making judgments of eyewitness accuracy, the question arises as to whether or not the variables in question actually serve as valid cues to the accuracy of eyewitnesses. This dual approach by eyewitness researchers is particularly important when considering the extent to which the research is to be used in giving expert testimony in courts of law. The general purpose of expert testimony is to assist the trier of fact, and if the trier of fact already has an understanding of how the variables affect eyewitness accuracy, the need for expert testimony is greatly diminished.

In our attempt to take a broad view of what has been learned from this research literature, we begin with some general observations that we think are well justified. We then turn to more specific observations and discuss some of the limitations to the conclusions that can be reached from this literature.

Perhaps the most general conclusion that can be reached from eyewitness experiments is that error in people's reports is easy to find. This general conclusion is well known and not particularly controversial. The apparent widespread use and appeal of the classroom demonstration, in which someone comes in and threatens the instructor and then the students have to give a description of the intruder, owes to the ease of replicating the basic finding that people are prone to make errors. Unfortunately, for those with only nodding familiarity with the eyewitness literature, this is where the understanding of the eyewitness issue tends to end. As a result, erroneous conclusions tend to be made. For instance, some are prone to conclude that eyewitness research shows that eyewitnesses are inherently unreliable. This is not an appropriate conclusion. The eyewitness literature reveals that both the type of error and the frequency of errors made by eyewitnesses rises and falls as a function of critical variables. Hence, under some conditions eyewitnesses can be highly reliable and under other conditions highly unreliable. It is these critical conditions that are the important subject of study.

VARIABLES CONTROLLING EYEWITNESS ACCURACY

Critical variables controlling eyewitness accuracy can be placed in three categories. First, there are variables that are "internal" to the eyewitness in the sense that they represent personality traits, attitudes, schemata, age, or other characteristics of the individual. Second, there are characteristics of the witnessing situation or stimulus event. Third, there are events that occur after the witnessed event, including the way in which the eyewitness's memory is tested, which affect the accuracy of the testimony. Empirical research exists in all three of these categories. It might be useful to note, however, that the first category, characteristics of the individual, is relatively much smaller in terms of its empirical base. This relative dearth of work on individual differences in eyewitnesses is likely to be due to several factors. We note, for instance, that it would be peculiar, to say the least, to give personality tests to eyewitnesses, and it is most doubtful that courts of law would ever find favor with such a proposal. The same would follow for most any other psychological test, including that of intelligence. As well, eyewitness researchers have not generally endorsed the idea that individual differences will matter much in the context of powerful situational and testing variables, assuming instead that most people will react in largely the same way. (The exception to this is the variable of age, where there is reasonable consensus that young children may be a special population that deserve to be singled out for separate analyses of their abilities as eyewitnesses.) A final reason why there is a dearth of research on individual differences in eyewitness performance is that individual differences fall into the class of estimator variables. Hence, unlike system variables, the system cannot control levels and frequencies of individual differences in a way that could improve eyewitness accuracy.

Characteristics of the Witness

Three characteristics of the eyewitness that have received attention are race, gender, and age, which are easily assessed without needing to administer a psychological test. Less work has been done with personality variables and intelligence, perhaps because of the need to administer psychological tests to assess these variables.

AGE. The largest part of the eyewitness literature that examines characteristics of the eyewitness is the literature on children versus adults as eyewitnesses. In fact, this literature is so large that numerous edited books have been devoted to children as eyewitnesses in recent years (e.g., Ceci, Ross, & Toglia, 1989; Ceci, Toglia, & Ross, 1987; Dent & Flin, 1992; Doris, 1991; Goodman & Bottoms, 1993). Because of the vastness of this literature, we can only touch on what we think are the major themes and general findings. In our view, these major themes and findings can be placed in two broad categories: the accuracy and completeness of the testimony accounts of children versus adults and the suggestibility of children versus adults. These two broad categories are not totally independent, of course, because suggestibility effects can influence accuracy, and because lack of completeness in children's reports can lead questioners to suggest memories to children.

At the risk of oversimplifying, we think that there is good evidence that young children tend to differ from adults both in the completeness of their reports of a witnessed event and in the accuracy of what they report. A fairly consistent pattern emerges from empirical studies: Young children tend to give much less information and slightly less accurate information under conditions of free recall and open-ended questions than do adults, and the differences in accuracy become even more pronounced under conditions allowing specific questions to be asked (e.g., Flin, Boone, Knox, & Bull, 1992; Laumann & Elliott, 1992; Leippe, Romanczyk, & Manion, 1991; Luus & Wells, 1992; Poole & White, 1991, 1993). This should not be particularly surprising given the fairly large literature that indicates that a variety of memory skills improve with age (e.g., see review by Kail, 1989).

Lineups and photospreads present difficulties for young children, but their difficulties are not qualitatively different from the difficulties experienced by adults. The primary condition for concern in eyewitness identification from lineups and photospreads is the condition in which the actual perpetrator is not present in the lineup or photospread. When the actual target is not among the members of the lineup, people have a great deal of difficulty making the correct response ("none of these") and tend instead to identify the person who resembles the perpetrator more than do the other lineup members (see Wells, 1984, 1988, 1993). In the case of young children, this propensity to make an identification even though the perpetrator is not in the lineup is especially pronounced when compared with adults (Beal, Schmitt, & Dekle, 1995; Dekle, Beal, Elliot, & Huneycutt, 1996; Parker & Caranza, 1989; Parker & Ryan, 1993). When the perpetrator is present in the lineup or photospread, children often can perform at levels that approximate the level achieved by adults. Deciding that a critical stimulus is absent is often more difficult than deciding that a critical stimulus is present. Hence, it is possible that the difference in adult versus child eyewitness performance is greater for perpetrator-absent than for perpetrator-present lineups because the perpetrator-absent lineups are tougher tests of an eyewitness's memory, thereby showing more clearly the weaknesses of a child's memory. On the other hand, the greater inclination of children to identify someone from a perpetrator-absent lineup could owe to the inherent suggestiveness of the perpetrator-absent lineup. In effect, presenting someone with a lineup or photospread involves a level of demand or suggestion that the perpetrator is present, or at least that the person giving the lineup believes that the perpetrator is among the people in the lineup; otherwise, why conduct the lineup?

Differences in the suggestibility of adult and child eyewitnesses has been a matter of considerable empirical attention in recent years. The data on the issue have been quite consistent in supporting the proposition that children are more suggestible than adults, and this is especially true of preschool children (Ceci & Bruck, 1993, 1995). This work complements other work indicating that under some circumstances young children (e.g., under 8 years of age) have more difficulty than older children and adults distinguishing between events that they have only imagined and those that they have actually experienced (e.g., Johnson & Foley, 1984). The greater memory suggestibility of children might owe primarily to the differences in their abilities to encode, store, retrieve, and monitor various types of information. In general, the weaker the memory trace, the greater the potential for suggestion effects (Pezdek & Roe, 1995). This type of reasoning has led some to argue that suggestion effects with children are severely diminished or even nonexistent when the event in question is a central, significant event, or when the child is a participant rather than a passive observer (e.g., Goodman, Rudy, Bottoms, & Aman, 1990). While acknowledging that children probably are less prone to suggestion effects when the matter involves a central event regarding their own bodies, Bruck, Ceci, Fancoeur, and Barr (1995) reported that 3-year-olds in one of their studies falsely asserted that their pediatrician had inserted a finger or stick into their genitals.

Recently, work by Brainerd, Reyna, and Brandse (1995) put an interesting new twist on false memories in young children by predicting that false memories in young children might actually be more stable (consistent, preserved) over time than true memories under some circumstances. Their reasoning was that true memory responses are supported by relatively unstable verbatim traces, while false memories are supported by relatively stable gist. Three experiments using 5- and 8-year-olds were supportive of the prediction. To the extent that this type of phenomenon holds up under other circumstances, those who work with child witnesses will need to rethink some of their assumptions about the meaning of consistency in children's reports in relation to whether a memory is true or false.

In contrast to the volume of work studying young children as eyewitnesses, much less work has been directed at how elderly eyewitnesses compare with younger adults. The empirical evidence thus far indicates that elderly people are somewhat more likely to make identification errors than are younger adults (Bartlett & Fulton, 1991; O'Rourke, Penrod, Cutler, & Stuve, 1989). Nevertheless, among older adults whose normal faculties of vision, hearing, or reasoning have not failed, there is little evidence that overall abilities as eyewitnesses are more than only slightly diminished by age per se (e.g., Smith & Winograd, 1978; Yarmey, 1984).

RACE. We think it is reasonable to conclude from the empirical literature that there is no support for the conclusion that members of one race are "better" eyewitnesses than another race. On the other hand, there are reasons to believe that characteristics of the witnessed event interact with race. Evidence indicates that people have less difficulty recognizing the faces of members of their own race than they do recognizing members of another race (see meta-analysis by Bothwell, Brigham, & Malpass, 1989).

GENDER. As with race of eyewitness, there is no consistent evidence to suggest that males are any better or worse as eyewitnesses than are females. On the other hand, evidence suggests that females might be more likely to notice and remember information relevant to their gender and males more likely to notice and remember information relevant to their gender (Powers, Andriks, & Loftus, 1979). Shapiro and Penrod's (1986) meta-analysis indicates that females may be more likely to make correct identifications and also more likely to make incorrect identifications, suggesting that females might be using a more lax criterion for recognition than males. At this point, it cannot be said that one gender is better than the other overall.

INTELLIGENCE AND PERSONALITY VARIABLES. The idea that intelligence might be related to eyewitness identification accuracy has received little or no support to date when subject samples fall within relatively normal ranges of intelligence (Brown, Deffenbacher, & Sturgill, 1977; Feinman & Entwistle, 1976). There is some evidence that personality characteristics might be related to eyewitness accuracy, however. In particular, work has been directed at looking for differences in eyewitness accuracy as a function of personality characteristics, such as self-monitoring. *Self-monitoring* refers to the tendency for some people to moderate their behavior in response to their social environment. One reason why self-monitoring might be related to eyewitness accuracy is that high self-monitors are thought to be more attentive to their social environment than are low-self-monitors. There is some evidence consistent with this hypothesis (Hosch, 1994; Hosch, Leippe, Marchioni, & Cooper, 1984). Field dependence and field independence might also moderate eyewitness identification accuracy. There is evidence that field independent eyewitnesses are more likely to make accurate lineup identifications than are field dependent eyewitnesses (Shapiro & Penrod, 1986). In addition, although apparently not related to eyewitness identification accuracy, individual differences in retrospective self-awareness seem to be related in a complex way to the relation between eyewitness identification accuracy and eyewitness confidence (see Kassin, 1985; Kassin, Rigby, & Castillo, 1991). There is also recent evidence to indicate that some people are more habitually susceptible to accepting postevent misinformation than are other people (Tomes & Katz, 1997).

Except for age, race, and gender, characteristics of the eyewitness have not played much of a role in the scientific literature on eyewitness accounts. This is especially true of personality variables. We note that the strength of these variables in terms of overall impact on eyewitness accuracy seems modest at best. When individual differences on personality variables are statistically significant in this work, the effect sizes tend to be small. It is quite possible that eyewitness researchers have underestimated the importance of personality characteristics of the eyewitness, however, owing to the tendency in much of this research to use relatively homogeneous subject populations. This is less of a problem with variables such as age because one must sample from relatively heterogeneous populations in order to examine age as a variable whereas tests of personality variables are often drawn from a college student sample. There might be a need for future work to focus on the moderating role of personalty variables using subject-witness populations that are more heterogeneous.

Characteristics of the Situation and Stimulus

Generally, characteristics of the situation and stimulus include such factors as duration of the incident, arousal during the witnessing of the event, race of the target, lighting, distance, opportunity to view, weapon focus, and other event characteristics that could affect the accuracy or completeness of the eyewitness's account.

RACE OF TARGET. We have already noted that race of the eyewitness is a factor that interacts with race of the target (Bothwell et al., 1989). In this sense, target race is a stimulus factor or characteristic of the situation that affects the accuracy of eyewitness identifications. As with race of the eyewitness, however, there is little evidence that race of the target exerts a main effect influence on the accuracy of eyewitness identifications. Studies that yield a main effect for target race are difficult to interpret. In the empirical work on the cross-race effect, little effort is taken to ensure that the samples of faces for one race are representative of that race as a whole. This situation is important to note because it leaves unanswered the question of whether any main effect differences between target races is due to general differences in the recognizability of the races or to the characteristics of the sample of target faces used in a particular study. This is not a problem for interpreting the interaction between target race and witness race, but it is a problem for the main effect differences that might surface in a given study, meaning that the main effect for race of face is largely uninterpretable at this point.

STRESS AND AROUSAL.   Some readers might think it odd that we place arousal and stress as characteristics of the situation or stimulus. After all, arousal and stress seem to be internal conditions particular to the eyewitness. Nevertheless, we presume that arousal and stress are triggered by the situation or by a particular stimulus in the witnessed situation, such as a threat or observation of violence. Indeed, we know that the observation of violence produces physiological arousal (Zillmann, 1971). Unfortunately, the status of our knowledge about the role of arousal is, in certain respects, limited. The principal limiting factors are threefold. First, it is difficult to induce the types and magnitudes of arousal and stress that have face validity for the types and magnitudes that can exist for some eyewitnesses. How, for instance, do we capture the arousal and stress of someone whose life is threatened or who is observing the commission of an actual murder? Second, there is some conceptual muddiness in distinguishing between arousal and stress, as well as between those constructs and anxiety, distraction, and so on. Third, the dominant theoretical model relating arousal to performance is curvilinear, as in the inverted U function of the Yerkes-Dodson curve. The idea is that arousal at low levels and at high levels impairs performance, and that there is some optimal level somewhere in between that produces the best performance. The reason that the inverted U model is problematic is that it is a theoretical model that is highly tolerant of results that show either increases in eyewitness performance as a function of increasing arousal or decreases in eyewitness performance as a function of increasing arousal. Increases in performance as a function of increasing arousal can be explained by assuming that one is testing the difference between low and moderate levels of arousal; decreases in performance as a function of increasing arousal can be explained by assuming that one is testing the difference between moderate and high levels of arousal. Without an operational definition of arousal level that is independent of the performance measure, the arousal-performance issue is a difficult one to test. The theoretical permissiveness of the inverted U model, combined with the difficulty of manipulating arousal at the levels that might exist in certain crime settings and the difficulty of maintaining distinctions between arousal, stress, and distraction, make the empirical and theoretical status of arousal a complex one at best.

Deffenbacher (1983) examined the experimental literature and concluded that there is evidence for the inverted U relation between arousal and eyewitness performance. Field studies of actual eyewitnesses, however, have not been so favorable to the idea that high arousal impairs eyewitness performance. MacLeod and Shepherd (1986), for instance, studied the reports of actual eyewitnesses to assaults for which there was physical injury or no physical injury to the victim. Of the 379 reports that were analyzed, no overall differences emerged, but there was a slight tendency for female eyewitnesses to report fewer details than male eyewitnesses when there was injury to the victim. Yuille and Cutshall (1986) reported a positive correlation between reports of arousal and accuracy of eyewitness reports among eyewitnesses to an actual shooting. Tollestrup, Turtle, and Yuille (1994) used victim versus bystander as a proxy for arousal and found few differences of note in their reports. Of course, it is quite possible that victims versus bystanders, crimes involving personal injury or not, and other proxy for arousal differ systematically on other dimensions (such as distance from the event or exposure duration) in ways that cancel or otherwise diminish any relation between arousal and eyewitness accuracy. It is also possible that arousal is not a particularly powerful variable in terms of its ability to either impair or facilitate eyewitness accuracy. The conceptual muddle between stress and arousal, in conjunction with evidence that stress interacts with a host of other factors (see Christianson, 1992), leaves us with no simple answers at this point. There is some evidence that stress might reduce the amount of information recalled but increase resistance to decay of memory over time (Yuille, Davies, Gibling, & Marxsen, 1994). A reduction in decay over time for stressful events might owe to the tendency of people to rehearse the event in their minds. But this does not mean that memory for events that are stressful, thought about a lot, salient, or significant are necessarily accurate.

The relative lack of clarity in the literature about the effects of stress and arousal on memory contrasts somewhat with the tendency of people to believe that certain events are so salient, meaningful, surprising, or important to the observer that some sort of indelible impression is left in memory. People report confidently on where they were, who was there, and various details for such events as the assassination of John Kennedy or the crash of the space shuttle *Challenger*. In fact, these vivid memories are of dubious validity. Neisser and Harsch's (1992) study of the *Challenger* explosion, for instance, showed that subjects' recollections of place, activity, time, and others who were present yielded only 30% correct answers, 27% partially incorrect answers, and 42% totally incorrect answers after 32 months. Confidence in the correctness of their answers was not significantly related to the accuracy of the answers. It might be more appropriate to conclude that significant events leave an impression of indelibility but not an indelible impression.

WEAPON FOCUS. Somewhat clearer than our conclusions about arousal are our conclusions about the idea of weapon focus. Numerous studies, using quite different methodologies, have yielded data indicating that eyewitnesses are influenced by the visual presence of a weapon, such as a gun or knife, in such a way that their memory for other details (including the perpetrator's face) is impaired (e.g., Kramer, Buckhout, & Eugenio, 1990; Loftus, Loftus, & Messo, 1987; Maas & Kohnken, 1989; Tooley, Brigham, Maas, & Bothwell, 1987).

EVENT DURATION. The duration of the witnessed event ought to be related to the completeness of eyewitness reports and perhaps to the accuracy of those reports. At the extremes, this relation would have to hold. Imagine a complex event that happened in only a few seconds versus one that unfolded over several hours. Somewhat surprisingly, there has been little empirical work in the eyewitness literature that uses duration of the event as a focal variable for study, perhaps because the relation is so obvious as to not require its demonstration. Cutler, Penrod, and Martens (1987b) included duration as a variable in order to look for possible interactions with other variables. Its role in eyewitness performance was restricted primarily to a main effect influence. Wells and Murray (1983) discussed several problems with duration and related variables or constructs (such as opportunity to view) in terms of their practical uses in actual cases. Among the problems are that these types of variables are difficult to measure in actual cases because one usually must rely on the very eyewitness whose memory is being called into question. People are not particularly accurate in estimating duration. Generally, people overestimate short temporal duration, especially when the event is complex or the person is stressed (Sarason & Stroops, 1978; Schiffman & Bobko, 1974). Often, these overestimations of short durations are on the order of 300% to 500%, as when a witness says that a culprit's face was in view for several minutes when in fact it was in view for only 20 or 30 seconds.

Postevent Factors

The largest part of the eyewitness literature has been concerned with factors that come into play after the critical event has happened. There are a number of reasons why eyewitness researchers have placed so much emphasis on postevent and testing factors. Perhaps chief among these reasons is that the factors that come into play after the critical event can potentially be brought under control in actual cases; factors such as characteristics of the witness and characteristics of the witnessed event, on the other hand, are fixed at levels that cannot be controlled in actual cases.

Hence, variables such as how eyewitnesses are questioned have received priority treatment by eyewitness researchers because it is assumed that advances in our understanding of such variables can lead to improvements in the accuracy of eyewitness reports.

THE PASSAGE OF TIME.   An eyewitness might be questioned almost immediately after he or she has witnessed an event, or there might be quite long delays before there is any attempt made to obtain an account from the eyewitness. The reasons for delay are numerous. For instance, the eyewitness might not have known that he or she was an eyewitness at the time of the event. Following a bombing in a midwestern city, for example, it might be hours or weeks before an automobile is traced to a car rental company. Attempts to obtain a description of the person who rented the car or administer a photospread to the person who dealt with the renter are thereby subject to the difficulties associated with the passage of time. It should not be surprising that eyewitnesses forget things over time (e.g., Flin, Boone, Knox, & Bull, 1992). It is somewhat more interesting to note how time interacts with other variables and the conditions in which there might actually be greater amounts of information recalled at a later time than at an earlier time (hyperamnesia). As for interactions with time, a number of variables have been identified. The most consistent of these is the interaction of time and suggestion. Generally speaking, the longer the delay between the witnessed event and an attempt to implant a suggestion (e.g., via a misleading question), the more effective the suggestion in distorting the eyewitness's report (Hoffman, Loftus, Greenmun, & Dashiell, 1992; Toland, Hoffman, & Loftus, 1991).

POSTEVENT MISINFORMATION.   The fact is that the passage of time itself might not be nearly as important as the events that occur during the retention interval. The work of psychologist Elizabeth Loftus and her colleagues has had a dramatic effect by focusing on the fact that people tend to incorporate into their testimony about an event information that was obtained from external sources during the retention interval. Importantly, this incorporation of postevent information can happen with false information as well as true information. The conditions under which false postevent information will be most likely to be incorporated into eyewitnesses' later reports have been fairly well identified. At this point, it seems safe to conclude that false postevent information is most likely to be incorporated into the eyewitnesses' later reports when the strength of the original memory trace is weaker rather than stronger, the misinformation is not recognized as being incorrect at the time, and the misinformation is delivered by a credible source (e.g., Belli, 1993; Belli, Windschitl, & McCarthy, 1992; Loftus, 1979; Okamoto & Sugahara, 1986; Toland et al., 1991). Less clear is the question of precisely what processes are operating and at what level these processes are operating in producing the misinformation effect. For instance, there are fundamental questions about whether the misinformation actually changes (e.g., replaces or modifies) the original memory trace, or whether it merely adds a second, competing memory trace (see McCloskey & Zaragoza, 1985). Questions have also been raised about whether the misleading information effect is merely a persuasion-type of phenomenon or a demand characteristic phenomenon in which the person reports the misinformation because the person trusts the misinformation more than his or her own memory, or does not want to contradict the source of the misinformation. It is beyond the scope of this chapter to describe fully the theoretical debate about the fate of the original memory trace or the psychological processes behind changes to people's reports of what they saw or heard. At some levels of analysis, it makes little difference whether the process is one in which the original memory trace is changed, or whether the process is governed by demand rather than the creation of a second memory. The fact that people's reports of what they had witnessed are affected by postevent misinformation (and that they seem to treat this misinformation as something that they actually saw or heard) is a matter of considerable significance and concern regardless of the precise psychological mechanisms that give rise to the effects.

Testing Conditions

By *testing conditions*, we mean all of the methods and procedures that are used to elicit information from eyewitnesses. Hence, for example, the wording of a question is a testing condition, the environment in which the questioning occurs is a testing condition, the way a lineup or photospread is constructed is a testing condition, and so on. This is a large part of the system variable eyewitness literature. In fact, this part of the eyewitness literature is so large that we can only touch on what we consider to be the major developments and conclusions.

Testing condition issues overlap with the misleading postevent information literature because one of the main ways in which misleading information can be effectively implanted is through the use of misleading or suggestive questions. Consider, for example, a misleading question of the form, "What was the man with the mustache doing with the young boy?" Assume that the man did not have a mustache. This form of the question might not have an effect on eyewitnesses' answers to the question itself (i.e., their description of what the man was doing might not be affected by the supposition of the mustache). Nevertheless, having asked this question could affect answers to subsequent questions (such as "Describe the man," see Loftus & Greene, 1980). Other questions can be suggestive in such ways that their wording affects answers to the question being asked. For instance, the question "How long was your discussion?" can elicit different estimates of duration than the question "How short was your discussion?" or "What was the duration of your discussion?" (see Yarmey, 1990). Again, the precise psychological processes giving rise to these effects are subject to some debate, but there is little debate remaining about the fact that question wording affects the testimony that people give about events that they have observed.

COGNITIVE INTERVIEW.   Ron Fisher and Edward Geiselman have conducted a number of studies examining different methods of getting eyewitnesses to recall information about an event that they have witnessed. Particularly problematic in many, if not most, cases is that eyewitness accounts of witnessed events are woefully incomplete. A nice summary of their work can be found in Fisher and Geiselman (1992) and Fisher (1995). In general, this work focuses on a contrast between the typical method for police interviews of eyewitnesses and the so-called cognitive interview. At this point, evidence indicating that the cognitive interview yields more correct information from eyewitnesses than does the standard police interview is persuasive enough that it might be useful to describe the basic protocol for the cognitive interview and discuss some of the ways that it is different from the typical witness interview conducted by police. The basic protocol for the cognitive interview is as follows (adapted from Fisher & Geiselman, 1992):

I. Introduction
   A. Control eyewitness's anxiety.
   B. Develop rapport.
   C. Tell eyewitness to actively volunteer information, not to wait passively for questions from the interviewer.
   D. Explicitly request detailed information.
   E. Tell eyewitness to not edit thoughts, also not to make up or fabricate answers.
   F. Tell eyewitness to concentrate intensely.
II. Open-ended Narration
   A. Recreate the general context.
   B. Request narrative description and do not interrupt.
   C. Pause after eyewitness speaks before going on to another question.
   D. Help eyewitness identify images.

    E. Develop a tentative probing strategy.

III. Probing Memory Codes

    A. Reemphasize concentration and recreate context.

    B. Ask eyewitness to close eyes and ask open-ended, framed question.

    C. Request detailed description and do not interrupt.

    D. Take detailed notes.

    E. Pause after eyewitness stops speaking.

    F. Exhaust image for information not in narrative, probe remaining images, reprobe earlier images.

    G. Probe concept codes.

IV. Review

    A. Review for eyewitness from notes taken by interviewer.

    B. Speak slowly and ask eyewitness to interrupt if more information can be given or if anything seems in error.

    C. Probe any new leads.

V. Close

    A. Collect background information.

    B. Remind eyewitness to call if she or he thinks of new information.

    C. Create positive last impression.

The cognitive interview is more detailed and requires more training than this simple description implies. Nevertheless, this outline helps make a few points about how the cognitive interview differs from what appears to be the typical police interview of eyewitnesses. Particularly important is the general idea of not interrupting the eyewitness and giving the eyewitness sufficient pause time to think further about the matter being recalled. Fisher's work with police officers indicates that their overall approach to questioning eyewitnesses is similar to their approach to questioning suspects and hostile witnesses. Their's is an aggressive, leading style of interrogation that does not work well with people who are actually trying to recall a prior event to the best of their abilities (Fisher, 1995). Notice as well that the cognitive interview encourages the use of imagery, encourages the blocking out of current stimuli (e.g., via the closing of the eyes), and, although not apparent in this description, encourages the eyewitness to recall the event in a variety of orders, not just the original temporal order. Which of the various characteristics of the cognitive interview are most important for obtaining more information from the eyewitness than the usual police interview is unclear at this point. It is possible that all of these features are important, and that their effects on the completeness of the eyewitness's report are additive. In any case, research on the cognitive interview demonstrates quite clearly that testing conditions make a difference in the amount of information that one gets from eyewitnesses (Gwyer & Clifford, 1997).

Whereas the cognitive interview attempts to reinstate the context of the witnesses' event mentally (through verbal instructions to the eyewitness), other research has examined reinstatements of the actual physical context of the witnessed event. Although the effects have been moderate—and sometimes reinstatement of physical context has not had any significant effect—it appears that context reinstatement can aid eyewitness identification performance to some extent under some conditions (Cutler, Penrod, & Martens, 1987a; Krafka & Penrod, 1985; Smith & Vela, 1992).

LINEUPS AND PHOTOSPREADS.   The testing conditions associated with lineups and photospreads have received particularly close attention because of the direct relation between the act of identifying someone from a lineup or photospread and the presumption of guilt. Many forms of eyewitness testimony are not closely associated with the ultimate issue of guilt but instead are merely elements of circumstantial evidence relating to the case (e.g., the color of a car, recall of a conversation). The identification of a suspect from a lineup, however, is often construed as direct evidence of guilt in the sense that if one believes that the eyewitness made an accurate identification, then the suspect is the culprit in question. An additional reason for eyewitness researchers' concerns about the testing conditions involved with lineups and photospreads comes from the observation that mistaken identification from lineups and photospreads is the principal cause of false conviction in actual cases that have been subjected to analysis (Rattner, 1988; Wells et al., 1998).

Systematic manipulations of lineup and photospread testing conditions have revealed sources of eyewitness identification error in three broad domains: instructions, structure, and procedure. A more detailed treatment of this literature can be found elsewhere (Wells, 1993), but the general conclusions can be readily summarized. In the domain of instructions, there is clear evidence that eyewitnesses must be told prior to viewing a lineup or photospread that the perpetrator might or might not be present (e.g., Malpass & Devine, 1981; Steblay, 1997) and warned to not guess (e.g., Hilgendorf & Irving, 1978). In the domain of structure, the evidence is clear that only one member of the lineup should be a suspect (Wells & Turtle, 1986), and that all members should match the general description of the culprit as described previously by the eyewitness (Lindsay & Wells, 1980; Luus & Wells, 1991; Wells, Rydell, & Seelau, 1993). Measures of how well the match-to-description criterion has been met have been developed (Doob & Kirshenbaum, 1973; Malpass, 1981; Malpass & Devine, 1983; Wells, Leippe, & Ostrom, 1979). In the domain of procedure, evidence shows that a dual lineup procedure is superior to a single lineup procedure (Wells, 1984), and that a sequential method of presenting lineup members is superior to the traditional simultaneous lineup procedure (e.g., Cutler & Penrod, 1988; Lindsay, Lea, & Fulford, 1991; Lindsay, Lea, Nosworthy, et al., 1991; Lindsay & Wells, 1985; Sporer, 1994).

Wells (1995) has noted how these testing condition variables have particularly strong effects, and that failure to set these instructional, structural, and procedural variables properly can produce considerably high rates of false identification. Particularly alarming is the fact that police receive little or no training on lineups and photospreads, there are no rules or laws that prevent constructing and conducting lineups and photospreads in ways that place an innocent suspect at risk, and courts are relatively insensitive to the ways that these subtle variations in lineups and photospreads have strong effects on the chances of mistaken identification.

Further complicating matters is the finding that the confidence with which an eyewitness makes a false identification can be quite high. Although a recent meta-analysis indicates that the mean confidence for accurate identifications from lineups and photospreads is higher than it is for inaccurate identifications (Sporer, Penrod, Read, & Cutler, 1995), the confidence levels of those who make false identifications overlap with those who make accurate identifications. More problematic is the fact that confidence-accuracy eyewitness identification studies have tested the confidence-accuracy relationship under what could be described as "pristine" conditions that might well overestimate the value of confidence as a cue to accuracy. In a dramatic illustration of this, Luus and Wells (1994) used a staged crime paradigm and gave "feedback" to eyewitnesses who had made false identifications from a photospread. After making the false identification, some eyewitnesses were told nothing (control), while others were told that a co-witness had identified the same person, or a co-witness had identified a different person, or a co-witness had said that the culprit was not in the photos. Later, when interviewed by a police officer, the eyewitnesses were asked how certain they were that they had correctly identified the actual culprit. Compared with the control condition, those who were told that their co-witness had identified the same person inflated their confidence to extremely high levels. Those who were told that their co-witness had identified someone else or that their co-witness had said that the culprit was not among the photos underwent profound drops in confidence. Once an eyewitness has made an identification in a real case, there are no prohibitions against police or prosecutors telling the eyewitness about co-witnesses, other evidence against the accused, and so on. Hence, even though there seems to be some diagnostic value to eyewitness confidence under controlled laboratory conditions, there are good reasons to believe that the confidence of an eyewitness on the witness stand is far removed from these clean laboratory conditions, and that the confidence of the eyewitness often is a reflection of information that comes from external sources rather than her or his memories.

Perhaps the clearest evidence that the confidence of an eyewitness is malleable can be found in the recent experiments reported by Wells and Bradfield (1998). After obtaining false identifications from 352 eyewitnesses, some were told, "Good, you identified the actual suspect in the case," others were told "Oh ... that is not the suspect ... the suspect is actually number ————," and others were given no feedback. Later, the eyewitnesses were asked to report how certain they recall having been at the time that they made their identification. Because witnesses were randomly assigned to feedback conditions *after* they had made their identifications, eyewitnesses in all three conditions were actually equally confident at the time of their identifications. However, those given the confirming feedback recalled having been quite certain at the time, while those given the disconfirming feedback recalled having been uncertain at the time. Moreover, those given confirming feedback following their identifications recalled having had a better view of the perpetrator, having paid more attention to the witnessed event, and having more easily made their identification decision than those who were given the disconfirming feedback.

The idea that eyewitness identification confidence is malleable as a function of suggestive postidentification influences is even more problematic in light of evidence that eyewitnesses are not able to report accurately on those influences. Figure 3.1 shows the effect of postidentification feedback on eyewitness confidence for eyewitnesses who reported that they were probably influenced by the feedback and those who reported that they were not influenced (from Wells & Bradfield, 1998, Experiment 2). Note that those who said that they were not influenced by the feedback manipulation nevertheless showed as much influence as did those who said that they were influenced. This is an important finding because it suggests that confidence inflation is not something on which eyewitnesses can make valid self-reports.

In the area of lineups and photospreads, there has been an attempt to articulate specific policy recommendations. Wells (1995), for instance, has described four rules that could clean up many of the problems with the ways lineups and photospreads are constructed and conducted. These

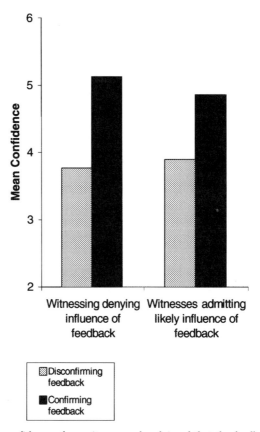

FIGURE 3.1. Mean confidence of eyewitnesses who claimed that the feedback manipulation affected versus did not affect their confidence as a function of feedback condition (from Wells & Bradfield, 1998).

four rules cover instructions to the eyewitness prior to viewing the lineup, the way distractors should be selected for lineups, how and when confidence statements should be obtained from eyewitnesses, and who should administer lineups and photospreads. Regarding the last point, Wells notes that lineups and photospreads are routinely administered by someone (usually the detective working the case) who knows which person in the lineup is the suspect. This is a particularly troublesome practice because of the numerous ways in which the lineup administrator can verbally and nonverbally influence the eyewitness's choice and confidence in that choice. As Wells notes, "all of the reasons for using double-blind procedures in behavioral experiments (Rosenthal, 1976) apply equally well to conducting lineups and photospreads" in actual criminal investigations (Wells & Seelau, 1995, p. 775).

THE RECOVERY OF REPRESSED MEMORIES

Increasingly over the last few years, eyewitness researchers and other memory scientists have turned their scrutiny toward a specific type of memory issue, namely the phenomenon of repression and subsequent recovery of the repressed episode(s) many years later. The idea that people might react to a traumatic event by pushing memory of it back into the unconscious, where it remains largely intact, and then somehow bring that memory forward years later in an accurate recollection has a long clinical history. A variety of cultural factors, including an increased awareness that childhood sexual abuse is more common than was once thought, has led to the use of popular therapy techniques with adults in which concerted attempts are made to get the person to recover repressed memories of childhood sexual abuse. Along with increased use of these therapy techniques have come detailed and vivid accounts of childhood sexual abuse from adults who had no recollections of childhood sexual abuse at all when they entered therapy. These results have produced considerable controversy and highly charged allegations over whether these memories are accurate portrayals of events that actually happened or are illusory memories created by the very procedures that were used to try to recover them.

THE OVERALL ISSUE

The issues regarding the concept of repression and the recovery of repressed memories are far too complex to represent as being merely a scientist versus practitioner debate or as the results of there being two distinct camps of thought. Nevertheless, it is useful to begin with an oversimplified portrayal of two extreme views that carve out the general domains of the debate. On the one hand are various researchers and theoreticians who have great difficulty reconciling the idea of repression and recovery (as defined earlier) with empirically grounded theories of how human memory does and does not work. These researchers note that there is no scientific evidence for the phenomenon of repression (e.g., Holmes, 1990), that many of the so-called memories recovered in therapy are of impossible events (e.g., Ofshe & Watters, 1994), that the procedures and techniques used in recovered memory therapy are quite similar to procedures that facilitate confusion between events actually experienced and those that were only imagined (e.g., Lindsay & Read, 1994), that illusory memories can be created experimentally (e.g., Loftus, 1993), and that it is difficult to dismiss the claims of thousands of parents who claim innocence regarding their adult offsprings' allegations of childhood sexual abuse and have sought help and information from the False Memory Syndrome Foundation (FMSF Scientific and Professional Advisory Board, 1994). On the other hand are advocates of the idea that people sometimes repress traumatic events, and that these events can be recovered from memory. Advocates of this position argue that it would be difficult to prove the phenomenon of repression to the satisfaction of some scientists, that traditional memory theory is designed to deal with events that fall in a more normal range of experience rather than the special memory phenomenon surrounding childhood sexual abuse, that proof of a few false claims does not undermine the validity of most recovered memories, that the procedures and techniques used in recovered-memory therapy are consistent with the procedures and techniques that would be most effective for helping someone recover a true memory, that the illusory memories that have been created in experiments are of trivial matters and are not like the traumatic events being reported by childhood sexual abuse victims, and that the alleged perpetrators contacting FMSF are in denial or are simply hiding their guilt. Needless to say, the scientific issues are difficult to assess because the sociopolitical context of the issues injects itself at almost every turn. The ideas that many professionals are career invested in recovered memory therapy, that attacks on the validity of recovered memories of childhood sexual abuse could result in further denial of the prevalence of childhood sexual abuse in our culture, and the sobering thought that victims could be denied an acknowledgment of their victim status combine to make the issue one of incredible controversy.

Most of those who question the validity of adulthood recovery of repressed memories of childhood sexual abuse are careful to distinguish between victims who have always remembered the abuse but have failed to report it for various reasons, and those who had no memory of abuse even when it was first suggested that perhaps they were sexually abused as a child. Hence, the issue has tended to focus more specifically on cases in which there is no memory of childhood sexual abuse for long periods of time, and the recollection is brought forth over a period of time by the use of various therapy techniques, such as journaling, dream interpretation, viewing videos that have an abuse theme, hypnosis, and even sodium pentathol.

The Development of Illusory Memories

Lindsay and Read (1994) have sketched one psychological process that could make the memory-recovery techniques that are used in therapy yield illusory memories. They point out that people tend to be able to distinguish between events that they have personally experienced and those that were only imagined by relying on certain cues. Events actually experienced, in contrast to events that were merely imagined, tend to be more vivid, detailed, and easier to generate (Johnson, 1988). To the extent that these qualities of memory are used to make judgments about whether or not a memory is real, misattributing an imagined memory to the occurrence of a real event can occur if the imagined memory is given these qualities (see Johnson, Hashtroudi, & Lindsay, 1993). Rehearsal of an imagined event, for instance, tends to make the event more detailed, vivid, and easier to generate; hence, it acquires more of the properties of real memories. In general, many of the factors that memory researchers have found contribute to the appearance of illusory memories—repetition of suggestions, credible sources of suggestion, communication of information that heightens the plausibility of the suggestions, encouragement to form and rehearse images of the alleged event, and encouragement to use lax criteria for deciding whether an image is a memory—are heavily used in therapy aimed at getting the patient to recall childhood sexual abuse. What begins as suggestion and imagination, according to this account, can become an illusory memory in which the person actually believes that the event(s) happened to them.

Evidence for Repression

The idea that children would react to traumatic events by repressing all memory of them is strongly held in some circles of therapists, but the empirical evidence is not particularly kind to the idea. Terr (1988, 1991), for instance, found that children's reaction to a single traumatic event was one of showing remarkably clear and detailed recollections, and that their reaction to repeated or prolonged traumatic events were spotty but nevertheless not at all like the idea of total amnesia. Along these lines, Loftus (1993) cited work by Malmquist (1986) in which 5- to 10-year-old children who witnessed the murder of their parents never showed signs of repression but instead seemed to not be able to get it out of their minds. There is some evidence that suggests that as many as 12% of a sample of adult women who, according to hospital records, were victims of sexual abuse (ranging from touching to intercourse) as a child, denied in adulthood having ever been sexually abused during childhood (Williams, 1994).

There could, of course, be reasons other than repression as to why these women denied or could not recall the childhood incident. Furthermore, even if one assumes that the incident occurred as stated in the hospital records, and that this 12% of the sample could not recall the incident, it begs the question of whether the actual memories are recoverable. The idea that the mental system has placed these particular memories into a part of the brain that doesn't decay like other memories, for instance, is difficult for many memory scientists to accept. In other words, showing that some people might have no memory for a traumatic event, or even a series of such events, does not mean that the memory is repressed and somehow preserved in such a way that it can be recovered intact at a later point (Holmes, 1990; Loftus & Ketcham, 1994).

MEMORY PERMANENCE

The general belief that information that enters the memory system is somehow permanent is not a belief that is backed by scientific evidence. Penfield's (Penfield & Perot, 1963) studies of brain stimulation and sup-posed flashbacks, for instance, and the use of hypnosis to recover memories do not stand up to close scrutiny as evidence that actual memories are being recovered using these techniques (see Loftus & Loftus, 1980, on the general issue of permanence; see Pettinati, 1988 on hypnosis). Although there is no scientific support for the proposition that memory is perma-nent, there also is no scientific proof that it is not permanent. It is always possible that there is a memory trace somewhere in the brain that is unavailable for retrieval, and that one sometimes retrieves an illusory memory in its place but the original memory remains stored intact never-theless. Hence, the issues can become increasingly complex when we consider that there might have been childhood sexual abuse, but the particular recollection of events is itself an illusory memory; that the abuse is something other than what is being recalled; or that the identity of the perpetrator is mistaken. Many critics of recovered memory therapy might be less concerned if there was an acknowledgment of the idea that these memories are subject to suggestion, error, and confusion just as other memories are.

THE CREDIBILITY OF RECOVERED MEMORIES

Additional ammunition for those who argue that adult recovery of long repressed childhood memories is illusory are cases in which patients recover memories of abuse from when they were 6 months old or younger. This stands in distinction to fact that infantile amnesia (no episodic memory before approximately the age of 2) has been so well accepted that scientists have primarily focused on *why* (rather than *whether*) people cannot recall events prior to the age of 2 (Fivush & Hammond, 1990). The fact that some people "recall" memories from the womb or from previous lives gives further ammunition to those who claim that these memories are illusory. The recovery of false memories of childhood sexual abuse has been dubbed the false memory syndrome. Nevertheless, finding that there are unbelievable and obviously false reports of childhood sexual abuse among those who recovered such memories using therapy does not in itself mean that all reports of adult recovered memories of childhood sexual abuse are false, but only that at least some apparently are.

It has been argued that there is not a solid scientific basis for the claim of a "false memory syndrome," that the scientific basis for implanting autobiographical memories may be as tenuous as the claims for recovery of repressed memories, and that claims about the extent to which risky methods are used by therapists are exaggerated (Pope, 1996). The issues surrounding the debate about the validity of recovered memories of repressed events are complex and easily spill over into highly charged sociopolitical concerns. Lindsay and Read's (1995) review of the scientific and clinical evidence on the issue appears to have some reasoned and reasonable conclusions. Against a backdrop of stressing that childhood sexual abuse occurs all too frequently, they argue that there is good evidence that illusory memories of abuse can be created, and that it would make sense to weight the validity of a recovered memory using five criteria. Specifically, they argue that one should consider evidence regarding the following:

(a) how memories were recovered (the more evidence of a prolonged, multifaceted, socially influenced search for memories, the greater the degree of skepticism); (b) the nature and clarity of the recovered memories (with more credence given to detailed recollections than to vague feelings, beliefs, dream images, or "body memories"); (c) the plausibility of the alleged events being forgotten (e.g., research indicates that people are particularly unlikely to forget repeated contact childhood sexual abuse extending into late adulthood or teenage years); (d) the plausibility of recovering the memories (e.g., research shows that the claims of recovering recollections of events before the age of 2 years should be treated with great skepticism); and (e) the base rate of the alleged type of abuse (the lower the base rate the greater the degree of skepticism). (p. 874)

We note that there are some interesting parallels between the skepticism conditions surrounding a recovered memory as described by Lindsay and Read and the skepticism conditions that have been discussed in the more traditional eyewitness literature. Regardless of whether one is dealing with a supposedly repressed memory or not, the issue arises as to what methods were used to elicit the memory. In the study of eyewitness identification, for instance, the failure to tell the eyewitness that the perpetrator might not be in the lineup is something that can trigger false identification, especially when the perpetrator is not in the lineup. Importantly, this instruction does not significantly undermine the eyewitness's ability to identify the perpetrator if he or she actually is in the lineup. Instead, it appears that warning the eyewitness that the perpetrator might not be in the lineup serves to help him or her distinguish between true recognition and mere resemblance. This leads us to wonder if a similar instruction might not prove useful in the context of recovered memory therapy. Specifically, we think it might be wise to inform clients about the possibility that they were not abused, and about the possibility that they could develop illusory memories. Perhaps this caution helps people maintain separation between imagined events and events that they actually experienced.

Although our discussion of the issue of repressed and recovered memories can provide readers with a feel for the issues, we have only scratched the surface of this multifaceted problem area. Those seeking a deeper analysis of the issues should examine a number of recent publications, including Goodman, Quas, Batterman-Faunce, Riddlesburger, and Kuhn (1994); Halperin (1996); Lindsay and Read (1994, 1995); Loftus (1993); Loftus and Ketcham (1994); Pendergrast (1996); and Pope (1996).

CONCLUSION

Our review of the traditional eyewitness literature and the literature on the recovery of repressed childhood memories leads us to see some key themes that run through this work. One major theme is that a memory report from an eyewitness can be false even though the eyewitness is genuinely certain that the memory is true. An eyewitness who identifies an innocent person from a lineup, for instance, can develop a great deal of confidence in this false recognition if she or he is supplied with other information supposedly corroborating the identification (Luus & Wells, 1994; Wells & Bradfield, 1998). Similarly, an event that was merely imagined can acquire the qualities of a real memory under certain conditions (Lindsay & Read, 1995), and false memories can actually be more persistent than true memories under some conditions (Brainerd et al., 1995). Hence, discriminating between accurate and inaccurate memories is a significant problem for both experts and practitioners.

Another major theme running through this work is that the conditions under which memories are elicited have a strong bearing on the validity of the memory report. The practice of having photospreads administered by someone who knows which member of the photospread is the suspect, for instance, leads to the possibility that the eyewitness's selection of someone from the photospread was based on the photospread administrator's verbal or nonverbal cues rather than on the eyewitness's memory (Wells & Luus, 1990). Similarly, the practice of therapists suggesting abuse scenarios to clients and accepting clients' feelings as valid memories to be further recovered leads to the possibility that these memory recovery techniques are creating illusory memories rather than recovering true memories.

We note one other common element in all of this work, namely, the practitioners who are attempting to make use of the memories of these witnesses typically are not trained in the area of memory. Police detectives, for instance, are the ones who question eyewitnesses and conduct lineups and photospreads, but they receive little or no training on memory interrogation (Fisher, 1995). Similarly, recovered memory therapists are not required to take advanced courses in human memory. Finally, as we stated at the outset of this chapter, the issues surrounding the validity of people's reports of events that they witnessed are not purely issues in memory. Understanding such phenomena as social influence and demand characteristics, for example, is at least as important as memory processes per se for assessing and controlling the validity of people's testimony.

REFERENCES

Bartlett, J. C., & Fulton, A. (1991). Familiarity and recognition of faces in old age. *Memory and Cognition, 19,* 229–238.

Beale, C. R., Schmitt, K. L., & Dekle, D. (1995). Eyewitness identification of children: Effects of absolute judgments, nonverbal response options, and event encoding. *Law and Human Behavior, 19,* 197–216.

Belli, R. F. (1993). Failure of interpolated tests in inducing memory impairment with final modified tests: Evidence unfavorable to the blocking hypothesis. *American Journal of Psychology, 106,* 407–427.

Belli, R. F., Windschitl, P. D., & McCarthy, T. T. (1992). Detecting memory impairment with a modified test procedure: Manipulating retention interval with centrally presented event items. *Journal of Experimental Psychology: Learning, Memory, and Cognition, 18,* 356–367.

Borchard, E. (1932). *Convicting the innocent: Errors of criminal justice.* New Haven, CT: Yale University Press.

Bothwell, R. K., Brigham, J. C., & Malpass, R. S. (1989). Cross racial identification. *Personality and Social Psychology Bulletin, 15,* 19–25.

Brainerd, C. J., Reyna, V. F., & Brandse, E. (1995). Are children's false memories more persistent than their true memories? *Psychological Science, 6,* 359–364.

Brown, E., Deffenbacher, K., & Sturgill, W. (1977). Memory for faces and the circumstances of the encounter. *Journal of Applied Psychology, 62,* 311–318.

Bruck, M., Ceci, S. J., Francoeur, E., & Barr, R. J. (1995). "I hardly cried when I got shot!": Influencing children's reports about a visit to their pediatrician. *Child Development, 66,* 193–208.

Ceci, S. J., & Bruck, M. (1993). The suggestibility of the child eyewitness: A historical review and synthesis. *Psychological Bulletin, 113*, 403–439.

Ceci, S. J., & Bruck, M. (1995). *Jeopardy in the courtroom: A scientific analysis of children's testimony.* Washington, DC: American Psychological Association Press.

Ceci, S. J., Ross, D. F., & Toglia, M. P. (Eds.). (1989). *Perspectives on children's testimony.* New York: Springer-Verlag.

Ceci, S. J., Toglia, M. P., & Ross, D. F. (Eds.). (1987). *Children's eyewitness memory.* New York: Springer-Verlag.

Christianson, S. A. (1992). Emotional stress and eyewitness memory: A critical review. *Psychological Bulletin, 112*, 284–309.

Clifford, B. R., & Bull, R. (1978). *The psychology of person identification.* London: Routledge & Kegan Paul.

Cutler, B. L., & Penrod, S. D. (1988). Improving the reliability of eyewitness identification: Lineup construction and presentation. *Journal of Applied Psychology, 73*, 281–290.

Cutler, B. L., & Penrod, S. D. (1995). *Mistaken identification: The eyewitness, psychology, and the law.* New York: Cambridge University Press.

Cutler, B. L., Penrod, S. D., & Martens, T. K. (1987a). Improving the reliability of eyewitness identifications: Putting context into context. *Journal of Applied Psychology, 72*, 629–637.

Cutler, B. L., Penrod, S. D., & Martens, T. K. (1987b). The reliability of eyewitness identification: The role of system and estimator variables. *Law and Human Behavior, 11*, 233–258.

Deffenbacher, K. (1983). The influence of arousal on reliability of testimony. In S. M. A. Lloyd-Bostock & B. R. Clifford (Eds.), *Evaluating witness evidence: Recent psychological research and new perspectives* (pp. 235–251). Chichester, UK: Wiley.

Dekle, D. J., Beal, C. R., Elliott, R., & Huneycutt, D. (1996). Children as witnesses: A comparison of lineup versus showup identification methods. *Applied Cognitive Psychology, 10*, 1–12.

Dent, H., & Flin, R. (Eds.). (1992). *Children as witnesses.* New York: Wiley.

Doob, A. N., & Kirshenbaum, H. (1973). Bias in police lineups—partial remembering. *Journal of Police Science and Administration, 1*, 287–293.

Doris, J. (Ed.). (1991). *The suggestibility of children's recollections.* Washington, DC: American Psychological Association Press.

Feinman, S., & Entwistle, D. R. (1976). Children's ability to recognize other children's faces. *Child Development, 47*, 506–510.

Fisher, R. P. (1995). Interviewing victims and witnesses of crime. *Psychology, Public Policy, and Law, 1*, 732–764.

Fisher, R. P., & Geiselman, R. E. (1992). *Memory-enhancing techniques for investigative interviewing: The cognitive interview.* Springfield, IL: Thomas.

Fivush, R., & Hammond, N. R. (1990). Autobiographical memory across the preschool years: Toward a reconceptualizing childhood amnesia. In R. Fivush & J. A. Hudson (Eds.), *Knowing and remembering in young children* (pp. 223–248). New York: Cambridge University Press.

Flin, R., Boone, J., Knox, A., & Bull, R. (1992). The effect of a five-month delay on children's and adult's eyewitness memory. *British Journal of Psychology, 83*, 323–336.

FMSF Scientific and Professional Advisory Board. (1994). *Frequently asked questions about the False Memory Syndrome Foundation.*

Goodman, G. S., & Bottoms, B. L. (1993). *Child victims, child witnesses: Understanding and improving testimony.* New York: Guilford Press.

Goodman, G. S., Rudy, L., Bottoms, B. L., & Aman, C. (1990). Children's concerns and memory: Issues of ecological validity in the study of children's eyewitness testimony. In R. Fivush & J. A. Hudson (Eds.), *Knowing and remembering in young children* (pp. 249–284). New York: Cambridge University Press.

Goodman, G. S., Quas, J. A., Batterman-Faunce, J. M., Riddlesburger, J., & Kuhn, J. (1994). Predictors of accurate and inaccurate memories of traumatic events experienced in childhood. *Consciousness and Cognition, 3,* 269–294.

Gwyer, P., & Clifford, B. R. (1997). The effects of the cognitive interview on recall, identification, confidence, and the confidence/accuracy relationship. *Applied Cognitive Psychology, 11,* 121–145.

Halperin, D. A. (Ed.). (1996). *False memory syndrome: Therapeutic and forensic perspectives.* Washington, DC: American Psychiatric Press.

Hilgendorf, E. L., & Irving, B. L. (1978). False positive identification. *Medicine, Science and the Law, 18,* 255–262.

Hoffman, H. G., Loftus, E. F., Greenmun, N., & Dashiell, R. L. (1992). The generation of misinformation. In F. Losel, D. Bender, & T. Bliesener (Eds.), *Psychology and law: International perspectives* (pp. 292–301). Berlin: Walter de Gruyter.

Holmes, D. (1990). The evidence for repression: An examination of sixty years of research. In J. Singer (Ed.), *Repression and dissociation: Implications for personality, theory, psychopathology, and health* (pp. 85–102). Chicago: University of Chicago Press.

Hosch, H. M. (1994). Individual differences in personality and eyewitness identification. In D. F. Ross, J. D. Read, & M. P. Toglia (Eds.), *Adult eyewitness testimony: Current trends and developments* (pp. 328–347). New York: Cambridge University Press.

Hosch, H. M., Leippe, M. R., Marchioni, P. M., & Cooper, D. S. (1984). Victimization, self-monitoring, and eyewitness identification. *Journal of Applied Psychology, 69,* 280–288.

Johnson, M. K. (1988). Discriminating the origin of information. In T. F. Oltmanns & B. A. Maher (Eds.), *Delusional beliefs* (pp. 34–65). New York: Wiley.

Johnson, M. K., & Foley, M. A. (1984). Differentiating fact from fantasy: The reliability of children's memory. *Journal of Social Issues, 40,* 33–50.

Johnson, M. K., Hashtroudi, S., & Lindsay, D. S. (1993). Source monitoring. *Psychological Bulletin, 114,* 3–28.

Kail, R. V. (1989). *The development of memory in children* (2nd ed.). New York: Freeman.

Kassin, S. M. (1985). Eyewitness identification: Retrospective self awareness and the confidence-accuracy correlation. *Journal of Personality and Social Psychology, 49,* 878–893.

Kassin, S. M., Rigby, S., & Castillo, S. R. (1991). The accuracy-confidence correlation in eyewitness testimony: Limits and extensions of the retrospective self-awareness effect. *Journal of Personality and Social Psychology, 61,* 698–707.

Krafka, C., & Penrod, S. (1985). Reinstatement of context in a field experiment on eyewitness identification. *Journal of Personality and Social Psychology, 49,* 58–69.

Kramer, T. H., Buckhout, R., & Eugenio, P. (1990). Weapon focus, arousal, and eyewitness memory. *Law and Human Behavior, 14,* 167–184.

Laumann, L. A., & Elliott, R. (1992). Reporting what you have seen: Effects associated with age and mode of questioning on eyewitness reports. *Perceptual and Motor Skills, 75,* 799–818.

Leippe, M. R., Romanczyk, A., & Manion, A. P. (1991). Eyewitness memory for a touching experience: Accuracy differences between adult and child witness. *Journal of Applied Psychology, 76,* 367–379.

Lindsay, D. S., & Read, J. D. (1994). Psychotherapy and memories of childhood sexual abuse: A cognitive perspective. *Applied Cognitive Psychology, 8,* 281–338.

Lindsay, D. S., & Read, J. D. (1995). "Memory work" and recovered memories of childhood sexual abuse: Scientific evidence and public, Professional, and personal issues. *Psychology, Public Policy, and Law, 1,* 846–909.

Lindsay, R. C. L., Lea, J. A., & Fulford, J. A. (1991). Sequential lineup presentation: Technique matters. *Journal of Applied Psychology, 76,* 741–745.

Lindsay, R. C. L., Lea, J. A., Nosworthy, G. J., Fulford, J. A., Hector, J., LeVan, V., & Seabrook,

C. (1991). Biased lineups: Sequential presentation reduces the problem. *Journal of Applied Psychology, 76*, 796–802.

Lindsay, R. C. L., & Wells, G. L. (1980). What price justice? Exploring the relationship between lineup fairness and identification accuracy. *Law and Human Behavior, 4*, 303–314.

Lindsay, R. C. L., & Wells, G. L. (1985). Improving eyewitness identification from lineups: Simultaneous versus sequential lineup presentations. *Journal of Applied Psychology, 70*, 556–564.

Lloyd-Bostock, S. M. A., & Clifford, B. R. (1983). *Evaluating witness evidence: Recent research and new perspectives.* New York: Wiley.

Loftus, E. F. (1979). *Eyewitness testimony.* Cambridge, MA: Harvard University Press.

Loftus, E. F. (1993). The reality of repressed memories. *American Psychologist, 48*, 518–537.

Loftus, E. F., & Greene, E. (1980). Warning: Even memory for faces may be contagious. *Law and Human Behavior, 4*, 323–334.

Loftus, E. F., & Ketcham, K. (1994). *The myth of repressed memory: False memories and allegations of sexual abuse.* New York: St. Martin's Press.

Loftus, E. F., & Loftus, G. R. (1980). On the permanence of stored information in the human brain. *American Psychologist, 35*, 409–420.

Loftus, E. F., Loftus, G. R., & Messo, J. (1987). Some facts about "weapon focus." *Law and Human Behavior, 11*, 55–62.

Loftus, E. F., & Palmer, J. C. (1974). Reconstruction of an automobile destruction: An example of the interaction between language and memory. *Journal of Verbal Learning and Verbal Behavior, 13*, 585–589.

Luus, C. A. E., & Wells, G. L. (1991). Eyewitness identification and the selection of distracters for lineups. *Law and Human Behavior, 15*, 43–57.

Luus, C. A. E., & Wells, G. L. (1992). The perceived credibility of child eyewitnesses. In H. Dent & R. Flin (Eds.), *Children as witnesses* (pp. 73–92). New York: Wiley.

Luus, C. A. E., & Wells, G. L. (1994). The malleability of eyewitness confidence: Co-witness and perseverance effects. *Journal of Applied Psychology, 79*, 714–724.

Maas, A., & Kohnken, G. (1989). Eyewitness identification: Simulating the "weapon effect." *Law and Behavior, 13*, 397–408.

MacLeod, M. D., & Shepherd, J. W. (1986). Sex differences in eyewitness reports of criminal assaults. *Medicine, Science, and Law, 26*, 311–318.

Malmquist, C. P. (1986). Children who witness parental murder: Post-traumatic aspects. *Journal of the American Academy of Child Psychiatry, 25*, 320–325.

Malpass, R. S. (1981). Effective size and defendant bias in eyewitness identification lineups. *Law and Human Behavior, 5*, 299–309.

Malpass, R. S., & Devine, P. G. (1981). Eyewitness identification: Lineup instructions and the absence of the offender. *Journal of Applied Psychology, 66*, 482–489.

Malpass, R. S., & Devine, P. G. (1983). Measuring the fairness of eyewitness identification lineups. In S. M. A. Lloyd-Bostock & B. R. Clifford (Eds.), *Evaluating witness evidence* (pp. 81–102). London: Wiley.

McCloskey, M., & Zaragoza, M. (1985). Misleading postevent information and memory for events: Arguments and evidence against memory impairment hypotheses. *Journal of Experimental Psychology: General, 114*, 1–16.

Neisser, U., & Harsch, N. (1992). Phantom flashbulbs: False recollections of hearing the news about *Challenger*. In E. Winograd & U. Neisser (Eds.), *Affect and accuracy in recall: Studies of "flashbulb" memories* (pp. 9–31). New York: Cambridge University Press.

Ofshe, R., & Watters, E. (1994). *Making monsters: False memories, psychotherapy, and sexual hysteria.* New York: Charles Scribner's.

Okamoto, S., & Sugahara, Y. (1986). Effects of postevent information on eyewitness testimony. *Japanese Psychological Research, 28*, 196–201.

O'Rourke, T. E., Penrod, S. D., Cutler, B. L., & Stuve, T. E. (1989). The external validity of eyewitness identification research: Generalizing across subject populations. *Law and Human Behavior, 13*, 385–395.

Parker, J. F., & Caranza, L. E. (1989). Eyewitness testimony of children in target-present and target-absent lineups. *Law and Human Behavior, 13*, 133–149.

Parker, J. F., & Ryan, V. (1993). An attempt to reduce guessing behavior in children's and adult's eyewitness identifications. *Law and Human Behavior, 17*, 11–26.

Pendergrast, M. (1996). *Victims of memory: Sex abuse accusations and shattered lives.* Hinesberg, VT: Upper Access.

Penfield, W. W., & Perot, P. (1963). The brain's record of auditory and visual experience. *Brain, 86*, 595–696.

Pettinati, H. M. (Ed.). (1988). *Hypnosis and memory.* New York: Guilford Press.

Pezdek, K., & Roe, C. (1995). The effect of memory trace strength on suggestibility. *Journal of Experimental Child Psychology, 60*, 116–123.

Poole, D. A., & White, L. T. (1991). Effects of question repetition on the eyewitness testimony of children and adults. *Developmental Psychology, 27*, 975–986.

Poole, D. A., & White, L. T. (1993). Two years later: Effect of question repetition and retention interval on the eyewitness testimony of children and adults. *Developmental Psychology, 29*, 844–853.

Pope, K. S. (1996). Memory, abuse, and science: Questioning claims about the false memory syndrome epidemic. *American Psychologist, 51*, 957–974.

Powers, P. A., Andriks, J. L., & Loftus, E. F. (1979). Eyewitness accounts of males and females. *Journal of Applied Psychology, 64*, 339–347.

Rattner, A. (1988). Convicted but innocent: Wrongful conviction and the criminal justice system. *Law and Human Behavior, 12*, 283–293.

Rosenthal, R. (1976). *Experimenter effects in behavioral research.* New York: Irvington Press.

Ross, D. F., Read, J. D., & Toglia, M. P. (Eds.). (1994). *Adult eyewitness testimony: Current trends and developments* (pp. 223–244). New York: Cambridge University Press.

Sarason, I., & Stroops, R. (1978). Test Anxiety and *The Passage of Time. Journal of Consulting and Clinical Psychology, 46*, 189–197.

Schiffman, H. R., & Bobko, D. J. (1974). Effects of stimulus complexity of the perception of short temporal durations. *Journal of Experimental Psychology, 103*, 156–159.

Shapiro, P. N., & Penrod, S. (1986). Meta-analysis of racial identification studies. *Psychological Bulletin, 100*, 139–156.

Shepherd, J. W., Ellis, H. D., & Davies, G. M. (1982). *Identification evidence: A psychological evaluation.* Aberdeen, Scotland: Aberdeen University Press.

Smith, A. D., & Winograd, E. (1978). Age differences in remembering face. *Developmental Psychology, 14*, 443–444.

Smith, S. M., & Vela, E. (1992). Environmental context-dependent eyewitness recognition. *Applied Cognitive Psychology, 6*, 125–139.

Sporer, S. L. (1994). Decision times and eyewitness identification accuracy in simultaneous and sequential lineups. In D. F. Ross, J. D. Read, & M. P. Toglia (Eds.), *Adult eyewitness testimony: Current trends and developments* (pp. 300–327). New York: Cambridge University Press.

Sporer, S., Penrod, S., Read, D., & Cutler, B. L. (1995). Choosing, confidence, and accuracy: A meta-analysis of the confidence-accuracy relation in eyewitness identification studies. *Psychological Bulletin, 118*, 315–327.

Steblay, N. (1997). Social influence in eyewitness recall: A meta-analytic review of lineup instruction effects. *Law and Human Behavior, 21,* 283–298.

Terr, L. (1988). What happens to early memories of trauma? A study of 20 children under age 5 at time of documented traumatic events. *Journal of the American Academy of Child and Adolescent Psychiatry, 27,* 96–104.

Terr, L. (1991). Childhood traumas: An outline and overview. *American Journal of Psychiatry, 148,* 10–20.

Toland, K., Hoffman, H., & Loftus, E. F. (1991). How suggestion plays tricks with memory. In J. F. Schumaker (Ed.), *Human suggestibility: Advances in theory, research, and application* (pp. 235–252). New York: Routledge.

Tollestrup, P. A., Turtle, J. W., & Yuille, J. C. (1994). Actual witnesses to robbery and fraud: An archival analysis. In D. F. Ross, J. D. Read, & M. P. Toglia (Eds.), *Adult eyewitness testimony: Current trends and developments* (pp. 144–162). New York: Cambridge University Press.

Tomes, J. L., & Katz, A. N. (1997). Habitual susceptibility to misinformation and individual differences in eyewitness memory. *Applied Cognitive Psychology, 11,* 233–251.

Tooley, B., Brigham, J. C., Maas, A., & Bothwell, R. K. (1987). Facial recognition: Weapon effect and attentional focus. *Journal of Applied Social Psychology, 17,* 845–859.

Wells, G. L. (1978). Applied eyewitness testimony research: System variables and estimator variables. *Journal of Personality and Social Psychology, 36,* 1546–1557.

Wells, G. L. (1984). The psychology of lineup identifications. *Journal of Applied Social Psychology, 14,* 89–103.

Wells, G. L. (1988). *Eyewitness identification: A system handbook.* Toronto: Carswell.

Wells, G. L. (1993). What do we know about eyewitness identification? *American Psychologist, 48,* 553–571.

Wells, G. L. (1995). Scientific study of witness memory: Implications for public and legal policy. *Psychology, Public Policy, and Law, 1,* 726–731.

Wells, G. L., & Bradfield, A. L. (1998). "Good, you identified the suspect": Feedback to eyewitnesses distorts their reports of the witnessing experience. *Journal of Applied Psychology, 83,* 360–376.

Wells, G. L., Leippe, M. R., & Ostrom, T. M. (1979). Guidelines for empirically assessing the fairness of a lineup. *Law and Human Behavior, 3,* 285–293.

Wells, G. L., & Loftus, E. F. (1984a). Eyewitness research: Then and now. In G. L. Wells & E. F. Loftus (Eds.), *Eyewitness testimony: Psychological perspectives.* New York: Cambridge University Pres.

Wells, G. L., & Loftus, E. F. (Eds.). (1984b). *Eyewitness testimony: Psychological perspectives.* New York: Cambridge University Press.

Wells, G. L., & Luus, E. (1990). Police lineups as experiments: Social methodology as a framework for properly conducted lineups. *Personality and Social Psychology Bulletin, 16,* 106–117.

Wells, G. L., & Murray, D. M. (1983). What can psychology say about the Neil v. Biggers criteria for judging eyewitness identification accuracy? *Journal of Applied Psychology, 68,* 347–362.

Wells, G. L., Rydell, S. M., & Seelau, E. P. (1993). On the selection of distractors for eyewitness lineups. *Journal of Applied Psychology, 78,* 835–844.

Wells, G. L., Small, M., Penrod, S., Malpass, R. S., Fulero, S. M., & Brimacombe, C. A. E. (1998). *Eyewitness identification procedures: Recommendations for lineups and photospreads.* A scientific review paper commissioned by the American Psychology-Law Society. (Available from the author.)

Wells, G. L., & Turtle, J. W. (1986). Eyewitness identification: The importance of lineup models. *Psychological Bulletin, 99,* 320–329.

Williams, L. M. (1994). Recall of childhood trauma: A prospective study of women's memories of child sexual abuse. *Journal of Consulting and Clinical Psychology, 62,* 1167–1176.

Wright, D. B., & McDaid, A. T. (1996). Comparing system and estimator variables using data from real lineups. *Applied Cognitive Psychology, 10,* 75–84.

Yarmey, A. D. (1979). *The psychology of eyewitness testimony.* New York: Free Pres.

Yarmey, A. D. (1984). Age as a factor in eyewitness memory. In G. L. Wells & E. L. Loftus (Eds.), *Eyewitness testimony: Psychological perspectives* (pp. 142–154). New York: Cambridge University Press.

Yarmey, A. D. (1990). Accuracy and confidence of duration estimates following questions containing marked and unmarked modifiers. *Journal of Applied Social Psychology, 20,* 1139–1149.

Yuille, J., & Cutshall, J. (1986). A case study of eyewitnesses' memory of a crime. *Journal of Applied Psychology, 71,* 291–301.

Yuille, J. C., Davies, G., Gibling, F., & Marxsen, D. (1994). Eyewitness memory of police trainees for realistic role plays. *Journal of Applied Psychology, 79,* 931–936.

Zillmann, D. (1971). Excitation transfer in communication-mediated aggressive behavior. *Journal of Experimental Social Psychology, 7,* 419–434.

4

Preventing Mistaken Convictions in Eyewitness Identification Trials

The Case against Traditional Safeguards

STEVEN D. PENROD AND BRIAN CUTLER

It is clear that eyewitness testimony and eyewitness identifications play important roles in the apprehension, prosecution, and adjudication of criminal offenders. Police rely on eyewitness statements in their initial investigations; eyewitness identifications from lineups and photospreads are common; and the eyewitness is probably the most common type of witness in criminal trials.

Despite the heavy reliance on eyewitnesses, the criminal justice system also recognizes an element of unreliability in eyewitness evidence. Cases of mistaken identification and conviction are well documented in the legal and popular literature, and such errors have been one motivation for the psychological study of eyewitness reliability. Much of this research has focused on factors that influence individual eyewitness performance (see Chapter 3, this volume). In this chapter, we examine research on decision makers "downstream" from the eyewitness, with particular em-

STEVEN D. PENROD • Law–Psychology Program, University of Nebraska, Lincoln, Nebraska 68588-0308. BRIAN CUTLER • College of Arts and Sciences, Florida International University, Miami, Florida 33199.

Psychology and Law: The State of the Discipline, edited by Ronald Roesch, Stephen D. Hart, and James R. P. Ogloff. Kluwer Academic/Plenum Publishers, New York, 1999.

phasis on the ability of jurors to differentiate accurate from inaccurate eyewitnesses and a secondary emphasis on the ability of attorneys and experts to aid jurors in their decision making.

THE EXTENT OF THE PROBLEM

At the outset it is fair to ask how often eyewitness evidence results in erroneous convictions? Several methods have been used to make such estimates. For example, Huff (1987) conducted a national survey of state attorneys general ($N = 54$) and in-depth surveys of criminal justice officials from Ohio (including judges, public defenders, and prosecutors; $N = 229$). Over 70% thought that erroneous convictions from all sources, not just eyewitness identifications, occurred in less than 1% of all felony convictions, although another 20% of the estimates fell into the 1%–5% range. For a second source of information about mistaken convictions, Huff also scoured major newspapers and 1,100 magazines and journals and located 500 known cases of erroneous conviction.

Even if one assumes, as did Huff, that the error rate is only .5%, the number of erroneous convictions may be staggering. We (Cutler & Penrod, 1995) used Department of Justice data (1983) to estimate there are probably 1.5 million convictions per year for serious offenses. If only .5% are erroneous, that yields 7,500 erroneous convictions per year for serious offenses. As Huff noted based on similar computations, "This level of accuracy is at once both reassuring and frightening—reassuring in the aggregate, but frightening to contemplate individual cases of injustice, even if they constitute a very small proportion of all convictions" (p. 103).

Several scholars, beginning with Borchard (1932), have studied the causes of erroneous convictions (see also Frank & Frank, 1957; Huff, 1987; Huff, Rattner, & Sagarin, 1986). Huff (1987) concluded, on the basis of the 500 cases of erroneous conviction he located, that the single leading cause of mistaken conviction (nearly 60% of the cases) was erroneous eyewitness identification. Based on the estimate of 7,500 cases of erroneous convictions from all sources, the archival data suggest there may be as many as 4,500 erroneous convictions per year arising mistaken identifications.

A third source of information about the likely rates of mistaken identifications is provided by experimental studies of eyewitness performance. Wells (1993) noted that across the many laboratory experiments on eyewitness identification, the false identification rates varied from nearly 0% to nearly 100%, and many of these false identifications are made with expressions of high levels of certainty. Although laboratory evidence demonstrates that false identifications can occur, this evidence does not squarely address accuracy rates in actual cases because laboratory experiments and crime simulations differ in many ways from actual crimes.

The research that is most relevant to accuracy rates in actual eyewitness identifications is probably that done in field experiments. Some researchers (Brigham, Maass, Snyder, & Spaulding, 1982; Krafka & Penrod, 1985; Pigott, Brigham, & Bothwell, 1990; Platz & Hosch, 1988) have conducted well-controlled experiments in realistic field settings. The primary purpose of these studies, as with laboratory experiments, has been to estimate the effects of particular factors on identification accuracy. For example, two of the experiments (Brigham et al., 1982; Platz & Hosch, 1988) were interested in the influences of witness and perpetrator race on identification accuracy. One (Krafka & Penrod, 1985) was concerned with identification procedures. Pigott et al.'s (1990) study examined the relation between accuracy of eyewitnesses' descriptions and their identifications. Despite variations in research foci, these studies were conducted in fairly realistic settings, and the identification accuracy rates they yielded are certainly better indications of the accuracy rates likely to be found in actual crimes—as compared with accuracy rates reported in laboratory experiments.

Brigham et al. (1982), for example, sent students into convenience stores and had them engage in unusual transactions with clerks that lasted from three to four minutes. Clerks were later asked to identify the customers from photoarrays. In their pilot work, Brigham et al. tested the clerks 24 hours later and found that less than 8% were able to identify the customers (comparable to guessing rates). Therefore, they modified the procedure to test after only 2 hours. A total of 73 clerks participated in the 2-hour time delay: 50 of their 146 identifications from target-present arrays (34.2%) were correct.

In the Krafka and Penrod (1985) experiment, a "customer" also entered convenience stores and made a purchase that lasted several minutes. Either 2 or 24 hours later the clerks attempted to identify the customer. Eighty-five clerks were shown either customer-present or customer-absent photoarrays. When the customer was present in the photoarray, 41% of the clerks correctly identified him. When the customer was absent from the photoarray, 34% falsely identified someone else's photograph as that of the customer.

Platz and Hosch (1988) also used a convenience store scenario with three accomplices who engaged clerks in lengthier than usual transactions. Identifications were tested using customer-present photoarrays 2 hours after the customers entered the stores. Each of 86 clerks attempted to identify all three customers—overall, 44.2% of the identifications were correct. The false identification rate could not be assessed because customer-absent photoarrays were not used.

Pigott et al. (1990) used local banks for their field study. Their accomplices attempted to cash a United States Post Office money order in which the amount of $10 was crudely altered to $110. All tellers refused to cash the money order despite arguments by the accomplice that the alteration was made by post office personnel. These interactions lasted approximately 90 seconds. Four to 5 hours later tellers were shown a customer-present or customer-absent photoarray. A total of 47 bank tellers participated, and among tellers shown a customer-present photoarray, 47.8% made a correct identification. Among tellers shown a customer-absent photoarray, 37.5% made a false identification.

In these four field experiments, data were gathered from 291 eyewitnesses administered 536 separate identification tests. The average percentage correct was 41.8% for correct identifications and 35.8% for false identifications. In short, identifications for persons seen briefly in nonstressful conditions and attempted after brief delays were frequently inaccurate—both in terms of failures to identify targets when present and in terms of identifications of innocent persons when targets were not present.

Although the scenarios used in these four studies may not resemble events in such crimes as armed robbery or murder, the scenarios do resemble many eyewitness situations. In contrast to some crime situations, the time during which the perpetrator was viewable was substantial and comparable to many crimes, and the time between the crime and identification was relatively brief compared with many criminal identifications.

The results from these field studies (and from laboratory experiments—see, e.g., Shapiro & Penrod, 1986) converge with those from archival studies in suggesting that miscarriages of justice arising from mistaken identifications may be entirely too common events. What accounts for these inaccuracies? We do not propose to address that question here—interested readers might wish to turn to more extensive reviews of the scientific literature found in volumes by Cutler and Penrod (1995); Ross, Read, and Toglia (1994); Sporer, Malpass, and Koehnken (1996); and Wells and Wright, and Bradfield (Chapter 3, this volume). Rather, we propose to focus on research that examines the efficacy of legal safeguards—particularly cross-examination—that are intended to minimize the likelihood that mistaken identifications will yield erroneous convictions. Along the way we will briefly consider the nature and quality of jury decision making, the effects of instructions given to jurors by judges, and the impact of eyewitness expert testimony.

In an effort to reduce the dangers of mistaken identification, the criminal justice system has designed safeguards that, in theory, protect the defendant. These include pretrial criteria designed to encourage the use of fair identification procedures, such as cross-examination of witnesses;

judicial instructions delivered to the jury at the conclusion of the trial; and the use of eyewitness experts—a less common safeguard (Penrod, Fulero, & Cutler, 1995).

A defense attorney in an identification case has two major opportunities to assist his or her client's case. The first comes during jury selection (the so-called voir dire of jurors) when the attorney can try to identify jurors who may be skeptical about eyewitness identifications or willing to critically evaluate an identification. The second major opportunity comes in the cross-examination of eyewitnesses, when, according to courts and commentators, a skillful attorney can expose the weaknesses of an identification. Can and do attorneys effectively use these tools?

VOIR DIRE AS A SAFEGUARD AGAINST MISTAKEN IDENTIFICATIONS

The primary purpose of voir dire is to identify and exclude potentially biased jurors (Wrightsman, Nietzel, & Fortune, 1993). In an eyewitness identification case, the fairness of the defendant's trial partly depends on the ability and willingness of jurors to scrutinize eyewitness testimony. Prospective jurors may vary in their willingness to trust eyewitnesses and hence their inclination to critically evaluate them. By carefully exercising causal and/or peremptory challenges, attorneys may be able to eliminate prospective jurors who are unable or unwilling to scrutinize eyewitness testimony.

Little research has examined the voir dire strategies that attorneys use in eyewitness cases, though considerable research has examined voir dire strategies in other types of cases. Fulero and Penrod (1990) reviewed lawyers' writings and empirical research on jury selection. Their review of trial practice manuals revealed a litany of theories about the use of jurors' demographic characteristics as predictors of jurors' verdict preferences. They concluded that the advice was often inconsistent and based on stereotypes unsupported by the empirical literature on jury selection. Fulero and Penrod also reviewed studies of attorneys' jury selection practices, focusing on characteristics that attorneys are interested in, the types of jurors they typically challenge, and the effects of their challenges. They concluded that attorneys tend to be interested in characteristics such as age, occupation, demeanor, gender, appearance, and race and tend to eliminate jurors based on simplistic profiles of dubious validity.

Fulero and Penrod (1990) concluded that general attitudes and demographics were weak predictors of juror verdicts. However, they noted that some case-specific attitudes are more powerful predictors of juror verdicts and noted work linking verdicts to (a) attitudes toward the death penalty (Moran & Comfort, 1986; Powers & Luginbuhl, 1987), (b) attitudes toward women in rape trials (Wier & Wrightsman, 1990), (c) attitudes toward drugs in controlled substance trials (Moran, Cutler, & Loftus, 1990), and (d) attitudes toward psychiatrists and the insanity defense predicted verdicts in insanity defense cases (Cutler, Moran, & Narby, 1992).

The effectiveness of voir dire as a safeguard in eyewitness cases rests on the assumption that case-specific attitudes can be reliably measured and can then be used to identify prospective jurors who differ in their willingness to scrutinize the testimony of eyewitnesses. In this arena, the most relevant study is that of Harby and Cutler (1994), who tested whether attitudes toward eyewitnesses can be reliably measured, and if so, whether these attitudes predict verdicts using trial simulation methodology.

Narby and Cutler first constructed a nine-item attitude inventory to assess predispositions to believe eyewitness testimony based on responses from 651 students and jury-eligible community residents and then examined the correlation between scores on the attitudes scale and the tendency to convict using a simulated jury trial. In one study, 62 undergraduates and 46 community residents (N = 108), all jury-eligible, completed the scale, viewed a simulated trial, and rendered verdicts. The correlation between the attitudes scale and verdict was nonsignificant (r = .14). This finding was replicated in a second study with 30 undergraduates and 27 community residents ($r = -.15$).

In sum, although case-specific attitudes may be the most successful class of predictors in studies of jury selection (Fulero & Penrod, 1990), it appears that some case-specific attitudes are weak predictors of perceptions of defendant culpability. Attitudes toward eyewitnesses may be one example, perhaps because of jurors' lack of experience with eyewitnesses. Of course, if attitudes toward eyewitnesses do not predict juror skepticism about eyewitness testimony, then voir dire may not be an effective method for identifying prospective jurors who might take a critical stance with respect to eyewitnesses.

CROSS-EXAMINATION AS A SAFEGUARD AGAINST MISTAKEN IDENTIFICATIONS

Cross-examination is probably the most relied-on safeguard against mistaken conviction. It is used in virtually every trial in which an eyewitness makes an identification. How effective is cross-examination in eyewitness identification cases? For a number of reasons, we doubt that it is.

In order for cross-examination to be effective, the following conditions must be met; the evidence suggests they are not:

1. Attorneys must have an opportunity to identify the factors that are likely to have influenced an eyewitness's identification performance in a particular case.
2. Attorneys must be aware of the factors that influence eyewitness identification performance.
3. Judges and juries must be aware during the trial, and consider during deliberations, the factors that influence eyewitness identification performance.

Attorney Opportunities to Develop Identification-Relevant Information for Cross-Examination

The first prerequisite for effective cross-examination is that attorneys have access to the information necessary for cross-examination. What opportunity does the attorney have to learn about the viewing conditions at the scene of the crime and the conditions surrounding the identification test?

Typically, attorneys design cross-examination to address two types of information: the conditions under which the event in question was witnessed and the manner in which identification tests were conducted. Because defense attorneys are not present at the crime, information about witnessing conditions must be obtained directly from the eyewitnesses or indirectly from the police who investigated the crime. The attorney usually has access to police reports and may also depose or examine investigators and eyewitnesses in pretrial hearings. And, attorneys may visit the crime scene and note physical factors that might influence an eyewitness's performance.

Most of the information used to develop cross-examination is obtained secondhand, and the quality of the information depends heavily on the quality of witnesses' memories and extent of cooperation of the eyewitnesses and investigators. Of course, a witness's memory for the crime, the perpetrator, and the conditions surrounding the event may be poor and of little value (beyond the fact they are poor) to the attorney.

Although the attorney is not present at the crime, he or she may be present at a subsequent identification test. Whether the attorney is or is not present at the identification test is sometimes a matter of law. In *U.S. v. Wade* (1967)—Justice Brennan in support of the conclusion that a suspect has a right to counsel at identification proceedings wrote: "A major factor contributing to the high incidence of miscarriage of justice from mistaken identification has been the degree of suggestion inherent in the manner in which the prosecution presents the suspect to witness for pretrial identification.... Suggestion can be created intentionally or unintentionally in many subtle ways" (p. 227).

Justice Brennan argued that one purpose of having the counsel present at lineups is to monitor the fairness of the procedure, as the defendant himself cannot be expected to do so: "*[E]ven though cross-examination is a precious safeguard to a fair trial, it cannot be viewed as an absolute ... assurance of accuracy and reliability.* Thus ... the first line of defense must be the prevention of unfairness and the lessening of the hazards of eyewitness identification of the lineup" (p. 235, emphasis added).

Three other cases in the late 1960s and early 1970s further defined the scope of the defendant's rights during an identification procedure. In *Stovall v. Denno* (1967), the Court acknowledged the suggestiveness of showups but decided they are permissible if exigent (pressing) circumstances require their use. In *Kirby v. Illinois* (1972), the majority held that the rule does not apply to identification tests conducted prior to a defendant's indictment. And in *United States v. Ash* (1973), the court rejected the notion that a photoarray was functionally equivalent to a live lineup and held that the right to counsel granted does not extend to photoarrays—in large part because improper procedures can be reconstructed at trial. The dissenting minority nonetheless emphasized that there are three important possible sources of suggestion in photoarrays: the photographs might suggest which of the pictures is that of the suspect, photographs may be displayed in a suggestive manner, and communications from the prosecutor may lead an uncertain witness to identify the "correct" photograph.

These cases are important not only because they define the defendant's rights, but also because they expose important assumptions about eyewitness and police behavior that can be tested empirically. It is clear, for example, that most justices *presume* defense attorneys know about threats to fairness and can identify suggestive practices if they see them. But, how frequently do defense attorneys attend identification tests involving their clients? Brigham and Wolfskeil (1983) surveyed Florida prosecutors, defense attorneys, and police officers on this question. They reported an attorney is seldom present at live lineups conducted prior to the first appearance of a defendant, usually present at live lineups conducted after first appearance, never present during photoarrays conducted prior to first appearance, and seldom present at photoarrays conducted after first appearance. These findings raise serious questions about attorneys' opportunities to develop information for cross-examination in the vast majority of identification proceedings.

At various points in these opinions, justices note that records of identification procedures can be kept. However, even if such records do permit better defense counsel insights into problems such as foil and clothing biases, and to a lesser extent, presentation biases, they will not reveal to defense attorneys the full array of problems associated with instruction and investigator biases.

In short, one of the weaker links in the argument that cross-examination is an effective safeguard against mistaken conviction is the assumption that defense attorneys have adequate opportunities to develop the information required for an effective trial strategy. In fact, attorneys must rely on the police to ask the right questions at the scene of the crime and to note the eyewitness's answers accurately. Investigating officers are, of course, relying on the eyewitness to report the viewing conditions accurately in the first place. Furthermore, the attorney is frequently absent from identification tests (though not by choice)—particularly photoarrays and identifications conducted at early stages of investigation. In such cases, the attorney must, once again, rely on the eyewitness, police officer, and defendant to report any suggestive elements of an identification test.

ATTORNEY KNOWLEDGE OF FACTORS INFLUENCING EYEWITNESS PERFORMANCE

A second prerequisite to effective cross-examination is that attorneys be knowledgeable about the psychology of eyewitness identification. In order to cross-examine an eyewitness effectively, an attorney must know what factors to look for. It certainly is common for an attorney to cross-examine the eyewitness, the conditions under which the event was witnessed, and the procedures used in the identification test. But do the questions asked by the attorney reflect a sound understanding of factors that influence eyewitness performance? Do attorneys ask about factors that are known to influence identification accuracy (e.g., the impact of disguise, weapon focus, lineup instructions, the manner in which lineup members are presented), while ignoring factors that are known not to predict identification accuracy (e.g., face recognition skills, training in witnessing, confidence)? With the exception of a few attorneys trained in cognitive and social psychology, there is little reason to expect that attorneys are familiar with the latest empirical literature on eyewitnesses. Are attorneys nonetheless sensitive to the factors that affect the encoding and storage of information as well as the suggestivity of identification tests?

Several researchers have surveyed attorneys to assess whether their knowledge of factors that influence eyewitness performance comports with what is known in the psychological literature. Brigham and Wolfskeil (1983) obtained responses from 89 public defenders, 69 state prosecutors, and 77 private defense attorneys from Florida. The survey was designed to ascertain the following about the respondents': (a) general background characteristics, (b) knowledge of legal procedures concerning eyewitness evidence, (c) estimates of the frequency of mistaken eyewitness identifications, (d) knowledge of factors that influence eyewitness identification accuracy, and (e) opinions about the weight that judges and jurors give to eyewitness evidence.

Most attorneys reported being involved with eyewitnesses less than once per week. Photoarrays were more commonly encountered than lineups—at least once a week by 59% of prosecutors and 25% of defense attorneys. Live lineups were encountered at least once per week by 23% of prosecutors and 9% of defense attorneys. Significantly, more prosecutors (84%) than defense attorneys (36%) felt that "90% or more" of identifications were probably correct. Prosecutors (75%) were more likely than defense attorneys (56%) to believe that eyewitnesses more commonly fail to identify guilty suspects than falsely identify innocent ones.

The survey also contained questions about factors that may be perceived to influence identification accuracy. Attorneys were asked about cross-race recognition. Consistent with the empirical literature, both groups of attorneys believed cross-race identifications to be less accurate than same-race identifications even though their estimates of the overall accuracy rates differed markedly.

Prosecutors and defense attorneys also tended to agree with each other on the influence of gender, education, and intelligence on identification accuracy. With respect to gender, over 60% of attorneys thought that males and females would perform comparably on identification tests. Over 60% thought that intelligent witnesses are more likely to be accurate. Most also thought that education was not related to identification accuracy. Attorney beliefs are consistent with the psychological literature on gender and education (Cutler & Penrod, 1995), but there is little empirical evidence supporting the relationship between intelligence and identification accuracy endorsed by the majority of attorneys.

Attorneys were also asked, in an open-ended format, what factors they believed to be related to identification accuracy. The characteristics most frequently mentioned by defense attorneys were the following: physical characteristics of the suspect (60%), lighting at the scene of the crime (39%), exposure duration during the crime (36%), proximity to the suspect at the crime (34%), and physical appearance of the suspect's body (33%). The most common characteristics mentioned by prosecutors were as follows: physical characteristics of the suspect (68%), lighting at the scene of the crime (60%), exposure duration during the crime (52%), whether or not the witness has a good memory (32%), and physical appearance of the suspect's body (32%). Most of these factors (lighting, opportunity to view the suspect at the scene of the crime, proximity of the suspect, exposure duration) are indeed potentially important factors. The physical characteristics of the suspect might refer to distinctiveness of appearance, which is also a reliable predictor of identification accuracy.

Based on the attorney's responses to this open-ended question, we generally conclude that on balance the factors mentioned by attorneys tend to be predictive of identification accuracy. But what of factors not mentioned by the attorneys? Potentially important factors such as weapon focus, disguises, changes in facial features, cross-race recognition, retention interval, and factors associated with suggestivity of identification tests did not rank on either prosecution or defense attorneys' "top 10" lists. It is possible that these factors present themselves with sufficient rarity that attorneys do not think of them or think they are less important than those factors they did mention.

It is notable that there is wide variability among defense and prosecuting attorneys concerning the top 10 factors. Across the two lists only two factors ("physical characteristics of the suspect" and "lighting at the scene of the crime") were mentioned by a majority of the respondents. Whatever the explanation for the absence of important factors from the "top 10" lists, these survey data only moderately support the notion that attorneys know what questions to ask.

Other survey questions assessed perceptions of how eyewitness testimony is used in court. When asked about how much weight judges and juries give to eyewitness evidence, 89% of defense attorneys but only 7% of prosecutors indicated "too much." Predictably, defense attorneys were significantly more favorably disposed toward expert psychological testimony on eyewitness identification. When asked whether "a psychologist's expert opinion should be considered in court when deciding the reliability of eyewitness identification," 11% of defense attorneys replied "never," 30% replied "rarely or only in unusual cases," 32% replied "fairly often," and 27% replied "routinely." For prosecutors, the responses were, respectively: 55%, 45%, 0%, and 0%.

Brigham and Wolfskeil's (1983) survey results suggested that attorneys are knowledgeable about some factors that influence eyewitness identification accuracy but less so about others, and there is little consensus about the relative importance of the factors about which they display some knowledge. Of course, it is impossible, on the basis of this survey, to determine whether attorneys do detect the problems they have identified when those problems present themselves in actual cases.

Rahaim and Brodsky (1982) also conducted a survey that tested attorneys' knowledge of factors that influence eyewitness identification accuracy. Respondents were 42 practicing lawyers, and although the questions employed were somewhat different, the pattern of results was similar.

Together, these two studies show that attorneys tend to be sensitive to some empirically supported eyewitnessing factors and less sensitive to others. Furthermore, the studies reveal substantial confusion about the influence of a number of factors—on only one item did more than 75% of the attorneys agree about a factor. For most questions, there was substantial disagreement among attorneys about the influence of particular factors.

The attorney knowledge research raises serious questions about the extent to which attorneys are familiar with the factors that influence eyewitness performance. Of course, attorneys who are not familiar with the threats to eyewitness reliability obviously cannot hope to undertake an effective examination of witnesses that will expose these threats.

Even a thorough knowledge of the factors that influence eyewitness performance is, unfortunately, no guarantee that an attorney can undertake effective examination of eyewitnesses and law enforcement personnel. Even the most cooperative witnesses and police officers may not remember critical information. And, although defendants do enjoy some rights to representation at postindictment lineups, counsel typically is not present at other identification proceedings.

Under these conditions—reliance on witness and police memories and limited access to identification proceedings—it appears that cross-examination in many criminal cases is built on a shaky foundation. Even when the foundation is solid, questions can still be raised about the third condition for effective cross-examination that we raised earlier: Will effective cross-examination of witnesses adequately alert juries (and/or judges) to threats to eyewitness reliability? And, will these decision makers give appropriate consideration to these threats when evaluating eyewitness evidence?

JURY DECISION MAKING AS A SAFEGUARD
AGAINST MISTAKEN IDENTIFICATIONS

Of course, even assuming that an attorney is quite sophisticated about the factors that influence eyewitness performance, there is no guarantee that cross-examination designed to underscore the threats to accurate identification will fall on receptive jury ears. If jurors do not appreciate that a factor such as cross-racial identification can influence eyewitness performance, there is little reason to elicit testimony about the factor during cross-examination of an eyewitness.

Effective cross-examination requires that juries be, or be made, sensitive to such factors. The attorney can argue during closing argument that particular factors enhance the likelihood of a false identification, but the jury may find such arguments implausible, especially if they perceive the attorney to be biased in favor of his or her client and find the arguments inconsistent with their commonsense understandings.

How well informed and receptive are juries? To answer this question we briefly consider three sets of studies. The first set comprises survey studies that assess lay knowledge by using multiple choice questions, as in the Brigham and Wolfskeil (1983) study of attorney sensitivity reported earlier. The second set examines the abilities of lay persons to predict the outcome of eyewitness identification experiments. The third set examines juror sensitivity to systematic variations in eyewitness evidence.

Survey Studies That Test Juror Knowledge About Eyewitness Reliability

Four different surveys, conducted in three countries and published in three articles, have examined juror knowledge about factors that influence eyewitness identification (Deffenbacher & Loftus, 1982; McConkey & Roche, 1989; Noon & Hollin, 1987). These studies use the same survey instrument but their samples vary. They include such populations as undergraduates, nonstudent adults, and law students. The studies used a questionnaire developed by Deffenbacher and Loftus (1982) that assess respondents' understanding of factors such as the influence of stress and violence on information recall, the influence of misleading questions on recall, the accuracy of time estimation, and to the influence of narrative versus closed-ended questions.

The somewhat diverse groups of subjects produced remarkably consistent results. American, English, and Australian respondents all appear to be somewhat sensitive to the influence of cross-race recognition and prior photoarray identifications on identification accuracy. They appear less sensitive to the negligible effects of training on identification accuracy and to the effects of witness age and retention interval. The surveys converge on the conclusion that prospective jurors are sensitive to some factors but less so to others and generally display high degrees of variability in their responses—which raises the question of how such disagreements are resolved by jurors. However, these survey studies examine only a limited number of variables.

PREDICTION STUDIES THAT TEST JUROR KNOWLEDGE
ABOUT EYEWITNESS RELIABILITY

Subjects in prediction studies are given descriptions of the methods used in eyewitness identification experiments and are then asked to predict the results (because the experiments have already been conducted, these are actually "postdiction" studies, but we will use the more familiar term, prediction). If subjects in these studies are sensitive to the factors that influence identification accuracy, they should be reasonably accurate at predicting study outcomes.

In one of the first of these experiments, Kassin (1979) gave students summaries of the experimental conditions employed in an experiment by Leippe, Wells, & Ostrom (1978). That experiment examined the influence of crime seriousness on identification accuracy. Subjects witnessed a staged theft and were led to believe, either before or after the theft, that the theft was high or low in seriousness (i.e., the item stolen was more or less valuable). The serious manipulation influenced identification accuracy among both eyewitnesses who knew the value of the stolen item prior to the theft (19% in the low-seriousness and 56% in the high-seriousness conditions correctly identified the thief) and those who learned of the stolen item's value after the theft (35% and 12.5%, respectively). Kassin's subjects predicted the first two cell means would be 66% and 65% and the second set 53% and 60%, respectively. Thus, Kassin's subjects were not sensitive to either the influence of crime-seriousness on identification accuracy or to overall levels of identification accuracy.

Wells (1984) reported several prediction studies. In one, students read the procedure section of the Leippe et al. (1978) study and were given one of two target cases to predict. In one case, the eyewitness was "completely certain" of his identification; in the other, the eyewitness was "somewhat uncertain." Leippe et al. found that confidence was unrelated to identification accuracy, but Wells's students predicted a .83 probability of a correct identification for the "completely certain" witness and a .28 probability of a correct identification for a "somewhat uncertain" witness. In short, not only did Wells's students believe confidence was related to accuracy, but they believed that it was very strongly related to accuracy.

In his second study, Wells had 80 students read a description of Malpass and Devine's (1981) study of instruction bias. In the original study identification data from vandal-absent conditions included 78% false identifications with biased instructions and 33% false identifications with unbiased instructions. Wells's students' predictions were 16% and 18%, respectively—thus these prospective jurors were not sensitive to a factor that clearly contributes to the suggestiveness of identification procedures: instruction bias.

Brigham and Bothwell (1983) gave their subjects descriptions of two experiments. One was Leippe et al.'s (1978) study of crime seriousness—in which subjects received a description of the high-seriousness, informed afterward condition. The second was Brigham et al.'s (1982) field study of cross-race recognition. Brigham and Bothwell found that respondents reliably overestimated the accuracy of eyewitness identifications. In Leippe et al.'s (1978) study, 12.5% of identifications were correct. However, survey respondents estimated that 70.6% would give correct identifications on average. In Brigham et al.'s (1982) field study, 32% of white clerks correctly identified black clerks, but survey respondents estimated that 51% had done so. Likewise, 31% of black clerks in the study correctly identified white customers, but survey respondents estimated that 70% had done so. Brigham and Bothwell's (1983) results reinforce the findings of Kassin (1979) and Wells (1984) and indicate that prospective jurors overestimate the accuracy of eyewitness identifications.

MOCK-JURY STUDIES OF JUROR DECISION MAKING— DIFFERENTIATING ACCURATE FROM INACCURATE EYEWITNESSES

We believe that the studies most relevant to the question of juror sensitivity are those that attempt to simulate the jury's actual task of evaluating eyewitness identifications. There are two distinct approaches to studying juror sensitivity: the first examines jurors' ability to discriminate between accurate and inaccurate eyewitnesses; the second examines mock-juror sensitivity to the factors that influence identification accuracy.

An example of the first type of study is an experiment by Wells, Lindsay, and Ferguson (1979) in which they staged a crime in view of witnesses who then attempted identifications from six-person photoarrays. Twenty-four witnesses who made accurate identifications and 18 who made inaccurate identifications then participated in a simulated cross-examination. For half of the eyewitnesses, the questions were leading, and for half they were nonleading. The identification testimony of these witnesses was then evaluated by 201 undergraduates who served as mock jurors. The mock jurors were asked whether they believed the identifications were correct. Wells et al. found that leading questions—typically used in cross-examination—may have a salutary effect on juror assessments of eyewitness performance. When the questions addressed to the witnesses were nonleading, inaccurate eyewitnesses were actually believed by more jurors (86%) than were accurate eyewitnesses (76%). In contrast, when questions were leading, accurate eyewitnesses were believed by more jurors (84%) than were inaccurate eyewitnesses (73%).

How good were the mock jurors at differentiating accurate and inaccurate eyewitnesses? Among jurors exposed to nonleading cross-examination, 76% correctly identified accurate eyewitnesses, but only 14% correctly identified inaccurate eyewitnesses. Among jurors exposed to leading cross-examination, 84% correctly identified accurate eyewitnesses, and 27% correctly identified inaccurate eyewitnesses. Thus, performance was not very encouraging: The 84% correct classification rate for accurate eyewitnesses is not profoundly worrisome, but the numbers for inaccurate eyewitnesses are quite disturbing because they suggest that nearly three out of four mistaken identifications would be believed.

Another worrisome finding was that the confidence of the eyewitness in his or her identification accuracy correlated significantly ($r = .53$) with whether the juror believed the eyewitness but nonsignificantly ($r = .05$) with the accuracy of the juror's decision. Thus, jurors were more likely to believe confident eyewitnesses, but confident eyewitnesses were no more likely to be accurate than less confident eyewitnesses.

A second study by Wells and Leippe (1981) involved 48 eyewitnesses to a staged theft who made positive identifications and were then cross-examined. The cross-examinations, which were videotaped, consisted of 21 questions, 11 of which pertained to peripheral details about which eyewitnesses were queried after the crime. Each of 48 eyewitnesses was subjected to one of two types of cross-examination. In one condition, eyewitnesses responded to each question and were not asked follow-up questions. In the "peripheral detail" condition, each time an eyewitness responded incorrectly to one of 11 peripheral detail questions, the attorney followed up, demonstrating that the eyewitness's answer was incorrect according to police records.

These videotaped cross-examinations were then evaluated by 96 undergraduate jurors who indicated their belief in the accuracy of the eyewitness's identification. Accurate eyewitnesses were believed by 75% of the jurors who viewed the control cross-examination, but they were believed by only 38% of the jurors who viewed the peripheral detail cross-examination. Inaccurate eyewitnesses were believed by 71% of the jurors who viewed the control cross-examination and 58% of jurors who viewed the peripheral detail cross-examination. Thus, cross-examination that focused on errors about peripheral details dramatically reduced jurors' belief of witnesses—unfortunately the effect was stronger for accurate eyewitnesses than it was for inaccurate eyewitnesses! This unfortunate set of results was further compounded by the fact that, in Wells and Leippe's study, eyewitness memory for peripheral details was inversely (though weakly) associated with identification accuracy.

A study by Lindsay and colleagues (Lindsay, Wells, & Rumpel, 1981) also tested jurors' abilities to discriminate accurate from inaccurate eyewitnesses by using methods similar to those of the two preceding studies. Once again, jurors gave witness identifications more credence than was merited by the performance of the witnesses. Witness confidence affected juror beliefs—77% of confident witnesses were believed versus 59% of low-confidence witnesses. Unfortunately, Lindsay et al. had found only a weak relationship between witness confidence and witness accuracy; thus the jurors were relying on less than fully diagnostic information when using confidence to gauge witness accuracy.

Lindsay, Wells, and O'Connor (1989) tested whether the findings from the 1981 research would generalize to a more realistic trial situation. Witnesses to a simulated crime tried to identify the perpetrator from target-present or target-absent photoarrays. One to 5 weeks later the eyewitnesses went, individually, to a courtroom where they were greeted by an experimenter and a "prosecutor" (a practicing attorney). The prosecutor spent 15 to 25 minutes discussing the case and the anticipated examination with the eyewitness. Then each eyewitness went through direct examination by the prosecutor, cross-examination by the defense attorney, and redirect examination by the prosecutor. All prosecutors obtained in-court identifications of the suspects. These proceedings were videotaped, and from the videotapes 16 "trials" were created using eight eyewitnesses who made correct identifications and eight whose identifications were false. Attorneys in this study varied in their level of experience: Half were experienced lawyers (averaging 12 years since passing the bar exam), and half were advanced law students with some legal aid experience.

The videotaped trials were shown to undergraduates, each of whom viewed one trial, rendered a verdict, and answered other questions about the trial. The conviction rate did not vary as a function of eyewitness accuracy (jurors could not differentiate accurate from inaccurate eyewitnesses). The degree of attorneys' experience also did not significantly influence verdicts, nor did attorney experience interact with eyewitness accuracy on the verdict. In short, the realism of the examination/cross-examination and the experience of the attorneys conducting these examinations did not change the conclusions from Wells et al.'s (1979, 1980, 1981) and Lindsay et al.'s (1981, 1986, 1989) earlier studies.

These studies converge on rather alarming conclusions about jurors' abilities: Jurors overestimate the accuracy of identifications (there are more convictions than there are accurate identifications); jurors fail to distin-

guish accurate from inaccurate eyewitnesses; and jurors tend to under-
value viewing conditions that are known to predict identification accuracy
and instead base their decisions in part on eyewitness memory for peripheral details and witness confidence—both of which tend to be poor predictors of identification accuracy.

TO WHICH ASPECTS OF AN EYEWITNESS IDENTIFICATION
ARE JURORS SENSITIVE?

In the preceding studies, jurors sometimes relied on inappropriate
information (e.g., answers to peripheral detail questions) in making their
assessments of eyewitnesses' reliability. It is this issue that we consider in
light of studies in which eyewitness evidence presented to mock jurors has
been systematically manipulated. The focus of these experiments is on
determining juror sensitivity to eyewitness factors that are known from
empirical research to influence (or not influence) eyewitness reliability.
What do jurors consider when making their decisions? In these experiments, it is juror sensitivity to these factors that is of interest rather than
ability to differentiate accurate from inaccurate witnesses.

In a series of four experiments, Lindsay, Lim, Marando, and Cully
(1986) examined factors that influence jurors' evaluations of eyewitnesses.
The first experiment examined the impact of the consistency of identification testimony across eyewitnesses. Lindsay et al. manipulated three factors: (a) the physical evidence (strong vs. weak evidence—a victim's purse
either found or not found in the defendant's possession) against the accused, (b) the number of eyewitnesses for the prosecution (0, 1, or 2), and
(c) the number of eyewitnesses for the defense (0, 1, or 2).

The physical evidence did not significantly influence verdicts (25% of
the subjects in the weak versus 33% of the subjects in the strong evidence
conditions were convicted). However, the number of eyewitnesses for
each side produced significant effects. The overall conviction rates were
10% for 0, 34% for 1, and 45% for 2 prosecution eyewitness conditions, and
41% for 0, 28% for 1, and 21% for 2 defense eyewitnesses. Convictions were
most likely when the prosecution's witnesses were unopposed (50%) and
least likely with unopposed defense witness testimony (2%), which suggests that the number of eyewitnesses is less important than whether or
not there is conflicting eyewitness identifications.

The second experiment examined the effects of defense witness testimony. Five conditions were tested using a videotaped enactment of an
assault trial: no additional evidence, a second eyewitness identification of
the defendant, a defense eyewitness who testified that the defendant was

not the perpetrator, an alibi witness for the defendant, and an alibi witness who was a relative of the defendant.

High conviction rates were obtained with two and one unopposed prosecution eyewitnesses (80% and 60%, respectively; this difference did not attain statistical significance). When an eyewitness testified the defendant was not the perpetrator or provided an alibi, significantly fewer jurors (27% in each condition) convicted. The alibi provided by the relative did not significantly reduce the conviction rate (57% guilty) in comparison which the no-defense-witness conditions. In short, jurors evaluated eyewitness identifications in light of other trial evidence.

The third Lindsay experiment examined the impact of inconsistent eyewitness testimony and defendant attractiveness on mock-juror decisions. Lindsay et al. presented to subjects an audiotaped simulated trial together with slides of the defendant and the eyewitness. In one condition, there were no inconsistencies in the eyewitness's testimony. In the inconsistent eyewitness condition, the witness testified that she originally said the criminal was blond but did not think that the defendant could be described as blond; did not know whether the defendant altered her hair color; and recalled the defendant's hair was dark at the lineup, but was still confident about her identification. Attractiveness was manipulated by showing slides of the defendant with attractive or unattractive makeup, hairstyle, and attire. The consistency of testimony did not significantly influence jurors' verdicts. On the other hand, the defendant was convicted by significantly fewer jurors when she was attractive (33%) than when she was unattractive (60%).

Lindsay et al.'s fourth experiment examined the impact of viewing conditions at the scene of the crime. An audiotaped burglary trial in which the defendant was identified by an eyewitness near the scene of the burglary was played for 60 undergraduates. In half of the trials, the crime occurred at 9:00 A.M. on a sunny day. For the other half, the crime occurred at 1:00 A.M., 60 feet from the nearest streetlight. Time-of-day condition was crossed with viewing durations of 5 seconds, 30 minutes, or 30 minutes with interaction with the burglar during that time. In all trials, the eyewitness was highly confident in his identification.

Exposure duration had a nonsignificant effect on verdicts and did not significantly interact with time of day: conviction rates were 45%, 40%, and 55% in the 5 seconds, 30 minutes, and 30 minutes plus interaction conditions, respectively. Jurors in the night condition convicted less often than jurors in the day condition (57% vs. 37%), but this difference was not statistically significant. These results indicate a lack of juror sensitivity to witnessing conditions that influence identification accuracy.

These findings are not entirely consistent with the results from the Lindsay, Wells, and Rumpel (1981) study reported earlier. In the earlier study, juror judgments of eyewitness accuracy were influenced by variations in witnessing conditions. It is possible the witnessing conditions were manipulated more powerfully in that study.

Berman, Narby, and Cutler (1995) also examined the effect of witness consistency on juror evaluations of eyewitnesses. In comparison with Lindsay et al., Berman et al. manipulated whether the witness gave inconsistent testimony on central versus peripheral information. Berman et al. hypothesized that jurors exposed to inconsistent eyewitness testimony would perceive the eyewitness as less credible and the defendant less culpable. Therefore, they would convict less often. They further hypothesized that inconsistent statements concerning central details would have a greater influence than inconsistent statements concerning peripheral details. Witnesses could be consistent or inconsistent on either peripheral or central facts.

Subjects viewed a 25-minute simulated examination and cross-examination of an eyewitness to a bank robbery. Inconsistencies were brought out during cross-examination. Conviction rates were 32% for peripheral-consistent and central-consistent, 12% for peripheral-consistent and central-inconsistent, 20% for peripheral-inconsistent and central-consistent, and 8% for peripheral-inconsistent and central-inconsistent. The main effect was significant for central details but nonsignificant for peripheral details. The interaction was also nonsignificant.

As predicted, jurors exposed to inconsistent eyewitness testimony perceived the eyewitness as less credible, the defendant as less culpable, and, at least when the inconsistencies concerned central details, they were less likely to convict. The difference between the Berman results and the Lindsay results may arise because Berman manipulated inconsistency on more central details than did Lindsay.

Although exposing inconsistencies in witness testimony may be an effective cross-examination strategy, it is not clear whether the strategy improves the quality of jurors' decisions. Eyewitness studies indicate that description accuracy, congruence, and consistency are *not* related to identification accuracy; hence, jurors probably should not rely on inconsistencies as a basis for devaluing eyewitness testimony (see Cutler & Penrod, 1995).

Bell and Loftus (1989) examined the influence of the level of detail in eyewitness testimony on juror assessments of eyewitnesses. Subjects in the first experiment read a description of a criminal trial. Within these summaries the degree of the detail provided by the prosecution witness was high versus low, the degree of detail provided by the defense witness was high versus low, and the degree of relationship between the detail and the perpetrator was high versus low. Level of detail was manipulated by using witness statements that contained either the gist of what happened or specific details about the event. Relatedness was manipulated by having the statements either concern the actions of the perpetrator or another party.

Detail of testimony significantly influenced subjects' verdicts. When the prosecution eyewitness's testimonial detail was high, 33% of mock jurors convicted versus 12% when detail was low. When the testimonial defense eyewitness's detail was high, 23% convicted; and 31% convicted when it was low. This difference was marginally significant. Relatedness did not significantly influence verdicts—the level of detail influenced jurors' judgments whether the testimony was or was not relevant to the defendant.

In their second experiment, Bell and Loftus's prosecution eyewitness always gave low-detail testimony; the defense eyewitness always gave testimony related to the perpetrator. Bell and Loftus manipulated the degree of detail in the defense eyewitness's testimony as they did in Experiment 1 and manipulated whether the prosecution eyewitness's testimony was verified. In the no-verification condition, the prosecution eyewitness was not asked about details provided by the defense eyewitness. In the verification condition, the witness was asked but replied that she could not remember the details.

Subjects were less likely to convict when the defense eyewitness gave highly detailed testimony (6% in the verification condition; 31% in the no-verification condition) than when the testimony was less detailed (47% and 25%, respectively). There was a significant interaction with verification: Level of detail had a much larger effect in the verification condition than in the no-verification condition. This pattern helps to supports Bell and Loftus's contention that jurors sometimes rely on superficial cues to evaluate eyewitnesses testimony.

We (Cutler, Penrod, & Dexter, 1990; Cutler, Penrod, & Stuve, 1988) have also used mock–jury experiments to examine factors that jurors use to evaluate identification evidence. Our simulated liquor store robbery trial was shown to 450 undergraduates and former jurors. Examination (direct and cross) of two prosecution witnesses served as a vehicle for disclosure of approximately 20 witness and identification factors that were discussed in the trial. Ten of these variables were systematically manipulated in the trial presentations (all two levels), while the remainder were held constant (all of the manipulated variables were selected because other research had demonstrated that they had an impact on or relationship to eyewitness accuracy). (We refer the interested reader to Cutler et al., 1988, for a more detailed description of the videotaped trial.) The two primary dependent measures were verdict (not guilty vs. guilty) and the subject's estimate of the probability that the identification was correct. Both dependent variables were equivalently influenced by the eyewitness factors.

The witness testified that, during the robbery, the robber wore either (a) a knit cap fully covering his hair or no hat; (b) that throughout the robbery a handgun was either outwardly brandished and pointed at her or hidden in the robber's jacket; (c) that the robber either threatened to kill her, manhandled her, fired his handgun into the floor, and pushed her to the floor before leaving or calmly and quietly demanded the money and then left; and (d) that the identification was made either 14 days after the robbery or 2 days after the robbery.

In half of the trials, the police officer who conducted the lineup testified that the witness was instructed to "choose the suspect from the lineup who you believe is the robber" or to "choose the suspect from the lineup who you believe is the robber or indicate that the robber was not in the lineup." In half of the videotapes, the witness testified that very few of the lineup members looked like the robber or that there were several lineup members who resembled the robber in physical appearance. She also testified that she was either 100% or 80% confident that she had correctly identified the robber.

The mean conviction rate in the trial was 63%; only one of the manipulated factors—confidence—influenced juror judgments (a 60% conviction rate in the low-confidence condition versus a 67% conviction rate in the high-confidence condition). The main effect for eligible and experienced versus undergraduate jurors was trivial and nonsignificant.

Weapon presence had a stronger impact on the judgments of eligible and experienced jurors than on the judgments of undergraduate jurors. Among the undergraduates, weapon presence produced a trivial effect on jurors' judgments, but eligible and experienced jurors were significantly more likely to convict if the weapon was present ($M = .66$) that if the weapon was hidden ($M = .54$). This finding indicates that neither group is appropriately sensitive to the weapon focus effect—existing research indicates that weapon presence undermines witness performance (Steblay, 1992).

In sum, the studies that have looked at juror sensitivity to eyewitnessing factors indicate that jurors are not appropriately sensitive to those factors. These studies, like the studies of attorneys and other types of jury studies, raise serious questions about the viability of traditional safeguards against mistaken identification.

CONCLUSIONS ABOUT TRADITIONAL SAFEGUARDS

The survey studies, the prediction studies, and the mock–juror experiments converge on the conclusion that jurors are generally insensitive to factors that influence eyewitness identification accuracy, that jurors often rely on factors (such as recall of peripheral details) that are not diagnostic of witness accuracy, and that jurors rely heavily on one factor—eyewitness confidence—that possesses only modest value as an indicator of witness accuracy.

The implications of these conclusions are profound. Even if attorneys were given the opportunity to gather the information necessary for effective cross-examination (and we have seen that such opportunities are rather limited), and even if attorneys knew which eyewitness factors to ask about when eliciting eyewitness identification information at trial (and we have seen research indicating they are not proficient at this), the effectiveness of cross-examination as a safeguard is still questionable in light of juror insensitivity to factors that are known to be diagnostic of eyewitness reliability.

This picture is a rather glum one. Defense attorneys are counted on as the primary bastions against erroneous convictions arising from mistaken eyewitness identifications. In theory, devices such as voir dire and cross-examination are intended to assure that defendants confronted by eyewitness identification evidence will have that evidence thoughtfully evaluated by jurors. And yet, as we have seen, there are serious flaws in this idealized picture.

We could go further. Defense attorneys are not the only courtroom actors who have a responsibility to assure that mistaken identifications do not lead to erroneous convictions. As officers of the court sworn to assure that justice is done in the courtroom, prosecutors also have a responsibility to assure that criminal prosecutions proceed on the basis of reliable trial evidence. We have no doubt that many prosecutors decline to prosecute cases based on "weak" identifications—which, we suspect, is highly synonymous with identifications in which the identifying witness is not very confident about the identification. However, given the weak relationship between witness confidence and witness accuracy and the range of threats to the diagnosticity of witness confidence (see Penrod & Cutler, 1995; Sporer, Penrod, Read, & Cutler, 1995), it is probably no more advisable for prosecutors to rely on witness confidence than it is for jurors to do so as a guide to witness accuracy. To the extent that prosecutors take other eyewitnessing factors into consideration (the Brigham & Wolfskeil, 1983, study reviewed earlier is instructive in this regard), there is little reason to believe that their judgments will be on a solider footing than that of defense attorneys.

We could go further still. Yet another officer with a responsibility to assure there are no convictions arising from mistaken identifications is the trial judge. One of the primary vehicles through which the judge exerts influence on jury decision making is through instructions delivered to the jury at the conclusion of the trial. Do these instructions work? Our review of the research on those instructions (Cutler & Penrod, 1995, chapter 17) indicates that standard instructions probably have an effect opposite to what is intended: They actually seem to desensitize jurors to diagnostic variations in trial evidence and make it less likely jurors will effectively differentiate between accurate and inaccurate eyewitnesses.

Is all lost? Clearly not: Jurors, attorneys, and judges are educable— though it appears there is substantial educating to be done. Is it possible to bring some light into the courtroom? One possible vehicle for increasing jury, attorney, and judge sensitivity to factors that threaten eyewitness reliability is the use of psychological experts in the courtroom. Elsewhere (Cutler & Penrod, 1995; Penrod & Cutler, 1989, 1992; Penrod et al., 1995) we have reviewed research—including our own—on the impact of expert testimony on jury decision making.

THE ALTERNATIVE: EXPERT TESTIMONY ON JUROR SENSITIVITY

Although courts have been and remain inhospitable to eyewitness expert testimony, a number of trial simulation experiments have looked at eyewitness expert effects, including Cutler, Dexter, and Penrod (1989); Cutler, Penrod, and Dexter (1989); Fox and Walters (1986); Hosch, Beck, and McIntyre (1980); Loftus (1980); Maass, Brigham, and West (1985); and Wells, Lindsay, and Tousignant (1980). These experiments yield some consistent findings with respect to expert testimony. The most important conclusions are that jurors are more skeptical of eyewitness identifications and fewer convictions are obtained if expert testimony is presented *and* eyewitnessing conditions are less than optimal.

One of the objections to eyewitness expert testimony has been that the testimony may simply make jurors more skeptical about all eyewitness identifications rather than making them sensitive to variations in witnessing and identification conditions that might threaten the reliability of identifications (McCloskey & Egeth, 1983). It was not clear from the early experiments whether reduced belief in eyewitnesses was due to improved sensitivity to factors that might have impaired the witnesses' ability to make a correct identification, to increased skepticism about all eyewitnesses, or to both. The experiments by Fox and Walters (1986), Hosch et al. (1980), and Maass et al. (1985) did not vary the presence of expert testimony and witnessing factors independently. Without variations in witnessing conditions, it is not possible to determine whether expert testimony enhances jurors' sensitivity to those conditions—skepticism and sensitivity are confounded. Fox and Walters varied the presence of expert testimony and eyewitness confidence simultaneously but found no substantial reduction in juror sensitivity to the weak relationship between confidence and identification accuracy. The only experiments that independently and simultaneously varied witnessing factors and the presence of expert testimony were those by Loftus (1980) and Wells et al. (1980), and both show trends toward improved sensitivity.

In contrast, the Cutler, Dexter, and Penrod (1989; Cutler, Penrod, & Dexter, 1989) experiments were designed to examine both sensitization and skepticism effects. Witnessing and identification conditions, witness confidence, and the presence of expert testimony were all varied orthogonally to secure independent tests of sensitivity and skepticism. They used a realistic trial simulation with rigorous cross-examination of the expert and found that jurors who did not hear expert testimony were much less sensitive to the factors that influence eyewitness memory than were jurors who heard the expert testimony. There were generally no skepticism effects. The expert testimony sensitized jurors to the importance of witnessing and identification conditions and the relative lack of importance of witness confidence.

The results from the studies of expert witness effects, together with the studies of juror sensitivity, underscore the fact that in the absence of expert testimony, jurors' decisions are (a) largely insensitive to factors known to influence eyewitness reliability, (b) appear to rely too heavily on eyewitness confidence when evaluating eyewitness accuracy, and (c) overestimate levels of eyewitness accuracy. The survey studies of lay knowledge about eyewitness reliability factors indicate that one source of juror insensitivity is simple lack of knowledge and confusion/disagreement about the influence of a number of eyewitnessing factors on eyewitness reliability. However, lack of knowledge and confusion are probably not the only sources of poor sensitivity. It is also possible that jurors are not making systematic use of the knowledge they do possess; jurors may be poor at using or integrating their knowledge when making their decisions.

Cutler, Penrod, and Dexter (1989) explored the problems of knowledge and integration. In their study, mock jurors demonstrated superior memory for the evidence surrounding the crime and the identification—a finding that indicates that memory cannot be blamed for the lack of effects that witnessing and identification conditions have on jurors' judgments.

Given that recall rates high without expert testimony, it is also likely that expert testimony does little to make up for witnessing conditions. Analyses of jurors' beliefs about eyewitness factors (in the absence of expert testimony) revealed that jurors believed disguise, retention interval, and lineup instructions all have appreciable effects on identification accuracy. However, jurors were unaware of the effects associated with weapon visibility. As noted before, jurors felt that witness confidence was an important determinant of identification accuracy.

If jurors were actually making use of their knowledge about the effects of disguise, retention interval, and biased lineup instructions, we would expect that knowledge to be reflected in their verdicts, their estimates of the likelihood that the eyewitness made a correct identification, and in other dependent measures, such as evaluations of the prosecution and defense evidence and witness credibility. Unfortunately, juror judgments did not reflect this knowledge—except when an expert testified.

When the expert testified, memory for the expert testimony was also very good. In addition to fostering sensitivity to disguise, retention interval, and lineup instructions, expert testimony also improved juror knowledge of the effects of weapon visibility and the weakness of the confidence-accuracy relationship.

In short, in the absence of expert testimony, jurors failed to make even minimal use of their knowledge of eyewitnessing factors and, instead, relied heavily on witness confidence in forming their judgments. However, when the expert testified jurors demonstrated significant sensitivity to witnessing and identification conditions in making judgments about the credibility of the eyewitness and about the strength of the prosecution's and defense's case. However, this expert-induced sensitivity still did not match the magnitude of the effects jurors claimed for these factors in their knowledge measures. Notably, the expert testimony reduced jurors's heavy reliance on witness confidence but did not increase jurors' general skepticism about the eyewitness's credibility.

Considered as a whole, the studies of juror knowledge and decision making indicate that expert psychological testimony can serve as a safeguard against mistaken identification. There is substantial evidence that jurors are insensitive to eyewitnessing and identification factors that influence eyewitness performance. Similarly, serious doubts can be raised about the ability of defense attorneys to foster juror sensitivity. Part of the problem is that laypersons and attorneys are not aware of, or are in disagreement about, the variety of factors that influence eyewitness performance. But a significant part of the problem is that jurors simply do not make use of the knowledge they do possess. Even when jurors appear to believe that a particular eyewitnessing factor is relevant and believe the factor substantially reduces the likelihood an eyewitness has made an accurate identification, the belief is not reflected in their evaluations of witness credibility or their verdicts. Rather, jurors rely heavily on witness confidence as a guide to witness accuracy. Unfortunately, confidence is not a particularly reliable indicator of eyewitness accuracy.

This picture changes when eyewitness expert testimony is presented to jurors. Despite the claims of some critics (e.g., McCloskey & Egeth, 1983), there is little empirical evidence that jurors are confused by the testimony. The existing studies of expert testimony effects indicate that it has the beneficial effect of educating jurors about factors that influence eyewitness identification and enhances their reliance on those factors when rendering decisions in eyewitness cases.

CONCLUSION

At the outset of this chapter, we noted that cases of mistaken identification and conviction are well documented in the legal and popular literature and by some estimates may reach as many as 4,500 per year. Such errors have motivated much psychological study of factors that influence eyewitness reliability (see Wells and Wright, & Bradfield, Chapter 3, this volume) and more recently motivated research on decision makers, such as attorneys and jurors, who must evaluate eyewitness identifications. In this chapter, we have looked closely at the ability of jurors to differentiate accurate from inaccurate eyewitnesses and the ability of attorneys and experts to aid jurors in their decision making. The picture that emerges is a somewhat gloomy one: Attorneys do not appear to possess all the knowledge necessary to assist them in such typical tasks as lineup construction and evaluation and cross-examination of witnesses. Jurors also seem incapable of differentiating between accurate and inaccurate eyewitnesses. Why are jurors so poor at this task? First, it is doubtful that laypersons understand the factors that typically influence eyewitness performance. Second, jurors seem to be oversensitive on witness confidence as a guide to witness accuracy. Unfortunately, witness confidence is not a particularly reliable guide to witness accuracy.

In contrast to the poor effectiveness of attorney and juror, expert testimony appears to be a promising adjunct to traditional safeguards. There is little evidence that jurors are confused by the testimony, while research indicates that it has the salutary effect of educating jurors about factors that influence eyewitness performance and enhances their reliance on those factors when rendering decisions. Furthermore, although attorneys have presumably devoted many (fruitless) years to the task of honing skills such as cross-examination of eyewitnesses, relatively little effort has been devoted to finding forms of expert testimony that maximize the educational effects of this testimony. Hence, it is likely that the full benefits of expert testimony about the problems of eyewitness reliability have not yet been realized.

REFERENCES

Bell, B. E., & Loftus, E. F. (1989). Trivial persuasion in the courtroom: The power of (a few) minor details. *Journal of Personality and Social Psychology, 56*, 669–679.

Berman, G. L., Narby, D. J., & Cutler, B. L. (1995). Effects of inconsistent eyewitness statements on mock-jurors' evaluations of the eyewitness, perceptions of defendant culpability and verdicts. *Law and Human Behavior, 19*, 79–88.

Borchard, E. M. (1932). *Convicting the innocent: Errors of criminal justice.* New Haven: Yale University Press.

Brigham, J. C., & Bothwell, R. K. (1983). The ability of prospective jurors to estimate the accuracy of eyewitness identifications. *Law and Human Behavior, 7*, 19–30.

Brigham, J. C., Maass, A., Snyder, L. D., & Spaulding, K. (1982). Accuracy of eyewitness identifications in a field setting. *Journal of Personality and Social Psychology, 42*, 673–680.

Brigham, J. C., & Wolfskeil, M. P. (1983). Opinions of attorneys and law enforcement personnel on the accuracy of eyewitness identification. *Law and Human Behavior, 7*, 337–349.

Cutler, B. L., Dexter, H. R., & Penrod, S. D. (1989). Expert testimony and jury decision making: An empirical analysis. *Behavioral Sciences and Law, 7*, 215–225.

Cutler, B. L., Moran, G., & Narby, D. J. (1992). Jury selection in insanity defense cases. *Journal of Research in Personality, 26*, 165–182.

Cutler, B. L., & Penrod, S. D. (1995). *Mistaken identifications: The eyewitness, psychology, and law.* New York: Cambridge University Press.

Cutler, B. L., Penrod, S. D., & Dexter, H. R. (1989). The eyewitness, the expert psychologist, and the jury. *Law and Human Behavior, 13*, 311–332.

Cutler, B. L., Penrod, S. D., & Dexter, H. R. (1990). Nonadversarial methods for sensitizing jurors to eyewitness evidence. *Journal of Applied Social Psychology, 20*, 1197–1207.

Cutler, B. L., Penrod, S. D., & Stuve, T. E. (1988). Juror decision making in eyewitness identification cases. *Law and Human Behavior, 12*, 41–55.

Deffenbacher, K. A., & Loftus, E. F. (1982). Do jurors share a common understanding concerning eyewitness behavior? *Law and Human Behavior, 6*, 15–30.

Fox, S. G., & Walters, H. A. (1986). The impact of general versus specific expert testimony and eyewitness confidence upon mock-juror judgment. *Law and Human Behavior, 10*, 215–228.

Frank, J., & Frank, B. (1957). *Not guilty.* London: Gallancz.

Fulero, S. M., & Penrod, S. D. (1990). The myths and realities of attorney jury selection folklore and scientific jury selection: What works? *Ohio Northern University Law Review, XVII*, 229–253.

Hosch, H. M., Beck, E. L., & McIntyre, P. (1980). Influence of expert testimony regarding eyewitness accuracy on jury decisions. *Law and Human Behavior, 4*, 287–296.

Huff, C. R. (1987). Wrongful conviction: Societal tolerance of injustice. *Research in Social Problems and Public Policy, 4*, 99–115.

Huff, C. R., Rattner, A., & Sagarin, E. (1986). Guilty until proven innocent. *Crime and Delinquency, 32*, 518–544.

Kassin, S. (1979). How adequate is human intuition for judging eyewitness testimony? In G. L. Wells & E. F. Loftus (Eds.), *Eyewitness testimony: Psychological perspectives* (pp. 256–272). New York: Cambridge University Press.

Kirby v. Illinois, 406 U.S. 682, 689 (1972).

Krafka, C., & Penrod, S. D. (1985). Reinstatement of context in a field experiment on eyewitness identification. *Journal of Personality and Social Psychology, 49,* 58–69.

Leippe, M. R., Wells, G. L., & Ostrom, T. M. (1978). Crime seriousness as a determinant of accuracy in eyewitness identification. *Journal of Applied Psychology, 63,* 345–351.

Lindsay, R. C. L., Lim, R., Marando, L., & Cully, D. (1986). Mock-juror evaluations of eyewitness testimony: A test of metamemory hypotheses. *Journal of Applied Social Psychology, 16,* 447–459.

Lindsay, R. C. L., Wells, G. L., & O'Connor, F. J. (1989). Mock-juror belief of accurate and inaccurate eyewitnesses: A replication and extension. *Law and Human Behavior, 13,* 333–339.

Lindsay, R. C. L., Wells, G. L., & Rumpel, C. M. (1981). Can people detect eyewitness identification accuracy within and across situations? *Journal of Applied Psychology, 66,* 79–89.

Loftus, E. F. (1980). Impact of expert psychological testimony on the unreliability of eyewitness identification. *Journal of Applied Psychology, 65,* 9–15.

Maass, A., Brigham, J. C., & West, S. G. (1985). Testifying on eyewitness reliability: Expert advice is not always persuasive. *Journal of Applied Social Psychology, 15,* 207–229.

Malpass, R. S., & Devine, P. G. (1981). Eyewitness identification: Lineup instructions and the absence of the offender. *Journal of Applied Psychology, 66,* 482–489.

McCloskey, M., & Egeth, H. (1983). Eyewitness identification: What can a psychologist tell a jury? *American Psychologist, 38,* 550–563.

McConkey, K. M.,& Roche, S. M. (1989). Knowledge of eyewitness memory. *Australian Psychologist, 24,* 377–384.

Moran, G., & Comfort, J. C. (1986). Neither "tentative" or "fragmentary": Verdict preference of impaneled felony jurors as a function of attitude toward capital punishment. *Journal of Applied Psychology, 71,* 146–155.

Moran, G., Cutler, B. L., & Loftus, E. F. (1990). Jury selection in major controlled substance trials: The need for extended voir dire. *Forensic Reports, 3,* 331–348.

Narby, D. J., & Cutler, B. L. (1994). Effectiveness of voir dire as a safeguard in eyewitness cases. *Journal of Applied Psychology, 79,* 274–279.

Noon, E., & Hollin, C. R. (1987). Lay knowledge of eyewitness behaviour: A British survey. *Applied Cognitive Psychology, 1,* 143–153.

Penrod, S. D, & Cutler, B. L. (1989). Assessing the need for and impact of eyewitness expert testimony on jury decision making. *Law and Contemporary Problems, 52,* 1001–1041.

Penrod, S. D., & Cutler, B. L. (1992). Eyewitnesses, experts, and jurors: Improving the quality of jury decision making in eyewitness cases. In J. Misumi, B. Wilpert, & H. Motoaki (Eds.), *Organizational and work psychology* (pp. 539–561). Hillsdale, NJ: Erlbaum.

Penrod, S. D., & Cutler, B. L. (1995). Witness confidence and witness accuracy: Assessing their forensic relation. *Psychology, Law & Public Policy, 5,* 817–845.

Penrod, S. D., Fulero, S., & Cutler, B. (1995). Expert psychological testimony on eyewitness reliability before and after Daubert. *Behavioral Sciences and the Law, 13,* 229–260.

Pigott, M. A., Brigham, J. C., & Bothwell, R. K. (1990). A field study of the relationship between quality of eyewitnesses' descriptions and identification accuracy. *Journal of Police Science and Administration, 17,* 84–88.

Platz, S. J., & Hosch, H. M. (1988). Cross racial/ethnic eyewitness identification: A field study. *Journal of Applied Social Psychology, 18,* 972–984.

Powers, T., & Luginbuhl, J. (1987, August). *Jurors' death penalty support and conviction prone-ness*. Paper presented at the 95th annual meeting of the American Psychological Association, New York.

Rahaim, G. L., & Brodsky, S. L. (1982). Empirical evidence versus common sense: Juror and lawyer knowledge of eyewitness accuracy. *Law and Psychology Review, 7,* 1–15.

Ross, D. F., Read, J. D., & Toglia, M. P. (Eds.). (1994). *Adult eyewitness testimony: Current trends and developments.* New York: Cambridge University Press.

Shapiro, P. N., & Penrod, S. D. (1986). Meta-analysis of facial identification studies. *Psychological Bulletin, 100,* 139–156.

Sporer, S. L., Malpass, R. S., & Koehnken, G. (Eds.). (1996). *Psychological issues in eyewitness identification.* Mahwah, NJ: Erlbaum.

Sporer, S. L., Penrod, S. D., Read, J. D., & Cutler, B. L. (1995). Gaining confidence in confidence: A new meta-analysis on the confidence-accuracy relationship in eyewitness identification studies. *Psychological Bulletin, 118,* 315–327.

Steblay, N. M. (1992). A meta-analytic review of the weapon focus effect. *Law and Human Behavior, 16,* 413–424.

Stovall v. Denno, 388 U.S. 293 (1967).

United States v. Ash, 413 U.S. 300 (1973).

United States v. Wade, 388 U.S. 218 (1967).

Wells, G. L. (1984). How adequate is human intuition for judging eyewitness testimony. In G. L. Wells & E. F. Loftus (Eds.), *Eyewitness testimony: Psychological perspectives* (pp. 256–272). New York: Cambridge University Press.

Wells, G. L. (1993). What do we know about eyewitness identification? *American Psychologist, 48,* 553–571.

Wells, G. L., & Leippe, M. R. (1981). How do triers of fact infer the accuracy of eyewitness identifications? Using memory for peripheral detail can be misleading. *Journal of Applied Psychology, 66,* 682–687.

Wells, G. L., Lindsay, R. C. L., & Ferguson, T. J. (1979). Accuracy, confidence, and juror perceptions in eyewitness identification. *Journal of Applied Psychology, 64,* 440–448.

Wells, G. L., Lindsay, R. C. L., & Tousignant, J. P. (1980). Effects of expert psychological advice on human performance in judging the validity of eyewitness testimony. *Law and Human Behavior, 4,* 275–285.

Wier, J. A., & Wrightsman, L. S. (1990). The determinants of mock-jurors' verdicts in a rape case. *Journal of Applied Social Psychology, 20,* 901–919.

Wrightsman, L. S., Nietzel, M. T., & Fortune, W. H. (1993). *Psychology and the legal system* (3rd ed.). Pacific Grove, CA: Brooks/Cole.

II

Forensic Assessment and Treatment

5

Forensic Assessment

ROBERT A. NICHOLSON

Our judicial system often relies on specialists to supply scientific and technical information to legal decision makers. Across disciplines, the application of principles gleaned from scientific investigation and professional experience to legal issues is commonly referred to as *forensics*, a term deriving from the Latin word *forensis* (of the forum—where courts were held in ancient Rome). Forensic psychological assessment, then, refers to the application of the principles and procedures of psychological assessment to address questions raised in legal contexts; it can be conceived as an interdisciplinary specialty within psychology that requires specialized training, experience, and scholarship (Golding, 1990). The purpose of this chapter is to survey and evaluate the state of this interdisciplinary specialty, including the status of professional practice as well as the conceptual and empirical foundation on which that practice is built.

Although the term *forensic psychologist* can refer to any psychologist who specializes in generating or communicating information appropriate for a legal forum (Grisso, 1987), information pertaining to psychological assessment is most likely to be provided by clinical psychologists. Hence, the emphasis throughout the chapter will be on assessments performed by clinical psychologists in legal contexts, also known as psycholegal assessment. The presentation that follows is divided into two major sections. The first discusses the history of forensic psychological assessment, including

ROBERT A. NICHOLSON • Department of Psychology, University of Tulsa, Tulsa, Oklahoma 74104.

Psychology and Law: The State of the Discipline, edited by Ronald Roesch, Stephen D. Hart, and James R. P. Ogloff. Kluwer Academic/Plenum Publishers, New York, 1999.

its emergence as a specialty area, and the charges made by scholars who question the reliability, validity and utility of forensic assessment and expert testimony. In the second section, I summarize key conceptual and empirical developments relevant to forensic psychological assessment during the past decade.

THE HISTORY OF FORENSIC PSYCHOLOGICAL ASSESSMENT

EMERGENCE AND GROWTH

For more than 30 years, psychologists have been recognized as expert witnesses in United States courtrooms (*Jenkins v. United States*, 1962; Perlin, 1977); and for more than 25 years, forensic psychologists have had a professional organization, the American Psychology-Law Society, to promote their discipline as an area of specialization (Grisso, 1991). Nevertheless, forensic psychological assessment emerged as a distinct interdisciplinary specialty little more than a decade ago.

Grisso (1987) noted that the publication of several psychological textbooks and monographs dedicated to forensic assessment and testimony during the mid-1980s appeared to represent the development of a formal body of specialized knowledge. In this regard, 1984 can be considered a landmark year in the history of the discipline. Of particular note, Amiram Elwork (1984a) edited a special issue of *Law and Human Behavior* on psycholegal assessment. He introduced it with his article: "Psycholegal Assessment, Diagnosis, and Testimony: A New Beginning" (Elwork, 1984b). Among the contributions to this special issue were validation studies of three psycholegal measures (Elwork, 1984b) or forensic assessment instruments (FAIs; Grisso, 1986)—the Interdisciplinary Fitness Interview (IFI; Golding, Roesch, & Schreiber, 1984), the Rogers Criminal Responsibility Assessment Scales (R-CRAS; Rogers, Wasyliw, & Cavanaugh, 1984), and the Mental State at the Time of Offense Screening Evaluation (MSE; Slobogin, Melton, & Showalter, 1984)—measures specifically designed to address questions raised by the courts. The special issue also included an examination of differences between judges and mental health professionals with regard to the weight given to psychological considerations in child custody cases (Lowery, 1984) as well as conceptual articles on competence to consent to treatment (Tepper & Elwork, 1984), the relationship between specific psychiatric diagnoses and legal insanity (Finkel & Sabat, 1984; Howe, 1984), the impact of insanity acquittal on treatment efficacy (Fein, 1984), and a model process for the conduct of forensic evaluations (Keilitz, 1984). Together, these articles reflected the discipline's efforts to grapple with thorny conceptual and procedural problems and to produce empirical evidence on assessments relevant to legal contexts.

Other events that year of the kind noted by Grisso (1987) suggested the development of a formal body of specialized knowledge and marked the emergence of forensic psychological assessment as a specialty area. Blau (1984) and Shapiro (1984) published comprehensive texts on forensic assessment and expert testimony. Grisso completed a draft of his NIMH-sponsored review of FAIs, *Evaluating Competencies* (Grisso, 1986), in which he proposed a conceptual model for developing such measures. Another comprehensive text on forensic evaluations—this one by Melton, Petrila, Poythress, and Slobogin (1987)—was completed that year and submitted to a publisher where, unfortunately, it was misplaced, eventually delaying its appearance for 3 years (N. Poythress, personal communication). In addition to the general texts on forensic evaluation, works focused on more specific topics or populations, such as informed consent (Lidz et al., 1984), the assessment of malingering and deception (Rogers, 1984a), and children, mental health, and law (Reppucci, Weithorn, Mulvey, & Monahan, 1984) arrived on our bookshelves.

The foregoing events reflected the extraordinary activity, excitement, and enthusiasm that characterized the nascent discipline. At the same time, the seeds of a later indictment of the field were being sown. Any summary of the events that marked 1984 as a watershed would be incomplete if it did not include a reference to the publication of *The Limits of Scientific Reasoning* by David Faust (1984). Although this work was not directed toward forensic audiences and did not attract much attention from forensic psychologists at the time, its publication nevertheless was a harbinger of later developments. In his monograph, Faust summarized research on human judgment and decision making and considered the implications of that research for the scientific enterprise. The evidence summarized in Faust's monograph obviously informed his later criticisms of forensic psychological assessment and expert testimony both individually (e.g., Faust, 1989a,b) and in collaboration with long-time critic Jay Ziskin (Faust & Ziskin, 1988, 1989; Ziskin & Faust, 1988).

Despite criticism from some quarters, forensic assessment has been and continues to be a growth industry, with rapidly expanding opportunities for practitioners. Evidence for this characterization can be drawn from several domains of law in which psychological assessment has been utilized, including juvenile, criminal, domestic/family, and civil law. Consider, for example, trends in the juvenile justice system. During the past 2 decades, every jurisdiction in this country has enacted laws to permit juveniles charged with serious offenses to be prosecuted and punished as adults (Ewing, 1990). Under the applicable statutes, certification to stand trial as an adult may be automatic for youths charged with the most severe offenses. For other serious offenses, certification of the juvenile is dependent on a determination by the court based on consideration of factors specified by statute. Forensic mental health professionals have come to play an important role in both types of situation, namely, in determining whether automatic certifications should be reversed and whether certifiable juveniles are amenable to treatment in the juvenile justice system.

Evidence from the criminal justice system also attests to growth in the practice of forensic assessment. All states have laws governing the pretrial psychological evaluation of criminal defendants and systems for delivery of forensic evaluation and treatment services. Although the issue of competence to proceed to adjudication is by far the most common question asked about defendants referred for pretrial evaluation, a defendant's mental state at the time of the offense and capacity to waive various rights are also the subject of assessment. Poythress, Otto, and Heilbrun (1991) noted that a growing population, rising crime rates, and increasing sophistication of the criminal bar all pointed toward growth in the "business" of pretrial evaluation. Moreover, during the past decade there has been a move toward decentralization of systems for pretrial service delivery in most states (Grisso, Cocozza, Steadman, Fisher, & Greer, 1994), expanding opportunities for psychologists and other mental health professionals to conduct such assessments. For example, in states that have adopted a private practitioner model, such pretrial assessments are now provided by a large number of community-based practitioners who are paid from a court fund or by means of contracts with the state department of mental health, whereas prior to decentralization such services would have been provided by a much smaller number of mental health professionals working on the state's inpatient forensic unit.

In the domain of domestic and family law, clinical psychologists continue to play a significant role in determinations of child custody and termination of parental rights (Committee on Professional Practice and Standards, 1994). Although mental health professionals probably conduct custody evaluations and provide expert testimony in only a small minority of all divorce cases (e.g., Melton et al., 1987), with a divorce rate that approaches 50%, the number of such evaluations conducted annually is nevertheless substantial (Otto & Collins, 1995). Notably, this is an area of expert testimony in which judges and attorneys apparently perceive psychologists rather than psychiatrists to be the experts of choice (LaFortune & Carpenter, 1996). Moreover, statutorily mandated mediation has been introduced in many jurisdictions, offering expanded roles for psychologists in divorce and custody proceedings. At the same time, allegations of child abuse or neglect, not limited to the context of divorce and custody proceedings, have grown dramatically, exhibiting an increase of more than 40% from 1985 to 1992 (Jenkins & Howell, 1994). Furthermore, many jurisdictions now allow expert testimony as to the conclusion that a child has been the victim of sexual abuse and also permit the child's statements to the expert to be entered into the record without testimony from the child (Golding, 1990), promoting increased solicitation of mental health professionals by attorneys.

The domain of civil law has witnessed an increasing demand for clinical neuropsychologists to enter the courtroom and testify in disability determination, worker's compensation, and personal injury cases (e.g., Kurlychek, 1984). In a recent survey, practicing clinical neuropsychologists cited "law" as the third most common referral source, trailing only neurology and psychiatry (Sweet, Moberg, & Westergaard, 1996). Furthermore, the courts have expanded the legal boundaries governing the kinds of injury deemed compensable (Hoffman & Spiegel, 1989; Weissman, 1985). Physical injury no longer constitutes a sine qua non; emotional injury can stand on its own as a basis for compensation without accompanying physical damage or loss of function. Stone (1993) recently noted that the introduction of the diagnosis of posttraumatic stress disorder (PTSD) into the official nosological system of the mental health professions, combined with the progressive expansion of the scope of third-party legal responsibility for negligent injury, threatened an "explosion of emotional injury adjudication" (p. 35). This possibility has also been enhanced by other developments. For example, in many states, the statute of limitations for lawsuits related to child sexual abuse has been extended to make this legal remedy available to victims who, as adults, experience a recovery of "repressed memories" (Loftus, 1993).

The foregoing examples, by no means an exhaustive list, illustrate our legal system's voracious appetite for information and convey some sense of the expanding opportunities for mental health professionals to perform assessments and provide expert testimony. Despite increasing demands by the courts for mental health expertise, the involvement of psychologists and psychiatrists as expert witnesses has not gone unchallenged and, indeed, has been sharply criticized by scholars from both the legal and mental health professions. Informed practice requires careful consideration of the merit, impact, and implications of such criticisms.

CHALLENGES: THE FAUST AND ZISKIN ASSAULT AND ITS AFTERMATH

Criticism of expert testimony is as old as expert testimony. Mental health professionals in particular have long been subjected to scathing attacks assailing not only the scientific foundation and credibility of their testimony but often their personal integrity as well. In fact, the special issue of *Law and Human Behavior* (Elwork, 1984a) described previously was organized partly as a response to the most frequently voiced criticisms (e.g., Bonnie & Slobogin, 1980; Morse, 1978; Ziskin, 1970), four of which were described in the lead article for the special issue (Elwork, 1984b). There, Elwork noted that the evidence presented by mental health professionals had been characterized as often unreliable or invalid, irrelevant to the legal questions being asked, incomprehensible to legal decision makers, and intrusive upon the authority of judges and juries. Grisso (1986) later described a similar set of criticisms, although he catalogued them in a slightly different way.

Perhaps the most acicular attacks on the courtroom role of psychiatrists and psychologists have come from within the mental health professions. Jay Ziskin's (1970) publication of the first edition of *Coping with Psychiatric and Psychological Testimony*, a compendium of evidence challenging the reliability and validity of mental health professionals' assessments and testimony, surprised and angered many forensic psychologists. The debate that followed was punctuated by visceral and sometimes vituperative exchanges between Ziskin and his critics, dividing the membership of the American Psychology-Law Society. Nevertheless, some participants later acknowledged that the debate, rather than destroying the nascent organization, had energized the membership and had given the society that Ziskin had founded a reason to survive (see Grisso, 1991).

Ziskin was later joined in his campaign against mental health expertise in the courtroom by David Faust, a practicing clinical psychologist with a longstanding interest in and extensive knowledge of the empirical literature on human judgment and decision making (e.g., Faust, 1984; Faust & Ziskin, 1988, 1989, 1992; Ziskin & Faust, 1988). Faust coauthored the fourth edition of the *Coping* text (Ziskin & Faust, 1988) and took the lead role in the most widely disseminated of their collaborative critiques, an article published in the prestigious journal, *Science* (Faust & Ziskin, 1988). There, they repeated the claim that most, if not all, of the testimony offered by psychologists and psychiatrists should be excluded from the courtroom. Although the authors acknowledged that they did not attempt an evenhanded analysis of the literature in their multivolume text, they failed to preface the abridged journal article with a similar caveat. Respondents to Faust and Ziskin have accused them of partisan scholarship (Matarazzo, 1990) and chastised them for abandoning the scientist's detached, dispassionate stance in favor of an advocacy role (Brodsky, 1989). Because of the notoriety that their review in *Science* has received, the commentary that follows highlights a few of the problematic issues related to the central thesis and evidence presented in that article.

The argument and evidence presented by Faust and Ziskin (1988) are problematic in several respects. Most important, their discussion of the admissibility of evidence from expert witnesses erred in its exclusive reliance on *Frye v. U.S.* (1923) and in its legal analysis of the principles set forth in the *Frye* ruling (Hoge & Grisso, 1992). Citing *Frye*, Faust and Ziskin described the essentials underlying "legal standards for expert status" as follows: (a) an expert must be able to state opinions with "reasonable medical certainty," which they translated as "pretty likely accurate"; and (b) the trier of fact should be able to reach a more valid conclusion with the expert's testimony than without it (Faust & Ziskin, 1988, p. 31). To the contrary, the "general acceptance" standard described in *Frye*, which was meant to apply to novel scientific evidence, targeted not the expert's opinion per se, but the theories and methods from which the expert's opinion was derived. As Hoge and Grisso (1992) noted, "But *Frye* does not mention accuracy, validity, or even 'general acceptance' of the opinion or conclusion that the expert reaches on the basis of these theories and methods" (p. 69). Moreover, "reasonable medical certainty" refers to the expert's confidence in his or her opinion and not to the accuracy or general acceptance of that opinion (Black, 1988). The subsequent U.S. Supreme Court decision in *Daubert v. Merrell Dow Pharmaceuticals* (1993) has further eroded the Faust and Ziskin position (see Melton, 1994, for an excellent discussion of *Daubert*), notwithstanding the fact that the full impact of *Daubert* on state courts remains to be seen. In short, flaws in their legal analysis effectively undercut Faust and Ziskin's (1988) conclusions regarding the exclusion of most mental health expert testimony from the courtroom.

Additionally, the Faust and Ziskin summary of evidence on the reliability and validity of psychiatric and psychological decision making was highly selective, a number of their assertions were potentially misleading. For example, with regard to the reliability of post-DSM-III psychiatric diagnoses, Faust and Ziskin (1988) argued, "A number of subsequent studies showed that rate of disagreement for specific diagnostic categories often equals or exceeds rate of agreement" (p. 31). At first blush, the assertion appears to be broad in scope, implying massive diagnostic errors even under the ostensibly more objective DSM-III criteria. Closer scrutiny reveals, however, that the claim is deceptively narrow. The key word is the adjective *specific*, a qualification that misrepresents diagnostic questions frequently addressed by forensic examiners. Although some referral questions may require the examiner to make fine diagnostic distinctions in order to assist the trier of fact, many do not. Diagnosis often constitutes a threshold issue in legal determinations (Halleck, Hoge, Miller, Sadoff, & Halleck, 1992). If establishing the presence or absence of a severe disorder such as a psychosis is sufficient to address the threshold question in such cases (e.g., a statutory definition of mental illness), it probably matters little whether the examinee suffers from schizoaffective disorder or bipolar disorder with mood-incongruent psychotic features.

The authors' assertion also illustrates the selectivity of the evidence used to support the charge of diagnostic unreliability. The three studies cited were drawn only from the literature on Axis II (personality) disorders; evidence regarding the generally higher diagnostic reliabilities for most Axis I disorders was omitted. Moreover, the authors failed to cite divergent evidence on the reliability of personality disorder diagnoses. A contemporaneous investigation incorporating the use of structured diagnostic interviews yielded substantially higher reliability estimates for most personality disorder diagnoses (Stangl, Pfohl, Zimmerman, Bowers, & Corenthal, 1985).

The Faust and Ziskin paper is reminiscent of an article that appeared in the same journal 15 years prior, David Rosenhan's (1973) abortive assault on psychiatric diagnosis, "On Being Sane in Insane Places." The article was described by Farber (1975) as an "instantaneous succes de scandale" (p. 589), an appellation appropriate for the Faust and Ziskin (1988) review as well. Fundamental flaws in the premises, research design, and interpretation of findings led Rosenhan's (1973) study to be dispatched as "pseudoscience" (Spitzer, 1975). However, in my opinion, Faust and Ziskin (1988) should not be dismissed as readily, despite the problematic nature of their legal analysis, selective citation of research, and misleading conclusions regarding the value of expert testimony by mental health professionals. Several considerations are relevant to this perspective, which is at odds with the views of some commentators (e.g., Hoge & Grisso, 1992). First, the long-term impact of the Faust and Ziskin collaborative efforts on the field of forensic assessment is likely to be salubrious. Just as Eysenck (1952) called on an earlier generation of psychotherapists to provide empirical evidence regarding treatment efficacy (and was assailed as a "mountebank" in the process), Faust and Ziskin (1988) challenged forensic psychologists to reexamine the content and empirical foundation of their courtroom testimony. The debate that followed the appearance of their article in *Science* has played a role in revitalizing the discipline, reacquainting those who perform assessment and courtroom testimony with the substantial literature on deficiencies in human judgment and reasoning and the limitations of our assessment methods. Arming attorneys is one sure method for promoting better preparation by mental health professionals who conduct forensic assessments. Although critical of the Faust and Ziskin approach, Brodsky (1991) has nevertheless expressed a similar view, noting that they have provided expert witnesses with "the impetus to reconsider the whats and hows" (p. 203) of forensic work.

Second, the Faust and Ziskin critiques have been accompanied by constructive efforts to advance the quality of forensic assessment and testimony. For example, Faust (1989a) edited an issue of *Behavioral Sciences and the Law* in which the collection of articles reviewed factors that promote errors in decision making, such as ignorance of base rates and hindsight bias (Arkes, 1989), and challenged some common but fallacious courtroom gambits used by expert witnesses, including claims about the expert's ability to weight and integrate numerous pieces of information obtained during an evaluation (Faust, 1989b) and the validity of decisions based on "years of clinical experience" (Dawes, 1989). These efforts have continued, as evidenced by the dissemination of practical steps for coping with the clinician's cognitive limitations and improving decision making, thereby enhancing clinical practice and the quality of the information provided to the courts (e.g., Borum, Otto, & Golding, 1993; Faust & Nurcombe, 1989).

Third, readers attempting to evaluate the merits of the differing perspectives on forensic expertise must carefully consider the possibility of bias and advocacy not only in the work of Faust and Ziskin but also in the work of the proponents of forensic assessment and testimony as well. Reviews purporting to offer more balanced coverage of the relevant literature (e.g., Garb, 1992; Matarazzo, 1990) soon appeared in response to the critical summaries by Faust and Ziskin. There is some merit to the claims of increased balance. Garb (1992) not only chronicled evidence supporting the reliability and accuracy of clinical and forensic judgments and predictions, he also acknowledged impediments to accuracy in human judgment, noted common judgmental errors (e.g., overreliance on the representativeness heuristic, failure to consider regression to the mean), and incorporated negative research findings (e.g., judgmental tasks not supported by the empirical literature) into his discussion. Nevertheless, the claim of evenhandedness should not be accepted uncritically. For example, Garb (1992) asserted that one of the more important inferences that can be drawn from histories and mental status exams is "judging when treatment can be of benefit" (p. 154), but he cited no evidence to support that claim. Unfortunately, the literature on assessment of treatability and prediction of treatment response in a variety of forensic contexts contradicts Garb's assertion: (a) although one investigation suggested that dimensions of treatability can be rated reliably by trained, motivated clinicians who have been given extensive information (Heilbrun et al., 1992), most research revealed substantial variability in treatability decisions (Greenland & Rosenblatt, 1972; Heilbrun et al., 1988; Jackson, 1986; Quinsey, 1975; Quinsey & Maguire, 1983; Webster, Menzies, & Jackson, 1982); and (b) there is little evidence that forensic mental health professionals are able to predict treatment response with more than modest accuracy (Ashford, 1988; Carbonell, Heilbrun, & Friedman, 1992; Cuneo & Brelje, 1984; Golding, 1992; Nicholson, Barnard, Hankins, & Robbins, 1994; Nicholson & McNulty, 1992; Rogers, 1992; Rogers & Webster, 1989). The moral is that consumers of this literature must guard against suspension of critical judgment as a function of his or her preference for the conclusions reached in a particular review.

Finally, the charge of selective citation leveled at Faust and Ziskin (1988) is an appropriate response to an article that is presented as a general indictment of the scientific foundation of the mental health professions and, hence, of what the professions have to offer the courts. However, if Faust and Ziskin (1988) is read more narrowly—as a critique of typical forensic practice—then the charge of selective citation may be less appropriate. For example, structured diagnostic interviews can be used profitably to reduce information variance and enhance the reliability of psychiatric diagnosis. Indeed, studies have demonstrated substantial discrepancies between research diagnoses based on structured interviews and diagnoses given in typical clinical practice, even for Axis I disorders; moreover, the discrepancies are greater for patients diagnosed in state hospitals and community mental health centers than for those diagnosed in university-affiliated hospitals (Fennig, Craig, Tanenberg-Karant, & Bromet, 1994). Acknowledging the weight of the evidence favoring structured interviews, Golding (1990) lobbied for their use forcefully and forthrightly: "If one is offering diagnostic testimony, it will no longer do to conduct a 'seat of the pants' mental status interview and offer testimony about the increased reliability of DSM-IIIR" (p. 300). Unfortunately, forensic practitioners seem reluctant to break with the past despite persuasive empirical evidence and the admonitions of leading scholars. In a recent study of 100 competency to stand trial reports, only 3 referenced a structured diagnostic interview as a source of information and basis for the examiner's opinion, even though virtually all of the reports cited symptoms of psychopathology and included a diagnostic summary (Skeem, Golding, Cohn, & Berge, in press). If structured interviews have not been adopted for use in forensic practice, then the Faust and Ziskin (1988) citations might reflect the realities of clinical practice more accurately than citation of research based on structured interviews. Although their review misrepresents the promise of forensic assessment (and even forensic assessment as it currently practiced by the best the discipline has to offer), it may not misrepresent forensic assessment and expert testimony at their point of greatest impact on the legal system—as practiced daily in front of judges in Biloxi, Louisville, Peoria, Little Rock, Waco, and Portland (Grisso, 1987).

To summarize, the fatal flaw in the Faust and Ziskin (1988) critique lies in their legal analysis of the principles governing admissibility of expert testimony. The circumscribed review of the literature that follows their legal analysis does serve to remind us that "we aren't exactly rocket scientists." Fortunately, we don't have to be. In *Daubert*, the Supreme Court rejected a narrow standard of admissibility in favor of the more liberal criteria embodied in the Federal Rules of Evidence (1974). Endorsing broad discretionary powers for trial judges in determining admissibility, Justice Blackmun noted that rules of evidence were structured "not for cosmic understanding" but to resolve specific legal disputes. Psychologists who seek to perform forensic assessment and offer expert testimony must give careful consideration to the issues, arguments, and evidence set forth in the works by Faust and Ziskin and in the responses to their charges by proponents of forensic assessment and testimony. Although we don't have to be rocket scientists, we are obligated not only to provide the courts the best that psychology has to offer but also to be candid about the limits of our science and our expertise. In this regard, challenges to the scientific foundation of forensic assessment demand more than criticism in kind; they demand an affirmative response. If the works that signaled the emergence of forensic psychological assessment as a distinct specialty indeed represented "the development of a formal body of specialized knowledge" (Grisso, 1987, p. 831), it is appropriate to ask about the content of this body of knowledge and, related to that question, whether the corpus has grown during the past decade. Has the conceptual and empirical foundation on which the practice of forensic assessment is built kept pace with the rapid expansion of opportunities offered by the legal system? The answers to such questions are crucial to the ultimate viability of the enterprise. Indeed, the author of one of the first texts on expert testimony by psychologists noted that the future of such testimony depended on the "content and quality of research in the behavioral sciences" (Blau, 1984, p. 16).

CONCEPTUAL AND EMPIRICAL DEVELOPMENTS: MAKING PROGRESS BUT LOSING GROUND

In the decade since forensic psychological assessment emerged as a specialty, its conceptual underpinnings have been strengthened considerably, accompanied by less substantial, but sometimes notable empirical advances. In the sections that follow, I summarize these developments, focusing on the advances that I perceive as fundamental to the scientific foundation on which the practice of forensic assessment is built. In particular, significant progress has been made in two broad domains during this period: (a) in the assessment of legal competencies, such as competency to stand trial and (b) in the detection of response distortion (e.g., malingering, defensiveness) during forensic assessment. In both of these areas, progress was marked by the publication of comprehensive, critical reviews of existing assessment methods and research strategies and by the articulation of conceptual models that provided a structure for the assessment process. Stimulated by these developments, studies of legal competencies and response distortion proliferated, with efforts directed toward validation of existing measures or construction of new methods of assessment. Although empirical progress often lagged behind conceptual developments, conceptual and empirical gains in some areas went hand in hand during the decade, solidifying the scientific foundation of forensic practice.

I recognize that the review that follows is necessarily selective, and that others might nominate a different set of developments. In self-defense, I echo a remark made by Morris Parloff as he commenced a review of research on the efficacy of psychotherapy. He likened his task to that of summarizing many years of research evidence while standing on one foot, adding, "It is inevitable that some will find that the foot I am standing on is theirs" (Parloff, 1980, p. 283).

ASSESSMENT OF LEGAL COMPETENCIES

Our understanding of legal competencies and our ability to conduct proper assessments of those competencies were enhanced greatly by the work of Tom Grisso, who laid a conceptual foundation for the assessment enterprise by proposing a model for the development and use of forensic instruments (Grisso, 1986). As the foregoing summary of the events of 1984 indicated, instruments for assessing psycholegal abilities were being actively researched prior to the publication of Grisso's model. Although earlier or concurrent work by other scholars contributed substantially to forensic research and practice in the assessment of specific legal competencies, Grisso (1986) developed a general conceptual model applicable to a wide range of legal competencies and then applied the model in an extensive, painstaking review of extant research on assessment instruments relevant to legal contexts. The following discussion presents an overview of Grisso's model, illustrates its application to a particular content domain, and summarizes research on forensic assessment instruments from several domains, with an emphasis on the empirical evidence that has accumulated since the publication of Grisso's model.

Conceptual Model for Assessment of Legal Competencies

According to Grisso (1986), two premises influenced the development of his conceptual model: "First, a conceptual model for assessments related to legal competencies must be based at the outset on an analysis of the law's view of competencies. Second, the model must be consistent with, and must promote, the scientific, empirical standards of mental health professionals' disciplines" (p. 12). The first premise in effect shifted the focus in forensic assessment away from the traditional topics of clinical evaluations—diagnosis, etiology, and treatment—and toward the specific issues raised by the courts in legal competency proceedings. Grisso (1986) was not the first to emphasize the law's view of legal competencies. Roesch and Golding (1980) had previously conducted a thoughtful analysis of case law in order to understand competency to stand trial as a legal construct. Before that, the work of Louis McGarry, Paul Lipsitt, and others at the Laboratory of Community Psychiatry (1974) and the checklists authored by Robey (1965) and Bukatman et al. (1971) had focused on sets of legally relevant abilities rather than the usual clinical signs and symptoms. Although the distinction between forensic assessments and traditional clinical assessments was not lost on forensic scholars, anecdotal evidence at the time suggested that many mental health professionals who were involved in the business of evaluating legal competencies failed to acknowledge the distinction and consequently performed assessments of competency much as they did intake and diagnostic interviews. Hence, Grisso's conceptual model was intended in part to serve an educational function.

The second premise was designed to ground the assessment process in empiricism: to promote the collection of reliable data in performing an assessment, the use of empirical findings to interpret the data, and the design and implementation of new investigations to improve the quality of both. In this regard, the model was designed to remind forensic assessors of their accountability.

In proposing a model for understanding and assessing legal competencies, Grisso (1986) endorsed the view that legal competencies could be likened to scientific constructs, hypothetical entities that cannot be operationally defined by a finite set of indicators (see also Roesch & Golding, 1980, pp. 12–13). As articulated by Meehl (1977), scientific constructs possess the following characteristics: (a) the correlation between a construct (e.g., anxiety) and any indicator of the construct (e.g., observer rating of speech dysfluency) is less than 1.0; (b) the list of indicators of the construct can be extended in such a way that we can never claim to have identified the entire set of possible indicators (i.e., a new indicator, such as the Beck Anxiety Inventory, can be developed or discovered and added to the list); and (c) the inner nature of the construct is unknown. In the early stages of scientific investigation, a construct is understood by virtue of its lawful relationships to other constructs and to observables in the theoretician's nomological network (Cronbach & Meehl, 1955). As scientific investigation proceeds, however, the inner nature of the construct can be discovered.

The investigator seeks to develop increasingly elaborate and detailed theoretical networks that further understanding of the trait in question and ultimately to discover and understand the trait's inner nature. These considerations suggest that legal constructs can be likened to scientific constructs only with regard to the first two characteristics described by Meehl (1977). Roesch and Golding's (1980) analysis of case law demonstrated that no single functional capacity could be equated with competency to stand trial, and that "no one set of facts could be considered dispositive of competency" (p. 13). With regard to the third characteristic, however, the correspondence between scientific and legal constructs breaks down. Unlike investigation of scientific constructs, the study of legal constructs is not directed toward elucidating their inner nature; instead, it must address established and evolving standards given by some combination of statutes, case law, and legal theory. Thus, the analogy between scientific and legal constructs is a useful one, but the similarities should not be overstated because such overstatement could lead to inappropriate expectations about the potential contributions of psychological science to our understanding of legal constructs.

Although statutes and case law depict a variety of specific legal competencies, Grisso (1986) argued that a common structure could be discerned across them. In his initial version of the model, Grisso (1986) described six characteristics common to legal competencies. A subsequent revision of the model identified five such characteristics, labeled *functional*, *causal*, *interactive*, *conclusory*, and *prescriptive* (Grisso, 1988). As articulated by Grisso, these five characteristics also constituted potential objectives in forensic assessment of legal competencies. Table 5.1 briefly describes these characteristics and illustrates how, as objectives of competency assessment, they serve to structure evaluations and provide guidance to forensic evaluators. (Adjudicative competence was selected as the specific competency at issue to provide a context for consideration of the model.)

According to the model, all legal competencies focus on the individual's *functional* abilities with regard to some behavior or capacity identified by law. In the context of adjudicative competence, these "legally relevant functional abilities" or "psycholegal abilities" refer to what a defendant can or cannot do, knows or does not know, believes or does not believe, as these impact the defendant's capacity to participate meaningfully in the legal proceedings against him or her.

Of course, for a defendant to be considered incompetent, any observed deficits in ability to function must be genuine. It is this consideration that points to the importance of discovering the probable explanation for any observed deficits in functional ability, which Grisso (1988) termed the *causal* characteristics of legal competencies. Thus, when impairments

TABLE 5.1. OBJECTIVES FOR EVALUATIONS OF ADJUDICATIVE COMPETENCE

Type of objective	Recommended status	Question addressed	Information needed
Functional	Essential	What are defendant's strengths and weaknesses in specific legal abilities?	Direct assessment of understanding and reasoning about trials and defense processes
Causal	Essential if deficits found	What is the most plausible explanation for the observed deficits?	Clinical observations and data on symptoms of mental disorder and possible causes of the observed deficits
Interactive	Useful but not essential	What is the significance of the deficits in light of demands of trial?	Nature of trial demands, expected nature of defense, comparison of deficits to demands
Conclusory	Not recommended	Is the defendant legally incompetent?	No new information needed
Prescriptive	Essential if deficits found	What is the potential for remediation of deficits?	Clinical observations and data to determine remediability, with what treatment, for how long, etc.

Source: T. Grisso (1988). *Competency to Stand Trial Evaluations: A Manual for Practice* (pp. 12–13). Sarasota, FL: Professional Resource Exchange, Inc. Copyright 1988 by Professional Resource Exchange, Inc. Reprinted with permission.

in functional capacity are identified, the forensic examiner must make an inference as to the nature and legitimacy of the impairment and its cause. Elsewhere (Nicholson, Briggs, & Robertson, 1988, p. 391), I have suggested that the examiner consider the following question: "Does the impairment reflect an actual and enduring incapacity, or is it illusory, the product of malingering, mulishness, or mere ignorance?" The relevance of psychiatric and psychological conditions to legal competency constructs can be asserted on these grounds; mental disorder and limited intellectual functioning are relevant precisely because they may influence an individual's legally relevant functional abilities and may explain an observed deficiency.

The *interactive* characteristic refers to the fact that legal cases vary on numerous dimensions and, as a result, place varying demands on defendants. For example, charges for which the prosecutor must prove a specific intent may require different functional capacities on the part of the defendant than do charges involving strict liability. Likewise, cases that proceed to trial may require different abilities than cases that are disposed of by means of a plea bargain. Assessments of legal competencies should take into account, insofar as possible, the specific demands placed on the defendant by the case at hand; in more complex cases, the defendant may be required to exhibit a greater degree of functional ability in order to be considered competent by the trier of fact than he or she would in a relatively simple, straightforward case. Nevertheless, Grisso (1988) cautioned that when the examiner's knowledge of the potential demands of a case is limited to personal speculation, this objective should be abandoned to prevent the credibility of the entire evaluation from being called into question. Moreover, some scholars have argued that one of the legal theories underlying the competency doctrine could be interpreted as requiring that a defendant be capable of "full participation" in a case, whether or not the defense strategy demands it (see Melton et al., 1987, p. 85).

The *conclusory* characteristic refers to an examiner's overall opinion as to a defendant's competency status. Grisso (1988) did not consider this a recommended objective of competency assessment because the ultimate decision about competency status is infused with considerations about morality and justice that lie outside the mental health professional's domain of expertise. Although most scholars appear to agree that psychologists (or other experts) should not answer the ultimate legal question in a report to the court or in courtroom testimony (Bonnie & Slobogin, 1980; Melton et al., 1987; Morse, 1978; Stone, 1984), that view has not gone unchallenged (Rogers & Ewing, 1989). Moreover, Federal Rules of Evidence do not prohibit ultimate issue testimony except with regard to a defendant's mental state at the time of an offense; many state statutes require that forensic examiners provide an opinion regarding the ultimate legal question at issue (or at least regarding penultimate issues that effectively determine the ultimate opinion). At the present time, the "ultimate issue" issue remains unresolved. Thus, the Specialty Guidelines for Forensic Psychologists do not proscribe ultimate opinion testimony but instead direct experts to (a) distinguish between their professional observations, inferences, and conclusions, on one hand, and legal facts, opinions, and conclusions, on the other and (b) explain the relationship between their testimony and the legal issues and facts of a case (see Committee on Ethical Guidelines for Forensic Psychologists, 1991, VII(F), p. 665). Nevertheless, for those mental health and legal professionals who are opposed to "ultimate issue" testimony, this characteristic of legal competencies and potential objective of competency assessments is viewed as an inappropriate intrusion on the authority of the trier of fact.

The characteristic of legal competencies labeled *prescriptive* by Grisso

(1988) directs the examiner to gather information relevant to the court's dispositional options, including a determination of whether a legitimate functional impairment or incapacity can be remediated, and if so, what treatment is needed and for how long. For the issue of competence to proceed to adjudication, this characteristic is consistent with the U.S. Supreme Court's decision in *Jackson v. Indiana* (1972), which required assessment of an incompetent defendant's capacity to be restored to competence and also set limits on the duration of commitment pursuant to a finding of incompetence.

In sum, Grisso's (1986, 1988) model provided a unifying conceptual framework for research and practice in forensic assessment of legal competencies. The model underscores the need for forensic examiners to assess directly an individual's knowledge, beliefs, and ability to function as described or implied by the statutes and case law relevant to a particular legal competency. There is also a corresponding emphasis on the need for forensic researchers to develop instruments specifically designed to assess legally relevant knowledge, beliefs, and capacities, and to explore the relationships between legal competencies and performance on nonforensic measures originally developed for use in psychological research and traditional clinical practice. In addition, the model highlights the relevance of psychological and psychiatric constructs to forensic practice and research. Information about an individual's status with regard to mental disorder, cognitive and intellectual functioning, and response style (e.g., defensive, malingering, random, etc.) can assist an examiner in determining whether or not there is a legitimate basis in fact for any observed deficit in the individual's functional abilities. Thus, the model recognizes distinctions between legal and psychological constructs but, at the same time, adumbrates possible linkages between them. The subsections that follow summarize, across different domains, existing evidence on the reliability and validity of forensic assessment instruments, the kinds of legally relevant measures Grisso's model encourages us to develop and use in forensic practice.

ADJUDICATIVE COMPETENCE

Research efforts to develop and validate legally relevant instruments for assessing adjudicative competence have a long history relative to most domains of psycholegal assessment. The earliest efforts consisted of checklists or topical questions that summarized the major factors to be considered in evaluating competency (e.g., Bukatman, Foy, & DeGrazie, 1971; Robey, 1965). Subsequently, interviews with varying degrees of structure (e.g., Golding et al., 1984; Laboratory of Community Psychiatry, 1974; Roesch, Webster, & Eaves, 1984) and quantifiable screening instruments (Barnard et al., 1991; Everington & Luckasson, 1992; Johnson & Mullett, 1987; Laboratory of Community Psychiatry, 1974; Lipsitt, Lalos, & McGarry, 1971; Wildman et al., 1978) were introduced. To date, eight such instruments have been developed and submitted to tests of their reliability and validity. The following discussion emphasizes developments subsequent to Grisso's (1986, 1992) earlier reviews as well as the integration of such developments with earlier research. We will begin with a summary of research on quantitative measures with explicit scoring criteria. Of these, two measures introduced since the publication of Grisso's (1986) comprehensive review, the Computer-Assisted Determination of Competence to Proceed instrument (CADCOMP; Barnard et al., 1991) and the Competence Assessment for Standing Trial for Defendants with Mental Retardation (CAST-MR; Everington & Luckasson, 1992) will be considered in somewhat more detail. Grisso (1992) provided only a cursory review of the initial data on the CAST-MR; additionally, the initial validation work on CADCOMP was not published in time to be incorporated into his review. Next, we will consider semistructured interviews, instruments that also permit some quantification of the components of competency but do not incorporate explicit rules for combining scores on individual items to generate a total score. Finally, the newest additions to the forensic examiner's armamentarium, the MacArthur Structured Assessment of the Competencies of Criminal Defendants (MacSAC-CD; Hoge, Bonnie, Poythress, Monahan, Eisenberg, & Feucht-Haviar, 1997) and its clinical version, the MacArthur Competence Assessment Tool-Criminal Adjudication (MacCAT-CA; Otto, Poythress, Nicholson, Edens, Monahan, Bonnie, Hoge, & Eisenberg, in press), will be introduced.

The oldest of the quantitative competency measures, the Competency Screening Test (CST), consists of 22 items that present hypothetical legal situations in a sentence completion format. Scores on individual items range from 0 to 2, with a higher score indicating a greater degree of competency. Based on an early validation study involving 43 subjects, the authors recommended a cutting score of 21 for classifying defendants as competent (Lipsitt et al., 1971). A manual (Laboratory of Community Psychiatry, 1974, Appendix) provided scoring criteria for each item along with examples of common responses. A number of authors (e.g., Brakel, 1974; Melton et al., 1987) have been sharply critical of the scoring criteria for the CST because of their tendency to classify defendants with a cynical or jaundiced view of the legal system as incompetent.

The GCCT, developed as a rapid, quantitative measure that would be easily understood by defendants (Wildman et al., 1978), is administered orally like a structured interview, but it also incorporates explicit scoring criteria for each item. The original version of the GCCT included 17 questions designed to sample a defendant's understanding of courtroom procedure, knowledge of the charge and possible penalties, and ability to communicate rationally with an attorney. Point totals for individual items vary, reflecting the authors' subjective weighting of the importance of the item to the competency construct. Item scores are summed to yield a total score of 50, with higher scores reflecting greater degrees of competency. This total score is multiplied by 2, producing a maximum score of 100. Based on their initial validation work, Wildman et al. (1978) recommended a cutoff score of 70 for classifying defendants as competent. The original form of the GCCT was modified by Will Johnson at Mississippi State Hospital and was labeled the GCCT-R (Johnson & Mullett, 1987). Four questions were added, weights given to some of the original items were changed, and the scoring criteria for questions about the charge and possible penalty were made more explicit. The maximum possible score and the recommended cutting score were not altered. Most investigators have referred to this version as the GCCT-MSH (Nicholson, Robertson, Johnson, & Jensen, 1988).

The CST and GCCT-MSH exhibit excellent interscorer reliability, reasonable item homogeneity, and good internal consistency (Johnson & Mullett, 1987; Nicholson, Briggs et al., 1988; Nicholson, Robertson et al., 1988; Randolph, Hicks, Mason, & Cuneo, 1982; Savitsky & Karras, 1984; Ustad, Rogers, Sewell, & Guarnaccia, 1996). In addition, with the exception of studies by Roesch and Golding (1980, Study 1 and Study 2; Schreiber, Roesch, & Golding, 1987), most investigations have found that the CST shows significant correlations with other competency criteria (Barnard et al., 1992; Daniel, Beck, Herath, Schmitz, & Menninger, 1984; Nicholson, Robertson et al., 1988; Nottingham & Mattson, 1981; Randolph et al., 1982; Shatin & Brodsky, 1979). Studies of the GCCT-MSH have consistently yielded significant correlations with independent criteria for competency (Bagby & Nicholson, 1992; Barnard et al., 1992; Gothard, Rogers, & Sewell, 1995; Gothard, Viglione, Meloy, & Sherman, 1995; Johnson, Nicholson, & Service, 1990; Nicholson, Robertson et al., 1988; Rogers et al., 1996; Ustad et al., 1996; Wildman, White, & Brandenburg, 1990). Furthermore, Nicholson and Johnson (1991) showed that performance on this instrument made a significant, independent contribution to prediction of competence status beyond that based on diagnosis, intellectual functioning, offense type, and background characteristics. Finally, the utility of the GCCT-MSH has recently been augmented by the development of an Atypical Presentation scale designed as a screen for feigned incompetence (Gothard, Rogers et al., 1995).

Analyses that examine how these competency instruments work are informative. In the case of the CST, some items appear to work better than others (Nicholson, Briggs et al., 1988), but correlates of the better predictors have not been identified. Furthermore, the factors that have emerged from factor analyses are not readily interpretable, are not stable across samples, and do not correspond to the original components of competency as outlined by the developers of the test (Bagby, Nicholson, Rogers, & Nussbaum, 1992; Laboratory of Community Psychiatry, 1974; Nicholson, Briggs et al., 1988). These limitations hinder the clinician's ability to use this test to draw inferences about impairment in specific psycholegal abilities.

In the case of the GCCT, all of the items show some correlation with a criterion; the best predictors appear to tap both cognitive ability and psychopathology (Bagby & Nicholson, 1992; Nicholson, Briggs et al., 1988). In addition, previous research has suggested that the GCCT is composed of three easily identifiable factors: General Legal Knowledge (knowledge of the roles of various courtroom participants), Specific Legal Knowledge (knowledge of the charge and possible penalties, ability to communicate with counsel), and Courtroom Orientation (location of personnel in the courtroom), which are stable across samples of pretrial defendants referred for evaluation of competency (Bagby et al., 1992; Nicholson, Briggs et al., 1988). The stability and generalizability of the dimensions underlying performance on the GCCT-MSH are important for forensic assessors who must attempt to draw inferences and provide the court with information about a defendant's functioning in specific areas of competency. Recently, some investigators have challenged the three-factor solution identified in earlier research (Rogers et al., 1996; Ustad et al., 1996). Notably, though, the sample characteristics in these recent studies differ from those in prior research. Previous factor analyses focused on defendants undergoing an initial evaluation of competence to proceed. In contrast, Ustad et al. (1996) examined defendants participating in a competency restoration program after being adjudicated incompetent; Rogers et al. (1996) examined defendants who were being housed on a mental health unit at a county jail but who had not necessarily been referred for an assessment of competency. In the latter study, almost one half of the sample scored above 90 on the GCCT-MSH, suggesting a distribution of scores that would be highly atypical for a sample of defendants referred for evaluation of competency. Because of these sampling differences, rejection of the three-factor model may be premature. Thus, additional research is needed to clarify the factor structure of the GCCT-MSH for different groups of defendants.

Regardless of the factor structure eventually judged to best fit the data from the various samples, a notable limitation of the measure is that the underlying factors identified in the studies to date do not correspond clearly to the competency construct as adumbrated by statute, case law, and legal theory. In particular, the instrument likely overemphasizes knowledge of courtroom personnel and their roles. Hence, the factors do not appear to reflect an adequate sampling of the domain of relevant abilities. An important next step in the evolution of this instrument would be the addition of items designed to assess the defendant's ability to make rational decisions about such crucial issues as entering a guilty plea, the quality of the defendant's relationship with his or her attorney, and other items that address the ability to consult with and assist counsel.

In contrast to the CST and GCCT, the recently developed CADCOMP was designed to provide broader coverage and a more comprehensive description of a defendant's functioning. Toward this end, CADCOMP employs interactive computer technology to collect relevant data from a defendant and produce a narrative report summarizing the findings (Barnard et al., 1991). Although designed to simulate the approach used by an experienced forensic psychiatrist conducting a competency assessment, CADCOMP was conceived as a screening or adjunctive component of a competency evaluation and can be administered by a trained technician. The instrument includes 272 items that solicit information about the defendant's background characteristics (e.g., demographics, educational attainment and experiences, psychiatric and legal history, etc.) as well as items that focus on psycholegal ability and psychopathology. The early research on CADCOMP documented high interrater reliability (88% agreement) and predictive validity (82%–86% agreement, depending on the criterion) of judgments based on the narrative report.

In subsequent research, Barnard et al. (1992) derived 18 scales from the CADCOMP item pool on rational/conceptual grounds. These scales describe the defendant's current psycholegal abilities (2 scales), current psychopathology (3 scales), postarrest behavior (2 scales), report of circumstances and behavior at the time of the alleged offense (4 scales), and educational, legal, and psychiatric history (5 scales). For purposes of assessing competency, the key scales are those assessing psycholegal ability and current psychopathology. The 4 original psycholegal ability scales include measures of the defendant's knowledge of the Adversarial Process (APR, 8 items) and appropriate Courtroom Behavior (CTB, 4 items) along with 2 measures of the defendant's relationship with his or her attorney (Active Relationship with Lawyer or ARL, 4 items; Perceived Relationship with Lawyer or PRL, 6 items). In addition, 1 scale deals with the period of the offense, Crime Awareness (CAW, 15 items), although not originally conceptualized as a psycholegal ability scale, has been treated as such in research on the reliability and validity of the CADCOMP scales. The scales assessing current psychopathology include Psychotic Features (PSY, 14 items), Cognitive Dysfunction (COG, 9 items), and Affective Disturbance (AFF, 3 items).

Together, these eight scales vary somewhat in the homogeneity of the items they contain. The mean interitem correlations ranged from .18 to .42 in a sample of pretrial defendants from Florida (Barnard et al., 1992), and from .18 to .38 in a sample from Oklahoma (Nicholson, Roach, & LaFortune, 1996). Thus, all of these scales had mean interitem correlations that approximate the range of .2 to .4 recommended by Briggs and Cheek (1986). Nevertheless, the differences across scales in item homogeneity and length resulted in considerable variability in estimates of internal consistency reliability. Alpha coefficients were greater than .70 for four scales in the Florida study and five scales in the Oklahoma study. The modest internal consistency reliabilities appear to be due in large part to the brevity of the scales.

In the Florida sample, two psycholegal ability scales, APR and CTB, and two psychopathology scales, PSY and COG, were significantly correlated with competency judgments (Barnard et al., 1992); three of these (with the exception of COG) were predictive of incompetent defendants' length of hospitalization (Nicholson, Barnard, Hankins, & Robbins, 1994). In the Oklahoma sample, APR, PSY, and COG were significantly correlated with competency judgments, although in each case the correlation was smaller than in the Florida sample (Nicholson et al., 1996).

Notably, in both validation studies, correlations between the CST or GCCT-MSH and competency judgments were as large or larger than the correlations for individual CADCOMP scales. However, using only the subscale scores for CADCOMP may put this instrument at a disadvantage in such a comparison. For example, each of the CADCOMP scales relevant to competency is considerably shorter and exhibits lower reliability than either the CST or GCCT-MSH. An alternative means of assessing CADCOMP's utility would involve creating a total score for the instrument by summing responses for all of the psychopathology and psycholegal items combined. Inasmuch as the CADCOMP assesses psychiatric status (whereas the CST and GCCT-MSH do not), computing a single score for this instrument might improve its predictive power relative to the other forensic tests.

In sum, although existing evidence on CADCOMP supports the continued development and investigation of this instrument, several issues need to be addressed. First, because CADCOMP can be administered by a trained technician, it has been touted as a screening instrument. However, validation studies have not been conducted in settings where screening for incompetency is necessary, a limitation that applies to virtually all of the research on the CST and GCCT-MSH as well. Second, the two psycholegal ability scales dealing with the defendant's relationship with an attorney were uncorrelated with competency judgments in both validation studies.

This result appears to be attributable to limitations of the scales themselves. Specifically, the items comprising those scales are nonpathological in content; a competent defendant can obtain a low score by not taking the initiative to contact her or his attorney, by reporting that they do not get along well, by voicing little trust in her or his attorney, and so on. Thus, these scales do not discriminate between defendants whose relationship with their attorney is impaired by virtue of a delusional belief system and those who are "merely dissatisfied" because they are represented by an overworked, undercompensated public defender. These scales should either undergo major revision or be deleted from the instrument entirely. Although deleting the scales would not compromise the predictive power of CADCOMP, there would be a reduction in the descriptive capability of the instrument. Hence, it would seem preferable to revise the scales or create new ones. Third, although homogeneity of the items was adequate for most scales, the internal consistency reliabilities for several scales were unacceptable. Reliability could be enhanced by adding items to the scales or by revising some of the more problematic items to increase their intercorrelation with other items on that same scale. This additional psychometric work on CADCOMP is necessary before a reasonable decision about its utility in competency evaluations can be made. Notably, the current scales for CADCOMP make use of fewer than one half of the total number of items on the instrument. It is possible that a set of scales with improved psychometric characteristics could be developed by making use of more of the CADCOMP item pool.

None of the instruments described thus far was developed for use in assessing defendants with mental retardation. Moreover, some evidence suggests that the CST (Chellsen, 1986) and perhaps the GCCT-MSH (Nicholson, Briggs et al., 1988) overdiagnose incompetence in defendants with mental retardation. The CAST-MR (Everington & Luckasson, 1992) was developed to meet the need for such a measure. Designed for use with individuals in the mild to moderate range of mental retardation, the instrument includes two sections that utilize a multiple-choice format and a third that uses an open-ended response format. The first section, *Basic Legal Concepts*, includes 25 items designed to assess a defendant's "knowledge of the criminal justice process" (Everington & Luckasson, 1992, p. 3), such as the roles and functions of various personnel. The second section, *Skills to Assist Defense*, includes 15 items to assess the defendant's "understanding of the client-attorney relationship" (Everington & Luckasson, 1992, p. 3). The third section, *Understanding Case Events*, includes 10 questions designed to assess the defendant's "ability to discuss the facts concerning the incident in a coherent manner and to understand the relationship between the alleged facts in the case and the subsequent arrest and charges" (Everington & Luckasson, 1992, p. 3). Multiple choice items are scored 0 or 1; open-ended questions are scored 0, ½ (for partial credit), or 1 (for full credit), yielding a maximum score of 50.

The manual that accompanies the CAST-MR provides data on the content validity of the scales (as rated by experts in criminal justice, mental retardation, and forensic psychology) and readability of the items (as assessed by six formal analyses of reading level). In addition, the manual reports promising, but as yet, preliminary and sketchy evidence on reliability and validity. Subjects and examiners for the CAST-MR research were recruited from sites in New Mexico, Ohio, Maryland, and Wisconsin. Two studies were conducted to assess interrater reliability for the open-ended questions and yielded averaged item agreement rates of 83% and 87%. However, the number and representativeness of the cases included in one or both of the reliability studies were unclear. Furthermore, the method of calculating reliability did not take into account the possibility of chance agreement, that is, the agreement that would have been expected simply on the basis of the examiner's base rate usage of score categories. The kappa coefficient, which corrects for chance agreement, would have provided a more accurate index of reliability. Of course, because interscorer reliability is probably relevant only for the 10 items in the third section of the instrument, this issue is perhaps not as crucial for the CAST-MR as it is for other measures.

Test-retest reliability, assessed in two small samples (total $n = 23$), appears excellent, with a correlation of about .90 over a 2-week period. However, because the subjects in these samples had no criminal charges, the reliability estimate must have been obtained only from Sections I and II of the instrument. Thus, we do not have an estimate of the stability of test scores based on administration of the entire test to an appropriate group of subjects from the target population, defendants with mental retardation.

Estimates of internal consistency reliability ranged from good to excellent. For example, in a sample of 93 defendants whose level of intellectual functioning (presence or absence of mental retardation) and competency status varied, alpha coefficients for Sections I, II, and III, were .91, .76, and .83, respectively. In another sample of mentally retarded defendants referred for competency assessment ($n = 35$), a comparable index (KR-20) yielded values of .92 for the total score and .84, .73, and .84 for the three sections of the test, again suggesting strong internal consistency reliability.

The construct validity of the measure was assessed by comparing scores of subjects who differed in level of intellectual functioning and competence status. The manual reports the percentage of items in Sections I and II answered correctly by 55 graduate students (98%), along with means and standard deviations on the total scale and three subscales for 46 defendants without mental retardation, 24 defendants with mental retardation who had not been referred for assessment of competency, 27 defendants with mental retardation who had been found competent, and 31 defendants with mental retardation who had been found incompetent. The rank ordering of means from highest to lowest followed this same order, a pattern of findings consistent with a priori hypotheses. Also promising was the finding that defendants found competent scored between one and two standard deviations higher than defendants judged incompetent. Nevertheless, the need for additional validation of the CAST-MR becomes apparent once it is recognized that of the 232 subjects included in the validation work to date, only 58 were from the population specifically targeted by the instrument, namely, defendants with mental retardation referred for assessment of competency. Moreover, these small samples render the results of the discriminant analyses reported in the manual meaningless. For example, in one of the studies, items from each of the sections of the test were used, in turn, to discriminate 12 competent and 11 incompetent defendants. In these analyses, the linear combination of items from Section I reportedly produced a classification rate of 100%. Given that there were more available predictors (items) than subjects in the criterion groups, this finding is a foregone conclusion. Equally disconcerting is the absence of a statement in the manual to the effect that examiners were blind to the competency status of the defendants they evaluated. If, in fact, examiners were not blind to defendants' competency status, the flaw would weaken the evidence for the validity of the CAST-MR. In sum, although the CAST-MR shows considerable promise, there is a pressing need to conduct additional research with larger samples of subjects using a prospective design and more appropriate indices of reliability and validity.

A possible limitation of the foregoing instruments is that the defendant's responses to test items are taken at face value in scoring. Only the GCCT-MSH has a scale for detecting feigned incompetence. And this was a recent addition (Gothard et al., 1995). The extent to which performance on these measures is affected by the defendant's test-taking style, including his or her degree of cooperation and truthfulness, is largely unexplored. Although structured interviews also rely on the defendant as information source, these measures potentially offer some advantage in that they allow the examiner to factor in the defendant's stylistic approach to the evaluation, to probe responses, and to modify ratings based on considerations other than the content of the defendant's verbal response to an item. The interviews also presumably offer broader coverage of the components of competency.

Three semistructured interviews permit some quantification of competency. Of these, the Fitness to Stand Trial Interview Test (FIT) has a larger data base than either of its better known counterparts, the CAI and the IFI; hence, the FIT will be the focus of the presentation here.[1] Developed by Roesch, Webster, and Eaves (1984) for use in the Canadian context, the original version of the FIT included 38 items in Likert format, which covered the domains of psycholegal ability and psychopathology. Three are summary items: one for the domain of psycholegal ability (Global Legal Fitness), one for the domain of psychopathology (Global Psychiatric Impairment), and one for the instrument as a whole (Final Judgment About Fitness). For each of the remaining items, the examiner rates the degree of incapacity observed as well as the importance of any impairment on that item to the overall decision about competency. Although Roesch et al. (1984) described the FIT as an extension of the CAI, the FIT shares significant features with the IFI as well, including coverage of the domain of psychopathology and the use of importance ratings in addition to ratings of incapacity.

The FIT shows good interrater agreement (McDonald et al., 1991; Roesch, Webster et al., 1984) and exhibits appropriate correlations with competency criteria (Bagby & Nicholson, 1992; Roesch, Webster et al., 1984), although the latter data are limited. As with the quantifiable screening tests, however, the most informative data on the FIT address the question of the instrument's construct validity. These investigations reveal some problematic characteristics. In one study, McDonald, Nussbaum, and Bagby (1991) found a mean interitem correlation among the legal items of .72, suggesting the possibility of a substantial halo effect. That is, raters may be unduly influenced by a single item; this influence may color their ratings of subsequent items. The possibility of a halo effect was also noted by Roesch, Jackson et al. (1984), based on the pattern of findings obtained in a study of ratings of videotaped interviews made by members of different professions. If there is a halo effect with the FIT, the rating format for the interview may contribute to the problem as it does not provide prompt questions or specific scoring criteria on the rating form. Notably, in a later study, Bagby et al. (1992) used a modified version of the FIT rating

---

[1]The FIT has since been revised to become the Fitness Interview Test–Revised (FIT-R; Roesch, Zapf, Eaves, & Webster, 1998) to reflect consideration of these criticisms and to assess three main areas that directly paralel changes that were made to the Canadian *Criminal Code* in 1992. Recent research has indicated that the FIT-R works well as a screening instrument for fitness to stand trial in Canada. Zapf and Roesch (1997) compared the decisions about fitness made on the basis of the FIT-R to the institution-based decisions about fitness made by mental health professionals at a forensic psychiatric institution in British Columbia. These authors found that there was a high rate of agreement (86%) between the FIT-R decisions and those made by the mental health professionals.

form that incorporated prompt questions for each item to be rated; this modification yielded a mean interitem correlation among the legal items of .42, suggesting a reduced halo effect. Factor analytic evidence on the construct validity of the FIT is also problematic because several factor analyses of FIT data have yielded inconsistent findings (Bagby et al., 1992; McDonald et al., 1991; Roesch, Webster et al., 1984). Specifically, these analyses have tended to yield a large first factor, a much smaller second factor, with frequent dual loadings of items on factors within samples and inconsistencies in the factor loadings across samples.

Findings based on the FIT may not generalize to the other structured interviews, but they at least raise the question of whether the interviews can deliver on their promises. If there is a substantial halo, then the specificity and breadth of coverage implied by the multiple rating format may be illusory. Furthermore, the format used by all of these instruments does not lend itself well to an examination of how these measures work. For each item rated, there are prompt questions provided in a handbook, but there is no scoring of responses to the recommended questions that would permit us to determine how the assessor arrived at the rating of an individual item.

Consideration of the limitations of both quantitative screening measures and the semistructured interviews suggests the need for a new generation of competency assessment instruments (Bagby et al., 1992; Grisso, 1991, 1992; Nicholson, 1992; Nicholson & Kugler, 1991), not only to improve assessment but also to increase our understanding of the competency construct. I have argued that such measures should incorporate multiple scales comprised of homogeneous items designed to assess specific components of the multifaceted construct. Toward this end, I have advocated the application of a bottom-up strategy of test construction that consists of two steps (e.g., Bagby et al., 1992; Nicholson, 1992). The first step is one of theory development, including the generation of hypotheses about the components of the factorially complex competency construct. The second step in the process involves the construction of homogeneous scales to assess each candidate component separately. The effect of the two steps is to produce a group of internally consistent measures, each of which relates to a particular aspect of the broader construct. This procedure permits the development of highly reliable measures without compromising the complexity of the construct under study. The realization of such a strategy would permit a focus not only on the broad dimension of competency, but also an equally sharp focus on the elements that comprise the broad dimension. Furthermore, it would permit conceptual analysis and hypothesis testing to proceed at the level of the components of competency.

Independent of my description of such a test construction strategy, the

MacArthur Research Network on Law and Mental Health followed a similar course in the development of a new measure, the MacSAC-CD (Hoge et al., 1997), and its clinical version, the MacCAT-CA. The foundation for the development of the MacArthur measure was laid by Richard Bonnie (1992, 1993) who articulated a theory of adjudicative competence that is more thorough and more sophisticated than previous attempts to conceptualize the construct. According to Bonnie, competence in the criminal context is not a unitary, open-ended construct. Rather, adjudicative competence should be viewed as comprising distinct, separable components: (a) competence to assist counsel (CAC), a foundational component derived from the legal rationales of dignity and reliability (accuracy, fairness); and (b) decisional competence (DC), a component derived from the legal rationale of autonomy that comes into play when certain decisions, reserved by law to the defendant, must be made, and then, only if the defendant is considered competent to assist counsel. The foundational component, CAC, encompasses such abilities as the capacity to understand the nature and purpose of criminal prosecution and punishment and the nature of the adversary process, especially the role of defense counsel; the capacity to understand the charges and appreciate one's own situation in relation to the charges and legal process; and the ability to relate to counsel and provide pertinent facts. DC encompasses the capacity to understand information associated with a particular legal decision, the ability to weigh and consider the information appropriately (e.g., the costs and benefits of various courses of action), the capacity to appreciate one's situation when facing a particular legal decision, and the ability to exercise a choice. According to Bonnie, the specific abilities encompassed by decisional competence depend on the particular decision facing the defendant and the context in which it arises. Indeed, in *Godinez v. Moran* (1993), and U.S. Supreme Court determined that the defendant's decision-making capacity was subsumed by the *Dusky* standard (*Dusky v. United States*, 1960) but did not delineate the abilities required for decisional competence.

In several respects, the structure of the MacSAC-CD departs from those used in previous measures of criminal competence (Hoge et al., 1997). First, most questions on the instrument are organized around a hypothetical vignette. This structure confers certain advantages: It serves to safeguard the defendant's Fifth Amendment right against self-incrimination; it permits the assessment of important capacities (e.g., the decision to plead guilty) prior to the availability of relevant information pertaining to the individual's case (e.g., a specific offer from the prosecutor). Although commentators (e.g., Nicholson, Briggs et al., 1988; Roesch & Golding, 1980) have been critical of hypothetical items on the CST (Lipsitt et al.,

1971) because they appeared to tax the cognitive capacities of many defendants, the problem with those items may have been due to the fact that the hypothetical frame of reference shifted from one item to the next. In contrast, because the hypothetical questions on the MacSAC-CD are organized around a single vignette, they do not require defendants to make item-by-item shifts in frame of reference. Second, the MacSAC-CD permits assessment of defendants' performances before and after disclosure of relevant information. After disclosure, defendants are asked to restate the information in their own words. This structure should assist in assessing defendants' latent capacities; that is, poor predisclosure performance followed by adequate postdisclosure responses should identify competent defendants who suffered from "mere ignorance." Third, in addition to predisclosure open-ended and post-disclosure paraphrase response formats, for each relevant item the MacSAC-CD incorporates a true-false response format following the postdisclosure request for paraphrase. The true-false format should assist in assessing the understanding of defendants whose verbal expressive capacities are limited or impaired.

Development of the MacSAC-CD was theory driven and involved the construction of scales designed to assess the two legal domains of competency as well as the psychological capacities—understanding, reasoning, and appreciation—underlying each domain (Hoge et al., 1997). The content of the Competence to Assist Counsel: Understanding (CAC:U) scale is similar to that assessed by other knowledge-based competency measures and covers such basic issues as the characteristics of criminal prosecution and defense, the nature of criminal charges, the consequences of conviction, and so on. The Competence to Assist Counsel: Reasoning (CAC:R) scale assesses the defendant's ability to recognize the information presented as more or less relevant to the legal case and to state why. The Competence to Assist Counsel: Appreciation (CAC:A) scale focuses on the defendant's own legal case rather than a hypothetical vignette and assesses whether the defendant has psychiatric symptoms (e.g., delusional beliefs) that may impair appreciation of the significance of his or her legal situation.

For Decisional Competence, two "understanding" scales were constructed, both based on the hypothetical vignette. One scale emphasizes the information needed to render a decision about pleading guilty (DC:U-PG); the other focuses on information necessary to make a decision about waiving a jury trial (DC:U-WJ). The first part of the Decisional Competence: Reasoning (DC:R) scale is also based on the vignette and assesses the defendant's capacity to request appropriate additional information, to conceive the legal effects and personal consequences of various alternatives, and to compare courses of action. The remainder of the DC:R scale measures the defendant's ability to assign relative values to alternatives consistently, to apply transitivity in thinking about alternatives, and to think using probabilities. A single item based on the vignette, Decisional Competence: Choice (DC:C), assays the defendant's capacity to express a choice about going to trial or pleading guilty. Finally, the Decisional Competence: Appreciation (DC:A) scale is based on the defendant's own legal case; it consists of only two items, each of which assesses the defendant's capacity to offer a plausible reason for an important legal decision (viz., pleading guilty and waiving a jury trial).

The preliminary reliability and validity data on MacSAC-CD are quite encouraging (Hoge et al., 1997). The initial field study involved three samples recruited in Virginia and Florida: (a) hospitalized incompetent defendants from state forensic units ($n = 159$), (b) randomly selected defendants who had been identified as mentally disordered (but not incompetent) and who were receiving mental health treatment in jail ($n = 113$), and (c) randomly selected defendants who had not been identified as mentally disordered and who were not receiving mental health treatment in jail ($n = 94$). The initial findings suggest adequate interscorer reliability (kappas range from .36 to .75, percent agreement from 75 to 88) and good internal consistency reliability (alpha coefficients range from .68 to .88). In addition, exploratory factor analysis of the scale scores yielded a three-factor solution consistent with the psycholegal capacities (understanding, reasoning, appreciation) hypothesized to underlie both CAC and DC. Construct validity was further demonstrated by expected differences across the three samples, appropriate correlations with measures of psychopathology and verbal cognitive functioning, the absence of correlations with a measure of perceived unfairness in the criminal justice system, and, in the hospitalized sample, modest correlations with clinical ratings of competence.

In sum, the MacSAC-CD represents a major contribution to the assessment of adjudicative competence. The combination of standardized administration, objective scoring, and broad (though not exhaustive) coverage of psycholegal domains is not matched by existing measures. According to the authors (Hoge et al., 1997), the MacSAC-CD was developed as a research instrument not for use in forensic practice. They note that the average time required by an experienced examiner for administration of the instrument is about 2 hours. For this reason, the MacCAT-CA, a much briefer clinical version that requires about 40 minutes to administer, has been developed and is currently undergoing field testing. In addition, research is underway to establish norms for the clinical instrument to enhance its utility. Although I applaud the authors' concern with the practical side of forensic assessment, I believe that it is a mistake to characterize the MacSAC-CD as a research instrument only; indeed, it may prove especially helpful in the assessment of restoration to competence and other "gray area" cases.

Criminal Responsibility

Two instruments for assessing criminal responsibility or mental state at the time of the offense—the MSE (Slobogin et al., 1984) and the R-CRAS (Rogers, 1984b)—were introduced more than a decade ago. The conceptual underpinnings, psychometric characteristics, and construct validity of these measures were thoroughly reviewed by Grisso (1986). Hence, the presentation here will be brief.

The R-CRAS, which was developed to standardize and organize insanity evaluations, consists of two parts. The first part includes 30 psychological and situational variables relevant to a judgment about the defendant's mental state at the time of the offense (e.g., severity of hallucinations at the time of the offense, level of intoxication, etc.), each of which is to be rated by the examiner based on a thorough review of available data. The R-CRAS manual provides a description of each item to be rated. In addition, the manual and the rating form provide anchors to assist the examiner in making discriminations on the rating scales, although for most items, the anchors are not linked to normative data. The manual also provides some guidance for data collection, including review of various documents (e.g., police reports, mental health records) and clinical interview of the defendant. The data collection process is not rigorously structured, but it will necessarily be guided by the content of the items to be rated by the examiner. The individual items are grouped into five clusters that can be treated as scales: patient's reliability, organicity, psychopathology, cognitive control, and behavioral control.

The second part of the R-CRAS provides explicit decision models for use with the American Law Institute (ALI; American Law Institute, 1962), M'Naghten, and GBMI standards, although according to the manual, only the ALI decision model is considered to have adequate reliability and validity data for clinical use. The examiner answers a series of summary questions that correspond to components of the particular insanity standard (e.g., the presence of an organic or major psychiatric disorder constitutes "mental disease or defect") or major issues to be considered in any insanity evaluation (e.g., malingering). Answers to the summary questions are based on a review of the examiner's ratings of individual psychological and situational variables, but the latter ratings are not combined quantitatively to arrive at an answer to the summary question. The summary items are laid out in decision tree format such that the examiner's responses to the items lead to an overall decision addressing the ultimate legal issue.

The MSE, which is characterized as a screening measure, was designed to permit an examiner to arrive at a decision about the presence of "significant mental abnormality" at the time of an offense that may have affected the defendant's actions and, hence, might constitute the basis for a defense of insanity or diminished capacity. When the examiner's judgment is affirmative, the defendant should be referred for a comprehensive evaluation. The MSE sensitizes examiners to the kinds of information needed to address the legal issue of a defendant's mental state at the time of an offense. Specifically, the instrument directs an examiner to gather (a) historical information regarding the presence of a number of psychiatric disorders relevant to criminal responsibility, (b) offense information from the defendant and from extrinsic sources, and (c) information regarding the defendant's mental status at the time of the evaluation. Although the MSE thus imposes some structure on the assessment of criminal responsibility, it does not require standardized administration. There is no formal scoring system to relate findings on components of the measure to overall judgments about whether the defendant suffered from "significant mental abnormality" at the time of the offense.

Of the two measures, the R-CRAS is by far the more thoroughly researched (see Rogers, 1984b, 1986; Rogers & Ewing, 1992; Rogers, Seman, & Clark, 1986). To date, studies of the R-CRAS have involved 385 defendants referred for assessment of criminal responsibility; 260 defendants from six forensic facilities were included in studies of the ALI decision model, and 125 defendants from three facilities were included a study of the M'Naghten and GBMI decision models. In studies of the ALI decision model, data on interexaminer agreement were obtained from independent evaluations of 76 cases conducted an average of almost 3 weeks apart. Reliabilities were extremely good for the six decision items relevant to the ALI standard; the mean rate of agreement was 90% (range, 85%–100%) and the mean kappa coefficient was .79 (range, .48–1.00). Reliability for the overall decision was even higher, with an agreement rate of 97% and a kappa of .94. In addition, interrater reliability for most of the individual items of the R-CRAS was at least adequate (mean $r = 0.58$). Unfortunately, the reported reliabilities for individual items were Pearson correlations rather than intraclass correlations. The intraclass correlation is the preferred index of reliability because it takes into account level differences as well as pattern differences across raters (Bartko & Carpenter, 1976). Also, it should be noted that interrater reliability for the M'Naghten and GBMI decision models and for five items relevant to those standards is unknown.

Perhaps the major limitation of research on the R-CRAS is that of criterion contamination. The central validity analysis in each study consisted of a comparison across criterion groups (e.g., sane vs. insane, sane vs. GBMI vs. insane) of scores on the relevant summary scales from the R-CRAS. Unfortunately, formation of the criterion groups was based on the overall clinical judgments of the same examiners who performed the R-CRAS ratings. Given the organization of the R-CRAS, such analyses are most appropriately viewed as analyses that support the internal structure rather than the criterion-related validity of the instrument.

Another criterion, the final court disposition, has been used in some research with the R-CRAS, but this criterion suffers from contamination as well. Because the examiners submitted a report or provided expert testimony in court regarding the results of the evaluations, the estimate of the rate of agreement between decisions based on the R-CRAS and court dispositions (88% of 93 cases) is likely to be inflated. Rogers and Ewing (1992) describe the difficulties posed by research on criterion-related validity of criminal responsibility measures, as well as the efforts to minimize criterion contamination in studies of the R-CRAS.

In a variation on the primary validation analyses involving the ALI decision model, four sets of discriminant analyses were used to assess whether the defendant's demographic characteristics, psychiatric history, legal history, or characteristics of the examination (e.g., location, profession of examiner) added to discrimination of criterion groups after the R-CRAS summary scales were entered into the analyses. These analyses, involving a minimum of 124 defendants, suggested that only two variables (the absence of a close interpersonal relationship outside the family after age 12 and a history of schizophrenia) made small, but statistically significant independent contributions to variance in the criterion. Similarly, in validation studies of the M'Naghten and GBMI decision models, involving 125 defendants, two sets of discriminant analyses were used to determine whether demographics (age, race, gender) and legal variables (current offense, fitness to stand trial) added to discrimination of the criterion groups after the R-CRAS summary scales were entered. None of the variables made an independent contribution to prediction of the criterion. The most important finding from these analyses can be stated succinctly: Decisions about criminal responsibility based on the R-CRAS items and decision model do not appear to be influenced by variables that, conceptually, should bear little relationship to such judgments (e.g., age, gender, race, current offense, site of evaluation, profession of examiner).

Empirical evidence on the MSE is limited, based on a single investigation of 36 cases randomly selected from admissions to a state hospital forensic unit in Virginia. There are no data on interrater agreement with regard to the major decision entailed by the MSE (presence of "significant mental abnormality"). The rate of agreement between examiners who used the MSE and forensic staff who conducted an independent evaluation was 72%. As is appropriate for a screening measure, all of the "errors" were false positives (i.e., defendants judged to have the basis for a potential insanity defense using the MSE were evaluated as sane by the forensic staff).

Existing reviews of the empirical evidence on the R-CRAS and MSE yield quite divergent conclusions. Meloy (1986) praised the R-CRAS, while Melton et al. (1987) and Golding and Roesch (1987) were sharply critical. For example, Melton et al. (1987) described the R-CRAS as "not without merit" (p. 147) but nevertheless underscored the limitations of the instrument and its research base. Golding and Roesch (1987) voiced similar concerns and also challenged some of the purported benefits of the R-CRAS, arguing that the reliability of judgments of insanity was also "quite high" in most studies that used no formalized interviews or rating scales. In contrast to their critical reviews of the R-CRAS, Golding and Roesch offered a positive appraisal of the MSE; Melton et al. discussed the screening measure without a single critical comment.

The absence of a critical evaluation of the MSE by Melton et al. (1987) and some of the specific arguments against the R-CRAS raised by Golding and Roesch (1987) suggest the possibility of bias in their summaries of the empirical evidence. For example, the claim (Golding & Roesch, 1987) that reliabilities comparable to those obtained for conclusions based on the R-CRAS have been observed in most studies without formalized interviews or rating scales is technically correct, but misleading because of the problematic nature of the cited evidence. For example, in one study (Fukunaga, Pawewark, Hawkins, & Gudeman, 1981), psychiatrists conferred before rendering their opinions; in another (Poythress & Stock, 1980), psychologists who had received several months of training and supervision in the same forensic facility simultaneously interviewed the defendant. Thus, the designs of these studies obviated structured assessment by minimizing information and criterion variance through other means. When assessed under more realistic conditions, interexaminer concordance on judgments of criminal responsibility from unstructured evaluations may be substantially lower, even with experienced examiners (e.g., Raifman, 1979). Moreover, Golding and Roesch (1987) misreported the reliability of an important R-CRAS item—one that calls for a rating of the extent to which loss of cognitive or behavioral control at the time of the offense was due to mental illness. Those authors reported that chance-corrected interrater agreement for the item was .49, while the R-CRAS manual reported a kappa coefficient of .89.

Tendentious summaries of the empirical evidence may partly reflect differences of opinion regarding the proper aim and scope of forensic assessment and the place of "ultimate issue" testimony in forensic work. Rogers endorsed such testimony and developed the R-CRAS to facilitate a conclusory opinion; in contrast, the project by Slobogin et al. (1984) had the narrower goal of developing a screening measure. Scholars who oppose ultimate opinions and testimony may be inclined to view the product of Rogers's ambitious efforts negatively and the more modest attempt by Slobogin et al. favorably. Indeed, a fundamental concern in the commentaries on the R-CRAS by Melton et al. (1987) and Golding and Roesch (1987) is that it does not substantially advance the forensic examiner's ability to offer testimony on the issue of insanity with a "reasonable degree of scientific certainty," as claimed by Rogers (1984b). Another factor impacting assessment of the R-CRAS is reflected in the concern that the availability of structured or standardized methods will deflect attention from "the critical need to develop a better fundamental understanding of the behavioral, perceptual, cognitive, affective, and judgmental correlates of various mental and especially personality disorders" (Golding & Roesch, 1987, p. 418).

No doubt there is a pressing need for research on such issues (e.g., Under what circumstances do psychotic individuals act on the basis of command hallucinations or delusions?). In fact, there is a growing empirical base that addresses these kinds of questions (e.g., Hustig & Hafner, 1990; Thompson, Stuart, & Holden, 1992), although significant gaps in our knowledge remain. In the interim, practicing forensic psychologists must decide how to proceed with the assessment of criminal responsibility "until the researcher comes." Examiners must decide whether or not to use either of the available measures, and if so, which one. Assuming comparable relevance of existing methods, the examiner's decision should be based on empirical evidence regarding the reliability and validity of a method in comparison with similar evidence for relevant alternatives. On this score, the available data support the use of the R-CRAS when compared with the MSE and traditional, unstructured assessments. Although forensic examiners should be well versed in the limitations of the R-CRAS, at the very least, the measure guides the data collection and decision-making processes and reduces information variance that contributes to unreliability in clinical judgment. Moreover, the R-CRAS is the only measure for which an examiner can point to even minimal data regarding interrater reliability and construct validity. Although the MSE does have promise as a screening measure that could enhance the efficiency of procedures for conducting insanity evaluations, the lack of data on interrater reliability and the meager validity data dictate that forensic examiners should be cautious about adopting the MSE for clinical use.

Some might argue that an examiner's position regarding ultimate issue testimony will direct the choice of instrument (as it apparently has impacted reviews of research). However, it should be noted that the R-CRAS does not have to be used to arrive at an opinion about the ultimate issue; an examiner may simply choose to describe the psychological and situational variables relevant to the ultimate issue for the court. Even so, the examiner who adopts this approach needs to be cognizant that some of the individual items on the R-CRAS incorporate elements of the ultimate legal issue and should therefore be omitted from the examiner's summary description.

Since the introduction of the MSE and R-CRAS more than a decade ago, there has been an increase in the quantity and quality of research on the insanity defense. We now have much more accurate information on the use and success of insanity pleas, the characteristics of successful NGRI acquittees, juror comprehension of insanity instructions and the factors that influence jury decision making, and the consequences of NGRI acquittal (e.g., Ogloff, Schweighofer, Turnbull, & Whittemore, 1992; Silver, 1995; Silver, Cirincione, & Steadman, 1994; see especially the volume by Steadman et al., 1993, whose painstaking efforts produced a multistate data base that is certainly the largest and best source of information on the insanity defense in the U.S.). In contrast, during this same time frame little progress has been made in the development and validation of methods for assessing criminal responsibility. With the exception of a validation study of the R-CRAS using the M'Naghten and GBMI standards (Rogers, Seman, & Clark, 1986), no empirical investigations of either the MSE or the R-CRAS have been conducted since Grisso's (1986) review. The difficulty and complexity of assessments of criminal responsibility, as well as gaps in the evidence regarding the reliability and validity of existing strategies, underscore the need for ongoing research designed to expand available technology and enhance the quality of these assessments.

CHILD CUSTODY/TERMINATION OF PARENTAL RIGHTS

Previous commentators have been sharply critical of assessments of child custody. For example, Melton et al. (1987) concluded that "there is virtually no scientific basis for provision of opinions about the kinds of questions that the courts must decide in divorce cases when children are involved" (p. 330). They further argued that there is no other area of forensic practice where "overreaching" in the opinions offered by mental health professionals "has been so common and so egregious" (p. 330). In part, problems in such assessments can be attributed to the misuse of standard, psychological measures for purposes of child custody decision making (e.g., Brodzinsky, 1993; Heilbrun, 1995). Grisso's (1986) earlier review was designed to shift the focus from traditional instruments to measures of parenting capacity and parental competence. However, several instruments specifically designed to assist forensic examiners in child custody assessments, including the Custody Quotient (Gordon & Peek, 1987), the Bricklin Perceptual Scales: Child-Perception-of-Parent Series (BPS; Bricklin, 1984), the Perception-of-Relationships Test (PORT; Bricklin, 1990a), the Parent Awareness Skills Survey (PASS; Bricklin, 1990b), and most recently, the Ackerman-Schoendorf Scales for Parent Evaluation of Custody (ASPECT; Ackerman & Schoendorf, 1992), were not available at the time of Grisso's (1986) review. The summary here will focus on the measures developed by Bricklin (1984, 1990a,b) and Ackerman and Schoendorf (1992). These instruments have been described as promising approaches (Brodzinsky, 1993), the manuals that accompany the instruments present initial reliability and validity data.

The BPS (Bricklin, 1984) was developed to measure a child's "gut-level, unconscious perceptions of parental behavior where this perception is, in largest part, based on the behavior's utility for the child" (p. 40). The 64 items (32 for each parent) assess the child's perception of his or her parents in four areas: competence (11 items), supportiveness (11 items), follow-up consistency (3 items), and possession of admirable traits (7 items). For each item, the examiner elicits verbal and nonverbal responses from the child. The nonverbal responses are obtained by reference to a continuum line anchored at the extremes by the phrases "very well" and "not so well" (e.g., "If this is Dad doing very well at ———, and this is Dad doing not so well, where on this line would Dad be?"). The child's nonverbal responses are considered more important than his or her verbal responses because the former are presumed to be less influenced by coaching or bribery and more likely to represent "gut-level, whole organism" responses. The parent who obtains a higher score on more items is declared the "parent-of-choice" (POC), "the parent better suited, in the perceptions of the child, to be the primary caretaking parent" (Bricklin, 1984, p. 39).

The PORT (1990a) was designed to measure the degree to which a child seeks psychological closeness (positive interactions) with each parent and the types of dispositions the child has had to develop to permit or accommodate interaction with each parent. The test utilizes seven tasks, including a child's figure drawings and placement of those figure drawings in various situations. The PORT scoring system yields a measure of the child's perception of his or her relationship with each parent and, based on those scores, identifies one or the other parent as the POC.

Serious questions can be raised about the quality of the reliability and validity data provided in the BPS and PORT manuals. Bricklin (1984, 1990a) accurately described the difficulties inherent in validation research in the child custody context and appropriately lamented the paucity of validity data on the BPS and PORT. However, his pointed critique of potential validation strategies contrasted sharply with a facile dismissal of deficiencies in the research offered to support the reliability and validity of the BPS and PORT. Indeed, the latter measures and supportive reliability and validity evidence are described with a zeal more characteristic of a psychic hotline, abdominal exerciser, or "no money down" infomercial than a psychological test manual. Thus, the manner in which the information on these measures is presented promotes greater confidence on the part of examiners than the data warrant.

A brief summary of reliability and validity data on the BPS should illustrate these concerns. First, no internal consistency reliabilities were reported, either for the total BPS or for the four subscales. Second, test-retest reliability data were available for only 12 subjects from adversarial cases. Furthermore, these 12 subjects required retesting because of delays in their custody hearings. Therefore, they were not randomly selected from the total pool of adversarial cases. According to the manual, there were no changes in the designated POC for the 12 cases. The manual acknowledges that changes in scores on individual items occurred but does not report stability coefficients for the total and subscale scores. Although the omission of this information can be justified (e.g., the stability coefficients lack generalizability and are of doubtful utility given the small and unrepresentative nature of the sample), such considerations apply to the reported stability of the POC index as well. Third, the basic validity data for the BPS were obtained from a small nonadversarial sample of volunteers (total $n = 21$). These subjects were selected because "extensive family, clinical and/or life history data were available" for a period of at least 2 years. Mental health professionals who had no knowledge of the child's BPS scores reviewed the available information and designated a primary care-taking parent. The two judges agreed with each other in 95% of the cases; in those cases, the rate of agreement between judges and the BPS was 100%. Other validity data reported in the manual include agreement rates between the BPS and various measures developed by the author, including the PORT, as well as the judges' decisions in cases in which the author testified. Finally, a supplement to the manual reports the results of a survey of practitioners who use the BPS. The 27 respondents reported rates of agreement between the BPS and what their recommendations would have been if based only on other sources of information (other tests, clinical/life history data, and a combination of the two) for 141 cases. With the exception of the original validity study involving independent judgments by mental health professionals in 21 nonadversarial cases, the remaining validity data are of questionable utility because of marked criterion contamination.

The findings presented in the BPS and PORT manuals are further compromised by egregious factual errors about fundamental measurement concepts. For example, the manual reports that the standard error of measurement (SEM) for the BPS is "zero" based on the initial validation study. How can this be? The concept of SEM is later described as "how the two distributions, the BPS scores and those of independent judges, compare" (Bricklin, 1990a). Because there were no cases of disagreement between the BPS and the judges in the 20 cases studied, the SEM is reported as 0! Ironically, the context for this erroneous description of the standard error of measurement is a discussion of the need to keep the statistics simple so that they can be easily understood by parents and judges, and so that attorneys will not misuse them.

Suggestions to practitioners about how to respond to questions during cross-examination are equally disturbing. For example, examiners are instructed to respond to questions about the stability of BPS findings as follows: "Quote the following reliability statistics: The research evidence indicates that in test-retest situations no significant changes were noted within a seven-month follow-up period. Were a score to change, it would be assumed that some significant shift in the child's perceptions took place" (p. 65). In other words, on the strength of the findings from 12 cases not representative of the sample of adversarial cases from which they were drawn, the examiner is encouraged to testify confidently about the stability of scores and to add a caveat that renders consideration of score stability meaningless. The author's suggestion for responding to questions about the content of the BPS also exemplifies the exaggerated claims made throughout the manual: "If the question comes up about why there are 11 items in two categories, 3 in another and 7 in the other, simply answer that this reflects the thinking of a consensus of mental health workers and also reflects the proportions of concerns shown in laws which have attempted to define *best interests of the child*" (Bricklin, 1984, p. 68; italics added for emphasis). I would submit that even Procrustes could not force statutory articulation of the "best interests of the child" into the four domains ostensibly tapped by the BPS, let alone in proportion to the number of items devoted to each domain (i.e., 34% competence, 34% supportiveness, 22% possession of admirable traits, and 9% follow-up consistency). A final, and perhaps most disconcerting, example is provided by the author's description of the unique contribution of "test data" to child custody determinations.

Judge ... if you had an elevated temperature and a doctor wanted to know what it was, he or she could simply ask you. Your answer would be an opinion.... This is basically what (whoever you are opposing) do in their interviews. They gather opinions. But I strongly suspect, your honor, that ... you would rather the doctor use a thermometer.... Test devices give much more accurate data than opinions.... I could ask you for hours on end what you think your temperature is, or I could find out what it is in less than two minutes. This is the value of test data. It tells what's really true, not what someone thinks is true—and it usually does this fairly rapidly. (Bricklin, 1984, pp. 64–65)

I will leave it to the reader to judge whether or not such a statement, if offered as expert testimony, would be considered consistent with our discipline's current specialty guidelines (Committee on Ethical Guidelines for Forensic Psychologists, 1991).

The other child custody measure to be considered is the ASPECT, a 56-item rating instrument designed to provide an overall summary index of parenting effectiveness (the Parent Custody Index or PCI) for each parent in a custody dispute. According to Ackerman (1995), the development of ASPECT began with a review of the psychological literature "to determine what criteria were being used to make custody recommendations by mental health professionals and how custody evaluations were currently being conducted" (p. 119). Each of the 56 items corresponds to a variable identified as being relevant for child custody determinations. Twelve of the items are considered to be critical items in that they are indicative of significant deficits in parenting capacity. The items are organized into three "standardized scales"—Observational, Social, and Cognitive-Emotional—devised "to quantify characteristics related to effective custodial parenting" (Ackerman, 1995, p. 119).

The Observational scale, which consists of 9 items, purportedly assesses the self-presentation and appearance of the parent. Some idea of the breadth of the scale can be seen in the fact that items tap parents' hygiene and grooming as well as their maturity and insight. The Social Scale, comprising 28 items, reportedly assesses the social environment provided by the parent and incorporates such considerations as the parents' involvement with the child, the possibility of physical or sexual abuse, and the parents' criminal history and potential for substance abuse. The Cognitive-Emotional scale includes 19 items and is intended to assess participants' cognitive and affective capacities for parenting, including parental psychopathology, ego strength, and social judgment.

The examiner responds to the 56 items for each parent in order to derive the summary index of parenting effectiveness or PCI. The examiner's answers to the individual items are based on information obtained from observations and interviews of the parents and children, each parent's responses to a parent questionnaire, and the results of psychological testing of both parents and children. The recommended battery of psychological tests includes the MMPI/MMPI-2, several projective tests (Rorschach, TAT or CAT, Draw-A-Family Test), and measures of intellectual functioning and school achievement. After the PCI for each parent is determined, the two scores can be plotted on a grid that yields an overall decision about which individual would make the better custodial parent.

Although the individual items of the ASPECT clearly target components of parenting capacity, the examiner's scoring of those items is based on information obtained from traditional clinical measures. Hence, careful consideration must be given to the link between item content and the underlying clinical information. In this regard, the limited reliability and validity of some of the recommended clinical measures (e.g., TAT or CAT, projective drawings) necessarily constrain the reliability and validity of inferences drawn from those measures and used to answer items on the ASPECT. Furthermore, the extent to which an inference needed to score an item on the ASPECT can legitimately be drawn from the recommended clinical measures must be subjected to scrutiny. The following example should illustrate this concern: One of the items on the ASPECT addresses the question of whether a parent has sufficient ego strength to meet the demands of parenting. An affirmative response is based on the finding that the parent scored above 45T on the Ego Strength (ES; Barron, 1953) scale of the MMPI or MMPI-2. Questions can be raised about the construct validity of the ES scale in general (Graham, 1993), its use an index of ego strength in the context of parenting (especially given the consistent gender differences observed on the ES scale), and the selection of 45T as the optimal cutoff score for classifying parents. Moreover, it is not entirely clear that the MMPI and MMPI-2 versions of ES measure the same construct. Of the 62 items included in the MMPI version of ES, 12 (19%) were deleted and others were modified (Butcher & Williams, 1992).

The reliability and validity data on the ASPECT are limited. The standardization sample consisted of a total of 100 couples seeking custody evaluations. These couples were not representative of the U.S. population. Psychologists in private practice participated as examiners, but no information about how they were selected or their demographic characteristics was provided. Interrater reliabilities were reported to be excellent, ranging from 0.92 on the Observational subscale to 0.96 on the PCI. However, internal consistency reliability, as indexed by alpha coefficients computed on 200 subjects in the standardization sample, was reasonable only for the PCI scale (0.76) and the Social subscale (0.72) but was poor for the Observational and Cognitive-Emotional subscales (0.50 for both). Not surprisingly, corrected item-total correlations were generally small for the three subscales, suggesting substantial item heterogeneity.

Ackerman (1995) argued that the ASPECT is considered content valid "because the questions were derived from the literature on custody issues" (p. 136). However, the wisdom of basing the selection of items on a review of the psychological literature in order to identify the variables being used by mental health professionals to make custody recommendations (see Ackerman, 1995) can be questioned. The most important step in the application of Grisso's model for developing forensic assessment instruments is the analysis of the law's view of the particular competency in question. Indeed, the history of child custody assessment, in particular, attests to the inadvisability of substituting the views of mental health professionals for an understanding of what statues, case law, and legal theory have to say about a legal construct (Goldstein, Freud, & Solnit, 1973; Lowery, 1984). A well-grounded understanding of the legal construct is a prerequisite for translation of that construct into psycholegal abilities that then become the targets for assessment. One by-product of the authors' focus on the psychological literature and the variables used by mental health professionals may be reflected in a recommended test battery that includes the gamut of traditional clinical measures—achievement tests, intelligence tests, objective personality measures, projective techniques, and clinical interviews. Apparently, in order for the examiner to complete the ASPECT, the entire test battery must be administered in every case.

Ackerman (1995) described two types of predictive validity studies that have been conducted with the ASPECT. The first involves "other psychologists administering the ASPECT but not tallying the results until after they have already formulated custody recommendations" (p. 136). The findings from this investigation were not described. The second type of predictive validity study involved comparing recommendations based on the ASPECT with judges' decisions in 56 custody cases. Overall, the rate of agreement was 75% (42 of 56 cases). However, in the 30 cases in which there was at least a 10-point difference in the PCI standard scores of the parents, the rate of agreement was 93.3%, as compared with an agreement rate of 53.8% in the 26 cases with less than a 10-point difference. The examiners in this study presumably based their recommendations to the court at least in part on the results of the ASPECT, rendering interpretation of study findings problematic and diminishing the value of the evidence as support for the predictive validity of the ASPECT.

Although the Bricklin measures and the ASPECT were developed specifically for use in child custody cases and are more relevant than traditional clinical measures to assessments in that legal context, Brodzinsky (1993) appropriately recommended caution in adopting these instruments for clinical use, noting that considerable questions remained regarding how best to validate the measures. To date, there are no studies examining the relationship between scores on these measures and independent criteria of parenting capacity in custody cases. In addition, there are no investigations assessing the outcome of decisions based on these measures. Examiners who may be considering one of these measures for use in performing child custody assessments should carefully review the test manuals and associated materials. Significant questions can be raised about each of the measures. Nevertheless, it is worth noting that the professional manual for the ASPECT (Ackerman & Schoendorf, 1992) more clearly specified the limitations of the instrument, made more circumspect claims about its utility, and generally provided a more scholarly appraisal of the measure than did the professional manuals for the BPS and PORT (Bricklin, 1984, 1990a).

Summary of Developments in the Assessment of Legal Competencies

Grisso's (1986, 1988) articulation of a conceptual model provides an extremely useful organizational framework for research and practice in assessment of legal competencies. Although representing a significant conceptual advance, the model constitutes only a starting point for research and practice. Indeed, Grisso (1992) noted a number of ambiguities and unresolved issues in application of the model. For example, the model does not specify whether instrument developers should focus on what the law says about a particular legal competency or on what the law should say; nor does it specify whether test developers should turn to statutes and case law or legal theory in order to understand the law's view of a particular competency. Moreover, the model does not indicate where in the psychological literature the test developer should look to find information about relevant psycholegal capacities. Test developers involved in the construction of new forensic assessment instruments should carefully and thoroughly articulate the targeted legal construct, relevant psycholegal abilities, and the hypothesized relationship between them. In addition, test developers should describe their efforts to resolve the ambiguities noted by Grisso (1992) and explain their rationale for the corresponding decisions during the course of test construction.

Clearly, the preceding review of research on forensic assessment instruments reveals uneven progress across the three domains. Significant progress appears to have been made in the assessment of adjudicative competence, while few gains have been achieved in the assessment of criminal responsibility and child custody. In the area of criminal responsibility, the development of the R-CRAS and MSE represented a step forward, but little has changed since the introduction of these tools more than a decade ago. Recently, Grisso (1996) identified some of the reasons for the limited advances in this arena, including the difficulty of identifying theoretical or operational definitions for the mental conditions to which legal standards for insanity refer; the complexity of the assessment task, which is necessarily retrospective and reconstructive; and the rapid, "kaleidoscopic" changes in insanity statutes following the acquittal of John Hinckley. In child custody assessment, the manuals that accompany these increasingly popular measures appear to raise more questions than they answer.

The explanation for the more substantial gains in assessment of adjudicative competence is straightforward. The legal standard for competence to stand trial has been fairly stable for more than 30 years. In addition, the standard is relatively more specific and easier to translate into psycholegal criteria than are the standards for criminal responsibility and, in particular, child custody. Furthermore, assessment of adjudicative competence, which focuses on an individual's present capacity, is a less complex evaluation than either the retrospective assessment of criminal responsibility or the assessment of custody placement "in the best interests of the child." The reduced complexity and relative brevity of pretrial competence assessments facilitate research on assessment methods. For example, validation studies that do not suffer from criterion contamination are typical in the domain of pretrial competence but virtually non-existent in the criminal responsibility and child custody domains. Most recently, the area of adjudicative competence has benefitted considerably from Richard Bonnie's (1990, 1992, 1993) articulation of a comprehensive and sophisticated theory of competence to proceed. Bonnie's work laid the foundation for development of a novel standardized and quantitative competence assessment tool by the MacArthur Research Network. Comparable elaborations of the crucial constructs in the other domains are simply not available at this time. This is particularly true of child custody but also relevant in the area of criminal responsibility, given the variety of forms that insanity standards take across jurisdictions. Stated differently, the amount of progress in each domain appears to mirror the degree of success in applying and working through Grisso's model of legal competencies. As the preceding review reveals, progress in a particular domain has been fostered by the (a) thorough explication of the appropriate legal construct, (b) translation (decomposition) of the legal construct into legally relevant functional abilities amenable to assessment, (c) identification of relevant clinical assessment instruments, and (d) theory-driven construction of specific forensic assessment tools.

A final distinction can be seen by contrasting the history of research and instrument development across the three domains. In the area of competence to proceed to adjudication, instrument development has often been supported by grants from governmental sources or private foundations: The National Institute of Mental Health (NIMH) supported the development of the CST and CAI as well as validation work on the IFI; the MacArthur Foundation supported the development of the Mac-SAC-CD; and NIMH is supporting research to establish norms for its clinical version, the MacCAT-CA. In addition, only one of the instruments (the CAST-

MR) has been released commercially, with the remainder being made available by the instrument developer for use in research and professional practice. Furthermore, for many of these competence measures, investigations of reliability and validity are not limited to those reported by test developers, but rather they have been conducted by independent groups of researchers around the country. In contrast, virtually all of the research on measures of criminal responsibility and child custody has been conducted by the developers of the instruments themselves. Moreover, particularly in the child custody domain, commercial publication and marketing of the instruments seem to have taken precedence over prefatory validation research.

CONCLUSIONS

Significant conceptual and empirical gains have been achieved during the past decade. Nevertheless, research on forensic assessment instruments and procedures has generally lagged behind conceptual advances, and neither of these developments has kept pace with the rapid expansion of opportunities for clinical psychologists to conduct forensic evaluations and provide expert testimony. The Red Queen's comment to Alice in *Through the Looking Glass*—"Now here, you see, it takes all the running you can do, to keep in the same place"—aptly characterizes the demand for conceptual and empirical progress created by burgeoning opportunities for forensic practice. From the practitioner's perspective, the scientific advances of the past decade do not yet provide an adequate foundation for addressing many issues germane to the referral questions submitted by attorneys and the courts. In this sense, we have been making progress but losing ground. Readers familiar with the quotation above will also recall the Red Queen's exhortations to Alice: "If you want to get somewhere else, you must run at least twice as fast as that!"

The vantage point of the researcher offers another perspective on the relationship between the science and practice of forensic assessment. Questions can be raised regarding the impact of conceptual and empirical achievements on the actual practices of those who conduct forensic evaluations. How knowledgeable are practicing clinicians of the empirical literature on forensic assessment, and to what extent does that knowledge impact the evaluations they conduct, the reports they write, and the courtroom testimony they provide? Systematic efforts to develop and provide educational and training programs to enhance the quality of forensic practice have been underway for some time, yet little attention has been given to the impact of such efforts. Indeed, Heilbrun and Collins (1995) noted that the long-standing and ongoing debate over the validity and utility of forensic assessment had taken place in the virtual absence of information on the actual practices of forensic mental health professionals. Recent investigations have sought to address this gap in the literature, either through surveys of forensic practitioners (e.g., Ackerman & Ackerman, 1997; Borum & Grisso, 1995; LaFortune & Carpenter, 1996) or direct examination of the content and quality of forensic reports (e.g., Heilbrun & Collins, 1995; Heilbrun, Warren, Rosenfeld, & Collins, 1994; Nicholson, LaFortune, Norwood, & Roach, 1995; Otto, Barnes, & Jacobson, 1996; Skeem et al., in press). Accumulated evidence of this kind should enable us to compare the promise of forensic assessment with current practice and to modify existing education and training efforts or develop new ones in order to foster the highest standards of professional practice.

REFERENCES

Ackerman, M. J. (1995). *Clinician's guide to child custody evaluations.* New York: Wiley.

Ackerman, M. J., & Ackerman, M. C. (1997). Custody evaluation practices: A survey of experienced professionals (revisited). *Professional Psychology: Research and Practice, 28,* 137–145.

Ackerman, M. J., & Schoendorf, K. (1992). *The Ackerman-Schoendorf Parent Evaluation of Custody Test (ASPECT).* Los Angeles: Western Psychological Services.

American Law Institute. (1962). *Model Penal Code.* Washington, DC: Author.

Arkes, H. R. (1989). Principles in judgment/decision making research pertinent to legal proceedings. *Behavioral Sciences and the Law, 7,* 429–456.

Ashford, J. B. (1988). Assessing treatability in drug offenders. *Behavioral Sciences and the Law, 6,* 139–148.

Bagby, R. M., & Nicholson, R. A. (1992). Psychometric evaluation of two scales for assessing fitness to stand trial. In F. Losel, D. Bender, & T. Bliesener (Eds.), *Psychology and law: International perspectives* (pp. 440–446). Berlin: Walter de Gruyter.

Bagby, R. M., Nicholson, R. A., Rogers, R., & Nussbaum, D. (1992). Domains of competency to stand trial: A factor analytic study. *Law and Human Behavior, 16,* 491–508.

Barnard, G. W., Nicholson, R. A., Hankins, G. C., Raisani, K. K., Patel, N. R., Gies, D., & Robbins, L. (1992). Itemmetric and scale analysis of a new computer-assisted competency assessment instrument (CADCOMP). *Behavioral Sciences and the Law, 10,* 419–435.

Barnard, G. W., Thompson, J. W., Freeman, W. C., Robbins, L., Gies, D., & Hankins, G. C. (1991). Competency to stand trial: Description and initial evaluation of a new computer-assisted assessment tool (CADCOMP). *Bulletin of the American Academy of Psychiatry and Law, 19,* 367–381.

Barron, R. (1953). An ego-strength scale which predicts response to psychotherapy. *Journal of Consulting Psychology, 17,* 327–333.

Bartko, J. J., & Carpenter, W. T. (1976). On the methods and theory of reliability. *Journal of Nervous and Mental Disease, 163,* 307–317.

Black, B. (1988). Evolving legal standards for the admissibility of scientific evidence. *Science,* *239*, 1508–1512.

Blau, T. (1984). *The psychologist as expert witness.* New York: Wiley.

Bonnie, R., & Slobogin, C. (1980). The role of mental health professionals in the criminal process: The case for "informed speculation." *Virginia Law Review, 66,* 427–522.

Bonnie, R. J. (1992). The competence of criminal defendants: A theoretical reformulation. *Behavioral Sciences and the Law, 10,* 291–316.

Bonnie, R. J. (1993). The competence of criminal defendants: Beyond Dusky and Drope. *University of Miami Law Review, 47,* 539–601.

Borum, R., & Grisso, T. (1995). Psychological test use in criminal evaluations. *Professional Psychology: Research and Practice, 26,* 465–473.

Borum, R., Otto, R., & Golding, S. L. (1993). Improving clinical judgment and decision making in forensic evaluation. *Journal of Psychiatry and Law, 21,* 35–76.

Brakel, S. J. (1974). Presumption, bias, and incompetency in the criminal process. *Wisconsin Law Review, 1974,* 1105–1130.

Bricklin, B. (1984). *Bricklin Perceptual Scales: Child Perception of Parent Series.* Furlong, PA: Village Publishing.

Bricklin, B. (1990a). *Perception of relationships Test (PORT).* Furlong, PA: Village Publishing.

Bricklin, B. (1990b). *Parent awareness skills survey (PASS).* Furlong, PA: Village Publishing.

Briggs, S. R., & Cheek, J. (1986). The role of factor analysis in the development and evaluation of personality scales. *Journal of Personality, 54,* 106–148.

Brodsky, S. L. (1989). Advocacy in the guise of scientific objectivity: An examination of Faust and Ziskin. *Computers in Human Behavior, 5,* 261–264.

Brodsky, S. L. (1991). *Testifying in court: Guidelines and maxims for the expert witness.* Washington, DC: American Psychological Association Press.

Brodzinsky, D. M. (1993). On the use and misuse of psychological testing in child custody evaluations. *Professional Psychology: Research and Practice, 24,* 213–219.

Bukatman, B. A., Foy, J. L., & DeGrazie, E. (1971). What is competency to stand trial? *American Journal of Psychiatry, 127,* 1225–1229.

Butcher, J. N., & Williams, C. L. (1992). *Essentials of MMPI-2 and MMPI-A interpretation.* Minneapolis: University of Minnesota Press.

Carbonell, J. L., Heilbrun, K., & Friedman, F. L. (1992). Predicting who will regain trial competency: Initial promise unfulfilled. *Forensic Reports, 5,* 67–76.

Chellsen, J. A. (1986). Trial competency among mentally retarded offenders: Assessment techniques and related considerations. *Journal of Psychiatry and Law, 14,* 177–185.

Committee on Ethical Guidelines for Forensic Psychologists. (1991). Specialty guidelines for forensic psychologists. *Law and Human Behavior, 15,* 655–665.

Committee on Professional Practice and Standards. (1994). Guidelines for child custody evaluations in divorce proceedings. *American Psychologist, 49,* 677–680.

Cronbach, L. J., & Meehl, P. E. (1955). Construct validity in psychological tests. *Psychological Bulletin, 52,* 281–302.

Cuneo, D. J., & Brelje, T. B. (1984). Predicting probability of attaining fitness to stand trial. *Psychological Reports, 55,* 35–39.

Daniel, A. E., Beck, N. C., Herath, A., Schmitz, M., & Menninger, K. (1984). Factors correlated with psychiatric recommendations of incompetency and insanity. *Journal of Psychiatry and Law, 12,* 527–544.

Daubert v. Merrell Dow Pharmaceuticals, 113 S. Ct. 2786 (1993).

Dawes, R. M (1989). Experience and validity of clinical judgment: The illusory correlation. *Behavioral Sciences and the Law, 7,* 457–467.

Dusky v. United States, 362 U.S. 402 (1960).

Elwork, A. (Ed.). (1984a). Psycholegal assessment, diagnosis, and testimony [Special issue]. *Law and Human Behavior, 8*(3 & 4).

Elwork, A. (1984b). Psycholegal assessment, diagnosis, and testimony: A new beginning. *Law and Human Behavior, 8*, 197–203.

Everington, C. T., & Luckasson, R. (1992). *Competence Assessment for Standing Trial for Defendants with Mental Retardation (CAST*MR) test manual*. Columbus, OH: International Diagnostic Systems, Inc.

Eysenck, H. J. (1952). The effects of psychotherapy: An evaluation. *Journal of Consulting Psychology, 16*, 319–324.

Ewing, C. P. (1990). Juveniles or adults? Forensic assessment of juveniles considered for trial in criminal court. *Forensic Reports, 3*, 3–13.

Godinez v. Moran, 113 St. C. 2680 (1993).

Farber, I. E. (1975). Sane and insane: Constructions and misconstructions. *Journal of Abnormal Psychology, 84*, 589–620.

Faust, D. (1984). *The limits of scientific reasoning*. Minneapolis: University of Minnesota Press.

Faust, D. (Ed.). (1989a). Judgment and decision processes. *Behavioral Sciences and the Law, 7*(4).

Faust, D. (1989b). Data integration in legal evaluations: Can clinicians deliver on their premises? *Behavioral Sciences and the Law, 7*, 469–483.

Faust, D., & Nurcombe, B. (1989). Improving the accuracy of clinical judgment. *Psychiatry, 52*, 197–208.

Faust, D., & Ziskin, J. (1988). The expert witness in psychology and psychiatry. *Science, 241*, 31–35.

Faust, D., & Ziskin, J. (1989). *Forensic neuropsychology: Challenging the assessment of brain damage*. Marina Del Rey, CA: Law and Psychology Press.

Fein, R. A. (1984). How the insanity acquittal retards treatment. *Law and Human Behavior, 8*, 283–292.

Fennig, S., Craig, T. J., Tanenberg-Karant, M., & Bromet, E. J. (1994). Comparison of facility and research diagnoses in first-admission psychotic patients. *American Journal of Psychiatry, 151*, 1423–1429.

Finkel, N. J., & Sabat, S. R. (1984). Split-brain madness: An insanity defense waiting to happen. *Law and Human Behavior, 8*, 225–252.

Frye v. United States. 293 F. 1013 (D.C. Cir., 1923).

Fukunaga, K., Pasewark, R., Hawkins, M., & Gudeman, H. (1981). Insanity plea: Interexaminer agreement and concordance of psychiatric opinion and court verdict. *Law and Human Behavior, 5*, 325–328.

Garb, H. N. (1992). The trained psychologist as expert witness. *Clinical Psychology Review, 12*, 451–467.

Golding, S. L. (1990). Mental health professionals and the courts: The ethics of expertise. *International Journal of Law and Psychiatry, 13*, 281–307.

Golding, S. L. (1992). Studies of incompetent defendants: Research and social policy implications. *Forensic Reports, 5*, 77–83.

Golding, S. L., & Roesch, R. (1987). The assessment of criminal responsibility: A historical approach to a current controversy. In I. B. Weiner & A. K. Hess (eds.), *Handbook of forensic psychology* (pp. 395–436). New York: Wiley.

Golding, S. L., Roesch, R., & Schreiber, J. (1984). Assessment and conceptualization of competency to stand trial: Preliminary data on the Interdisciplinary Fitness Interview. *Law and Human Behavior, 8*, 321–334.

Goldstein, J., Freud, A., & Solnit, A. J. (1973). *Beyond the best interests of the child*. New York: Free Press.

Gordon, R., & Peek, L. (1987). *The Custody Quotient*. Dallas, TX: The Wilmington Institute.

Gothard, S., Rogers, R., & Sewell, K. W. (1995). Feigning incompetency to stand trial: An investigation of the George Court Competency Test. *Law and Human Behavior, 19*, 363–373.

Gothard, S., Viglione, D., Meloy, J. R., & Sherman, M. (1995). Detection of malingering in competency to stand trial evaluations. *Law and Human Behavior, 19*, 493–506.

Graham, J. R. (1993). *MMPI-2: Assessing personality and psychopathology* (2nd ed.). New York: Oxford University Press.

Greenland, C., & Rosenblatt, E. (1972). Remands for psychiatric examination in Ontario, 1969–1970. *Canadian Psychiatric Association Journal, 17*, 387–401.

Grisso, T. (1986). *Evaluating competencies: Forensic assessments and instruments*. New York: Plenum Press.

Grisso, T. (1987). The economic and scientific future of forensic psychological assessment. *American Psychologist, 42*, 831–839.

Grisso, T. (1988). *Competency to stand trial evaluations: A manual for practice*. Sarasota, FL: Professional Resource Exchange.

Grisso, T. (1991). A developmental history of the American Psychology–Law Society. *Law and Human Behavior, 15*, 213–231.

Grisso, T. (1992). Five-year research update (1986–1990): Evaluations for competence to stand trial. *Behavioral Sciences and the Law, 0*, 353–366.

Grisso, T. (1996). Pretrial clinical evaluations in criminal cases: Past trends and future directions. *Criminal Justice and Behavior, 23*, 90–106.

Grisso, T., Cocozza, J. J., Steadman, H. J., Fisher, W. H., & Greer, A. (1994). The organization of pretrial forensic evaluation services: A national profile. *Law and Human Behavior, 18*, 377–394.

Halleck, S. L., Hoge, S. K., Miller, R. D., Sadoff, R. L., and Halleck, N. H. (1992). The use of psychiatric diagnoses in the legal process: Task force report of the American Psychiatric Association. *Bulletin of the American Academy of Psychiatry and Law, 20*, 481–499.

Heilbrun, K. (1995). Child custody evaluation: Critically assessing mental health experts and psychological tests. *Family Law Quarterly, 29*, 63–78.

Heilbrun, K., Bennett, W. S., Evans, J. H., Offutt, R. A., Reiff, H. J., & White, A. J. (1988). Assessing treatability in mentally disordered offenders: A conceptual and methodological note. *Behavioral Sciences and the Law, 6*, 479–486.

Heilbrun, K., Bennett, W. S., Evans, J. H., Offutt, R. A., Reiff, H. J., & White, A. J. (1992). Assessing treatability in mentally disordered offenders: Strategies for improving reliability. *Forensic Reports, 5*, 85–96.

Heilbrun, K., & Collins, S. (1995). Evaluations of trial competency and mental state at the time of the offense: Report characteristics. *Professional Psychology: Research and Practice, 26*, 61–67.

Heilbrun, K., Warren, J., Rosenfeld, B., & Collins, S. (1994). The use of third party information in forensic assessments: A two-state comparison. *Bulletin of the American Academy of Psychiatry and Law, 22*, 399–406.

Hoffman, B. F., & Spiegel, H. (1989). Legal principles in the psychiatric assessment of personal injury litigants. *American Journal of Psychiatry, 146*, 304–310.

Hoge, S. K., Bonnie, R. J., Poythress, N., Monahan, J., Eisenberg, M., & Feucht-Haviar, T. (1997). The MacArthur Adjudicative Competence Study: Development and validation of a research instrument. *Law and Human Behavior, 21*, 141–179.

Hoge, S. K., & Grisso, T. (1992). Accuracy and expert testimony. *Bulletin of the American Academy of Psychiatry and Law, 20*, 67–76.

Howe, E. G. (1984). Psychiatric evaluation of offenders who commit crimes while experiencing dissociative states. *Law and Human Behavior, 8*, 253–282.

Hustig, H. H., & Hafner, R. J. (1990). Persistent auditory hallucinations and their relationship to delusions and mood. *Journal of Nervous and Mental Disease, 178*, 264–267.

Jackson, M. A. (1986). Psychiatric decision-making for the courts: Judges, psychiatrists, lay people? *International Journal of Law and Psychiatry, 9,* 507–520.

Jackson v. Indiana. 406 U.S. 715 (1972).

Jenkins v. United States. 307 F.2d 637 (1962).

Jenkins, P. H., & Howell, R. J. (1994). Child sexual abuse examinations: Proposed guidelines for a standard of care. *Bulletin of the American Academy of Psychiatry and Law, 22,* 5–17.

Johnson, W. G., & Mullett, N. (1987). Georgia Court Competency Test–R. In M. Hersen & A. S. Bellack (Eds.), *Dictionary of behavioral assessment techniques.* New York: Pergamon.

Johnson, W. G., Nicholson, R. A., & Service, N. (1990). The relationship of competency to stand trial and criminal responsibility. *Criminal Justice and Behavior, 17,* 165–189.

Keilitz, I. (1984). A model process for forensic mental health screening and evaluation. *Law and Human Behavior, 8,* 355–369.

Kurlychek, R. T. (1984). The contributions of forensic neuropsychology. *American Journal of Forensic Psychology, 2,* 147–150.

Laboratory of Community Psychiatry (1974). *Competency to stand trial and mental illness.* New York: Jason Aronson.

LaFortune, K. A., & Carpenter, B. N. (March, 1996). Attorneys' perceptions of the usefulness of extrajudicial procedures and mental health evaluations in domestic court. Paper presented at the biennial convention of the American Psychology-Law Society, Hilton, Head, SC.

Lidz, C., Meisel, A., Zerubavel, E., Carter, M., Sestak, R., & Roth, L. (1984). *Informed consent: A study of decisionmaking in psychiatry.* New York: Guilford Press.

Lipsitt, P. D., Lelos, D., & McGarry, A. L. (1971). Competency for trial: A screening instrument. *American Journal of Psychiatry, 128,* 137–141.

Loftus, E. F. (1993). The reality of repressed memories. *American Psychologist, 48,* 518–537.

Lowery, C. (1984). The wisdom of Solomon: Criteria for child custody from the legal and clinical points of view. *Law and Human Behavior, 8,* 371–380.

Matarazzo, J. (1990). Psychological testing versus psychological assessment: Validation from Binet to the school, clinic, and courtroom. *American Psychologist, 45,* 999–1017.

McDonald, D. A., Nussbaum, D. N., & Bagby, R. M. (1991). Reliability, validity, and utility of the Fitness Interview Test. *Canadian Journal of Psychiatry, 36,* 480–484.

Meehl, P. E. (1977). Specific etiology and other forms of strong influence: Some quantitative meanings. *Journal of Medicine and Philosophy, 2,* 33–53.

Meloy, J. R. (1986). Review of Rogers Criminal Responsibility Assessment Scales. *Bulletin of the American Academy of Psychiatry and Law, 14,* 99–100.

Melton, G. B. (1994). Expert opinions: "Not for cosmic understanding" (pp. 59–96). In B. D. Sales & G. Van den Bos (eds.), *Psychology in litigation and legislation.* Washington, DC: American Psychological Association.

Melton, G. B., Petrila, J., Poythress, N. G., & Slobogin, C. (1987). *Psychological evaluations for the courts: A handbook for mental health professionals and lawyers.* New York: Guilford Press.

Melton, G. B., Weithorn, L. A., & Slobogin, C. (1985). *Community mental health centers and the courts: An evaluation of community-based forensic services.* Lincoln: University of Nebraska Press.

Morse, S. J. (1978). Crazy behavior, morals, and science: An analysis of mental health law. *Southern California Law Review, 51,* 527–654.

Nicholson, R. A. (August, 1992). Defining and assessing criminal competencies. Paper presented as part of a symposium, K. Heilbrun (Chair), *Advances in forensic mental health assessment,* at the annual convention of the American Psychological Association, Washington, DC.

Nicholson, R. A, Barnard, G. W., Hankins, G. C., & Robbins, L. (1994). Predicting outcome of hospitalization for incompetent defendants. *Bulletin of the American Academy of Psychiatry and Law, 22,* 367–377.

Nicholson, R. A., Briggs, S. R., & Robertson, H. C. (1988). Instruments for assessing competency to stand trial: How do they work? *Professional Psychology: Research and Practice, 19,* 383–394.

Nicholson, R. A., & Johnson, W. G. (1991). Prediction of competency to stand trial: Contribution of demographics, type of offense, clinical characteristics, and psycholegal ability. *International Journal of Law and Psychiatry, 14,* 287–297.

Nicholson, R. A., & Kugler, K. E. (1991). Competent and incompetent criminal defendants: A quantitative review of comparative research. *Psychological Bulletin, 109,* 355–370.

Nicholson, R. A., LaFortune, K. A., Norwood, S., & Roach, R. L. (August, 1995). Quality of pretrial competency evaluations in Oklahoma: Report content and consumer satisfaction. Paper presented as part of a symposium, *Assessing the content and quality of forensic evaluations,* R. K. Otto, Chair, at the annual convention of the American Psychological Association, New York, NY.

Nicholson, R. A., & McNulty, J. L. (1992). Outcome of hospitalization for defendants found incompetent to stand trial. *Behavioral Sciences and the Law, 10,* 371–384.

Nicholson, R. A., Roach, R. L., & LaFortune, K. A. (August, 1996). Assessing defendants' competence to proceed: Validation of the CADCOMP. Paper presented as part of a symposium, *Recent developments in the assessment of competence to proceed,* R. A. Nicholson, Chair, at the annual convention of the American Psychological Association, Toronto, Ontario.

Nicholson, R. A., Robertson, H. C., Johnson, W. G., & Jensen, G. (1988). A comparison of instruments for assessing competency to stand trial. *Law and Human Behavior, 12,* 313–321.

Nottingham, E. J., & Mattson, R. E. (1981). A validation study of the Competency Screening Test. *Law and Human Behavior, 5,* 329–335.

Ogloff, J., Schweighofer, A., Turnbull, S., & Whittemore, K. (1992). How much do we really know? A review of the empirical research on the insanity defense. In J. R. P. Ogloff (Ed.), *Law and psychology: The broadening of the discipline* (pp. 171–207). Durham, NC: Carolina Academic Press.

Otto, R. K., Barnes, G., & Jacobson, K. (March, 1996). The content and quality of criminal forensic evaluations in Florida. Paper presented at the biennial meeting of the American Psychology-Law Society, Hilton Head, SC.

Otto, R. K., & Collins, R. P. (1995). Use of the MMPI-2/MMPI-A in child custody evaluations. In Y. S. Ben-Porath, J. R. Graham, G. C. N. Hall, R. D. Hirschman, & M. S. Zaragoza (Eds.), *Forensic applications of the MMPI-2* (pp. 222–252). Thousand Oaks, CA: Sage.

Otto, R. K., Poythress, N. G., Nicholson, R. A., Edens, J. F., Monahan, J., Bonnie, R., Hoge, S. K., & Eisenberg, M. (In press). Psychometric properties of the MacArthur Competence Assessment Tool–Criminal Adjudication (MacCAT-CA). *Psychological Assessment.*

Perlin, M. (1977). The legal status of the psychologist in the courtroom. *Journal of Psychiatry and Law, 5,* 41–54.

Parloff, M. (1980). Psychotherapy and research: An anaclitic depression. *Psychiatry, 43,* 279–293.

Poythress, N. G., Otto, R. K., & Heilbrun, K. (1991). Pretrial evaluations for criminal courts. *Journal of Mental Health Administration, 18,* 198–208.

Poythress, N., G., & Stock, H. (1980). Competency to stand trial: A historical review and some new data. *Journal of Psychiatry and Law, 8,* 131–146.

Quinsey, V. L. (1975). Psychiatric staff conferences of dangerous mentally disordered offenders. *Canadian Journal of Behavioural Science, 7,* 60–69.

Quinsey, V. L., & Maguire, A. (1983). Offenders remanded for a psychiatric examination: Perceived treatability and disposition. *International Journal of Law and Psychiatry, 6*, 193–205.

Raifman, L. J. (1979, October). Interrater reliability of psychiatrists' evaluation of criminal defendants' competency to stand trial and legal sanity. Paper presented at the meeting of the American Psychology–Law Society, Baltimore, MD.

Randolph, J. J., Hicks, T., Mason, D., & Cuneo, D. J. (1982). The Competency Screening Test: A validation study in Cook County, Illinois. *Criminal Justice and Behavior, 9*, 495–500.

Reppucci, N., Weithorn, L., Mulvey, E., & Monahan, J. (Eds.). (1984). *Children, mental health, and the law.* Beverly Hills, CA: Sage.

Robey, A. (1965). Criteria for competency to stand trial: A checklist for psychiatrists. *American Journal of Psychiatry, 122*, 616–623.

Roesch, R., & Golding, S. L. (1980). *Competency to stand trial.* Urbana, IL: University of Illinois Press.

Roesch, R., Jackson, M. A., Sollner, R., Eaves, D., Glackman, W., & Webster, C. D. (1984). The Fitness to Stand Trial Interview Test: How four professions rate videotaped fitness interviews. *International Journal of Law and Psychiatry, 7*, 115–131.

Roesch, R., Webster, C. D., & Eaves, D. (1984). The Fitness Interview Test: A method for examining fitness to stand trial. Toronto, Ontario: Research report of the Centre for Criminology, University of Toronto.

Roesch, R., Zapf, P. A., Eaves, D., & Webster, C. D. (1998). *The Fitness Interview Test–Revised.* Burnaby: BC: Mental Health, Law, and Policy Institute. (Available from Ronald Roesch, Mental Health, Law, and Policy Institute, Simon Fraser University, Burnaby, BC, Canada, V5A 1S6.)

Rogers, R. (1984a). *Rogers Criminal Responsibility Assessment Scales.* Odessa, FL: Psychological Assessment Resources.

Rogers, R. (1984b). Towards an empirical model of malingering and deception. *Behavioral Sciences and the Law, 2*, 93–111.

Rogers, R. (1986). *Conducting insanity evaluations.* New York: Van Nostrand Reinhold.

Rogers, R. (1992). Treatability of mentally disordered offenders: A commentary on Heilbrun et al. *Forensic Reports, 5*, 97–101.

Rogers, R., & Ewing, C. P. (1989). Ultimate issue proscriptions: A cosmetic fix and plea for empiricism. *Law and Human Behavior, 13*, 357–374.

Rogers, R., & Ewing, C. P. (1992). The measurement of insanity: Debating the merits of the R-CRAS and its alternatives. *International Journal of Law and Psychiatry, 15*, 113–123.

Rogers, R., Seman, W., & Clark, C. C. (1986). Assessment of criminal responsibility: Initial validation of the R-CRAS with the M'Naghten and GBMI standards. *International Journal of Law and Psychiatry, 9*, 67–75.

Rogers, R., Ustad, K. L., Sewell, K. W., & Reinhart, V. (August, 1996). Incompetency to stand trial: Dimensions of the GCCT and the Dusky standard. Paper presented at the annual meeting of the American Psychological Association, Toronto, Ontario, Canada.

Rogers, R., Wasyliw, O. E., & Cavanaugh, J. L. (1984). Evaluating insanity: A study of construct validity. *Law and Human Behavior, 8*, 293–303.

Rogers, R., & Webster, C. D. (1989). Assessing treatability in mentally disordered offenders. *Law and Human Behavior, 13*, 19–29.

Rosenhan, D. L. (1973). On being sane in insane places. *Science, 179*, 250–258.

Savitsky, J. C., & Karras, D. (1984). Competency to stand trial among adolescents. *Adolescence, 19*, 349–358.

Schreiber, J., Roesch, R., & Golding, S. (1987). An evaluation of procedures for assessing competency to stand trial. *Bulletin of the American Academy of Psychiatry and Law, 15*, 187–203.

Shapiro, D. (1984). *Psychological evaluations and expert testimony: A practical guide to forensic work.* New York: Van Nostrand Reinhold.

Shatin, L., & Brodsky, S. H. (1979). Competency for trial: The Competency Screening Test in an urban hospital forensic unit. *Mount Sinai Journal of Medicine, 46*, 131–134.

Silver, E. (1995). Punishment or treatment: Comparing the lengths of confinement of successful and unsuccessful insanity defendants. *Law and Human Behavior, 19*, 375–388.

Silver, E., Cirincione, C., & Steadman, H. J. (1994). Demythologizing inaccurate perceptions of the insanity defense. *Law and Human Behavior, 18*, 63–70.

Skeem, J. L., Golding, S. L., Cohn, N. B., & Berge, G. (In press). The logic and reliability of evaluations of competence to stand trial. *Law and Human Behavior*.

Slobogin, C., Melton, G. B., & Showalter, C. R. (1984). The feasibility of a brief evaluation of mental state at the time of the offense. *Law and Human Behavior, 8*, 305–321.

Spitzer, R. L. (1975). More on pseudoscience in science and the case for psychiatric diagnosis: A critique of D. L. Rosenhan's "On being sane in insane places" and "The contextual nature of psychiatric diagnosis." *Archives of General Psychiatry, 33*, 459–470.

Stangl, D., Pfohl, B., Zimmerman, M., Bowers, W., Corenthal, C. (1985). A structured interview for the DSM-III personality disorders: A preliminary report. *Archives of General Psychiatry, 42*, 591–596.

Steadman, H. J., McGreevy, M. A., Morrissey, J. P., Callahan, L. A., Robbins, P. C., & Cirincione, C. (1993). *Before and after Hinckley: Evaluating insanity defense reform*. New York: Guilford Press.

Stone, A. A. (1984). *Law, psychiatry, and morality: Essays and analysis*. Washington, DC: American Psychiatry Press.

Stone, A. A. (1993). Post-traumatic stress disorder and the law: Critical review of the new frontier. *Bulletin of the American Academy of Psychiatry and Law, 21*, 23–36.

Sweet, J. J., Moberg, P. J., & Westergaard, C. K. (1996). Five-year follow-up survey of practices and beliefs of clinical neuropsychologists. *The Clinical Neuropsychologist, 10*, 202–221.

Tepper, A. M., & Elwork, A. (1984). Competence to consent to treatment as a psycholegal concept. *Law and Human Behavior, 8*, 205–223.

Thompson, J. S., Stuart, G. L., & Holden, C. E. (1992). Command hallucinations and legal insanity. *Forensic Reports, 5*, 29–43.

Ustad, K. L., Rogers, R., Sewell, K. W., & Guarnaccia, C. A. (1996). Restoration of competency to stand trial: Assessment with the Georgia Court Competency Test and the Competency Screening Test. *Law and Human Behavior, 20*, 131–146.

Webster, C. D., Menzies, R., & Jackson, M. A. (1982). *Clinical assessment before trial: Legal issues and mental disorder*. Toronto: Butterworths.

Weissman, H. N. (1985). Psycholegal standard and the role of psychological assessment in personal injury litigation. *Behavioral Sciences and the Law, 3*, 135–147.

Wildman, R. W., II, Batchelor, E. S., Thompson, L., Nelson, F. R., Moore, J. T., Patterson, M. E., and de Laosa, M. (1978). The Georgia Court Competency Test: An attempt to develop a rapid, quantitative measure of fitness for trial. Unpublished manuscript, Forensic Services Division, Central State Hospital, Milledgeville, GA.

Wildman, R. W., II, White, P. A., & Brandenburg, C. A. (1990). The Georgia Court Competency Test: The baserate problem. *Perceptual and Motor Skills, 70*, 1055–1058.

Zapf, P. A., & Roesch, R. (1997). Assessing fitness to stand trial: A comparison of institution-based evaluations and a brief screening interview. *Canadian Journal of Community Mental Health, 16*, 53–66.

Ziskin, J. (1970). *Coping with psychiatric and psychological testimony*. Marina del Rey, CA: Law and Psychology Press.

Ziskin, J., & Faust, D. (1988). *Coping with psychiatric and psychological testimony* (4th ed.). Marina del Rey, CA: Law and Psychology Press.

6

Predicting Violence in Mentally and Personality Disordered Individuals

KEVIN S. DOUGLAS
AND CHRISTOPHER D. WEBSTER

An inmate who has spent the last five years incarcerated for aggravated sexual assault comes before a parole board asking to be considered for release. A person suffering from schizophrenia murdered his parents and was found not guilty by reason of insanity and now, some years later, stands before a release review board. A 14-year-old girl allegedly has attacked a classmate with a knife and a prosecutor now petitions to raise her to adult court. A police officer escorts a young man acting in a threatening manner to a psychiatric emergency service. In each of these instances an important decision must be made that pits the right of the individual not to be arbitrarily detained or punished against the rights of members of society to be safe from potentially violent persons.

How are these decisions made? To what extent are psychologists and psychiatrists asked to comment on such matters, and are they under increasing pressure as the years pass to offer more and more such opinions in the context of an ever-broadening range of issues? What factors do these

KEVIN S. DOUGLAS • Department of Psychology, Simon Fraser University, Burnaby, British Columbia, V5A 1S6, Canada. CHRISTOPHER D. WEBSTER • University of Toronto, Toronto, Ontario M5T 1R8, Canada.

Psychology and Law: The State of the Discipline, edited by Ronald Roesch, Stephen D. Hart, and James R. P. Ogloff. Kluwer Academic/Plenum Publishers, New York, 1999.

decision makers consider? What should they be taking into account? What does psychology contribute to the making of fair and justifiable decisions, and how can this be assessed? The present chapter addresses these and related questions. The common thread that runs through all of the examples, and other situations similar to them is that a determination of the likelihood of future violence—or risk assessment—is required. Shah (1978) earlier identified 15 points in the criminal justice and mental health systems that demand such assessments. Since the time of Shah's observation, many others have appeared. These are not necessarily restricted to the mental health and criminal justice domains. School boards, business corporations, universities, immigration boards, and many other organizations have been forced in recent years to develop policies and procedures in an attempt to estimate and divert threats to their integrity and well-being.

An important question is begged by these junctures in the criminal justice, mental health and other systems: To what extent can mental health professionals accurately forecast the probability of violent behavior? This query has spurred a great deal of research and debate. Until recently, it was commonly asserted that predictions of violence are woefully inaccurate (Ennis & Litwack, 1974; Kozol, Boucher, & Garofalo, 1972; Monahan, 1981; Steadman & Cocozza, 1974; Thornberry & Jacoby, 1979). According to Cocozza and Steadman (1976), there was, at least by the standards of the mid-1970s, "clear and convincing evidence" for the inaccuracies of psychiatric predictions of violence. Yet, in the past 5 or 10 years, improved research methodology has demonstrated that, while risk assessments remain far from perfect, they may be appreciably better than previous studies may have led us to believe.

The present chapter chronicles what is currently known about assessing for the risk of violence. After first considering why it is that the frequency of risk assessments is on the rise, we turn our attention to recent scientific advances in the area. This discussion centers around methodological and statistical issues, factors that have been identified as relating to violence and its prediction, and systematized assessment schemes that have evolved in attempts to proffer reliable and valid risk assessments. We conclude with a look to the future and to recently emerging conceptual and theoretical matters.

THE RISE OF RISK

Violence is a salient public health issue. One striking example of this lies in the fact that for African Americans between 15 and 34 years of age, the leading cause of death is homicide (United States Department of Health and Human Services, 1991). Violence has of late been construed not so much as crime per se, but rather as a national health crisis (see, generally, Monahan & Steadman, 1994b). The prevention and prediction of violence, then, is a task in which many researchers, clinicians, politicians, and mental health and correctional authorities have come to invest a good deal of energy and resources. Assessments of risk for various types of violence have yet to establish themselves as solidly founded enterprises; yet they are being called for with more frequency than in the past. Although risk assessments were not employed abstemiously in previous years, they tended to be conducted as a matter of routine practice without much effort being expended to show their accuracy (e.g., Pfhol, 1978).

The point of the following section is to offer some explanations for the current proliferation of risk evaluations. Inadequately funded and weakly coordinated deinstitutionalization exercises, media attention to exceptionally violent crimes and the accompanying public outcries, and society's apparent fear of mentally ill people as violent, often fueled by television and movie plots, may be seen as spurring the demand for risk assessments. Case law has evolved, particularly in the United States, which has fostered the accrual of predictions of violence, as has statutory law. Likely in response to these kinds of pressures, in addition to recognition that the task may not be as formidable as it once was considered, academics and researchers have devoted more and more resources to the study of risk assessment in recent years.

Systemic Reorganization

Moved by the seemingly humanitarian spirit of recent years, deinstitutionalization has dramatically lowered the numbers of mentally ill people held in psychiatric facilities. In turn, there has been a corresponding increase in numbers of homeless people (Teplin, 1984), many of whom are seriously mentally ill (Dennis, Buckner, Lipton, & Levine, 1991). A fair number of these people are repeatedly admitted to psychiatric facilities. Given that "dangerousness" to others is now an element of commitment laws in every state (Miller, 1992), it is not difficult to see how the prevailing ethos drives the demand for risk assessments. Although, mercifully, people are seldom hospitalized for untoward periods of time as in the past, they are admitted much more frequently (Bachrach, 1993). And, as Dvoskin and Steadman (1994) pointed out, once these persons have been released into the community, the task of managing their behavior, including violent behavior, is extremely taxing and difficult. Deinstitutionalization, as we shall later see, produced changes in the law which have contributed to the call for risk assessments.

The deinstitutionalization movement certainly introduced the average American and Canadian citizen to mental illness, and the bizarre behavior it may sometimes beget. Not altogether surprising is that the public tends to fear mentally ill people largely on the grounds that they are seen as dangerous (Link & Cullen, 1986; Link, Cullen, Frank, & Wozniak, 1987). This fear may stem from the same sentiment which seems to pervade American and Canadian societies—the demand for a retributive, punitive criminal justice system and the perception that the courts are too lenient with criminals (Blumstein & Cohen, 1980; Roberts & Doob, 1990). Such forces may be seen possibly to have contributed to legislative reforms (to be delineated later) aimed at the early identification of criminal behavior, which entail assessments of risk.

Media attention to heinous crimes and to failed predictions by parole boards and the like may exacerbate the public's dissatisfaction with law and policy makers regarding violent offenders. Vitriolic articles in newspapers revile the seemingly glaring mistakes of correctional officials. They say things like "only a group of morons could fail to see that a determined wife killer had just been given a potential seven-day jump on his victim. A parole board had failed to see this" (Stall, 1994, p. A14). It is a matter of debate whether strident headlines merely reflect or, rather, drive public opinion. However this may be, they depict a public that has become more and more dissatisfied with the apparent inability of decision makers to predict violence. This, in turn, and in concert with social forces of the kind sketched above, is pressuring law and policymakers to improve risk assessments (e.g., National Parole Board of Canada, 1994). As well, case and statutory laws, which are at least partially rooted in these social factors, exert their own influence on the surging assessment "market."

CASE LAW

Despite the shortcomings of risk assessment that were well spelled out in the 1970s and 1980s (e.g., Kozol et al., 1972; Monahan, 1981), courts have seemed more, not less, interested in recruiting mental health professionals to assess for future risk of violent behavior. An American judge, in defending the constitutionality of the *Bail Reform Act* (1984) and the violence predictions it entails, claimed that "there is nothing inherently unattainable about a prediction of future criminal conduct" (*United States v. Salerno*, 1987, p. 751). In *Barefoot v. Estelle* (1983), the constitutionality of violence predictions was considered in the context of jurors making decisions about future violent behavior of defendants to whom, on this basis, the death penalty would be applied. The Supreme Court of the United States acknowledged the argument that psychiatrists were unable to predict future violence accurately, but refuted its unconstitutionality, stating that although "psychiatric predictions of violence are wrong in at least two out of every three cases ... it makes little sense, if any, to subject that psychiatrists, out of the entire universe of persons who might have an opinion on this issue, would know so little about the subject that they should not be permitted to testify" (p. 896–897). In *Schall v. Martin* (1984), a similar issue arose with respect to a statute permitting the pretrial detainment of young offenders who were judged to be dangerous to others. The Supreme Court of the United States again supported the validity of the statute.

Canadian courts have echoed this messages. In *Re Moore and the Queen* (1984), it was submitted to the Ontario Supreme Court that, given the inaccuracies of predictions of violence made by psychiatrists, to allow such evidence in court violated the tenets of fundamental justice that all evidence must be of probative weight. The Court, while agreeing that risk assessments are often erroneous, held that such assessments should be allowed because courts ultimately determine dangerousness, and because parole boards would be able to correct errors made at earlier stages.

The sentiment underlying these rulings stems in part from a precedent-setting case, *Tarasoff v. Regents of the University of California* (1976). In this case, a graduate student at the University of California was in therapy at the university clinic. In the course of therapy he indicated a desire to kill a young woman—Tatiana Tarasoff. The psychologist alerted the campus police and his supervisor to his suspicions. The police saw the young man and opined that he was not dangerous. Two months later, however, he stabbed Tarasoff to death. Tarasoff's family sued the psychologist for malpractice, and in 1974, the Supreme Court of California ruled that the psychologist was negligent in failing to perform a duty to warn Tarasoff. In *Tarasoff* (1976) the court alerted its original decision, indicating a duty to take whatever steps reasonable to protect the potential victim. *Tarasoff* entrenched in case law the idea that mental health workers ought to have the capacity to isolate and act on information that may have a bearing on future violent conduct.

This case has been precedent for many others in the United States, several of which have expanded the duty to protect. In *Peck v. Counseling Service of Addison County* (1985), the duty was extended to include protection of property and to apply to all mental health professionals, not merely clinical psychologists. In *Currie v. United States* (1986), the court ruled that the duty applied even in cases where an identifiable victim was not present. This decision extended the duty to cover all foreseeable victims. In

Lipari v. Sears, Roebuck & Company (1980), the duty was broadened to impose a responsibility upon mental health professionals to protect society at large from potentially dangerous clients, even in such cases where the client does not know who may be a victim of his or her actions. It may now also be likely that school psychologists can be held liable for violence perpetrated by their students (deGroot, 1994). The duty to protect in Canadian jurisprudence exists in similar fashion, though it is less well defined and perhaps less onerous (e.g., Birch, 1992).

Tarasoff and cases that have followed have made the duty to protect a salient issue among mental health professionals (Appelbaum, 1985). This may have fostered an increased fear of malpractice litigation and the practice of defensive psychotherapy (Appelbaum, 1988). Without doubt, it has placed the necessity of being able accurately to assess risk for violence in a spotlight it had not previously occupied. Given the continuing emerging import of the concept of "dangerousness" that was spawned by *Tarasoff* and its progeny, legislative activity has been directed towards the incorporation of dangerousness into its laws and policies.

Legislative Developments

As noted above, since the 1970s, every American state has adopted civil commitment criteria which include "dangerousness." To admit or release persons from psychiatric hospitals, some of whom, as pointed out earlier, are repeatedly evaluated, requires assessments of risk to be made. Canadian civil commitment laws, which vary province by province, generally demand that mentally ill persons be threats to themselves or to society before they may be admitted.

In other American legislation, the *Bail Reform Act* (1984) incorporated the issue of public protection, which necessitates predictions of violence. *Salerno* upheld the constitutionality of this legislation which had been challenged on grounds that it was not possible to predict violence accurately. In 1991, Washington State enacted the *Sexually Violent Predators Act*, which permits, postsentence, the indefinite commitment of sex offenders who are deemed to be at high risk for sexually violent and predatory behavior. Likewise, spurred by public outcry at a brutal sex murder (Skaggs, 1995), Kansas enacted its own *Sexual Predator Act* in 1994. The *California Assembly Bill 2900* defined the duty of psychotherapists to report potentially violent clients to putative victims and to law enforcement agencies (Mills, Sullivan, & Eth, 1987). It should be noted that the "three strikes and you're out" legislation in California, while not requiring risk assessments by correctional and mental health professionals, is founded on past criminality, known to be one of the most robust risk markers for future violence.[1] The underlying assumption is that if a person commits (and is convicted of) three offenses, the probability that he or she will commit another offense is so great as to warrant life incapacitation.

Canadian legislative developments, too, are setting the stage for a continued burgeoning of risk assessments. The legislation that governs criminal responsibility was changed in 1991 by *Bill C-30*. People detained in forensic psychiatric units must now be assessed for release more frequently than in the past. The bill, parts of which admittedly remain unproclaimed, has made a finding of criminal nonresponsibility as a function of mental disorder less onerous than heretofore (Roesch et al., 1997). This legislation has resulted in the insanity defense being raised more often than previously (Ogloff, 1991), which, of course, requires more and more risk assessments before people can be released. Before this bill, danger to others was not explicitly outlined in the law as an issue to address before release could be granted. The (unproclaimed) section even creates a new category called "dangerous mentally disordered accused." Changes to other Canadian legislation, such as the *Dangerous Offender Act* of 1977 (Part XXIV of the *Criminal Code of Canada*) and the *Corrections and Conditional Release Act* (1992) have ensured for correctional and mental health professionals an expanded role in the assessment of risk to others.

As Monahan (1996) pointed out, professional organizations have paralleled legal precedents. The American Bar Association (1989) proposed that mentally ill people who have been found not criminally responsible by virtue of their mental illness should be committed to psychiatric institutions if they pose a danger to others. Both the American (1992) and Canadian Psychological Associations (1988) dictated that one of the few conditions under which it is permissible, and in some cases ethically required, to breach client–therapist confidentiality is when there is reasonable grounds to suspect that the client poses risk of harm to others.

RESEARCH

Given the plethora of social and legal contributants to the rise of risk assessments in the mental health, legal, correctional, and other systems, it should come as little surprise that much academic and research energy is being devoted to the improvement of prediction accuracy. If the assessment of risk were not a topic of major clinical importance in the first three-quarters of this century, it has certainly become one in the last quarter.

---

[1] It is interesting to reflect that risk assessment schemes, such as those considered later in this chapter, are often criticized on the grounds that they consider too few variables. Such law, seen as a kind of violence assessment scheme in its own right, is apt to consider a sole factor.

Several lines of research, which will be considered subsequently, have invigorated the research community by demonstrating that, while far from perfect, risk assessments can be performed at levels notably better than chance. A sense of guarded optimism is emerging among researchers. More and more studies are being conducted by more and more researchers, new theory is being developed, and better methodological and statistical procedures are being employed. This has led to risk assessment coming to occupy one of the principal research areas in forensic psychology, psychiatry, and other mental health professions. As one example, the MacArthur Foundation is providing very extensive funding to leading researchers in the area. This kind of support is allowing for the conduct of what promises to be by far the most comprehensive research project to date (see Steadman et al., 1994, 1998).

EARLY STUDIES

The literature prior to 1970 was reasonably clear in making the case that mental health professionals, particularly psychiatrists, were simply unable to predict violence with any appreciable degree of accuracy (Stone, 1985). At the time, there was good reason for this pessimism, in that the extant research, what little of it there was, consistently pointed up this inadequacy. Steadman and Cocozza (1974) had capitalized on the decision of the United Sates Supreme Court in *Baxstrom v. Herold* (1966) to release mentally ill offenders from the Dannemora State Hospital for the Criminally Insane. Over 900 such individuals from Dannemora and another similar institution were released outright or transferred to institutions less secure than those in which they had previously been held. Roughly half of these people found their way into the community. This presented a rare research opportunity. Although young age and prior criminality were related to future arrests, for every correct prediction made from these variables, there were two predictions of dangerousness which were not borne out. It is important to note that all of these patients were considered dangerous, yet of 98 patients released to the community, only 20 were arrested over a 4-year period, and of these, only 7 committed violent offenses.

A similar opportunity, made possible by the decision in *Dixon v. Attorney General of the Commonwealth of Pennsylvania* (1971) to transfer mentally ill offenders from a prison hospital to a civil hospital, was presented to Thornberry and Jacoby (1979). Over 400 of these individuals were eventually released into the community and followed up for an average of 3 years. There were 60 patients (14.5%) who were either arrested or rehospitalized for involvement in a violent incident. Again, age (below 50) was the strongest predictor, although a full 82% of people below 50 were *not* violent at follow-up.

Two important lessons were learned from the *Baxstrom* and *Dixon* studies: (a) violence was being remarkably overpredicted (the "false positives" problem to be explained later); and (b) there were relatively low base rates of violence during the follow-up periods. Monahan (1981) drew these problems to the attention of researchers and other interested parties in his now classic monograph, *Predicting Violent Behavior: An Assessment of Clinical Techniques*. He called for a "second generation" of studies on the prediction of violent behavior. In this monograph, and other papers which followed (Monahan, 1984, 1988), he argued that while mental health professionals may not be particularly adept at forecasting violence, this may stem not from a lack of ability but rather from a lack of understanding and knowledge. He urged the next generation of researchers to conduct studies with shorter-term follow-up periods than were used previously, more clearly defined predictor variables, and more comprehensive methods of detecting violence (e.g., use of multiple sources rather than simple official arrest data, which grossly underestimate the prevalence, or base rate, of violence, with attendant overestimation of dangerousness).

Researchers have heeded Monahan's calls. Since the early or mid-1980s, a great many studies have been conducted on the prediction of violence. The remainder of this chapter will focus on these, and, in particular, those of the last 10 years. We begin with an introduction to the basic statistical terminology and techniques common to the area and to new procedures that show some promise for simple and telling presentation of results. The discussion then turns to matters of current predictive accuracy and to what factors actually predict violent behavior.

RECENT RESEARCH ADVANCES

DISTINGUISHING BETWEEN PREDICTING GENERAL CRIMINALITY AND VIOLENT BEHAVIOR

At the outset, it is important to note that there have been two general lines of research that are concerned about the prediction of some type of illegal or deviant behavior. The one of main interest to this chapter is the prediction of violence, whether it results in official arrests or not. A second line of research is devoted to general recidivism; that is, researchers are interested in official re-arrests for any type of offense, whether violent or otherwise. Often this latter kind of research is sponsored by government correctional and parole agencies, and is conducted by researchers in their employ. Although we will not be discussing this second line of prediction research, it is not surprising that many of the factors which will later be discussed predict both general recidivism and violent behavior. There are, however, some important differences and issues (see Menzies & Webster, 1995).[2] Fortunately there are now several informative reviews of this corpus (e.g., Gendreau, 1995; Porporino & Motiuk, 1995).

ADVANCES IN METHODOLOGICAL AND STATISTICAL TECHNIQUES

The purpose of this section is to provide the reader with a grounding in methodological and statistical concepts routinely employed in risk assessment research and with an indication of how accuracy of findings tends to be portrayed. We also describe some techniques that though used quite commonly in other areas, are new to the risk assessment field.

Methodological Issues

Several types of designs are commonly employed in risk assessment studies (i.e., retrospective; prospective; longitudinal; case cohort; epidemiological). Regardless of the particular design, some approaches have been put forth to maximize predictive accuracy (Monahan, 1981, 1984, 1988; Monahan & Steadman, 1994a). Obviously, strategies used to promote sound research design in many contemporary research areas (i.e., adequate sample size; control for nuisance variables; proper statistical techniques; appropriately randomized or matched groups, and the like) may be considered prerequisite to conducting research in risk assessment. The following comments will therefore be directed to issues which may have particular relevance to the specific topic at hand.

One of the most salient problems is that only rarely is there opportunity properly to follow-up predictions. People who are rated very high as a result of a risk assessment interview or instrument typically are not released into the community. Their opportunities for being violent become circumscribed. Although being able to release from institutions all members of a group deemed potentially violent would be the most methodologically obvious and sound procedure, it is also usually administratively, legally, and ethically impossible. For this reason, researchers are normally limited to working with samples of people in which variance in

---

[2] It is worth noting that in Canada, correctional authorities tend to use an overall measure of recidivism—the General Statistical Information on Recidivism (Nuffield, 1982)—to predict specifically violent behavior.

violence potential is truncated. This necessarily deflates predictive accuracy and is a very limiting constriction. Yet, as some researchers have recently shown, there is ample reason to continue the attempt to construct instruments and apply them to groups of people, most of whom will secure eventual release (e.g., Harris, Rice, & Quinsey, 1993; Menzies, Webster, & Sepejak, 1985a,b). This makes sense given the reality of the correctional and forensic systems. Because there are people who will never be released, there is little practical point in developing schemes for post-release violence using these people (see Dietz, 1985).[3] In circumstances calling for the prediction of within-institution violence, it is of course necessary to develop procedures with "lifers" included in the sample.

Monahan and Steadman (1994a; see also Monahan, 1988) have identified three major weaknesses in violence prediction research that, ideally, should be accounted for in any risk assessment study. They make a fourth point, addressed shortly, that applies generally to those who conduct research in the area. The first point addresses impoverished predictor variables. They emphasize the complicated nature of violent behavior, in general, and among mentally disordered people, in particular. Many factors are involved relating to the individual's background, social setting, and psychological and biological makeup (Blackburn, 1995). Given this complexity, researchers should really not be taken aback by exceedingly small correlations between narrowly defined, circumscribed predictor variables used in isolation and subsequent violent behavior in a variety of contexts. Multiple predictors, informed and enriched by theory, that address various dimensions of behavior on several planes of analysis are required. Domains that should be covered include those of the physiological/neurological, psychological, situational, and historical nature. These aspects must be dissected finely enough to prevent the loss of meaning inherent in gross categories (e.g., a category of mentally ill versus not mentally ill is too broad and should be replaced by terms that describe specific psychiatric symptomatologies).

The second issue raised by Monahan and Steadman parallels the first but concerns the criterion variable—violence. It is not enough to request the official criminal records of study participants. As already noted, this will ordinarily provide a gross underestimate of the frequency of violent behavior. The convictions a person does incur often will not reflect the actual violent incident, due sometimes to plea bargaining. Moreover, the underrepresentation of true violence via arrest data procure low base

---

[3]Yet, it is acknowledged that which persons do or do not get released depends on swings in public sentiment, legislative changes, availability or otherwise of putatively effective treatment programs, and myriad other factors.

rates, that, as described in the following section, precludes high predictive accuracies. These problems hold for any type of official data obtained from police, hospital, court, mental health clinics, or other sources. All that can be hoped for is the detection of enough violence to permit conventional statistical analyses. Ideally, multiple sources of official records are combined with interviews of the patients or offenders, as well as with people or agencies who are familiar with the study sample participants. Even records within institutions may underestimate violence. Fifty percent more assaults were identified in a sample of psychiatric patients by using both officially recorded incidents and chart reviews, rather than by official reports alone (Convit, Isay, Gadioma, & Volavka, 1988). Using official records only, Mulvey, Shaw, and Lidz (1994) detected violence in 73 of 629 (12%) patients they followed up. When patient self-reports and collateral information were added, the base rate rose dramatically to 47% (n = 293). As dramatically, Steadman et al. (1998) showed that, in the MacArthur risk assessment project, when violence were measured by agency reports alone, the one year base rate was 4.5%, but when participant and collateral reports were added, the cumulative percentage was 27.5. Rice and Harris (1995) reported that the correlational index used in their analyses (ϕ) increased by 37.5% (from .25 to .40) when base rates increased from 15% to 50%. Douglas and Hart (1998) found in a meta-analysis of the research on the relationship between psychosis and violence that studies which used a combination of interviews and official records to detect violence found stronger relationships between psychosis and violence than studies which used one or the other alone.

Another source of weakness in criterion variables stems from their definitions (Monahan & Steadman, 1994a). Often researchers will simply measure "violent/not violent." This sort of measurement is inadequate by itself. Although it is often helpful to address violence first on a global level, it is important to determine which types of violence may be best predicted by what sorts of factors. Researchers are inveighed to code violence with enough precision to allow comparisons to be made between the predictive accuracies of factors for types, severities, situational aspects, and targets of violent behavior (see, generally, Mulvey & Lidz, 1995).

Finally, the settings that are studied may constrict the occurrence of violent behavior. Most studies, as drawn to our attention by Monahan and Steadman (1994b), are concerned with violence that occurs either in the institution or in the community, not both. Both settings place limits either on whether violence will occur or on the abilities of researchers to detect it. Although violence is especially apt to be detected in an institution, it may in fact sometimes be less likely to occur there than elsewhere because patients are watched very closely. When patients' affect, hostility, or agitation escalates, they are likely to be placed in seclusion or restraint with attendant reduction in probability of committing a violent act. Conversely, most patients or prisoners who are released into the community represent, at least in the eyes of the releasing agency, a relatively low risk for violence. The community sample may be restricted by virtue of a selection bias. To exacerbate this difficulty, although violence may be more likely to occur in the community than in institutions given the unstructured and often unsupervised context, its identification is less probable, even if researchers are not hampered by limited resources. To remedy the problem of low-risk samples, researchers may include only people who are suspected to have a high basal probability for violence (e.g., young males, alcohol and drug abusers). As Monahan and Steadman (1994a) observed, however, although this procedure will likely enhance predictive accuracy, it also introduces an element of artificiality into the study in that predictions must often be made for people without these particular demographic characteristics. This approach also prevents from the start any study of risk markers in large numbers of people who do not possess certain demographic features.

Once these methodological concerns have been addressed, the researcher is left with the problem of measuring the accuracy of assessments. The following section will describe common indexes of predictive accuracy, some problems which have been noted with these, and some new, and perhaps better, procedures.

Indexes of Statistical Accuracy

Table 6.1 presents a 2 × 2 contingency arrangement. From such a table the core indexes of predictive accuracy are derivable. Although in much prediction-outcome research people employ techniques that are ubiquitous in social sciences, such as chi-square, analysis of variance, multiple regression, and discriminant function analysis, researchers should be urged to present their raw data in frequency format so that these indexes can be configured (Hart, Webster, & Menzies, 1993). These frequencies should be stated outright or made easily available to colleagues who might wish to examine them.

The definitions of the key predictive accuracies defined in Table 6.1 follow: The *base rate* is, as the name suggests, the percent of the criterion variable, in our case violence, which is present in the sample. The *relative improvement over chance* (RIOC) refers to, in the case of predictions, the extent to which both positive and negative predictions are accurate, after taking into account the baserate and prior probabilities that these predictions would be correct if left to chance alone. A *false positive* (FP) occurs when a person is predicted to be violent but in fact is not. This may come to

TABLE 6.1. INDEXES OF ACCURACY DERIVABLE FROM A 2 × 2 CONTINGENCY TABLE

		OUTCOME	
		Violent	Not Violent
PREDICTION	Violent	A	B
	Not Violent	C	D

Accuracy Indexes	Formulae
Base rate	(A+C) / (A+B+C+D)
Relative improvement	
Over chance	Kappa (K)
False positive	Cell B
False negative	Cell C
True positive	Cell A
True negative	Cell D
Specificity (true negative rate)	D / (D+B)
Sensitivity (true positive rate)	A / (A+C)
False positive rate	B / (B+D)
Positive predictive power	A / (A+B) x 100%
Negative predictive power	D / (D+C) x 100%
Odds ratio	(AxD) / (BxC)

light when, against advice or expectations a person, considered dangerous, is released from an institution and proves later to be nonviolent. Yet, as noted above, it may also stem from failure to detect violence when it does occur. A *true positive* (*TP*) is sometimes called a "hit," and means that a person predicted to be violent did, in fact, act violently. A *false negative* (*FN*) results when, having been predicted to be nonviolent, a person acts violently; a *true negative* (*TN*) is the term applied when a person predicted to be nonviolent does not act violently.

The relationship between these four measures is often of main interest to researchers and readers. The *true negative rate* (*specificity*) refers to the likelihood that a person who was identified as nonviolent actually will be nonviolent, whereas the *true positive rate* (*sensitivity*) is the index named for the probability that predictions of violence are made for people who actually are violent or would be if given the chance. The *false positive rate* is the proportion of nonviolent people who are wrongly predicted to be violent. In a similar vein, *positive predictive power* (*PPP*) is the percentage of people who were correctly predicted to be violent; *negative predictive power*

(*NPP*) is the percent of people who were correctly predicted to be non-violent. Finally, the *odds ratio* refers to the odds that persons will be violent, given that they were predicted to be so. For example, an odds ratio of 2 is equivalent to stating that people predicted to be violent are twice as likely actually to be violent as those predicted not to be violent. An odds ratio of 2 or 3 is typically considered to indicate a large effect size (Fleiss, Williams, & Dubro, 1986).

INNOVATIONS IN PORTRAYING ACCURACY

Some authors have highlighted the disadvantages of statistics derived from a 2×2 table. Hart et al. (1993), for example, pointed out how the term *false positive* has been used inconsistently between researchers. In the specific case they cite, this discrepancy has potentially dramatic implications for confusing our understanding of the research corpus. In particular, Monahan (1981) had reviewed the literature in terms of *percent false positives* (B/A+B in Table 6.1), while Otto (1992), in his comparison of first- and second-generation studies (the former being those that Monahan [1981] had summarized), used a different formula (B/B+D) to derive the *false positive rate*. These indexes of accuracy are not the same, and comparisons made between them under the impression that they are equivalent may be erroneous and misleading. In fact, Otto (1992) concluded from his review that there was reason to be more optimistic about our abilities to predict violence than had been warranted in the past. As Hart et al. (1993) pointed out, however, the degree of improvement between first- and second-generation research after the definition of false positive had been equated was not as great as Otto's (1992) conceptualization had allowed us to believe. Hart et al. (1993) also recommend, as many studies fail to do so, that PPP, NPP, and overall *chance-corrected* accuracy be reported routinely.

In addition to these problems with 2×2 table data, the values of the traditional methods of portraying accuracy (FP, FN, TP, TN) vary depending on the prevalence of violence in the sample and on the criterion or threshold of defining "high risk." They also are dependent on one another, so that by minimizing error in one quarter (e.g., false negatives), error increases in another (e.g., false positives). As Mossman (1994a) noted, because these indexes are base-rate dependent, they may obscure true predictive performance.

The relative improvement over chance (RIOC) measure of accuracy may obfuscate which of a number of assessors of violence is the most accurate. As Mossman (1994a) explained, with low base rates of violence in a sample of people for whom violence is being predicted, one assessor may use a low criterion threshold to make a positive prediction of violence.

This assessor would, then, have a higher RIOC than a judge who had a high criterion threshold for making a determination of future violence, which would seem to imply greater accuracy. However, the converse may be true, or the two judges may perform at the same level of accuracy. That is, by using a low threshold for violence to base prediction on, false negatives are minimized. However, doing so would also cause to such a judge erroneously predict many people to be violent, who, if they were released from a confining institution, would not act violently. The second assessor, in contrast, by using a high threshold, would minimize false positive errors. Either judge may be deemed more accurate than the other depending on the manner in which error is defined (i.e., false positives or false negatives). Similarly, the values of PPP, NPP, and *kappa* will change across administrations of the same test if the base rates also change (Mossman, 1994b).

To avoid such problems in the interpretation of predictive accuracy, several commentators (Douglas, Ogloff, Nicholls, & Grant, 1998; Mossman, 1994a,b; Rice & Harris, 1995; Rice, 1997) have advocated a procedure adopted from signal detection theory called *Receiver Operating Characteristic (ROC)* analysis, which is less dependent on base rates than are the previous indexes and allows comparisons of accuracies obtained under various thresholds or definitions of "high risk." Earlier we discussed how base rates that deviate from 50% necessarily lower such indexes as correlation coefficients (Rice & Harris, 1995). The term "receiver operating characteristic" took its name because it describes the detection, or prediction, "characteristics" of the test, and the "receiver" of the data can "operate" at any given point on the curve (Metz, 1978). ROCs are meant to be applied to data that are comprised of a continuous predictor variable and a dichotomous dependent measure. They take the form of a figure (see Figure 6.1 for an example) with the sensitivity (true positive rate [TPR]) of the predictor plotted as a function of the false positive rate (FPR [1-specificity]) (Mossman & Somoza, 1991). For any given level of specificity, the receiver knows the sensitivity. Each point on the curve (which corresponds to a cutoff on the predictor) represents a different trade-off between sensitivity and specificity (Metz, 1984).

The area under the curve (AUC) of the ROC graph can be taken as an index for interpreting the overall accuracy of the predictor. Areas can range from 0 (perfect negative prediction), to .50 (chance prediction), to 1.0 (perfect positive prediction). The interpretation of the AUC is as follows: A given area represents the probability that a randomly chosen person who scores positive on the dependent measure (i.e., is actually violent) will fall above any given cut-off on the predictor measure, and that an actually nonviolent person will score below the cut-off (Mossman & Somoza, 1991).

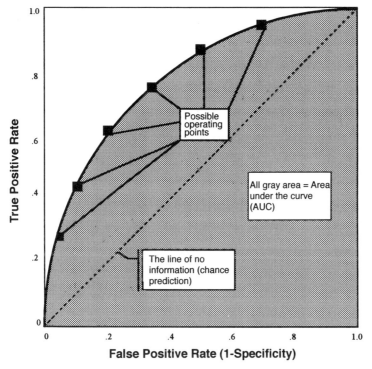

FIGURE 1. A Sample Receiver Operating Characteristic (ROC) Curve.

Thus, an area of .75 means that there is a 75% chance that an actually violent person would score above the cut-off for violence on the predictor, and an actually nonviolent person would score below the cut-off, regardless of the base rate of violence in the study. To use ROCs, a curve is plotted which pits sensitivity against sensitivity at various cut-off levels of some risk assessment instrument. The resulting area under the curve (AUC) is interpreted as an index of predictive accuracy. The interpretation is framed as follows: AUC is the probability that an assessor, using predetermined methods and thresholds, would rate a randomly selected violent person as being more likely to be violent than a randomly selected nonviolent person. An AUC of .5 would be chance performance, whereas an AUC of 1.0 would be perfect classification of violent people as violent. Rice and Harris (1995) have shown how ROCs are preferable to other indexes of predictive accuracy across various base rates of the criterion measure (i.e., violence) in that the most appropriate (i.e., maximally accurate) cut-off score for a predictive measure can be determined as a function of the costs of errors of both the false positive and negative types. Across various base rates, the AUC remained relatively stable for the predictive instrument in use, whereas other indexes varied.

On conceptual grounds, some have argued that we abandon entirely reliance on 2×2 tables and Yes/No predictions to derive measures of accuracy. Probabilistic statements are put forth as a preferable method of conceptualizing accuracy statements because they more accurately reflect our true ability to forecast violence (Monahan & Steadman, 1996; Webster, Harris, Rice, Cormier, & Quinsey, 1994). Assessments may be expressed in terms of regression weights or correlations or, as some have started to do, in *survival curves* and *ranges* of probability statements.

As an example of the former, Serin and Amos (1995) investigated the role psychopathy plays in whether offenders would be violent after release from incarceration. Three hundred offenders were followed for roughly 5.5 years. Survival curves were plotted with time on the X-axis, and the percent of people who have been violent (or not violent) on the Y-axis. When various groups are plotted at the same time, a survival curve provides an easily interpretable demonstration of which groups were more likely to be violent at various times. In the study by Serin and Amos (1995), groups rated as psychopaths, nonpsychopaths, and mixed psychopaths (moderate score on the Psychopathy Checklist-Revised [Hare, 1991]) were included in the same graph. Psychopaths were most likely to be violent at any time point. An appeal of survival curves, in addition to the ease of interpretation, is that comparisons can be made between groups over time. It is possible to discover valuable information about how the pattern of violence differs between groups, something apt to prompt theoretical advances. Two groups, for example, might look the same viewed cross-sectionally at, say, 5-year follow-up, but one group, on the whole, might have acted violently much earlier than the other. Such a finding would, in turn, have implications for the management of violence in different groups of people being released into the community (e.g., to apply intensive supervision earlier versus later).

An example of the latter method of displaying ranges of probabilities may be found in Harris et al. (1993). These investigators gathered a wealth of demographic, clinical, and offense-related data from the files of over 600 mentally disordered offenders who had been released into the community with attendant opportunity to reoffend. After narrowing the pool of potential predictor variables to the strongest 12, they created nine "bins" or categories of risk level. Each bin had a correspondent probability of violence attached to it, resulting in ranges of probability statements being offered. The data in the Harris et al. (1993) study revealed that if a person scored in the highest bin, the most accurate forecast of violence that could be offered was a 100% chance of future violent behavior. If the score fell into the lowest bin, it would be most accurate to estimate between 5% and 15% chance of future violence. The ranges offered at each bin (except for the ninth bin) indicated the 95% confidence intervals which accompanied each level. So, at the fifth bin, there was a 95% chance that a person whose score fit into this bin would have a probability of being violent of roughly .35 (35%). Harris et al. (1993) showed a clear and steady rise of risk in the curve from low left to high right. The advantage of this approach is its appeal to the eye; even statistically unsophisticated readers can appreciate the correspondence between prediction and outcome.

A further emerging trend has been the scoring of risk variables in three point categories (i.e., 0 = absence of variable; 1 = suggestion of or mild presence of the variable; 2 = definite presence of variable). This kind of scoring is used in Hare's (1991) Psychopathy Checklist-Revised (PCL-R). The logic is that in over 20 or so variables, appreciable variability in scores may be obtained; then ranges of probability statements can be made, or survival curves constructed. Examples of violence risk assessment schemes that use this format for scoring include the HCR-20 (Webster, Douglas, Eaves, & Hart, 1997), the Sexual Violence Risk-20 (SVR-20; Boer, Hart, Kropp, & Webster, 1998) and the Spousal Assault Risk Assessment Guide (SARA); Kropp, Hart, Webster, & Eaves, 1998).

A technique that has not yet found its way into the risk assessment field, but that may be expected to do so, is Item Response Theory (IRT). This technique has emerged as a popular and important test validation procedure in the measurement field (Embretson, 1996). It also has been applied to the construct of psychopathy (Cooke & Michie, 1997). IRT analysis has several attractive features. It provides an analysis of the items of a scale in terms of the strength of their relationship to the underlying latent trait or construct that the scale purports to measure (i.e., violence risk).[4] As Cooke and Michie (1997) explain, IRT allows examination of the probability of response to an item as a function of the level of the underlying trait or construct. Such a function permits, if desired, the elimination of items that do not convey significant information about the construct. This analysis also can help to chose items that have either important predictive characteristics across the whole test or around a selected cut-off point. IRT is also very useful in terms of identifying biased items (called *differential-item functioning* in IRT terminology). These are items that, generally, behave differently in psychometric terms as a function of specified characteristics such as gender. Although IRT has not yet become established in the risk assessment field, it certainly can offer valuable analytic strategies.

---

[4] It should be pointed out that whether "violence risk" is an underlying construct is a theoretical and conceptual matter that is not assumed and would have to be argued.

Methodological Gaps

Obviously, all methodological and statistical ideals are rarely achieved in any given applied study. It is, though, now possible to combine the results of studies so as to maximize the benefit of strong design features. Nevertheless, problems pervade the research in this area. As explained by Monahan and Steadman (1994b), there is little consensus among researchers concerning the definitions of predictor and outcome variables. While one group of researchers may conceptualize mental illness, for example, as any Axis I DSM-IV disorder, other investigators may include only psychotic disorders, while still others may only include mental illness as a risk marker if the psychosis is actively florid and indicated by certain features. Similarly, violence may be defined by some as anything from threats to homicide, while others are interested only in particular sorts of incidents (e.g., sexual or domestic assaults).

The procedure by which study participants are chosen varies markedly across projects. Procedural differences may arguably make cross-study comparisons untenable, because groups of participants may differ systematically along some unknown dimension. Although it is important to attempt generalizations across samples, ideally, sample characteristics are well known and prespecified. The problem lies in the interpretation of inconsistent findings (e.g., a variable relates to violence in Study A but not B). To what do we attribute this inconsistency? Something inherent in the unreliability of the variable itself, known differences between groups, or unknown differences?

The issues that relate to the lack of consensus within the research community make direct comparisons of results across studies difficult. A possible remedy is for researchers to code the same construct (i.e., mental illness) in more than one way so that comparisons can be made with similar and dissimilar construals of the same variable. Although it would be unwise to suggest that all research efforts conform to uniform definitions of variables (which would not permit for the exploration of different aspects or facets of these variables), some effort does need to be expended in fostering reliable between-study contrasts. As a first step in this direction, researchers need to be willing to share their detailed coding manuals and protocols with one another.

ADVANCES IN SUBSTANTIVE KNOWLEDGE

The previous section served to ground readers in the somewhat tedious necessities of statistical and methodological terminologies, concepts, weaknesses, and procedures. It also highlighted several contentious issues concerning the appropriateness of various statistical measures. In what follows, we summarize recent literature with the goal of identifying factors that seem most strongly to relate to violence. After describing these variables in general, the next following sections will deal with the integration of these variables into particular schemes used for the prediction of violence.

THE CLINICAL VERSUS ACTUARIAL DISTINCTION

Over time researchers and clinicians have proposed hundreds of variables that conceivably might predict violence. Similarly, there are many ways to conceptualize categories of predictors. We have chosen here a traditional dichotomy in the risk assessment area around which to center our discussion—static/historical versus clinical/dynamic. In this chapter we adhere to the established dichotomy but, as we explain later, chose to consider future adjustment and risk management as a third category. Before proceeding with this, it is necessary to comment on the distinction between static/historical and clinical/dynamic risk factors. The division stems directly from the long-standing actuarial versus clinical decision-making debate. This controversy has persisted over 4 decades after first being brought to light by Paul Meehl (1954). Static variables are features about the individual or the situation that do not change, and they link to the actuarial side of the debate. Dynamic variables, in contrast, are defined as features about the individual, such as emotional, psychiatric, or attitudinal experiences, which are subject to fluctuation. Projections about future risk management issues include such variables as anticipated stress levels, compliance with medications, feasibility of treatment plans, and expected levels of support and supervision.

In what follows, we discuss literature relevant to 20 factors. Ten of the variables considered by us are relatively fixed in nature. We refer to them as historical factors. They are as follows: (a) previous violence, (b) young age at first violence, (c) relationship instability, (d) employment instability, (e) substance abuse, (f) major mental disorder, (g) psychopathy, (h) early maladjustment at home or school, (i) personality disorder, and (j) prior release or detention failure or unauthorized absences. A further five variables center around clinical concepts, and are as follows: (a) lack of insight, (b) negative attitude, (c) psychiatric symptomatology, (d) behavioral and affective instability, and (e) unresponsiveness to treatment. The final five variables are risk management variables that are oriented to the future—to estimating risk of violence in particular social and physical environments. They are as follows: (a) lack of release plan feasibility, (b) access to victims, weapons, drugs and alcohol, (c) lack of support and supervision, (d) non-compliance with the release plan, and (e) stress. This notion of a 3-stage assessment process, based on past, present, and future, has been discussed and published previously by us (Douglas, Webster, Eaves, Wintrup, & Hart, 1996; Webster, Douglas, Eaves, & Hart, 1997a, 1997b; Webster, Eaves, Douglas, & Wintrup, 1995). The so-called HCR-20 scheme (Webster et al., 1995; HCR-20 Version 2, Webster et al., 1997a) is used here mainly as a way of ordering the discussion. In this document, based on consultations with researchers, clinicians, and administrators, we urge that the prediction task be completed in an orderly and systematic manner. It goes without saying that factors other than those listed here will be of obvious importance in some instances.

A word is necessary concerning the actuarial–clinical prediction controversy. Grove and Meehl (1996) describe that statistical (or actuarial, or mechanical) prediction "involves a formal, algorithmic, objective procedure (e.g., equation) to reach the decision" (p. 293). Clinical prediction "relies on an informal, 'in the head,' impressionistic, subjective conclusion, reached (somehow) by a human clinical judge" (Grove & Meehl, 1996, p. 294). It certainly is the case that actuarial prediction, when pitted against global clinical judgment, has the more impressive record in terms of predictive accuracy. As Hart (1998) points out, however, actuarial prediction may have shortcomings within the risk assessment field, such as failing to account for crucial yet idiosyncratic risk markers that may not be included in an actuarial scheme, lacking the flexibility to be incorporated into an ongoing assessment process that includes emphasis on risk management, and tending to focus upon a narrow range of usually static risk factors.

We have commented upon this debate to emphasize that, in the present chapter, the term clinical, when used to describe types of variables, does not have the same meaning as clinical decision making. It refers here to types of variables that can fluctuate or are dynamic. In Meehl's (1954; Grove & Meehl, 1996) usage, clinical refers to the process of prediction, and not to what types of variables are used. Clinical variables, as we define them, can actually be used in either actuarial or clinical prediction models. Similarly, static variables, which are sometimes misleadingly called actuarial variables, are variables that do not fluctuate, but could also be used in either actuarial or clinical prediction models.

As will become evident in this and subsequent sections, the bulk of current evidence supports static variables as most strongly predictive of violence. This finding parallels Meehl's (1954) condemnation of clinical decision making as subjective and less accurate and consistent than actuarial predictions. In the risk assessment paradigm, actuarial factors and predictive techniques are generally considered superior to clinical predictions of violence (Dawes, Faust, & Meehl, 1989; Monahan, 1984, 1988; see also, generally, Webster et al., 1994).[5] Yet, it is important to acknowledge that carefully designed studies have shown that clinical predictions of violence can obtain appreciable accuracy (Lidz, Mulvey, & Gardner, 1993). In the Lidz et al. (1993) study, it was difficult to determine which method outperformed the other because actuarial predictions yielded better sensitivity than clinical predictions but poorer specificity.

As one example of actuarial superiority, McNiel, Binder, and Greenfield (1988) compared the predictive accuracies of clinicians to actuarial discriminant function equations based on past violence, age, gender, diagnosis, and the like. Clinical predictions were retrieved from the files of some 250 civilly committed involuntary psychiatric inpatients who were judged by the presiding clinicians to be either a danger to others or not to be so. Actuarial predictions were similarly obtained from file data. Physical attacks on others during the first 3 days of hospitalization were used as the criterion for violence. The findings revealed that of those predicted to be violent by clinicians, 27% were actually violent (i.e., true positive rate of 27%). This corresponds to an improvement over chance of only 9%, and a false positive rate of 73%. Using the actuarial equations, the improvement over chance was 27%, with a true positive rate of 46% and a false positive rate of 55%. The sensitivity of clinical predictions was greater than for actuarial predictions (63% versus 23%), which indicates that clinical judgments identified more patients who were actually violent. However, this came at the huge expense of having three-quarters of patients predicted to be violent actually not behaving violently.

RISK MARKERS

In what follows, we discuss in some detail variables whose relationship with violence are supported by research. We start with historical or static variables, and then discuss clinical variables, defined by their dynamic (fluctuating) nature. The final set of risk markers we discuss are called risk management variables. These tend to be future and situationally oriented, and deal with projections of circumstances that may aggravate or, conversely, mitigate, violence risk.

---

[5]Yet, the present authors are very aware of the fact that what now pass for actuarial variables may have strong grounding in clinical practice. A good example is the notion of psychopathy, first delineated by the psychiatrist Hervey Cleckley (1941) in his book, *The Mask of Sanity*, and later operationalized and given numerical shape by psychologist Robert Hare (1991).

Static Factors

PAST VIOLENT BEHAVIOR.   A history of previous violence, whether leading to arrest, hospitalization, or neither, is a relatively robust predictor, one which has really never been disputed as bearing on the probability of future violent acts. It was one of the variables found to predict violence during studies conducted in the late 1960s and 1970s (see Cocozza, Melick, & Steadman, 1978; Kozol et al., 1972) and has been reliably found to associate with future violence in more recent empirical work (Ball, Young, Dotson, Brothers, & Robbins, 1994; Binder & McNiel, 1990; Klassen & O'Connor, 1988a, 1989; McNiel & Binder, 1989, 1994a,b; McNiel et al., 1988; Swanson, 1994). Past violent behavior also appears to predict future violence that may occur in considerably different contexts, as demonstrated by McNiel et al. (1988), whose study found that the strongest predictor of violence perpetrated by involuntarily detained psychiatric inpatients in the first few days of hospitalization was violence in the community during the few weeks prior to commitment.

YOUNG AGE.   With rare exceptions, the younger a person is, the greater the likelihood of their acting violently (see Menziers & Webster, 1995, for an exception). During the age of "first generation" risk assessment research, when, for the most part, researchers were busy demonstrating the difficulties entailed in predicting violence, young age consistently emerged as a reasonably notable predictor of violence (Cocozza et al., 1978; Steadman & Cocozza, 1974). Monahan (1981), in his influential text, attested to the strength of young age as a predictor of violence after having reviewed the extant research. As with previous violence, young age has continued to be substantiated throughout the 1980s (Kay, Wolkenfeld, & Murrill, 1988; Sepejak, Menzies, Webster, & Jensen, 1983; Steadman & Felson, 1984) and the 1990s (Bartels, Drake, Wallach, & Freeman, 1991; Cirincione, Steadman, Robbins, & Monahan, 1992; Harris et al., 1993; Swanson, 1994; Wessely, Castle, Douglas, & Taylor, 1994). There are dozens of other studies that have found a relationship between young age and violent behavior. One surprising finding worth mentioning comes from a study by Lindqvist and Allebeck (1990), who found that in a large group ($N = 644$) of released schizophrenic patients, while patients aged 21–29 were more likely to be violent than those aged 30–49, so too were people between the ages of 50 and 59. There is also the point that individuals who score high on psychopathy, as measured by Hare's (1991) revised Psychopathy Checklist (PCL-R), may not "burn out" as had been thought previously (Harris, Rice, & Cormier, 1991).

Combining this category with the previous one, many researchers have found that the younger a person is at their first violent incident, the greater their chances of behaving violently in the future (Harris et al., 1991, 1993; Hodgins, 1983; Lattimore, Visher, & Linster, 1995; Rice, Harris, Lang, & Bell, 1990). Similarly, being hospitalized before the age of 18 has been shown to predict violence (Ball et al., 1994; Klassen & O'Connor, 1988a).

RELATIONSHIP INSTABILITY.   The inability to form lasting partnerships or the tendency to persist in abusive, unstable, and hostile relationships could parallel a generic conflict-oriented approach to interaction with any persons. Being unmarried, for example, correlated with subsequent violence at $r = .18$ in the Harris et al. (1993) investigation, at .16 for non-schizophrenics and .20 for schizophrenics in the study by Harris et al. (1991), and at .15 in Klassen and O'Connor's (1988b) work. It contributed to an overall prediction model used with a combined group of psychiatric patients and prison inmates by Shaffer, Waters, and Adams (1994). Men who are violent toward their spouses are at an elevated risk for being violent to others as well (Saunders, 1992; Stuart & Campbell, 1989). Offenders with mental illness may have an added potential for relationship instability or the inability to form relationships (Feder, 1991).

EMPLOYMENT INSTABILITY.   The logic underlying this variable is analogous to relationship patterns, in that persons who are unable to sustain employment due to personality style or attitude may have traits that spill over into other aspects of their lives. In a combined group of psychiatric patients and prison inmates, vocational instability (defined as being unemployed for more than 3 of 12 months preceding incapacitation) contributed significantly to an overall model of violence prediction (Shaffer et al., 1994). Menzies & Webster (1995) found that of 11 demographic variables, unemployment at time of arrest was 1 of 4 that predicted violent recidivism ($\beta = .18$) in a group of accused persons who had been previously referred by the courts for psychiatric evaluation. In a longitudinal study of schizophrenic patients by Wessely et al. (1994), employment acted as a buffer to criminal conviction. Klassen and O'Connor (1988c) noted that vocational patterns tended to be less stable among those psychiatric patients who were violent rather than nonviolent. Motiuk (1996) has observed that unstable employment is an important risk factor for general recidivism among persons released from Canadian penal institutions. The employment patterns of mentally ill offenders may be less stable than those without such illnesses (Feder, 1991).

SUBSTANCE USE.   Abusing or being dependent on alcohol or other drugs dramatically increases the chance that a person will be violent. Perhaps the best evidence we have for this association stems from an epidemiological survey of over 10,000 community residents (Swanson,

1994). In this study, the odds for being violent (defined as hitting, weapon use, fighting, and the like), given abuse of substances, were roughly 10 times the odds of being violent when no such diagnosis was applied, even after other variables were statistically controlled. These odds were substantially greater than those produced by major mental disorder, race, age, or other factors. One of the strongest findings to emerge so far from the MacArthur risk assessment project is that while psychiatric patient status was not itself independently related to community violence, substance abuse was (Steadman et al., 1998). There also appeared to be an interaction between substance abuse and patient status. Patients were no more likely to be violent than community control participants, although patients who reported symptoms of substance abuse were more likely than community participants who reported symptoms of substance abuse to be violent.

Hoffman and Beck (1985) included heroin or opiate dependence in their risk assessment analyses and their final model was quite successful at distinguishing between offenders who would incur subsequent serious charges. In a more general vein, Haywood et al. (1995) found that alcohol and drug problems experienced postrelease for psychiatric patients was a very strong predictor (partial β = .50) of return to hospital. Several studies have observed very high substance abuse rates (35%–57%) among inmates, including violent inmates in comparison to nonviolent inmates (Hodgins, 1990; Taylor, 1986; Yarvis, 1990), an effect that may be even stronger when antisocial personality disorder is a co-occurring diagnosis (Abram, 1989; Tiihonen & Hakola, 1994). Violent psychiatric inpatients (Blomhoff, Seim, & Friis, 1990) and outpatients (Bartels et al., 1991; Klassen & O'Connor, 1988a) are more likely than their nonviolent counterparts to have substance abuse problems.

Not all studies have found strong effects. For example, a relatively weak correlation (r = .13) was found between violence and alcohol abuse by Harris et al. (1993). Some investigators have found no relationship between substance abuse and violence (McNiel et al., 1988), or a reduced level of substance abuse among groups of mentally ill offenders in comparison to offenders without mental illnesses (Feder, 1991).

It is tempting to draw causal connections between substance abuse and violent behavior and perhaps to assert that being intoxicated lowers inhibitions, distorts logical thinking, and induces behavior and affective instability. Yet, such a causal mechanism must not be taken for granted. People who are likely to be violent may also be likely to abuse substances, but both of these factors may be caused by some third variable (e.g., antisocial attitudes and values; attempts at self-medication).

MAJOR MENTAL DISORDER.   Generally, having a major mental disorder, elevates the risk for violent behavior. Douglas and Hart (1998), in a meta-analysis of the research on the relationship between major (psychotic) disorders and violence, found that the odds for violence increased several times if a diagnoses of schizophrenic or affective psychoses was given in studies. In Swanson's (1994) epidemiological study of over 10,000 community participants, diagnoses of schizophrenia or schizophreniform illnesses produced likelihoods of violence some five times greater then if no diagnosis were given.

In the MacArthur study, one with very good methodology, Steadman et al. (1998) reported that persons were not at elevated risk for violence as a function of major mental disorder. This category was defined to include schizophrenia, schizophreniform disorder, schizoaffective disorder, depression, dysthymia, mania, cyclothymia, and other psychotic disorders. As mentioned earlier, there was an elevated rate of violence among patients with co-occurring substance abuse compared with community participants with substance abuse. Possible future reports from the MacArthur project that divide the major mental disorder group into more fine subgroups (e.g., schizophrenic only; manic only), and then investigate the relationship between these groups and violence, will be instructive.

Studies of prison inmates point to an association between mental disorder and violence. Feder (1991) found that prison inmates with mental illness were more likely to have been convicted for a violent index offense and to have a history of violence than inmates without mental illness. Similarly, Cote and Hodgins (1992) observed in their sample of 460 Canadian inmates, that those who had been convicted of murder had a higher prevalence of major mental disorder than did inmates convicted of other offenses. Taylor's (1986) assessment of all live-sentenced prisoners in London, England, revealed that 20% had diagnoses of either definite or probable schizophrenia. Estimates of the prevalence of major mental disorder in American jails places it at two to three times higher than in the general population, even after controlling for demographic factors such as age, sex, and the like (Teplin, 1990). A quarter of participants in Hodgins' (1990) study of close to 500 inmates suffered from a major mental disorder. Of 100 murderers, Yarvis (1990) found that 29% of such people had diagnoses of either schizophrenia (21%) or affective disorders (8%), and another 22% suffered from some other mental disorder.

Results from longitudinal studies of mentally disordered samples provide some support for the association between major mental disorder and violence. Wessely et al. (1994), in a study of all schizophrenics ($N = 538$) and matched nonschizophrenic controls who had had their first contact with certain mental health services in a section of London, England, over a 20-year-period, calculated that the rate ratio associated with the violence of men as a function of diagnosis of schizophrenia was 3.8. For women schizophrenics, the rate ratio for violence was not elevated. Lindqvist and

Allebeck (1990), in a 14-year follow-up study of 644 schizophrenic patients released from hospital in Stockholm, Sweden, in a period of 1 year, determined that the rate of violent arrests was 4 times greater for schizophrenic patients than for the general population. Most of the violence was assault or threat-related, and was seldom excessively brutal. In a sample of psychiatric outpatients, however, homicidal attempts were disproportionately common in schizophrenic patients in comparison with those who had other diagnoses (Asnis, Kaplan, van Praag, & Sanderson, 1994).

A study of psychiatric inpatients revealed that those with schizophrenia were 10 times more likely to be violent than patients with other diagnoses (Karson & Bigelow, 1987). In a sample of over 1600 psychiatric patients, Rossi et al. (1986) found that paranoid schizophrenia was overrepresented in patients who engaged in fear-inducing or assaultive behavior. Diagnostic information was more predictive of assaultiveness than was demographic information. A study of all psychiatric referrals from the Tokyo prosecutor's office revealed that people with psychotic mental disorders were more likely to have been charged with violent offenses rather than other offenses (Inada, Minagawa, Iwashita, & Tokui, 1995).

Although many studies on this topic focus on schizophrenia or other psychoses, Collins and Bailey (1990) were specifically interested in the potentially elevated risk of violence that mood disorders may engender. Results, based on structured psychiatric interviews with 1140 incarcerated male inmates, revealed that dysthymia was associated with robbery and frequent fighting since age 18, after controlling for sociodemographic and substance-related factors. Depression and depressive symptoms were also disproportionately elevated in people with histories of fighting. Manic diagnoses tend to predict inpatient psychiatric violence in studies by McNiel and Binder (see Binder & McNiel, 1988; McNiel & Binder, 1994a,b, 1995).

Major mental disorder is related to violence. However, on this gross level, it is less reliable and strong a predictor of violence and less useful in terms of explaining the link between the constructs than is specific psychiatric symptomatology (which will be addressed in the section on dynamic predictors of violence). For example, although some have found moderately strong relationships between, say, schizophrenia and violence (Binder & McNiel, 1988) or mania and violence (McNiel et al., 1988), others have found no relationship (Palmstierna & Wistedt, 1989), while yet others still have found negative associations (Harris et al., 1993; $r = -.17$; Rice, Quinsey, & Houghton, 1990).[6] One recent meta-analysis of predictors of violence reported no relationship between mental illness and violent or non-violent

[6]This may well be because in these studies those with a primary diagnosis of schizophrenia were pitted against those with a main diagnosis of personality disorder.

recidivism (Bonta, Law, & Hanson, 1998). However, this study used relatively few studies that included mental illness and violence ($n = 11$) and
focused entirely on mentally disordered offenders who were released from
correctional institutions, excluding population-based studies, civil psychiatric samples, or forensic psychiatric samples (except one). However, the
majority of research appears to support a relationship between major
mental disorder and violence (see Douglas & Hart, 1998).

PSYCHOPATHY.   Over a half-century ago, Hervey Cleckley (1941) described a certain personality style which he named psychopathy. Robert
Hare (1991, 1993, 1996) has since refined and clarified the construct, and
provided a psychometrically reliable and valid instrument to assess it—
the Psychopathy Checklist-Revised (Hare, 1991). Psychopathy can be par-
celed into behavioral and affective/interpersonal factors. Psychopaths, as
conceptualized by Hare, are grandiose, glib persons who demonstrate
superficial charm. They are callous, remorseless, and unable to experience
the normal range and depth of emotional experience, which precludes
empathy. Impulsive, reckless, manipulative, and dishonest, psychopaths
do not accept responsibility for their behaviors. Psychopaths "leech" from
others parasitically and have either no or poorly thought out long-term
future plans. Not unexpectedly, psychopathic individuals tend to have
criminal records that are both diverse and long-standing, frequently stemming from adolescence.

If this description of a psychopath seems like a recipe for violence, this
impression is not a false one. There is abundant empirical evidence that
people who score high on the PCL-R (typically, of a possible 40 points,
above 30 or sometimes 25) are more likely to engage in general criminal
and violent behavior, and are more likely than their counterparts to have
parole or conditional release revoked and at earlier times. Two recent
meta-analytic reviews of the literature on psychopathy and violence provide support for at least a moderate (Hemphill, Hare, & Wong, 1998) to
large-sized (Salekin, Rogers, & Sewell, 1996) association with violence.
Serin and Amos (1995) found that psychopaths were five times more likely
to recidivate violently than were nonpsychopaths, and they reoffended
significantly sooner after release from prison. In a study by Harris et al.
(1991) psychopaths recidivated violently at a rate of 77%, versus 21% of
nonpsychopaths. Psychopaths also may be at elevated probability for
using weapons, threats, and instrumental violence (Serin, 1991). Not surprisingly, in comparison to nonpsychopaths, psychopaths are more likely
to commit offenses that are not accompanied by strong emotional arousal,
and their offenses are also likely to be motivated by material gain (Wiliam-
son, Hare, & Wong, 1987). Their crimes are motivated more by instrumen-

tal (i.e., money or power) goals rather than by emotionally driven hostile or reactive goals (Cornell et al., 1996).

Even in mentally disordered offenders, the construct of psychopathy was found by Harris et al. (1993) to be their single most powerful predictor of future violence (r = .34). Rice and Harris (1992) found that the relationship between psychopathy and violence was stronger in a subsample of schizophrenics (r = .30) that nonschizophrenics (r = .19). Using the recently developed "Screening Version" of the PCL-R (PCL:SV; Hart, Cox, & Hare, 1995), Hill, Rogers, and Bickford (1996) found an appreciably sized relation between PCL:SV total scores and inpatient aggression among forensic psychiatric inpatients (β = .28). Hill et al. (1995), in a supplementary analysis, entered into a regression equation, among other variables, a dichotomous psychopathy variable—"psychopath/not psychopath," based on a cutoff score of 19 (out of a possible total of 24). Impressively, this was the only variable to enter the regression equation, and it accounted for nearly half of the variance in aggression (R^2 = .48; β = .69). Douglas et al. (1998) found, in a sample of 193 released civil psychiatric patients, that those who scored above the median of the PCL:SV were 13 times more likely to perpetrate violent criminal offenses in the community than those scoring below the median.

A modified version of the original PCL was developed by Forth, Hart, & Hare (1990) and used to study previous and future violence in a Canadian group of incarcerated seriously violent young offenders (mean age = 16.3).[7] The PCL score correlated $-.25$ with age at first arrest, .27 with number of past violent offenses, and .46 with the number of charges within the institution for violence or aggression. Concerning recidivism, although PCL scores were unrelated to nonviolent convictions, they bore a moderately strong correspondence to the number of violent rearrests or reconvictions (r = .26). Psychopathy has also been found to predict sexual recidivism (r = .23; Quinsey, Rice, & Harris, 1995). In this same study, PCL-R scores predicted violent recidivism at .33.

What seems fair to conclude is that psychopaths, in comparison with nonpsychopaths, are at an increased risk for acting violently and for doing so more quickly and in more diverse ways and across various settings, whether they are mentally disordered, sex offenders, young offenders, or just "regular" nonmentally ill offenders.

EARLY MALADJUSTMENT AT HOME OR SCHOOL.   There are many factors relating to childhood experiences that predict violence. For example,

---

[7]It is important to point out that while there has been some research using the PCL or PCL-R with young offenders, the diagnosis of psychopathy is still, to date, generally reserved for people over 18 years of age.

being separated from parents before the age of 16 was found to correlate at .25 with violence by Harris et al. (1993). These same researchers found that maladjustment in elementary school, such as being truant, expelled, or having failing grades, also was related to violence as an adult (r = .31) nearly as strongly as psychopathy was. Childhood problems have been noted to predict adult violence in other studies by this group of researchers (Harris et al., 1991; Rice & Harris, 1992). Experiencing severe and cruel parental discipline as a child has been found to correlate with violence as an adult in an inpatient sample of people with bipolar illness (r = .45; Yesavage, 1983a). Participants in Klassen and O'Connor's (1989) study suffered similar pasts, marred by poor early family quality (defined by severity of punishment, how well parents met needs, whether injured by adult, and whether parents fought physically with each other and others). A group of violent psychiatric inpatients was compared to a nonviolent group by Convit et al. (1988); differences were found between them concerning *early family deviance,* as the authors termed it. On the whole, violent patients had a greater amount of familial psychiatric hospitalization, substance abuse, and physical abuse within their nonintact childhood families. Physical violence in the family of origin distinguished violent psychiatric inpatients from those who were nonviolent (Blomhoff et al., 1990). Smith and Thornberry (1995) found that more severe childhood maltreatment is related to more serious juvenile delinquency.

PERSONALITY DISORDER.   In the Harris et al. (1993) study, having any personality disorder elevated the probability of future violence (r = .26; see also Harris et al., 1991, in which a correlation of .14 was found). In a civil psychiatric sample, Douglas, Ogloff, & Nicholls (1997) found that a diagnosis of any personality disorder increased the odds of violence after release from hospital by some 3.5 times, and a diagnosis of antisocial personality traits or disorder elevated the odds by 4.5 times. Yarvis (1990), in addition to finding a high prevalence of mental disorder in a sample of 100 murderers, also detected that 74% of individuals in the sample had a personality disorder. Heading the list, not surprisingly, was antisocial personality disorder[8] at 38%, followed by borderline personality (18%), and a host of other personality disorders (18%). Snyder, Pitts, and Pokorny (1986), using a large sample of nearly 5,000 Veteran Hospital inpatients,

---

[8]Antisocial Personality Disorder (APD), as defined in the *Diagnostic and Statistical Manual of Mental Disorders* (4th ed.) (DSM-IV; American Psychiatric Association, 1994), differs importantly from, though overlaps with, psychopathy. APD almost entirely is characterized by behavioral factors, and hence is similar to the behavioral aspects of psychopathy. However, APD lacks the affective and interpersonal qualities of psychopathy. For this reason, APD is more common than psychopathy.

found that the presence of borderline personality traits, but not necessarily the disorder, elevated the probability of a patient acting violently both in the community and the hospital. Taylor's (1986) study of life-sentenced offenders indicated a lower (33%) although still substantial prevalence of personality disorder.

Antisocial personality disorder seems to carry pervasively strong effects on a person's life, which may obscure the influence of other factors, such as mental illness. For example, Hodgins and Cote (1993) found in their study of 451 randomly selected federal inmates from penitentiaries in Quebec, Canada, that, regardless of whether these inmates had a major mental disorder, those with antisocial personalities were much more likely than those without to (a) have a juvenile arrest record, (b) be younger the first time they were sentenced to a penitentiary, and (c) have more total convictions. Curiously, whether mentally disordered or not, those with antisocial personalities were no more likely to have a greater number of violent convictions in their pasts. From the large-scale NIMH Epidemiological Catchment Area survey, Robins, Tipp, and Przybeck (1991) observed that 85% of some 600 people diagnosed with antisocial personality disorder had histories of some sort of violent behavior. In a Canadian epidemiological survey, Bland and Orn (1986) found that roughly half of those with antisocial personality disorder had histories of violence toward family members, and this proportion increased sharply to over 80% when substance abuse also was involved.

PAST ATTEMPTED OR ACTUAL ESCAPES AND VIOLATIONS OF CONDITIONAL RELEASES. It is not surprising that people who are apt to behave in violent ways are also more probable to act in other antiauthority manners, such as attempting to escape from incarceration or violating the terms of parole or other types of conditional release. Harris et al. (1993) found that this factor was moderately related to violence ($r = .24$; see also Harris et al., 1991). As part of a larger battery of items, being on escape status predicted reconviction for a serious offense (Hoffman & Beck, 1985). Inpatients in a forensic psychiatric hospital who were judged to be an escape risk were more likely to behave violently while in the institution (Ball et al., 1994). A history of actual or attempted escapes in medium security inmates was correlated with violence during the first 6 months of their incarceration ($r = .28$; nonsignificant due to small N; Cooper & Werner, 1990).

Dynamic/Clinical Factors

The previous section was devoted to factors which tend to be relatively stable and have received some degree of substantiation so far as their predictive power is concerned. This section on "dynamic" risk markers is concerned with characteristics of individuals that may be more fleeting and transitory. Here we are concerned with affective, attitudinal, and psychiatric features of persons' mental and behavioral repertoires, which tend to fluctuate over time, whether for minutes, hours, or some longer period. It is important to issue the caveat that these variables, at least so far as they are currently described and understood, lack the predictive strength of historical variables. Yet, when measured carefully with attention to interrater reliability, dynamic variables do relate to violent behavior. Similarly, global opinions of future risk for violence, when offered carefully by some individual clinicians, have been found to relate to violence with enough strength to warrant further exploration (Menzies, Webster, McMain, Staley, & Scaglione, 1994). In an exceptionally well-designed and well-executed study intended to assess the accuracy of clinical predictions, Lidz et al. (1993) found that clinicians' general predictions exceeded chance and fared no worse than actuarial judgments. Whatever else might be said, it seems reasonable to think that we are further ahead than 30 years ago when the "triad" of enuresis, firesetting, and cruelty to animals was being offered as a guide to clinical thinking on the topic (Hellman & Blackman, 1966).

LACK OF INSIGHT. This factor includes the extent to which an individual realizes that he or she has a mental or personality disorder and is in need of treatment, and appreciates his or her own potential for violence and the broader social consequences of the mental disorder (Amador et al., 1993). It may be only indirectly that this variable links to violence. Lack of insight, for example, may reduce the probability that an individual will faithfully adhere to medication regimes; this, in turn, may lead to the exacerbation of violence-inducing psychiatric symptoms of the sort we will discuss later.

Insight, although usually construed as an individual's ability to introspect, may well be applied to his or her understanding of others' functioning as well. Much of the research in this area has been conducted on aggressive adolescents. Dodge, Price, Bachorowski, & Newman (1990) administered a measure of hostile attributional biases to a group of incarcerated adolescent males from a maximum security institution. Scores on this measure reflected the degree to which the participants attributed hostile intent to others where none unambiguously existed, and were correlated with measures of conduct disorder and reactive aggression. Importantly, they were also related to the number of violent crimes committed ($r = .20$). The boys in the highest quartile of violent crimes showed 58% more hostile attributions than the lowest group. As Dodge et al. (1990) reported, this bias is quite pervasive among violent youth. Slaby & Guerra

(1988) found that violent youths were more likely to endorse the legitimacy of aggression and to believe that aggression increases self-esteem and helps to avoid a negative self-image. Members of this group also felt that victims do not suffer from the violence inflicted on them, and that victims deserve the aggression they receive. Incarcerated violent offenders were found to attribute the cause of their offense to external factors (including the victims) rather than to themselves and to justify their behavior on the basis of some victim characteristic (Henderson & Hewstone, 1984).

NEGATIVE ATTITUDE AND PERSONALITY STATES. Certain aspects of an individual's personality and attitudinal repertoire may predispose him or her to violence. Several of these may reflect long-standing personality traits, perhaps stemming from psychopathy or antisocial personality disorder, and normally will have been included under static/historical variables. Yet, the subitems we will now consider may best be construed as dynamic states prone to wax and wane over time.

Anger has been reasonably well defined and studied as it relates to violence. Novaco perhaps has contributed the greatest amount of theoretical and psychometric understanding of the construct of anger. Novaco (1994) reported on the development of his newest scale designed to assess anger, the Novaco Anger Scale, and on its ability to predict violence. The measure reflects Novaco's theoretical understanding of anger, and is comprised of four factors: cognitive; arousal; behavioral; intensity and generality. Subsumed by these factors are such subscales of anger as suspicion, rumination, hostile attitude, intensity, somatic tension, irritability, impulsive and aggressive reactions, and physical confrontations.

In a retrospective analysis of psychiatric patients, Novaco's (1994) scale correlated .34 with the number of convictions for violent crimes. The hostile attitude subscale correlated .36, and the duration subscale .37. Various other subscales produced correlations above .30. These relations were stronger than for other measures of anger (except for the Caprara Rumination Scale: .33). In a prospective analysis, correlations were not as strong. In comparison to several other measures of anger and hostility, the impulsive reaction subscale of Novaco's measure was the only to achieve a significant correlation (.26) with physical assault. It should be pointed out that while these correlations are not exceedingly large, they are comparable to correlations between violence and other constructs that are considered strong in the risk assessment area (e.g., psychopathy correlated .34 with violence in the study by Harris et al., 1993, higher than any other variables).

Selby (1984) found that not only did violent offenders score higher on the Novaco Anger Inventory (NAI; an earlier version of the measure described previously) than did nonviolent offenders, but also that a 25-item scale abstracted form the NAI was able to classify with 90% accuracy violent versus nonviolent offenders. Anger was found by Kay et al. (1988) to be strongly related to physical aggression in a sample of 208 male and female psychiatric inpatients (β = .46). Welsh and Gordon (1991) found support for the relationship between trait anger and aggressive behavior. Kennedy, Kemp, and Dyer (1992) put forth that anger (and fear) mediates the relationship between paranoid delusions and violence.

Another such variable is hostility. Menzies and Webster (1995), deriving a clinically based scheme on foundations laid by Megargee (1976), found, as part of a larger battery of items, that trained assistants' ratings of mentally disordered defendants' hostility were moderately strong predictors of future community violence (β = .36) and violence in the hospital (β = .30). These same investigators found that lower levels of both capacity for empathy and guilt were related to violent outcomes summed across settings (β = .37 and .27, respectively). Furthermore, low levels of passive-aggressiveness predicted violence in the community (β = -43) and across settings (β = $-.26$). Others have reported an association between violence and hostility (Kay et al., 1988).

Three decades ago, Megargee and colleagues developed a scale called Overcontrolled-Hostility (O-H) for the Minnesota Multiphasic Personality Inventory (MMPI). This they based on theoretical reasoning which held that many violent and murderous offenders were extremely unassertive and hence unable to express their anger and hostility (Megargee, Cook, & Mendelsohn, 1967). Bottling extreme hostility inside oneself, the theory holds, may result in the periodic explosive outburst of violence. Quinsey, Maguire, and Varney (1983) indeed found that murderers who scored high on the O-H scale were less assertive than murderers who fell low on the O-H scale, offenders without histories of violent offenses, and community controls. Selby (1984) demonstrated that violent offenders scored high on both the O-H MMPI scale and on the Buss-Durkee Hostility Inventory.

PSYCHIATRIC SYMPTOMATOLOGY. Evidence has already been provided for the association between psychiatric disorder in general (particularly schizophrenia and mania) and violence (Douglas & Hart, 1998; Swanson, 1994; though see Teplin, Abram, & McClelland, 1994, who found no relationship between major mental disorder and violence in released offenders). In their meta-analysis, Douglas and Hart (1998) determined that when studies used symptom, rather than the broader category of diagnosis, as the unit of measurement, the association between psychosis and violence was stronger. Some research has attempted to offer more specific explanations for this connection. Link, Andrews, and Cullen (1992) determined, based on psychiatric diagnostic interviews with over 500 community members and over 200 psychiatric patients, that patients had an enhanced level of all types of violence measured (e.g., self-report arrests, official arrests, hitting others, fighting, weapon use, and hurting others badly), even after variables such as age, gender, education, race, and the like had been controlled for statistically. Investigating this apparent connection further in regression analyses, controlling for psychotic symptoms, the relationship between patient status and violence disappeared, meaning that it was active psychosis that accounted for the increase in violence. Odds ratios for hitting others, fighting, and weapon use were 2.2, 4.0, and 1.9, respectively. When analyses were run separately for the patient group and the never-treated community group, psychotic symptoms predicted violence significantly in both groups.

Based on the same data set, Link and Stueve (1994) conducted more refined analyses in an attempt to identify the active ingredient that produces the connection between psychotic symptoms and violence. Their hypotheses were centered around the "principle of rationality within irrationality" (p. 143), which holds that within the (objectively irrational) subjective experience produced by florid psychosis, behaviors may be carried out that are very rational to the person afflicted with psychosis. To operationalize this concept, Link and Stueve (1994) proposed that symptoms that override a person's sense of self-control (i.e., feeling that external forces control one's thoughts, or that thoughts are put into one's mind by outside forces) or threaten a person's sense of safety (i.e., feeling that others are out to harm one), though irrational to the observer, create a context for people afflicted with them in which it is rational to act on these feelings by being violent. These symptoms are called "threat/control-overide" (TCO) symptoms. Other types of symptoms, though equally indicative of psychosis, were postulated to bear no relation to violence. The data fully supported Link and Stueve's hypotheses. People who experienced TCO symptoms were at a greater risk for violence than those who experienced other symptoms, or none at all. This finding held regardless of whether a person was a patient or a community member. Odds ratios could be calculated from the data offered by Link and Stueve (1994). When patient status was the independent variable, odds ranged from 1.9 to 3.9, depending on the type of violence. When TCO symptoms were the predictor variables, odds ranged from 10.3 to 19.2.

Recently, Swanson and colleagues tested the TCO hypothesis using the ECA data from over 10,000 people (Swanson, Borum, Swartz, & Monahan, 1996). For analyses, this variable was coded dichotomously, such that people who had any TCO symptom(s) were put into one category, and those with none into another. People with TCO symptoms were 2.9 times more likely to have been violent since the age of 18 than those without. However, when analyses were confined to the previous year, TCO symptoms did not relate to violence because the effects of substance abuse (odds = 6.4) were very strong. Swanson et al. (1996) reported the probability of acting violently since age 18 as a function of combinations of diagnoses and levels of TCO symptoms. For people with major mental disorder plus substance abuse and TCO symptoms, there was a reported 86% chance of violence; for people with major mental disorder and TCO symptoms, there was a 63% chance; for people with major mental disorder and non-TCO symptoms, the level dropped to 39%; for those with mental disorder and no active symptoms, it diminished to 26%; and for persons with no disorder and no symptoms, it settled at 17%.

Clearly, TCO psychotic symptoms and the principle of rationality within irrationality appear to possess a fair deal of explanatory power with respect to the psychosis/violence connection. Other avenues of research not dealing with these constructs seem to support the proposition that psychiatric symptoms predict violence. Many studies have found that items and factors on the Brief Psychiatric Rating Scale (BPRS; Overall & Gorham, 1962) that relate to psychotic symptoms (e.g., hallucinatory behavior, disorganized thought, odd beliefs) correlate at a moderate strength with violent behavior or differentiate between violent and nonviolent groups (Krakowski & Czobor, 1994; McNiel and Binder, 1994a; Tanke & Yesavage, 1985). In a study of schizophrenic outpatients, patients who demonstrated hallucinations and/or delusions, paranoia, disorganization of thought, or suicidiality were more likely to be violent than those who did not experience such states (Bartels et al., 1991). The odds of violence occurring based on the presence of such factors, calculated by this chapter's authors, ranged from 3.7 for suicidality to 44.8 for paranoia, with hallucinations/delusions (11.0) and disorganized thought (16.5) having intermediate, though substantial, odds. Support for the relationship between specific symptoms such as delusions or hallucinations and violence has been obtained elsewhere (Noble & Rodger, 1989; Taylor, 1985). Assessors also will want to be attentive to the potential presence of sadistic fantasies and homicidal ideation (MacCulloch, Snowden, Wood, & Mills, 1983).

Concerning delusions specifically, a recent informative study has shed some light on factors that may lead people to act on their delusions (Buchanan et al., 1993). According to the self-report of the study participants, they were more likely to act on delusions when they felt frightened, sad, or anxious because of their beliefs. Also, having sought out evidence in support of their beliefs and thinking that evidence existed to support their beliefs increased the chances of acting on delusions. The possible connection between feelings of fright and anxiety to TCO symptoms is interesting, in that feelings of fright and anxiety may very well arise from feeling out of control or that others intend harm.

It may be with this particular topic of psychiatric symptomatology that clinicians are most apt to draw "illusory correlations" between a particular symptom and violent behavior. For instance, although the link between command hallucinations and violence seems relatively well fixed in clinical lore, its connection to violence in the research is quite variable. On review of nearly 800 files from psychiatric inpatients, 151 patients were identified who had experienced auditory hallucinations, and of these, 58 had had command hallucinations (Hellerstein, Frosch, & Koenigsberg, 1987). There were no significant differences in assaultive behavior among groups with no auditory hallucinations, auditory but noncommand hallucinations, and command hallucinations. Another study found that those suffering command hallucinations were less likely to be violent than other patients (Thompson, Stuart, & Holden, 1992).

Junginger (1990) studied command hallucinations and violent behavior in psychiatric inpatients and outpatients and found a relationship, albeit a relatively weak one. Of 51 participants who had experienced command hallucinations, 20 (39%) had complied with them. Eight (16% of total) such cases were deemed *dangerous* by Junginger (1990), and this term applied to either self or other harm or to overdose of medications. Fewer than half of those people experiencing command hallucinations complied with them, under one-sixth resulted in dangerous behavior, and this behavior was not comprised solely of danger to others. Rogers, Nussbaum, and Gillis (1988), after reviewing some half-dozen studies, concluded that a small but consistent proportion (about 5%) of people with antisocial command hallucinations act on them. Indirect support for the relationship between violence and command hallucinations comes from a study that compared forensic psychiatric inpatients who suffered from command hallucinations, noncommand hallucinations, or no hallucinations (Rogers, Gillis, Turner, & Frise-Smith, 1990). The content of the command hallucinations was rated as being more aggressive than noncommand hallucinations, and many command hallucinations had some sort of criminal content. Furthermore, 80% of patients with commands admitted to obeying them at some point in the recent past. Nearly half of such patients apparently acted on commands frequently. The results of Rogers et al. (1990) do not, however, permit a definitive statement regarding whether the presence of command hallucinations increases the frequency of violent behavior. Although there seems to be some link between command hallucinations and violence, it is surely not a robust one, and, to date, its prevalence as identified through research is unreliable. In their meta-analysis of the literature, Douglas and Hart (1998) found that command hallucinations did not strongly elevate the risk for violence.

Being suicidal may elevate one's risk to harm others. Asnis et al. (1994) found that attempts at homicide by psychiatric outpatients were more common in those with a history of suicide attempts. Similarly, a group of violent psychiatric inpatients had a significantly greater prevalence of violent suicide attempts (39.1%) than did a nonviolent group (19.4%; Convit et al., 1988). In a study of male forensic psychiatric inpatients, Hillbrand (1995) noted that patients with histories of suicide attempts and current self-injurious behavior were more likely to be verbally and physically aggressive toward people and destructive of property in the hospital than patients with one or none of these characteristics. This effect held after controlling statistically for age, length of hospitalization, and effects of medication. There were no differences in psychiatric diagnoses among the groups. Other researchers have found that lifetime aggression scores are greater in suicide victims than they are in nonsuicidal controls (Brent et al., 1994). Finally, in the United States, there are roughly 1,000 to 1,500 murder-suicides each year, often involving young, jealous, paranoid, dependent, substance-abusing males who kill female partners and then end their own lives (Palermo, 1994).

Although there is quite solid evidence for the link between specific symptomatology and violence, some commentators have wisely pointed out that sometimes such relationships may be more apparent that real. The "misidentification syndrome" provides an instance of this. The syndrome involves a delusion in which a person misidentifies somebody they do not know as a person they do know—or vice versa—who has inexplicably changed in appearance. A link between the syndrome and violent behavior has been indicated several times (De Pauw & Szulecka, 1988; Silva, Leong, & Weinstock, 1992), Dinwiddie and Yutzy (1993) pointed out, however, that most of this research is anecdotal because only those patients with the syndrome who are violent may end up in hospital, and rarely is there a comparison group of psychotic people without such syndromes. Whether misidentification syndrome increases the odds of violence is therefore unclear.

BEHAVIORAL AND AFFECTIVE INSTABILITY. The core element of impulsivity is the lack of control over affect, behavior, or cognition. Impulsivity may spawn reactivity to provocation or frustration. The inability to regulate behavior in response to impulses or thoughts may lead to violent behavior that otherwise may not occur. Barratt (1994) has contributed a good deal of empirical and theoretical work to the study of impulsivity. His Barratt Impulsiveness Scale was constructed to include three a priori factors: (a) motor impulsiveness, (b) cognitive impulsiveness, and (c) non-planning impulsiveness. A fair number of groups have been compared using this measure. Prisoners, as a generic group, scored higher than various other groups (e.g., community controls, college students, psychiatric inpatients, substance abusers) on all three factors (Barratt, 1994). *Impulsive aggression*, defined by Barratt as lacking the self-control necessary to refrain from acting on a "hair-trigger" temper, may include acting without thinking, a genetic predisposition toward impulsivity and aggression, lack of behavioral control, and, quite possibly, some neurochemical imbalances. Barratt also claims that impulsive aggression is closely tied to anger and hostility. The concept of "lifestyle impulsivity," meaning a pervasive impulsiveness that affects most areas of a person's life and precipitates recklessness and disruptiveness, has been found reliably and clearly to distinguish recidivistic from nonrecidivistic offenders (Prentky, Knight, Lee, & Cerce, 1995). Those high in lifestyle impulsivity were roughly three times more likely to commit subsequent offenses of a variety of types than those low in impulsivity. Hollander and Stein (1995), in an edited book, documented the many ways in which impulsivity contributes to various types of violence. Webster and Jackson (1997) have similarly published a book that contains useful chapters on the relationship between impulsivity and violence.

UNRESPONSIVENESS TO TREATMENT.   The degree to which an individual responds to treatment efforts is of prime interest to clinicians. Some patients' symptoms remit in response to medication. Others resist the effects of medication and patients remain seriously disturbed. Although some persons may attain the skills necessary to function adaptively in society, others may not have the capacity to do so. Some with the capacity may not have the desire. For that reason, in addition to medication responsiveness, it is important to assess a person's attitude toward being treated. Some individuals may protest against the attempts of clinicians to provide neuroleptic or other remediation. Although their symptoms may decrease in severity, and they may attend therapy sessions, once they are no longer under the watchful eye of their "captors," they may no longer continue with some or all treatment strategies. Haywood et al. (1995) found that patients who did not comply with medication regimes after having been released into the community were at elevated risk to return to hospital.

Psychopathy is relevant to the issue of treatability. Psychopathic individuals are notoriously difficult to treat. Whether this stems from their constitutional makeup, personality traits, or the fact that there has yet to be a treatment strategy that has been properly operationalized and tested is unclear (see Ogloff & Douglas, 1995). What is not in debate is the fact that existing research has yet to demonstrate a treatment approach that reduces the violence of psychopaths, let alone attenuates the traits of psychopathy. In fact, some investigations have demonstrated that conventional treatment approaches, such as those carried out in prison, may make matters worse. That is, psychopaths who have received treatment in prison may be more likely to recidivate than psychopaths who have not received treatment (Ogloff, Wong, & Greenwood, 1991). Already skilled at manipulation, deceit, and conning, psychopaths who spend time in treatment may actually refine the interpersonal skills which are integral to these endeavors. To speculate, well-intentioned therapeutic efforts may lead them to try ever more ambitious scams and crimes. Yet, given their fundamental impulsivity, lack of forethought, and poor planning skills, they also may be no more likely to evade detection than they ever were.

Risk Management (Future Situational) Variables

LACK OF RELEASE PLAN FEASIBILITY.   Whether there exist community agencies and staff members willing and able to work with patients and prisoners after they have been released into the community may bear relation to whether those released can exist nonviolently in society. The issue here is relatively simple—many community agencies may be reluctant to assume responsibility for the housing and supervision of patients and prisoners because of their violent and disruptive track records. If, at time of release, suitable housing and monitoring has not been secured for these individuals, difficulties in adapting to society may be likely. Plans, if developed but not well thought out and tailored to individuals' particular needs, may be ineffectual. Estroff and Zimmer (1994), using a sample of released psychiatric patients, found higher incidences of violence in patients who received less care from mental health professionals than those who received more attention (see following section). Bartels et al. (1991) observed a relationship between the violent behavior of released patients and inadequate housing and difficulties in handling such tasks as finances and meals. Release plans ought to be individualized to meet needs of particular persons. This conclusion carries with it the implication that uniform release plans are unlikely to help all people. It is probable that people at low risk to commit violence need relatively small amounts of intense supervision and structure built into their release plans. Andrews et al. (1990) proposed the "Risk/Needs Responsivity" principle, which holds that high risk patients and prisoners need a correspondingly high level of service delivery in order to prevent recidivism. Furthermore, not all people are responsive to the same treatment strategies. As Ogloff and Douglas (1995) explained in their discussion of the treatment of high-risk offenders, it is essential that treatment plans target the changeable aspects of individuals that predispose them to violence. Targeted treatment is required for each person, based on an assessment of risk markers and treatment needs.

Supporting these concepts is a study that showed that low-risk offenders who were placed in an "intensive supervision" probation program were more likely to recidivate than low-risk offenders who were supervised under less stringent conditions (Andrews, Kiessling, Robinson, & Mickus, 1986).

ACCESS TO VICTIMS, WEAPONS, DRUGS, AND ALCOHOL. If the environment into which the individual is discharged (e.g., skid row hotel) permits easy access to weapons, drugs, alcohol, and victims, the potential for violence may be greater than if the situation were controlled for these. This may be particularly relevant if the individual has committed previous acts of violence with a weapon or under the influence of substances. Environments that are similar to past situations in which the individual acted violently are to be eschewed in the planning of release decisions. As one example of this concept, Gendreau (1995) reports, on the basis of his meta-analysis of the literature, that having antisocial peers elevates the potential that individuals will behave in antisocial ways themselves. It seems only reasonable to expect, based on well-established principles (Skinner, 1953), that situations that have induced antisocial and violent conduct in the past will do so in the future. Though this point seems perfectly evident, it is nonetheless remarkable how often it is routine practice to release prisoners and patients into exactly the same circumstances as before they were institutionalized.

LACK OF SUPPORT AND SUPERVISION. The inability to adapt to the standards and norms of a society places persons at elevated risk for myriad difficulties. Under this broad category is included lack of social skills, lack of social and financial supports, and such extremes as homelessness. These factors may be linked to appreciable stress and frustration and, in some cases, violent behavior. Estroff and Zimmer (1994) provided both a cogent synopsis of the literature in the area of social supports for mentally ill people, as well as a study designed to address many of the weaknesses and gaps in previous research. They point out that social factors may serve both insulative and precipitative functions with respect to violence among mentally ill people. Past research, they argue, has been too narrow and exclusive, ignoring many factors (e.g., the nature of the relationship between mentally ill perpetrators of violence and their victims, living arrangements, life histories) that may very well be crucial to understanding the role played by social influences. In many ways, their criticism of the research parallels that offered by Monahan (1988; discussed earlier; Monahan & Steadman, 1994b) concerning impoverished predictor and criterion variables.

In their study, Estroff and Zimmer (1994) followed 169 severely mentally ill people for 18 months after release from psychiatric institutions, conducted six interviews (five of which were in person) with patients over this time, and, for 59 patients, interviewed other persons knowledgeable about their lives. They collected information bearing on social, demographic, clinical, and historical factors. Twenty-three people (13.6%) were violent during the follow-up period, and an additional 33 (22%) threatened violence. People whose social networks comprised few mental health professionals, and those whose networks consisted of many family members were at increased risk to be violent. Concerning threatening behavior only, as the number of people in a person's network increased, so too did the chance of uttering threats. Patients who felt threatened or perceived hostility in their relatives and friends were apt to threaten violence (though not to act violently). People who lived with unrelated others were more likely than those living alone to utter threats. Most of the targets of violence or threats were known to the patients (77%) and were typically mothers. Close to 40% of the 87 victims had been named by patients as members of their social circles. These researchers have reported elsewhere that being financially dependent on one's relatives was associated with violent acts and threats (Estroff, Zimmer, Lachicotte, & Benoit, 1994). To some extent, given the thorough follow-up procedure, it is surprising that Estroff and Zimmer (1994) did not find more relationships between violence and social variables. Variables tended to be predictive of threats of violence rather than actual violence. It is worth noting that their findings, though important, were limited at outset due to the low base rate (14%) of violence.

The finding that threats of violence increased as size of social circle increased may appear counterintuitive. It may be expected that the more people individuals have in their social circles, the less chance there is that they will be aggressive. This finding underscores the importance that family members and friends, in addition to being merely present, be patient, tolerant, sympathetic, and, preferably, somewhat knowledgeable about the condition with which their relative or friend is afflicted. If they are merely present, or, worse, are hostile or in some other manner provocative, then they may be more likely to be victims rather than supporters. Seen in this way, the presence of family and friends, if they are unsupportive or otherwise unhelpful, might warrant consideration as an aggravating factor under the previous item entitled "access," rather than as a mitigating factor under the present one.

Other researchers have addressed some of the same questions as Estroff and Zimmer (1994). Bartels et al. (1991), for example, measured various aspects of the social environment in their sample of schizophrenic outpatients. Patients who behaved violently had difficulties in several basic social areas, including housing, finances, meals, and daily activities. Draine and Solomon (1994) followed up a group of mentally ill offenders who were released from prison into an environment lacking stable housing. Although recidivism in general, not merely violent recidivism, was the dependent measure, the results were instructive, and there is no reason to suspect that they would differ dramatically for violent recidivism. Variables that differentiated those who were returned to prison from those who were not included subjective quality of life as poor and fewer case management services. The latter finding is consistent with the already-mentioned principle called Risk/Need Responsivity (for empirical support, see Andrews et al., 1990). This principle holds that service level must be commensurate with risk level, such that high-intensity, high-frequency services are necessary for high-risk offenders. It may have been the case in Draine and Solomon's (1994) finding that high-risk people were not being delivered services of high enough intensity or frequency.

In a series of studies, Klassen and O'Connor have found that current aspects of a patient's relationship to his or her family predict violence (Klassen & O'Connor, 1988a,b,c, 1989). Feeling let down by and dissatisfied with parents and siblings and frequent arguments with family members seem to relate to an elevated potential for violence in the community.

Typically, social dysfunction, as the term implies, is associated with the inability to adjust to social demands and pressures. However, some investigators have studied parallel dynamics within institutions. In a study of psychiatric inpatients, for example, those who were unable to adapt to the "social" characteristics of the ward (i.e., daily exercises, grooming, social interaction, and recreational activities) were more likely to assault others than were patients who were better adjusted ($r = .41$; Krakowski, Jaeger, & Volavka, 1988). As with the study by McNiel et al. (1988) which demonstrated the continuity of behavior between the community and the institution, the work of Krakowski et al. (1988) implied that this may extend to adjustment to the individual's "social" environment.

NONCOMPLIANCE WITH MEDICATION OR OTHER TREATMENT. The noncompliance factor overlaps with nonresponsiveness to treatment (dealt with previously) but here refers specifically to estimated compliance with treatment once a person is living in the community. Typically the desire, motivation, and ability to comply with treatment regimes is taken to indicate a degree of understanding on the individual's part that without such treatment, he or she may run into troubles, for example, by decompensating and behaving violently. Noncompliance with medication has been found to be a very strong predictor of return to hospital in psychiatric patients (Haywood et al., 1995). In this investigation, the relationship was of considerable strength (partial β = .44). A clear effect for noncompliance on violence was obtained in a sample of schizophrenic outpatients (Bartels et al., 1991). Violent patients were much more likely to have evinced noncompliance (71%) than those who were merely threatening (29%) or irritable (21%), or displayed no aggression or hostility whatsoever (17%).

A good deal of the difficulty is that treatment programs, both those in institutions and those in the community, tend to lack organization, purpose, and intensity. They can look better on paper than in practice. Patients may, in fact, not have much to comply with. Even if they do show up for the 2-hour group sessions each week, it is not in the least reasonable to think that the benefits, if any, should permeate the remaining 166 hours. It is not possible in this chapter to deal with the literature on treatment even though the two matters are vitally connected. Several recent reviews, though, are at hand (Harris & Rice, 1997; Rice, Harris, Quinsey, & Cyr, 1990; Webster, Hucker, & Grossman, 1993).

STRESS. Much of the preceding discussion on future situational risk factors leads logically to a consideration of the stressfulness of living conditions and its contribution to violent behavior. Perhaps as a result of these aforementioned factors, stress experienced by people released into the community may rise, which in turn may lead to violent behavior (Guerra, Huesmann, Tolan, Van Acker, & Eron, 1995; Hall, 1987; Klassen & O'Connor, 1994). Lack of support from friends, family members, and community agencies; inadequate release plans; difficulties in housing, finances, and daily living tasks; and deterioration of one's mental state arising from noncompliance with medication may all induce stress levels which decrease the individual's ability to cope with the demands of people and society at large. Monahan (1981) suggested that potential sources of stress from three general areas—family, employment, and peers—should be examined. In line with this, assessors of risk should concern themselves not just with the degree of conflict in relationships, financial security, employment opportunities and demands, but also with the difficult task of estimating how well or how poorly individuals will cope with the impending deaths of close relatives, serious illnesses they must face, conviction of relatives on serious charges, death of children, and the like (e.g., being a victim of violence). Felson (1992) found that stress and physical aggression were related in samples of adult excriminal offenders, released psychiatric patients, and high school students. It is important to note, however, that the relationship between the two was mediated by whether a person was also the target of violence. That is, stress predicted the perpetration of violence only when study participants were also victims of violence.

RISK ASSESSMENT SCHEMES: PUTTING IT ALL TOGETHER

We chose in this review to structure our discussion around important constructs that relate to violence rather than to concentrate on certain risk assessment schemes that have appeared in the literature. The principal reason for this decision was that most schemes include some combination or variation of the items listed in this chapter. It seemed that by canvassing the items rather than the tools which employ them, a more thorough explication of risk markers could be obtained. Nonetheless, it is important to point out several risk assessment schemes that have been developed. Borum (1996), in an important article on the clinical practice of violence risk assessment, described how, despite advances in research on risk assessment, "there have been virtually no systematic efforts to incorporate this information into a useful, empirically based framework for clinical assessment" (p. 947). He described the valuable function that risk assessment schemes can serve in both improving the clinical practice of risk assessment as well as risk assessment technology. We refer the reader to the original sources for more thorough descriptions of the devices and their psychometric properties.

The first risk assessment scheme to be discussed is the HCR-20 violence risk assessment scheme (Webster et al., 1995, 1997). This guide was designed to be integrated into clinical practice, yet to be rooted in empirically validated risk factors. It contains 20 violence risk markers under 3 scales—Historical, Clinical, and Risk Management. Although the HCR-20 can be used as an actuarial scale, it is forwarded as a guide or protocol for structured (as opposed to global, impressionistic) clinical decision making (see Hart, 1998). Its risk markers were chosen from a comprehensive review of the empirical and professional literature rather than from a calibration study on a single sample. As such, it should have potential applicability to a wide range of settings for which violence risk assessment is relevant (i.e., forensic psychiatric; civil psychiatric; correctional).

Although there have been several samples within which the HCR-20 has been tested, most reports are unpublished given the instrument's relative recency. There have been 2 civil psychiatric samples that have given rise to several reports and presentations. Douglas et al. (1998) found AUC values that ranged from .76 to .80 in a sample of 193 released psychiatric patients. In this study, scores above the median of the HCR-20 elevated the odds of later violence by 6 to 13 times. The HCR-20 tended to produce somewhat larger and more consistent effect sizes than the PCL:SV. Nicholls, Ogloff, and Douglas (1997) found that, in general, the HCR-20 worked as well for women as it did for men. In another civil psychiatric sample of 131 different patients, Ross, Hart, and Webster

(1998) reported AUC values that ranged from .68 to .75 for community violence.

There have been 4 samples of forensic psychiatric patients that have focused on validity data. Strand, Belfrage, Frannson, and Levander (in press) found in their sample of 40 Swedish forensic patients that the HCR-20 AUC for violent criminal recidivism was .80. Further, the mean difference between recidivistic and nonrecidivistic groups produced a Cohen's d of 1.19, which is a large effect size (Cohen, 1988). Surprisingly, the C and R items were most able to differentiate recidivists from nonrecidivists. Another Swedish sample of 404 forensic patients compared the VRAG and the H scale of the HCR-20 (Grann, Belfrage, & Tengstron, 1998). For the H scale, the AUC value was .71, and for the VRAG it was .68. This finding replicated in a subsample of personality-disordered patients. In a schizophrenic subsample, the AUC for the H Scale dropped to .66, and the VRAG's AUC was not greater than chance. How the full HCR-20 would have performed, particularly in light of Strand et al.'s (in press) findings, is an interesting question.

In a Canadian sample of 80 forensic psychiatric patients, Wintrup (1996) observed that the HCR-20 and PCL-R both correlated at approximately .30 with various types of postrelease violence, but the HCR-20 correlated more strongly with subsequent forensic ($r = .38$) and civil rehospitalization ($r = .45$) than did the PCL-R ($rs = .25$ and 36, respectively). In a different Canadian sample of 175 forensic patients, Douglas, Klassen, Ross, Hart, and Webster (1998) focused on concurrent validity. They observed that the HCR-20 was strongly related to the PCL-R and Brief Psychiatric Rating Scale (BPRS; Overall & Gorham, 1962). However, the Historical Scale of the HCR-20 correlated much more strongly with the PCL-R than did the C and R Scales. In turn, the C and R scales were strongly related to the BPRS, whereas the H Scale was unrelated. This pattern of correlations makes conceptual sense, given the content of the various scales. The HCR-20 also was related to various measures of past violence and other antisocial behavior, with scores above the median elevated the odds of violence by 2 to 4 times.

In the only prison or correctional sample to date, Douglas and Webster (in press) found in a retrospective sample that the H Scale[9] correlated with past violence at $r = .50$; the C Scale did so at $r = .30$, the PCL-R did so at $r = .41$, and the VRAG did so at $r = .20$.[10] Scores above the median of the

[9]Item H1 (Previous Violence) was removed from analysis to avoid artificial inflation of coefficients.
[10]The R Scale of the HCR-20 could not be coded because most prisoners had not yet been considered for release.

HCR-20 elevated the odds for various indexes of past violence and anti-social behavior by an average of 4 times. Hierarchical regression analyses tended to show that the HCR-20 added incremental validity to the PCL-R and VRAG.

In terms of reliability, Belfrage (in press) had 6 clinicians rate the same 43 forensic patients on the HCR-20. Overall multivariate interrater reliability, using Kendall's W, was .81. Estimates of interrater reliability using Pearson r are .82 (Ross et al., 1998), and .80 (Douglas & Webster, in press). Douglas, Hart et al. (1998) found that ICC_1 = .80 and ICC_2 = .89 in their forensic sample and Douglas, Ogloff et al. (1998) found ICC_1 = .80 in their civil psychiatric sample. In terms of internal consistency of full scale scores, Cronbach's alpha was reported by Belfrage (in press) to be .95, and by Douglas, Klassen et al. (1998) to be .79.

Harris, Rice, and Quinsey (1993) developed an actuarial tool called the Violence Risk Appraisal Guide (VRAG) from a sample of 618 Canadian mentally disordered offenders. Comprised of 12 variables[11] the VRAG's multiple correlation with community violence was a respectable .46. The extent to which this scale generalizes to other samples is not yet clear. These authors attempted to cross-validate the VRAG on a sample of sex offenders. They found that it possessed similar predictive accuracy for the nonsexual violent recidivism of sex offenders, but in fact did quite poorly for the prediction of sexual recidivism (Rice & Harris, 1997). The VRAG has been adopted into a risk device called the Violence Prediction Scheme (VPS; Webster, Harris, Rice, Cormier, & Quinsey, 1994), which also includes, tentatively, a subscheme for evaluating clinical factors called the ASSESS-LIST. One commentator (Monahan, 1995) has remarked of it: "[T]he Violence Prediction Scheme is so far superior to anything previously available that not to seriously consider its use, at least on an experimental basis, in other jurisdictions would be a difficult choice to justify" (p. 447).

Based on numerous studies on inpatient violence by psychiatric patients, McNiel and Binder (1994b) proposed a 5-item screening tool for the assessment of risk of inpatient violence.[12] The following indexes of predictive accuracy for the dependent variable of physical attack were obtained

[11]These were, along with their univariate correlations with violence: (a) psychopathy, .34; (b) separation from parents under the age of 16, .25; (c) victim injury in index offense, −.16; (d) DSM-III diagnosis of schizophrenia, −.17; (e) never married, .18; (f) elementary school maladjustment, .31; (g) female victim in index offense, −.11; (h) failure on prior conditional release, .24; (i) property offense history, .20; (j) age at index offense. −.26; (k) alcohol abuse history, .13; (l) DSM-III diagnosis of personality disorder, .26.
[12]These items, dichotomously coded, were (a) history of physical attacks and/or fear-inducing behavior in the two weeks prior to admission; (b) absence of suicidal behavior in the two prior weeks; (c) presence of schizophrenic or manic diagnoses; (d) male gender; and (e) currently married or living together.

from the validation sample of 338 patients: sensitivity 55%; specificity 64%; FP rate 68%; FN rate 18%; positive predictive power 41%; negative predictive power 82%; and total predictive value 62%. The relative improvement over chance was 25%. When the dependent variable was any aggressive behavior, the relative improvement over chance increased somewhat, to 28%. This instrument demonstrated reasonable statistical properties and, as a brief screening tool, could serve a useful function to direct resources to those patients for whom the risk of violence would appear greatest.

Also conducting research with psychiatric patients as participants, but concentrating on violence after release into the community, Klassen and O'Connor have carried out several well-designed prospective calibration and validation studies (Klassen & O'Connor, 1988a,b,c, 1989). Factors typically relating to violence include hospitalization prior to age 18, past arrests and violence, poor early family quality, never having been married, and poor family relations. These domains of variables have correctly classified 85% of patients according to whether they were violent or not. A cross-validation study (Klassen & O'Connor, 1989) correctly classified 76%, and classification rates of 88% and 93% within subgroups of schizophrenic and nonschizophrenic patients, respectively, have been obtained (Klassen & O'Connor, 1988c), although there were some differences between the subgroups in terms of which items were related to violence.

Gardner, Lidz, Mulvey, and Shaw (1996) concerned themselves with predictive efficiency. That is, they tested two methods of risk assessment designed to be less cumbersome and resource-consuming than traditional, large-scale risk assessment measures. Using a sample of 714 psychiatric emergency room patients, these researchers compared the predictive utility of regression trees (sequence of yes/no decisions based on actuarial factors) and a two-stage screening method designed to focus assessment resources on patients who present initially as relatively high risk. The first stage uses information that hospitals collect as a matter of routine (i.e., drug use, age, prior violent incidents). Without delving into the statistical complexities, both the regression tree and screening method performed at levels significantly greater than chance. Although they did not perform better than traditionally longer assessment batteries, they were as accurate; arguably, they were also easier to use in clinical practice and less time and money-consuming.

A VIEW TO THE FUTURE:
RECENT THEORETICAL AND CONCEPTUAL ADVANCES

The past two decades or so have witnessed a barrage of research aimed at predicting violence. Progress has been made. We are aware of many constructs which correlate with violence, and, by measuring such factors, we typically can achieve fairly respectable correlations with violence, classification of violent offenders, prediction of violence, and the like. Studies are typically conducted with more or less similar methodologies. The problem at hand is conceptualized without much variation across research efforts—that is, a host of factors known or suspected to predict violence is measured; violence is indexed in the institution, the community, or both; and the results are cross-tabulated. It may be wise, however, to question whether steadfast adherence to such a model will appreciably increase our abilities to forecast future violence. If we measure even more variables, will we account for ever increasing amounts of variance in violence? It seems unlikely that the average multiple correlation will suddenly jump from .45 to .75 any time soon. Our ability to measure the various constructs we routinely employ is limited, which in turn necessarily restricts the levels our correlations attain. Continued definition and study of extant risk markers will likely maintain, or even increase somewhat, the current level of predictive ability. More progress remains to be achieved than has already been made, and we recommended continued vigilant efforts to improve measurement, methodology, and statistical procedures. Yet, we cannot end this survey of risk assessment without offering some speculations about how the task might be conceptually reconstructed in ways that may enhance our ability not only to predict violence but also to understand it.

First, there has already been a notable shift from predicting violence and dangerousness to managing it in the community (Heilbrun, 1997). The management approach to issues of violence risk appears to be favored over others among both researchers and clinicians (Heilbrun et al., 1998). Becoming interested in what happens to people after release will direct attention toward potentially important factors that may very well lead to subsequent violence. Studies cited in this chapter that employ interviews with participants who are in the community are consistent with this notion. This approach could be framed as one of assisting people on a more or less routine basis in adapting to community living. Not only would this lead to greater understanding of what sorts of events precipitate future violent conduct but it would also tie the risk assessment strategy closely to the management and prevention of violence.

A related idea, "conditional prediction," is put forth by Mulvey and Lidz (1995). Its goal is to identify precisely conditions on which violence depends. Situational aspects are highlighted. It is important to know when violence will occur, under which circumstances, against whom it will expressed, and in what form. Previous research adopted a "cue-utilization" approach that strives to identify variables, typically about the individual, and then tries to match them up with violent conduct (Monahan & Stead-man, 1994a). This method, Mulvey and Lidz (1995) asserted, forces the consideration of only certain variables to the exclusion of others, usually situational or environmental in nature. Deriving prediction models that include primarily historical variables such as age and previous violence, may perform reasonably well statistically but may be of little assistance to clinicians who must decide, or help others to decide, whom should be released. Clinicians must individualize their risk assessments and assess the environments into which clients will be discharged. They must try to discern with whom patients and prisoners will be interacting, and against whom they may aggress. Arguably, research that is modeled after clinicians' decisions and that focuses on the circumstances into which clients will be released may lead to improved predictions. Mulvey and Lidz (1995) argue that predictions should be framed in conditional terms (e.g., if this person goes off medications, which is likely to happen if he or she experiences stress from family members, then the potential for violence will increase).

The HCR-20 Scheme (Webster et al., 1995; 1997), in addition to including 10 Historical (static) items and five Clinical (dynamic) factors, possesses five Risk Management (situational) items, which include potential stressors likely to be experienced (along with anticipated compliance with medication; support and supervision by family, friends, and community agencies; feasibility of release plan; and access to possible victims and weapons). Systematic inclusion of these factors can allow for the type of conditional prediction called for by Mulvey and Lidz (1995). Research has shown that these R factors are related to violence in the community (Douglas et al., 1998; Strand et al., in press).

Because most research is devoted to content-related issues (e.g., which variables predict violence), there is a dearth of investigation into process-related factors. For example, does it matter who predicts violence? Some investigators have compared the predictive accuracies of psychologists, psychiatrists, nurses, and other such groups (Webster et al., 1984) or have focused on the items these groups tend to consider in the offering of risk assessments (Menzies & Webster, 1995). Various writers recommend certain strategies for improving predictive accuracy. These entail establishing the base rates of violence for particular groups, knowing the relevant legal and procedural rules under which a prediction is offered, framing predictions in probabilistic rather than dichotomous terms, clarifying assessment questions, removing obvious potential biases from the assessment, and the like (Monahan, 1981; Webster et al., 1995; Webster & Polvi, 1995). Very few of these guidelines have actually been subjected to direct empirical scrutiny in the risk assessment sphere. In general, process-oriented variables have received little attention, although they may have much to offer.

Another fruitful area to explore in an attempt to elevate our understanding about predictive ability lies in distinguishing between causes and mere correlates of violence. The bulk of risk assessment research largely ignores the causation issue and focuses solely on prediction or correlation. Although we do not dispute the importance of prediction research, it could well serve researchers to begin the task of differentiating mere predictors from causes. Understanding how violence is driven will enrich prediction. It is as though we do not yet possess that kind of conceptual sophistication with its attendant vocabulary.

Searching for psychological causes of violence promises to be no easy task. For example, an array of research evidence for the relationship between violence and substance abuse was presented earlier. Does this mean that substance abuse causes violence? The answer is less than clear. It could very well do so. Yet, deep-seated antisocial personality traits may induce violence *and* substance abuse. Similarly, there is evidence for genetic and biological bases to both violence and substance abuse. It could be possible that certain genetic and biological combinations cause both. In these cases,violence and substance abuse would be correlated, and assume no causal link. To determine potential causes of violence, the investigator needs to identify, on conceptual grounds, factors that bear strong theoretical, logical, and conceptual links to violence and aggression. Some possibilities include psychopathy, anger, and impulsivity (see Monahan & Steadman, 1994a). Each of these constructs is logically and coherently related to violence. Support for a casual relationship stems not only from empirically demonstrated connections between violence and these items but also from their core theoretical postulates. Each major system of psychological theory may have key constructs that could bear a potential logical link to violence. Psychodynamic theory has a well-developed literature on hatred, rage, and sadism. Without trying to validate key psychodynamic postulates such as libidinal drives, castration anxiety, and the like, the concepts and their development could be investigated empirically. Cognitive models promote mediational systems that intervene between an event in the world and influence a person's reaction to it. Previous research has been presented on the connection between hostile attributional biases and violence. Other such links could be forged. Behavioral reinforcement and social learning theories have by no means been exhausted (Patterson & Yoerger, 1993). Biological models have provided a wealth of research on violence.

Other areas that need development, as described by Borum (1996), are the state of clinical practice guidelines for risk assessment, and the system-atized development of training programs. Concerning the first point, Borum argues that the state of the discipline of risk assessment has reached a point that should allow professional agreement on certain key issues related to assessment and management of risk. Examples of guidelines may include setting minimum competency practice standards. Other sorts of guidelines may apply to institutions. That is, when patients or clients are seen to be high risks for violence, there ought to be a set response or "action template" to deal with such cases. Concerning the latter point re-garding training, Borum makes the point that wide-spread training in risk assessment is a desirable goal, given its ubiquity. He suggests that violence risk assessment and management could be declared a proficiency area within the American Psychological Association, and that graduate train-ing programs ensure that they provide teaching and training in risk assess-ment in some regard. The recommendations of Borum would serve to advance the practice and profession of violence risk assessment.

Finally, it may be worthwhile to approach the risk assessment task from various theoretical perspectives. Earlier we described receiver–operating characteristics. This statistical procedure was initially employed in signal detection theory and physics. Its adoption was portrayed as a step forward in the statistical realm of risk assessment because other techniques are sensitive to base rates, problems with which pervade the risk assessment area. A similar argument could be forwarded concerning Item Response Theory. Recently, chaos theory (Barton, 1994; Haynes, 1995; Heiby, 1995a, 1995b) and the concept of phase–space functions (Haynes, Blaine, & Meyer, 1995) have been introduced into psychological assess-ment. Generally, these models assume that behavior and its causes fluctu-ate greatly in terms of magnitude, form, and frequency or rate. Aspects of behavior are dynamic and nonlinear and such capriciousness is difficult to assess or predict, but also creates difficulty in establishing causes of the behavior. Implications that may flow from chaos theory include the use of statistics for detecting nonlinear associations, close and frequent tracking of changes in behavior, and putative precipitants, across many small time periods, and clear, careful, and thorough theoretical postulates about the behavior to be assessed. This last point stems from the concept of behavior being highly determined by so-called initial conditions that may consist of prior expressions of the behavior as well as other factors. With insufficient or incorrect specification of initial conditions, prediction is doomed to fail. Of course, this treatment of chaos theory is very rough and limited. It is offered merely as one example of how risk assessment may come to be reconceptualized as we move into the twenty-first century.

REFERENCES

Abram, K. M. (1989). The effect of co-occurring disorders on criminal careers: Interaction of antisocial personality, alcoholism, and drug disorders. *International Journal of Law and Psychiatry, 12*, 133–148.

Amador, X. F., Strauss, D. H., Yale, S. A., Flaum, M. M., Endicott, J., & Gorman, J. M. (1993). Assessment of insight in psychosis. *American Journal of Psychiatry, 150*, 873–879.

American Bar Association. (1989). *ABA criminal justice mental health standards.* Chicago: Author.

American Psychiatric Association. (1994). *Diagnostic and statistical manual of mental disorders* (4th ed.). Washington, DC: American Psychiatric Association.

American Psychological Association. (1992). Ethical principles of psychologists and code of conduct. *American Psychologist, 47*, 1597–1611.

Andrews, D. A., Kiessling, J. J., Robinson, D., & Mickus, S. (1986). The risk principle of case classification: An outcome evaluation with young adult probationers. *Canadian Journal of Criminology, 28*, 377–384.

Andrews, D. A., Zinger, I., Hoge, R. D., Bonta, J., Gendreau, P., & Cullen, F. T. (1990). Does correctional treatment work: A clinically relevant and psychologically informed meta-analysis. *Criminology, 28*, 369–404.

Appelbaum, P. S. (1985). *Tarasoff* and the clinician: Problems in fulfilling the duty to protect. *American Journal of Psychiatry, 142*, 425–429.

Appelbaum, P. S. (1988). The new preventative detention: Psychiatry's problematic responsibility for the control of violence. *American Journal of Psychiatry, 145*, 779–785.

Asnis, G. M., Kaplan, M. L., van Praag, H. M., & Sanderson, W. C. (1994). Homicidal behaviors among psychiatric outpatients. *Hospital and Community Psychiatry, 45*, 127–132.

Bachrach, L. L. (1993). The biosocial legacy of deinstitutionalization. *Hospital and Community Psychiatry, 44*, 523–524.

Bail Reform Act, 98 U.S. C. §202 (1984). USC 3141, Sec. 202, p. 1976.

Ball, E. M., Young, D., Dotson, L. A., Brothers, L. T., & Robbins, D. (1994). Factors associated with dangerous behavior in forensic inpatients: Results from a pilot study. *Bulletin of the American Academy of Psychiatry and the Law, 22*, 605–620.

Barefoot v. Estelle, 463 U.S. 880 (1983).

Barratt, E. S. (1994). Impulsiveness and aggression. In J. Monahan & H. J. Steadman (Eds.), *Violence and mental disorder: Developments in risk assessment* (pp. 61–79). Chicago, Ill: University of Chicago Press.

Bartels, S. J., Drake, R. E., Wallach, M. A., & Freeman, D. H. (1991). Characteristic hostility in schizophrenic outpatients. *Schizophrenia Bulletin, 17*, 163–171.

Barton, S. (1994). Chaos, self-organization, and psychology. *American Psychologist, 49*, 5–14.

Baxstrom v. Herald, 383 U.S. 107 (1966).

Belfrage, H. (in press). Implementing the HCR-20 scheme for risk assessment in a forensic psychiatric hospital: Integrating research and clinical practice. *Journal of Forensic Psychiatry.*

Bill C-30: An act to amend the Criminal Code (mental disorder) and to amend the National Defense Act and the Young Offenders Act in consequence thereof. (1991). S. C., 1991, c. 43.

Binder, R. L., & McNiel, D. E. (1988). Effects of diagnosis and context on dangerousness. *American Journal of Psychiatry, 145*, 728–732.

Binder, R. L., & McNiel, D. E. (1990). The relationship of gender to violent behavior in acutely disturbed psychiatric patients. *Journal of Clinical Psychiatry, 51*, 110–114.

Birch, D. E. (1992). Duty to protect: Update and Canadian perspective. *Canadian Psychology, 33*, 94–101.

Blackburn, R. (1995). Violence. In R. Bull & D. Carson (Eds.), *Handbook of legal psychology* (pp. 357–373). Chichester, UK: Wiley.

Bland, R., & Orn, H. (1986). Family violence and psychiatric disorder. *Canadian Journal of Psychiatry, 31,* 127–137.

Blomhoff, S., Seim, S., & Friis, S. (1990). Can predictions of violence among psychiatric inpatients be improved? *Hospital and Community Psychiatry, 41,* 771–775.

Blumstein, A., & Cohen, J. (1980). Sentencing of convicted offenders: An analysis of the public's view. *Law and Society Review, 14,* 223–261.

Boer, D. P., Hart, S. D., Kropp, P. R., & Webster, C. D. (1998). *Manual for the Sexual Violence Risk—20.* Vancouver: British Columbia Institute Against Family Violence.

Bonta, J., Law, M., & Hanson, R. K. (1998). The prediction of criminal and violent recidivism among mentally disordered offenders: A meta-analysis. *Psychological Bulletin, 123,* 123–142.

Borum, R. (1996). Improving the clinical practice of violence risk assessment: Technology, guidelines, and training. *American Psychologist, 51,* 945–956.

Brent, D. A., Johnson, B. A., Perper, J., Connolly, J., Bridge, J., Bartle, S., & Rather, C. (1994). Personality disorder, personality traits, impulsive violence, and completed suicide in adolescents. *Journal of the American Academy of Child and Adolescent Psychiatry, 33,* 1080–1086.

Buchanan, A., Reed, A., Wessely, S., Garety, P., Taylor, P., Grubin, D., & Dunn, G. (1993). Acting on delusions. II: The phenomenological correlates of acting on delusions. *British Journal of Psychiatry, 163,* 77–81.

Canadian Psychological Association. (1988). *Canadian code of ethics for psychologists: Companion manual.* Old Chelsea, Quebec: Author.

Cirincione, C., Steadman, H. J., Robbins, P. C., & Monahan, J. (1992). Schizophrenia as a contingent risk factor for criminal violence. *International Journal of Law and Psychiatry, 15,* 347–358.

Cleckley, H. (1941). *The mask of sanity.* St. Louis, MO: Mosby.

Cocozza, J. J., Melick, M. E., & Steadman, H. J. (1978). Trends in violent crime among ex-mental patients. *Criminology, 16,* 317–334.

Cocozza, J. J., & Steadman, H. J. (1976). The failure of psychiatric predictions of dangerousness: Clear and convincing evidence. *Rutgers Law Review, 29,* 1084–1101.

Cohen, J. (1988). *Statistical power analysis for the behavioral sciences* (2nd ed.). Hillsdale, NJ: Lawrence Erlbaum Associates.

Collins, J. J., & Bailey, S. L. (1990). Relationship of mood disorders to violence. *Journal of Nervous and Mental Disease, 178,* 44–47.

Cooke, D. J., & Michie, C. (1997). An item response theory analysis of the Hare Psychopathy Checklist-Revised. *Psychological Assessment, 9,* 3–14.

Convit, A., Isay, D., Gadioma, R., & Volavka, J. (1988). Underreporting of physical assaults in schizophrenic inpatients. *Journal of Nervous and Mental Disease, 176,* 507–509.

Convit, A., Jaeger, J., Lin, S. P., Meisner, M., & Volavka, J. (1988). Predicting assaultiveness in psychiatric inpatients: A pilot study. *Hospital and Community Psychiatry, 39,* 429–434.

Cooper, R. P., & Werner, P. D. (1990). Predicting violence in newly admitted inmates: A lens model analysis of staff decision making. *Criminal Justice and Behavior, 17,* 431–447.

Corrections and Conditional Release Act. S.C. 1992, c. 20.

Cornell, D., Warren, J., Hawk, G., Stafford, E., Oram, G., & Pine, D. (1996). Psychopathy in instrumental and reactive violent offenders. *Journal of Consulting and Clinical Psychology, 64,* 783–790.

Cote, G., & Hodgins, S. (1992). The prevalence of major mental disorders among homicide offenders. *International Journal of Law and Psychiatry, 15,* 89–99.

Criminal Code of Canada. R. S. C. 1985, c. C-47.

Currie v. United States, 644 F. Supp. 1074 (1986).

Dawes, R. M., Faust, D., & Meehl, P. E. (1989). Clinical versus actuarial judgment. *Science, 243,* 1668–1674.

deGroot, G. (1994). Are school psychologists liable for student actions? *American Psychological Association Monitor, 25,* 1, 58.

Dennis, D. L., Buckner, J. C., Lipton, F. R., & Levine, I. S. (1991). A decade of research and services for homeless mentally ill persons. *American Psychologist, 46,* 1129–1138.

De Pauw, K. W., & Szulecka, T. K. (1988). Dangerous delusions: Violence and the misidentification syndromes. *British Journal of Psychiatry, 152,* 91–96.

Dietz, P. E. (1985). Hypothetical criteria for the prediction of individual criminality. In C. D. Webster, M. H. Ben-Aron, & S. J. Hucker (Eds.), *Dangerousness: Probability and prediction, psychiatry and public policy* (pp. 87–102). New York: Cambridge University Press.

Dinwiddie, S. H., & Yutzy, S. (1993). Dangerous delusions? Misidentification syndromes and professional negligence. *Bulletin of the American Academy of Psychiatry and the Law, 21,* 513–521.

Dixon v. Attorney General of the Commonwealth of Pennsylvania, 325 F.Supp. 966 (M.D. Pa. 1971).

Dodge, K. A., Price, J. M., Bachorowski, J., & Newman, J. P. (1990). Hostile attributional biases in severely aggressive adolescents. *Journal of Abnormal Psychology, 99,* 385–392.

Douglas, K. S., & Hart, S. D. (1998). *Psychosis as a risk factor for violence: A quantitative review of the research.* Manuscript under review.

Douglas, K. S., Hart, S. D., Webster, C. D., & Eaves, D. (1998). *HCR-20 violence risk assessment scheme: Psychometric properties in a forensic psychiatric sample.* Manuscript under review.

Douglas, K. S., Ogloff, J. R. P., & Nicholls, T. L. (1997, June). *The role of personality disorders in community violence among civil psychiatric patients.* Paper presented at the Fifth International Congress of the Disorders of Personality, Vancouver, B.C., Symposium Moderator: C.D. Webster.

Douglas, K. S., Ogloff, J. R. P., & Nicholls, T. L., & Grant, I. (1998). *Assessing risk for violence among psychiatric patients: The HCR-20 risk assessment scheme and the Psychopathy Checklist: Screening Version.* Manuscript under review.

Douglas, K. S., & Webster, C. D. (in press). The HCR-20 violence risk assessment scheme: Concurrent validity in a sample of incarcerated offenders. *Criminal Justice and Behavior.*

Douglas, K. S., Webster, C. D., Eaves, D., Wintrup, A., & Hart, S. D. (1996, March). *A new scheme for the assessment of dangerousness and the prediction of violence.* Paper presented at the biennial meeting of the American Psychology-Law Society, Hilton Head, SC.

Douglas, K. S., Webster, C. D., & Wintrup, A. (1996, August). *The HCR-20 risk assessment scheme: Psychometric properties in two samples.* Paper presented at the annual conference of the American Psychological Association, Toronto, Ontario, Canada.

Draine, J., & Solomon, P. (1994). Jail recidivism and the intensity of case management services among homeless persons with mental illness leaving jail. *The Journal of Psychiatry and Law, 22,* 245–261.

Dvoskin, J. A., & Steadman, H. J. (1994). Using intensive case management to reduce violence by mentally ill persons in the hospital and community psychiatry. *Hospital and Community Psychiatry, 45,* 679–684.

Embretson, S. E. (1996). The new rules of measurement. *Psychological Assessment, 8,* 341–349.

Ennis, B. J., & Litwack, T. R. (1974). Psychiatry and the presumption of expertise: Flipping coins in the courtroom. *California Law Review, 62,* 693–752.

Estroff, S. E., & Zimmer, C. (1994). Social networks, social support, and violence among persons with severe, persistent mental illness. In J. Monahan & H. J. Steadman (Eds.), *Violence and mental disorder: Developments in risk assessment* (pp. 259–295). Chicago, Ill: University of Chicago Press.

Estroff, S. E., Zimmer, C., Lachicotte, W. S., & Benoit, J. (1994). The influence of social networks and social support on violence by persons with serious mental illness. *Hospital and Community Psychiatry, 45,* 669–679.

Feder, L. (1991). A comparison of the community adjustment of mentally ill offenders with those from the general prison population. *Law and Human Behavior, 15,* 477–493.

Felson, R. B. (1992). "Kick 'em when they're down": Explanations of the relationship between stress and interpersonal aggression and violence. *Sociological Quarterly, 33,* 1–16.

Fleiss, J., Williams, J. B. W., & Dubro, A. F. (1986). The logistic regression analysis of psychiatric data. *Journal of Psychiatric Research, 20,* 145–209.

Forth, A. E., Hart, S. D., & Hare, R. D. (1990). Assessment of psychopathy in male young offenders. *Psychological Assessment: A Journal of Consulting and Clinical Psychology, 2,* 342–344.

Gardner, W., Lidz, C. W., Mulvey, E. P., & Shaw, E. C. (1996). A comparison of actuarial methods for identifying repetitively violent patients with mental illness. *Law and Human Behavior, 20,* 35–38.

Gebotys, R. J., & Roberts, J. V. (1987). Public views of sentencing: The role of offender characteristics. *Canadian Journal of Behavioural Science, 19,* 479–488.

Gendreau, P. (June, 1995). *Predicting criminal behaviour: What works?* Paper presented at the annual meeting of the Canadian Psychological Association, Charlottetown, Prince Edward Island, Canada.

Grann, M., Belfrage, H., & Tengström, A. (1998). *Actuarial assessment of risk for violence: Predictive validity of the VRAG and the historical part of the HCR-20.* Manuscript under review.

Grove, W. M., & Meehl, P. E. (1996). Comparative efficiency of informal (subjective, impressionistic) and formal (mechanical, algorithmic) prediction procedures: The clinical-statistical controversy. *Psychology, Public Policy, and Law, 2,* 293–323.

Guerra, N. G., Huesmann, L. R., Tolan, P. H., Van Acker, R., & Eron, L. D. (1995). Stressful events and individual beliefs as correlates of economic disadvantage and aggression among urban children. *Journal of Consulting and Clinical Psychology, 63,* 518–528.

Hare, R. D. (1991). *Manual for the Hare Psychopathy Checklist-Revised.* Toronto: Multi-Health Systems.

Hare, R. D. (1993). *Without conscience: The disturbing world of the psychopaths among us.* Toronto: Pocket Books.

Hare, R. D. (1996). Psychopathy: A clinical construct whose time has come. *Criminal Justice and Behavior, 23,* 25–54.

Harris, G. T., & Rice, M. E. (1997). Mentally disordered offenders: What research says about effective service. In C. D. Webster & M. A. Jackson (Eds.), *Impulsive people: Approaches to assessment and treatment.* New York: Guilford.

Harris, G. T., Rice, M. E., & Cormier, C. A. (1991). Psychopathy and violent recidivism. *Law and Human Behavior, 15,* 625–637.

Harris, G. T., Rice, M. E., & Quinsey, V. L. (1993). Violent recidivism of mentally disordered offenders: The development of a statistical prediction instrument. *Criminal Justice and Behavior, 20,* 315–335.

Hart, S. D. (1998). The role of psychopathy in assessing risk for violence: Conceptual and methodological issues. *Legal and Criminological Psychology, 3,* 121–137.

Hart, S. D., Cox, D. N., & Hare, R. D. (1995). *The Hare psychopathy checklist: Screening version (PCL:SV).* Toronto, Ontario: Multi-Health Systems.

Hart, S. D., Webster, C. D., & Menzies, R. J. (1993). A note on portraying the accuracy of violence predictions. *Law and Human Behavior, 17,* 695–700.

Haynes, S. N. (1995). Introduction to the special section on chaos theory and psychological assessment. *Psychological Assessment, 7,* 3–4.

Haynes, S. N., Blaine, D., & Meyer, K. (1995). Dynamic models for psychological assessment: Phase space functions. *Psychological Assessment, 7*, 17–24.

Haywood, T. W., Kravitz, H. M., Grossman, L. S., Cavanaugh, J. L., Davis, J. M., & Lewis, D. A. (1995). Predicting the "revolving door" phenomenon among patients with schizophrenic, schizoaffective, and affective disorders. *American Journal of Psychiatry, 152*, 856–861.

Heiby, E. M. (1995a). Chaos theory, nonlinear dynamic models, and psychological assessment. *Psychological Assessment, 7*, 5–9.

Heilbrun, K. (1997). Prediction versus management models relevant to risk assessment: The importance of legal decision-making context. *Law and Human Behavior, 21*, 347–359.

Heilbrun, K., Philipson, J., O'Neill, M., Paninopolous, M., Strohman, L., & Bowman, Q. (1998, August). *Expert and practitioner approaches to communicating violence risks.* Paper presented at the annual convention of the American Psychological Association, San Francisco.

Hellerstein, D., Frosch, W., & Koenigsberg, H. W. (1987). The clinical significance of command hallucinations. *American Journal of Psychiatry, 144*, 219–221.

Hellman, D., & Blackman, J. (1966). Enuresis, firesetting and cruelty to animals: A triad predictive of adult crime. *American Journal of Psychiatry, 122*, 1431–1435.

Hemphill, J. F., Hare, R. D., & Wong, S. (1998). Psychopathy and recidivism: A review. *Legal and Criminological Psychology, 3*, 139–170.

Henderson, M., & Hewstone, M. (1984). Prison inmates' explanations for interpersonal violence: Accounts and attributions. *Journal of Consulting and Clinical Psychology, 52*, 789–794.

Hill, C. D., Rogers, R., & Bickford, M. E. (1996). Predicting aggressive and socially disruptive behavior in a maximum security forensic hospital. *Journal of Forensic Sciences, 41*, 56–59.

Hillbrand, M. (1995). Aggression against self and aggression against others in violent psychiatric patients. *Journal of Consulting and Clinical Psychology, 63*, 668–671.

Hodgins, S. (1983). A follow-up study of persons found incompetent to stand trial and/or not guilty by reason of insanity in Quebec. *International Journal of Law and Psychiatry, 6*, 399–411.

Hodgins, S. (1990). The prevalence of mental disorders among penitentiary inmates in Quebec. *Canada's Mental Health, 38*, 1–5.

Hodgins, S., & Cote, G. (1993). The criminality of mentally disordered offenders. *Criminal Justice and Behavior, 20*, 115–129.

Hoffman, P. B., & Beck, J. L. (1985). Recidivism among released federal prisoners: Salient factor score and five-year follow-up. *Criminal Justice and Behavior, 12*, 501–507.

Hollander, E., & Stein, D. J. (Eds.). (1995). *Impulsivity and aggression.* Toronto: Wiley.

Howell, D. C. (1992). *Statistical methods for psychology* (3rd ed.). Boston: PWS-Kent.

Inada, T., Minagawa, F., Iwashita, S., & Tokui, T. (1995). Mentally disordered criminal offenders: Five years' data from the Tokyo district public prosecutor's office. *International Journal of Law and Psychiatry, 18*, 221–230.

Junginger, J. (1990). Predicting compliance with command hallucinations. *American Journal of Psychiatry, 147*, 245–247.

Karson, C., & Bigelow, L. B. (1987). Violent behavior in schizophrenic inpatients. *Journal of Nervous and Mental Disease, 175*, 161–164.

Kay, S. R., Wolkenfeld, F., & Murrill, L. M. (1988). Profiles of aggression among psychiatric patients II: Covariates and predictors. *Journal of Nervous and Mental Disease, 176*, 547–557.

Kennedy, H. G., Kemp, L. I., & Dyer, D. E. (1992). Fear and anger in delusional (paranoid) disorder: The association with violence. *British Journal of Psychiatry, 160*, 488–492.

Klassen, D., & O'Connor, W. A. (1988a). Crime, inpatient admissions, and violence among male mental patients. *International Journal of Law and Psychiatry, 11*, 305–312.

Klassen, D., & O'Connor, W. A. (1988b). Predicting violence in schizophrenic and non-schizophrenic patients: A prospective study. *Journal of Community Psychology, 16*, 217–227.

Klassen, D., & O'Connor, W. A. (1988c). A prospective study of predictors of violence in adult male mental health admission. *Law and Human Behavior, 12,* 143–158.

Klassen, D., & O'Connor, W. A. (1989). Assessing the risk of violence in released mental patients: A cross-validation study. *Psychological Assessment: A Journal of Consulting and Clinical Psychology, 1,* 75–81.

Klassen, D., & O'Connor, W. A. (1994). Demographic and case history variables in risk assessment. In J. Monahan & H. J. Steadman (Eds.), *Violence and mental disorder: Developments in risk assessment* (pp. 229–258). Chicago, Ill: University of Chicago Press.

Kozol, H. L., Boucher, R. J., & Garofalo, R. F. (1972). The diagnosis and treatment of dangerousness. *Crime and Delinquency,* 371–392.

Krakowski, M. I., & Czobor, P. (1994). Clinical symptoms, neurological impairment, and prediction of violence in psychiatric inpatients. *Hospital and Community Psychiatry, 45,* 700–705.

Krakowski, M., Jaeger, J., & Volavka, J. (1988). Violence and psychopathology: A longitudinal study. *Comprehensive Psychiatry, 29,* 174–181.

Kropp, P. R., Hart, S. D., Webster, C. D., & Eaves, D. (1998). *Manual for the Spousal Assault Risk Assessment Guide* (3rd ed.). Toronto: Multi-Health Systems.

Lattimore, P. K., Visher, C. A., & Linster, R. L. (1995). Predicting rearrest for violence among serious youthful offenders. *Journal of Research in Crime and Delinquency, 32,* 54–83.

Lidz, C. W., Mulvey, E. P., & Gardner, W. (1993). The accuracy of predictions of violence to others. *Journal of the American Medical Association, 269,* 1007–1111.

Lindqvist, P., & Allebeck, P. (1990). Schizophrenia and crime: A longitudinal follow-up of 644 schizophrenics in Stockholm. *British Journal of Psychiatry, 157,* 345–350.

Link, B. G., Andrews, H., & Cullen, F. T. (1992). The violent and illegal behavior of mental patients reconsidered. *American Sociological Review, 57,* 275–292.

Link, B. G., & Cullen, F. T. (1986). Contact with the mentally ill and perceptions of how dangerous they are. *Journal of Health and Social Behavior, 27,* 289–303.

Link, B. G., & Stueve, A. (1994). Psychotic symptoms and the violent/illegal behavior of mental patients compared to community controls. In J. Monahan & H. J. Steadman (Eds.), *Violence and mental disorder: Developments in risk assessment* (pp. 137–159). Chicago, Ill: University of Chicago Press.

Lipari v. Sears, Roebuck and Company, 497 F. Supp. 185 (1980).

MacCulloch, M. J., Snowden, P. R., Wood, P. J. W., & Mills, H. E. (1983). Sadistic fantasy, sadistic behaviour, and offending. *British Journal of Psychiatry, 143,* 20–29.

McCorkle, R. C. (1993). Research note: Punish and rehabilitate? Public attitudes toward six common crimes. *Crime and Delinquency, 39,* 240–252.

McNiel, D. E., & Binder, R. L. (1989). Relationship between preadmission threats and later violent behavior by acute psychiatric inpatients. *Hospital and Community Psychiatry, 40,* 605–608.

McNiel, D. E., & Binder, R. L. (1994a). The relationship between acute psychiatric symptoms, diagnosis, and short-term risk of violence. *Hospital and Community Psychiatry, 45,* 133–137.

McNiel, D. E., & Binder, R. L. (1994b). Screening for risk of inpatient violence: Validation of an actuarial tool. *Law and Human Behavior, 18,* 579–586.

McNiel, D. E., & Binder, R. L. (1995). Correlates of accuracy in the assessment of psychiatric inpatients' risk of violence. *American Journal of Psychiatry, 152,* 901–906.

McNiel, D. E., & Binder, R. L., & Greenfield, T. K. (1988). Predictors of violence in civilly committed acute psychiatric patients. *American Journal of Psychiatry, 145,* 965–970.

Meehl, P. E. (1954). *Clinical versus statistical prediction.* Minneapolis, MN: University of Minnesota Press.

Megargee, E. I. (1976). The prediction of dangerous behavior. *Criminal Justice and Behavior, 3,* 3–22.

Megargee, E. I., Cook, P. E., & Mendelsohn, G. A. (1967). Development and evaluation of an MMPI scale of assaultiveness in overcontrolled individuals. *Journal of Abnormal Psychology, 72,* 519–528.

Menzies, R., & Webster, C. D. (1995). Construction and validation of risk assessments in a six-year follow-up of forensic patients: A tridimensional analysis. *Journal of Consulting and Clinical Psychology, 63,* 766–778.

Menzies, R. J., Webster, C. D., McMain, S., Staley, S., & Scaglione, R. (1994). The dimensions of dangerousness revisited: Assessing forensic predictions about violence. *Law and Human Behavior, 18,* 1–28.

Menzies, R. J., Webster, C. D., & Sepejak, D. S. (1985a). Hitting the forensic sound barrier: Predictions of dangerousness in a pre-trial psychiatric clinic. In C. D. Webster, M. H. Ben-Aron, & S. J. Hucker (Eds.), *Dangerousness: Probability and prediction, psychiatry and public policy* (pp. 115–143). New York: Cambridge University Press.

Menzies, R. J., Webster, C. D., & Sepejak, D. S. (1985b). The dimensions of dangerousness: Evaluating the accuracy of psychometric predictions of violence among forensic patients. *Law and Human Behavior, 9,* 35–56.

Metz, C. E. (1978). Basic principles of ROC analysis. *Seminars in Nuclear Medicine, 8,* 283–298.

Metz, C. E. (1984). Statistical analysis of ROC data in evaluating diagnostic performance. In D. E. Herbert & R. H. Myers (Eds.), *Multiple regression analysis: Applications in the health sciences* (pp. 365–384). Washington, DC: American Institute of Physics.

Miller, R. D. (1992). Need-for-treatment criteria for involuntary civil commitment: Impact in practice. *American Journal of Psychiatry, 149,* 1380–1384.

Mills, M. J., Sullivan, G., & Eth, S. (1987). Protecting third parties: A decade after Tarasoff. *American Journal of Psychiatry, 144,* 68–74.

Monahan, J. (1981). *Predicting violent behavior: An assessment of clinical techniques.* Beverly Hills, CA: Sage.

Monahan, J. (1984). The prediction of violent behavior: Toward a second generation of theory and policy. *American Journal of Psychiatry, 141,* 10–15.

Monahan, J. (1988). Risk assessment of violence among the mentally disordered: Generating useful knowledge. *International Journal of Law and Psychiatry, 11,* 249–257.

Monahan, J. (1992). Mental disorder and violent behavior. *American Psychologist, 47,* 511–521.

Monahan, J. (1996). Violence prediction: The last 20 and the next 20 years. *Criminal Justice and Behavior, 23,* 107–120.

Monahan, J., & Steadman, H. J. (1994a). Toward a rejuvenation of risk assessment research. In J. Monahan & H. J. Steadman (Eds.), *Violence and mental disorder: Developments in risk assessment* (pp. 1–17). Chicago, Ill: University of Chicago Press.

Monahan, J., & Steadman, H. J. (Eds.). (1994b). *Violence and mental disorder: Developments in risk assessment.* Chicago, Ill: University of Chicago Press.

Monahan, J., & Steadman, H. J. (1996). Violent storms and violent people: How meteorology can inform risk communication in mental health law. *American Psychologist, 51,* 931–938.

Mossman, D. (1994a). Assessing predictions of violence: Being accurate about accuracy. *Journal of Consulting and Clinical Psychology, 62,* 783–792.

Mossman, D. (1994b). Further comments on portraying the accuracy of violence predictions. *Law and Human Behavior, 18,* 587–594.

Mossman, D., & Somoza, E. (1991). ROC curves, test accuracy, and the description of diagnostic tests. *Journal of Neuropsychiatry and Clinical Neurosciences, 3,* 330–333.

Motiuk, L. (1996). Targeting employment patterns to reduce offender risk and need. *Forum on Corrections Research, 8,* 22–24.

Mulvey, E. P., & Lidz, C. W. (1995). Conditional prediction: A model for research on dangerousness to others in a new era. *International Journal of Law and Psychiatry, 18,* 129–143.
Mulvey, E. P., Shaw, E., & Lidz, C. W. (1994). Why use multiple sources in research on patient violence in the community? *Criminal Behaviour and Mental Health, 4,* 253–258.
National Parole Board of Canada. (1994). *Risk assessment training project.* Ottawa, Canada: Author.
Nicholls, T. L., Ogloff, J. R. P., & Douglas, K. S. (1997, August). Comparing risk assessments with female and male psychiatric outpatients: Utility of the HCR-20 and Psychopathy Checklist: Screening Version. In J. R. P. Ogloff (Chair) *Involuntary civil commitment— patient characteristics, review panel decision making, and risk assessment.* Symposium conducted at the annual convention of the American Psychological Association, Chicago.
Noble, P., & Rodger, S. (1989). Violence by psychiatric in-patients. *British Journal of Psychiatry, 155,* 384–390.
Novaco, R. W. (1994). Anger as a risk factor for violence among the mentally disordered. In J. Monahan & H. J. Steadman (Eds.), *Violence and mental disorder: Developments in risk assessment* (pp. 21–59). Chicago, Ill: University of Chicago Press.
Nuffield, J. (1982). *Parole decision-making in Canada: Research towards decision guidelines.* Ottawa: Ministry of Supply and Services Canada.
Ogloff, J. R. P. (1991). *The use of the insanity defense in British Columbia: A qualitative and quantitative analysis.* Ottawa: Canada.
Ogloff, J. R. P., & Douglas, K. S. (1995). *The treatment of high risk offenders: A literature review and analysis.* Completed under contract #19011-00-002. Ottawa, Canada: Department of Justice.
Ogloff, J. R. P., Wong, S., & Greenwood, A. (1991). Treating criminal psychopaths in a therapeutic community program. *Behavioral Sciences and the Law, 8,* 81–90.
Otto, R. K. (1992). Prediction of dangerous behavior: A review and analysis of "second-generation" research. *Forensic Reports, 5,* 103–133.
Overall, J. E., & Gorham, D. R. (1962). The brief psychiatric rating scale. *Psychological Reports, 10,* 799–812.
Palermo, G. B. (1994). Murder-suicide—an extended suicide. *International Journal of Offender Therapy and Comparative Criminology, 38,* 205–216.
Palmstierna, T., & Wistedt, B. (1989). Risk factors for aggressive behaviour are of limited value in predicting the violent behaviour of acute involuntarily admitted patients. *Acta Psychiatrica Scandinavica, 81,* 152–155.
Patterson, G. R., & Yoerger, K. (1993). Developmental models for delinquent behavior. In S. Hodgins (Ed.), *Mental disorder and crime* (pp. 140–172). London: Sage.
Peck v. Counseling Service of Addison County, 499 A.2d 422 (1985).
Pfohl, S. J. (1978). *Predicting dangerousness: The social construction of psychiatric reality.* Lexington, MA: Lexington Books.
Porporino, F. J., & Motiuk, L. L. (1995). The prison careers of mentally disordered offenders. *International Journal of Law and Psychiatry, 18,* 29–44.
Prentky, R. A., Knight, R. A., Lee, A. F. S., & Cerce, D. D. (1995). Predictive validity of lifestyle impulsivity for rapists. *Criminal Justice and Behavior, 22,* 106–128.
Quinsey, V. L., Maguire, A., & Varney, G. W. (1983). Assertion and overcontrolled hostility among mentally disordered murderers. *Journal of Consulting and Clinical Psychology, 51,* 550–556.
Quinsey, V. L., Rice, M. E., & Harris, G. T. (1995). Actuarial prediction of sexual recidivism. *Journal of Interpersonal Violence, 10,* 85–105.
Re Moore and the Queen, 10 C.C.C. (3d) 306 (1984).
Rice, M. E. (1997). Violent offender research and implications for the criminal justice system. *American Psychologist, 52,* 414–423.

Rice, M. E., & Harris, G. T. (1997). Cross-validation and extension of the Violence Risk Appraisal Guide for child molesters and rapists. *Law and Human Behavior, 21*, 231–241.

Rice, M. E., & Harris, G. T. (1995). Violent recidivism: Assessing predictive validity. *Journal of Consulting and Clinical Psychology, 63*, 737–748.

Rice, M. E., & Harris, G. T. (1992). A comparison of criminal recidivism among schizophrenic and nonschizophrenic offenders. *International Journal of Law and Psychiatry, 15*, 397–408.

Rice, M. E., Harris, G. T., & Cormier, C. A. (1992). The evaluation of a maximum security therapeutic community for psychopaths and other mentally disordered offenders. *Law and Human Behavior, 16*, 399–412.

Rice, M. E., Harris, G. T., Lang, C., & Bell, V. (1990, Fall–Winter). Recidivism among male insanity acquittees. *Journal of Psychiatry and Law*, 379–403.

Rice, M. E., Harris, G. T., Quinsey, V. L., & Cry, M. (1990). Planning treatment programs in secure psychiatric facilities. In D. N. Weisstub (Ed.), *Law and mental health: International perspectives* (vol. 5) (pp. 162–230). New York: Permagon Press.

Rice, M. E., Quinsey, V. L., & Houghton, R. (1990). Predicting treatment outcome and recidivism among patients in a maximum security token economy. *Behavioral Sciences and the Law, 8*, 313–326.

Roberts, J. V., & Doob, A. N. (1990). News media influences on public views of sentencing. *Law and Human Behavior, 14*, 451–468.

Robins, L. N., Tipp, J., & Przybeck, T. (1991). Antisocial personality. In L. N. Robins & D. Reiger (Eds.), *Psychiatric disorders in America* (pp. 258–290). New York: Free Press.

Roesch, R., Ogloff, J. R. P., Hart, S. D., Dempster, R. J., Zapf, P. A., & Whittemore, K. (1997). The impact of Canadian Criminal Code changes on assessments of fitness to stand trial and criminal responsibility. *Canadian Journal of Psychiatry, 42*, 509–514.

Rogers, R., Gillis, J. R., Turner, R. E., & Frise-Smith, T. (1990). The clinical presentation of command hallucinations in a forensic population. *American Journal of Psychiatry, 147*, 1304–1307.

Rogers, R., Nussbaum, D., & Gillis, R. (1988). Command hallucinations and criminality: A clinical quandary. *Bulletin of the American Academy of Psychiatry and the Law, 16*, 251–258.

Ross, D. J., Hart, S. D., & Webster, C. D. (1998). *Facts and fates: Prediction and management of hospital and community aggression using the HCR-20*. Unpublished manuscript.

Rossi, A. M., Jacobs, M., Monteleone, M., Olsen, R., Surber, R. W., Winkler, E. L., Wommack, A. (1986). Characteristics of psychiatric patients who engage in assaultive or other fear-inducing behaviors. *Journal of Nervous and Mental Disease, 174*, 154–160.

Salekin, R. T., Rogers, R., & Sewell, K. W. (1996). A review and meta-analysis of the Psychopathy Checklist and Psychopathy Checklist—Revised: Predictive validity of dangerousness. *Clinical Psychology: Science and Practice, 3*, 203–215.

Saunders, D. G. (1992). Woman battering. In R. T. Ammerman & M. Hersen (Eds.), *Assessment of family violence: A clinical and legal sourcebook* (pp. 208–235). New York: Wiley.

Schall v. Martin, 104 S.Ct. 2403 (1984).

Selby, M. J. (1984). Assessment of violence potential using measures of anger, hostility, and social desirability. *Journal of Personality Assessment, 48*, 531–543.

Sepejak, D., Menzies, R. J., Webster, C. D., & Jensen, F. A. S. (1983). Clinical predictions of dangerousness: Two-year follow-up of 408 pre-trial forensic cases. *Bulletin of the American Academy of Psychiatry and the Law, 11*, 171–181.

Serin, R. C. (1991). Psychopathy and violence in criminals. *Journal of Interpersonal Violence, 6*, 423–431.

Serin, R. C., & Amos, N. L. (1995). The role of psychopathy in the assessment of dangerousness. *International Journal of Law and Psychiatry, 18*, 231–238.

Sexual Predator Act. (1994). Kan. Stat. Ann. §59-29a01 to -29a15.

Sexually Violent Predator Act. (1991). Wash. Rev. Code Ann. §71.09.010-71.09.902 (West 1975 & Supp.).

Shaffer, C. E., Waters, W. F., & Adams, S. G. (1994). Dangerousness: Assessing the risk of violent behavior. *Journal of Consulting and Clinical Psychology, 62*, 1064–1068.

Shah, S. A. (1978). Dangerousness and mental illness: Some conceptual, prediction and policy dilemmas. In C. Frederick (ed.), *Dangerous behavior: A problem in law and mental health* (NIMH DHEW Publication No (ADM) 78-563, pp. 153–191). Washington, DC: Superintendent of Documents, U.S. Government Printing Office.

Silva, J. A., Leong, G. B., & Weinstock, R. (1992). The dangerousness of persons with misidentification syndromes. *Bulletin of the American Academy of Psychiatry and the Law, 20*, 77–86.

Skaggs, C. C. (1995). Kansas' sexual predator act and the impact of expert predictions: Psyched out by the *Daubert* test. *Washburn Law Journal, 34*, 320–344.

Skinner, B. F. (1953). *Science and human behavior.* New York: Macmillan.

Slaby, R. G., & Guerra, N. G. (1988). Cognitive mediators of aggression in adolescent offenders: I. Assessment. *Developmental Psychology, 24*, 580–588.

Smith, C., & Thornberry, T. P. (1995). The relationship between childhood maltreatment and adolescent involvement in delinquency. *Criminology, 33*, 451–481.

Snyder, S., Pitts, W. M., & Pokorny, A. D. (1986). Selected behavioral features of patients with borderline personality traits. *Suicide and Life-Threatening Behavior, 16*, 28–39.

Stall, B. (1994). Reason to be afraid. *Vancouver Sun.* July 19, A14.

Steadman, H. J., & Cocozza, J. J. (1974). *Careers of the criminally insane: Excessive social control of deviance.* Lexington, MA: Lexington Books.

Steadman, H. J., & Felson, R. B. (1984). Self-reports of violence. *Criminology, 22*, 321–342.

Steadman, H. J., Monahan, J., Appelbaum, P. S., Grisso, T., Mulvey, E. P., Roth, L. H., Robbins, P. C., & Klassen, D. (1994). Designing a new generation of risk assessment research. In J. Monahan & H. J. Steadman (Eds.), *Violence and mental disorder: Developments in risk assessment* (pp. 297–318). Chicago, Ill: University of Chicago Press.

Steadman, H. J., Mulvey, E., Monahan, J., Robbins, P. C., Appelbaum, P. S., Grisso, T., Roth, L. H., & Silver, E. (1998). Violence by people discharged from acute psychiatric inpatient facilities and by others in the same neighborhoods. *Archives of General Psychiatry, 55*, 393–401.

Stone, A. A. (1985). The new legal standard of dangerousness: Fair in theory, unfair in practice. In C. D. Webster, M. H. Ben-Aron, & S. J. Hucker (Eds.), *Dangerousness: Probability and prediction, psychiatry and public policy* (pp. 13–24). New York: Cambridge University Press.

Strand, S., Belfrage, H., Fransson, G., & Levander, S. (in press). Clinical and risk management factors in risk prediction of mentally disordered offenders: More important that actuarial data? *Legal and Criminological Psychology.*

Stuart, E. P., & Campbell, J. C. (1989). Assessment of patterns of dangerousness with battered women. *Issues in Mental Health Nursing, 10*, 245–260.

Swanson, J. W. (1994). Mental disorder, substance abuse, and community violence: An epidemiological approach. In J. Monahan & H. J. Steadman (Eds.), *Violence and mental disorder: Developments in risk assessment* (pp. 101–136). Chicago, Ill: University of Chicago Press.

Swanson, J., Borum, R., Swartz, M., & Monahan, J. (1996). Psychotic symptoms and disorders and the risk of violent behavior in the community. *Criminal Behaviour and Mental Health, 6*, 317–338.

Tanke, E. D., & Yesavage, J. A. (1985). Characteristics of assaultive patients who do and do not provide visible cues of potential violence. *American Journal of Psychiatry, 142*, 1409–1413.

Tarasoff v. Regents of the University of California, 551 P2d. 334 (1976).

Taylor, P. J. (1985). Motives for offending among violent and psychotic men. *British Journal of Psychiatry, 147*, 491–498.

Taylor, P. J. (1986). Psychiatric disorder in London's life-sentenced offenders. *British Journal of Criminology, 26*, 63–78.

Teplin, L. A. (1984). Criminalizing mental disorder: The comparative arrest rate of the mentally ill. *American Psychologist, 39*, 794–803.

Teplin, L. A. (1990). The prevalence of severe mental disorder among male urban jail detainees: Comparison with the epidemiologic catchment area program. *American Journal of Public Health, 80*, 663–669.

Teplin, L. A., Abram, K. M., & McClelland, G. M. (1994). Does psychiatric disorder predict violent crime among released jail detainees? *American Psychologist, 49*, 335–342.

Thompson, J. S., Stuart, G. L., & Holden, C. E. (1992). Command hallucinations and legal insanity. *Forensic Reports, 5*, 29–43.

Thornberry, T. P., & Jacoby, J. E. (1979). *The criminally insane: A community follow-up of mentally ill offenders.* Chicago, Ill: University of Chicago Press.

Tiihonen, J., & Hakola, P. (1994). Psychiatric disorders and homicide recidivism. *American Journal of Psychiatry, 151*, 436–438.

United States Department of Health and Human Services. (1991). *Healthy people 2000: National health promotion and disease prevention objectives.* Washington, DC: U.S. Government Printing Office.

United States v. Salerno, 481 U.S. 739 (1987).

Webster, C. D., Dickens, B. M., & Addario, S. M. (1985). *Constructing dangerousness: Scientific, legal and policy implications.* Toronto, Ontario: University of Toronto Centre of Criminology.

Webster, C. D., Douglas, K. S., Eaves, D., & Hart, S. D. (1997a). *HCR-20: Assessing risk for violence* (Version 2). Vancouver, British Columbia, Canada: Mental Health, Law, and Policy Institute, Simon Fraser University.

Webster, C. D., Douglas, K. S., Eaves, D., & Hart, S. (1997b). Assessing risk of violence to others. In C. D. Webster & M. A. Jackson (Eds.), *Impulsivity: Perspectives, principles, and practice* (pp. 251–277). New York: Guilford.

Webster, C. D., Eaves, D., Douglas, K. S., & Wintrup, A. (1995). *The HCR-20 scheme: The assessment of dangerousness and risk.* Vancouver: Simon Fraser University and Forensic Psychiatry Services Commission of British Columbia.

Webster, C. D., Harris, G. T., Rice, M. E., Cormier, C., & Quinsey, V. L. (1994). *The violence prediction scheme: Assessing dangerousness in high risk men.* Toronto: University of Toronto: Centre of Criminology.

Webster, C. D., Hucker, S. J., & Grossman, M. G. (1993). Clinical programmes for mentally ill offenders. In K. Howells & C. R. Hollin (Eds.), *Clinical approaches to the mentally disordered offender* (pp. 87–109). Chichester, UK: Wiley.

Webster, C. D., & Jackson, M. A. (Eds.), *Impulsivity: Theory, assessment, and treatment.* New York: Guilford.

Webster, C. D., & Polvi, N. (1995). Challenging assessments of dangerousness and risk. In J. Zisken & D. Faust (Eds.), *Coping with psychiatric and psychological testimony* (5th ed., Vol. 2, pp. 1371–1399). Los Angeles: Law and Psychology Press.

Webster, C. D., Sepejak, D. S., Menzies, R. J., Slomen, D. J., Jensen, F. A. S., & Butler, B. T. (1984). The reliability and validity of dangerous behavior predictions. *Bulletin of the American Academy of Psychiatry and the Law, 12*, 41–50.

Welsh, W. N., & Gordon, A. (1991). Cognitive mediators of aggression: Test of a causal model. *Criminal Justice and Behavior, 18*, 125–145.

Wessely, S. C., Castle, D., Douglas, A. J., & Taylor, P. T. (1994). The criminal careers of incident cases of schizophrenia. *Psychological Medicine, 24*, 483–502.

Williamson, S., Hare, R. D., & Wong, S. (1987). Violence: Criminal psychopaths and their victims. *Canadian Journal of Behavioural Sciences, 19,* 454–462.

Wintrup, A. (1996). *Assessing risk of violence in mentally disordered offenders with the HCR-20.* Unpublished master's thesis, Simon Fraser University, Burnaby, British Columbia, Canada.

Yarvis, R. M. (1990). Axis I and axis II diagnostic parameters of homicide. *Bulletin of the American Academy of Psychiatry and the Law, 18,* 249–269.

7

Forensic Treatment

A Review of Programs and Research

KIRK HEILBRUN AND PATRICIA GRIFFIN

The field of forensic treatment has received relatively little attention in the research and practice literature. Although this is particularly true for forensic treatment delivered in the community (Heilbrun & Griffin, 1993, 1998), it is also apparent that the entire area of forensic treatment has received far less attention than has forensic assessment (Ogloff, Roberts, & Roesch, 1993).

In this chapter, we will begin by discussing definitional issues surrounding the terms forensic, treatment, jurisdiction, setting, and outcome. Next, we will review the existing literature on forensic treatment, concentrating in particular on empirical studies. From these results and other descriptions of various forensic treatment programs and the process of forensic treatment, we will draw implications for standards of treatment. When the literature is clear in a given area, we will describe a standard as established. When there is disagreement or relatively little information, but it appears that a standard may be developing, we will describe it as emerging. Finally, we will discuss the implications of these findings on forensic treatment for three areas: policy, clinical practice, and need for further research.

KIRK HEILBRUN AND PATRICIA GRIFFIN • Department of Clinical and Health Psychology, Law–Psychology Program, Allegheny University of the Health Sciences, and School of Law, Villanova University, Philadelphia, Pennsylvania 19102-1192. PATRICIA GRIFFIN • 8503 Flourtown Avenue, Wyndmoor, Pennsylvania 19038.

Psychology and Law: The State of the Discipline, edited by Ronald Roesch, Stephen D. Hart, and James R. P. Ogloff. Kluwer Academic/Plenum Publishers, New York, 1999.

DEFINITION AND METHOD

FORENSIC

The phrase "mentally disordered offender" has been used to describe individuals in the following categories: (a) Incompetent to Stand Trial (IST), (b) Not Guilty by Reason of Insanity (NGRI), (c) Mentally Disordered Sex Offender, and (d) Mentally Ill (jail or prison) Inmate transferred to a secure treatment facility (Monahan & Steadman, 1983; Steadman, Monahan, Hartstone, Davis, & Robbins, 1982). Others have offered definitions that have expanded on these categories (e.g., "to be evaluated for trial competence") and included other categories as well (e.g., "defective delinquent") (Kerr & Roth, 1986). In the present chapter, our definition of "forensic" will include the categories of Incompetent to Stand Trial, Not Guilty by Reason of Insanity, and Mentally Ill Inmate Transfer. This last category will be fairly broad because it has a different meaning according to setting and jurisdiction. In Great Britain, for example, a recent treatment review has included (a) those showing the "coincidence of mental disorder and antisocial behavior" as well as (b) mentally disordered individuals in any legal context, as affected by that law (Eastman, 1993). In such cases, we will come as close as possible to describing the treatment of the individuals in our three selected categories. At times, this will be impossible because the treatment of forensic patients in some settings involves a high degree of integration with the treatment of nonforensic patients. We will not discuss the treatment of sexual offenders, inmates without mental disorder (or those treated in population of jail or prison), or juveniles, as each has a sizeable and distinct literature that we could not hope to include without greatly expanding the length of this chapter.

TREATMENT

We will consider treatment services of three kinds: traditional, contemporary, and targeted. *Traditional* mental health treatment services involve standard kinds of mental health interventions (such as diagnostic assessment for treatment planning purposes, medication, milieu therapy, and group and individual therapy for inpatients; medication, case management, and group and individual therapy for outpatients) that might be delivered to nonforensic or forensic patients in need of mental health intervention. *Contemporary* treatment services include psychoeducational, skills-based services, and behavioral interventions comprising approaches, such as psychosocial rehabilitation, that have become increasingly well regarded during the last 10 years in the United States. Finally, *targeted* treatment services include those interventions that are designed to address functional deficits relevant to legal standards (such as anger control or impulse control relevant to nonviolent, responsible behavior required for legal compliance with conditional release criteria).

JURISDICTION

Forensic treatment is directly affected by the law of the jurisdiction in which it occurs. Particularly relevant are statutes and administrative codes pertaining to hospital commitment and release; such standards are important in determining who is hospitalized, who has the authority to make the decision to hospitalize, and for what legal status, how long, and under what conditions will hospitalized persons return to the community. Furthermore, if there is a provision within the law for conditional release, this provision is also relevant to the conditions to which a released individual must conform in the community and the potential consequences for violating such conditions.

Clearly, then, it is important to consider the particular jurisdiction within which the forensic treatment takes place. Beyond making this point and specifying the jurisdiction when discussing a particular program, however, the scope of this chapter limits us from a more detailed analysis. Because we will review examples of treatment programs in the United States, Canada, the United Kingdom, and the Netherlands, such a discussion would entail addressing the structure of legal systems as they differ across countries and varying standards within different areas of the same country. Although this cannot be done here, we will offer examples of how the law of a particular jurisdiction can affect a given treatment program.

SETTING

The next relevant consideration in a review of forensic treatment involves the setting in which that treatment is delivered. In this chapter, we will consider the following settings: hospital (high security and medium-to-low security), prison, and the community (conditional release and parole or probation). We will provide examples of treatment programs in each of these settings and discuss important considerations and standards for how forensic treatment might differ according to the setting in which it is delivered.

Outcomes

Finally, we will consider the goals for forensic treatment in the following categories: (a) *clinical* (focused on remission of symptoms and improvement in overall functioning), (b) *legal* (designed to specifically address functional deficits that are directly relevant to legal standards), and (c) *hybrid* (designed to improve both clinical symptomatology and functional deficits). This will be a useful way of considering treatment goals (and, if available, treatment outcome data). It is certainly true that a single program may offer different forms of treatment that would be considered differently using these criteria. One of our purposes in discussing treatment goals and outcomes using these dimensions, however, is to address the question of the extent to which published descriptions of forensic treatment involve traditional treatment (i.e., clinical) in specialized settings, and the extent to which programs have integrated legal standards into treatment goal setting by incorporating forms of treatment that directly address functional deficits (i.e., legal) or address both symptomatology and deficits (i.e., hybrid).

EMPIRICAL INVESTIGATIONS OF FORENSIC TREATMENT

Hospital Settings

Much of the available empirical and descriptive information on hospital-based forensic treatment has been described in a 1993 special issue of the *International Journal of Law and Psychiatry* (Poythress, 1993). Many of the descriptions in this section were published in that special issue.

Great Britain

Inpatient treatment to forensic patients in Great Britain is provided in Special Hospitals. A recent description (Eastman, 1993) provided a breakdown of the categories under which the 1,740 British Special Hospital patients were committed: (a) 61% were detained as mentally ill, (b) 25% were detained as psychopathic disorder, (c) 9% were detained as mentally impaired, and (d) 4% were detained as severely mentally ill. One noteworthy aspect of these categories involves the psychopathic disorder classification. This apparently includes a variety of personality disorders—it is not limited to the North American conception of psychopathy—but does mean that there is an explicit commitment category for individuals who do not suffer from severe mental illness. Not surprisingly, individuals with "psychopathic disorders" have often proved difficult to treat and tend to remain hospitalized for longer periods of time. For example, among male patients admitted to Broadmoor between 1982 and 1984 ($N = 187$), 25% of those with a psychopathic disorder were discharged within 4 years, while 53% remained after 8 years. Longer length of stay was associated with more violent offenses and a greater likelihood of having committed a sexual offense. By contrast, 41% of patients with "mental illness" were discharged within 4 years, while 42% remained after 8 years (Dell, Robertson, & Parker, 1988).

Treatment outcome was evaluated by using rearrest following hospital discharge. Thus, approximately 50% of psychopaths reoffended within 3 years, with half of these rearrests for violent offenses. Approximately two thirds of the "mentally impaired" (mentally retarded) individuals were also reconvicted following hospital discharge (Bartlett, 1993).

United States

ATASCADERO STATE HOSPITAL (CALIFORNIA). Several model forensic hospital treatment programs were described in the 1993 issue of the *International Journal of Psychiatry*, the first being the program at Atascadero State Hospital in California (Marques, Haynes, & Nelson, 1993).[1] Atascadero serves patients in different legal categories. The first category is NGRI (173 patients, which constituted 20% of the total hospital census and 8% of annual admissions to the hospital); NGRI acquittees had a reported mean length of stay of 2.8 years on discharge.[2] The second category is Mentally Ill Inmates (346 patients, constituting 39% of census and 34% of the annual admissions, with a mean length of stay of 1.1 years). Those in this category were convicted inmates transferred from a Department of Corrections

---

[1]It should be noted that much of the forensic treatment in California has recently shifted from Atascadero to Patton State Hospital (A. Wursten, personal communication, August, 1995).

[2]An omnipresent problem in calculating length of stay for populations confined for indeterminate periods is the issue of whether only those patients who have been discharged should be included in the calculations (which has the effect of underestimating length of stay because those who have been hospitalized for very long periods of time are not included), or whether the entire population should be considered (which introduces the difficulty of how to consider those patients who have been recently admitted as well as those hospitalized for a long period). The least problematic solution to this problem is for the researcher to calculate and report length of hospital stay figures for three separate groups: (a) individuals who have been discharged, (b) recently admitted patients who have been hospitalized for less than the modal length of hospitalization, and (c) individuals who have been hospitalized longer than the modal period. Unfortunately, this is rarely done; length of stay figures are typically calculated only from the first subgroup, with no discussion of the problems associated with using only this figure.

facility, not mentally ill individuals transferred from local jails.[3] The third category, Incompetent to Stand Trial defendants, was composed of 230 patients with a mean length of stay of 6 months. This total was described as 26% of the daily census; IST individuals were 47% of the annual admissions. Following revocation of a 1981 California law, Atascadero no longer received committed Mentally Disordered Sex Offenders. However, a total of 33 such individuals remained (4% of census, with a mean length of stay of 3.0 years). Mentally Disordered Offenders, who are end-of-sentence inmates ($N = 15$, 2% of annual admissions) are individuals committed to Atascadero after getting out of prison who are (a) mentally ill, (b) convicted of a violent offense, and (c) will not stay in remission without treatment. Finally, the Sex Offender Treatment and Evaluation Project, a federally funded treatment project for sexual offenders, included 40 patients (5% of census and 2% of annual admissions, with a mean length of stay of 1.9 years).

Primary diagnoses for patients at Atascadero include a large majority (70%) of major mental disorders (schizophrenia, affective disorders, and other psychoses). The primary offense for Atascadero patients was typically (72%) an offense against persons, a much higher figure than the base rate for this category within the California Department of Corrections (DOC) (45%). Conversely, property offenses were underrepresented among Atascadero patients relative to DOC inmates (16% vs. 30%, respectively) as were drug offenses (4% vs. 22%).

Treatment services in different areas were described. Traditional clinical services included medication and family therapy, while contemporary clinical services included (a) cognitive restructuring, biofeedback, and psychoeducation and retraining in memory and attention for neurologically impaired individuals; (b) social and independent living skills training for chronically psychotic individuals; and (c) substance abuse treatment in three phases—dependency, recovery, and relapse—taking

---

[3]Whether a forensic hospital accepts jail transfers (i.e., mentally ill jail inmates in need of acute hospitalization) can have a great impact on the nature of the treatment provided by that hospital and also on the larger system. For example, the state of Virginia has a provision for transferring mentally ill jail inmates to a secure forensic hospital for acute hospitalization, while the state of Florida does not. Our experience in both of these states suggests that the high rate of Virginia jail transfer admissions (typically 600–700 admissions yearly to a unit with an average daily census of 150), even with the short length of stay for most of these mentally ill inmates (modal period of hospitalizations between 8 and 10 days), had the effect of sharply decreasing the number of Incompetent for Trial admissions. Florida, by contrast, had no jail transfer provision for violent felons. Since the only pretrial mechanism for getting a mentally ill inmate transferred to a forensic hospital was adjudication as Incompetent to Stand Trial, this was a far more frequent kind of admission in Florida than Virginia.

about 9 months to complete. Targeted legal treatment services included behavioral approaches to restoring trial competence, including role playing and mock trials. Finally, targeted hybrid treatment, addressing both symptoms and legally relevant deficits, included conditional release aftercare as part of the Conditional Release Program (CONREP), the California approach since 1986 to monitoring insanity acquittees in the community.

THE CENTER FOR FORENSIC PSYCHIATRY (MICHIGAN). Michigan's Center for Forensic Psychiatry (Clark, Holden, Thompson, Watson, & Wightman, 1993) serves populations in several legal categories. First, they perform outpatient evaluations of defendants' competence to stand trial and criminal responsibility, performing 1,228 such evaluations in 1986.[4] Second, they admit and treat defendants who have been adjudicated incompetent to stand trial (there were 286 such admissions in 1986, with an average of 62 IST defendants, constituting 40% of the census, present at the time of the article). Third, they admit and treat defendants who have been found NGRI, with an average monthly census of 74 NGRI acquittees being treated following commitment.

No explicit philosophy of, or orientation to, treatment is described at the Center for Forensic Psychiatry. Treatment approaches include those that we would classify as traditional clinical services: milieu therapy, individual and group therapy, activities therapy, and seclusion/restraint. They also include services that might be considered as contemporary hybrids: more time-limited, educationally focused services delivered to IST defendants and case management and broader rehabilitative services to NGRI acquittees. No formal attempt to assess treatment outcomes are described, although length of stay data are available.

KIRBY FORENSIC PSYCHIATRIC CENTER (NEW YORK). Kirby's Forensic Psychiatric Center, as described by Wack (1993), is similar to Michigan's

---

[4]Forensic hospitals often make a distinction between "outpatient" evaluations, which involve bringing the defendant to the hospital in the custody of the authorities and having them remain up to a day while seeing one or more staff members as part of the evaluation process; however, these defendants are not admitted to the hospital. Inpatient evaluations, by contrast, involve formal admission to the hospital; may involve a length of stay of many days, depending on the nature of the evaluation; and also require formal admissions procedures and counting that individual on the hospital's census. Both outpatient and inpatient evaluation are inefficient ways of delivering forensic assessment services (see Grisso, Cocozza, Steadman, Fisher, & Green, 1994) when mental health professionals in the community are able to deliver comparable services, but inpatient evaluations are particularly inefficient. One of the consequences of such practices is that staff resources that could otherwise be devoted to treatment are diverted to evaluation, weakening the program's overall capacity to deliver relevant treatment services.

Forensic Center in two of the primary categories of patients it serves: those who are IST (61%), and those who are NGRI (23%). Although Kirby apparently does not provide outpatient forensic evaluations, they do offer services to patients in two additional categories: civilly committed without charges (10%) and unrestorably IST (6%). Before describing specific treatment services, Wack offered several overarching principles that are used to guide service delivery. An explicit attempt is made to integrate security and treatment needs. A therapeutic community model is employed. Each patient is involved in a minimum of 20 hours of weekly treatment under the provisions of New York law. Issues of the limits of confidentiality and informed consent are addressed with each patient on admission. There is an attempt to provide such explanations and subsequent services in ways that are culturally and ethnically sensitive.

Treatment planning is facilitated by diagnostic evaluation, as is customary in such secure inpatient settings. An unusual aspect of treatment planning, however, is an explicit assessment of the risk of future violence toward others that includes (a) a history of the types, characteristics, frequency, patterns, and victims of past violence; (b) risk-enhancing and -reducing environmental and situational factors; and (c) current functioning and mental state in light of these two areas, yielding an estimate of current risk.

Treatment services include some that would be described as traditional clinical, such as medication, educational services, vocational training, and recreational activities. They also include services that would be classified as contemporary hybrids, such as cognitive-behavioral groups and skills groups on a variety of topics: AIDS education, parenting, activities in daily living, and substance abuse treatment, among them. Finally, Kirby offers targeted legal services, such as competency training groups.

One final aspect of the treatment program at Kirby that clearly facilitates program development is the ongoing evaluation of programs through research. Kirby has a formal research component, sharing two forensically trained researchers with the Nathan Kline Institute for Psychiatric Research, a joint venture of the New York Office of Mental Health and New York University.

TAYLOR HARDIN SECURE MEDICAL FACILITY (ALABAMA).   Taylor Hardin is a forensic hospital in Alabama that is smaller than other inpatient forensic hospitals described earlier, consistent with the needs of Alabama. As described by Dixon and Rivenbank (1993), it has 100 beds; patients are designated as being in either evaluation or treatment status, with the great majority (over 87% between 1982 and 1987) being admissions for pretrial evaluations. Over 90% of such evaluations addressed the issues of competence to stand trial and mental state at the time of the offense. Among the patients who are admitted in the treatment category are included those who are IST, NGRI, or DOC transfers.

Like Kirby, Taylor Hardin provides a formal approach to assessing future violence risk for patients who might be transferred or released to a less secure setting. This approach, called Violent Behavior Analysis (VBA), involves the administration of a semistructured interview (in conjunction with a record review) focusing on previous acts of violence. The VBA is administered just prior to a transfer or possible release.[5]

Treatment services in various categories are described. Among the traditional clinical services offered are medication and reality orientation group. Contemporary clinical services include mental illness awareness group and relaxation training. Among the contemporary hybrids are social skills training group, medication education group, substance abuse group, and reality therapy group. Adult basic education, which might be described as a traditional hybrid service, is also provided; finally, one targeted legal service—competency education group—is offered. No treatment outcome data were provided as part of this description.

NORRISTOWN STATE HOSPITAL (PENNSYLVANIA).   In an evaluation of a skills-based treatment program for incompetent for trial defendants, Siegel and Elwork (1990) compared results obtained from random assignment with either the experimental or the control condition. Didactic information about court procedures and the roles of courtroom personnel, as well as a problem-solving task that was relevant to each participant's case, were components of the treatment condition. Significant differences were noted on relevant knowledge and the percentages of each group considered competent by hospital staff after 45 days, suggesting that *targeted legal*

---

[5]An adaptation of the Violent Behavior Analysis, which was developed by Norman Poythress while he was clinical director at Taylor Hardin, has been used in Virginia. Renamed the Analysis of Aggressive Behavior (AAB), it is used (like the VBA) with NGRI acquittees to assess the appropriateness of a possible transfer or conditional release by attempting to determine whether significant risk factors for violence toward others are still present. However, unlike the VBA, Virginia's AAB is administered immediately following admission, so that risk factors may be addressed in treatment and planning throughout hospitalization as well as around the time of transfer or release. An updated version of the AAB is obtained when such transfer is considered, so that decision makers can assess the progress that has been made in addressing risk factors and, hence, reducing the risk of future violent behavior.

treatment services could have significant value for increasing relevant knowledge and decreasing length of hospitalization for IST defendants.

Canada

QUEBEC. There are three levels of hospitals for treating mentally disordered offenders in Quebec, as described by Hodgins (1993). The first is the secure psychiatric hospital, which includes inpatient beds, aftercare, and psychiatric services. The second is the nonsecure psychiatric hospital; the third is the general hospital.[6] What we have described as traditional clinical services are delivered in nonsecure psychiatric and general hospitals. Hodgins notes that aggressive behavior, risk, criminal history, and alcohol/drug use are rarely considered in such settings. Nonetheless, NGRI and unfit defendants are often treated in general hospitals, with the court making the decision about placement.

The secure hospital in this system is the Institut Philippe Pinel in Montreal. Like some of the other hospitals discussed (e.g., Taylor Hardin in Alabama), Pinel performs inpatient evaluations of fitness to stand trial and criminal responsibility; in addition, it also evaluates sentencing options. Treatment is provided to individuals who are unfit or NGRI and to some NGRI acquittees who were previously released from Pinel and are readmitted on a voluntary basis.[7] Traditional clinical services include medication and education. Contemporary hybrid services, such as vocational training, social skills and life skills training, stress management, and sex education, are also offered. Aftercare for discharged patients is always available. A more recent move involves typically making such services

---

[6]This system for delivering forensic treatment services is not unique to Canada and may appear unusual when compared with some of the other programs described in this chapter (as a function of the authors' choice to describe the larger system rather than a single hospital). This does raise an important point, however. Forensic treatment services are not delivered exclusively in secure hospitals. It is informative to consider the range of facilities across the entire forensic system in which services are delivered to obtain a representative view of forensic treatment in a given jurisdiction.

[7]One of the system-level characteristics of a forensic treatment system concerns the extent of control that is exercised over NGRI acquittees after they have left a secure psychiatric setting. The option of conditional release, which is available in some jurisdictions, allows the decision maker to release an acquittee to a less secure setting but still retain the authority to monitor that individual's performance in a number of important areas. For those who violate conditions of conditional release involuntary rehospitalization may be implemented. The voluntary rehospitalization option is rarely available, in our experience, but deserves consideration. It would allow an acquittee who is experiencing problems with his or her mental state to enter a hospital staffed with mental health professionals who know his or her history and treatment needs. More efficient treatment and a shorter period of rehospitalization might be the result.

mandatory, enforcing compliance with their conditions through keeping the warrant in place.

Satellite services in this jurisdiction are offered through the Centre de Psychiatrie Legale de Montreal (CPLM), located in the center of the city, not at Philippe Pinel. In 1990, a total of 231 new files (23% court ordered, the remainder voluntary) and referrals from probation and parole (46% of overall total) were served. It was rare to receive referrals from family, or self-referrals (only 9% of the total were in this category). The CPLM provided consultation to the Montreal jail and also ran a Dangerousness Clinic featuring multidisciplinary team consultation and workshops. No treatment outcome data are provided as part of this description.

PENETANGUISHENE MENTAL HEALTH CENTRE (ONTARIO).   The program at the forensic hospital at Penetanguishene, as described by Rice and Harris (1993), differed in one significant way from the programs described thus far—in its use of empirical data to reorganize, plan, and develop treatment services for forensic inpatients. During the years 1986–1987, the hospital underwent a reorganization that was based on the administration of a 70-item checklist addressing the problems experienced (both in the hospital and in the community) by each of the 189 patients hospitalized at that time. The information obtained through this approach revealed many serious, important problems that were not traditional psychiatric symptoms and could best be addressed by teaching skills in relevant areas. Cluster analysis was used to simplify the overall patient population into clinically homogeneous subgroups; these subgroups were then used in making recommendations for clinical and administrative reorganization (Rice & Harris, 1988).

In 1991, Oak Ridge (the inpatient forensic hospital at Penetanguishene) had a census of 122 (with 77 NGRI acquittees, 13 unfit defendants, 28 prison transfers, and 4 individuals to be assessed). Four units were functioning: (a) a behavior therapy unit (using a token economy, but other treatment largely eclectic), (b) a social management unit (higher functioning, nonassaultive patients), (c) a rehabilitation unit (with many who refuse treatment participation, including much individual therapy, skills training, and vocational training), and (d) a forensic assessment unit (for newly admitted patients and pretrial evaluations). Some traditional clinical services (such as medication, individual therapy, and group therapy) were provided across all four units. There were also a number of treatment modalities that would be considered contemporary hybrids (e.g., token economies, skills training, and vocational training). As well, the empirically based organization of the hospital was very unusual, and commendable, among forensic inpatient treatment programs.

Furthermore, the treatment appeared to be well integrated with the other necessary components of inpatient forensic programs, assessment and decision making. Although the committing court made the decision about who would be admitted to Oak Ridge, the hospital was organized so that much of the forensic assessment and treatment-planning was done early in the hospital stay on a single unit. There was also a review board that had ultimate responsibility within the hospital for release decisions. The hospital's organizational structure seemed to lend itself easily to tracking an individual's progress through the evaluation process, treatment at different levels of progress, and (ultimately) the request for release. Finally, it should be noted that although no treatment outcome data were offered as part of this article, the researchers based at Penetanguishene have been quite active in publishing data relevant to treatment outcome and recidivism (e.g., Rice & Harris, 1995).

One intriguing example involved their retrospective evaluation of a therapeutic community, a peer-operated program run between 1968 and 1978, involving up to 80 hours weekly of group therapy (Rice, Harris, & Cormier, 1992). Using a matched group, quasiexperimental design, they measured the impact of the program on criminal recidivism over an outcome period that averaged longer than 10 years. When compared with no program (in most cases, prison), they found that program participants had lower recidivism rates when they were nonpsychopaths (as measured by Hare's original [1980] Psychopathy Checklist) but higher recidivism rates when they were psychopaths. Such results suggested a differential impact of treatment on recidivism risk, depending on level of psychopathy.

In a comprehensive review of how effective service is informed by research, Harris and Rice (1994a, pp. 23–24) reached several conclusions:

1. *Some drugs are powerfully effective in relieving the symptoms of psychotic disorders.* Although effective neither for all symptoms nor for all patients, neuroleptics and antidepressants have profoundly altered the treatment of mental patients. Because there is no effective drug for many problems and symptoms, however, and because some patients resist taking known drugs or do not improve as a result of taking them, drug treatment cannot represent a complete solution to the difficulties experienced by persons diagnosed with mental disorders.

2. *Effective services for persons with psychotic mental disorders need to be comprehensive.* Comprehensive services entail an emphasis on teaching and learning, opportunities for patients to share responsibilities, efforts to prevent social isolation by actively promoting client-clinician interaction, clarity of staff roles and purpose, and stable staffing.

3. *Four main outcomes have been studied: symptom number and severity, rehabilitative outcome (social, vocational functioning), humanistic outcome (happiness), and public safety (violence, antisocial conduct).* Although these out-

comes don't march in lock step, comprehensive services demonstrably make improvements in each of these outcomes.

4. *The principles of effective service apply both to institutional and to community-based programs.* However, effective community programs also employ assertive approaches to service delivery, give practical advice and training for families, and help with money and housing. Much has been written about case management for mental patients in the community. It is clear that case management is not a single clinical entity; it is manifested in a number of different styles or models, ranging from the advocate and service broker model to the full-service and support model. It is also clear that the effectiveness of case management depends on the interventions arranged for or provided directly by case managers. To the extent that case-managed interventions embody the characteristics of effective service generally and eschew ineffective or counterproductive activities, case management can enhance treatment effectiveness.

Harris and Rice (1994b) have also discussed the contributions of the research literature for treatment planning designed particularly for violent and criminal patients. Although cautioning that the field is "insufficiently developed" to draw empirically based conclusions, they did offer the following "sensible advice" based on a review of controlled treatment studies for criminal offenders (p. 472):

1. *Risk:* More intensive service should be provided to higher-risk cases.
2. *Needs:* Service should target criminogenic needs; that is, personal characteristics that contribute to the commission of crime. Known criminogenic targets include changing antisocial attitudes, promoting familial affection and supervision, increasing self-control, replacing lying and aggression with prosocial skills, reducing substance abuse, and improving interpersonal and vocational skills. Inappropriate targets include self-esteem, increasing the cohesiveness of antisocial peer groups, and focusing on intrapsychic forces not empirically linked with criminality.
3. *Style of treatment:* Behavioral or cognitive-behavioral treatments consistently produce larger treatment effects than other styles of treatment (nondirective, punitive, insight-oriented, psychodynamic, evocative and relationship-dependent therapies). There is no guarantee that these same principles apply to treatment for violent (as opposed to general criminal) behavior. However, in the absence of evidence to the contrary, we propose that these principles be applied in selecting treatments for violent clients (Harris & Rice, 1994b, p. 472).

The Netherlands

In The Netherlands, there is one central intake unit, the Meijers Institut, and seven regional hospitals that provide forensic treatment, according to the description provided by Derks, Blankstein, and Hendricks (1993). The total census, including the Meijers Institut and these seven regional hospitals, was 450 patients at the time their description was written. The Meijers Institut uses several criteria in determining placement, including level of security needed, gender, bed availability, and type of treatment needed. Three broad treatment modalities are considered at this stage: (a) psychodynamic individual therapy, (b) cognitive-behavioral training, and (c) sociotherapy. If the patient acts aggressively or otherwise adjusts poorly to placement in the first hospital selected, then reselection (a return to Meijers for placement in another hospital) can occur.

It is not clear what legal categories are held by patients treated at Meijers and, subsequently, at least one regional hospital. No treatment outcome data were presented as part of the Derks et al. article. However, it is clear that the range of treatment orientations and associated services is quite broad within this system. This range may be partly a function of the fact that several of the regional hospitals are private, while the others are run by the state (state-run hospitals being far more typically in forensic systems). For example, the Dr. Henri van der Hoeven Klinieck and the Pompe Kliniek, both private, rely on therapeutic community models to deliver traditional clinical services. Individual psychotherapy is featured prominently among such services. At the Pompe Kliniek, the orientation for such therapy is described as psychodynamic, based on object relations theory, a very unusual orientation to observe in a forensic treatment program.[8] There are also more contemporary services offered, which might be

---

[8]Behavioral, cognitive-behavioral, and reality therapy orientations are much more commonly seen among forensic treatment providers. There appear to be several reasons for this. First, the empirical evidence suggests that behavioral and cognitive-behavioral interventions are more effective than psychodynamic approaches in criminal and quasi-criminal populations. Second, there is a large subpopulation of the severely mentally ill within forensic populations, for whom psychodynamic assumptions about etiology and treatment needs are poorly applicable. Third, the emphasis on observable behavior as an important source of problem definition and index of treatment progress is integrated more easily into other modalities but not necessarily into psychodynamic therapy, where the assumption is that enhanced understanding and intrapsychic change (the more important components of therapeutic change) will eventually result in different patterns of behavior. Fourth, therapy with forensic patients involves elements of coercion (almost without exception, forensic hospitalization is involuntary) and suspension of belief (in which the therapeutic stance involves saying, "It is important to talk and think differently about antisocial behavior, but it is equally important to change that behavior; behavior change without associated cognitive change might represent progress, under some circumstances, but cognitive change without associated behavior change almost never does"). Such coercion and suspension of belief can be incorporated readily into a number of therapeutic orientations, but it is very difficult to do so with psychodynamic therapeutic approaches.

either clinical or hybrids, depending on the treatment goals (e.g., family therapy, vocational training, "practical training").

Finally, it is noteworthy that two of the regional hospitals, both high security, offer contrasting services and treatment approaches. The van Mesdag Kliniek, the final resort hospital for difficult patients, features high-intensity psychoanalytically oriented individual therapy, while the State Institute "Veldzicht" is behaviorally oriented, providing cognitive restructuring with treatment plans based on detailed analyses of the crime.

COMMUNITY-BASED FORENSIC TREATMENT

We will now turn to a discussion of community-based forensic treatment (CBFT), from which we will draw on previous discussions of this topic (Heilbrun & Griffin, 1993, 1998). We will describe characteristics of programs and patients in nonjail community settings, using the same contours employed in discussing forensic hospital treatment in the previous section. We will continue to describe patients who are NGRI and will add mentally disordered offenders on parole or probation. However, because there is virtually no published information on the treatment of individuals IST in the community, we will exclude this legal category. We will also exclude jail and prison transfers for similar reasons, although some recent work has been performed in this area (e.g., Ogloff, Roesch, & Hart, 1993; Ogloff, Tien, Roesch, & Eaves, 1991).

During recent years, there has been a trend toward treating forensic patients in the community as well as in high-security, geographically remote institutions, as deinstitutionalization for civilly committed patients has grown over the past 3 decades. A chapter on forensic treatment must address treatment that is being delivered in the community because it has become more common, but also because CBFT plays an important part in the comprehensive delivery of treatment and other forensic services. Our discussion of CBFT will cover forensic treatment services delivered in the community—in particular, in halfway houses, outpatient clinics, and crisis stabilization units.

UNITED STATES

The descriptive and evaluative literature on community treatment of NGRI and parole/probation patients has come primarily from Illinois, Oregon, and Maryland, but we have also included material from California, Connecticut, Florida, New York, and Oklahoma.

Illinois

Descriptive data from Illinois have been provided on treatment done through the Isaac Ray center in Chicago (Rogers & Cavanaugh, 1981) with two groups of potentially violent patients: those on probation for violent crimes, and those acquitted by reason of insanity and subsequently released from institutions. In its first 2 years of operation, the Isaac Ray Center accepted 54 patients and refused 27; all who were accepted had committed crimes of violence (with 61% charged with murder or attempted murder). A total of 87% had a primary diagnosis of schizophrenia or affective disorder. The center's treatment was eclectic and problem oriented, employing both biological and psychosocial interventions. The treatment goals included clinical (a reduction in psychopathology), hybrid (development of healthy and responsible interpersonal relationships), and legal (a reduction of the potential for future violent behavior). Follow-up was made over a period of 1 to 2 years, during which clinical services were gradually reduced. Brief hospitalizations were employed, particularly on reemergence of symptomatology similar to that seen during prior episodes of violent behavior. Cavanaugh and Wasyliw (1985) have provided a more detailed description of the treatment of forensic patients through the Isaac Ray Center. They followed 44 NGRI outpatients in treatment during a 2-year period from July 1981 to June 1983. Rehospitalization was needed for 25% of the patients during the study period, which is consistent with rates reported by other investigators. The Schedule for Affective Disorders–Change Version (SADS-C) and Symptom Check List (SCL-90) reflected gradual clinical improvement over time, with better adjusted individuals less likely to be rehospitalized. Medication noncompliance was another major contributor to rehospitalization. There were only two rearrests during the 19-month outcome period: one for shoplifting, another for refusing to comply with a court order for outpatient treatment.

In another study using these data, Rogers, Harris, and Wasyliw (1983) concluded that it was important to use multiple sources of data over time in assessing the treatment progress of NGRI acquittees in the community. This was important for two reasons: (a) there was variability in other-observed versus self-reported symptoms, and (b) a small subgroup of patients at high risk for decompensation was identified more readily through the use of multiple sources of information. In this study, the level of disturbance and risk for decompensation for the more severely impaired patients would have been underestimated by self-report data alone. Although the particular importance of third-party information in forensic *assessment* has been discussed elsewhere (Heilbrun, 1988; Heilbrun, Rosenfeld, Warren, & Collins, 1994; Melton, Petrila, Poythress, & Slobogin, 1997), the present study suggests that third-party information may be very important in planning and assessing the effectiveness of forensic *treatment* as well.

Another Illinois study (Rogers & Wettstein, 1984) sought to distinguish patients who were not rehospitalized from those who were. Gender and criminal charge were important, with males and homicide acquittees more likely to be rehospitalized. Global functioning and number of symptoms were also found to distinguish these groups, with greater initial psychopathology and the lower functioning associated with greater likelihood of rehospitalization.

Oregon

CBFT services in Oregon are delivered to patients under the supervision of the Psychiatric Security Review Board (PSRB), which was created by the Oregon legislature in 1977 to supervise Oregon defendants found "not responsible due to mental illness." This board is explicitly a public safety model, with the prevention of violent behavior in the community a primary goal (Bloom & Bloom, 1981; Rogers, Bloom, & Manson, 1984). Because the board is assured that it will promptly learn about violations of release conditions or deterioration in a person's mental functioning, it did not need to be convinced that a patient was rehabilitated before it granted a conditional release. When the patient was stabilized and a realistic plan for conditional release was formulated, then the patient could be released to the community (Rogers & Bloom, 1985). This model clearly has important implications for hospital as well as community-based treatment, with the more realistic treatment goal of improved adjustment ensured through careful monitoring substituted for rehabilitation.

One CBFT program treating clients under PSRB jurisdiction (Bloom, Williams, Rogers & Barbur, 1986), located in Portland, delivered services to PSRB clients through a large community hospital day treatment program. Traditional clinical services were offered (e.g., group and individual therapy), as were contemporary hybrids (e.g., social skills, time management training, and vocational training). This program could initially accept or reject patients referred by the PSRB; it also provided services to individuals on parole or probation. Patients could also be dropped from this program for a variety of reasons, with the mean period of treatment for those successfully completing the program being 63 months, but the mean for those dropped only 9 months. Patients were often dropped from the program after a relatively short time, consistent with the observation of community treatment providers that patients who have difficulty adjusting to conditional release often show problems after a short time.

This study also compared those accepted for treatment ($N = 110$) at the day treatment program with those who were not accepted ($N = 51$). These groups did not differ on demographic characteristics, crime seriousness, or DSM-III Axis I diagnosis. The group that was not accepted had a significantly greater frequency of Antisocial Personality Disorder diagnosis. Even the treated group, however, frequently had substance abuse (50%) and personality disorder (40%) diagnoses. Within the treated group, a comparison of those remaining in treatment ($N = 21$) with those revoked from conditional release ($N = 46$) indicated that the revoked group was involved in more crises, with a greater percentage requiring staff home visits, crisis intervention services, and hospitalization. There was also a difference in living situations, with the revoked group spending 41% of their time living in sheltered housing and 55% in independent living, while the successful group spent only 13% of their time living in sheltered housing and 86% of their time living independently. These percentages might suggest that independent living favorably affected the likelihood of continuing in treatment and complying with conditional release requirements. In addition, it might mean that better adjusted patients, with more personal and family resources, were less likely to show a deterioration in mental condition and were thus better risks for succeeding on conditional release.

Maryland

Treatment information on NGRI acquittees has also come from Maryland. Insanity acquittees released from the state forensic hospital were required under Maryland law to undergo a 5-year conditional release period. A residential treatment program, Hamilton House, was located on the grounds of a state hospital in Maryland, Clifton T. Perkins Hospital Center; a total of 27 Hamilton House residents, formerly patients at Perkins, were followed over a 22-month period. Four individuals (15%) were rearrested during this time, although none of the arrests were for offenses as serious as the original crimes for which the men were acquitted by reason of insanity; none of the rearrests occurred while the residents were in Hamilton House. By contrast, 11 of the 27 residents (40.5%) were rehospitalized during this period (Goldmeier, Sauer, & White, 1977; Goldmeier, White, Ulrich, & Klein, 1980).

Another Maryland study (Silver, 1983) indicated that 43% of conditionally released NGRI acquittees went to a halfway house. Of the 65 acquittees involved in court-mandated outpatient treatment, 24% were rearrested (primarily for misdemeanors), and 11% were rehospitalized.

Evaluative data from Maryland (Spodak, Silver, & Wright, 1984) described the outcomes for NGRI acquittees ($N = 86$) over a 15-year period following their release from hospitalization. Of these, 56% were arrested and 30% convicted of subsequent crimes. A later Maryland study described predictors for the success of insanity acquittees conditionally released to community-based treatment (Cohen, Spodak, Silver, & Williams, 1988). A longitudinal investigation of 127 male insanity acquittees who had been released from Clifton T. Perkins Hospital Center between 1967 and 1978 was performed. All the patients had been discharged from the hospital on conditional release and living in the community for an average of 10.8 years. A control group of convicted subjects ($N = 127$) was also obtained, as was a third group of mentally disordered prisoners ($N = 135$) treated at Perkins between 1969 and 1981. Using discriminant analysis, the authors reported that NGRI acquittees who successfully completed conditional release were more likely to have been married, working at the time of the offense, arrested for less severe offenses, functioned well or very well prior to hospitalization, adjusted well to hospitalization, been assessed by hospital clinical staff as considerably improved, and had a Global Assessment Scale (GAS) (Endicott, Spitzer, Fleiss, & Cohen, 1976) score of 50 or better on release. Predictors were also developed for rearrest. NGRI acquittees who were not arrested during their conditional release period had adjusted well to the hospital, had been assessed by clinical staff as considerably improved at the time of discharge, had a GAS score at release of 50 or more, and had functioned well or very well prior to arrest for the acquitted offense. They were less likely to be heroin addicts; they were only children or the youngest child in their families. The rates for successfully completing conditional release (49%) and avoiding arrest (46%) were given, but it was not clear from the article whether these were representative of the overall NGRI population in Maryland during this period.

Florida

The description of a community-based forensic services program in Palm Beach County, Florida (Dvoskin, 1989), demonstrated that the successful integration of assessment and treatment services for NGRI acquittees and individuals on parole and probation requires both administrative coordination and specialized service delivery. This study is a useful description of essential community forensic services and the strengths and weaknesses of a good community forensic program.

In a later article, Dvoskin and Steadman (1994) elaborated on these issues in discussing the importance of using intensive case management to reduce violence by mentally ill persons in the community. The elements of this contemporary hybrid treatment include small caseloads, 24-hour availability of case managers, and strong linkages to the criminal justice system and to agencies that provide a broad range of interventions (services in the areas of mental health, substance abuse, and social needs).

California

Follow-up data have been reported on NGRI acquittees ($N = 79$) conditionally released in California (Lamb, Weinberger, & Gross, 1988). The median age was 33; 89% were male. They had been mostly charged with and acquitted of crimes against persons (67%)—almost all (99%) were felonies. The median length of forensic hospitalization prior to beginning court-mandated community outpatient treatment was 20 months. A total of 38 acquittees (48%) had their conditional release revoked at least once during the 5-year follow-up period of community-based treatment. Rearrests were noted for 16% of acquittees during this period (13% for violent crimes), with hospitalization in nonforensic facilities for 34%. The authors suggested that unsuccessful outcomes could have been prevented with greater structure and supervision. This conclusion is consistent with our views and those of others (e.g., Rogers et al., 1984): Structure, monitoring, and (if necessary) rehospitalization can reduce the risk of criminal recidivism for NGRI acquittees in the community. Such services are crucial to the effective delivery of community-based forensic treatment and could be considered either contemporary hybrid or targeted legal.

Further evidence for the importance of conditional release in CBFT has been provided (Wiederanders, 1992) by comparing 191 acquittees placed on conditional release with 44 individuals released from hospitalization with no aftercare following the expiration of their commitment terms. The conditionally released group had a significantly lower community-period arrest rate than did the unconditionally released group. Survival rate analyses, with dependent variables of time until arrest and time until revocation, indicated that revocations made during the first 8 months following discharge reduced the likelihood of arrest within the conditionally released group. A subsequent study (Wiederanders & Choate, 1994) provided further information about the community adjustment of a larger sample of released NGRI acquittees ($N = 306$). Twelve dimensions, measured in a psychometrically respectable fashion (Cronbach's alpha $> .70$ for all except one), were obtained: employment, social supports, substance abuse, independence and compliance, unobtrusiveness, self-confidence, self-confidence, responsibility, paranoia, psychosis, anxiety and depression, risk and dangerousness, and blunted affect. Clients who reoffended or were rehospitalized were significantly different on all dimensions than clients who remained successfully in the community.

New York

There are also follow-up data available on the outcomes of NGRI acquittees (*N* = 331) released to the community in New York State between 1980 and 1987 (McGreevy, Steadman, Dvoskin, & Dollard, 1991). The follow-up period averaged 3.8 years. During this period, 22% of the NGRI acquittees were rearrested; the majority (64%) of the arrests were for misdemeanors, and the great majority (92%) were for minor felonies or less. Some 11% of the group were arrested more than once. A smaller percentage of individuals were rehospitalized (5%), although petitions for recommitment were filed on 12% of the sample. The following key features of a successful conditional release program were described: (a) centralized responsibility, (b) a uniform system of treatment and supervision, and (c) a network of community services. These features would be equally applicable to the monitoring and treatment of individuals on parole or probation and emphasize the importance of integrating decision making, treatment (with a combination of traditional clinical, contemporary hybrid, and targeted legal services), and treatment compliance-enhancement strategies, such as careful monitoring.

Oklahoma

Norwood, Nicholson, Enyart, and Hickey (1992) have described community outcomes for insanity acquittees in Oklahoma. Rates of rearrest, rehospitalization, and contact with community mental health centers were cited for three groups of released NGRI acquittees treated between May 1979 and November 1983: (a) those released at first court review (*N* = 9), (b) those released following recommendation by the hospital (*N* = 16), and (c) those who were AWOL (*N* = 5). The numbers of individuals rearrested during the follow-up period (averaging 960.5 days) were different among the groups (33% vs. 19% vs. 80%, respectively), although statistical comparisons would not have been meaningful because of the low numbers. Rehospitalization rates were less discrepant (33% vs. 38% vs. 20%, respectively), but the number of individuals contacting community mental health centers showed clear differences (44% vs. 81% vs. 20%, respectively).

Minnesota

Reid and Solomon (1981) have described two residential rehabilitation programs for individuals on parole or probation. The first is housed in a dormitory on the grounds of a state hospital within walking distance of schools, a college, vocational schools, and downtown Rochester, Minnesota. The program had strong community ties from its inception in 1969; included on its board of directors were law enforcement and correctional officers, mental health professionals, educators, and lay persons. Individuals in this program generally lack employment and money management skills, most are school dropouts, and approximately 40% have learning disabilities. Well over 50% are severe drug abusers. Treatment is facilitated by a written contract, often used in community-based forensic treatment, that is clear, easily monitored, and addresses the goals for each individual. Reality oriented, confrontational group meetings with peers (a contemporary hybrid treatment) are mandatory. About 75% of the adult clients successfully completed the program, and postdischarge follow-up indicated that 35% had no arrests, 40% had mild encounters with law, and 25% had moderate to severe encounters (Tyce, Olson, & Amdahl, 1980).

Reid and Solomon (1981) described a second residential program in Minnesota, Portland House. Founded in Minneapolis in 1973 under the auspices of local Lutheran Social Services, it has been largely supported by $30 per diem payments from each client. Fewer than 20 young adult males (ages 18–30) live in a large house in a residential neighborhood, with community educational and vocational resources readily available. There are four to five full-time nonmedical staff, several resident counselors, and trained volunteers. The goals of this program involve (a) reversing antisocial behavior, and (b) establishing relations with the community in terms of employment, social interaction, interpersonal relationships, and improved self-esteem. Clients participate in regular group and individual therapy, take a money management course, maintain family ties, and work with other residents. About 50% of the accepted offenders complete this program, with the more serious offenders more likely to complete the program. Of the 50% who did successfully complete the program, the rate of postdischarge arrest over a 1–6-year period was 10%.

Wisconsin

A study of the complex offender project in Dane County, Wisconsin, tested the hypothesis that deviant behavior could be altered via training of more acceptable and socially constructive ways of behaving (Kloss, 1978). Complex offenders (defined as persons with psychological problems as well as a history of legal involvement) treated through this project were randomly selected as subjects for the Koss study if they met the following criteria: (a) on probation, with no pending charges; (b) age 18–30; (c) have at least one previous conviction; and (d) have a poor employment record. A total of 106 individuals (mean age of 21, 15% female, 14% minority group members) were seen three times weekly for 20 months. Comparisons between treatment and control groups supported the conclusion that this form of intensive, goal-oriented, training-based community treatment of mentally disordered offenders was an effective approach to treatment with this population. Although such an approach was described as more costly than probation, it was still less expensive than incarceration. Once again, this study demonstrated that intensive monitoring, which could be described as an essential part of forensic treatment in the community, is effective in improving treatment compliance and outcome.

Connecticut

One study of a program treating substance abusers (Schottenfeld, 1989) described a free-standing, satellite clinic of a regional community mental health center affiliated with the Yale University Psychiatry Department. Approximately 110 patients are evaluated per month. Some 26% are referred by probation officers, 24% for outstanding DWI charges, 9% for other pending legal difficulties, and the remaining 41% are self-referred. This study demonstrates two CBFT phenomena: (a) treatment programs are often integrated, accepting individuals with differing legal status, rather than treating only NGRI acquittees or individuals on parole or probation; and (b) programs may be constructed to address primarily clinical symptoms (with traditional clinical services predominating), or they may address a range of symptoms and functional behaviors. In the case of this program, the primary issue being addressed is substance abuse, a very common problem particularly within the parole/probation group.

CANADA

British Columbia

In a study of all defendants acquitted by reason of insanity in British Columbia between November 1975 and January 1984 ($N = 188$), a total of 124 individuals were identified who had been hospitalized and subsequently discharged to the community at least once (Golding, Eaves, & Kowaz, 1989). Rehospitalization occurred an average of 2.38 times for the 62.9% of the cohort that was rehospitalized, while no rehospitalization was needed for the remaining 37.1%. Outpatient supervision took place over an average of 47.7 months before absolute discharge. The common element for community treatment for this sample, therefore, was monitoring under the terms of the hospital conditional release, which might also be called target hybrid treatment.

SUMMARY OF CBFT PROGRAMS AND PATIENTS

Descriptions of CBFT programs for NGRI acquittees emphasize the treatment of psychopathology and the management of aggressive behavior. In order to meet both goals, programs may refuse to accept high-risk patients, who are generally regarded as more antisocial individuals. Empirical accounts of factors distinguishing between successful and unsuccessful acquittees on conditional release use rearrest and rehospitalization as outcome criteria. Factors predicting successful outcome in both areas include better functioning prior to hospitalization, rated as improved by hospital clinical staff, and a GAS score of 50+ at the time beginning CBFT. Rearrest rates on conditional release ranged from 2% to 16%, with higher rates (42%–56%) seen on long-term follow-up after conditional release is terminated. Rehospitalization rates while on conditional release were both higher and more variable, ranging from 11% to 78%, with most estimates between 11% and 40%. Higher rates of rehospitalization were associated with lower rates of rearrest when clear external control, such as a Psychiatric Security Review Board, was utilized. The Oregon model appeared exemplary from several perspectives, including public safety orientation, appropriate external control, and facilitation of research and evaluation.

CBFT programs treating individuals on parole or probation may be either outpatient clinics or residential (halfway house) facilities. The clinics tended to offer both assessment and treatment services to individuals in a variety of legal categories, including pretrial, parole, probation, and sometimes insanity acquittees. Certain clinics offering substance abuse treatment also accepted self-referred (voluntary) clients, underscoring the heterogeneity of the client population for such programs. Facilities providing residential treatment reported rates of successful completion ranging from 50%–75%, with posttreatment arrest rates typically reported as one form of outcome measure. Clinics and residential programs shared the necessity of treating individuals on an involuntary basis.

INTEGRATION: PRINCIPLES OF FORENSIC TREATMENT

Based on the descriptions of the forensic treatment programs given in this chapter and the previously described principles of community-based forensic treatment (Griffin, Steadman, & Heilbrun, 1991), it is possible to identify two sets of principles relevant to forensic treatment. The first set, which we will call *established principles*, consists of those that seem sufficiently well-established so as to be recognized by (if not fully incorporated into) most forensic treatment programs. The second set—*emerging principles*—

consists of those which, although not consistently accepted, have shown sufficient promise to be recognized on a preliminary basis.

Established Principles

1. *There should be distinct consideration of assessment, treatment, and decision-making functions.* Forensic treatment programs provide two kinds of assessment: for treatment planning purposes and for legal decision-making purposes. Treatment planning assessment is directly relevant to subsequent treatment services, while assessment for legal decision-making purposes may not be. The two should be considered as conceptually distinct. Likewise, because virtually all forensic treatment is delivered with involuntary patients, there will be a decision as to whether the assessment data and treatment progress justify the patient's transfer to a less restrictive setting. Again, this step should be considered distinct from assessment and treatment.

2. *Forensic treatment should address clinical symptomatology and functional deficits and should be structured according to the legal status of the patient.* In addition to clinical symptoms, forensic patients show functional deficits that interfere with the capacity to perform relevant legal tasks. Just as the particular legal tasks and related functional abilities vary according to legal status, so should the treatment designed to remediate the deficits and restore the individual's capacity to perform the tasks.

3. *Shorter term, focused clinical and psychoeducational interventions should be used with defendants who are hospitalized as incompetent to stand trial or transferred from correctional facilities for emergency treatment.* The combination of psychotropic medication, training to improve performance in area of legally relevant functional deficits, and communication with staff from the transferring facility to improve adjustment on return should successfully address the majority of such referrals. In turn, these interactions should allow forensic treatment programs to meet the desirable goal of returning the patient to the transferring agency as quickly as possible.

4. *Longer term, multimodal interventions should be used with patients (e.g., NGRI acquittees) who will return to the community following their release from secure hospitalization.* When the goal is more broadly rehabilitative, and discharged patients will be living in a setting that requires improved symptomatology, better global functioning, and lowered risk for violent and other antisocial behavior, then intervention strategies should be more extensive and more intensive.

5. *Communication is essential for success. Such communication must encompass individuals within the mental health and criminal justice systems.* In particular, it must include institution to community and case manager or

probation/parole officer to court, therapist, and living supervisor or family member. The role of the case manager or probation officer in coordinating such communication is very important. Without such an individual's willingness and ability to obtain and communicate relevant information in a timely fashion, it is inevitable that some CBFT clients will present a greater risk for violating the conditions of community living and possibly breaking the law as well.

6.   *There must be an explicit balance between individual rights, the need for treatment, and public safety.* This balance must be operationalized and clearly articulated to clients prior to their entering community-based treatment. The recommended model for CBFT is oriented explicitly toward public safety. In part, this orientation is a recognition of political reality. Funding for CBFT programs providing community services to individuals involved in criminal behavior, who also have mental problems, is unlikely to be obtained solely on the basis of treatment needs. Rather, the argument that such programs are likely to deter criminal behavior, with documentation of this experience in other communities, is more likely to be persuasive. However, a program that does not balance public protection with respect for human dignity and the delivery of needed services does no more than serve a monitoring function. It is important to have this balance carefully considered, operationalized, and clearly articulated to staff, clients, and others who have contact with the program.

7.   *It is helpful to use a demonstration model in assessing risk of aggression toward others and treatability in the community.* A CBFT treatment plan should demonstrate a logical connection between the risk factors for target behavior classes, such as aggression, the pattern of clinical symptoms, and the interventions delivered. The judgments concerning risk and treatment outcome are not always facilitated by the availability of empirical data on large groups of CBFT clients, so it is usually necessary to rely on historical information and a theoretical and logical fit on a case-by-case basis.

8.   *Clarify the legal requirements in areas such as confidentiality and duty to protect, specific reporting demands (e.g., child abuse), and malpractice.* A priori legal consultation is an essential ingredient for any CBFT program. Emergency response procedures for critical incidents (such as threats of violence, criminal behavior, or refusal to take prescribed medication) should be specified before such incidents occur. Ready access to legal advice should also be available to clinicians who work with these clients, given the kind of questions that can require immediate legal consultation.

9.   *Set, practice, and monitor sound risk management procedures.* Such procedures should include being aware of risk assessment and the law of the jurisdiction, obtaining recent records, questioning patients and relevant others directly about violent acts and thoughts, and communicating

this information to responsible decision makers. It should also include special handling of difficult cases, consultation from colleagues, and follow-up on lack of compliance with treatment. Documenting the source, content, and data of significant information on risk, as well as the content, rationale, and date of actions taken to prevent violence, is important. Finally, the development of feasible guidelines for handling risk, subjecting these guidelines to clinical and legal review, educating staff in their use, and auditing their compliance are all encouraged. Tampering with the record or making public statements of responsibility following a violent incident are strongly discouraged, however (Monahan, 1993).

10. *Practice principles promoting health care adherence* (Meichenbaum & Turk, 1987; Wexler, 1991). Develop a contract with CBFT clients before treatment has begun. Clients should be provided with clear information regarding the conditions to which they must adhere and the consequences for violating these conditions. Frequent components of such a contract include medication compliance, attendance at scheduled sessions with therapists and case mangers, abstinence from alcohol and drug use (and blood or urine screening, if indicated, to monitor adherence), disallowance of weapons possession, housing (including where the person will live, applicable rent and how it will be paid, adherence to housing rules), and the consequences for violating conditions. More specific conditions—no contact with the victim, employment, specialized forms of treatment and monitoring, and transportation—can be included as needed. Agreement with this contract involves making a public commitment to the CBFT program. The family should be involved, if they are available and willing.

EMERGING PRINCIPLES

1. *Hiring of qualified mental health staff in jails and prisons must be increased.* When correctional facilities offer reasonable mental health care (either on site or through an agreement with a proximate facility), there is less need to transfer inmates to expensive, oft-remote, high-security forensic programs.

2. *The epidemiology of forensic populations is weak.* It is difficult to design effective forensic treatment programs without good data on the course and prevalence of clinical disorders and relevant functional deficits that are associated with forensic patients in different legal categories.

3. *Treatment outcome studies that use clinical and behavioral outcomes must be linked to the goal of comprehensive, integrated, high-quality forensic treatment services.* Measures of outcome have frequently been limited to variables such as rearrest and rehospitalization in forensic research. Sensi-

tive measures that address functioning through direct observation are needed as well.

4. *The use of contemporary forms of treatment should be expanded.* The use of psychosocial rehabilitation, relapse prevention, and multimodal treatments addressing anger and impulse control are examples of treatments that have been developed and used successfully with nonforensic populations. Their more structured nature and associated measurable outcomes lend themselves better to the outcome research (noted in Principle 3).

5. *The task of lowering violence risk through treatment should be considered a separate treatment goal for forensic patients who will return to the community following discharge.* Although some efforts have been directed toward describing violence risk reduction through treatment (e.g., Roth, 1987; Wack, 1993), this is a very important area for virtually every forensic treatment program. Moreover, such programs are ideal sites to develop and refine treatment approaches to violence.

6. *Use of review board and other administrative review mechanisms should improve decision making regarding privileging and release.* Even when the court retains jurisdiction over all decisions regarding the privileging (e.g., grounds privileges, community visits) of forensic patients, it is still desirable to have a level of administrative review between treatment providers and decision makers. This protects programs from the consequences of poor recommendations and shields treatment providers (to some extent) from the pressures that can be experienced from both treating and making decisions about the same patients. When internal mechanisms are not in place or fully satisfactory, then the use of outside consultants can serve a comparable purpose.

7. *Conditional release is an effective way of balancing the public safety and individual liberty considerations, and the importance of treatment compliance, upon release from a secure setting into the community.* The impact of conditional release has been to decrease arrests while increasing the rate of rehospitalization among discharged NGRI acquittees. Continued monitoring in the community and the prospect of immediate response in the event of a problem also means that hospital treatment programs can afford to release patients earlier, given a reasonable conditional release plan, than they otherwise might have.

IMPLICATIONS FOR POLICY, PRACTICE, AND RESEARCH

Policy

Several implications for policy relevant to forensic treatment emerge from the discussion in this chapter. First, it seems clear that standards for admission to and release from forensic treatment programs (whether contained in statute or administrative code) should be structured according to the legal status of the patient. This establishes a precedent for the structuring of a forensic treatment program within the larger forensic system and reflects the importance of relevant legal considerations in setting goals.

The balance between individual rights, treatment needs, and public safety considerations should be made as explicit as possible. Although a failure to meaningfully incorporate each of these elements into the overall structure of a forensic system will inevitably weaken it, the relative emphasis assigned to each will vary between jurisdictions. Without some explicit standards for achieving this balance, however, it will fluctuate considerably depending on the judge, treatment program, treatment team, and individual clinician. Some greater degree of uniformity is needed.

For several reasons, it is important to clarify the legal requirements and associated policy in relevant areas for treatment agents and programs. First, assessment, treatment, and decision making associated with the risk of patients' violence toward others should be integral elements of a treatment program. Failing to address how these elements relate to legal obligations to protect the public promotes a passive stance toward achieving the necessary balance between public safety, individual liberty interests, and treatment. Second, the failure to anticipate the possibility that a discharged patient may, despite all efforts to the contrary, be involved in an incident in which someone is seriously hurt—that a case may "go bad" in a highly visible way—is to increase the prospect that a forensic program or system will be dismantled in the event of such a disaster. Third, forensic treatment programs should be leaders in the development and implementation of sound risk management procedures through the use of administrative review boards, conditional release, and the proactive awareness of and compliance with professional risk management standards.

PRACTICE

It should be clear from our discussion that there is no single ideal forensic treatment program. One of the influences on the structure of a good program will be the legal status of patients admitted. Short-term treatment modalities are appropriate for patients whose legal status requires immediate restoration and return as its goal, while longer term treatments are indicated for discharged patients who will not be returning to a high-security setting but rather will be back in the community (even if continued court jurisdiction and monitoring will remain in place). To implement these kinds of treatment most effectively at all levels, it is important to promote effective communication across mental health and criminal justice systems, between clinical and legal professionals, and between those who interact with patients in varying treatment and monitoring roles.

Even considering recent improvements in conceptual and empirical approaches to assessing violence risk (Monahan, 1981, 1993; Monahan & Steadman, 1994), the best-integrated and most defensible approach to integrating risk reduction and treatment is a demonstration model. When programs allow patients to demonstrate improvements in symptoms, treatment compliance, and responsible, nonviolent behavior across a series of decreasingly restrictive sets of conditions, then these results present one of the best arguments for risk reduction. Moreover, the duration and size of each of the steps (moving, for example, from a highly restrictive admissions ward with no freedom of movement to a less restrictive ward that permits a patient to request escorted grounds privileges) can be controlled by the design of the program and the individualized judgment of the treatment team and the review board.

One of the crucial determinants of the improvement of forensic patients and the maintenance of treatment gains is treatment compliance. Particularly following transfer into less restrictive settings in which it becomes more difficult to respond immediately to violent or threatening behavior, it is very important that patients continue to comply with treatment. In order to lower violence risk through treatment, forensic patients must out of necessity agree to continue to participate in relevant, stipulated treatment without unilateral withdrawal or nonattendance. A system's implementation of principles promoting health care compliance can help to achieve this goal.

Finally, it is important to use the full range of treatment modalities that have been developed during the last decade. By employing treatments such as recently developed psychotropic medications, psychosocial rehabilitation, skills-based psychoeducational interventions designed to improve relevant areas of deficits, and relapse prevention, it is likely that treatment response in a forensic program will be enhanced.

RESEARCH

Finally, there are several important research implications that seem clear from the discussion in this chapter. There is virtually no good epidemiologic research on forensic patients in hospital and community settings using large samples and common measures across different jurisdictions. It would help promote the standardization of treatment outcome research to provide such research, focusing on clinical symptoms and relevant functional deficits. The use of research approaches employed in community psychology (Roesch, 1995) could be helpful in this regard. A particular focus on the problems of individuals with co-occurring diagnoses (often substance abuse and a mental health diagnosis) and their associated treatment needs would be helpful.

A second, related research goal involves the implementation of comprehensive integrated, high-quality treatment services whose effectiveness can be measured. This goal can best be realized through treatment outcome studies that are performed over a period of time following subjects' discharge into the community, using clinical symptoms, treatment compliance, and risk-relevant behavioral outcome measures. Although outcome measures such as rearrest and rehospitalization should continue to be employed, much more treatment-relevant data will be provided when more sensitive outcome variables are employed.

Finally, there is the important question of the accuracy of decisions that are made at various points in the process of evaluation and treatment of forensic patients. It has been anecdotally observed (but not empirically demonstrated), for example, that the use of a review board will increase the uniformity and improve the accuracy of decisions about privileging and release.

REFERENCES

Bartlett, A. (1993). Rhetoric and reality: What do we know about the English Special Hospitals? *International Journal of Law and Psychiatry, 16,* 27–51.

Bloom, J. L., & Bloom, J. D. (1981). Disposition of insanity defenses in Oregon. *Bulletin of the American Academy of Psychiatry & the Law, 9,* 93–100.

Cavanaugh, J., & Wasyliw, O. (1985). Adjustment of the Not Guilty by Reason of Insanity (NGRI) outpatient: An initial report. *Journal of Forensic Sciences, 30,* 24–30.

Clark, C., Holden, C., Thompson, J., Watson, P., & Wightman, L. (1993). Treatment at Michigan's Forensic Center. *International Journal of Law and Psychiatry, 16,* 71–81.

Cohen, M. I., Spodak, M. K., Silver, S. B., & Williams, K. (1988). Predicting outcome of insanity acquittees released to the community. *Behavioral Sciences & the Law, 6,* 515–530.

Dell, S., Robertson, G., & Parker, E. (1988). *Sentenced to hospital: Offenders in Broadmoor.* Oxford: Oxford University Press.

Derks, F., Blankstein, J., & Hendrickx, J. (1993). Treatment and security: The dual nature of forensic psychiatry. *International Journal of Law and Psychiatry, 16,* 217–240.

Dixon, J., & Rivenbark, W. (1993). Treatment of Alabama's Taylor Hardin Secure Medical Facility. *International Journal of Law and Psychiatry, 16,* 105–116.

Dvoskin, J. (1989). The Palm Beach County, Florida, forensic mental health services program: A comprehensive community-based system. In H. J. Steadman, D. W. McCarty, & J. P. Morrissey (Eds.), *The mentally ill in jail: Planning for essential services* (pp. 178–197). New York: Guilford Press.

Dvoskin, J., & Steadman, H. J. (1994). Using intensive case management to reduce violence by mentally ill persons in the community. *Hospital and Community Psychiatry, 45,* 679–684.

Eastman, N. (1993). Forensic psychiatric services in Britain: A current review. *International Journal of Law and Psychiatry, 16,* 1/2, 1–27.

Endicott, J., Spitzer, R., Fleiss, J.,& Cohen, J. (1976). The global assessment scale. *Archives of General Psychiatry, 33,* 766–771.

Golding, S. L., Eaves, D., & Kowaz, A. M. (1989). The assessment, treatment and community outcome of insanity acquittees: Forensic history and response to treatment. *International Journal of Law and Psychiatry, 12,* 149–179.

Goldmeier, J., Sauer, R., & White, E. (1977). A halfway house for mentally ill offenders. *American Journal of Psychiatry, 34,* 45–49.

Goldmeier, J., White, E. V., Ulrich, C., & Klein, G. A. (1980). Community intervention with the mentally ill offender: A residential program. *Bulletin of the American Academy of Psychiatry & the Law, 8,* 72–81.

Griffin, P. A., Steadman, H. J., & Heilbrun, K. (1991). Designing conditional release systems for insanity acquittees. *Journal of Mental Health Administration, 18,* 231–241.

Grisso, T., Cocozza, J., Steadman, H., Fisher, W., & Greer, A. (1994). The organization of practical forensic evaluation services: A national profile. *Law and Human Behavior, 18,* 377–393.

Harris, G. T., & Rice, M. E. (1994a). *Mentally disordered offenders: What research says about effective service.* Penetanguishene, Canada: Mental Health Centre Research Reports.

Harris, G. T., & Rice, M. E. (1994b). The violent patient. In M. Hersen & R. T. Ammerman (Eds.), *Handbook of prescriptive treatments for adults* (pp. 463–4886). New York: Plenum Press.

Heilbrun, K. (1988, March). *Third-party information in forensic assessment: Much needed, sometimes collected, poorly guided.* Paper presented at the Mid-Winter Meeting of the American Psychology-Law Society/Division 41, Miami, FL.

Heilbrun, K., & Griffin, P. (1993). Community-based forensic treatment of insanity acquittees. *International Journal of Law and Psychiatry, 16,* 133–150.

Heilbrun, K., & Griffin, P. (1998). Community-based forensic treatment. In R. Wettstein (Ed.), *Treatment of the mentally disordered offender* (pp. 168–210). New York: Guilford.

Heilbrun, K., Rosenfeld, B., Warren, J., & Collins, S. (1994). The use of third-party information in forensic assessments. *Bulletin of the American Academy of Psychiatry and the Law, 22,* 399–406.

Hodgins, S. (1993). Mental health treatment services in Quebec for persons accused or convicted of criminal offenses. *International Journal of Law and Psychiatry, 16,* 179–194.

Kerr, C., & Roth, J. (1986). Populations, practices, and problems in forensic psychiatry facilities. *Annals of the American Academy of Political and Social Science, 484,* 127–143.

Kloss, J. (1978). The impact of comprehensive community treatment: An assessment of the Complex Offender Project. *Offender Rehabilitation, 3,* 81–108.

Lamb, H., Weinberger, L., & Gross, B. (1988). Court-mandated community outpatient treatment for persons found Not Guilty by Reason of Insanity: A five-year follow-up. *American Journal of Psychiatry, 145,* 450–456.

Marques, J., Haynes, R., & Nelson, C. (1993). Forensic treatment at Atascadero State Hospital. *International Journal of Law and Psychiatry, 16,* 57–70.

McGreevy, M. A., Steadman, H. J., Dvoskin, J. A., & Dollard, N. (1991). New York State's system of managing insanity acquittees in the community. *Hospital and Community Psychiatry, 42,* 512–517.

Meichenbaum, D., & Turk, D. (1987). *Facilitating treatment adherence: A practitioner's guidebook.* New York: Plenum Press.

Melton, G., Petrila, J., Poythress, N., & Slobogin, C. (1997). *Psychological evaluations for the courts: A handbook for mental health professionals and attorneys* (2nd edition). New York: Guilford Press.

Monahan, J. (1981). *Predicting violent behavior: An assessment of clinical techniques.* Beverly Hills: Sage.

Monahan, J. (1993). Limiting therapist exposure to *Tarasoff* liability: Guidelines for risk containment. *American Psychologist, 48,* 242–250.

Monahan, J., & Steadman, H. (Eds.). (1983). *Mentally disordered offenders: Perspectives from law and social science.* New York: Plenum Press.

Monahan, J., & Steadman, H. (Eds.). (1994). *Violence and mental disorder: Developments in risk assessment.* Chicago: University of Chicago Press.

Norwood, S., Nicholson, R. A., Enyart, C., & Hickey, M. L. (1992). Insanity acquittal in Oklahoma: Recommendations for program planning and social policy. *Forensic Reports, 5,* 5–28.

Ogloff, J. R. P., Roberts, C. F., & Roesch, R. (1993). The insanity defense: legal standards and clinical assessment. *Applied and Preventive Psychology, 2,* 163–178.

Ogloff, J. R. P., Roesch, R., & Hart, S. D. (1993). Screening, assessment, and identification of services for mentally ill offenders. In H. J. Steadman & J. J. Cocozza (Eds.), *Providing services for mental illness and related disorders in America's prisons* (pp. 61–90). Seattle, WA: National Coalition for the Mentally Ill in the Criminal Justice System.

Ogloff, J. R. P., Tien, G., Roesch, R., & Eaves, D. (1991). A model for the provision of jail mental health services: An integrative, community-based approach. *Journal of Mental Health Administration, 18,* 209–222.

Poythress, N. J. (1993). Forensic treatment in the United States: A survey of selected forensic hospitals: Introduction. *International Journal of Law and Psychiatry, 16,* 53–55.

Reid, W. H., & Solomon, G. F. (1981). Community-based offender programs. In W. H. Reid (Ed.), *The treatment of antisocial syndromes* (pp. 76–94). New York: Van Nostrand Reinhold.

Rice, M. E., & Harris, G. T. (1988). An empirical approach to the classification and treatment of maximum security psychiatric patients. *Behavioral Sciences & the Law, 6,* 497–514.

Rice, M. E., & Harris, G. T. (1993). Ontario's Maximum Security Hospital at Penetanguishene: Past, present, and future. *International Journal of Law and Psychiatry, 16,* 195–215.

Rice, M. E., & Harris, G. T. (1995). Violent recidivism: Assessing predictive validity. *Journal of Consulting and Clinical Psychology, 63,* 737–748.

Rice, M. E., Harris, G., & Cormier, C. (1992). Evaluation of a maximum security therapeutic community for psychopaths and other mentally disordered offenders. *Law and Human Behavior, 16,* 399–412.

Roesch, R. (1995). Creating change in the legal system: Contributions from community psychology. *Law and Human Behavior, 19,* 325–343.

Rogers, J., & Bloom, J. D. (1985). The insanity sentence: Oregon's Psychiatric Security Review Board. *Behavioral Sciences & the Law, 3,* 69–84.

Rogers, J., Blooom, J. D., & Manson, S. (1984). Oregon's new insanity defense system: A review of the first five years, 1978 to 1982. *Bulletin of the American Academy of Psychiatry & the Law, 12,* 383–402.

Rogers, R., & Cavanaugh, J. (1981). A treatment program for potentially violent offender patients. *International Journal of Offender Therapy and Comparative Criminology, 25,* 53–59.

Rogers, R., Harris, M.,& Wasyliw, O. (1983). Observed and self-reported psychopathology in NGRI acquittees in court-mandated outpatient treatment. *International Journal of Offender Therapy and Comparative Criminology, 27,* 143–149.

Rogers, R., & Wettstein, R. (1984). Relapse of NGRI outpatients: An empirical study. *International Journal of Offender Therapy and Comparative Criminology, 28,* 227–235.

Roth, L. (Ed.). (1987). *Clinical treatment of the violent person.* New York: Guilford Press.

Schottenfeld, R. S. (1989). Involuntary treatment of substance abuse disorders—Impediments to success. *Psychiatry, 52,* 164–176.

Siegel, A., & Elwork, A. (1990). Treating incompetence to stand trial. *Law and Human Behavior, 14,* 57–65.

Silver, S. B. (1983). *Treatment and aftercare of insanity acquittees in Maryland: Testimony before the Subcommittee on Criminal Law of the Committee on the Judiciary, United States Senate* (Serial No. J-97-122, pp. 374–383). Washington, DC: U.S. Government Printing Office.

Spodak, M., Silver, S. B., & Wright, C. (1984). Criminality of discharged insanity acquittees: Fifteen year experience in Maryland reviewed. *Bulletin of the American Academy of Psychiatry & the Law, 12,* 373–382.

Steadman, H., Monahan, J., Hartstone, E., Davis, S., & Robbins, C. (1982). Mentally disordered offenders: A national survey of patients and facilities. *Law and Human Behavior, 6,* 31–38.

Tyce, F. A., Olson, R. O., & Amdahl, R. (1980). P.O.R.T. of Olmsted County, Minnesota. In J. Masserman (Ed.), *Current psychiatric therapies* (pp. 151–157). New York: Grune & Stratton.

Wack, R. (1993). Treatment services at Kirby Forensic Psychiatric Center. *International Journal of Law and Psychiatry, 16,* 83–104.

Wexler, D. B. (1991). Health care compliance principles and the insanity acquittee conditional release process. *Criminal Law Bulletin, 27,* 18–41.

Wiederanders, M. (1992). Recidivism of disordered offenders who were conditionally vs. unconditionally released. *Behavioral Sciences and the Law, 10,* 141–148.

Wiederanders, M., & Choate, P. (1994). Beyond recidivism: Measuring community adjustments of conditionally release insanity acquittees. *Psychological Assessment, 6,* 1–6.

III

Issues in Civil Law

8

Civil Law

Employment and Discrimination

JANE GOODMAN-DELAHUNTY

This chapter reviews empirical work pertinent to the laws on employment and discrimination.[1] The crux of employment discrimination litigation entails proof of some of the most elusive and intangible human motives and reactions: bias and prejudice on one hand; psychological impairment and injury on the other hand. These topics have long been of interest to psychologists. The contribution of the discipline of psychology in cases involving employment and discrimination has been very uneven. Some aspects of employment discrimination, such as affirmative action and sexual harassment, have been quite thoroughly researched. Other aspects, such as disability discrimination, remain largely unexamined. The intent of this chapter is to summarize psychological research and literature that bears on this topic and to identify gaps in our knowledge of these issues. In addition, it will propose some research questions for future study.

[1]The views expressed in this chapter are those of the author and do not necessarily reflect those of the U.S. Equal Employment Opportunity Commission or any other government agency. Appreciation and credit is due to Nancy Jasmine Abdel-Sayed, a student at the University of South Carolina School of Law and a summer intern at the U.S. Equal Employment Opportunity Commission, who provided valuable research assistance.

JANE GOODMAN-DELAHUNTY • Administrative Judge, U.S. Equal Employment Opportunity Commission, Los Angeles District Office, Roybal Federal Building, Fourth Floor, 255 East Temple Street, Los Angeles, California 90012.

Psychology and Law: The State of the Discipline, edited by Ronald Roesch, Stephen D. Hart, and James R. P. Ogloff. Kluwer Academic/Plenum Publishers, New York, 1999.

Few matters affect people as intensely as events in the workplace. One reason for this is that employee and employer relationships endure for the greater part of our lives. Moreover, because employment is fundamental to the economic structure of our society, employment relationships hold a prominent position affecting our livelihood and well-being. Disputes over conduct in the workplace are often as intense, protracted, and traumatizing as the most vitriolic divorce. The relationship between employers and employees is regulated by a panoply of common law doctrines, statutes, judicial pronouncements, and administrative agency findings. Laws prohibiting employment discrimination represent one small portion of the corpus of legislation that governs the employee–employer relationship. They are intended to guarantee a minimum of security to wage earners to be free from adverse action because of discriminatory conduct by the employer.

In considering the evolution of employment discrimination law, it is helpful to know that although the first bill proposing a ban on employment discrimination was introduced to Congress in 1942, the Civil Rights Act of 1964 passed only 22 years later (Burstein, 1992). The act, also known as Title VII, prohibits discrimination in employment on the basis of race, color, national origin, gender, and religion. Public employers, private employers with more than 15 employees, employer's agents, labor unions, and employment agencies are bound by Title VII.

The adoption of EEO legislation was a critical step in the United States's attempts to end employment discrimination during an era in which social scientific theories about discrimination surfaced (Burstein, 1992). Following *Brown v. Board of Education* (1954), in which psychological conclusions based on empirical studies regarding the detrimental impact of racial segregation on self-esteem were endorsed by the U.S. Supreme Court, courts were receptive to evidence provided by social scientists. Civil rights groups engaged in concerted action to secure changes in the law (Epp, 1990) and made frequent use of social science in discrimination cases.

Conduct that comprises a discriminatory adverse action varies from case to case. Although initially, the major thrust of the legislation was to prevent discriminatory termination of an employee, today, all phases of the employment relationship, whether the employee is temporary or permanent, part time or full time, may be the subject matter of employment discrimination litigation. Restricted opportunities to develop and maintain employment can cause considerable hardship with disastrous consequences. One consequence of the recent economic shrinkage is a high incidence of "job discontinuances," causing widespread job insecurity and competition as opportunities for career advancement diminish (Opotow, 1996). Thus, the facts of a particular situation that are being contested can entail circumstances surrounding the employer's decision whether to post a vacancy (denial of the opportunity to apply for a position), the screening and rating of applicants for a job vacancy (nonhire or nonpromotion), training, evaluation, compensation, benefits, demotion, the decision to discharge an employee, or the extent to which an employee's decision to quit a job was prompted by untenable discriminatory conduct. Most recently, the U.S. Supreme Court affirmed that events after the termination of the employment relationship may also form the basis of a discrimination-based claim, if, for example, biased comments that detrimentally affect that individual's prospective employment are made about a former employee to a new, prospective employer.

The scope of this chapter is confined to employment and discrimination. Accordingly, it does not include a review of studies on general employment issues, such as the costs of employment litigation. This chapter does not address developments in the workplace that involve claims for workplace stress or management assessments of the propensity for violence in the workplace, except where these may be related to discrimination claims. Similarly, studies of employee overwork or burnout, workload allocation, efficacy of management, leadership styles, or partnership between workers and managers are not addressed.

SOURCES OF ANTIDISCRIMINATION LAW

As noted earlier, the major federal legislation that prohibits adverse action by an employer based upon discrimination is Title VII. Other major federal sources of antidiscrimination legislation include the Equal Pay Act (1963); the Civil Rights Act of 1866 (42 U.S.C. Sections 1985 and 1986 regarding racial discrimination); the Civil Rights Act of 1871 (42 U.S.C. Sections 1981 and 1985, prohibiting discrimination under color of state law); the Age Discrimination in Employment Act of 1967 (ADEA), which protects individuals over age 40; and the Americans With Disabilities Act of 1990 (ADA, 1991), which outlaws discrimination based on psychological or physiological impairments or disabilities. In general, the purpose of these laws is to protect individuals from discriminatory treatment based on (a) immutable characteristics, such as those discernible from an individual's appearance or name (e.g., ethnicity, race, gender, national origin, age, physiological disability) and (b) the exercise or expression of political or religious freedoms held inviolate by the U.S. Constitution and the Bill of Rights (e.g., religion, retaliation for opposing apparent discrimination or for participating in the legal process established to eliminate unlawful discrimination). Related federal legislation and executive orders that influence antidiscrimination conduct are Executive Orders 11246 (1964–1965; affirmative action), the Immigration Reform and Control Act (IRCA, 1986), and more recently, the Administrative Dispute Resolution Act of 1995 (ADRA).

In addition to the foregoing federal statutes and orders, numerous state antidiscrimination statutes offer similar, but not necessarily identical, guarantees to combat discrimination against specific identifiable or cognizable groups. Often, state or local regulations are more far reaching and protective of individual rights than federal legislation and may include prohibitions against discrimination based on sexual orientation and marital status. Most federal and state antidiscrimination laws include anti-retaliation provisions, prohibiting an employer from acting in reprisal or retaliation against an employee who engages in protected conduct by participating in the claiming process or as a witness on behalf of another employee or by protesting or opposing allegedly discriminatory practices.

Employment discrimination claims can be brought in state or federal court under the foregoing regulations; claims may also be premised on tort or contract law (e.g., on grounds that adverse conduct by the employer violates public policy or breaches an implied or express contract). The doctrine of employment at will, unique to the United States, developed in the late 19th and early 20th centuries, permitting employers to terminate employees without notice, for good cause, bad cause, a cause that is morally wrong, or no cause at all (Franczak, 1995), leaving employees little recourse (Dertouzos & Karoly, 1992). Some 55–65 million members of the American workforce are subject to arbitrary discharge under the doctrine of employment at will; approximately 5 million are terminated each year. A claim of wrongful, discriminatory termination may be accompanied by related tort claims of intentional infliction of emotional distress, false imprisonment, defamation, fraud, assault, battery, negligence, or whistle-blowing.

When state law is the basis of the discrimination claim, courts generally rely on the federal law for guidance. The major point is that the legislative bases enumerated earlier are by no means exhaustive. A maze of laws exists that applies to and may be implicated in a discrimination action.

CONDUCT PROHIBITED BY DISCRIMINATION LAWS

What comprises actionable discriminatory conduct in the workplace? One intriguing facet of employment discrimination litigation is that there are many diverse ways in which actions alleged to be adverse can occur.

Employees may litigate over the disparate imposition of discipline or performance evaluations that an employee contends are intentionally lower than warranted. Nowadays, litigation ensues in an effort to prevent the employer from establishing grounds and a record to support subsequent termination.

Precisely who is protected by the antidiscrimination laws and the conduct that comes within their purview has evolved over time. The scope of protection now extends to certain conduct, groups, and categories of persons never considered when the original legislation was drafted. In fact, gender as a protected status was never part of the contemplated legislation; it was added as a prohibited basis at the last minute of the battle of the filibuster in an effort to ensure the failure of the act. Despite this inauspicious beginning, considerable litigation based on gender ensued as female employees entered nontraditional occupations, in cases challenging the height, weight, and physical agility requirements for positions such as firefighter, police officer, or logger, for example. The plain language and text of Title VII is silent regarding sexual harassment and discrimination based on pregnancy. Both come within the ambit of gender-based discrimination. The number of sexual harassment claims has increased annually since this issue was recognized as being within the purview of Title VII. Obviously, the initial legislation never foresaw "reverse discrimination" claims, such as those by White males alleging discriminatory treatment on grounds that female or minority co-workers are favored.

Past litigation has addressed whether sexual orientation or sexual preference comes within the scope of the federal antidiscrimination laws, and, in general, the courts have held that it does not. The limited existing research on discrimination based on sexual orientation suggests that gay, lesbian, and bisexual individuals are subjected to higher rates and more extreme forms of harassment and victimization than are heterosexual individuals (Herek, Gillis, Cogan, & Glunt, 1997). Federal courts were divided on the issue of same-sex harassment. Some courts permitted the claims where homosexuality was involved but not among heterosexuals; others rejected the claims on grounds that the harassment did not occur because of the employee's sex (Stone-Harris, 1996). In 1998, the U.S. Supreme Court held that same-sex harassment was prohibited by Title VII (*Oncale v. Sundowner Offshore Services, Inc.*, 1998).

Political issues abound in the discrimination arena, adding both confusion and intensity to the debates. For example, there is some tension in the areas of overlap between policies underlying the Immigration Reform and Control Act of 1986 (IRCA) and those underlying Title VII. Specifically, the more disincentives and penalties there are for employers to hire illegal aliens under IRCA, the more this body of law promotes discrimination against minority groups that include many illegal aliens (e.g., among the Haitians or those in the Hispanic communities). In Fiscal Year 1995, more than 11,000 illegal aliens were removed from jobs in work sites across the United States of America (U.S. Immigration and Naturalization Service, 1996). Enforcement of IRCA, ostensibly to eradicate child labor and the exploitation of illegal aliens in sweatshops and so forth, can engender discrimination against individuals authorized to work in the United States, many of whom may have been born and raised within its borders.

THE PREVALENCE OF WORKPLACE DISCRIMINATION CHARGES

The agency charged with the enforcement of federal antidiscrimination laws is the United States Equal Employment Opportunity Commission (EEOC), one of the smaller and more beleaguered federal agencies, employing fewer than 3,000 employees nationwide. Records of discrimination charges filed with the EEOC show a steady increase in the total number of individual claims filed from 1990 (62,135) to 1994 (91,189), dropping somewhat in 1996 and 1997 (77,990 and 80,680, respectively).

EEOC reports do not take into account state claims filed or employment discrimination claims filed on other bases. EEOC statistics show that claims on the basis of race or national origin are the most common, accounting for approximately one third of the total number of individual charges. Of this group, in 1996, only very few, 3.3%, were "reverse discrimination" charges, filed by White males or females claiming that minorities were favored to their detriment. Gender-based discrimination complaints represented 29%, less than one third, of the total number of charges filed. In FY 1994, 14,420 sexual harassment complaints were filed; approximately 1,000 more were filed in FY 1996. Numbers of age- and disability-based claims filed are approximately even, each accounting for about one fifth of the individual charges filed. A relatively small number of claims, approximately 2%, are filed annually on the basis of religion.

Since FY 1993, when the EEOC began accepting charges filed on the basis of physiological or psychological disability, approximately one fifth of the total number of charges have been filed on that basis; 23% of the charges filed in FY 1995, 1996, 1997. Of 50,000 ADA complaints filed by 1996, approximately 6,000 were for psychological disabilities, separate and apart from learning disabilities. Of that group, 25% alleged failure to accommodate.

Claims of discriminatory termination or discharge (firing) account for the largest proportion of bias cases filed with the EEOC annually. In FY

TABLE 8.1. U.S. EQUAL EMPLOYMENT OPPORTUNITY COMMISSION
CHARGE STATISTICS, FY 1990–1997

Protected basis	1990	1992	1994	1995	1996	1997
Race	29,121	29,042	31,656	29,986	26,287	29,199
	46.7%	40.3%	34.8%	34.3%	33.8%	36.2%
National origin	7,236	7,126	7,414	7,035	6,687	6,712
	11.6%	9.9%	8.1%	8.0%	8.6%	8.3%
Gender	19,160	22,784	27,255	27,454	24,774	25,862
	30.7%	31.6%	29.9%	31.4%	31.8%	21.1%
Religion	1,147	1,337	1,546	1,581	1,564	1,709
	1.8%	1.9%	1.7%	1.8%	2.0%	2.1%
Age	14,719	19,264	19,571	17,401	15,665	15,785
	23.6%	26.7%	21.5%	19.9%	20.1%	19.6%
Retaliation	7,579	10,932	14,415	15,342	14,412	18,113
	12.1%	14.4%	15.8%	17.5%	18.5%	22.5%
Disability	na	999	18,808	19,778	17,954	18,108
		1.3%	20.7%	22.6%	23.1%	22.4%
Total charges	62,135	73,302	91,189	87,529	77,990	80,680

Note: Because some individuals file charges on multiple bases, the total number of charges filed in a given year, which reflects total individual charges, will be less than the sum of total charges on the protected bases listed. EEOC began enforcing the Americans with Disabilites Act on July 26, 1992.
Source: U.S. Equal Opportunity Commission.

the largest proportion of bias cases filed with the EEOC annually. In FY 1994, 48,138 firing and layoff claims were received. Complaints of discriminatory working conditions accounted for 15,029 charges, distinguished from claims of harassment for reasons other than sex, of which 11,657 complaints were filed. Claims of discriminatory promotion and hiring accounted for 8,060 and 7,252 claims, respectively. Wage-based discrimination was alleged 6,482 times in FY 1994.

Over time, the standards the plaintiff must meet to prevail in individual discrimination claims have become more stringent (e.g., *St. Mary's Honor Center v. Hicks*, 1993). Thus, although there are more claims filed than before, including more nonmeritorious claims, it is more difficult for plaintiffs with bona fide discrimination claims to prevail. In FY 1994, the EEOC itself filed only 357 lawsuits, leading one commentator to note that "the primary function of the EEOC appears to be to process a large number of cases that the agency determines have no merit" (Selmi, 1996).

Many early discrimination cases were class actions or "pattern and practice" claims in which social scientific and statistical evidence was presented on behalf of the plaintiffs. By the mid-1980s, under the Reagan Administration, the EEOC abandoned class action litigation and enforced "one-on-one" or individual claims only. Class actions, once the mainstay of employment litigation, vanished from the scene (Donohue & Siegelman, 1991). In 1997, under EEOC Commissioner Casellas and the Clinton Administration, this policy was reversed; pattern-and-practice class action litigation is being revived in the public interest.

Tracking and counting employment claims is difficult, and an accurate picture of the prevalence of discriminatory conduct in the workplace is more difficult to discern. Some data exist regarding the incidence of claims filed in federal district court. For instance, in the 15-year period between July 1, 1972 and March 31, 1987, 92,090 employment discrimination claims were filed in federal district court (Siegelman & Donohue, 1990). Employment litigation is notably the fastest growing area of civil litigation in the federal system, with approximately 81% of the litigation relating to termination (Copus, 1996). The federal employment discrimination caseload grew dramatically in the 20 years between 1970 and 1990, at a rate several times faster than the rest of the federal civil caseload (Donohue & Siegelman, 1991). Given the fact that most lawyers prefer to file employment discrimination claims in state rather than federal court and combine those claims with common law tort claims, at least in part because of the availability of more extensive damages, the strong implication is that comparable data for the civil caseload in state courts reflects filing patterns that exceed those in federal district court.

In sum, the developments outlined here have created circumstances in which employment discrimination litigation is increasing dramatically, but the outcome of the cases is unpredictable and risky for all parties. The participation of psychologists and other social scientists in discrimination cases and their contributions to this field of law outside of the courtroom have fluctuated over the past 35 years. An outline of the major available legal theories of discrimination that highlights the areas in which contributions for psychology may have the most salience follows.

LEGAL THEORIES OF WORKPLACE DISCRIMINATION

THEORIES OF LIABILITY FOR WORKPLACE DISCRIMINATION

One of four available legal theories underlies most claims of employment discrimination. Disparate treatment and adverse impact are the two broad theories of liability for workplace discrimination that are the best known. They have been permitted since the Civil Rights Act of 1964 was enacted:

"Disparate treatment" [occurs when] ... the employer simply treats some people less favorably than others because of their race, color, religion, national origin.... Claims of disparate treatment may be distinguished from claims that stress "disparate impact." The latter involve employment practices that are facially neutral in their treatment of different groups but that in fact fall more harshly in one group than another and cannot be justified by business necessity. (*International Brotherhood of Teamsters v. United States*, 1977, p. 335)

A third theory of discrimination, aimed at eliminating a hostile workplace environment or instances of employee harassment by co-workers or supervisors and managers, has become increasingly popular in the past decade.

Fourth, the antidiscrimination laws require special consideration in the form of reasonable accommodation in response to requests by employees regarding their needs for special consideration for (a) religious observance and (b) psychological and physiological impairments. Claims of disparate treatment, disparate impact, and harassment may be brought with respect to any protected basis, that is, on grounds of race, color, gender, national origin, age, disability, religion, and reprisal. Issues of reasonable accommodation arise only in cases concerning religion and disability.

DISPARATE TREATMENT

Disparate treatment claims require proof of discriminatory intent on the part of the employer. This intent can be established by means of direct or indirect, circumstantial evidence or statistical plus anecdotal (direct) evidence. Direct evidence is that which evinces an improper motive, such as comments revealing bias or prejudice based on age, gender, race. Where direct evidence is produced, to avoid liability, the employer must affirmatively prove by a preponderance of the evidence that the discriminatory motive was of no consequence; that the same employment decision would have been made absent the discriminatory factor (*Price-Waterhouse v. Hopkins*, 1989).

More frequently, proof of discriminatory intent is established through indirect or circumstantial evidence showing that illegal considerations of age, gender, race, disability, and so on motivated the employer.[2] The employer can defend by showing that legitimate, nondiscriminatory reasons motivated the adverse treatment at issue. Subjective reasons, expla-

[2]For example, to establish a *prima facie* case of hiring discrimination, the plaintiff must establish that he or she is (a) a member of a protected group, (b) applied for and was qualified for the position for which the employer was seeking applicants, (c) was rejected, and (d) the position remained vacant, while the employer continued to seek applicants with the plaintiff's qualification (*McDonnell-Douglas Corp. v. Green*, 1973).

nations, or criteria are not per se unlawful.[3] In rebuttal, the plaintiff must show that the employer's stated reason is a pretext for discrimination. The plaintiff retains the burden of proof and ultimately must show that the adverse action taken was motivated by discriminatory intent. The model for circumstantial proof of discriminatory intent was established in *McDonnell-Douglas Corp. v. Green* (1973). Statistical evidence may be used as part of the circumstantial proof to establish an inference of discriminatory intent or to show that the employer's stated reason lacks credibility and is a pretext for discrimination.

In *St. Mary's Honor Center v. Hicks* (1993), the U.S. Supreme Court held that to prevail the plaintiff must not only raise an inference of discriminatory intent by introducing direct or indirect evidence, but the plaintiff must also show that discriminatory intent in fact motivated the decision in issue. Merely showing that the employer's stated reason lacks credulity is not adequate. Thus, the burden on plaintiffs in disparate treatment cases was heightened. The Court held that if an employer's explanation for its conduct lacked credulity, this did not necessarily establish discriminatory intent. The plaintiff must prove that discrimination was the actual motivation for the adverse action in issue. One consequence of the more exacting standard is that more employment discrimination claims are dismissed on summary judgment; another is that fewer attorneys are willing to represent plaintiffs on a contingent fee basis.

Adverse Impact

The adverse impact theory or analysis covers situations in which the defendant employer treats all employees or job applicants equally, but the result or consequence of that equal treatment is the disproportionate exclusion of members of a protected class. In *Griggs v. Duke Power Co.* (1971), Black employees challenged the use of intelligence tests, specifically the Wonderlic Personnel Test and the Bennett Mechanical Comprehension Test, as a prerequisite for promotion or transfer to positions for which they were otherwise qualified on grounds that the tests did not measure the ability to perform jobs or a category of jobs for which they were used. The Supreme Court distinguished claims of disparate treatment from claims of disparate impact, holding that "good intent or absence of discriminatory intent does not redeem ... testing mechanisms that operate as 'built-in headwinds' for minority groups" (p. 432) and extended the application of the Civil Rights Act to "practices that are fair in form, but discriminatory in

---

[3]More intense scrutiny of the subjective criteria is applied when the explanation is proffered by someone who is not a member of the plaintiff's protected group. (*Page v. Bolger*, 1981).

operation" (p. 431). Once a disproportionate impact of the tests was demonstrated, the employer had to justify their use by proving the tests were job related and required by business necessity (i.e., that they had validity).

The elements of proof in a disparate impact case were outlined by the Court in *Albemarle Paper Company v. Moody* (1975), a case in which an industrial psychologist was retained to validate the use of general ability tests as a prerequisite to employment. In cases of disparate or adverse impact, intentional discrimination is inferred based on circumstantial evidence. The policy or practice in issue may be a facially neutral practice, the impact of which is demonstrated to fall more harshly on members of protected than unprotected groups. Subjective employment practices, such as word-of-mouth recruiting, lack of objective job qualifications, and subjective criteria in hiring and promotion, may be scrutinized under a disparate impact analysis (*Watson v. Fort Worth Bank & Trust*, 1988). In addition to proving a cognizable disparate impact, the plaintiff must prove that a specific identified employment practice, whether subjective or objective, caused the disparate impact. Once a showing of the disparity is made, the burden of proof shifts to the employer, who must then prove that the practice in issue is justified by business necessity. There is no requirement that the challenged practice be essential or indispensable to the employer's practice to pass muster, but a mere insubstantial justification in this regard will not suffice. The plaintiff can rebut this showing by establishing that the same goal or objective can be achieved by means of a less discriminatory alternative.

Historically, adverse impact cases relied on statistical evidence to show that a particular employment practice has a significant impact. In a disparate treatment case, statistical evidence represents circumstantial evidence of intentional discrimination. In the early years, to establish a disparate impact case, a plaintiff merely had to demonstrate a statistical disparity in a job category or the workforce, and the employer had to show that the practice was a bona fide requirement or business necessity. In 1977, three cases were issued in which the use of statistical evidence was addressed, and as a consequence, the standard changed.

STATISTICAL PROOF OF DISCRIMINATION

In *International Brotherhood of Teamsters v. United States* (1977), the Court held that statistics were competent evidence to prove discrimination. In that case, the statistics consisted merely of differences in the proportions of Blacks and Whites in the total workforce with regard to certain job strata. In *Hazelwood School District v. United States* (1977), a standard deviation from the mean in the relevant labor market was used to predict the expected racial proportion in the workforce, and the concept of a qualified relevant labor market was endorsed. The statistical analyses required could be quite simple. In *Furnco Construction Corporation v. Waters* (1978), the Court held that an employer could present rebuttal statistical evidence to show there was no discriminatory violation in its conduct or practices.

In the 1980s the perspective changed. From *Connecticut v. Teal* (1982) came the principle that "bottom-line" disparities in overall hiring or promotion rates were insufficient to prove disparate impact. In that case, four Black employees failed to achieve a passing cutoff score on a written test to qualify them as eligible permanent state employees. The passing rate for Blacks was 68% of that for Whites, but the actual promotion rate for eligible Blacks exceeded that for eligible Whites. The Supreme Court held that the bottom-line statistical disparities did not preclude the plaintiffs "from establishing a *prima facie* case of employment discrimination, nor did it provide the employer with a defense to such a case" (p. 2526). In other words, simple work force disparities in proportional comparisons are inadequate (*Lopez v. Laborers International Union Local 18*, 1993). The extent to which statistical disparities will be regarded as adequate varies from case to case. The Supreme Court elected not to adopt a benchmark that three standard deviations were required to demonstrate that the observed disparities had statistical significance (Schwartz & Goodman, 1992). Thereafter, courts focused on whether, when statistically significant disparities were observed, a causal connection had been demonstrated between the disparities and the practices at issue. Statistical proofs became more sophisticated, and the cases reflect discussions of one-tailed versus two-tailed tests, hypergeometric models, and so on (see, for example, *EEOC v. Federal Bank of Richmond*, 1983).

In the face of legal rulings that no inference of discrimination will be drawn from mere statistical proof of imbalances in an employer's workforce, the plaintiff must prove what caused the disparities. Traditional statistical approaches include psychometric analysis and multiple regression. An alternate survey data analysis approach was outlined by Schwartz and Goodman (1992).

The psychometric approach entails a presentation of evidence establishing that employment criteria used by the employer are job related and consistent with business necessity. For example, in selecting candidates for hire or promotion, selection criteria must be job related and valid predictors of job performance. Validity generalization analyses may be presented where tests shown to be valid or job related in one job performance are generalized to another. The relevance of a generic validity generalization study to the particular circumstances presented by a particular case is often in question. Haney and Hurtado (1994) noted that the practice of validity generalization "pushes the notion of merit about as far (or further than) it can go" (p. 229).

The multiple regression approach entails accounting for factors that best predict an employer's decisions (i.e., job relevant qualifications versus prohibited considerations, such as age, gender, race). Arguments often center on the use of proxy variables, omitted variables, or unmeasurable variables and the probative value of the data, given some omissions. When multiple regression analyses are used, the courts will ignore the statistics if certain measurable relevant variables are omitted (*EEOC v. Sears, Roebuck & Company*, 1988). Multiple regression models remain the most commonly used statistical models.

The survey data analysis method avoids some of the problems encountered in multiple regression analyses by directly gathering information about factors that could cause the decisions in issue and testing the effect of these factors on decisions. A common employer defense to patterns of disparate promotion rates of males versus females was that females were not interested in promotion to the higher paying jobs or the jobs with more responsibility (Schultz, 1990; Schultz & Petterson, 1992). To test whether this defense really represents the interests of management rather than that of the plaintiff class, a survey designed to test the impact of interest goals on advancement opportunities of females can be devised. To meet the plaintiff's burden to show causation of nonpromotion, a survey instrument can be used to assess the extent to which management decisions are determined by employee interest versus stereotyped attitudes that females are less willing to put in the effort and time needed to secure promotions to managerial level jobs; assessments that women were less able than men to work in management; and the belief that women should be oriented to home and family, not work (Schwartz & Goodman, 1992). In other words, the survey method examines employer decision making more directly by focusing on such elements as the attitudes of the employer, the environment at work, and the interests of the affected employees in the protected categories at issue.

In general, use of statistical proofs and has declined (Howard, 1994). In part, this is because of judicial rulings in the face of vast quantities of competent statistical evidence that anecdotal testimony is needed "to bring the numbers to life" (*EEOC v. Sears, Roebuck & Company*, 1988). Other judicial responses to the plaintiff's statistical evidence that discouraged plaintiffs were holdings that even when the evidence was competent, it failed to establish discriminatory intent or requisite causation (Kaye, 1990).

Furthermore, after the 1970s, the EEOC halted its program of litigating class action "pattern-and-practice" claims of discrimination in hiring, promotion, compensation, or termination cases.

In 1991, the Glass Ceiling Act of 1991 was incorporated into the 1991 Civil Rights Act as Title II. The purpose of the act was to eliminate barriers to the advancement of women and minorities to management and decision-making positions in business and to promote workforce diversity (Sections 202(A) and (B)). A 21-member Glass Ceiling Commission was established for 4 years to study the problem and prepare recommendations to the president and Congress on ways to increase opportunities and eliminate artificial barriers to the advancement of women and minorities (Section 203). The commission concluded that artificial barriers continue to impede equal access of women and minorities to advancement in high-level corporate management. The status of any recommendations is uncertain in light of nationwide state initiatives to end preferential treatment of women and minorities and a review of all federal affirmative action programs (Bureau of National Affairs, Inc., 1995, p. S-90).

HOSTILE WORKPLACE ENVIRONMENT DISCRIMINATION

In 1980, the U.S. Equal Employment Opportunity Commission promulgated guidelines prohibiting harassment in the workplace on grounds that an employer has an affirmative duty to maintain a working environmentfree from harassment, intimidation, or insult. The guidelines prohibited harassment on the basis of race, color, religion, national origin, age, sex, and gender as a violation of Section 703 of Title VII, or the ADEA. An employer has an affirmative duty to take positive action to eliminate such practices or remedy their effects (*EEOC v. Murphy Motor Freight Lines, Inc.,* 1980; *Rogers v. EEOC,* 1971). Harassment claims require a plaintiff to establish that slurs and other verbal or physical conduct based on an employee's protected status (a) have the purpose or effect of creating and intimidating, hostile, or offensive working environment; (b) have the purpose or effect of unreasonably interfering with an individual's work performance; or (c) otherwise adversely affect an individuals' employment opportunities (U.S. EEOC, 1980a).

The hostile workplace environment theory has been applied to co-worker conduct that comprised racially based, national-origin based, religion-based, gender-based, and reprisal-based harassment (Hartstein & Wilde, 1994). This theory has also been applied to reverse discrimination claims (e.g., White males referred to by Black co-workers as "White asses," and "White boys," who sat in an area referred to by co-workers as "Georgetown," *Turner v. Barr,* 1992).

To establish a *prima facie* case of racial harassment, for example, an employee must prove (1) he or she belongs to a protected group based on race and/or color; (2) he or she was subjected to unwelcome or offensive comments, jokes, acts, and other verbal or physical conduct of a racial nature in the workplace; (3) the conduct complained of substantially interfered with his or her work performance, creating an intimidating, hostile, or offensive working environment; and (4) his employer knew or should have known of the conduct complained of and failed to take prompt remedial action (*Harris v. International Paper Co.*, 1991).

To prove whether the conduct is unwelcome and offensive, the plaintiff must show not only that he or she subjectively found the conduct offensive, but also that a reasonable person in the same protected group would find the comments or conduct offensive. Thus, in some jurisdictions, the objective standard is that of a "reasonable Black person," a "reasonable person of Hispanic national origin," or a "reasonable woman," and so on. The plaintiff must allege conduct that a reasonable person would consider sufficiently severe or pervasive to alter the conditions of employment and create an abusive working environment (*Canada v. Boyd Group*, 1992; *Harris v. Forklift Systems, Inc.*, 1993; *Oncale v. Sundowner Offshore Services, Inc.*, 1998).

Reasonable Accommodation

Employees who request accommodation because they wish to observe religious holidays, or because they have a physical or psychological disability are entitled to special consideration under Title VII and the Americans With Disabilities Act. In response to such requests, employers have a duty to accommodate religious needs and disabilities unless accommodation imposes an undue hardship or burden on the conduct of the employer's business. In a religious observance case, the term *religion* has been held to include all aspects of religious observance and practice, as well as moral or ethical beliefs that occupy the role of religion in a person's life. Political or social ideologies, however, are not protected by Title VII. To establish a religious discrimination *prima facie* case, the plaintiff must prove that (1) a sincerely held, *bona fide* religious belief conflicts with or prevents compliance with an employment requirement; (2) the employer was informed of the conflict; and (c) the plaintiff suffered adverse treatment because of refusal to comply with the employment requirement. The burden is then on the employer to prove that good faith efforts were made to accommodate the plaintiff's beliefs, and if these efforts were unsuccessful, to demonstrate that reasonable accommodation was not possible without an undue hardship (*Anderson v. General Dynamics*, 1978).

In the case of disabled employees, reasonable accommodation may include (a) making facilities accessible and usable by disabled persons; (b) restructuring and/or creating jobs part-time or modified work schedules; (c) reassignment; (d) acquisition or modification of examinations, the provision of readers and interpreters, and other similar actions. Thus, reasonable accommodation mandates that certain individuals receive preferential treatment in the workplace because of religion and physical or psychological disabilities.

REPRISAL AND RETALIATION

The antidiscrimination laws prohibit employers from taking adverse action against employees because they oppose what appears to be a Title VII violation, or because they participate in the EEO process, either as a claimant or, for example, as a witness on someone else's behalf. To establish a *prima facie* case of reprisal, an employee must show that he or she (a) engaged in protected opposition to Title VII discrimination or participated in a Title VII proceeding; (b) received adverse treatment from the employer; and (c) there was a causal connection between the protected activity and the adverse treatment (*Wrighten v. Metropolitan Hospitals, Inc.*, 1984). Thus, reprisal cases can be brought under a disparate treatment or a harassment model.

LEGAL RELIEF AND REMEDIES
FOR WORKPLACE DISCRIMINATION

TRADITIONAL RELIEF

The policy underlying traditional relief available to victims of discrimination under Title VII is to make them whole. Under the Civil Rights Act of 1964, make-whole relief included back pay, possible front pay, and various types of injunctive relief. Reinstatement can be ordered, as can retroactive raises or promotions to which the plaintiff is entitled. Other potential relief that may be awarded includes lost fringe benefits, sick leave pay, vacation pay, medical benefits, lost overtime, shift differential pay, pensions, retirement bonuses, and travel allowances. Damages recoverable under the Equal Pay Act and the Age Discrimination in Employment Act include liquidated damages, or double the lost back pay, unless the employer acted reasonably and in good faith.

The 1991 Civil Rights Act made available attorney fees, expert fees, and compensatory and punitive damages to plaintiffs under the federal antidiscrimination laws, purportedly to attract more personal injury lawyers to this field (Copus, 1996). Depending on the size of the employer, combined punitive and compensatory damages are limited to $50,000 for employers with fewer than 101 employees, to $100,000 for employers with between 101 and 200 employees, $200,000 for employers with between 201 and 500 employees, and $300,000 for employers with more than 500 employees. The "caps" or maximum dollar amounts recoverable as compensatory and punitive damages under federal law do not exist under most state antidiscrimination laws. Consequently, most practicing attorneys prefer to bring suit in state court.

COMPENSATORY DAMAGES

The 1991 Civil Rights Act authorizes compensatory damages in cases of intentional discrimination in violation of Title VII of the Civil Rights Act of 1964, the Rehabilitation Act of 1973, and Title I of the Americans With Disabilities Act of 1990. Compensatory damages are not available in disparate impact cases, nor in cases under the ADA in which an employer has made a good faith effort to provide reasonable accommodation to an employee. The availability of compensatory and punitive damages under the 1991 Civil Rights Act was particularly significant for racial or sexual harassment victims; previously, neither reinstatement nor front pay were possible remedies to the injuries. Without doubt, these innovations legitimized claims for pain and suffering, emotional distress, anguish, and so on, as consequences of unlawful discriminatory conduct.

Under the law, serious psychological harm is not required to establish a violation of Title VII resulting from discrimination or a hostile or abusive workplace environment (*Harris v. Forklift Systems, Inc.*, 1993). The plaintiff must produce evidence of actual injury caused by discriminatory conduct (*Bolden v. SEPTA*, 1994). The plaintiff must establish (a) a reasonable probability, rather than a mere possibility, that damages due to emotional distress were in fact incurred; (b) the extent of the actual injury; and (c) that such harm resulted from the discriminatory conduct (*Gore v. Turner*, 1977).[4] The employer bears the burden to show that the plaintiff failed to take

---

[4]For instance, in a case in which a plaintiff testified that she had suffered emotional distress and lost income, a jury award of $25,000 was reduced to $2,940 by the court on grounds that the plaintiff produced no evidence that her peers thought any less of her, of her loss of income, or of physical suffering, or that she had sought counseling for any emotional distress (*Spence v. Board of Education of Christian School District*, 1986).

reasonable steps to mitigate his or her damages (*Booker v. Taylor Milk Co.*, 1995; *Blum v. Witco Chemical Corp.*, 1987).

There is no legal requirement that emotional distress be diagnosable in order to be compensable. Expert testimony, while advisable, is not mandatory (*Bolden v. SEPTA*, 1994). Potential injuries and defenses are set forth in McDonald and Kulick (1994). Damages for emotional harm include intangible injuries, such as emotional pain and suffering, inconvenience, mental anguish, loss of enjoyment of life, and injury to professional standing, character, and reputation. Emotional harm may manifest itself as sleeplessness, anxiety, stress, depression, marital strain, humiliation, emotional distress, loss of self-esteem, excessive fatigue, or a nervous breakdown (U.S. EEOC, 1992). Emotional trauma and damage caused by other events cannot be recovered, but exacerbation of a preexisting psychological injury caused by discriminatory conduct is compensable.

PUNITIVE DAMAGES

Punitive damages are awarded against a private employer who acts "with malice or with reckless indifference to the federally protected rights of an aggrieved person" (Civil Rights Act of 1991, Section 102(b)(1)). The purpose of punitive damages is to punish the employer and deter future discriminatory conduct. Relevant considerations include the character of the defendant's acts, the nature and extent of harm likely to occur from the employer's conduct, the nature and extent of harm actually suffered, and the financial wealth of the defendant (*TXO Production Corp. v. Alliance Resources Corp.*, 1993).

To determine whether conduct supports an award of punitive damages, the EEOC recommends consideration of (a) the egregiousness of the conduct; (b) the nature, extent, and severity of harm to the plaintiff; (c) the duration of the discriminatory conduct; (d) the existence and frequency of similar past discriminatory conduct by the employer; (e) whether or not the employer attempted to cover up the conduct; (f) the response of the employer once notified of the offensive conduct; and (g) the existence of threats or deliberate retaliatory action against the plaintiff. Regarding the defendant's financial status, the EEOC identified the following factors: (a) the revenues and liabilities of the business; (b) the fair market value of the employer's assets; (c) the amount of liquid assets on hand, including what the employer can reasonably borrow; (d) the employer's projected future earnings and the future resale value of the employer's business; and (e) the affiliation of the employer with, or status as a subsidiary of, a larger entity that could provide it with additional financial resources.

The Right to a Jury Trial

When Title VII was adopted, no provision was made for jury trials on grounds that popular sentiment would be against employees suing for discrimination. By the mid-1990s, juror sentiments in employment litigation were notably antiemployer, based in part on perceptions that corporate America's loyalty to its workers had declined. One 8-year study of jury verdicts in employment cases revealed that plaintiff employees prevailed in jury trials approximately 57% of the time (Copus, 1996). The 1991 amendments to the 1964 Civil Rights Act permit jury trials in federal district court regarding discrimination claims if a complaining party seeks compensatory or punitive damages (Section 102(c)(1)). Jurors are not informed of the caps or limits on awards for compensatory or punitive damages (Section 102(c)(2)).

Affirmative Action

One noteworthy trend in the courts since the early 1980s is the restriction of affirmative action on a voluntary basis and as a legal remedy for past discrimination. Affirmative action is not, and has never been, binding on private educational institutions and employers who do not conduct business with the government (Executive Order 11,246). The order, signed by President Johnson, applies only to the federal government and federal contractors. Its application in this regard was restricted by the U.S. Supreme Court, as noted later. In August 1985, the Reagan Administration abandoned the use of affirmative action goals and timetables to remedy past discrimination (Pettigrew & Martin, 1987). Private entities may engage in voluntary affirmative action to promote equal opportunity in the workplace (Wittig, 1996).

In 1994, the Bureau of Labor Statistics of the U.S. Department of Labor reported that women comprised 46% of the workforce, Blacks 7.1%, and Hispanics 4.6%. Almost all the cleaners and servants (95.8%) were women. The analyses revealed that Blacks and Hispanics experienced more unemployment, more part-time work, lower wages, and were more susceptible to removal than their White counterparts. More Hispanics than Blacks or Whites were in occupations with employment of relatively short duration, such as laborer and service jobs. Despite gains in educational level and test scores, "In almost any measure of success in the job market, Blacks and Hispanics continue to lag behind Whites" (Bureau of National Affairs, Inc., 1995, p. S-38).

As a legal remedy, affirmative action must follow a court order based on a judgment of liability finding discrimination has been rendered (i.e., once a violation of the law has been proven). In *City of Richmond v. J. A. Croson Co.* (1989), a provision of a remedy imposed by a lower court requiring a 30% set-aside by a city municipality for minority contractors was struck down as improper affirmative action because it was not narrowly tailored to remedy a finding of past discrimination. Finally, in *Adarand Constructors v. Pena* (1995), the U.S. Supreme Court rejected the government's rationale for benign racial classifications and struck down a federal program that awarded prime contractors a bonus for awarding subcontracts to disadvantaged business enterprises, assuming those belonged to minority contractors.[5]

Thereafter, the EEOC issued guidelines for both voluntary and court-ordered remedial affirmative action, stating that affirmative action did not permit the use of quotas and is lawful "only when it is designed to respond to a demonstrated and serious imbalance in the workforce, is flexible, time-limited, applies only to qualified workers, and respects the rights of non-minorities and men" (Bureau of National Affairs, Inc., 1995, p. S-97).

The foregoing legal overview demonstrates that both liability and damages in employment discrimination law are in a state of flux, providing many opportunities for collaboration between lawyers and social scientists to contribute to the growth and development of law on these topics. Some of the major research contributions by psychologists in the past that bear on workplace discrimination are reviewed in the following sections.

PERCEPTIONS OF FAIRNESS
AND EQUITY IN THE WORKPLACE

Various researchers have noted the importance of perceived fairness in assessing attitudes about social justice in the workplace (Kravitz et al., 1997; Rasinski, 1987). In some instances, measures of prejudice have been confounded with fairness considerations (Kravitz et al., 1997). Theoretically, perceived fairness has only recently been studied as a mediating variable regarding attitude formation. To date, some research has been

---

[5] Adarand, a rejected nonminority subcontractor, claimed his nonselection violated Title VI of the Civil Rights Act of 1964 and the Equal Protection Clause of the Fifth Amendment. The Court subjected government affirmative action programs to strict judicial scrutiny, the most exacting standard of review, requiring that the classification serve a compelling government interest and be narrowly drawn. What comprises sufficient evidence of past discrimination to meet this standard and thereby justify affirmative action is somewhat unclear (Murrell & Jones, 1996). Justices Scalia and Thomas maintained that an affirmative action program can never survive strict scrutiny; Justice O'Connor suggested that a program aimed at pervasive, continuing discrimination might survive.

conducted on cognitive factors that may influence perceptions of fairness or discrimination in the workplace; other studies have examined cultural differences that affect the way people think about and react to workplace events. These are fertile areas for consideration, drawing, for example, on studies on the "just world" hypothesis, perceptions of distributive justice, cognitive illusions, and cross-cultural findings on relative individualism and collectivism. Certain implications of perceptions of distributive, procedural, and retributive justice for gender, race, or national origin discrimination in the workplace were summarized by Tyler, Boeckmann, Smith, and Huo (1997). For example, members of all ethnic groups focused on procedural fairness issues in assessing their supervisors' decisions. These researchers concluded that "a focus on the fairness of procedures is a phenomenon that exists in very different social and cultural groups" (Tyler et al., 1997, p. 251).

Illusions of Distributive Justice

Theories of social perceptions regarding equity and deprivation demonstrated that comparing one's reward with the rewards of others is the basis of social comparison theory. This approach is explicitly reflected in the law encompassed within the *prima facie* elements of proof in a disparate treatment case outlined earlier. Four types of relative deprivation pertinent to workplace discrimination, some of which have been the focus of extensive empirical research, were distinguished by Crosby (1984). First, personal deprivation exists when an individual receives less than he or she desires or deserves. Second, in-group deprivation or collective relative deprivation exists when an individual's groups receives less than the individual desires and believes the group deserves (Tougas & Veilleux, 1988). Third, ideological deprivation exists when a group with which the individual sympathizes receives less than the individual desires or believes it deserves (Tougas & Beaton, 1993). Fourth, backlash exists when the individual resents the fact that others have received positive outcomes (Lynch, 1992).

Illusions of distributive justice exist because of misleading perceptions of factual distributions. Previous research has demonstrated that individuals perceive the distribution of social goods, including those available in the workplace, in relation to the extent that they are in command of those goods. Most individuals believe they are rewarded by just standards, perceiving their own standing and income on a distorted continuum. For example, in past studies as many as 94% of the subjects reported their income as "average," a statistical impossibility.

Some preliminary work on perceived disparities was conducted in

Israel by comparing the perceptions of women working in male-dominated versus female-dominated jobs. Women working in female-dominated jobs had a strong awareness of being the target of discrimination. Women in male-dominated jobs, even though disparities existed, did not complain of disparities because they regarded themselves as part of the privileged group. Thus, they were more likely to deny deprivation. Working in a gender atypical job promoted comparisons with others outside of the working group; working in a gender typical job promoted comparisons with others in the same job (Moore, 1990). Whether these findings generalize to situations in which the ratio of minority and majority employees within a department is disparate, leading to predictions about the frequency of racially based claims in the workplace, is unknown.

One problem facing researchers and practitioners who venture into the labyrinth of employment discrimination litigation is a conceptual muddle among issues of fairness, equity, equality of opportunity, affirmative action, and absence of discrimination. Unfairness or inequity in the workplace is not synonymous with unlawful discrimination. Even for those who understand the differences and make appropriate distinctions, the problem does not end. The likelihood is that less well versed participants will continue to use the terms and concepts interchangeably. Thus, it is critical to distinguish fair employment treatment from nondiscriminatory treatment. Antidiscrimination legislation and laws provide no guarantee of fair or equal treatment. They simply outlaw adverse or inequitable treatment motivated by illegal bias or prejudice based on race, color, national origin, gender, religion, age, disability, or reprisal. Consequently, a legal determination that employer conduct was not discriminatory in motive does not necessarily imply that the action taken was fair or equitable. Many employers whose challenged conduct is determined to be nondiscriminatory erroneously infer they are fair and evenhanded in their treatment of employees.

THE MYTH OF MERIT-BASED DECISION MAKING IN THE WORKPLACE

Laypeople frequently assert "discrimination" when an employer does not apply merit-based decision-making principles in reaching the adverse decision at issue. Many employees are disappointed to learn that there is no constitutional right to merit-based decisions in the workplace (Fallon, 1980), and that the antidiscrimination laws do not mandate fair or equitable treatment. Numerous cases arise because what occurred is manifestly unfair, evincing poor judgment, sloppy management, administrative or judgmental errors, rudeness, favoritism, nepotism, and so on, but the conduct, although unpleasant, does not amount to unlawful discrimination. Unfortunately, many employees who have been treated unfairly or inequitably or in violation of principles of merit have no legal recourse. Often, legal opinions in employment discrimination decisions conclude that what transpired violated sound employment policy and practice, contravened guidelines, and was manifestly unprincipled, but that the preponderance of the evidence failed to establish that the actions were perpetrated because of prohibited discriminatory animus.

The core of the problem, according to Haney and Hurtado (1994), is the myth of merit-based decisions regarding the hiring or promotion of employees: Assumptions are made that merit exists, that it is tangible, immutable, and measurable in a unitary way. Merit-based selections are almost universally positively evaluated (Kravitz et al., 1997). Haney and Hurtado (1994) have discussed how the emphasis on merit, often undeclared, leads to an undue focus on the selection phase in employment decisions rather than on other aspects of the employment process, such as the training of employees on the job. Critics of antidiscrimination legislation, including affirmative action, often assume that merit-based decision making is uniformly unproblematic (Belz, 1991; Cohen, 1991). However, as other scholars have noted, what constitutes merit is generally subject to dispute (Burstein, 1992; Fallon, 1980), and assessing merit based on error rates, productivity, or other factors, is exceedingly difficult (Burstein, 1992; Haney & Hurtado, 1994). Surprisingly few employers whose actions are challenged can demonstrate fairness in their decision-making process based on measurements of merit (Burstein & Pitchford, 1990). Often, merit and ability, or competencies, are treated as if they are synonymous (Haney & Hurtado, 1994). For many Americans, meritocracy and equality are negatively correlated and are not seen as compatible (Peterson, 1994).

DISTRIBUTIVE AND PROCEDURAL FAIRNESS:
AFFIRMATIVE ACTION AND EQUAL OPPORTUNITY

Various commentators have noted that few issues are as poorly understood as affirmative action (Crosby, 1994; Nordin, 1989). Considerable variance in the understanding of affirmative action has been empirically documented (Kravitz et al., 1997). Many people erroneously believe that affirmative action is "preferential selection" or treatment, while others operationalize affirmative action as quotas, recruitment of minorities and women, or the elimination of discrimination in the workplace (Kravitz et al., 1997). Although use of quotas is illegal unless imposed by a court in rare and specific circumstances to remedy proven discrimination in the past, many persons believe that the imposition of quotas favoring females or minorities is a prevalent form of affirmative action (Pratkanis & Turner, 1996). Because negative perceptions of affirmative action are often confounded with reactions to antidiscrimination laws, they cannot be ignored. Thus, researchers must take care to distinguish the principle and the practice of affirmative action and to distinguish affirmative action and equal employment opportunity (Crosby, 1994).

Equal opportunity and affirmative action differ in some fundamental respects. Crosby (1994) noted that affirmative action is proactive; takes cognizance of demographic markers, such as race, gender, and age; regards the world as currently unfair; downplays the role of intentions; and focuses on the system. By comparison, equal opportunity is passive and reactive, ignores demographic markers, imagines the world is fair, highlights the role of intentions in human affairs, and focuses on the individual.

Many individuals who may believe they are motivated by values such as equality or fairness, in fact, apply a "fairness" heuristic (i.e., a subjective assessment of the fairness in a situation that they then use as an organizing principle in responding to those issues). One study demonstrated that the relationship between individual values and individual attitudes toward affirmative action was mediated by assessments of procedural fairness (Lind, 1992).

The significance of differences in the perceived fairness of affirmative action versus equal opportunity has been empirically demonstrated (Kravitz et al., 1997). Several studies confirmed that perceived fairness is a highly influential mediating variable in determining a person's assessment of an affirmative action program (Kravitz, 1995; Murrell, Dietz-Uhler, Dovidio, Gaertner, & Drout, 1994). Perceived fairness has been identified as the key variable in reactions both to affirmative action, in general, and to a particular affirmative action policy (Dovidio & Gaertner, 1996; Peterson, 1994).

Recently, further research indicated that racism is one of the leading causes of opposition to affirmative action (Kravitz, 1995; Pratkanis & Turner, 1996; Sidanius, Pratto, & Bobo, 1996). Research by Murrell et al. (1994) confirmed that support for affirmative action and equal opportunity were significantly negatively correlated, and that support for the latter was overall far stronger. Conflict arises because there is support for affirmative action on grounds of attitudes toward distributive fairness; and opposition on the basis of attitudes toward procedural fairness (Peterson, 1994). Some studies have confirmed that accurate perceptions of affirmative action are related to positive perceptions of the policy (Belliveau, 1996). At a minimum, these findings underscore the importance of including considerations of affirmative action when investigating alleged discrimination in the workplace.

The issues posed by equal employment opportunity goals and affirmative action goals have been much obscured by public controversy and misunderstanding (Kneel, 1991). There is evidence that affirmative action can assist target group members; no empirical data show that it harms organizations. However, individuals identified as selected under affirmative action programs are perceived as less competent by themselves and by others, unless unambiguous controverting information about their competence is apparent (Kravitz et al., 1997).

FAIRNESS IN OBJECTIVE TESTING

Psychometric tests have long been used by employers for personnel selection or promotion. One employment practice in which social scientists have played a significant role involves fairness in employment testing. Under Title VII, once a plaintiff alleges that a specific practice disqualifies members of a protected class disproportionately, the employer must prove that the challenged practice is job related or justified by business necessity. Proof of the job-relatedness of an employment practice is accomplished by *validation*, a term drawn from personnel psychology to demonstrate "the relationship between a test instrument or other selection procedures and performance on the job" (U. S. EEOC, 1978). Three methods of establishing validity or the job-relatedness of a practice are recognized in the EEOC guidelines on Uniform Selection Procedures: (a) criterion-related validity, (b) content validity, and (c) construct validity (U. S. EEOC, 1978). Implementing documents regarding the guidelines included questions and answers about their application and joint revisions by the EEOC, the Office of Personnel Management, and the Departments of Treasury and Labor (U. S. EEOC, 1978, 1979, 1980a). In practice, however, criterion-related validity (an empirical demonstration that the employment screening practice in issue predicts successful performance on the job) and content validity (the test or practice representatively samples significant parts of the job) were the proofs regularly used. Proof of construct validity was rarely applied in employment cases because the regulations stated it had to be accompanied by a criterion-validity study demonstrating the successful performance of the job, and because conducting a criterion-validity study was already an arduous and extensive undertaking. Thus, employers preferred to confine their efforts to the criterion-validity study (Copus, 1996; Guardians Association of the New York City Police Department, 1980).

A controversy developed over test validation when some psychometricians took issue with the interpretation of the guidelines followed by the courts, namely that validation by any one of the three identified methods was acceptable. The psychologists favored the view that all three validation methods were subsets of construct validation (Bersoff, 1982). The Uniform Guidelines, issued in 1966, have not been amended. Interestingly, when the 1991 Civil Rights Act amendments were drafted, imposing the requirement that employers in disparate impact cases demonstrate that the challenged job practice was both job related and consistent with business necessity, industrial psychologists protested that this was "too stringent," and that psychology could not show a substantial relationship between an employment practice and job performance (Moses, 1990).

A protracted testing controversy erupted surrounding the psychometric practice of adjusting cutoff scores on standardized tests. Various standardized tests were widely employed, such as the General Aptitude Test Battery (GATB), used by the U.S. Department of Labor in about 40 states. The use of combined gender norms compromised prediction accuracy, so the test developers recommended separate gender norms.[6] Similar adaptations were made for minority group testees. When minority or female test takers tend to score below majority or male test takers on a test that does not predict job performance perfectly, most of the people with low scores who would perform adequately on the job will be minority or female applicants. The practice of gender or race norming uses different cutoff scores on the same tests for female versus male and minority versus majority racial group members.

Some employers eliminate the disparate impact of a test by lowering the minimum test scores for the protected group with the lowest scores. This testing practice was critically questioned in the 1980s following a public furor over employers' disparate treatment of males and females and minority and nonminority employees (Wittig, 1996). Hostility toward perceived preferential selection stimulated many backlash measures in the employment arena. Males and nonminorities contended that use of different cutoff scores based on gender, race, or ethnic origin was an unlawful form of preferential selection, favoring females and minority racial groups. In response, a National Academy of Sciences blue-ribbon panel was commissioned to study the use and scoring of general aptitude tests. Their investigation highlighted the fact that the validity of the GATB was lower for Blacks than for Whites. In fact, not only did the predictive validity for

---

[6]As Kaye (1996) explained: "When one regresses job performance on variables that are proxies for productivity, one obtains an equation that predicts performance on the basis of these proxies. This ordinary regression equation is usually thought to establish that the use of the proxies in selecting or compensating employees is fair if, on the average, minority and majority applicants with the same predictors do equally well on the job. In 'reverse regression,' one regresses a predictor on job performance. This addresses the question of whether minority and majority applicants who perform equally well on the job have, on the average, the same predictors" (p. 1258, n. 9).

the two groups differ, but it was low—even for Whites. Use of different cutoff scores did not address the validity issues (Wittig, 1996). Nonetheless, the panel recommended that scores of historically low-scoring minorities be judged against norms for their racial groups (Hartigan & Wigdor, 1989).

As the controversy progressed, some psychologists argued that use of the test results as predictors of success was compromised by the use of combined gender norms and was better with gender norms separated. The NAS panelists recommended that this practice be adhered to when it would improve measurement validity and accuracy. Although affirmative action considerations had no place in the discussion, the public debate over race and gender norms in employment testing centered on the assumption that uses of different subgroup norms was implemented to accomplish "affirmative action" decision making. The debacle escalated and culminated in the adoption as part of 1991 Civil Rights Act of provisions amending the Civil Rights Act of 1964, prohibiting employers from engaging in the practice of race norming or gender norming:

> It shall be an unlawful employment practice for a respondent in connection with the selection or referral of applicants or candidates for employment or promotion, to adjust the scores of, use different cutoff scores for, or to otherwise alter the results of, employment related tests on the basis of their race, color, religion, sex, or national origin. (Section 106)

This provision, a political coup for "antiquota" activists and opponents of affirmative action, resulted in a standoff of sorts between psychology and law regarding employment testing. The 1991 prohibition against adjustments to test scores for groups based on gender, culture, or socioeconomic factors runs counter to NAS panel recommendations after examining the issues associated with subgroup norms in-depth to promote fairness in testing.

Not all social scientists agree about the appropriate scientific technique to promote fairness in testing and the relative weight of performance versus prediction fairness. For example, one panel of experts concluded that there was no professional statistical consensus on the relevance or validity of reverse regression (Fienberg, 1989). In light of the fact that the widespread use of standardized testing produces discriminatory results, Haney (1993) criticized psychologists and the American Psychological Association on grounds that they were reticent to acknowledge the nature and scope of discriminatory testing practices and reluctant to advocate (much less require) the kind of rigorous testing standards and regulation of test use needed to reduce discriminatory practices. Ironically, the prohibition against race norming and gender norming leaves employers vulnerable to allegations of disparate impact by various protected subgroups.

To avoid such claims, many employers have abandoned the use of objective tests.

Empirical investigations of prejudice and discrimination have continued over 4 decades. However, inquiries have focused on one or two areas, leaving others relatively untouched. Most studies on the effect of prejudice have examined racism rather than sexism (Kravitz et al., 1997); many gender discrimination studies have addressed sexual harassment. Thus, the research literature on racism and sexual harassment is well developed in comparison with that on ageism and reprisal-based discrimination. Only since the passage of the ADA has research on disability discrimination commenced. Accordingly, the following sections focus on findings that bear on racial prejudice and sexual harassment in the workplace.

MODERN RACISM IN THE WORKPLACE

Background to Current Issues and Research

Some empirical efforts to assess the efficacy of antidiscrimination legislation on race discrimination have been conducted by sociologists and economists. For example, Burstein and Edwards (1994) examined whether the equal employment opportunity laws had made a lasting difference to the earnings of Blacks by examining the content of 2,081 appellate decisions published between 1965 and 1985. They determined that judicial decisions had a lasting impact of Blacks' earnings and concluded that litigation may be an effective agent of social change. Other scholars credit the Civil Rights Act of 1964 for substantially increasing the percentage of jobs held by women, Blacks, and Hispanics from 1972 to 1992 (Blumrosen, 1995). Nonetheless, economic disparities between Black and White families persist after more than 30 years of antidiscrimination legislation. Trends in corporate restructing, such as downsizing, disproportionately impact minorities, particularly Blacks (Murrell & Jones, 1996). Hispanics are underrepresented in higher status positions and overrepresented in lower status positions compared with Americans with Western European backgrounds (Bureau of National Affairs, Inc., 1995; Jiobu, 1990). The income gap between Hispanics and Whites is approximately 12% in low-status positions and 22% in higher status positions, increasing with education (Dovidio, Gaertner, Anastasio, & Sanitioso, 1992). In sum, the barriers to racial minorities are less visible but no less substantial. Researchers have concluded that discrimination, not just the legacy of discrimination, continues (Crosby & Cordova, 1996).

Psychologists have held widely differing opinions over the conceptual and operational definitions of racism (Kravitz et al., 1997). An examination of shifts in psychological concerns regarding prejudice in the 20th century distinguished the following seven changes in the concerns of researchers over time: (a) demonstrating that ethnic minorities are intellectually inferior, (b) explaining why majority members concluded that minorities were intellectually inferior, (c) specifying "universal" mental phenomena responsible for prejudice, (d) finding persons who have "authoritarian" personalities, (e) understanding how social influence operates, (f) discovering how social roles and group dynamics jointly determine prejudice, and (g) identifying the mental antecedents of prejudice and between-groups conflict (Duckitt, 1994).

Most recently, social scientific studies have examined intergroup conflict and the underlying attitudes that lead to such conflicts by studying interethnic prejudice in group interactions. The thrust of contemporary research on prejudice, racially motivated prejudices in particular, has been to show how normal cognitive and motivational processes can contribute to the development, maintenance, and perpetuation of discrimination (Dovidio et al, 1992). In other words, research has examined biases in the way people acquire, process, and store information about their own versus other groups through the processes of social categorization and stereotyping and the circumstances that foster the manifestation of such biases (Gaines & Reed, 1995). For instance, studies of prejudiced versus unprejudiced individuals revealed that racial prejudice influenced the extent to which attributions for stereotype-confirming or disconfirming behaviors occurred.[7]

INSTITUTIONAL BARRIERS TO RACIAL MINORITIES

Various social scientists have noted that statistics are often cited to evaluate the extent of gaps or disparities in employment, but rarely are they used to identify barriers to women and minorities. In a landmark nationwide survey of 4,078 private and public sector employers, practices used in recruiting and filling job vacancies were identified by Braddock and MacPartland (1987) as institutional barriers faced by racial minorities, African Americans, and Hispanics when (a) applying as a job candidate, (b) entering a new job, (c) being evaluated for on-the-job performance, and (d) reaching the job promotion stage. Their research revealed that most employment decisions are made based on informal and inexpensive strat-

---

[7]In reviewing the analysis of U.S. Supreme Court opinions in discrimination cases, Nacoste (1997) argued that the Court was operating on the theory that use of group membership as a criterion for a decision tends to reinforce common, negative group stereotypes.

egies, such as word-of-mouth recruiting, even for upper level jobs, although recruitment methods varied more at those levels. Because minorities are not often connected to the social networks relied on by employers as recruitment channels, they miss the chance to be hired for many better jobs. The survey also revealed that many employers avoid hiring minorities at the job-entry stage when positions require academic achievement and thinking skills. Whites are favored in lower level positions where interpersonal skills are important and in upper level positions. For lower, middle, and upper level jobs, job references and recommendations play a significant role, as does previous employment experience. Regarding internal promotions, unless public posting occur, minorities are unlikely to be approached and offered positions or invited to apply, as are their White counterparts. The most important information relied on for internal promotions in performance evaluations. Thus, minorities face difficulties in penetrating systemic institutional exclusionary barriers. Other more recent studies have confirmed that hiring decisions continue to favor White male applicants over other equally qualified candidates. For instance, a study by the Urban Institute in which pairs of applicants for low-skill, entry-level positions were matched in all respects except race showed that the White applicants received more favorable treatment than Blacks in the hiring process, and that this trend increased as the job level became more advanced (Turner, Fix, & Struyk, 1991).

FORMS OF CONTEMPORARY RACISM

Some researchers have argued that what has changed over the years is not the *presence* of prejudice and discrimination but the *form* of the prejudice, which has become more subtle and indirect. For instance, survey research has demonstrated that many White Americans believe discrimination is a problem of the past and that Blacks have only themselves to blame for their economic disadvantage (Kravitz et al, 1997). Two contemporary forms of racial prejudice have been distinguished: aversive racism and symbolic racism. Aversive racism, most common among liberals and those who embrace egalitarianism, is characterized by subtle, rationalized discrimination, manifested in avoidance, fear, or disgust. Symbolic or modern racism, most common among political conservatives, is characterized by indirect and symbolic actions, ostensibly to preserve such values as personal freedom, asserting, for example, that protected classes have received more benefits socially and economically than they deserve (Dovidio & Gaertner, 1996). Aversive racists do not regard minorities as inferior, but regard Whites as superior. Their biases emerge when what is right or wrong is not clearly defined, or when a negative response can be rationalized or justified. Those justifications may be directed at language or cultural differences, not at a specific ethnic group (Dovidio et al, 1992). Individuals who manifest aversive and symbolic racism generally perceive that discrimination is no longer a social problem and believe they are nonprejudiced. Symbolic racism is a strong predictor of negative reactions to affirmative action (Jacobsen, 1985; Sears, 1988).

CONTEXTUAL STUDIES OF INTERGROUP BIASES

Many of the common criticisms of social psychological research have been leveled at research on racial prejudice, namely, that verbal judgments rather than overt actions have been measured (Gaines & Reed, 1995). In response to such criticisms, researchers conducted contextually rich studies simulating events and conduct that occur in the workplace. For example, Dovidio and Gaertner (1996) studied intergroup relations in a variety of contexts, ranging from situations in which evaluative judgments were made about employment candidates and their competence to emergency helping behavior toward members of other racial groups. They concluded that changes in public norms and socially desirable conduct have diminished the extent to which prejudices are directly revealed and overtly declared, but that antidiscrimination laws and social changes have not eliminated the underlying attitudes that produce discrimination. Rather, they submitted that racism has become more subtle in response to the social constraints against discrimination. They also noted that aversive racism is most likely to occur in situations in which the criteria for evaluation are ambiguous and permit subjective factors to enter into the decision making.

Some confirmation of the impact of these mechanisms comes from studies of the ways in which negative social stereotypes of oppressed or stigmatized groups create obstacles to achievement for members of those groups. For instance, Steele (1997) demonstrated how the presence of negative stereotypes of intergroup relations impeded academic performance and achievement for African Americans and for women studying quantitative subjects. Another illustration comes from a study of racial factors in a common workplace task, issuing performance evaluation ratings or work products. Whites favored other Whites over people of color in rating the same work product. Through measurements of response latencies and priming tasks, the investigators observed that negative characteristics were more commonly associated with members of the other race, particularly Blacks, than with Whites. They also found that subjects rated White male supervisors systematically higher than White female or Black male partners in terms of competence. In other words, perceived relative status was more significant than actual competence. The subjects held biased perceptions of relative competence, rating high-ability Black partners as less intelligent and high-ability White females as no more intelligent. Majority members were reluctant to believe that Black males or White females could demonstrate as much competence as they did (Dovidio & Gaertner, 1991, 1993). In sum, both on rating tasks and on choosing tasks, the prejudices emerged. Meta-analyses of rater race effects in assessing performance evaluations in 88 studies confirmed that Whites favor Whites and Blacks favor Blacks (Kraiger & Ford, 1985). Moderating variables in 77 studies showed that racial discrepancies in ratings by Whites were greater in the field than in the laboratory, and when the proportion of Black employees in the workforce was relatively small (Kraiger & Ford, 1985).

Research drawing on attribution theory has confirmed that individuals who scored high on a scale assessing prejudice toward Blacks rated the quality of applications by Black versus White job applicants significantly differently, favoring the White applicants, while individuals who scored low on the prejudice scale rated the applicants from different racial groups equally (Munro, 1997). Ratings of a Hispanic manager were significantly less favorable when the manager displayed a nonnormative, Hispanic managerial style versus a normative, Anglo managerial style (Ferdman, 1989).

Studies of justice perceptions have recently begun to examine identification and group salience vis-à-vis workplace issues (Huo, Smith, Tyler, & Lind, 1996). For example, Queller and Major (1997) investigated the effects of intergroup comparison in perceptions of a hiring decision. Focusing on intergroup differences, such as ways in which female undergraduates differed from male undergraduates, led participants to rely on assessments driven by procedural fairness. Participants who focused on intergroup similarities, such as listing ways in which female undergraduates were similar to male undergraduates, relied on assessments driven by distributive fairness. These findings confirmed what Tyler et al. (1997) noted, namely, that when interactions occur within group boundaries, people are more concerned about relational issues; when interactions occur across group boundaries, outcome issues may loom more prominently and be more influential. Thus, when people are perceived as outsiders, based on a different nationality, ethnicity, or gender, for example, the interactions are more instrumental than they are when the conflicts are with people perceived as in-group members. Accordingly, when people identify with their work organization, they weight managers' decisions more relationally and less instrumentally. In one study in which employees were first classified as assimilators, biculturalists, separatists, and alienated based on the degree to which they identified with the superordinate work organization and their ethnic subgroup, the researchers found that separatists reacted to their supervisors' decisions in instrumental terms, focusing on what they won oor lost. By comparison, those who identified with the work organization, assimilators and biculturalists, deferred to supervisors whom they perceived as neutral and trustworthy (Huo et al., 1996).

One concern to emerge among researchers of contemporary racism is that because some prejudices are unconscious and unintentional, there is no longer a good fit between the antidiscrimination laws prohibiting intentional discrimination and the phenomenon of racial bias and prejudice that operates to limit the opportunities and advancement of nonmajority employees in the workplace. For instance, aversive racists are largely insulated from legal liability for their conduct. Specifically, with respect to the phenomenon of stereotyping, a controversy has developed as to whether this process is conscious or unconscious. If unconscious, presumably unintentional, employment decisions based on stereotyping might not demonstrate prohibited racial animus under the more common disparate treatment model of liability. However, the case that stereotyping is intentional was made by Fiske (1987). Nonetheless, the issue has been raised that "there now exists a fundamental 'lack of fit' between the jurisprudential construction of discrimination and the actual phenomenon it purports to represent" (Krieger, 1995).

SEXUAL HARASSMENT IN THE WORKPLACE

BACKGROUND TO CURRENT ISSUES AND RESEARCH

The magnitude and meaning of gender differences has intrigued psychologists (Buss, 1995; Eagly, 1995a,b; Hyde & Plant, 1995; Maracek, 1995). Psychological researchers have been somewhat slower to examine gender discrimination in the workplace (Frazier & Hunt, 1988). As noted earlier, gender as a protected class had an inauspicious beginning under Title VII (Whalen, 1985). Some aspects of gender protection have been systematically delimited since the Civil Rights Act was implemented. For example, the doctrine of comparable worth, which sought to provide increased compensation for females in relatively undervalued jobs filled predominantly by women, was not endorsed by the U.S. Supreme Court under Title VII (*County of Washington v. Gunther*, 1981). Thereafter, the Ninth Circuit reversed a finding of liability under a comparable worth theory, holding that employer reliance on prevailing discriminatory labor markets does not constitute intentional discrimination (*American Federation of State, County, and Municipal Employees v. Washington*, 1985). As a consequence, the theory of comparable worth has been virtually eliminated from the corpus of equal employment opportunity law. Against this backdrop, somewhat surprisingly, the legal doctrine of sexual harassment emerged—and flourished by comparison.

The first Congressional hearings on sexual harassment among federal sector employees were conducted in 1979. The following year, Congress commissioned a study of sexual harassment in the federal workplace (U.S. Merit Systems Protection Board, 1981). Although Title VII does not expressly prohibit harassment, in 1980 the Equal Employment Opportunity Commission published regulatory guidelines prohibiting sex discrimination, including harassment because of sex, on grounds that harassing conduct interfered with the terms, conditions, and privileges of employment (U. S. EEOC, 1980b). Six years later, in *Meritor Savings Bank FEB v. Vinson* (1986), the U.S. Supreme Court gave clear approval to legal theories prohibiting sexual harassment in the workplace, acknowledging two types of claims: *quid pro quo* and hostile workplace environment discrimination.

Data gathered by the EEOC show that gender discrimination complaints account for just under one third of all EEO charges filed (29%). Sexual harassment complaints have made up an increasing proportion of the gender-based complaints filed with federal and state antidiscrimination agencies. In 1990, for example, of a total of approximately 20,000 gender claims filed, about one third (6,127) were sexual harassment complaints. By contrast, in 1997, 64% of 24,728 gender claims (15,889 claims) were sexual harassment as opposed to disparate treatment/unequal pay/ pregnancy act claims. The percentage of males filing sexual harassment claims has increased from 8% in 1990 to 12% in 1997. In raw numbers, this means 1,844 sexual harassment claims were filed by men in FY 1996.

THEORIES OF HARASSMENT:
QUID PRO QUO AND HOSTILE WORKPLACE ENVIRONMENT CLAIMS

A claim for sexual harassment requires a victim to prove by a preponderance of the evidence that (a) he or she was subjected to unwelcome sexual conduct, physical or verbal in nature (e.g., sexual advances, requests for sexual favors, sexual cartoons, drawings, gestures, jokes, derogatory comments); (b) submission to such conduct was explicitly or implicitly a term or condition of the individual's employment; and (c) the conduct had a purpose or effect of unreasonably interfering with an individual's work performance or creating an intimidating, hostile, or offen-

TABLE 8.2. SEXUAL HARASSMENT CHARGES FILED,
FY 1990–1997

Complainant gender	1990	1992	1994	1996	1997
Males and females	6,127	10,532	14,420	15,342	15,889
Females	92%	91%	90%	90%	88%
Males	8%	9%	10%	10%	12%

Source: U.S. Equal Employment Opportunity Commission Charge Statistics, FY 1990–1996.

sive work environment. Different standards of liability and different defenses apply depending on whether the harasser is, on the one hand, a supervisor with immediate authority over the employee, or on the other hand, a co-worker, customer, independent contractor, or other supervisor. With respect to harassment by a supervisor, affirmative defenses are available only when the action did not result in any tangible employment harm. Tangible employment actions fall within the special province of the supervisor. Where the harasser is not a supervisor with immediate authority over the employee, a negligence standard applies, and employers are liable only if they knew, or should have known, of the harassment and failed to take prompt and effective remedial action. Physical or psychological harm inflicted by a co-worker does not qualify as a "tangible employment action" (*Burlington Industries v. Ellerth*, 1998; *Faragher v. Boca Raton*, 1998).

In a *quid pro quo* claim, the underlying facts generally involve some type of sexual coercion regarding unwelcome sexual favors. The plaintiff must establish that job benefits were conditioned on receipt of sexual favors, that is, that the harassment affected tangible aspects of compensation, terms, conditions, or privileges of employment. Examples include situations in which sexual favors are requested in exchange for a bonus, a salary increase, or a positive performance evaluation. An employee who is denied benefits, such as assignments or promotions, because he or she refused or rejected the sexual attention of a supervisor, or because those benefits were given to a less qualified employee who had a sexual relationship with a supervisor may also bring a claim. In *quid pro quo* cases, no separate job detriment need be proven because the fact that the harasser conditions certain benefits on sexual favors is egregious. When a supervisor's harassment culminates in tangible employment action, such as hiring, firing, failing to promote, reassignment with significantly different responsibilities, or a decision causing significant change in benefits, the employer is vicariously liable, and no affirmative defense is available.

When a supervisor's harassment does not culminate in a tangible employment action, the employer is vicariously liable unless the employer exercised reasonable care to prevent and promptly correct any sexually harassing behavior and the employee unreasonably failed to take advantage of any preventive or corrective opportunities provided by the employer or to avoid harm otherwise (*Burlington Industries v. Ellerth*, 1998; *Faragher v. Boca Raton*, 1998).

In a hostile work environment claim, the plaintiff must establish that the harassment was so severe and pervasive that it unreasonably altered or interfered with the individual's work performance and created a hostile, intimidating, or offensive work environment. The conduct in issue need not be of a sexual nature so long as gender is a substantial factor motivating the conduct. In some instances, where males or females work in positions outside of traditional sex roles, they may be harassed in ways that are not sexual but which would not have occurred but for their gender. This is gender-based harassment. Even when an employer is an "equal opportunity harasser," if the conduct is gender driven, a violation may be found (*Chiapuzio v. BLT Operating Corp.*, 1993).

A "totality of circumstances test" is applied to evaluate factors in determining whether the conduct in issue creates an abusive work environment by focusing on the severity and frequency or pervasiveness of the conduct. The U.S. Supreme Court determined that Title VII does not prohibit "genuine but innocuous differences in ways men and women routinely interact with members of the same sex and of the opposite sex," and elaborated upon its view that standards for judging hostility are sufficiently demanding to ensure that Title VII does not become a "general civility code," (*Faragher v. Boca Raton, Fla.*, 1998). Ordinary tribulations of the workplace, such as the sporadic use of abusive language, gender-related jokes, and occasional teasing, do not amount to a discriminatory change in the terms and conditions of employment (Lindemann & Kadue, 1992). In addition, the nature of the conduct is considered (i.e., whether physical threats or verbal abuse occurred). Thus, if the incidents are rare but involve unwanted physical touching, liability may attach. Several incidents of nonphysical conduct, involving sexual joking, comments, pictures, and so on, may also result in liability. The context in which the conduct occurred is examined, as is the cumulative effect of that conduct. The victim need not suffer psychological injury or harm nor economic damages before a claim is actionable (*Harris v. Forklift Systems, Inc.*, 1993).

In hostile workplace environment claims, even if there is clear evidence that unwanted sexual conduct of a nature sufficiently severe or pervasive to comprise actionable harassment occurred, if the employer acts promptly and adequately after receiving notice of the complaint and takes steps to eliminate the harassment, liability can be avoided (*Kauffman v. Allied Signal, Inc.*, 1992). This provision in the law has placed great emphasis on the employer's response to complaints of harassment once on notice, particularly on the quality of the investigation of sexual harassment complaints (Abell & Jackson, 1996).

One unresolved controversial legal issue concerns the perspective from which the totality of circumstances is to be assessed in a hostile workplace environment case. The standard presently incorporates both subjective and objective components. In other words, the victim must personally be offended by the conduct, and the conduct must also be offensive to a reasonable person or victim. The latter objective component insures against claims by hypersensitive individuals or claims based on petty slights.

With respect to the objective component, in the Third, Eighth, and Ninth Circuit Courts of Appeal, and the New Jersey Supreme Court, for example, the perspective of a reasonable woman or victim applies (*Andrews v. City of Philadelphia*, 1990; *Burns v. McGregor Electronic Industries, Inc.*, 1993; *Ellison v. Brady*, 1991; *Fuller v. City of Oakland*, 1995; *Lehmann v. Toys 'R' Us, Inc.*, 1993). In the Fourth, Fifth, and Sixth Circuit Courts of Appeal, and the Michigan Supreme Court, *Harris v. Forklift Systems, Inc.* (1993), is interpreted as mandating the reasonable person standard (*Davis v. Monsanto Chemical Co.*, 1988) (race case); *DeAngelis v. El Paso Municipal Officers Association*, 1995; *Radtke v. Everett*, 1993). The reasonable woman test was not adopted based on empirical research establishing that males and females perceived the events differently. Rather, the standard was derived based on the judicial determination that many women were offended by conduct that many men considered unobjectionable, that women shared common concerns that men did not share, and that a sexblind standard tended to be male-biased and to systematically ignore the experience of women. Other court have pointed out that the reasonable woman standard may entrench the sexist attitudes it attempts to eliminate (*Radtke v. Everett*, 1993).

The difference between the reasonable person and reasonable woman standard has been described as the distinction between a gender-neutral and a gender-specific standard, i.e., one that takes the gender of the victim into account. Support for the reasonable woman standard is generally premised on the assumption that "women often think sexual harassment has occurred in situations in which men feel that it has not" (DeBruin, 1998, p. 115). Four possible vantage points in issue are (a) the perspective of a reasonable person, (b) the perspective of a reasonable woman, (c) the perspective of a reasonable victim, male or female; and (d) the perspective of a reasonable employee (*Harris v. Forklift Systems, Inc.*, 1993). In cases in which the reasonable person standard is employed, jurors are instructed to

JANE GOODMAN-DELAHUNTY

look at the evidence from the perspective of a reasonable person's reaction to a similar environment under similar circumstances. They are also instructed not to view the evidence from the perspective of an overly sensitive person and to evaluate the total circumstances and determine whether the alleged harassing behavior could be objectively classified as the kind of behavior that would seriously affect the psychological well-being of a reasonable person.

By contrast, in courts in which the reasonable woman standard pertains, the focus in evaluating the severity and pervasiveness of the conduct in issue is the perspective of a female, not necessarily of the victim of sexual harassment. Jurors are likely to be instructed to take into account the experiences and perceptions of women and to avoid stereotyped notions of acceptable behavior. In determining whether a severe and extensive hostile environment existed, they must consider the evidence from the perspective of a reasonable but not oversensitive female and determine whether a reasonable woman would have been offended by the conduct in question (American Bar Association, 1993).

In its most recent opinions on elements of a hostile workplace sexual harassment claim, two of which involved female victims and one, a male victim, the U.S. Supreme Court did not explicitly endorse the reasonable woman standard, but stated, "a sexually objectionable environment must be both objectively and subjectively offensive, one that a reasonable person would find hostile or abusive, and one that the victim did in fact perceive to be so" (*Harris v. Forklift Systems, Inc.*, 1993, p. 510; *Oncale v. Sundowner Offshore Services, Inc.*, 1997; *Faragher v. Boca Raton, Fla.*, 1998). This standard reflects the EEOC policy guidance that recommends an objective standpoint of a reasonable person, adding that the reasonable person standard should consider the victim's perspective and not stereotyped notions of acceptable behavior, suggesting that the victim's gender should be considered (U. S. EEOC, 1990). The ambiguity of the prevailing standard has practical implications for both judges and juries who must serve as fact finders in harassment cases (Brown & Germanis, 1994).

FORMS OF SEXUALLY HARASSING CONDUCT

The major contributions of social science to the law on sexual harassment fall into three distinct areas or categories: (a) data on behaviors most people regard as sexual harassment and gender differences in this consensus; (b) data on individual characteristics that affect whether conduct is perceived as sexually harassing; and (c) data on contexts or situations that affect whether conduct is perceived as sexually harassing (Frazier, Cochran, & Olson, 1995).

Relatively little is known about the consensus among lay people as to what behaviors make up sexual harassment, or how prevalent they are. The first category of research provides data on behaviors that most people regard as sexual harassment and encompasses questions about defining and measuring sexual harassment. Researchers conducted various studies measuring perceptions of sexual harassment by means of surveys or by asking subjects to rate events described in a brief scenario.

One of the first studies of the prevalence of sexual harassment in the federal workplace, conducted in 1981, revealed that 42% of the women surveyed and 15% of the men surveyed claimed to have experienced one or more incidents of sexual harassment in the past 24 months (U.S. Merit Systems Protection Board, 1981). More recent studies of the incidence of sexual harassment on the federal workplace, replicating the 1981 Merit Systems Protection Board survey in 1987 and 1994, using the same instrument, revealed that the percentages of females and males reporting incidents of sexual harassment within 24 months of the survey had remained consistent (U.S. Merit Systems Protection Board, 1981, 1995).

Some limitations on early studies of assessments of the scope of the sexual harassment problem were the failure to provide subjects with an adequate definition of sexual harassment or definitions that did not approximate legal definitions (Frazier et al., 1995). Where legal definitions were used, no distinction was made between actionable and nonactionable harassment (Arvey & Cavanaugh, 1995). In addition, the survey approach used by some researchers was criticized because self-reports of incidents of harassment were not validated and were susceptible to memory distortions. Furthermore, no information was gathered about how recently the events recalled occurred or about the sexual experience of the respondents. Finally, in many of the studies samples of convenience were used, primarily undergraduate students, which limited the generalizability of the results. The Sexual Experiences Questionnaire developed by Fitzgerald et al. (1988) is the most widely used instrument for assessing sexual harassment experiences (Arvey & Cavanaugh, 1995). To date, with the exception of the Merit Systems Protection Board surveys of federal employees, the emphasis in sexual harassment research has been on the harassment of females by male supervisors or peers. The handful of recent studies on the sexual harassment of males sheds additional light on the phenomenon and may also have implications for the adoption of the reasonable person/ victim/woman standard. For instance, a study of males and females in the armed services revealed that for males, the most common form of sexual harassment was sexual hostility expressed in crude or offensive remarks. Relatively few males were subjected to unwanted sexual attention. Females experienced gender harassment, sexual hostility, sexist hostility, and unwanted sexual attention. The incidence rate of reported harassment among males was lower than that among females (36% of the males versus 76% of the females who responded had experienced one or more types of sexual harassment in the past 12 months; Fitzgerald, Drasgow, Magley, & Waldo, 1997).

As sexual harassment research evolved, investigators adopted the convention of identifying unwanted sexual attention in the following categories: (a) rape or assault; (b) pressure for sexual favors; (c) touching, cornering, pinching; (d) suggestive looks and gestures; (e) letters, phone calls; (f) pressure for dates; (g) sexual teasing, jokes, remarks; (h) whistles, calls; and (i) attempts to persuade to participate in other sexual activities (Bastian, Lancaster, & Reyst, 1996). A 1996 Department of Defense survey of approximately 47,000 active duty military members revealed that unwanted sexual attention in the past 12 months was reported by 22% of the personnel: 64% of women and 17% of men. Most commonly reported were behaviors that might comprise a hostile workplace environment, namely, sexual teasing, jokes or comments (reported by 44% of the females and 10% of the males), and sexually suggestive looks, gestures, or body language (reported by 37% of the females and 7% of the males). A substantial number of the respondents who had said they had experienced one or more harassing behaviors in the past 12 months, 52% of the women and 9% of the men, did not regard at least some of the behaviors they checked as forms of sexual harassment (Bastian et al., 1996). This finding highlights problems jurors may experience in applying the law when lay definitions of sexual harassment and legal definitions do not overlap (Baird, Bensko, Bell, & Viney, 1995).

One significant finding to emerge is that males are more likely to be harassed by males than females are by other females, and that in approximately 70% of those cases, the perpetrators are co-workers rather than managers or supervisors (Waldo, Berdahl, & Fitzgerald, 1998). Male employees surveyed in a variety of employment settings reported experiencing four types of harassing conduct, listed in descending order of reported frequency: (a) lewd and obscene comments, most frequently by other males, often taking the form of pressure to enforce masculine stereotypes (e.g., when males appeared effeminate or performed tasks less typical of the male gender role, such as picking up children from the day-care center, etc.); (b) negative gender-based comments, most often from females; (c) unwanted sexual attention from males or females; and (d) sexual coercion by males or females, or by a male supervisor to harass a female co-worker. Thus, the kinds of sexual harassment most commonly experienced by males appear to differ in their nature and frequency from the kinds of sexual harassment most commonly experienced by females (Waldo et al., 1998).

Data gathered by researchers of sexual harassment demonstrate that there are some behaviors regarded as sexual harassment by almost every-one, such as sexual touching and sexual propositions (Frazier et al., 1995). In cases in which there is physical harassing conduct of a sexual nature (touching, groping, rubbing, patting), there is a strong consensus that the behavior is sexual harassment. Often, researchers have called this type of harassment "sexual coercion"; generally, it fits within the *quid pro quo* legal model. By comparison, behaviors such as requests for dates, staring, flirt-ing, use of coarse language, and sexual jokes, which may be part of a non-*quid pro quo* hostile workplace environment, are not universally re-garded as harassment.

With respect to the ways in which males versus females perceive sexual behavior, and whether it comprises sexual harassment, most gen-der differences appear when the conduct is ambiguous or less severe in nature (i.e., when verbal comments or jokes, sexual looks, flirting, and nonsexual touching are involved). These data are consistent with findings in other general gender studies, which revealed beliefs that women differ from men in role behaviors, occupations, and physical characteristics (Deaux, 1995). The gender of mock jurors has usually emerged as the strongest predictor of decisions or verdicts regarding harassment (Wiener, Watts, Goldkamp, & Gaspar, 1995). Most typically, however, the gender effects are moderate. For instance in the foregoing study by Wiener et al. (1995), gender explained 10% of the variance in mock-juror judgments about hostile work environment harassment; women found more evi-dence for unwelcome, severe, and pervasive conduct than did men.

More recently, researchers have explored many factors that might be covariates, such as richness of the stimulus materials, the sexual harass-ment experience of the respondents, sexism attitudes, self-identification with victims, case context variables, victim traits, the power relationships between the harasser and the harassee, the general workplace environ-ment, and the type of occupation of the victim. Frazier et al. (1995) and Gutek and O'Connor (1995) have pointed out that although gender differ-ences have emerged consistently, the magnitude of gender differences in perceived sexual harassment is not as large nor as consistent as was earlier declared. A meta-analysis by Blumenthal (1998) based on 111 studies in-volving a total of 34,350 subjects and 83 combined effect sizes, produced a mean gender unweighted effect size of .172 (Mdn = .151). This analysis confirmed that a small but stable gender gap exists in the perception of sexual harassment, and that it persists across certain cultures and stimulus types. Moderating variables were (a) contextualized materials, which ten-ded to diminish the effect; (b) when the study was conducted, as recent studies enhanced the gender effect; and (c) the nature of the subjects, in that the effect was more pronounced among students than among working subjects.

Various models have been posited to account for the findings of gender differences, but there has been little agreement as to the nature of a gender gap regarding perceptions of sexual harassment and its significance. A "sex role spillover" explanation for harassment, theorizing that employees are categorized according to their gender role rather than their occupational role, and that this categorizing can produce a sexualized workplace, one where employees are perceived as potential sexual partners, was posited by Gutek (1993). These processes are hypothesized to increase when the work group sex ratios and occupational sex ratios are skewed (Gutek & Morasch, 1982). Expert testimony along these lines has been admitted in some sexual harassment cases (*Jenson v. Eveleth Taconite Company*, 1993; *Robinson v. Jacksonville Shipyards, Inc.*, 1991). Other social scientists have applied attribution theory and person-environment interaction frameworks (Wiener, Hurt, Russell, Mannen, & Gaspar, 1997; Williams, Brown, Lees-Haley, & Price, 1995) to account for the gender gap.

Persistent findings of gender differences have led some researchers, such as Wiener (1995), to support the use of the reasonable woman standard over the reasonable person standard because men and women perceive social sexual conduct differently. Other researchers, such as Gutek and O'Connor (1995), have argued that the reasonable woman standard has little practical value because the sex differences are relatively small and disappear when the alleged harassment is either very severe or very mild. Preliminary research on mock-jury decisions applying either a reasonable woman or a reasonable person standard produced mixed results (Gutek, O'Connor, & Melancon, 1997; Wiener, 1995). Johnson (1993) contended that the "reasonable person of the same sex as the victim" standard is unworkable for juries because (a) male jurors cannot determine what a reasonable woman would think without relying on stereotypes, (b) employing experts to testify as to a reasonable woman's perspective is inconsistent with the reasonableness standard itself, and (c) expert testimony on a reasonable woman's perspective usurps the role of the jury in applying social norms to the case at hand. Another common objection to the reasonable victim standard is that it is too subjective and too fragmented to be practical. Legally, the difference between the two standards remains somewhat hypothetical.

THE INFLUENCE OF INDIVIDUAL AND SOCIAL FACTORS ON SEXUAL HARASSMENT

Empirical investigations of the second category of data, individual characteristics that affect whether conduct is perceived as sexually harassing, produced findings that the status of the harasser makes a difference (i.e., the power relationship or status differences of the harasser and the victim make a difference). In other words, subjects rate cases in which the harasser is a supervisor or manager as more egregious than those in which the harasser is a co-worker or peer (Blumenthal, 1998). The law already distinguishes between these two contexts and attaches liability to cases where the harasser is a manager or supervisor without requiring the plaintiff to report the conduct to a superior. In some states, such as California, a standard of strict liability applies to any conduct by supervisors.

Another topic identified as worthy of investigation is the influence of personal and social factors (i.e., individual and organizational factors in a workplace setting). For example, the failure by many victims to report the harassment or to protest the unwelcome conduct has been examined because it has a bearing on one *prima facie* element of a sexual harassment claim. A defending employer may contend that an employee who failed to complain of sexual harassment or to report it did not find it unwelcome or offensive. Fitzgerald, Swan, and Fischer (1995) analyzed responses of victims to harassment experiences and the phenomenon of underreporting incidents of sexual harassment. They found that the most common reason for failure to report was fear of reprisal or retaliation. In fact, reporting incidents of harassment is often followed by negative outcomes. In some instances, the conduct in issue was not reported because it was ambiguous in nature, thus it was difficult to recognize and describe as a sexually harassing event. For example, harassment may initiate in the context of a joke or amidst other legitimate work-related interaction that includes touching. In those instances, failure to object may be the most normal response. In general, assertive responses increased with the severity of the harassment experienced. Courts have accepted expert testimony on the reluctance of female victims of sexual harassment to complain because of factors such as fear of reprisal, loss of privacy, and the diminished self-worth of the victim (*Bohen v. City of East Chicago*, 1986; *Snider v. Consolidated Coal Co.*, 1992).

Studies in the third category, those examining the contexts or social influences that promote or inhibit sexual harassment, have included experiments varying the occupation of the victim and the situational and individual factors that promote or discourage harassment. For example, Pryor, Giedd, and Williams (1995) assessed causes of sexual harassment by examining situational and individual factors. Among the significant situational factors they found that promoted or inhibited harassing behaviors were the local organizational norms and what was tolerated by management. In their studies, significant correlations were found between perceived harassment and perceived tolerance in management responses to harassing behavior.

Regarding "person factors" that increased or diminished the likelihood of harassment, Pryor and his colleagues examined the propensity to harass by developing the "Likelihood to Harass Scale" or "LHS" using college males as subjects and measures of sexual violence, gender roles, and sexual behaviors. They found that high scores on the LHS are related to numerous measures of sexual aggression and to stereotypic male gender masculinity values, including antifemininity, status, toughness, and hypermasculinity. Other correlates are dominance (desire to control one's sexual partner), novelty (sex to avoid boredom), recognition (sex to impress others), and hedonism (sex for personal gratification). Sexual harassers hold strong preexisting associations between dominance and sexuality. High LHS scores are not correlated with love and affection. Men with high LHS scores found it easy to generate reasons to harass and were also aware of constraints on such behavior. Individual predispositions to harass were acted on only when the social norms permitted. A significant finding was that "group contagion" of harassing behaviors occurred when men found other men held similar views of women (i.e., when they felt disinhibited) (Pryor & Whalen, 1997).

Gutek (1993) reported that environments that promote harassment include those where (a) pinups of women in other than professional roles were displayed at work; (b) the workforce was sex-segregated, making sole or token females appear "out of role"; (c) occupational roles may prime sexually (e.g., cocktail waitressing versus nursing); (d) sexual advances were part of normal workplace exchanges, with more females reporting harassment; and (e) individuals in positions of power were less likely to pay attention to actions of subordinates and to resort to stereotypes when making judgments.

Subsequent research by Bargh and Raymond (1995) studied the impact of automatic cognitive processing that accounts for many denials of sexual harassment. Males primed regarding power who had an automatic power-dominance-sexuality link rated a female significantly more attractive than those who did not. These males were also those likely to harass or exploit females. Similar findings emerged in studies by Rudman and Borgida (1995), which showed the effects of viewing TV commercials that depict women as sexual objects on men's thoughts about and behavior toward women whom they met later in the context of an interview for a job. These commercials primed the men to behave in sexualized ways toward the women; they also influenced the way these men interpreted a candidate's behavior during the interview. Both men with a proclivity to harass and men without this predisposition were influenced in the same way by the commercials. The studies showed how cognitive processes mediate the effects of commercials on men's behavior. Thus, an employer who provides an atmosphere that is tolerant of verbal, pictorial, or behavioral conduct that depicts females as sexual objects is setting an environment in which sexual harassment is evoked and fostered. One noteworthy feature of this research is that it addressed the issue of causation. Stereotypes of women may be elicited or promoted by the environment. Once "primed" sexually, stereotypes become more accessible. Thereafter, more physical observations rather than content observations are recalled by masculine men. Recent research by Greenwald and Banaji (1995) showed that even when individuals consciously deny that they are being affected by negative stereotypes, their decision making is nonetheless biased by cognitive processes that rely on stereotypes.

Borgida, Rudman, and Manteufel (1995) studied workplace conditions that promote stereotyping and reported that stereotyping is more likely when (a) the target is isolated or one of a small number in an otherwise homogenous group, (b) the target is in a group that is in a nontraditional occupation, (c) the workplace environment is sexualized, and (d) the evaluative criterion is ambiguous or target individuating information is ambiguous.

In studies to examine the impact of these contextual variables, Fiske and Glick (1995) distinguished benevolent and hostile sexism and paternalistic from competitive motives. In follow-up studies, they distinguished benevolent from hostile sexism and ambivalent harassment that may contain components of both forms of sexism. Subtypes of stereotypes of women fall into three distinct clusters: "sexy" (concerned with own appearance), "nontraditional" (demanding, ambitious, intelligent, independent), and "traditional" (conforming, passive, dependent, uncritical, stupid). The fit between stereotypes of women and jobs promotes discrimination and sexual harassment. The most consistent female stereotype is one inconsistent with terms to describe a career woman who is intelligent, determined, goal oriented, knowledgeable. The associations with the stereotypes are usually sexually negative (i.e., seductress, vamp, tart, sex bomb, flirt, socializes with men not women).

More recent research by Burgess and Borgida (1997) built upon those distinctions by assessing the reactions of subjects to traditional versus nontraditional occupations, varying three female subtypes (weak, iron ladies, sex objects) and the type of conduct in issue. Their findings confirmed that occupation of the target interacts with perceived harassment and showed that sexism not gender *per se* may account for biased conduct. In other words, women who score high on a sexism scale because they hold stereotypes about females behave more like other sexists, a group that includes males, than like other females who do not score high on the sexism scale. These findings provide encouraging news for those who have struggled with same-sex discrimination claims. In these studies, for instance, women in male-dominated, nontraditional occupations were less likely to be judged victims of sexual harassment. The researchers speculated that perhaps this was because women in these occupations evoked stereotypes of "the iron lady," less vulnerable and more powerful than other women. Research is under way examining the link between stereotype activation and sex role spillover, the content of cognitions that might be associated with gender differences, and the attributes of harassers and victims (Burgess & Borgida, 1997; Wiener et al., 1997).

Organizational characteristics that create a certain climate that may promote or inhibit sexual harassment were identified in studies of the armed forces (Fitzgerald et al., 1977). The first factor was the gender ratio. As the ratio of males and females approached parity, the frequency of sexual harassment diminished monotonically. The second factor was the attitude toward sexual harassment by the organizational leadership. Where leaders made it clear that sexual harassment would not be tolerated, and might be punished, there was less sexual harassment than in organizations in which harassment was tolerated by management.

DIRECTIONS FOR FUTURE RESEARCH

One drawback in summarizing the past findings and assessing future directions for researchers of employment discrimination is the gulf and disparate focus that has existed between researchers of individual versus group phenomena (Brewer, 1997). For example, researchers of individual and interpersonal processes have studied stereotyping, unconscious judgment and evaluation of others, ingroup favoritism, and aversive racism. Researchers of group process, by comparison, have studied such topics as social categorization and identity, institutional racism, and collective action (Brewer, 1994). Within each subfield, insular subgroups have investigated distinctive topics, such as cognition, affect or attitude, and behavior or conduct. Researchers with different approaches to the problem have worked independently in isolation. Only very recently have some of these groups met in an effort to bridge gaps and synthesize the research (Zanna & Olson, 1994).

In the past, psychological factors and considerations have been excluded from the debate about employment discrimination (Jones, 1997). Social psychologists, in particular, have not been involved in the policy debates regarding intergroup relations because of the inaccessibility of their findings, and because the findings have not been well linked to practice or public policy (Brewer, 1997). Researchers studying individual and interpersonal processes of cognition, attitude, affect, and behavior, and researchers of group and collective processes need to collaborate and develop unified theories. Researchers who study biases related to race, gender, age, disability, and so on need to focus on commonalities that underlie discrimination against all groups as well as manifestations of unique forms of prejudice against specific groups.

Among the underresearched substantive topics are issues related to age discrimination, discrimination against Latinos and Hispanics, discrimination based on psychological and physiological disabilities, and reprisal and retaliation actions. Given the burgeoning groups of individuals over age 40 in the workplace, it is surprising that there has not been more research on age-based stereotyping and more claims of age-based discrimination. Psychologists have been actively studying ageism, but relatively few studies have addressed events in the workplace. The paucity of psychological research on the biases of Anglo (non-Hispanic White) Americans toward Hispanics, in comparison to the amount of research concerning attitudes toward Blacks, has been noted previously (Dovidio et al., 1992). This deficit is more alarming in light of the extent (approximately 25 million in 1990) and relative rate of growth of the Hispanic population, 60% versus 11% for the U.S. populations as a whole. The Americans with Disabilities Act of 1992 is commonly regarded as a "work in progress," thus research on various aspects of this law is still in its infancy.[8] Reprisal and retaliation claims can build on findings in whistle-blowing studies in general (e.g., Miceli & Near, 1992), although studies of retaliatory discrimination per se are the exception rather than the rule.

Major gaps in the types of research conduced on employment discrimination fall into four broad categories. First, systemic or institutional factors that operate as barriers at the hiring, evaluation, and promotional phases of employment need to be addressed, including the glass-ceiling phenomenon and the impact of assumptions about workplace decision making. Second, studies on effective ways to reduced discrimination and remove barriers to equal employment need to be conducted. Third, research is needed on all aspects of the consequences of employment discrimination, including injuries and damages that follow workplace discrimination. Fourth, additional research is needed on the influence of aspects of the discrimination claims process.

SYSTEMIC AND INSTITUTIONAL FACTORS IN EMPLOYMENT DISCRIMINATION

Further study is needed to assess systemic and institutional circumstances and factors that cause discrimination. As Pettigrew and Martin (1987) acknowledged, modern racism is complex, necessitating clarifica-

---

[8]Research on factors such as the average cost of reasonable accommodation and uses of mediation in disabilities cases has been conducted by Blanck (Blanck, 1994).

tion of some fundamental assumptions about the legal standards to (a) the workplace, (b) forms of prejudice, and (3) the legal standards to establish discrimination. For example, in the future, more explicit acknowledgement of the role of meritocracy in employment decision making is vital. Similarly, to the extent that issues about the intentionality of stereotyping remain unresolved, additional clarification of the applicability of stereotyping in proving intentional employment discrimination is warranted.

As noted earlier, glass-ceiling allegations by women and minorities are likely to resurface. Researchers who have examined barriers to the career progress of women isolated five causal factors: (a) internal attributes (subjective) versus human capital attributes that are job relevant (objective); (b) societal norms regarding gender roles based on marital status, number of children; (c) organizational features (e.g., jobs that are male or female dominant); (d) mechanisms within the workplace that facilitate career progress (e.g., an "old boys" network); and (e) gender bias by decision makers (Melamed, 1995). Using a slightly different approach, Gutek (1993) identified four models to account for the fact that few women make it to the top: (a) individual deficit model; (b) structural factors of the work organization; (c) sex roles; and (d) intergroup model, regarding relationships between males and females. Studies conducted in Britain on the "glass-ceiling" phenomenon examined whether factors accounting for the gender gap in career success of males and females manifested in salary and managerial levels. Factors such as personality differences, job-relevant human capital attributes, demographic characteristics, career choices, labor market forces, and organizational structural features explained some of the variance in career success, but 55% of the variance was attributed to gender discrimination (Melamed, 1995).

Noteworthy is the similarity of many of the foregoing factors to those factors identified by Braddock and MacPartland (1987) as comprising barriers to the advancement of Black employees in the workforce. Future investigations of glass-ceiling discrimination based on gender and race will address some of the structural, institutional barriers highlighted by commentators and researchers that perpetuate discrimination in the workplace.

REDUCING DISCRIMINATION IN THE WORKPLACE

One major generalizable variable that emerged in past studies is the importance of the attitude of employer leadership in establishing a context that either encourages, tolerates, or diminishes discriminatory conduct. People look to authority figures to define who are "outsiders." Hostility to outside groups is a culturally learned phenomenon, evident in children as early as 3 years of age (Fishbein, 1996). Similarly, anti–affirmative action attitudes are culturally learned. Leaders' definitions of the outsiders play a role in removing obstacles and creating change (Steele, 1997). Problems associated with cultural diversity arise when cultural differences are used "as a means of categorization and defining group boundaries" (Tyler et al., 1997, p. 262).

A handful of preliminary studies of racism and sexual harassment that have applied some of these principles in the workplace have produced encouraging results. Gaertner and Dovidio (1986) found that when norms for appropriate behavior are clearly defined, Whites are consistently as positive in their behavior toward Blacks as toward Whites. Regarding sexual harassment, Pryor, LaVite, and Stoller (1993) reported that harassment reports in the military were significantly higher when the commanding officer was indifferent or neutral on the subject of sexual harassment or encouraged it. They concluded that when local norms suggest that sexually harassing conduct is tolerated, some men will behave accordingly. Effective intervention requires altering the behavior of top management (Bastian, Lancaster, & Reyst, 1996).

One key finding to emerge from the studies by Tyler et al. (1997) is that the extent to which individuals identify both with subgroups and super-ordinate groups can determine when relational justice indicators will dominate in their response to authorities. These studies build on previous work by Tajfel (1982) and others showing that the salience of group identity fosters differential treatment and stereotyping. Individuals who identify both with subgroups and superordinate groups react to the superordinate authority based on procedural justice assessments. Accordingly, Tyler et al. (1997) recommended that efforts be focused on ways to promote identification with superordinate groups to decrease conflict in the workplace and elsewhere. Strategies to achieve these goals include (a) promoting socialization in organizational workplace cultures, (b) increasing task interdependence and common goals among employees, and (c) increasing the use of fair procedures and decision making in the workplace.

Ten years ago, several researchers acknowledged the need for alternative remedies to those that existed to prevent or alleviate discrimination. For instance, Braddock and MacPartland (1987) recommended that (a) managers be instructed in the operation of modern forms of racism; (b) workplace teams be structured so that members of different groups develop common goals and interdependence, that is, through task and team redesign; and (c) minorities be provided workplace or on-the-job training to develop competencies; and (d) measures of competencies on the job be developed to evaluate employee performance. A decade later, most of their suggestions and recommendations remain untested.

With the passage of time, it is evident that more researchers have pointed to the need to conduct studies on methods employers can implement to reduce the salience of intergroup boundaries; strategies to produce decategorization or to increase individuating information about members of other ethnic, cultural, or gender groups in the workplace; and ways to enhance development of a common workteam identity. For example, Dovidio et al. (1992) proposed that if performance evaluations and bonuses were tied to a superordinate unit that included employees from various subgroups, this strategy might diffuse biases and aversive racism. Cooperative learning and interdependence was advocated by Fishbein (1996), while diversity in workteams was advocated by Jackson and Ruderman (1996). In sum, these recommendations form the basis for a research agenda for psychologists in the future.

DAMAGES FLOWING FROM EMPLOYMENT DISCRIMINATION

Given the fact that monetary damages for psychological harm and injury in federal employment discrimination cases have been available only since the implementation of the Civil Rights Act in November, 1991, little research on this topic has been conducted to date. Regarding damages caused by sexual harassment, Burns (1995) contended that the profound nature of sex-based harm is seldom recognized and little understood. Per Feldman-Schorrig (1994), the most common psychiatric disorders that may be caused by sexual harassment are, in order of frequency, (a) adjustment disorders, (b) mood disorders, (c) anxiety disorders, and (d) post-traumatic stress disorder. Types of injury or harm that accompany sexual harassment were examined in a recent study of the armed forces (Schneider, Swan, & Fitzgerald, 1997). The reported consequences of sexual harassment included (a) negative impacts on the employee's job, such as decreased job satisfaction and productivity, lower levels of commitment, and less satisfaction with co-workers; (b) psychological detriment (e.g., stress, anxiety, depression); and (c) physical detriment (e.g., headaches, gastrointestinal problems, sleep disturbances). Some evidence of gender differences was gathered. Female victims were more likely to report experiencing anxiety, distress, and intense discomfort, while male victims were more likely to regard the events as trivial, welcome, and pleasant (Waldo et al., 1998).

Some guidance on evaluating compensatory and punitive damages was issued by the EEOC (U.S. EEOC, 1992). Factors to consider in evaluating emotional damages include (a) whether and to what extent the plaintiff was subject to overt discrimination; (b) whether and to what extent the plaintiff was subject to public humiliation; (c) whether the plaintiff sought professional assistance; (d) whether the plaintiff's testimony on damages was corroborated by other witnesses; (e) whether other factors or trauma that may have caused the plaintiff's damages were present; (f) whether the plaintiff's susceptibility to emotional harm was reasonable (objective); (g) whether a subjective susceptibility to emotional harm existed (e.g., the existence of prior abuse or preexisting mental conditions that may have rendered the plaintiff more vulnerable to psychological harm); (h) what the length of time the plaintiff suffered the harm was; (i) what length of time the pain or harm is likely to continue; and (j) what the length of time between the discriminatory conduct and the manifestation of the psychological injury was (Goodman-Delahunty & Foote, 1995).

Several questions related to the role and use of expert testimony on damages warrant study. Little is known about what jurors make of experts' testimony on damages in discrimination cases (Greene & Goodman-Delahunty, 1995). Preliminary research has demonstrated that the offensiveness of the conduct perceived as sexual harassment is a critical variable in determining whether an employee will report the harassing events (McDonald & Lees-Haley, 1995). Similar factors may influence the magnitude of damages awarded to compensate a plaintiff.

Whether expert testimony makes a substantial difference to a plaintiff who seeks compensation for a protracted emotional injury is unknown. Results in a pencil-and-paper study of awards to a plaintiff discriminated against on the basis of age (Raitz, Greene, Goodman, & Loftus, 1990) indicated that mock-jury awards fell in ranges close to those provided by the experts, and that these awards were significantly higher than awards in a no-expert condition.

Many employers believe that juries who serve in employment discrimination cases are biased in favor of plaintiff employees and against corporate employers. One survey revealed that in approximately 75% of Californian employment claims tried before a jury, the plaintiff employees won their cases, recovering an average of $300,000 to $450,000 in damages (Franczak, 1995; St. Andean, 1992). Jury awards for psychological impairment are regarded as so unpredictable and excessive and costs of employment litigation so extensive (they range from $20,000 to $200,000, per St. Andean, 1992), that many employers prefer to avoid litigation and jury trials in particular. Employers, who are often risk averse, tend to spend more on claim prevention—to avoid having employees file claims—than they spend litigating claims (Dertouzos & Karoly, 1992).

PROCEDURAL ASPECTS THAT INFLUENCE DISCRIMINATION CHARGES

Few researchers have studied factors that influence whether or not employees perceive themselves as disadvantaged or adversely treated, and, if they do, factors that influence whether they file a charge of discrimination. Where discrimination excludes certain individuals from the workplace, they may have no insight into the discriminatory conduct at play, may not perceive they were victims of discrimination, and thus may not make any charges or complaints. The extent to which victims fail to report discriminatory conduct, and whether this conduct differs from cases in which individuals do make reports is unknown. How generalizable the failure of female sexual harassment victims to report harassing events may be to victims of race, age, national origin, disability discrimination, and so on is also unknown.

Another factor that may influence the willingness of victims to litigate is the extent to which employee claims are shaped by events that occur once the employee makes an initial internal report of harassment or some other form of discrimination to his or her employer. In many cases, before an employee can seek legal relief, he or she must fulfill a number of administrative prerequisites, which may entail an investigation of the claim by on-site personnel, such as the human resources manager or the union, followed by an investigation by an external consultant. External consultants may be EEOC or agency employees working in the public interest or attorneys or other professionals knowledgeable about employment discrimination. In one study, management personnel who handled internal EEO complaints in 10 large organizations were interviewed about complaints of incumbent employees before EEO complaints were filed externally or litigation commenced (Edelman, Erlanger, & Lande, 1993). The complaint handlers generally construed the law as a requirement of fair treatment, often interpreted as consistent treatment of employees. In most instances, the frame of the complaints was transformed from that of a legal right to a right to resolution of the complaint.

The extent to which employers and employees opt for private, pre-litigation, or pretrial resolution of discrimination complaints in-house or before a neutral third party, such as a mediator or arbitrator, is increasing. Many employers incorporated arbitration clauses in their employee manuals and agreements (Copus, 1996). Following recent challenges to this practice, courts in several circuits have held that mandatory arbitration of employment discrimination claims is unlawful, and that the right to a jury trial and the right to discovery and punitive damages in such cases cannot be removed by contracts (*Gibson v. Neighborhood Health Clinics, Inc.,* 1997; *Harmon v. Philip Morris, Inc.,* 1997; *Nelson v. Cyprus Bagdad Copper Corp.,* 1997). Nonetheless, certain discrimination claims, such as disability claims for reasonable accommodation and sexual harassment claims, may be more amenable to resolution through private dispute resolution vehicles than others.

The controversy over mandatory arbitration of employment disputes highlighted some negative factors associated with these practices. However, empirical data on this issue are lacking. Research conducted by Lind, Huo, and Tyler (1994) examined African-American, Asian-American, Hispanic-American, and European-American preferences for persuasion, negotiations, mediation, and arbitration to resolve conflicts. They found that although the European Americans were more individualistic, and the other three groups more collectivistic, procedural fairness concerns were widely shared. Differences that existed in preferences were attributable to views as to which procedure was most fair, not whether fairness was important. Attention to ethnic and gender differences in procedural justice judgments in the workplace and with regard to employment discrimination warrants further study.

CONCLUSION

Ten years ago, the symbolic value of affirmative action was thought by some to be its greatest asset (Katz & Proshansky, 1987). Nowadays, similar comments are made about equal opportunity laws. One researcher commented how sobering it was that "the major debate between those who have studied the impact of EEO legislation and affirmative action most systematically is between those who believe that EEO enforcement has had a modest effect, and those who believe it has had virtually none" (Burstein, 1992, p. 913). Today, a third perspective can be added to the debate, namely, that of those who contend that the classifications incorporated into the EEO legislation and the jurisprudence of discrimination have served to institutionalize and perpetrate intragroup biases and prejudices and to inhibit assimilation and group harmony (Chang, 1996).

Recent advances in the study of intergroup relations and perceptions of social justice are most timely, as a new era gets under way to address equal opportunity and affirmative action in the workplace. Indications are that psychology has much to offer in reducing conflicts in the workplace based on findings about the efficacy of promoting the multiculturalism and the diversity of individuals and multicultural shared values (Brewer, 1997). The dynamic nature of the law prohibiting discrimination provides a fertile opportunity for psychologists to engage in interdisciplinary collaboration and contribute to the growth and development of the law on this topic.

REFERENCES

Abell, N. L., & Jackson, M. N. (1996). Sexual harassment investigations—cues, clues and how-to's. *The Labor Lawyer, 12,* 17–56.

Adarand Constructors v. Pena, 115 S. Ct. 2097 (1995).

Administrative Dispute Resolution Act of 1995, 5 U.S.C. §§ 571–583 (1995).

Age Discrimination in Employment Act, 29 U.S.C. § 201 (1967).

Albemarle Paper Company v. Moody, 422 U.S. 405 (1975).

American Bar Association. (1993). *ABA model jury instructions in employment cases.* Chicago, IL: American Bar Association Litigation Section.

American Federation of State, County and Municipal Employees v. Washington, 77 F.2d 1401 (9th Cir. 1985).

Americans With Disabilities Act of 1990, Pub. L. No. 101-336, § 12101 *et seq.* (1991).

Anderson v. General Dynamics, 589 F.2d 397 (9th Cir. 1978).

Andrews v. City of Philadelphia, 895 F.2d 1469 (3rd Cir. 1990).

Arvey, R. D., & Cavanaugh, M. A. (1995). Using surveys to assess the prevalence of sexual harassment: Some methodological problems. *Journal of Social Issues, 51,* 117–138.

Baird, C. L., Bensko, N. L., Bell, P. A., & Viney, W. (1995). Gender influence on perceptions of hostile environment sexual harassment. *Psychological Reports, 77,* 79–82.

Bargh, J. A., & Raymond, P. (1995). The naive misuse of power: Nonconscious sources of sexual harassment. *Journal of Social Issues, 51,* 85–96.

Bastian, L. D., Lancaster, A. R., & Reyst, H. E. (1996). *Department of Defense: 1995 sexual harassment survey.* Arlington, VA: Defense Manpower Data Center.

Belliveau, M. A. (1966). The paradoxical influence of policy exposure on affirmative action attitudes. *Journal of Social Issues, 52,* 99–104.

Belz, H. (1991). *Equality transformed: A quarter century of affirmative action.* New Brunswick, NJ: Transaction.

Bersoff, D. N. (1982). Regarding psychologists testily: The legal regulation of psychological assessment. In C. J. Scheirer & B. L. Hammonds (Eds.), *The Master Lecture Series: Psychology and the law* (pp. 37–88). Washington, DC: American Psychological Association.

Blanck, P. D. (1994). *Communicating the Americans With Disabilities Act. Transcending compliance: A case report on Sears, Roebuck & Co.* Washington, DC: Annenberg Washington Program in Communications Policy Studies of Northwestern University.

Blum v. Witco Chemical Corp., 829 F.2d 367 (3rd Cir. 1987).

Blumenthal, A. J. (1998). The reasonable woman standard: A meta-analytic review of gender differences in perceptions of sexual harassment. *Law and Human Behavior, 22,* 33–58.

Blumrosen, A. W. (1995). Draft report on reverse discrimination commissioned by Labor Department. In Bureau of National Affairs, Inc., *Affirmative action after* Adarand: *A legal, regulatory, legislative outlook (Daily Labor Report, 147,* pp. S45–51). Washington, DC: Author.

Bohen v. City of East Chicago, 622 F. Supp. 1234 (N.D. Ind. 1985), *rev'd in part* on other grounds, 799 F.2d 1180 (7th Cir. 1986).

Bolden v. SEPTA, 31 F.3d 29 (3rd Cir. 1994).

Booker v. Taylor Milk Co., 64 F.3d 860, 864 (3rd Cir. 1995).

Borgida, E., Rudman, L. A., & Manteufel, L. L. (1995). On the courtroom use and misuse of gender stereotyping research. *Journal of Social Issues, 51,* 181–192.

Braddock, J. M., II, & McPartland, J. M. (1987). How minorities continue to be excluded from equal employment opportunities: Research on labor market and institutional barriers. *Journal of Social Issues, 43,* 5–39.

Brewer, M. B. (1994). The social psychology of prejudice. Getting it all together. In M. Zanna & J. Olson (Eds.), *The psychology of prejudice: The Ontario Symposium* (Vol. 7, pp. 315–329). Hillsdale, NJ: Erlbaum.

Brewer, M. B. (1997). The social psychology of intergroup relations: Can research inform practice? *Journal of Social Issues, 53,* 197–211.

Brown v. Board of Education, 347 U.S. 483 (1954).

Brown, B. B., & Germanis, I. L. (1994). Hostile environment sexual harassment: Has *Harris* really changed things? *Employee Relations Law Journal, 19,* 567–578.

Bureau of National Affairs, Inc. (1995, August). *Affirmative action after* Adarand: *A legal, regulatory, legislative outlook* (*Daily Labor Report, 147*, pp. S1–101). Washington, DC: Author.

Burgess, D., & Borgida, E. (1997). Sexual harassment: An experimental test of sex-role spillover theory. *Personality and Social Psychology Bulletin, 23*, 63–75.

Burlington Industries, Inc. v. Ellerth, U.S. Supr. Ct. No. 97-569 (June 26, 1998).

Burns v. McGregor Electronic Industries, Inc., 989 F.2d 959 (8th Cir. 1993).

Burns, S. E. (1995). Issues in workplace sexual harassment law and social science research. *Journal of Social Issues, 51*, 193–210.

Burstein, P. (1992). Affirmative action, jobs, and American democracy: What has happened to the quest for equal opportunity? *Law and Society Review, 26*, 901–922.

Burstein, P., & Edwards, M. E. (1994). The impact of employment discrimination litigation on racial disparity in earnings: Evidence and unresolved issues. *Law and Society Review, 28*, 79–111.

Burstein, P., & Pitchford, S. (1990). Social-scientific and legal challenges to education and test requirements in employment. *Social Problems, 37*, 243–257.

Buss, D. M. (1995). Psychological sex differences: Origins through sexual selection. *American Psychologist, 50*, 164–168.

Canada v. Boyd Group, 809 F. Supp. 771 (D. Nev. 1992).

Chang, W. C. (1996). Toward equal opportunities: Fairness, values and affirmative action programs in the U.S. *Journal of Social Issues, 52*(4), 93–98.

Chiapuzio v. BLT Operating Corp., No. 92-CV-0277-B (July 29, 1993).

City of Richmond v. J. A. Croson Co., 488 U.S. 469 (1989).

Civil Rights Act of 1866, 42 U.S.C. §§ 1985, 1986 (1866).

Civil Rights Act of 1871, 42 U.S.C. §§1983, 1985, as amended (1986).

Civil Rights Act of 1964, 42 U.S.C. § 2000e *et seq.*, as amended (1964).

Civil Rights Act of 1991, Pub. L. No. 102-106, § 106 (1991).

Cohen, C. (1991). Racial preference in the factory. In R. Nieli (Ed.), *Racial preference and racial justice: The new affirmative action controversy* (pp. 279–312). Washington, DC: Ethics and Public Policy Center.

Connecticut v. Teal, 457 U.S. 440 (1982).

Copus, D. A. (1996). *Employment law 101 deskbook: The essential foundation in the law for business executives, human resource professionals, and employment counsel.* Larkspur, CA: National Employment Law Institute.

County of Washington v. Gunther, 452 U.S. 161 (1981).

Crosby, F. J. (1984). Relative deprivation in organizational settings. In B. M. Staw & L. Cummings (Eds.), *Research in organizational behavior* (Vol. 6, pp. 51–93). Greenwich, CT: JAI Press.

Crosby, F. J. (1994). Understanding affirmative action. *Basic and Applied Social Psychology, 15*, 13–41.

Crosby, F. J., & Cordova, D. I. (1996). Words worth of wisdom: Toward an understanding of affirmative action. *Journal of Social Issues, 52*, 33–49.

Davis v. Monsanto Chemical Co., 858 F.2d 345 (6th Cir. 1988).

DeAngelis v. El Paso Municipal Police Officers Association, 51 F.3d 591 (5th Cir. 1995).

Deaux, K. (1995). How basic can you be? The evolution of research on gender stereotypes. *Journal of Social Issues, 51*(1), 11–20.

DeBruin, D. A. (1998). Identifying sexual harassment: The reasonable woman standard. In S. G. French, W. Teays, and Laura M. Purdy (eds.), *Violence against women* (pp. 107–122). Ithaca, NY: Cornell University Press.

Dertouzos, J. N., & Karoly, L. A. (1992). *Labor market responses to employer liability.* Santa Monica, CA: Rand's Institute for Civil Justice.

Donohue, J. J., & Siegelman, P. (1991). The changing nature of employment discrimination litigation. *Stanford Law Review*, *51*, 983–1033.

Dovidio, J. F., & Gaertner, S. L. (1981). The effects of race, status and ability on helping behavior. *Journal of Social Psychology Quarterly*, *44*, 192–203.

Dovidio, J. F., & Gaertner, S. L. (1983). The effects of sex, status and ability on helping behavior. *Journal of Applied Social Psychology*, *13*, 191–205.

Dovidio, J. F., & Gaertner, S. L. (1996). Affirmative action, unintentional racial biases, and intergroup relations. *Journal of Social Issues*, *52*, 51–75.

Dovidio, J. F., Gaertner, S. L., Anastasio, P. A., & Sanitioso, R. (1996). Cognitive and motivational bases for bias: The implications of aversive racism for attitudes towards Hispanics. In S. Knouse, P. Rosenfeld, & A. Culbertson (Eds.), *Hispanics in the workplace* (pp. 75–106). Newbury Park, CA: Sage.

Duckitt, J. (1994). *The social psychology of prejudice*. Westport, CT: Praeger.

Eagly, A. H. (1995a). Reflections on the commenters' views. *American Psychologist*, *50*, 169–171.

Eagly, A. H. (1995b). The science and politics of comparing men and women. *American Psychologist*, *50*, 145–158.

Edelman, L. B., Erlanger, H. S., & Lande, J. (1993). Internal dispute resolution: The transformation of civil rights in the workplace. *Law and Society Review*, *27*, 497–534.

EEOC v. Federal Bank of Richmond, 689 F.2d 633 (4th Cir. 1983).

EEOC v. Murphy Motor Freight Lines, Inc., 488 F. Supp. 381 (D. Mn. 1980).

EEOC v. Sears, Roebuck & Company, 839 F.2d 302 (7th Cir. 1988).

Ellison v. Brady, 924 F.2d 872 (9th Cir. 1991).

Epp, C. R. (1990). Connecting litigation levels and legal mobilization: Explaining interstate variation in employment civil rights litigation. *Law & Society Review*, *24*(1), 145–163.

Equal Pay Act, 29 U.S.C. § 206(d) (1963).

Executive Order No. 11246, 3 C.F.R. 339 (1964–1965).

Fallon, R. H., Jr. (1980). To each according to his ability, from none according to his race: The concept of merit in the law of antidiscrimination. *Boston University Law Review*, *60*, 815–877.

Faragher v. Boca Raton, Fla., U.S. Supr. Ct. No. 97-282 (June 26, 1998).

Feldman-Schorrig, S. P. (1994). Special issues in sexual harassment cases. In J. J. McDonald & F. B. Kulick (Eds.), *Mental and emotional injuries in employment litigation* (pp. 332–390). Washington, DC: Bureau of National Affairs, Inc.

Ferdman, B. M. (1989). Affirmative action and the challenge of color-blind perspective. In F. A. Blanchard & F. J. Crosby (Eds.), *Affirmative action in perspective* (pp. 169–176). New York or Berlin: Springer-Verlag.

Fienberg, S. E. (ed.). (1989). *The evolving role of statistical assessments as evidence in the courts* (Report of the Panel on Statistical Assessments as Evidence in the Courts). New York: Springer-Verlag.

Fishbein, H. (1996). *Peer prejudice and discrimination*. Boulder, CO: Westview Press.

Fiske, S. T. (1987). On the road: Comment on the cognitive stereotyping literature in Pettigrew and Martin. *Journal of Social Issues*, *43*, 113–118.

Fiske, S. T., & Glick, P. (1995). Ambivalence and stereotypes cause sexual harassment: A theory with implications for organizational change. *Journal of Social Issues*, *51*, 97–115.

Fitzgerald, L. F., Drasgow, F., Magley, V. J., & Waldo, C. (1997, August). *Sexual harassment in the armed forces: A test of an integrated model*. Paper presented at the 105th Convention of the American Psychological Association, Chicago, IL.

Fitzgerald, L. F., Shullman, S. L., Bailey, N., Richards, M., Swecker, J., Gold, A., Ormerod, A. J., & Weitzman, L. (1988). The incidence and dimensions of sexual harassment in academia and the workplace. *Journal of Vocational Behavior*, *32*, 152–175.

Fitzgerald, L. F., Swan, S., & Fischer, K. (1995). Why didn't she just report him? The psychological and legal implications of women's responses to sexual harassment. *Journal of Social Issues, 51,* 117–138.

Franczak, M. S. (1995). The Model Employment Termination Act (META): Does it violate the right to trial by jury? *Journal on Dispute Resolution, 10,* 441–467.

Frazier, P. A., Cochran, C. C., & Olson, A. M. (1995). Social science research on lay definitions of sexual harassment. *Journal of Social Issues, 51,* 21–38.

Frazier, P. A., & Hunt, J. (1998). Research on gender and the law: Where have we been and where are we going? *Law and Human Behavior, 22,* 1–16.

Fuller v. City of Oakland, 47 F.3d 1522 (9th Cir. 1995).

Furnco Construction Corporation v. Waters, 438 U.S. 567 (1978).

Gaertner, S. L., & Dovidio, J. F. (1986). The aversive form of racism. In J. F. Dovidio & S. L. Gaertner (Eds.), *Prejudice, discrimination, and racism* (pp. 61–89). Orlando, FL: Academic Press.

Gaines, S. O., & Reed, E. S. (1995). Prejudice: From Allport to DuBoios. *American Psychologist, 50,* 96–103.

Gibson v. Neighborhood Health Clinics, Inc., 121 F.3d 1126 (7th Cir. 1997).

Goodman-Delahunty, J., & Foote, W. (1995). Compensation for pain, suffering, and other psychological injuries: The impact of *Daubert* on employment discrimination claims. *Behavioral Sciences and the Law, 13,* 183–206.

Gore v. Turner, 563 F.2d 159 (5th Cir. 1977).

Graham, H. D. (1990). *The civil rights era.* New York: Oxford University Press.

Greene, E., & Goodman-Delahunty, J. (1995). Diagnosis of psychological impairment in employment discrimination claims. *Behavioral Sciences and the Law, 13,* 459–476.

Greenwald, A., & Banaji, M. (1995). Implicit social cognition: Attitudes, self-esteem and stereotypes. *Psychological Review, 102,* 4–27.

Griggs v. Duke Power Co., 401 U.S. 324 (1971).

Guardians Association of the New York City Police Department v. Civil Service Commission, 630 F.2d 79 (2nd Cir. 1980), cert. denied, 452 U.S. 940 (1981).

Gutek, B. (1993). Changing women's status in management. *Applied Psychology: An International Review, 42,* 301–311.

Gutek, B. A., & Morasch, B. (1982). Sex ratios, sex role spillover, and sexual harassment of women at work. *Journal of Social Issues, 38,* 55–74.

Gutek, B. A., & O'Connor, M. O. (1995). The empirical basis for the reasonable woman standard. *Journal of Social Issues, 51,* 151–166.

Gutek, B. A., O'Connor, M. O., & Melancon, R. (1997, May). *Factors affecting perceptions of sexual harassment using realistic, detailed scenarios.* Presentation at the Annual Meeting of the American Psychological Society, Washington, DC.

Haney, C. (1993). Psychology and legal change: The impact of a decade. *Law and Human Behavior, 17,* 371–398.

Haney, C., & Hurtado, A. (1994). The jurisprudence of race and meritocracy: Standardized testing and "race-neutral" racism in the workplace. *Law and Human Behavior, 18,* 223–248.

Harmon v. Philip Morris, Inc., No. 71605, 1997 WL 537654 (Ohio Ct. App., Aug. 28, 1997).

Harris v. Forklift Systems, Inc., 114 S. Ct. 567, 510 U.S. 17 (1993).

Harris v. International Paper Co., 765 F. Supp. 1509 (D. Me. 1991).

Hartigan, J. A., & Wigdor, A. K. (1989). *Fairness in employment testing.* Washington, DC: National Academy Press.

Hartstein, B. A., & Wilde, T. M. (1994). The broadening scope of harassment in the workplace. *Employee Relations Law Journal, 19,* 639–653.

Hazelwood School District v. United States, 433 U.S. 299 (1977).

Herek, G. M., Gillis, J. R., Cogan, J. C., & Glunt, E. K. (1997). Hate crime victimization among lesbian, gay, and bisexual adults. *Journal of Interpersonal Violence, 12,* 195–215.

Howard, W. M. (1994, April). The decline and fall of statistical evidence as proof of employment discrimination. *Labor Law Journal*, 208–220.

Huo, Y. J., Smith, H. J., Tyler, T. R., & Lind, E. A. (1996). Superordinate identification, subgroup identification, and justice concerns: Is separatism the problem; is assimilation the answer? *Psychological Science, 7*, 40–45.

Hyde, J. S., & Plant, E. A. (1995). Magnitude of psychological gender differences: Another side of the story. *American Psychologist, 50*, 159–161.

Immigration Reform and Control Act of 1986, Pub. L. No. 99-603, § XX, 100 Stat. 3359 (1986).

International Brotherhood of Teamsters v. United States, 431 U.S. 344 (1977).

Jackson, S., & Ruderman, M. (Eds.). (1996). *Diversity in workteams*. Washington, DC: American Psychological Association.

Jacobsen, C. K. (1985). Resistance to affirmative action: Self-interest or racism? *Journal of Conflict Resolution, 29*, 751–329.

Jenson v. Eveleth Taconite Company, 824 F. Supp. 847 (D. Minn. 1993).

Jiobu, R. M. (1990). *Ethnicity and inequality*. Albany: State University of New York Press.

Johnson, P. (1993). The reasonable woman standard in sexual harassment law: Progress or illusion? *Wake Forest Law Review, 28*, 619–669.

Jones, J. M. (1997). *Prejudice and racism*. New York: McGraw-Hill.

Katz, I., & Proshansky, H. M. (1987). Rethinking affirmative action. *Journal of Social Issues, 43*, 99–104.

Kauffman v. Allied Signal, Inc., 970 F.2d 178 (6th Cir. 1992).

Kaye, D. H. (1990). Improving legal statistics. *Law and Society Review, 25*, 1255–1275.

Kneel, R. (1991). Ethnic tribalism and human personhood. In R. Kneel (Ed.), *Racial preference and racial justice: The new affirmative action controversy* (pp. 61–104). Washington, DC: Ethics and Public Policy Center.

Kraiger, K., & Ford, J. K. (1985). A meta-analysis of ratee race effects in performance ratings. *Journal of Applied Psychology, 70*, 56–65.

Kravitz, D. A. (1995). Attitudes toward affirmative action plans directed at Blacks: Effects of plan and individual differences. *Journal of Applied Social Psychology, 25*, 2192–2220.

Kravitz, D. A, Harrison, D. A., Turner, M. E., Levine, E. L., Chaves, W., Brannick, M. T., Denning, D. L., Russell, C. J., Conrad, M. A. (1997). *Affirmative action: A review of psychological and behavioral research*. Bowling Green, OH: Society for Industrial and Organizational Psychology.

Krieger, L. H. (1995). The content of our categories: A cognitive bias approach to discrimination and equal employment opportunity. *Stanford Law Review, 47*, 1161–1248.

Lehmann v. Toys 'R' Us, Inc., 626 A.2d 445 (N. J. 1993).

Lind, E. A. (1992). The fairness heuristic: Rationality and "relationality" in procedural evaluation. Paper presented at the Fourth International Congress of the Society for the Advancement of Socio-Economics, Irvine, CA.

Lind, E. A., Huo, Y. J., & Tyler, T. R. (1994). ... And justice for all: Ethnicity, gender and preferences for dispute resolution procedures. *Law and Human Behavior, 18*, 269–290.

Lindemann, B., & Kadue, D. (1992). *Sexual harassment in employment law*. Washington, DC: Bureau of National Affairs.

Lopez v. Laborers International Union Local 18, 987 F.2d 1210 (5th Cir. 1993).

Lynch, F. R. (1992). Race unconsciousness and the white male. *Society, 29*, 30–35.

Maracek, J. (1995). Gender, politics and psychology's way of knowing. *American Psychologist, 50*, 162–163.

McDonald, J. J., Jr., & Kulick, F. B. (1994). *Mental and emotional injuries in employment litigation*. Washington, DC: Bureau of National Affairs.

McDonald, J. J., Jr., & Lees-Haley, P. R. (1995). Avoiding "junk science" in sexual harassment litigation. *Employment Relations, 21,* 51–71.

McDonnell-Douglas Corp. v. Green, 411 U.S. 792 (1973).

Melamed, T. (1995). Barriers to women's career success: Human capital, career choices, structural determinants, or simply sex discrimination. *Applied Psychology: An International Review, 44,* 295–314.

Meritor Savings Bank FEB v. Vinson, 477 U.S. 57, 106 S. Ct. 2399 (1986).

Miceli, M. P., & Near, J. P. (1992). *Blowing the whistle: The organizational and legal implications for companies and employees.* New York: Lexington.

Moore, D. (1990). Discrimination and deprivation: The effects of social comparisons. *Social Justice Research, 4*(1), 49–64.

Moses, S. (1990). Civil right bills worry some I/O psychologists: Effects on testing, selection are questioned. *APA Monitor,* p. 24.

Munro, G. D. (1997, May). *Judgments of outgroup and ingroup members employment qualifications: The role of antiblack prejudice.* Poster presented at the annual convention of the American Psychological Society, Washington, DC.

Murrell, A. J., Dietz-Uhler, B. L., Dovidio, J. F., Gaertner, S. L., & Drout, C. (1994). Aversive racism and resistance to affirmative action: Perceptions of justice are not necessarily color blind. *Basic and Applied Social Psychology, 15,* 71–86.

Murrell, A. J., & Jones, R. (1996). Assessing affirmative action: Past, present, and future. *Journal of Social Issues, 52,* 77–92.

Nacoste, R. W. (1996). How affirmative action can pass Constitutional and social psychological muster. *Journal of Social Issues, 52,* 133–144.

Nelson v. Cyprus Bagdad Copper Corp., 118 F.3d 756 (9th Cir. 1997).

Nordin, V. (1989). Affirmative action. In M. Chamberlain (Ed.), *Women in academe* (pp. 165–191). New York: Russell Sage.

Oncale v. Sundowner Offshore Services, Inc., 118 S. Ct. 998 (1998).

Opotow, S. (1996). Affirmative action, fairness, and the scope of justice. *Journal of Social Issues, 52,* 19–24.

Page v. Bolger, 645 F.2d 227 (4th Cir. 1981), *cert. den.* 454 U.S. 892 (1981).

Peterson, R. S. (1994). The role of values in predicting fairness judgments and support of affirmative action. *Journal of Social Issues, 50,* 95–115.

Pettigrew, T. F., & Martin, J. (1987). Shaping the organizational context for Black American inclusion. *Journal of Social Issues, 43,* 41–78.

Pratkanis, A. R., & Turner, M. E. (1996). The proactive removal of discriminatory barriers: Affirmative action as effective help. *Journal of Social Issues, 52,* 111–132.

Price-Waterhouse v. Hopkins, 490 U.S. 228 (1989).

Pryor, J. D., Giedd, J. L., & Williams, K. B. (1995). A social psychological model for predicting sexual harassment. *Journal of Social Issues, 51,* 69–94.

Pryor, J. D., LaVite, C. M., & Stoller, L. M. (1993). A social psychological analysis of sexual harassment: The person/situation interaction. *Journal of Vocational Behavior, 42,* 68–83.

Pryor, J. D., & Whalen, N. (1997). A typology of sexual harassment: Characteristics of harassers and social circumstances under which sexual harassment occurs. In W. O. Donohue (Ed.), *Sexual harassment: Theory, research, and treatment.* Needham Heights, MA: Allyn & Bacon.

Queller, S., & Major, B. (1997, May). *Effects of group focus on attention to distributive vs. procedural fairness.* Poster presented at the annual convention of the American Psychological Society, Washington, DC.

Radtke v. Everett, 501 N.W. 2d 155 (Mich. 1993).

Raitz, A., Greene, E., Goodman, J., & Loftus, E. F. (1990). Determining damages: The influence of expert testimony on jurors' decision making. *Law and Human Behavior, 14*(4), 385–395.

Rasinski, K. A. (1987). What's fair is fair—or is it? Value differences underlying public views about social justice. *Journal of Personality and Social Psychology, 53*, 201–211.

Rehabilitation Act, 29 U.S.C. 794 *et seq.*, as amended (1973, 1978).

Robinson v. Jacksonville Shipyards, Inc., 760 F. Supp. 1486 (M. D. Fla. 1991).

Rogers v. EEOC, 454 F.2d 234 (5th Cir. 1971), *cert. denied*, 406 U.S. 957 (1972).

Rudman, R. A., & Borgida, E. (1995). The afterglow of construct accessibility: The behavioral consequences of priming men to view women as sexual objects. *Journal of Experimental Social Psychology, 31*, 493–517.

Schneider, K. T., Swan, S., & Fitzgerald, L. F. (1997). Job-related and psychological effects of sexual harassment in the workplace: Empirical evidence from two organizations. *Journal of Applied Psychology, 82*, 401–415.

Schultz, V. (1990). Telling stories about women and work: Judicial interpretation of sex segregation in the workplace in Title VII cases raising the lack of interest argument. *Harvard Law Review, 103*, 1749–1843.

Schultz, V., & Petterson, S. (1992). Race, gender, work, and choice: An empirical study of the lack of interest defense in Title VII cases challenging job segregation. *University of Chicago Law Review, 59*, 1073–1177.

Schwartz, D. J., & Goodman, J. (1992). Expert testimony on decision processes in employment cases. *Law and Human Behavior, 16*, 337–355.

Sears, D. O. (1988). Symbolic racism. In P. A. Katz & D. A. Taylor (Eds.), *Eliminating racism: Profiles in controversy* (pp. 53–84). New York: Plenum Press.

Selmi, M. (1996). The value of the EEOC: Reexamining the agency's role in employment discrimination law. *Ohio State Law Journal, 57*, 1–26.

Sidanius, J., Pratto, F., & Bobo, L. (1996). Racism, conservativism, affirmative action, and intellectual sophistication: A matter of principled conservativism or group dominance? *Journal of Personal and Social Psychology, 70*, 476–490.

Siegelman, P., & Donohue, J. J. (1990). Studying the iceberg from its tip: A comparison of published and unpublished employment discrimination cases. *Law & Society Review, 24*(5), 1133–1170.

Snider v. Consolidated Coal Co., 973 F.2d 555 (7th Cir. 1992), *cert. denied*, 506 U.S. 1054 (4th Cir. 1993).

Spence v. Board of Education of Christian School District, 806 F.2d 1198 (3rd Cir. 1986).

St. Andean, T. J. (1992). The Model Employment Termination Act: Fairness for employees and employers alike. *Labor Law Journal, 43*, 495.

St. Mary's Honor Center v. Hicks, 509 U.S. 502, 113 S. Ct. 2472 (1993).

Steele, C. M. (1997). A threat in the air: How stereotypes shape intellectual identity and performance. *American Psychologist, 52*, 613–629.

Stone-Harris, R. (1996). Same-sex harassment—The next step in the evolution of sexual harassment law under Title VII. *St. Mary's Law Journal*, 269–327.

Tajfel, H. (1982). Social psychology of intergroup attitudes. *Annual Review of Psychology, 33*, 1–39.

Tougas, F., & Beaton, A. M. (1993). Affirmative action in the workplace: For better or for worse. *Applied Psychology: An International Review, 42*, 253–264.

Tougas, F., & Veilleux, F. (1988). The influence of identification, collective relative deprivation, and procedure of implementation on women's response to affirmative action: A causal modeling approach. *Canadian Journal of Behavioural Science, 20*, 15–28.

Turner v. Barr, 806 F. Supp. 1025 (D. D. C. 1992).

Turner, M. A., Fix, M., & Struyk, R. J. (1991). *Opportunities denied, opportunities diminished: Racial discrimination in hiring.* Washington, DC: The Urban Institute Press.

TXO Production Corp. v. Alliance Resources Corp., 113 S. Ct. 2711 (1993).

Tyler, T. R., Boeckmann, R. J., Smith, H. J., & Huo, Y. J. (1997). *Social justice in a diverse society*, Boulder, CO: Westview.

U. S. Equal Employment Opportunity Commission. (1966, August 24). *Guidelines on employee selection procedures*. Washington, DC: Author.

U. S. Equal Employment Opportunity Commission. (1978, September 25). *Uniform guidelines, supplementary information*. Washington, DC: Author.

U. S. Equal Employment Opportunity Commission. (1979, March 2). *Questions and answers to clarify and provide a common interpretation of the uniform guidelines on employee selection procedures*. Washington, DC: Author.

U. S. Equal Employment Opportunity Commission. (1980a). *Guidelines on discrimination because of national origin*. Washington, DC: Author.

U. S. Equal Employment Opportunity Commission. (1980b). *Guidelines on discrimination because of sex*. Washington, DC: Author.

U. S. Equal Employment Opportunity Commission. (1985). *Uniform guidelines for validation of tests*. Washington, DC: Author.

U. S. Equal Employment Opportunity Commission. (1990). *Policy guidance on current issues in sexual harassment*. Washington, DC: Author.

U. S. Equal Employment Opportunity Commission. (1992, July 14). Compensatory damages and punitive damages available under Section 102 of the Civil Rights Act of 1991. *EEOC Enforcement Guidance*. Washington, DC: Author.

U. S. Immigration and Naturalization Service. (1996). *Worksite enforcement: Reducing the job magnet*. Washington, DC: Author.

U. S. Merit Systems Protection Board. (1981). *Sexual harassment in the federal workplace—Is it is problem?* Washington, DC: Author.

U. S. Merit Systems Protection Board. (1995). *Sexual harassment in the federal workplace: Trends, progress, continuing challenges*. Washington, DC: Author.

Waldo, C. R., Berdahl, J. L., & Fitzgerald, L. F. (1998). Are men sexually harassed? If so, by whom? *Law and Human Behavior, 22*, 59–80.

Watson v. Fort Worth Bank & Trust, 487 U.S. 977, 108 S. Ct. 2777 (1988).

Weaver v. Casa Gallardo, Inc., 922 F.2d 1515 (11th Cir. 1991).

Whalen, C., & B. (1985). *The longest debate*. Cabin John, MD: Seven Locks Press.

Wiener, R. L. (1995). Social analytic jurisprudence in sexual harassment litigation: The role of social framework and social fact. *Journal of Social Issues, 51*, 167–180.

Wiener, R. L., Hurt, L. E., Russell, B., Mannen, K., & Gasper, C. (1997). Perceptions of sexual harassment: The effects of gender, legal standard, and ambivalent sexism. *Law and Human Behavior, 21*, 711–794.

Wiener, R. L., Watts, B. A., Goldkamp, K. H., & Gasper, C. (1995). Social analytic investigation of hostile workplace environments: A test of the reasonable woman standard. *Law and Human Behavior, 19*, 263–281.

Williams, C. W., Brown, R. S., Lees-Haley, P. R., & Price, J. R. (1995). An attributional (causal dimensional) analysis of perceptions of sexual harassment. *Journal of Applied Social Psychology, 25*, 1169–1183.

Wittig, M. A. (1996). Taking affirmative action in education and employment. *Journal of Social Issues, 52*, 145–160.

Wrighten v. Metropolitan Hospitals, Inc., 726 F.2d 1346 (9th Cir. 1984).

Yates v. Avco Corp., 819 F.2d 630 (6th Cir. 1987).

Zanna, M., & Olson, J. (Eds.). *The psychology of prejudice: The Ontario Symposium*. Hillsdale, NJ: Erlbaum.

9

Best Interests of the Child

New Twists on an Old Theme

MARSHA B. LISS
AND MARCIA J. McKINLEY-PACE

King Solomon may have been the first judge to determine a child's custody; the standard he verbalized focused on equity, the sharing by each of two women in the physical custody of the child. In reality, King Solomon was testing the two women in order to determine which woman was the true mother and what was in the *best interests* of the child. So too, in the 1990s, judges in family law courts around the United States have had to make decisions about children's lives in new and unusual situations. These decisions cover a wide range of issues (see Elrod, 1994, 1995, for a comprehensive review of court decisions and state statute revisions). Some are adoption cases, others, custody or visitation cases. Some are brought by one or more of the numerous adults vying for the custody of a child; in others, older children themselves have brought the cases to court. Some cases involve the creation of new families; others, the dissolution of what were once intact families or relationships. Some types of cases did not even

Note: This chapter represents the opinions and research of the authors and does not necessarily represent the views of the United States Department of Justice or George Mason University.

MARSHA B. LISS • Child Exploitation Section, U.S. Department of Justice, 1331 F Street, NW, Sixth Floor, Washington, DC 20530-0001. MARCIA J. McKINLEY-PACE • Department of Psychology, George Mason University, Fairfax, Virginia 22030.

Psychology and Law: The State of the Discipline, edited by Ronald Roesch, Stephen D. Hart, and James R. P. Ogloff. Kluwer Academic/Plenum Publishers, New York, 1999.

exist prior to the last decade. Despite the wide range of issues they address, however, these cases share several common dimensions. In each case, the judge has had to invoke a definition or concept of the family and choose a standard for defining the child's "family." In some cases, but certainly not all, psychologists and other mental health professionals have been involved in evaluations and decision making.

The decision-making process used by courts has evolved over time in response to societal developments. Over the years, the definition of a family has taken many forms and been shaped by numerous factors, including biology, psychological ties, and societal influences (Schwartz, 1993). Traditionally, the family was defined by biology and consisted of two married parents and their offspring; maintaining family ties was critical for the economic survival of the individuals and the family unit. Adoption was seen as an alternative, though clearly less desirable form of family (Bartholet, 1993). Prior to urbanization, extended families (including multiple generations of grandparents, aunts, uncles, and cousins) beyond the nuclear family were also common (Schwartz, 1993).

The family has undergone numerous changes since that time. Today, the traditional nuclear family constitutes a smaller percentage of families in the United States (Furstenberg & Cherlin, 1991) and extended families play a smaller and smaller role in children's lives. Instead, for various reasons, including new reproductive technologies and an increased numbers of divorces, more families are headed by single parents or have taken other new forms. Many of these new "families" are considered "blended"— combinations of parts of prior existing families that are brought together in new living constellations (Schwartz, 1992, 1993). Some children may experience a succession of varying family relationships or developing stages of the family (Gindes, 1995): intact nuclear, extended, separated, single parent, blended, separated, and blended again. In addition, the roles of parents and primary caretakers have changed, frequently requiring courts to make custody determinations involving third parties as caregivers.

As the courts face more and more of these nontraditional situations, the standards that they have relied on in the past to make decisions are no longer adequate. As a result, increasingly the definition of family is also being shaped by judicial factors. Thus, the concepts of family that determine many family law cases come from myriad sources, including statutory and case law, mental health evaluations (if any), and courts views of the importance of biological, psychological, and societal factors. Unfortunately, these definitions of family rarely consider the psychological literature on children and families. It is also important to note that, except in cases where parental rights were formally and irrevocably terminated, family law courts retain jurisdiction to modify custody determinations, thus making the decisions important but not permanent and leaving the court door open for further litigation; thus, custody issues are still ripe for change until the child reaches the age of majority.

This chapter reviews the psychological research relevant to the decisions facing family law judges.[1] We begin by describing the legal standards that courts have used throughout the years in making decisions about child custody and visitation, focusing especially on the current best-interests standard for decision making. Next, we describe recent family law cases that have riveted the country and dominated the headlines and how the best interests standard has been applied to these cases. Finally, we illustrate how the psychological literature can contribute to an understanding of what is in children's best interests, thus impacting how these cases are resolved.

HISTORICAL STANDARDS

Over the years, the standards used to determine child custody and visitation have evolved to reflect changing social and economic circumstances (Jacob, 1988). Under English common law, for example, children were considered property (Bratt, 1979). More specifically, because women could not own property, children were considered their fathers' property, and fathers were thus presumed to be entitled to child custody. Over the years, a number of factors interacted to eliminate the property standard, at least in name. Feudalism eroded and was replaced by industrialization. America established its own legal traditions. Most importantly, women and children began to gain greater power. The early women's rights movement first brought women greater political power, including the right to own property. Similarly, the 19th century also brought changes in societal beliefs about children. As early theories of child development were increasingly accepted, children were viewed not as property but as evolving human beings (Aries, 1965). A combination of these factors led to the emergence of the tender years doctrine, which suggested that children should be in their mother's custody during the early formative years (Roth, 1975). Under the tender years doctrine, the mother was presumed to be the better parent, and the good mother was the ideal. As a result, in those cases when a mother lost custody to a father or a third party, it was presumed that there was something terribly wrong with the mother; that she was unfit.

---

[1]The present review is not intended to be comprehensive. It does not consider all topics related to the role of psychology in family law or all family law topics. For instance, cases and research dealing with racial and religious issues, reproductive techniques, and on custodial concerns are not included.

Over time, a shift in social and economic circumstances worked to minimize this preference for maternal custody. The women's rights movement of the 20th century led to a decrease in sexual stereotyping and a greater range of choices for women and men. Women began to emphasize their professional as well as family goals; in turn, began to be more involved with family roles, not just with professional roles. As a result, during the 1970s fathers increasingly began to seek child custody. These developments, combined with a new awareness of the importance of fathers in their children's lives, led courts to reject the maternal preference standard. Instead, family law courts were now put in the unenviable position of determining which of two seemingly fit parents should have custody of the child (Mnookin, 1975).

CURRENT STANDARD

With more and more parents disputing the custody of their children, the emphasis began to move from the parents to the child. Courts were asked to make determinations of what decision would be in the child's best interests (Grossberg, 1985). The resulting best-interests standard simply stated that courts should make custody determines solely on what was in a child's future best interests and not on the gender of the custodial parents. The power differential of the parents, traditional family configurations, and adversarial posturing of the parties are not important considerations under this standard, although the percentage of time the child spends with each parent is a factor in calculating the economics of child custody in terms of child support. Most states have since incorporated the best interests standard into their custody statutes, although their definitions of the types of custody arrangements vary considerably. Some of these states have adopted the guidelines outlined in the Uniform Marriage and Divorce Act (9a U.L.A. 91, 1976) for determining what is in the child's best interests. This act states that courts should consider the following criteria in determining children's best interests: the wishes of the child's parents; the wishes of the child; the interaction and relationships between the child and his parent, his siblings, and any person who may significantly affect the child's best interest; the child's adjustment to his home, school, and community; and the mental and physical health of all involved individuals. In cases where there is family abuse, substance abuse, or other contraindications for custody for one of the parents, the court may have an relatively easy decision-making process. In fact, recently, some states have amended their child custody statutes so that judges either must or may take incidents of domestic violence within the family into consideration (Family Violence Project, 1995). However, it is far harder for courts to resolve cases where both parents are fit, psychologically attached to the child, and have been active caregivers but are unwilling to share custody. In such cases, is it in the best interests of the child to award custody to only one of these competent parents, or should some combination of parenting roles be devised? Does the former suggest that in fact one of the parents is really more competent, or does it mean the noncustodial parent is less than perfect? Interestingly, judges report that the most important determinative factors in reaching custody decisions are the desires of adolescents, custody investigations by court or probation department staff, parties' testimony, and court-appointed mental health professionals' reports (Reidy, Silver, & Carlson, 1989). The younger the child, the less likely the judge was to take the child's wishes into consideration.

Although seemingly laudable, the best interests standard has had some unfortunate consequences. First, the best interests standard at times has inadvertently led to increased acrimony during chid custody disputes. When parents advocate for why it would be in the child's best interests to live with them, they often focus on the other parent's deficits, many of which are related to sexual activity (Emery, 1994). The prevailing party is then essentially rewarded by the court (with custody decisions in their favor) for revealing every bad comment or action made by the other parent during the course of the intact relationship (Emery, 1994). In these cases, the parent without deficits usually wins custody of the child over the parent with deficits—even if the parent with deficits had previously had stronger psychological ties to the child. Unfortunately, the ensuing custody disputes are often bitter, leading to more sole custody (rather than joint custody) awards because it is difficult for courts to imagine the parents being able to have amicable conversations to discuss visitation and developmental tasks.

The child's best interests originally were determined on a case-by-case basis (Cochran, 1991). Generally, a second limitation to the best interests standard is its vagueness. As a result of its vagueness, courts have been able to interpret the best-interests standard in many different ways, sometimes in response to societal beliefs and sometimes based only on their personal beliefs. For example, in the early years of the best interests standard, many courts assumed that remaining with the mother would be in the child's best interests because mothers were naturally superior caregivers (Grossberg, 1985). In fact, a 1985 survey of California judges found that 85% still favored maternal custody, even after the passage of gender-neutral custody legislation (Weitzman, 1985). Even more recently, a 1994 survey of court decisions in Utah indicated that custody awards to fathers were no more common than they were under the tender years doctrine (Bahr, Howe, Mann, & Bahr, 1994).

The vagueness of the best interest standard eventually led many states to enact custody statutes that specified a preferred custody arrangement that would go into effect unless one parent could demonstrate that the arrangement would *not* be in the child's best interests. As noted earlier, this type of reasoning may have unfortunately led to further custody litigation, especially in cases involving domestic violence (Liss & Stahly, 1993).

APPLICATION TO DIVORCE CASES

In divorce cases, states have established two primary preferences established by law: the primary caretaker preference and the joint custody preference.

Primary Caretaker Preference

Under this preference, courts will award custody to the parent who has been the child's primary caretaker (Cochran, 1991). Among the duties that indicate that a parent is the primary caretaker are preparing and planning meals; bathing, grooming, and dressing; purchasing, cleaning, and care of clothes; medical care; arranging for social interactions; arranging alternative care; attending to the child's nighttime needs (putting her to bed, attending to her in the middle of the night, waking her in the morning); disciplining; educating; and teaching (*Garska v. McCoy*, 1981). If neither parent can demonstrate that she or he has been the primary caretaker, there is no preference in determining custody; the award must be made on a case-by-case basis.

Under the primary caretaker rule, mothers are not automatically preferred over fathers in terms of custody determinations. For example, in its opinion rejecting the maternal preference, the New York Family Court stated, "Studies of maternal deprivation have shown that the essential experience for the child is that of mothering—the warmth, consistency, and continuity of the relationship rather than the sex of the individual who is performing the mothering function" (*Watts v. Watts*, 1973, p. 290). Despite its gender-neutral nature, however, the primary caretaker standard still results in greater number of awards to mothers than to fathers simply because women are more often children's primary caretakers (Cowan & Cowan, 1988). The primary caretaker rule is thought to be in the child's best interests for several reasons. First, it is an easy rule to apply. Therefore, it is likely to discourage litigation because both parents will know the likely outcome of any litigation (Cochran, 1991). This will reduce conflict within the family. In addition, litigation in courts that have this preference will focus on determining who the primary caretaker was, rather than on parental deficits. In addition, the primary caretaker preference will ensure continuity in the child's relationship with the primary caretaker. As the

Minnesota Supreme Court stated, "Continuity of care with the primary caretaker is not only central and crucial to the best interest of the child, but is perhaps the single predictor of a child's well-being about which there is agreement" (*Pikula v. Pikula*, 1985, p. 712). Some recent challenges to the primary caretaker concept have been asserted in cases where the mother works outside the home (*Smith v. Ireland*, 1994).

Joint Custody Preference

In states where there is not a preference toward awarding custody to the primary caretaker, courts typically award joint custody. In this arrangement, parents share legal custody and/or physical custody of the child. Joint legal custody refers to shared parental rights and responsibilities (including decision-making power) and is easily obtained in custody discussions. Parents with joint physical custody (often called shared parenting) share not only legal guardianship of the child, but also the child's time (Emery, 1994). Children in joint physical custody arrangements spend approximately the same amount of time with each parent (Emery, 1994). Joint custody (of either type) is becoming an increasingly common option. As of 1991, all but nine states had statutes allowing or encouraging joint custody (Folberg, 1991). Some states actually favor joint custody, while others regard it as only one possible option. Through the 1980s, legal reviews of the experiment with joint custody questioned its use. In addition, although it is difficult to assess the types of custody awards in the majority of cases (because family law cases do not usually reach appellate courts and are neither cited nor published), there is evidence to suggest that courts are beginning to choose this option more frequently (Freed & Walker, 1991).

Joint custody has been touted by some as the savior of children's relationships with both parents (e.g., Cochran & Vitz, 1983) and criticized by others as requiring parents to communicate in ways they were incapable of during the intact relationship (e.g., Scott & Derdeyn, 1984). Regardless, its development is noted for contributing to the concept of the child's best interests; it promotes psychological parenting by both parents and the involvement of all members of the family. In addition, joint custody may be economically advantageous because it decreases the need for child support payments by the generally nonprimary custodial parent.

ADOPTION CASES

The discussion thus far has focused around divorce custody cases. In addition to custody cases, family law courts must also make decisions regarding children's adoption. Generally, the history behind adoption law mirrors that of custody law. The early concept of children as property resulted in orphans being indentured to new parents, the transportation of dependent children from the eastern states to the western states via the "orphan train movement" to assist in farm work, and children of unmarried women being sold on the "black market" (Cole & Donley, 1990). Later, when the adoption of infants (rather than older children) became more common, adoption agencies attempted to convince parents that they could guarantee them of a perfect child, without physical, emotional, or mental defects (Cole & Donley, 1990). In fact, until the 1960s, it was common to keep infants, especially those of questionable lineage, in "study homes" for 6 to 12 months after birth for observation. Children with known pathology were considered unadoptable (Cole, 1985). The social and economic changes of the 1960s and 1970s influenced adoption law in ways similar to custody law. Most importantly, courts began to focus on the best interests of the child. This new emphasis led to a recognition of the importance of placing children early and with minimal delay and uncertainty, to the growing practice of letting birth parents and adoptive parents work together to choose the degree and type of contact and information shared between them, and to a willingness to give adoptees access to information about their background, even over the birth parents' objections (Cole & Donley, 1990).

There are several methods of adoption. In the majority of cases, birth parents relinquish their parental rights to an adoption agency. The agency then screens, selects, and places the child with an adoptive couple or individual. Usually, children adopted through agencies will not be placed with adoptive parents until legally freed by *both* biological parents. Although children could once be placed for adoption at the mother's request, recent laws have shifted attention to fathers' rights. As a result, married biological fathers are presumed to have parental rights equal to those of the mother, and unmarried fathers are given the option of denying paternity and/or waiving right to be notified about the adoption procedure. In some cases, the birth parents and adoptive parents may bypass the agency; this is called independent adoption. In independent adoptions, birth parents will either personally select the adoptive parents or hire an attorney or private adoption agency to do this for them. After birth, adoptive parents will take the infant home and file a petition to adopt with the court. The birth parents must sign a consent-to-adopt form. At any point until this form has been signed, the birth parents have the right to change their minds. Finally, in all types of adoption cases, there may be another 6-to-12-month waiting period until the adoption is finalized.

In the majority of adoption cases, everything goes smoothly. Birth parents surrender their rights in a timely way and do not contest the adoption. Occasionally, however, one of birth parents will contest. This is especially common in cases of independent adoption, in which the biological parents have not relinquished custody before placement. It may also occur in agency adoptions if the father has not relinquished custody. If the biological parents do choose to contest the adoption, courts nearly always rely on statutory or case law in requiring adoptive parents to relinquish custody of the child.

RECENT HEADLINE CASES

Today, the best interests standard continues as the backbone of most states' custody laws. As discussed, the best interests standard is commendable for its ultimate goal: placement of the child in the most favorable environment for its growth and development. Moreover, some recent state court trends toward establishing preferences for child custody decisions have overcome some of the previous criticisms that the best-interests standard is vague. However, not all case decisions reflect this trend. In addition, the best interests standard may not be sufficiently developed to address many of the other types of custody situations facing courts in the late 1990s.

As a result of the vagueness of the best interests standard, statutes invoking it vary from state to state. Thus, perhaps, more can be learned about how the best-interest standard work in practice than in theory. Examinations of the trends in case law is very difficult in family law cases. Very few family law cases reach the appellate courts or the state supreme courts, let alone the United States Supreme Court. Therefore, the reader should note that although it is interesting to examine the headline cases that have been reviewed by the higher courts or reported in the media, the vast number of family law cases are neither published nor easily accessible for investigation, which makes the trends found in higher court decisions and media published cases potentially misleading.

CUSTODY RELATIONS AFTER DIVORCE OR SEPARATION

There are innumerable examples of custody disputes between divorcing or splitting couples. In most of these cases, settlements eventually are reached, and the court itself will endorse the decisions selected by the parents. In some situations, however, the disputes become acrimonious and the court must intervene. In others, both parties appear to be providing psychological parenting from which the child would benefit, without any adverse factors that could be held to be detrimental to the child.

For instance, a Massachusetts court (*Raymond v. Raymond*, 1994) was faced with parents who both wanted custody and a pair of twins who wanted to be with both parents. As not everyone could win, the court made a Solomonic decision to make everyone at least somewhat happy; each parent was awarded custody of one of the twin 10-year-old girls. Interestingly, although the court took the parents' requests into consideration, and each parent got at least half of what they wanted, the girls did not get their wish—to remain together.

Some splitting couples are not married, and this only makes the custody decision more difficult. The court most configure a family arrangement in the absence of the traditional bonds of marriage and presumptions of paternity. Jennifer Ireland (*Smith v. Ireland*, 1994) was a college student when she gave birth to her daughter; she placed the girl in day care while she attended classes. Jennifer was the primary custodial parent until her daughter's unemployed biological father sought custody. The trial court found in favor of the father, stating that he would be able to provide more time with the girl; interestingly, the court did not make a qualitative statement about the time, only a quantitative one. Here, the trial court determined that even though the existing psychological parenting was not insufficient or detrimental, the child should be cared for in a more traditional living arrangement with the father and his family. In the fall of 1995, this decision was overturned and the girl returned to Jennifer and her day care setting pending the lower court's findings (*Ireland v. Smith*, 1995).

ADOPTION CASES

In two of the most debated adoption cases, Baby Jessica (*DeBoer v. Warburton*, 1995) and Baby Richard (*Doe v. Kirchner*, 1995), the baby's father had either left the mother or been disinterested in the pregnancy; in both cases, a couple sought to adopt the baby and the baby was placed in their care during the finalization of the adoption. In both cases, the biological father reappeared some time later and sought to have the adoption orders revoked. During each of these cases, the child's future was kept in limbo until all possible appeals had been made. Babies Jessica and Richard stayed with their prospective adoptive parents only to later have their custody awarded to their biological parents. In both cases, the headlines portrayed crying children and distraught prospective adoptive parents, with jubilant biological parents whisking the children away. What the headlines did not portray was the set of procedural issues that led to the unfortunate protracted delay in the resolution of the cases and the prospective adoptive parents' refusal to move on with their lives and allow the children to move on with theirs. And is was these procedural issues on which the courts based much of their deliberations. In these cases, the system may be thought to have failed; the emphasis on procedural questions may have left the interests of the children per se lost in the shuffle. In addition, these cases may be read as supporting a biological basis for custody decision making, when the decisions may really have been made on the basis of procedural due process.

Although these may be the most headlined cases, they are not indicative of the majority of adoption custody cases. In most cases, if the procedural guidelines are followed by all parties, and the parties adhere to adverse decisions, the child's custody and future will be established. For example, in a case which sounds similar to that of Babies Jessica and Richard, Baby Emily (*In Re the Adoption of EAW*, 1995) became embroiled in a custody dispute between her adoptive prospective parents and her recently returned biological father. In this case, however, the judge noted that the procedural requirements were satisfied by the adoptive parents and not the biological father, and that Emily had established a psychological parenting relationship with the adoptive parents. Even more important from a psychological perspective, the judge's determination that it was in Emily's best interests to remain with the adoptive parents was based in part on the *emotional* as well as the financial and physical abandonment by her biological father. So, unlike Jessica and Richard, the family of which Emily is now a part was constituted and sanctioned by the court and social service agencies.

A recurring theme in these headline cases is the juxtaposition of biology and psychology. A biological parent has ties formed during conception but may not have any other relationship with the child. A psychological parent, on the other hand, may or may not have a biological tie to the child but has developed an affective connection with the child based on postbirth experiences. Despite the concerns of the mental health community, some recent cases appear to have relied on the biological background in determining the child's future. At the same time, it is clear that procedural irregularities influence decision making; in those cases where everything went according to schedule, and each party was afforded their proper rights (as with Baby Emily), the child's custody seemed to favor the psychological or residential parent. In those cases where the overall system did not work according to the proscribed plan, then the biological connection was favored (Babies Jessica and Richard).

SUITS BY OLDER CHILDREN

Two cases involving older children are also of note in determining if there is a best interest standard for children. In Gregory K.'s case (*Kingsley v. Kingsley*, 1993), a young boy sought to divorce his biological parents and be adopted by another couple. Gregory did not claim that he was abused or maltreated, but that he would be better off in a warmer, nurturing environment than with his biological family. This case was hailed as a children's rights case, although it is unclear what standard of the best interests of the child was articulated. Kimberly Mays (*Twigg v. Mays*, 1993) also created headlines when it was revealed that she and another baby had been switched at birth. Kimberly's "mother" had died, and she was living with the only father she had known until her adolescence. When they found out about the switch, Kimberly's biological parents sought custody. Kimberly wished to remain with the parent who had raised her, that is, the psychological parent. The Twiggs' request was also turned down by the courts, which concluded that Kimberly did not have to be turned over to her biological parents and could remain with her psychological parent, her "father." in both Kimberly and Gregory's cases, the court chose the psychological over the biological parent. Furthermore, in Gregory's case, the psychological parental choice was outside the definitions of the family.

Lastly, in North Carolina, Sonya Kinney (*The News & Observer*, 1995) was a deaf child whose father refused to learn sign language to communicate with her. Sonya sought to live with her teacher and sign language interpreter. The court found in Sonya's favor, changing her custody arrangement despite her biological parent's objection. It did not, however, terminate the parental rights of the biological parents altogether; instead, it changed the physical custodial relationship.

In each of these cases, the biological parents' interests took second place to the child's best interests, and the courts endorsed the desires of the child. In two of the cases, Gregory K. & Sonya Kinney, the psychological parenting relationship with the primary caretakers were also put aside in determining the best interests of the adolescent.

PSYCHOLOGICAL LITERATURE

The cases just discussed are only a small fraction of the thousands of cases heard and decided by family law courts every day. Even this small sample, however, reveals the wide range of possible decisions that can be made in such cases—all in the name of the child's best interests.

Unfortunately, the mental health community has little input in the majority of family law cases. Occasionally, psychologists will testify as child custody evaluators or expert witnesses, sometimes resulting in a battle of experts who have different perspectives of the best interests of the child. Just as often, though, the psychological perspective is not represented, and courts are left to make the important decision of what would be in the child's best interests on their own. This section illustrates how existing psychological literature can contribute to an understanding of the best interests standard. It should be noted, however, that this standard is vague not only from a legal point of view, but also from the psychological point of view. The field of psychology has not advanced to the point that experts can reliably predict future outcomes for particular children (Emery, 1994; Reppucci & Crosby, 1993). Even if accurate predictions were possible, however, it would still be unclear what alternatives are best for a child (Mnookin, 1975). Mnookin (1975) summarized this position when he stated that a child's best interests "is not demonstrable by scientific proof, but is instead fundamentally a matter of values" (p. 164). Despite these limitations, however, psychological literature may still offer courts and other decision makers some hints of the factors that should be considered in determining best interests.

RESEARCH ON PSYCHOLOGICAL FACTORS

Psychological research may assist family court judges in decision making in a number of ways. For example, both theory and research on stability and continuity and on resilience may assist decision makers in setting goals for the decisions they make. Other bodies of research, while not directly addressing the issues facing courts, may assist judges in making decisions that are in children's best interests. For example, research on attachment, children's definitions of the family, and sibling and extended family relationships may all provide critical information for difficult decisions. Finally, a growing body of literature is directly addressing the issues that courts face today. By examining the effects of joint custody, adoption, and adolescent identity, for example, researchers are bridging the gaps between law and psychology, between theory and application. This section briefly reviews these disparate bodies of research to demonstrate how they impact on family law decisions.

STABILITY AND CONTINUITY

One of the most well accepted principles of developmental psychology is that children benefit from stability and continuity in their lives, especially in their relationships with parents, siblings, extended family members, and other significant figures with whom the child has relationships. Various lines of research demonstrate the negative effects of a lack of stability and continuity. For example, many studies on the effects of divorce have indicated that children from divorced families have more negative outcomes than children from never-divorced families. Among the negative outcomes that have been linked to divorce are externalizing problems, lower academic self-concepts and reduced achievement motivation, precocious sexual activity, early marriage, an increased likelihood of divorce, and poor relationships with parents (Kelly, 1993; Wallerstein, 1991; Wallerstein & Blakeslee, 1989). Despite the long line of research on divorce, some intervening variables have not been as effectively studied. For example, children of divorced parents are frequently exposed to a number of disruptions in their lives, including changes in parental involvement in their lives and economic changes, including relocations, changes in school and peers, an increased number of hours spent in day care, and mothers returning to work (Emery, 1994; Kelly, 1993; Wallerstein, 1991). It has frequently been noted that what appear to be the effects of divorce may instead result from these other disruptions in children's lives. In any case, the divorce literature appears to indicate that a lack of continuity and stability in children's lives—whether due to divorce or the changes brought about by divorce—may have negative consequences.

Yet another line of research demonstrating the importance of stability and continuity examines the effects of parental death on children. This research indicates that although not as severe as children's reactions to divorce (Grusec & Lytton, 1988), children who experience parental death may also suffer a variety of negative outcomes. Specifically, they are more likely than their peers to experience troubled behavior of various kinds, personality changes, and a sense of vulnerability. Furthermore, grieving children frequently experience all of the signs of depression, including sleep disturbances, decreased appetite, social withdrawal, sadness, crying, and irritability (Garmezy, 1983). These reactions may persist into adulthood. Some studies have suggested that children who experience parental death are more likely to experience later psychiatric disorder, especially depression (Brown & Harris, 1978).

The literature on divorce and bereavement are only two of the lines of research that consistently demonstrate that stability and continuity in relationships promotes healthy development. Similar findings have resulted from research on children who have been separated from their mothers due to hospitalization, children whose lives are disrupted by war (Garbarino, Kostelny, & Dubrow, 1991), and children subjected to numerous foster home and institutional placements (Garmezy, 1983). Thus, one might conclude that the best interests standard would make explicit reference to stability and continuity.

Resilience

In addition to demonstrating the importance of stability and continuity, research in the area of developmental psychology also indicates that there are a number of factors that may influence children's adaptation to stress. The child's age, sex, and developmental status, for example, are only a few of the factors that may influence the impact that a stressor has on the child's life (Garmezy, 1983). In addition to these variables, there are also other less concrete variables present in children who are resilient to negative outcomes. These individuals possess some combination of individual, familiar, or societal factors that can protect them from even extreme stress (Cicchetti & Garmezy, 1993).

Unfortunately, the study of resiliency is new and suffers from several difficulties inherent in new lines of research. Specifically, researchers define *resilience* in different ways, which may lead to very different conclusions. For example, studies examining risk factors in psychological development and resiliency have employed different ranges and degrees of risk and different understandings of what constitutes adaptive outcomes (Cicchetti & Garmezy, 1993). In addition, resilience is probably not a static trait, but one that is situationally determined. Individuals may be resilient in one domain of their lives at one time period in their lives—or may be resilient to a variety of stressors over the course of the life span. This makes resiliency an inherently difficult concept to study and also limits the generalizability of the findings in this area (Cicchetti & Garmezy, 1993).

Nevertheless, despite these limitations, initial studies of resilience have led to a number of findings that may be useful to judges making decisions about child custody. One of the most intriguing lines of resiliency research stems from the Kauai Longitudinal Study, a study of all children born on Kauai during 1955. During the initial study, researchers identified 201 infants at risk for developmental problems who were exposed to moderate to severe perinatal stress, born into poverty, and lived in family environments characterized by chronic discord, parental alcoholism, or mental illness (Werner, 1993). Over the years, the researchers examined these individuals' functioning in a variety of domains of development, using a number of different sources of information. They concluded that despite the risks they were exposed to during childhood, approximately one-third of these individuals grew into competent, caring, confident adults (Werner, 1993). These resilient individuals shared a number of important characteristics (Werner, 1993). First, resilient individuals often had temperamental characteristics that helped them to elicit positive responses from caretakers and peers. Second, they also had skills and values that led them to efficiently use whatever abilities they had. Third, the caretakers of resilient children were more likely to have characteristics and caregiving styles that fostered the children's sense of competence and self-esteem. Resilient children were also more likely to have other support adults in their lives.

Research on the psychological effects of contested divorces on children further emphasizes the importance of resilience. Wolman and Taylor (1991) unexpectedly found that children who were the subject of contested custody cases scored higher than most children in the general population on measures of an internal locus of control. In addition, they showed less separation anxiety and more positive family concepts than children who came from uncontested custody cases. One can speculate that these patterns are the result of the need to find a comfortable space within the family and survive the custody dispute. Additionally, as in adoption cases, the contested nature of the custody discussion may be perceived by the children as indicating a greater feeling of being wanted.

The application of the concept of resiliency to the best-interests standard is difficult because it is unclear if resiliency can be easily measured. However, all assessments of children's psychological health inherently reflect children's resiliency.

ATTACHMENT

The research on resiliency clearly indicates that stability and continuity, especially in relationships with significant others, may be among the factors that make children resilient to the other stressors in their lives. These findings are consistent with research on attachment. An understanding of attachment is essential to many of the cases currently facing family law courts, especially those involving contested adoptions.

Attachment can be defined as the "strong, affectional tie we feel for special people in our lives that leads us to feel pleasure and joy when we interact with them and to be comforted by their nearness during times of stress" (Berk, 1994, p. 414). There is a substantial body of psychological literature that suggests that the development of a healthy attachment is one of the principle "tasks" of early childhood, and that without this attachment, a number of poor developmental outcomes are more likely. During early childhood, infants who have not developed a secure attachment to their parents will be more anxious, less involved and confident in exploring their environments, and have poorer relationships with their peers. Later in childhood, these children have less effective problem-solving abilities, poorer social skills, lower self-confidence, more behavior problems, poorer familial and peer relationships, and more problems in adjusting to school (Bretherton, 1985; Sroufe, 1983). There have been suggestions that the effects of not forming a healthy attachment may continue even into adulthood, although the research on long-term effects of attachment are fraught with methodological difficulties.

Although the majority of research on attachment has examined the attachment between children and their mothers, there is a smaller body of research examining children's attachment to other significant people in their lives. Researchers have found that children also form attachments to fathers (e.g., Lamb, 1977), siblings (Grusec & Lytton, 1988), and others. One early study reported on the attachments among a group of young children whose parents were killed in Nazi Germany (Freud & Dann, 1951). These children met in the concentration camps and became the sole source of stability in each other's lives. After the war ended and they were brought to England, the children clung to each other and were upset when separated from each other. Thus, consideration of the child's attachment to all significant individuals could be incorporated into a determination of the best interests of the child.

Sibling Relationships

Research on siblings' attachment relationships represents only a fraction of the research on the importance of sibling relationships throughout the life span. Other lines of research have demonstrated that siblings not only rely on each other for companionship, emotional support, and assistance with everyday tasks (Berk, 1994), but that sibling relationship are also important in the development of social competence (Howe, 1991; Howe & Ross, 1990) and problem solving (Azmitia & Hesser, 1993). During adolescence, siblings may provide compensating emotional support for individuals who have difficulty in making friends (East & Rook, 1992). Even in late adulthood, siblings may serve as an important support. Siblings report feeling closer to their siblings as they age and may even care for each other in late adulthood (Cicirelli, 1985).

Sibling relationships may be especially important to children when parents are unavailable (Grusec & Lytton, 1988). In fact, continuity of the sibling relationship after divorce may be important in assuring better outcomes for children (Foster, 1987), even more so than a stable physical environment (Atkinson, 1984). For example, after the trauma of divorce, siblings can turn to each other for support (Nichols, 1986).

Kaplan, Hennon, and Ade-Ridder (1993) recently examined sibling custody arrangements in the context of a family system theory model. They suggest that split custody (when one parent takes custody of one child and the other parent, another child) may have a number of detrimental effects. First, it may disrupt the formation of the sibling relationship, preventing siblings from forming supportive bonds. Not only may this deprive siblings of a form of support during the aftermath of divorce, but research also indicates that the degree of closeness experienced later in life is related to the extent of contact early in life (Cicirelli, 1982). Thus, being separated in early childhood may affect the quality of siblings relationships throughout life (Scott, 1990). A second possible consequence of being separated in childhood involves disruption of the entire family system. When siblings are separated, the family will experience stress. Boundaries will be redefined, and children's roles in the new family structures will shift. The ambiguity and changes in these roles may disrupt the sense of responsibility, self-concept, and self-esteem that these roles normally provide (Ahrons & Rodgers, 1987).

RELATIONSHIPS WITH EXTENDED FAMILY

In earlier times, the extended family included the grandparents, aunts, uncles, and second-tier cousins among others. Although most extended family relatives have not figured prominently in court cases, some grandparents have been quite vocal. This has been true in adoption cases, as well as the terminating of couple relationships (Schwartz, 1984; Thompson, Scalora, Limber, & Castrianno, 1991). For example, at least one court allowed visitation by the paternal grandparents of the child of an unmarried couple even though the couple did not maintain a relationship after the birth of the child (*Bishop v. Pillar*, 1994). Additionally, as a result of one recent case (*Campbell v. Campbell*, 1995), the Utah Court of Appeals found the state's statute providing grandparents with the opportunity to seek time with their grandchildren, in divorced as well as intact families, was rationally related to the state's interest in promoting family relationships and sources of support for children. Although such cases are not common, most states allow grandparents to petition for visitation only in disrupted families, such as when a couple separates and the grandparents (and grandchildren) wish to continue the affective family ties (Thompson et al., 1991). Most states have statutes endorsing or even requiring grandparent visitation in both intact and separated families; however, the manner in which these statutes are implemented varies considerably (Burns, 1995). The issue of grandparent visitation with children who have been adopted varies even more widely. In most adoptions, this option may not be available because the child will become part of another family, and the ties to the former grandparents will be served totally (Schwartz, 1984). Open adoptions, however, allow biological and adoptive families to maintain contact, although these situations make the definition of the family more complex. In some states, visitation by biological grandparents with children who have been adopted may be statutorily permitted (Burns, 1995).

The psychological research on the effects of the grandparent-grandchild relationship in both parties' lives indicates that the grandparenting role is highly individualized (Thompson et al., 1991). Some grandparents enjoy regular contact with their grandchildren, including surrogate care in some case (Gottfried & Gottfried, 1994), while other grandparents prefer a more distant relationship (Cherlin & Furstenberg, 1986). Thus, it is unsurprising that the importance of this relationship also varies. The importance of the grandparent to the grandchild may also vary according to other factors: race, with some researchers reporting the relationship as being more active and hence significant in Black families (Bengtson, Rosenthal, & Burton, 1990); grandparental style (Cherlin & Furstenberg, 1986); other family dynamics, most notably the parent-grandparent bond (Johnson, 1983); and geographic proximity and frequency of contact (Thomas & King, 1990). Thus, it appears that the relationships between grandparents and grandchildren can take a variety of forms and meanings in all parties' lives. When it is a close relationship in a child's life, grandparents may provide the sense of stability and continuity that is so important for children, ultimately contributing to the resilience that may buffer against future stressors.

It is important to note that decisions involving grandparent visitation rights require courts to craft decisions taking into account at least three competing interests: the compelling state interests, the parents' interests, and the best interests of the child. Unfortunately, although current custody evaluation guidelines provide direction for mental health professionals' reports and their usage by courts, they do not deal directly with visitation by extended family members (American Psychological Association, 1994).

DEFINITIONS OF THE FAMILY

Another factor that may prove critical in defining best interests is children's definitions of the family. One recent study of children's definitions of family indicates that even if children include residential and biological factors in their definitions, affective ties were the most pervasive element (Newman, Roberts, & Syre, 1993). In fact, although they also used biological ties and coresidence in their definitions of family, it was the affective relationships between individuals that was most salient to children. These ties appear to be defining features in children's definitions of *family*. Children's endorsement of definitions of the family that go beyond their biological makeup and beyond the walls of their homes echoes the concept of the psychological parent or perhaps the psychological relative.

Children of all ages found the contractual relationships related to court actions to be confusing and perhaps immaterial (Newman, Roberts, & Syre, 1993). In fact, these young people may have endorsed the psychological extended family, including not just those parental figures with psychological or affective connections, but also those who may not reside with them and may be part of the custodial parents' networks.

JOINT CUSTODY

In addition to research that may indirectly assist decision makers, psychologists have also researched the consequences of the decisions being made. For instance, one topic of considerable research in recent years has been the effects of joint custody. Early examinations of joint custody highlighted families in which the shared parenting relationship was constructed by the parties themselves. Often these parents stood out as somewhat different from the norm; they tended to be middle class, highly educated, older, and with sufficient incomes. The fathers had flexible schedules and tended to spend considerably more time with their young children than most other fathers did (Greif, 1979; Phear, Beck, Hauser, Clark, & Whitney, 1984; Steinman, 1981; Steinman, Zemmelman, & Knoblauch, 1985). As these arrangements became more accepted by the legal system, they were also endorsed by mental health professionals. Initially, this seemed reasonable; the parents were pleased, the children were pleased, and it made the job of the courts much easier. Furthermore, several studies indicate advantages in joint custody arrangements, including decreased conflict, increased compliance with child support awards, greater family cohesion, better adjustment, and fewer deviant behaviors (Crosbie-Burnett, 1991; Irving & Benjamin, 1991; Kelly, 1993). Joint custody is not only preferred by children of divorce, but also by the majority of parents of both sexes (Crosbie-Burnett, 1991).

Soon the notion of joint custody became more widespread, and courts and family law practitioners sought to use it frequently and not just when some unusual couple wanted that kind of situation. In itself, this was not a bad development, but it appeared to have expanded unchecked and been applied to families who are very different than the original proponents of the idea. Commentators have noted that some courts began to impose joint custody on families who not only did not want joint custody, but who also strongly wanted the sole custody agreements (Folberg, 1991). Unfortunately, the trend toward the presumption of joint custody ignores the psychological literature that suggests that there are certain circumstances in which joint custody is unsuccessful.

Not only have some researchers failed to find significant differences between joint custody and sole custody families, but some have also noted that joint custody can have negative consequences for children and families in certain circumstances (Johnston, Kline, & Tschann, 1991). Thus, the presumption of joint custody for all families may be ignoring important situations in which joint custody is contraindicated. In addition to the parties' opposition to joint custody (Elkin, 1991), there are also numerous other parental and child variables that distinguish families that succeed in joint custody arrangements from those that fail. Research by Steinman et al. (1985) indicated, for example, that the parents who are successful in maintaining joint custody arrangements maintain respect and appreciation for the bond between their children and the other parent; can maintain some degree of objectivity throughout the divorce process; can empathize with the child and the other parent; establish new role boundaries; have generally high self-esteem, flexibility, and openness to help; and can shift expectations from that of mate to that of coparent. In contrast, parents who failed in the joint custody arrangement could not separate their hostility toward the other parent from the child, were overwhelmingly angry and felt the need to punish the spouse, had a history of physical abuse and substance abuse, had a fixed belief that the other parent was a "bad parent," and could not separate their own needs from those of the child (Steinman et al., 1985). Furthermore, children who adapt well to change appear to be more likely to fare successfully in joint custody arrangements than those who do not (Saposnek, 1983), probably because joint physical custody requires frequent changes (i.e., switching between homes and sometimes even between schools). This adaptability appears to be more frequently found at younger ages, when children are not also coping with the demands of school and peers. In addition, children may be better able to cope with the changes required by joint custody when other aspects of their lives are stable (Steinman et al., 1985).

Most recently, Bender (1994) reviewed joint versus sole custody in terms of relitigation rates, adjustment, compliance, and attachment issues. Bender found that adjustment by both mothers and children are higher in joint custody families, relitigation rates are lower, and compliance with terms of the agreement or consent decree are higher. Furthermore, joint custody holds the potential for greater attachment to both parents than other arrangements. Many of these factors have been noted by judges who favor joint custody only when the parents express a willingness to enter into such an arrangement, the degree of bitterness and anger between the parents is minimal, the parents are both psychologically stable, and the quality of the parent-child relationships is good. Demographic variables, however, are not critical (Reidy et al., 1989). The literature on joint custody continues to grow and show changes in patterns of success; this topic will need to be reviewed and expanded, involving a greater number of variables inherent in the custody arrangements, before final comments can be made on the breadth of its utility for American families.

SPECIAL CONCERNS OF ADOLESCENTS

The cases of Gregory, Kimberly, and Sonya raise other questions regarding children's input and what has also been called children's rights. The related work in this section refers to the decisions older children and adolescents make and the relationship of these decisions and processes to those of adults. Earlier literature on medical decisions found primarily that by the fourth-grade level children reach conclusions similar to those of adults, although the bases for their decisions often differ (Grisso & Vierling, 1978; Weithorn, 1980). The response to these findings has been to afford adolescents greater input into decisions about their lives, including certain legal actions (e.g., access to contraception).

In addition, as children get older they are allowed to make an increasing number of decisions and have an increasing number of rights until they reach full adulthood. These social and legal rites of passage are based on the belief that as adolescents develop their reasoning approaches that of adults. For instance, since the decision *In Re Gault* (1967), adolescents have been provided access to attorneys and judicial processes comparable with those of adults. Similarly, as adolescents approach adulthood, they are accorded an increasing number of privileges under the law, including the right to drive, make contracts, work, and receive information on contraception (Liss & Studley, 1983). One might argue that if adolescents are allowed to make independent decisions regarding many activities in their lives, they should also be allowed to have input into custody decisions.

Adolescents' rights and abilities in decision making, however, are contrasted with parental and state interests in the children's best interests. Adolescence traditionally has been described, in both positive and negative terms, as a period of transition. In this regard, it is important to note that adolescents with strong parental attachments go through their transitions with less anxiety and depression than do other adolescents (Papini, Roggman, & Anderson, 1991). Furthermore, according to Hauser et al. (1984) "enabling" parents contribute significantly to adolescent development. Therefore, one might conclude that enabling parents, with whom adolescents have strong attachments, are important for youth. It would be in the adolescents' best interests to live with such individuals—who might not be their actual parents.

Special Concerns in Adoption

One of the most enduring findings in adoption is that adopted children are overrepresented in psychological treatment (Brodzinsky, 1990). What is unclear, however, is whether adoptive children have more psychological problems, whether knowing they have special family relationships makes them more sensitive to issues, and whether adoptive parents are more willing to explore psychological treatment assistance for typical adolescent issues. Several explanations have been provided by researchers working on adoption issues. Deeg (1989) believed that unless the relationship with the biological mother is established, the child will suffer from the loss of the object to which the child was cathected while in utero, that is, the mother. Brodzinsky (1990) developed a model to account for adoptees' vulnerability and response to stress factoring in biological, cognitive, coping, environmental, and person variables dimensions. Schwartz (1994) noted that the issue of a lack of blood ties to custodial parents may create a lack of concern for children. However, she also noted that some literature indicated that the choice to parent and the desire for the child may create more positive outcomes and expectations on the parts of the parents. Furthermore, once the biological ties issue is set aside, "rearing one's nonbiological children is more similar to than different from rearing one's biological children" (Schwartz, 1994). In the future there is likely to be additional data from studies of open adoptions.

RESEARCH ON DECISION-MAKING PROCESS FACTORS

Another emerging trend, beginning in the 1980s and burgeoning in the 1990s, relates to *how* custodial decisions are made rather than the substantive decisions themselves. The most researched trend in this area is mediation, a form of alternative dispute resolution. The theory behind mediation is that the parties can avoid the escalating confrontations and costs of litigation when they work with a neutral party to solve their conflicts (Emery, 1994). Unlike arbitration, the mediator does not make any final decisions for the parties but enables them to problem solve together. The mediator may be an attorney, a mental health professional, or a layperson. Due to the complexities of family law dilemmas, often an attorney and a mental health professional will work jointly as co-mediators (Emery, 1994).

It has been hypothesized that mediation can result in more positive outcomes for parents and children (Kitzmann & Emery, 1994). Unfortunately, because it is such a new concept, few studies have examined this claim. Those who have studied it have not found much support (Emery, 1994; Kitzmann & Emery, 1994). However, although research has not found direct relationships between the method of dispute resolution and child outcomes, there may be several indirect effects between these variables. First, mediation may work to restrict marital conflict (Emery, 1994). In addition, mediation also results in greater satisfaction with the divorce process among both fathers and mothers (Bautz, & Hill, 1991), in increased awards of joint physical custody awards (Bruch, 1992), and in greater compliance with child support payments (Bautz & Hill, 1991). Because these variables have all been linked with parental involvement, which in turn results in better outcomes for children, it is hypothesized that mediation may be indirectly related to outcomes (Bautz & Hill, 1991). Related research shows that parent-child mediation leads to adolescent empowerment and sense of competence and partnership in the family (Shaw & Phear, 1988). Parent–child mediation promotes adolescent involvement in family activities and decreases adolescent rebellion. Thus, incorporating mediation into the decision-making process in adolescent custody disputes may be in the adolescents' best interests.

Despite these potential advantages, in some situations mediation is not only undesirable, but may also even be harmful. For example, when domestic violence, child abuse, or substance abuse have resulted in drastic inequalities between partners, a truly consensual mutual decision may be impossible (Thoennes, Salem, & Pearson, 1995). Furthermore, such situations may be dangerous for the victim because they give the abuser increased access to the victim (Thoennes et al., 1995). It is important to note that other commentators have found support for the use of mediation in domestic violence custody cases, although not for all litigants (Pearson, 1993). Other situations in which mediation may be problematic are cases involving one parent's severe mental illness, mental retardation, or substance abuse (because the parent will not be able to adequately represent themselves in mediation); or child abuse (because such allegations are obviously of great importance in determining custody) (Emery, 1994).

Mediation has been hailed as a panacea for custody disputes and, at the same time, disparaged for the lack of finality and the range of practitioner skills; yet, there is an aspect of mediation that appears unexplored: the inclusion of children in the process. Commentators have noted several reasons for *not* including children in the mediation process. For example, Emery (1994) said that although he initially favored involving children in mediation, his experiences had led him to change this view. He now believed that involving children in mediation does not only give them the *right* to have a choice about family functioning, but it also appears to instill the *responsibilities* of these decisions. Because these are decisions that parents are struggling with, he believed that it was not appropriate to give children this grave responsibility (Emery, 1994). Wallerstein and Kelly (1980) also agreed that children should not be involved in the mediation process, although for different reasons. Specifically, they asserted that children below the age of adolescence are not good judges of what is in their own best interests, and that their preferences, therefore, should not be relied on in making custody decisions. Another possible reason that mediators may be reluctant to involve children in mediation is that they view their roles as facilitators and not judges or even arbitrators. Thus, they are wary of involving other parties for fear of developing biases in their neutral roles and of crossing the boundary into evaluation. This is especially true for the mental health professionals who in their own practices may be both therapists and evaluators.

Although mediation in family law custody cases is a topic that must still be subjected to empirical research, it is important that mediators not dismiss children's involvement without examining the situation. In fact, one commentator (Sasposnek, 1983) recommended examining children's involvement on a case-by-case basis. Mediators may especially want to consider involving adolescents in mediation because it is clear that older children and adolescents often make the same decisions as adults, albeit sometimes for different reasons (Grisso & Vierling, 1978; Weithorn, 1980). This observation provides an additional rationale for their inclusion in the mediation process. Lastly, children who are involved in family decision making and feel wanted through the process of family consultation, fare better than children who lack this experience. This suggests that parental disputes are not the only factor for children to avoid. In addition, it is important for children to be heard. Further evidence of the power of mediation for adolescents comes from the parent-child mediation literature (Phear et al., 1984), which finds that when youth are exposed to mediation skills, they are more involved in the resolution process and feel that they have been considered.

APPLICATION OF RESEARCH TO RECENT CASES

When the headline cases discussed earlier are reviewed with the psychological evidence in mind, it is difficult to say that courts always act with children's best interests in mind. For example, although Jessica and Richard's fathers had legitimate claims to their custody, was it in their best interests to separate the children from their nonbiological, but psychological, parents? In fact, as Schwartz (1993) noted, regardless of the eventual decisions, even the lengthy delays in finalizing Jessica and Richard's situations clearly were not in their best interests. in the end, these decisions appear to rely more on the legal procedures and rights of the parents to their children than on the child's best interests. Yet, in Baby Emily's case, essentially the same set of circumstances led to the conclusion that she would be better off with those individuals who had been raising her, whom she would know as family. The psychological literature suggests that children's best interests would be served by maintaining stability and continuity in their relationships. Interestingly, there appears to be a lack of stability and consistency in the decisions in custody cases! Perhaps alternative methods of meeting both the parents' rights and the child's best interests (e.g., open adoption) could be sought, rather than putting children at risk for the negative outcomes that may accompany disruptions early in their lives.

Perhaps the courts' instincts in these cases will prove the literature (on stability, attachment, and disruption) wrong, and Jessica and Richard will be able to adjust to their new situations. One hopes that Jessica and Richard possess the inner resilience that will help them cope with the difficult transitions to their new families and homes. Although the literature on resilience has not traditionally been used in terms of custody decisions, the concept is worth exploring now and in future work. In such decisions, notions of stability and continuity must be weighed against the available evidence on resilience. However, it should be noted that many explorations of resilience point out that it is the presence of *stable* relationships in a child's life that make them resilient. Thus, the concepts of stability and resilience may be inextricably intertwined.

The concept of stability must also be considered when addressing custody issues following divorce or separation. Before courts make decisions that separate children from their siblings and from their extended families, careful consideration must be given to other alternatives. This is imperative when these relationships are particularly supportive, for example, following divorce, or when they offer children the stability and continuity that is so important in their lives.

Joint custody provides another arena in which to examine stability and continuity. Joint custody may now be a preferred custody option in postdivorce custody disputes, yet several recent cases illustrate that courts are all too willing to overlook this preference in the name of the child's best interests and overlook other research—such as that on stability and continuity—in the process. For example, in the case of Maranda Ireland, who had two parents who wanted her, the trial court defined best interests in terms of the simple quantity of time spent with biological relations. Similarly, one might wonder what the circumstances were for a decision to separate twins rather than award joint custody and perhaps satisfying both parents and both children.

The issue of change with respect to one parent's desire to move also appears in the custody literature. Most of the time, this situation arises when the custodial parent decides to make a significant geographical move, out of the child's school area and neighborhood. Absent a showing of actual harm, many courts have chosen to award custody to the former noncustodial parent, the one who would be remaining in the child's neighborhood, allowing a continuation of the child's activities and relationships with peers. In fact, many family law practitioners will now include a clause about moving in the custody agreements. The clause usually provides for a drastic change in custody or visitation if one parent moves. The underlying goal is actually to discourage parental moves that could impact on the child's stability of environment. The psychological response to this rationale shows merit in the judicial assumptions. As earlier discussed, children may face a number of difficulties when exposed to disruptions in their lives.

It is particularly important to maintain stability and continuity in the relationships that are most important to the child. The psychological literature on attachment and on the empirical definitions of family may prove especially useful for this purpose. Specifically, defining the family in terms of affective relationships may provide an increased number of support systems for the child. This expanded definition can also be applied to some of the developing dilemmas facing family law courts. For instance, following the death of their biological mother, and in opposition to the explicit guardianship clauses in her will, custody of the Porter boys was awarded their biological father, who had been absent from their lives since birth (*McGuffin v. Overton & Porter*, 1995). If the notion of an affective psychological family had been applied in such a case, the boys would have continued to live with their mother's partner, the other psychological parent, and not the biological parent with whom they had no affective connection. Kimberly Mays's situation also endorses this concept; Kimberly sought to stay with her affective or psychological parent regardless of the biological basis of parentage.

In all of the cases involving older children, the adolescents put forth their own best interests in having the most supportive environments and the continued stability of their lives. In Gregory's case, it is unlikely that his mother would have been termed *unfit* under the fitness standards, but his choice of psychological parents was in his best interests. Likewise, Sonya would fare better with someone who communicated with her in the only way she could communicate, even though this clearly overturned her family's rights to have physical custody of her. Kimberly Mays apparently felt that living with her psychological parents, rather than her biological parents, would be in her best interest, although she has since changed her mind. Applying these findings to the actions of Gregory, Kimberly, and Sonya, the psychological literature would support the court's actions in even hearing the cases and then working toward supporting the children's actions. However, perhaps there are other situations that would have been more advantageous. For example, if Gregory, Kimberly, and Sonya had been able to assert their rights in a mediation setting, perhaps their cases would never have made headlines. Lack of publicity would have spared them and their families the pain of public scrutiny.

DIRECTIONS FOR FUTURE RESEARCH

As with many topics in psychology, custody decisions and the definition of the best interests standard are ripe for research investigation. There are, however, many obstacles to research in this area which make it formidable for those committed to the questions. For instance, custody decisions involve emotionally charged situations, with many players and respective sets of personal values. Either imposing participation or active recruitment of participation for traditional empirical research is fraught with ethical issues too numerous to describe. Therefore, researchers are left with cells of designs that are not randomly nor empirically filled or are missing control groups (Trombetta, 1989), leaving the field open to a great deal of criticism from both researchers and philosophers alike. In addition, many of the questions about the viability, predictability, and validity of the factors that are invoked in the name of the best interests standard can only be examined using significant samples in longitudinal designs. The cost, measures, and confidentiality issues that are part of such endeavors are daunting. And then there are the troublesome question of trying to define the outcome: What is the correct way to determine whether the custody arrangement is working?

In cases such as Baby Richard and Baby Jessica, mental health professionals have expressed concern about each child's welfare. If researchers were to administer psychological tests to these children every 5 years or so, would the mental health professionals' concerns be justified or nullified? Psychologically, one might predict disaster and poor social adjustment; however, if the children and parents have received appropriate psychological counseling through the adjustment period, then there might not be any problems. Would such a result be interpreted to mean that it may be in the children's best interests to be separated from their psychological parents and primary caretakers? Or would such findings be an endorsement of the value of clinical mental health services? Similar findings in research would generate multiple explanations.

It is important to understand that parallel methodological concerns have been noted in the studies of joint custody. Recall that many early studies showed that joint custody was favorable for families; however, the pioneering families were highly unusual demographically and different than the growing number of families requesting such determinations from courts in later years. Meta-analyses of the custody literature are also difficult to accomplish for several reasons: definitions of success vary greatly, qualitative differences between custodial arrangements further impede comparisons of measurements, and individual perceptions of the arrangements may also vary within a family, let alone across families (Trombetta, 1989). Thus, custody decisions indicate the difficulty in generalizing from samples to the population at large. Similarly, studies of adoption are needed to examine issues such as attachment to biological and adoptive parents and relationships to siblings and other members of the extended family.

CONCLUSION

The continuing question is: What is the definition of the best interests standard? Clearly it is applied differentially in different cases and in separate courts. Sometimes statutory language may account for the differences. Although the evolution of the best interests standard is clear and the underlying premise laudable, some direction in applying this vague term is necessary. Review of cases in which the child's best interest has been invoked would help define the term and lead toward some consistency in applying it to families.

The state of the discipline of the nexus of family law and psychology is one hopes at a turning point in the late 1990s. Several developments over the past half century have been questioned. These include the widespread use of joint custody even for families who have not chosen this option and who have not exhibited cooperative efforts to resolve disputes. Research has continued on the effects of joint custody; further long-term studies of indicated and contraindicated situations will be of great importance.

Mediation, too, although hailed by some, has also been criticized for its efforts. Mediation is also not advised for some families. Earlier we suggested that mental health professionals working as mediators consider incorporating the child into the mediation setting. This should provide empowerment for the child in custody much like the impact of allowing the input of adolescents in parent-child mediation.

Although research is needed to understand the issues and concerns about custody, the impact of separation from biological parents, and the weight of various factors used in defining the best interests of the child standard, it is important to realize that family law will continue to march on, and decisions will need to be made long before results of longitudinal studies or experiments in custody arrangements can provide information for decision-making solutions. It is hoped that as social scientists and legal scholars reach consensus on the effects of changes in family structures, the impact of psychological factors in parenting, and the role of evaluations and mediation in making custody decisions, their conclusions will be available for application and implementation by courts. Ideally, social scientists will arrive at conclusions in a timely manner for many families.

The definition of the best interests of the child still appears vague. Perhaps it is best summarized by Sorkow (1991) as a retrospective conclusion that "only the passage of time and the development of the child will determine if the trial judge was correct in defining the best interests of the child" (p. 387). Similarly, the status of the research will be determined with the passage of time and further examination of families involved in custody arrangements. As put by Trombetta (1989), "So, is shared parenting working? Probably not as well as it will be working 50 years from now" (p. 19).

REFERENCES

Ahrons, C. R., & Rodgers, R. H. (1987). *Divorced families: A multidisciplinary view*. New York: Norton.

American Psychological Association. (1994). Guidelines for child custody evaluations in divorce proceedings. *American Psychologist, 49,* 677–680.

Aries, P. (1965). *Centuries of childhood*. New York: Random House.

Atkinson, J. (1984). Criteria for deciding child custody in the trial and appellate courts. *Family Law Quarterly, 18,* 1–42.

Azmitia, M., & Hesser, J. (1993). Why siblings are important agents of cognitive development: A comparison of siblings and peers. *Child Development, 64,* 430–444.

Bahr, S. J., Howe, J. D., Mann, M. M., & Bahr, M. S. (1994). Trends in child custody awards: Has the removal of maternal preference made a difference? *Family Law Quarterly, 28,* 247–267.

Bartholet, E. (1993). *Family bonds*. Boston: Houghton-Mifflin.

Bautz, B. J., & Hill, R. M. (1991). Mediating the breakup: Do children win? *Mediation Quarterly, 8,* 199–210.

Bender, W. N. (1994). Joint custody: The option of choice. *Journal of Divorce and Remarriage, 21*(3/4), 115–131.

Bengtson, V., Rosenthal, C., & Burton, L. (1990). Families and aging: Diversity and heterogeneity. In R. H. Binstock & L. K. George (Eds.), *Handbook of aging and the social sciences* (3rd ed., pp. 263–280). San Diego, CA: Academic Press.

Berk, L. E. (1994). *Child development*. New York: Allyn & Bacon.

Bishop v. Pillar, 637 A.2d 976 (Pa. 1994).

Bratt, C. (1979). Joint custody. *Kentucky Law Journal, 67,* 271–308.

Bretherton, I. (1985). Attachment theory: Retrospect and prospect. In I. Bretherton & E. Waters (Eds.), Growing points of attachment theory and research. *Monographs of the Society for Research in Child Development, 50*(Serial No. 209).

Brodzinsky, D. M. (1990). A stress and coping model of adoption adjustment. In D. M. Brodzinsky & M. D. Schechter (Eds.), *The psychology of adoption* (pp. 3–24). New York: Oxford University Press.

Brown, G. W., & Harris, T. (1978). *Social origins of depression: A study of psychiatric disorder in women.* New York: Free Press.

Bruch, C. S. (1992). And how are the children? The effects of ideology and mediation on child custody law and children's well-being in the United States. *International Journal of Law and the Family, 2,* 106–126.

Burns, E. M. (1995). Grandparent visitation rights: Is it time for the pendulum to fall? *Family Law Quarterly, 25,* 59–81.

Campbell v. Campbell No. 930790-CA (Utah Ct. App., May 18, 1995).

Cherlin, A. J., & Furstenberg, F. F., Jr. (1986). *The new American grandparent: A place in the family, a life apart.* New York: Basic Books.

Cicchetti, D., & Garmezy, N. (1993). Prospects and promises in the study of resilience. *Development and Psychopathology, 5,* 497–502.

Cicirelli, V. G. (1982). Sibling influence throughout the life span. In M. E. Lamb & B. Sutton-Smith (Eds.), *Sibling relationships: Their nature and significance across the life span* (pp. 267–284). Hillsdale, NJ: Erlbaum.

Cicirelli, V. G. (1985). The role of siblings as family caregivers. In W. J. Sauer & R. T. Coward (Eds.), *Social support networks and the care of the elderly: Theory, research, and practice* (pp. 93–107). New York: Springer.

Cochran, R. F. (1991). Reconciling the primary caretaker preference, the joint custody preference, and the case-by-case rule. In J. Folberg (Ed.), *Joint custody and shared parenting* (pp. 218–240). New York: Guilford Press.

Cochran, R. F., & Vitz, P. Z. (1983). Child protective divorce laws: A response to the effects of parental separation on children. *Family Law Quarterly, 327.*

Cole, E. S. (1985). Adoption: History, policy, and program. In J. Laird & A. Hartman (Eds.), *A handbook of child welfare* (pp. 638–666). New York: Free Press.

Cole, E. S., & Donley, K. S. (1990). *The psychology of adoption.* New York: Oxford University Press.

Cowan, P. A., & Cowan, C. P. (1988). Changes in marriage during the transition to parenthood: Must we blame the baby? In G. Y. Michaels & W. A. Goldbergs (Eds.), *The transition to parenthood* (pp. 114–154). New York: Cambridge University Press.

Crosbie-Burnett, M. (1991). Impact of joint versus sole custody and quality of co-parental relationship on adjustment of adolescents in remarried families. *Behavioral Sciences and the Law, 9,* 439–449.

DeBoer v. Warburton, 164 Ill.2d 468, 649 N.E.2d 324 (1995).

Deeg, C. F. (1989). On the adoptee's cathexis of the lost object. *Psychoanalysis and Psychotherapy, 7*(2), 152–161.

Doe v. Kirchner, 115 S.Ct. 891, 103 L.Ed. 873, 63 USLW 3598 (January 28, 1995).

East, P. L., & Rook, K. S. (1992). Compensatory patterns of support among children's peer relationships: A test using school friends, nonschool friends, and siblings. *Developmental Psychology, 28,* 163–172.

Elkin, M. (1991). Joint custody: In the best interest of the family. In J. Folberg (Ed.), *Joint custody and shared parenting* (pp. 11–15). New York: Guilford Press.

Elrod, L. D. (1994). Summary of the year in family law. *Family Law Quarterly, 28,* 485–514.

Elrod, L. D. (1995). A review of the year in family law. *Family Law Quarterly, 29,* 541–572.

Emery, R. (1994). *Renegotiating family relationships: Divorce, child custody, and mediation.* New York: Guilford Press.

Family Violence Project of the National Council of Juvenile and Family Court Judges. (1995). Family violence in child custody statutes: An analysis of state codes and legal practice. *Family Law Quarterly, 29,* 197–227.

Folberg, J. (Ed.). (1991). *Joint custody and shared parenting.* New York: Guilford Press.

Foster, B. C. (1987). Children and siblings. In A. Thomas & J. Grimes (Eds.), *Children's needs: Psychological perspectives* (pp. 548–553). Washington, DC: National Association of School Psychologists.

Freed, D. J., & Walker, T. B. (1991). Family law in the fifty states: An overview. *Family Law Quarterly, 24,* 309–405.

Freud, A., & Dann, S. (1951). An experiment in group upbringing. *Psychoanalytic Study of the Child, 6,* 127–168.

Furstenberg, F. F., Jr., & Cherlin, A. J. (1991). *Divided families.* Cambridge: Harvard University Press.

Garbarino, J., Kostelny, K., & Dubrow, N. (1991). *Growing up in a war zone.* Lexington, MA: Lexington.

Garmezy, N. (1983). Stressors in childhood. In N. Garmezy & M. Rutter (Eds.), *Stress, coping, and development in children* (pp. 43–84). NY: McGraw-Hill.

Garska v. McCoy, 278 S.E.2d 357 (W. Va. 1981).

Gindes, M. (1995). Guidelines for child custody evaluations for psychologists: Overview and commentary. *Family Law Quarterly, 29,* 39–50.

Gottfried, A. E., & Gottfried, A. W. (Eds.). (1994). *Redefining families: Implications for children's development.* New York: Plenum Press.

Greif, J. (1979). Father, children, and joint custody. *American Journal of Orthopsychiatry, 49,* 311–319.

Grisso, T., & Vierling, L. (1978). Minors' consent to treatment: A developmental perspective. *Professional Psychology, 9,* 412–427.

Grossberg, M. (1985). *Governing the hearth.* Chapel Hill: University of North Carolina Press.

Grusec, J. E., & Lytton, H. (1988). *Social development: History, theory, and research.* New York: Springer-Verlag.

Hauser, S. T., Powers, S., Jacobson, A., Noam, G., Weiss, B., & Follansbee, D. (1984). Family contexts of adolescent ego development. *Child Development, 55,* 195–213.

Howe, N. (1991). Sibling-directed internal state language, perspective taking, and affective behavior. *Child Development, 62,* 1503–1512.

Howe, N., & Ross, H. S. (1990). Socialization, perspective taking, and the sibling relationship. *Developmental Psychology, 26,* 160–165.

In Re the Adoption of EAW, Docket #93-3040 (Florida State Supreme Court).

In Re Gault, 387 U.S. 1 (1967).

Interpreter gains custody of deaf girl. (1995, June 2). *The News & Observer,* p. A4.

Ireland v. Smith, 542 N.W.2d 344, 214 Mich. App. 235 (November 7, 1995).

Irving, H. H., & Benjamin, M. (1991). Shared and sole-custody parents: A comparative analysis. In J. Folberg (Ed.), *Joint custody and shared parenting* (pp. 114–131). NY: Guilford Press.

Jacob, H. (1988). *The silent revolution.* Chicago: University of Chicago Press.

Johnson, C. L. (1983). A cultural analysis of the grandmother. *Research on Aging, 5,* 547–567.

Johnston, J. R., Kline, M., & Tschann, J. M. (1991). Ongoing postdivorce conflict in families contesting custody: Do joint custody and frequent access help? In J. Folberg (Ed.), *Joint custody and shared parenting* (pp. 117–184). New York: Guilford Press.

Kaplan, L., Hennon, C. B., & Ade-Ridder, L. (1993). Splitting custody of children between parents: Impact on the sibling system. *The Journal of Contemporary Human Services, 74*(3), 131–144.

Kelly, J. B. (1993). Current research on children's postdivorce adjustment. *Family and Conciliation Courts Review, 31*, 29–49.

Kingsley v. Kingsley, 623 So.2d 780, 18 Fla. L. Weekly D1852 (August 18, 1993).

Kitzmann, K. M., & Emery, R. E. (1994). Child and family coping one year after mediated and litigated child custody disputes. *Journal of Family Psychology, 8*, 150–159.

Lamb, M. E. (1977). Father-infant and mother-infant interaction in the first year of life. *Child Development, 48*, 167–181.

Liss, M. B., & Studley, C. (1983, August). *Attaining legal adult status in the 50 states.* Paper presented at the Annual Meeting of the American Psychological Association, Anaheim, CA.

Liss, M. B., & Stahly, G. B. (1993). Domestic violence and child custody. In M. Hansen & M. Harway (Eds.), *Battering and family therapy: A feminist perspective.* Newbury Park, California: Sage.

McGuffin v. Overton & Porter, WL 621740 (Mich. Ct. App., October 20, 1995).

Mnookin, R. (1975). Child custody adjudication: Judicial functions in the face of indeterminancy. *Law and Contemporary Problems, 39*, 226–292.

Newman, J. L., Roberts, L. R., & Syre, C. R. (1993). Concepts of family among children and adolescents: Effect of cognitive level, gender, and family structure. *Developmental Psychology, 29*, 951–962.

Nichols, W. C. (1986). Sibling subsystem therapy in family system reorganization. *Journal of Divorce, 9*, 13–31.

Papini, D. R., Roggman, L., & Anderson, J. (1991). Early-adolescent perceptions of attachment to mother and father: A test of the emotional-distancing and buffering hypotheses. *Journal of Early Adolescence, 11*(2), 258–275.

Pearson, J. (1993). Ten myths about family law. *Family Law Quarterly, 27*, 279–299.

Phear, W. P. C., Beck, J. C., Hauser, B. B., Clark, S. C., & Whitney, R. A. (1984). An empirical study of custody agreements: Joint versus sole legal custody. *Journal of Psychiatry and Law, 11*, 419–441.

Pikula v. Pikula, 374 N.W.2d 705–712 (1985).

Raymond v. Raymond, No. 92D-1730 C1 (Plymouth County Cir. Ct., 1994).

Reidy, T.J., Silver, R. M., & Carlson, A. (1989). Child custody decisions: A survey of judges. *Family Law Quarterly, 23*, 75–87.

Reppucci, N. D., & Crosby, C. A. (1993). Law, psychology, and children: Overarching issues. *Law and Human Behavior, 17*, 1–10.

Roth, A. (1975). The tender years presumption in child custody disputes. *Journal of Family Law, 15*, 423.

Saposnek, D. T. (1983). *Mediating child custody disputes.* San Francisco: Jossey-Bass.

Saposnek, D. T. (1991). A guide to decisions about joint custody: The needs of children of divorce. In J. Folberg (Ed.), *Joint custody and shared parenting* (pp. 29–40). New York: Guilford Press.

Schwartz, L. L. (1984). Adoption custody and family therapy. *American Journal of Family Therapy, 12*, 51–58.

Schwartz, L. L. (1986). Unwed fathers and adoption custody disputes. *American Journal of Family Therapy, 14*, 347–355.

Schwartz, L. L. (1992). Children's perceptions of divorce. *The American Journal of Family Therapy, 20*, 324–332.

Schwartz, L. L. (1993). What is a family? A contemporary view. *Contemporary Family Therapy, 150*, 429–442.

Schwartz, L. L. (1994). The challenge of raising one's nonbiological children. *The American Journal of Family Therapy, 22*, 195–207.

Scott, E. S., & Derdeyn, A. P. (1984). Rethinking joint custody. *Ohio State Law Journal, 45*, 455–474.

Scott, J. P. (1990). Sibling interaction in later life. In T. H. Brubaker (Ed.), *An overview of family relationships in later life* (2nd ed., pp. 86–99). Newbury Park, CA: Sage.

Shaw, M., & Phear, W. P. (Eds.). (1988). *Parent-child mediation.* NY: Institute for Judicial Administration.

Smith v. Ireland, Docket #93-385 (Macomb County, Mich., June 27, 1994).

Sorkow, H. R. (1991). Best interest of the child: By whose definition? *Pepperdine Law Review, 18,* 383–387.

Sroufe, A. (1983). Infant-caregiver attachment and patterns of adaptation in preschool: The roots of maladaptation. In M. Perlmutter (Ed.), *Minnesota Symposia on Child Psychology* (*Vol. 16,* pp. 41–83). Hillsdale, NJ: Erlbaum.

Steinman, S. B. (1981). The experience of children in a joint custody arrangement. *American Journal of Orthopsychiatry, 51,* 403–415.

Steinman, S. B., Zemmelman, S. E., & Knoblauch, T. M. (1985). A study of parents who sought joint custody following divorce: Who reaches agreement and sustains joint custody and who returns to court. *Journal of the American Academy of Child Psychiatry, 24*(5), 554–562.

Thoennes, N., Salem, P., & Pearson, J. (1995). Mediation and domestic violence: Current policies and practices. *Family and Conciliation Courts Review, 33,* 6–29.

Thomas, J. L., & King, C. M. (1990, August). *Adult grandchildren's views of grandchildren: Racial and gender effects.* Paper presented at the Annual Meeting of the American Psychological Association, Boston, MA.

Thompson, R. A., Scalora, M. J., Limber, S. P., & Castrianno, L. (1991). Grandparent visitation rights: A psycholegal analysis. *Family and Conciliation Courts Review, 29,* 9–25.

Trombetta, D. (1989). Shared parenting as joint physical custody. *Family and Conciliation Courts Review, 27,* 17–20.

Twigg v. Mays, WL 330624 (Fla. Cir. Ct., 1993).

Wallerstein, J. S. (1991). The long-term effects of divorce on children: A review. *Journal of the American Academy of Child and Adolescent Psychiatry, 30,* 349–359.

Wallerstein, J. S., & Blakeslee, S. (1989). *Second chances.* NY: Ticknor & Fields.

Wallerstein, J. S., & Kelly, J. B. (1980). *Surviving the breakup: How children and parents cope with divorce.* New York: Basic Books.

Watts v. Watts, 77 Misc. 2d 178, 181, 350 N.Y.S.2d, 285, 287 (1973).

Weithorn, L. A. (1980). Developmental factors and competence to consent to treatment. In G. B. Melton (Ed.), *Legal reforms affecting child and youth services.* New York: Haworth.

Weitzman, L. J. (1985). *The divorce revolution.* New York: Free Press.

Werner, E. E. (1993). Risk, resilience, and recovery: Perspectives from the Kauai Longitudinal Study. *Development and Psychopathology, 5,* 503–515.

Wolman, R., & Taylor, K. (1991). Psychological effects of custody disputes on children. *Behavioral Sciences and the Law, 9,* 399–417.

IV

Ethics and Professional Issues

—————————— 10 ——————————

Preparing for Two Cultures

Education and Training in Law and Psychology

DONALD N. BERSOFF

It would be interesting to speculate what it says about the discipline of law and psychology in the United States that its putative parent, Hugo Munsterberg, was a German nationalist who was cajoled into emigrating to this country by William James, became president of the American Psychological Association one year after he arrived here, attempted to arouse sympathy among the American people for the German cause during World War I, never became an American citizen (Keller, 1979), and whose work, *On the Witness Stand* (Munsterberg, 1908), was so vilified by legal scholars (e.g., Wigmore, 1909) that it almost irreparably damaged the nascent attempt to apply the behavioral sciences to the law. In fact, it took 20 years and the legal realism movement before any such serious interdisciplinary work reappeared, primarily collaborative efforts by social scientists and law professors (Loh, 1981; Schlegel, 1979).

PERIODIC FLIRTATION OR STABLE RELATIONSHIP?

Although the work of the legal realists in the 1920s was significant (Schlegel, 1995), it was not until almost half a century after the publication

DONALD N. BERSOFF • School of Law, Villanova University, Pennsylvania 19085; Department of Clinical and Health Psychology, Medical College of Pennsylvania–Hahnemann University of the Health Sciences, Philadelphia Pennsylvania 19102.

Psychology and Law: The State of the Discipline, edited by Ronald Roesch, Stephen D. Hart, and James R. P. Ogloff. Kluwer Academic/Plenum Publishers, New York, 1999.

of Munsterberg's much maligned text that the most noteworthy modern event responsible for stimulating interest in the application of social science research to legal issues occurred. That event, of course, was *Brown v. Board of Education* (1954), the seminal decision that held that separate but equal public school facilities violated the equal protection rights of African-American children. Although the works by social scientists that the Supreme Court cited in support of its decision in what is probably the law's most famous footnote were themselves severely criticized (e.g., Cahn, 1955; Tomkins & Oursland, 1991; Van den Haag, 1960), *Brown* brought renewed vitality to those advocating for the use of psychological data in judicial and legislative decision making. In fact, just 3 years after *Brown* was decided—and 50 years after the publication of *On the Witness Stand*—at the Association of American Law Schools (AALS) 1957) annual meeting, the eminent University of Chicago legal scholar and jury researcher, Harry Kalven, was persuaded to assert that "undoubtedly this is a high point in the periodic flirtation between law and social science" (Kalven, 1958, p. 94).

The resurgence of interest by the legal profession in law and psychology was not restricted to purely scholarly and academic activities. A second speaker at the AALS Conference, Caleb Foote, avidly lobbied for applying information from the behavioral sciences to practical aspects of the law, particularly to domestic relations, adult and juvenile criminal law, and the confluence of criminal and mental health law. In fact, in many ways, Foote's advocacy of data-oriented forensic decision making coincided with the creation of the scientist-practitioner model of professional training developed at the Boulder Conference in 1949 (Raimy, 1950):

> Perhaps the most serious defect of some efforts to integrate behavioral-science material in law teaching has been the inclusion of only the findings which behavioral scientists have reached, without the data on which they are based. This precludes student's comparative evaluation of the research methods of the various disciplines and grossly oversimplifies the problem of law-science interaction by giving [no idea of the complicated statistical techniques that are inherent] in research. (Foote, 1958, p. 84)

I do not plan to provide the reader with an extended history of the many attempts to integrate law and the social sciences throughout this now waning century. A great many sources are already available for tracing the uneven nature of these attempts (e.g., Bersoff & Glass, 1995; Kolasa, 1972; Loh, 1984; Melton, Monahan, & Saks, 1987; Monahan & Walker, 1985; Monahan & Walker, 1994; Ogloff, Tomkins, & Bersoff, 1996; Saks, 1989; Schlegel, 1995; Tanford, 1990). Nevertheless, there are four observations about this history that may have relevance to education and training in psychology and law.

First, despite its cyclical nature, there has been a century-long interest by the law in the social and behavioral sciences, not only stimulated by experimentalists like Munsterberg, but also clinicians as eminent as Freud (1906/1959). This has resulted in two somewhat orthogonal lines of training. There are those whose interests are mainly devoted to exploring the application of psychology to the legal process or the legal system itself. Complementing them are those whose interests are focused on understanding and analyzing the ways in which the law defines and regulates the activities of psychologists, whether in research or clinical practice (Grisso, Sales, & Bayless, 1982).

Second, as the allusion to a "periodic flirtation" implies, the law's "ambivalen[ce] about social science" (Kalven, 1958, p. 96) has almost a "manic-depressive quality" (Kalven, 1958, p. 95) about it. Twenty-five years later, I used a comparable analogy:

> It is relatively clear ... that the relationship between ... psychologists and the courts is less than perfect. In fact, if that relationship were to be examined by a Freudian, the analyst would no doubt conclude that it is a highly neurotic, conflict-ridden ambivalent affair (I stress affair because it is certainly no marriage). (Bersoff, 1986, p. 155)

Third, perhaps one can locate the cause of this ambivalence in the hypothesis "that lawyers and social scientists come from two different cultures" (Saks, 1989, p. 1115). By and large, lawyers and scientists have different interests, major in different areas as undergraduates, develop different cognitive approaches to solving problems, possess different attitudes toward confrontation and argument, arrive at the truth in different ways, and are exposed to different styles of education during their post-baccalaureate training (see Goldberg, 1994; Haney, 1980, for an extended discussion of some of these differences). Or to use Michael Saks' more pithy comment, "Law students are typically smart people who do not like math ... [and] most social scientists have little appreciation of the breadth and content of the law" (Saks, 1989, pp. 1115–1116).

Psychologists value the methods of science in aiding them to understand, predict, and control behavior. The law, to the contrary, particularly the judicial system, does not find experimental data dispositive in deciding crucial issues, such as the meaning or reach of the Constitution (Bersoff, 1986; Tomkins, & Oursland, 1991). In law, constitutional history, values, and precedent—what might be called normative philosophy—will outweigh empirical considerations either when the data possess only statistical and not social significance, or when constitutional norms persuade the courts that such norms are in conflict with the data. For example, in a 1976 sex discrimination case, the Supreme Court stated, "Providing broad sociological propositions by statistics is a dubious business, and one that inevitably is in tension with the normative philosophy that underlies the Equal Protection Clause" (*Criag v. Boren*, 1976, p. 204).

More recently, Chief Justice Rehnquist wrote an opinion in which the Court was asked to decide whether "death-qualified" jurors act more favorably to the prosecution than do non–death-qualified jurors (*Lockhart v. McCree*, 1986). Death qualification is a process that eliminates prospective jurors from deciding the guilt or innocence of a defendant in a first degree murder trial if they have moral or religious scruples that would prevent them from voting for the imposition of the death penalty under any and all circumstances, assuming they found the defendant responsible for committing first degree murder. After reviewing a wealth of social psychological studies supporting the hypothesis that death-qualified jurors did act more favorably to the prosecution at the guilt phase (thus raising questions about the fairness of the trial under the Fifth and Fourteenth Amendments and the right to a representative and impartial jury under the Sixth Amendment), Justice Rehnquist stated:

> We will assume for purposes of this opinion that the studies are both methodologically valid and adequate to establish that "death qualification" in fact produces somewhat more "conviction prone" juries than "non-death-qualified" juries. We hold, nonetheless that the Constitution does not prohibit the States from "death-qualifying" juries in capital cases. (*Lockhart v. McCree*, 1986, p. 173)

Thus, the Supreme Court, proclaiming as it did in *Criag* that "it is unrealistic to expect either members of the judiciary or state officials to be well versed in the rigors of experimental or statistical technique" (*Craig v. Boren*, 1976, p. 204), often relies on "common human experience" (*Parham v. J.R.*, 1979, p.609) rather than data. As one commentator noted, "Dominant legal thought is nothing but some more or less plausible common-wisdom banalities, superficialities, and generalities" (Kelman, 1981, pp. 671–672). Or, even more acerbically, "most legal policy debates are resolved through a heated exchange of quotations. The idea of going out and obtaining data to resolve those issues that are empirical often does not enter the minds of legal policy makers" (Saks, 1989, p. 1115).

If graduate students in psychology adopted the pervasive thinking and predominant mode of inquiry of law students, they would never be allowed to complete their doctoral programs. As a result, "Students who desire training in law and psychology have a formidable task ahead of them.... There are inherent difficulties in mastering two, independent disciplines which have languages (i.e., terminologies), methods, and epistemologies of their own" (Tomkins & Ogloff, 1990, pp. 206–207). In short, those who seek to combine law and psychology must "bridge ... two cultures" (Saks, 1989, p. 1116).

These major differences in cognition and process evoke my fourth and final comment on history. There is significant disagreement about whether a successful rapprochement is possible between law and psychology. Saks (1989) expressed "little expectation" (p. 1116) that a bridge between the two cultures would be constructed in the foreseeable future. Other educators are more optimistic about the prospects, particularly if training can produce people who speak not only the separate languages of law and psychology but a third language combining the two: "Training in law/psychology allows the students and graduates to draw upon and focus on the perceived strengths of each discipline, and combine them into a whole that is greater than the sum of its parts" (Hafemeister, Ogloff, & Small, 1990, p. 271).

PLAUDITS AND PROBLEMS

SOURCES OF OPTIMISM

Whether or not scholars and practitioners in law and psychology become "comfortable guest[s]" (Melton, 1987a, p. 494) in each other's professional homes, develop the facility to speak "trilingually," or simply become consumers of an evanescent and relatively short-lived fad, there is little doubt that law and psychology has piqued a great deal of interest in the past 20 years. In reviewing the data obtained from a 1982 survey to determine how many psychology departments offered law-related courses, Grisso et al. (1982) concluded: "The picture derived from these results is of a rapidly growing field, that in its infancy, is exploring in every direction the potential and existing relationships between psychology and the law" (p. 273). Five years later, Melton reinforced this judgment, asserting that, "Psycholegal studies may be fairly termed as psychology's new growth industry" (Melton, 1987b, p. 681).

As we tread expectantly toward the millennium there is, indeed, sound evidence to support the conclusion that this is an expansive time in law and psychology, stimulating students to become part of this burgeoning enterprise. There are now over 1,900 members of the American Psychology-Law Society (Division 41 of the American Psychological Association [APA]), with an active, strong, and vital student section. At the present time, there are at least four highly regarded joint programs awarding law degrees and doctorates in psychology, each attracting the very best law and graduate students (Ogloff et al., 1996). The Law and Society Association and the American Academy and Board of Forensic Psychology, the latter with over 125 diplomates, are strong, growing organizations. *Law and Human Behavior*, *Behavioral Sciences and Law*, and *Criminal Justice and Behavior*, among other important journals in the field, were joined in

1995 by *Psychology, Public Policy, and the Law,* an APA published, law school-sponsored, peer reviewed journal, edited by Bruce Sales, the founder of the first J.D./Ph.D. Program in Law and Psychology in the United States. There is now a Psych-Law Listserv on the Internet, which despite some dross, has become a rich source of opinion, resources, and comment. In the midnineties, of 11 members of the APA Board of Directors, two had dual degrees in law and psychology, as does one of the heads of APA's four directorates. Five prominent members of the Federal Judicial Center, the research arm of the federal courts, have dual degrees, including four who graduated from a joint J.D./Ph.D. program. At least three prestigious law schools have psychologists as members of their tenured full-time faculty (Melton et al., 1987). Two Master Lecture Series presented during APA conventions in the last dozen years have been devoted exclusively to law and psychology (Sales & VandenBos, 1994; Schierer & Hammonds, 1983). Undergraduate offerings on the topic are often the most popular course in psychology departments. The field has been able to attract well-known, thoughtful, and prolific law professors who now focus almost exclusively on our enterprise. And, law and psychology has been the subject of two major scholarly reviews of the field's contributions to science (Monahan & Loftus, 1982; Tapp, 1976).

SOURCES OF CONCERN

On the other hand, this is also a time of ferment, turmoil, and anxiety in the education and training of future scholars, practitioners, and researchers in law and psychology. It is very likely that funding for graduate students (i.e., tuition waivers and stipends) will disappear before the decade concludes and the century ends. At this point, no one can predict the fate of the National Institutes of Health, including the National Institute of Mental Health, or the National Science Foundation and the grants they provide to support the bulk of law/psychology research. And, in the search for ever-diminishing funds, researchers will inevitably be constrained by their benefactors, thus further constricting the areas of investigation in which educators, trainers, and their students engage. Practicum sites and institutions providing pre- and postdoctoral internships are cutting back, reducing the number of slots for training.

In our courtrooms, psychology is still seen as a mysterious, inexact discipline with little consensus in adopting an overarching scientific theory to guide its endeavors (*Berger v. Board of Psychologist Examiners,* 1975), populated by hired guns who will switch sides and proffer opinions for the right fee and the greatest notoriety (Bersoff, 1995a). New, often unvalidated "psychological" syndromes seem to proliferate every day, and new theories for mitigating responsibility for one's actions abound (Dressler, 1987; Morse, 1984, 1995). Despite decades of research, our field still has no definitive method for determining whether someone will become violent, for delineating the extent of the relationship between violence and mental illness, or whether memories are false, uncovered, or repressed. And, the Supreme Court, despite the best efforts of psycholegal scholars, remains woefully naive and unsophisticated, if not downright hostile, to the application of social science research to empirically based constitutional questions (Bersoff & Glass, 1995; Saks & Baron, 1980; Tremper, 1987).

Even more relevant to our topic, there is a whole host of issues directly related to the training and teaching of future scholars and practitioners in law and psychology. At the undergraduate level, there is little consensus as to the subject matter that should be communicated (cf. e.g., Bartol, 1983; Ellison & Buckhout, 1981; Foley, 1993; Horowitz & Willging, 1984; Wrightsman, Nietzel, & Fortune, 1998). There is indecision as to whether the thrust of investigation and teaching should be on the relationship of psychology to law, or whether we should apply the methods of the behavioral sciences to the study of law as a social instrument. The background and training of instructors varies widely. And all of this may explain why, despite the fact that law and psychology courses are so popular, so few undergraduates, proportionately, are attracted to pursuing the field at the graduate level.

Undergraduate programs at least pay for themselves through large enrollments. But those at the graduate level are faced with having to prove to financially anxious administrators and boards of trustees that their programs—whether focused on forensic training or social science—are justified, both from economic and scholarly perspectives.

In the forensic arena, there is little agreement about whether there is enough time in graduate school to teach students everything they need to know to become competent clinicians—the core of psychology, research design and statistical methods, clinical assessment, basic but relevant legal principles, as well as the complexities of competency, insanity, and custody evaluations. The question remains whether the primary focus of forensic training in graduate school should be that of educating applied professionals to perform clinical functions or social scientists whose primary foundation is research, with practical training postponed until the postdoctoral years. I address these troubling issues in more detail in a later section of this chapter.

With regard to graduate education in the social sciences, the issues are equally weighty. Students who wish to pursue research in law and psychology, like their forensic counterparts, must be trained in two disciplines. One can question whether there is enough time in graduate school to accomplish that goal, and whether there are enough legally sophisticated psychology faculty to provide the proper training. One possible solution is for graduates to pursue a masters of legal studies at law schools that admit doctoral-level professionals to study for a year, a sort of "finishing school" for psycholegal scholars. This may be a viable option, but there are currently few law schools that provide such training.

As at the undergraduate level, there is no consensus as to what should be taught in law-oriented social science programs. Though psycholegal studies are almost a century old, it has been slow to expand beyond the borders of eyewitness identification and the behavior of juror and juries (Saks, 1986). In contrast to teaching about memory, perception, and the dynamics of groups, we have only begun to explore the contributions of psychometrics, cognitive psychology, and development psychology through the life span, among others, to issues raised by the legal system (Bersoff, 1995b). And, we may be concentrating mistakenly on the trial process rather than on those fora where most crucial legal decisions are made, such as state and federal administrative agencies, state legislatures, and Congress, and during pretrial and posttrial proceedings.

With regard to practical training, I would guess that there is almost universal agreement that graduate education in clinically oriented J.D./ Ph.D. joint programs and doctorate-only forensic programs must contain relevant predoctoral practicum and internship experiences (particularly if they seek accreditation of these programs from APA). Many would argue, however, that one additional year in a postdoctoral internship or residency in a forensic setting is essential to becoming a competent forensic clinician. Yet, there are relatively few such facilities available. And, even if they were to be developed, there is no consensus whether they should admit all professional psychologists or limit participation to those who will specialize in forensic psychology. It is unclear at this point what the impact will be of the policy adopted by the APA Council of Representatives in 1995 (Joint Interim Committee, 1995a,b) regarding the development of identifiable specialties and proficiencies in psychology (I have some thoughts about this later in this chapter), and whether the nascent movement by APA to accredit postdoctoral programs will extend to forensic facilities.

The most ambitious and lengthy form of graduate training remains, of course, joint programs that culminate in students being awarded the J.D. in law and the Ph.D. or Psy.D. in psychology. As we enter the third decade since the creation of the first of these joint efforts (Melton, 1990), there is still sharp disagreement about the worth of such programs (e.g., Freeman & Roesch, 1992; Melton, 1987b). There are concerns about whether the contributions they make are justified by their costs, both temporal and financial. And, as yet there are no mutually accepted common curricular requirements among the four of them, nor agreement that they should seek accreditation by the APA, or even that they should continue to exist. I devote considerable attention to these issues in a subsequent section of this chapter.

In this era of a glut of law school graduates and the terrifying effect of managed health care on professional employment, allowing insurers to hold down costs in part by using nondoctoral providers, an overarching question is whether these training programs can place their graduates in academic and clinical settings. With diminished funding for faculty and research, it is possible we are leading our students down a primrose path to nowhere or, at best, to government agencies, profit-oriented businesses that produce research on demand, or law firms where billable hours and bottom lines predominate.

Relatively neglected in a consideration of law and psychology training is the role of continuing education. At this time in the development of the profession, most clinicians who provide forensic services are not trained in graduate school but in weekend or one-day seminars and workshops. Yet, there is very little, if any, regulation of these experiences or scrutiny of the credentials of those who provide them. And, as in graduate forensic programs, there is a great deal of concentration in these continuing education courses on courtroom testimony to the neglect of pretrial processes, such as discovery (involving rules regarding depositions and the exchange of documents).

Most forensic clinicians who teach continuing education courses do so to their professional colleagues. As a result, continuing education efforts, by and large, neglect members of the legal profession. Lawyers are fundamentally ignorant about basic mental health principles, the vagaries and shortcomings of the *Diagnostic and Statistical Manual* (American Psychiatric Association, 1994), the limits of assessment data, and the principles of science, experimentation, and research design (I discuss impending progress on this issue in this chapter's final substantive section). Furthermore, as anyone who has practiced law or served as an expert witness knows, there are state and federal judges who, like members of the U.S. Supreme Court, prefer to make decisions based on instinct, gut feelings, or their own, often circumscribed experience, rather than on carefully considered, methodologically sound data, even when the questions to be decided are essentially empirical. Teaching judges is crucial, but it has been perhaps the least successful of our efforts at continuing education.

This litany of issues should both concern and excite the interested reader. Whether the relationship between law and psychology is characterized as a flirtation, an affair, a shameless seduction, an ambivalent and conflicted interaction, or a genuine and mature interest in the positive attributes of each other, the field is alive, full of ferment, and open to a whole new generation of students. At the same AALS meeting at which Kalven and Foote spoke, University of Pennsylvania Law Professor Leo Levin made an assertion that can still provide the rallying cry (though uttered 40 years ago) for students and teachers alike who populate the arcane interdisciplinary field of law and psychology:

> If it is true that there is a vast undeveloped potential for law in empirical research in the behavioral sciences, then it is essential that we develop a supply of individuals trained in the law who have the desire and the ability, the sophistication and discrimination to actualize this potential. (Levin, 1958, p. 89)

THE NATIONAL INVITATIONAL CONFERENCE

Rallying cries can arouse the faithful to achieve a goal, but they do little to provide the means for doing so. By 1995, it seemed time to address the several serious issues concerning the nature and direction of law and psychology as a transdisciplinary, jurisprudential, practical, and research enterprise, perhaps even to develop models of training from undergraduate through postdoctoral education, to create more regular and formal means to disseminate knowledge about training programs, and simply to reflect on the history of law and psychology, its current status, and what we anticipate the field will look like in the 21st century.

These were the purposes of the National Invitational Conference on Education and Training in Law and Psychology held from May 25–28, 1995, at Villanova Law School, located in suburban Philadelphia (Bersoff et al., 1997). Now more popularly known as the "Villanova Conference," it was attended by 48 invited participants, chosen after self- and other-nomination from over 100 applicants. The participants were primarily identified with one of eight major areas: (a) undergraduate education; (b) graduate social science programs; (c) graduate forensic programs; (d) joint degree programs; (e) practical training, including predoctoral practica, internships, and postdoctoral experiences; (f) continuing education; (g) law school teaching; and (h) student issues. The conference was funded by the APA, the American Psychology-Law Society, the American Academy of Forensic Psychology, the Florida Mental Health Institute, and Villanova Law School. It was organized by a steering committee comprised of Jane Goodman-Delahunty, Thomas Grisso, Valerie Hans, Norman Poythress, Ronald Roesch, and myself as Chair.

ISSUES AND GOALS

As the conference began, I attempted in my keynote address (Bersoff, 1995b) to stimulate participants to focus on three overarching points and to try to achieve five discrete goals. The first overarching point was a plea to develop means for evaluating what educators and trainers in law and psychology do all along the continuum—from undergraduate programs through postdoctoral training and continuing education. As a field, particularly because our training is so lengthy and often out of the mainstream, we have a responsibility to our students, ourselves, and our profession to provide data validating our own enterprise, just as in our roles as psycholegal scholars and forensic clinicians, we expect others to provide such data about theirs. Second, I requested that participants ponder why law and psychology is so ethnocentric a discipline. Why such a result, despite that fact that we are part of an international community of law and psychology academics and practitioners? A considerable amount of validation, evaluation, and generalizability of our data come from our international colleagues, and a significant amount of training in our field occurs around the globe, from Canada to Australia and points in between. Yet, we rarely acknowledge the work of our counterparts not only in North America, but in such countries as Great Britain, Germany, The Netherlands, South Africa, and the Scandinavian countries. The third, and most pressing point is our own national ethnocentrism. Law and psychology as an educational enterprise has been woefully inadequate, perhaps even derelict, in its efforts to attract ethnic and racial minorities to the field (see Haney, 1993). We have done reasonably well as a profession attracting women throughout our short history (Grisso, 1991), although even conceding this point, women remain relatively underrepresented. But, when those trained in law and psychology meet at conventions there are few, if any, men and women of color or with physical disabilities. It is my view that our field needs more diversity, not only in the subject matters it addresses, but in thought, perception, and scholarly contributions if it is to confront and help solve the full range of issues facing it (see also Roesch, 1995).

In more mundane terms, the five goals of the eight working groups at the conference were to (a) identify those aspects of education and training that worked well in the past and/or are current successes; (b) identify ongoing problems that remain unresolved; (c) develop strategies for addressing those problems; (d) delineate among those strategies, the ones with the most potential for being practical, implementable, and effective; and (e) recommend possible model curricula, programs, and levels of training. Finally, like any good keynote speaker, I tried to energize the participants with some rousing final words:

> In attempting to achieve these goals, I hope you will engage in two not necessarily incompatible tasks. First, let your thinking soar—fantasize, ideate wildly, anticipate and plan for the future, develop ideal models, conceptualize freely. Identify and develop an educational philosophy or group of contrasting philosophies that may

undergird training and education in law and psychology. Second, adapt the products of your imagination to real life, practical solutions. Let us try to make what is thinkable, doable. (Bersoff, 1995b)

Despite this evocative rhetoric, not every dream, purpose, or goal can be realized in a 3 day conference no matter how hard working or illustrious the participants. Only time will tell how successful the Villanova Conference was. But, I can report that the participants did end up with, among other accomplishments, a first attempt to delineate levels and models of training and with a number of specific, planned products. I will save a detailed discussion of the levels of training for a later section of this chapter and reserve for this space a brief description of five planned or currently in-progress product outcomes.

FIVE OUTCOMES: SURVEYS, VIDEOTAPES, ARTICLES, BOOKS, AND COGPPAL

Everyone involved in forensic training acknowledges that practical forensic experience is necessary at the predoctoral level. But, it remains unclear precisely what experiences and facilities are available for such training at the present time. There have been earlier surveys and informational articles attempting to identify and describe these facilities (e.g., Fenster, Litwack, & Symonds, 1975; Fowler & Brodsky, 1978; Goldenberg, 1978; Heilbrun & Annis, 1988; Kaslow & Abrams, 1976; Lawlor, Siskind, & Brooks, 1981; Levine, Wilson, & Sales, 1980; Otto, Heilbrun, & Grisso, 1990; Poythress, 1979; Roesch, Grisso, & Poythress, 1986). For example, in a 1975 survey of 85 APA-approved internship sites responding (of 120), 13% reported having forensic experiences as an integral part of their training, 14% reported offering optional experiences, and 28% reported having both regular and optional experiences (Levine et al., 1980). In a more particularized survey done 4 years later, of 76 (of 127) internship sites responding, 70% reported providing forensic evaluation training, and 77% reported providing treatment experience with forensic populations, but the surveyors concluded "that growth has been haphazard, uncoordinated, and unplanned" (Lawlor et al., 1981, p. 402). In what appears to be the most recent attempt to gather information, Heilbrun and Annis (1988) in 1985 surveyed 103 forensic inpatient facilities. Of the 68 sites responding, 41% provided predoctoral internships, and 43% offered practicum training to graduate students.

As helpful as these surveys are, they are outdated and somewhat unsystematic. Therefore, an ad hoc group of conference participants identified with forensic training and practice are developing surveys to (a) canvass the directors of clinical training programs to determine which among them offer predoctoral practica and assessment experiences related to forensic psychology, (b) determine which of the predoctoral internships listed in the *Association of Psychology Practicum and Internship Centers Directory* (Cantrell & Hall, 1995) offers forensic experiences, and (c) request information from relevant sources concerning the availability of postdoctoral training in forensic psychology, information missing from the prior surveys. The ad hoc group hopes to compile the information from these surveys into a directory to be completed by 1997.

Although textbooks and articles on law and psychology abound, there is a dearth of practical and visual material for use in training at all levels of the education continuum. Therefore, from my perspective, one of the more exciting proposals to emanate from the Villanova Conference is to develop a series of videotapes in which well-known experts in particular fields of law and psychology would appear, present didactic material, and demonstrate fundamental techniques. For example, one production might instruct students in the legal principles regarding competency to stand trial, differentiate it from an insanity evaluation, and show an experienced clinician actually performing a competency evaluation, using the most methodologically sound and valid procedures. Some of these tapes would be geared to undergraduate courses (perhaps demonstrating issues related to eyewitness identifications or jury selection) and some to graduate and practicum students and interns. The APLS Training and Education Committee has taken responsibility for developing these tapes.

An article describing the major issues and outcomes from the Villanova Conference developed by each of the eight working groups was published in the *American Psychologist* (Bersoff et al., 1997). The conference organizers are also planning to develop a full length text useful for undergraduates, graduate students, and already-trained scholars and practitioners. Although the book will report on the conference, it is designed to discuss more fully a wide band of general issues in law and psychology training. The chapters will identify current problems and issues in each of the substantive areas covered in the conference—undergraduate education, graduate social science programs, graduate forensic programs, joint degree programs, predoctoral practica and internships, postdoctoral training, law school education, and continuing education, with each group addressing relevant student issues. Chapter authors will also describe the usefulness of training for psychologists, in general, and inform readers of what can be done with the training (e.g., potential occupations and roles that may result from concentrating on law and psychology as an undergraduate or a graduate student).

For perhaps the first time in history, the directors of the four clearly identified joint J.D. doctoral programs in law and psychology met for extended discussions at the Villanova Conference. We were able to share thoughts and concerns; compare curricula, program structure, and training philosophies; and inform each other of the employment placements enjoyed by our respective graduates. As a result of this experience, we decided to form the Council of Graduate Programs in Psychology and Law (COGPPAL) and to invite other directors of graduate social science programs in law and psychology to attend as well. The group plans to meet at least once each year and to eventually develop a model curriculum in psycholegal studies that will be debated and revised. My own personal vision for the Villanova Conference was the history-making Boulder Conference (Raimy, 1950) at which was developed the scientist-practitioner model of professional education in clinical psychology, a model that still has major impact on that field. I have hopes that the Villanova Conference will have a similar influence on education and training in law and psychology for the first half of the 21st century. It took 4 years to obtain the imprimatur of the APA to cosponsor the conference, to raise the money to fund it, to select and invite participants to it, and to structure it so that it would have the greatest possibility for success. The Conference was perhaps the only time in the next several decades that the field will be able to gather together, formulate ideas, and translate those ideas into implementable plans. I would like those who follow us to read the record of the conference proceedings in 2050 and say that its participants provided definitive models for education and training in law and psychology that survived for 5 decades.

THE CONTINUING CONTROVERSY ABOUT JOINT PROGRAMS

Although there appears to have been a plan to develop a joint J.D./ Ph.D. program in law and the social sciences at Northwestern University in the early 1970s (Kolasa, 1972), it is acknowledged that the first law and psychology program began at the University of Nebraska in 1974 (Melton, 1990). Since that time, the Nebraska program and the others that followed in the 1970s have generated a considerable amount of comment, criticism, and controversy. Despite this extended attention, and because "without doubt, the most extensive psycholegal training is to be found in joint-degree psychology-law doctorate programs" (Freeman & Roesch, 1992, p. 568), they are worth analyzing in some detail.

DEFINITIONS AND AIMS

I will limit discussion to those joint programs that fit the following criteria:

1. Students are enrolled simultaneously in a J.D. program at an accredited law school and a doctoral program (either Ph.D. or Psy.D.) in psychology.
2. The program is led by an individual designated as its director or coordinator.
3. The program contains an identifiable and integrative law and psychology curriculum in addition to ensuring that students complete all formal requirements toward the J.D. and doctoral degrees.

Roesch et al. (1986) elucidated three specific aims of these programs that are helpful in defining them. One is the epistemological aim. Joint programs, they suggest, teach more than the content of the two distinct disciplines of law and psychology. "Joint degree students may [also] learn a mode of thought and inquiry which is *neither* legal nor scientific, but an amalgam or synthesis or elements of both" (Roesch et al. 1986, p. 91); that is, these students are "trilingual." Second, is the aim of producing graduates who can further certain social objectives:

> Joint-degree programs seek to produce professionals and researchers who will respond to unmet needs of society. One of these presumed needs is for professionals who can analyze policy and implement policy change, in areas where human behavior and functioning are the central policy concern. Another is for the researcher who can provide scientific information, acquired, analyzed, and interpreted in ways which speak as clearly and directly as possible to legal and policy concerns. Finally, some joint-degree students are expected to devote their careers, or portions of them, to teaching future joint-degree students. (Roesch et al., 1986, p. 91)

The third aim is for their students to develop a unique professional identity. Given their dual perspectives, graduates from joint degree programs "can be expected to produce a different vision of objectives and solutions to problems" (Roesch et al., 1986, pp. 91–92) compared with their counterparts trained solely in law or psychology.

These limiting criteria and specific aims create two important distinctions. First, these programs do not encompass joint programs offering nondoctoral graduate degrees, like a master of arts in psychology or the master of legal studies, a 1-year degree granted by law schools that does not prepare students to practice law (see Ogloff et al., 1996; Tomkins & Ogloff, 1990, for a compilation of these programs). Second, as I have defined them, joint programs are differentiated from dual degree programs. Dual degree programs are neither conceptually organized nor coordinated. Administrators may allow students to enroll for both degrees, but the universities that offer them take a predominantly laissez-fire attitude toward the students. Students become responsible for arranging the curriculum and integrating what they have learned. Both of these kinds of programs are, in turn, distinguished from the approach of individuals who have on their own pursued degrees in law and psychology, at different times and often at separate institutions.

Using the criteria I have stated, only four programs in North America currently meet the definition of a joint program (although each university may have its own idiosyncratic nomenclature). They are the programs at the University of Nebraska, the University of Arizona, the Medical College of Pennsylvania–Hahnemann University (MCPHU) and Villanova Law School (VLS), and Widener University. At one point, the Johns Hopkins University Department of Psychology and the University of Maryland School of Law also had a joint program (that I coordinated), but is has since been discontinued (Tomkins & Ogloff, 1990). The MCPHU-VLS program is different from the other three because it is the only one whose students are enrolled simultaneously at two, albeit cooperative, universities. The Widener Program is distinguished by two facts. First, its director, Amiram Elwork, is the only program head who is trained solely in psychology (at the University of Nebraska), and it is the only one to offer the Psy.D. rather than the Ph.D.

The graduates of joint degree programs are different from many of the current leaders in law and psychology who attained both degrees but at different schools and at different times. As a personal example, I obtained my Ph.D. from New York University in 1965, practiced psychology for 8 years, and graduated from Yale Law School in 1976. Steven Penrod, now the director of the Nebraska program, received his doctorate in social psychology from Harvard in 1979 after obtaining his law degree from Harvard in 1974. Bruce Sales, the founding director of the Nebraska program and now the head of the joint program at the University of Arizona, received his Ph.D. from the University of Rochester in 1971 and his J.D. from Northwestern University in 1973. It is interesting to note, therefore, that none of the current directors of the four formal joint programs I have identified were trained in joint programs.

The four programs vary in the kinds of lawyer-psychologists they train. Some may prepare primarily researchers who concentrate in social, developmental, or experimental psychology; some may prepare students primarily for health and mental health policy positions; some are devoted solely to producing scientist-practitioners who concentrate their efforts in clinical psychology; and some may have more than one purpose. "Although the specific training goals of the programs may vary, they share the common goal of training scholars and practitioners interested in research and policy careers who will produce theoretically and methodologically sophisticated research integrating the psychology, law, and policy interface" (Ogloff et al., 1996, p. 217). "They tend to produce lawyer-psychologists who can bring the information base, research methods, and concerns of psychology to bear upon questions of law and policy" (Roesch et al., 1986, p. 89).

BENEFITS AND COSTS

Given their aims, goal, and purposes, there appear to be many advantages of joint degree training programs. "It is believed that providing students with standard and complete training in law, in psychology, and in law and psychology, gives them an understanding and insight into the field of psychology and law that is comprehensive and unique" (Ogloff et al., 1996, p. 217). The uniqueness of this training permits graduates to pursue careers in settings that singly trained graduates would find it difficult or impossible to enter (Hafemeister et al., 1990; Melton, 1987b, 1990). It is more likely, for example, that joint degree alumni would become mental health policy administrators, identify and investigate areas of law that do not bear an obvious link to psychology (Ogloff et al., 1996), or "contribute to the formal education of legal professionals" (Otto et al., 1990, p. 222).

Despite these benefits and the fact that joint training programs are now almost a quarter of a century old, since their inception commentators have been skeptical of, if not concerned and critical about, them. For example, a commonly noted disadvantage of joint programs "is the enormous commitment of time and effort it requires" (Hafemeister et al., 1990, p. 281). There is no gainsaying the fact that all joint programs require from 6 to 7 years to complete (including, for those enrolled in J.D./Ph.D. programs specializing in clinical psychology, a full-time 1-year internship). It is also true that students must find the means to pay tuition to two institutions at the same time, although some programs, such as the MCPHU-VLS programs, have developed innovative financial arrangements that obviate the need for students to pay law school tuition or take out loans while they pursue both degrees.

Because students must take the full sequence of law school courses to become eligible for the J.D., they may despair that some of their training is wasteful. For example, they may find such courses as Trusts and Estates, Corporations, Antitrust Law, or Federal Income Tax—which most law schools require or strongly recommend—relatively useless (Poythress, 1979), although I believe these and similar courses may offer unmined opportunities for psycholegal analysis and research. If readers will forgive another personal note, as an example, the first paper I ever presented in law and psychology was a presentation at APA on the application of contract law principles to the practice of psychotherapy (Bersoff, 1974).

The most pervasive concerns have come from those who train forensic psychologists. There is a view that "good courtroom consultation does not require extensive legal training and that if legal training either inhibits or replaces the consultant's psychological perspectives it can limit his or her contributions" (Dillehay & Nietzel, 1986, p. 168). Particularly because of the breadth and length of legal training, Otto et al. (1990) asserted that "there is little reason to believe that both degrees are necessary for competent forensic practice" (p. 220). Certainly, given the scarcity of joint programs and the limited number of applicants admitted each year (from one to six, depending on program and area of training), "such programs ... may never meet the needs of a sizable number of psychologists who desire or are destined to practice in the forensic area" (Poythress, 1979, p. 617). For students whose goals for forensic practice are clear, it may be more efficient to enroll in doctoral programs whose aims and curricula are designed to produce forensic clinicians (see Fenster et al., 1975; Freeman & Roesch, 1992; Poythress, 1979, for examples).

As the founder of one joint program and the current director of another, I, of course, believe that the advantages of integrated training outweigh its cost for the appropriate student. There is a concern, however, I have about joint programs that has been largely ignored. One of the great values of joint training is that it produces people who are comfortable and conversant in two divergent languages—that of science and that of law. Thus, graduates have the potential of serving as translators for the respective members of these two jargon-filled and technical fields. Graduates of J.D./doctoral programs can translate legal principles for psychologists, helping them to understand the meaning and implications of such relevant concepts as due process, equal protection, informed consent, and insanity and the impact of the legal system on the practice of psychology. Conversely, these graduates can help inform law students, law professors, lawyers, and judges about the meaning of such legally relevant terms as falsifiability, Type I and Type II errors, multivariate analysis, test validity, psychosis, or the applicability of research on memory, perception, and group dynamics to such legal problems as eyewitness identification, the constitutionality of nonunanimous juries, or the validity of certain exculpatory "syndromes."

The problem with realizing this role is that entry into law and psychology, respectively, is controlled by different criteria. By and large, a graduate of any APA-accredited professional program, with an internship from an APA-accredited facility, particularly with a proven record of research, will be eligible for employment in most academic institutions. Law, on the other hand, with a longer history, traditionally has been a highly elitist profession. Entry as an associate into the large, most prestigious law firms or as a professor behind the ivy-covered walls of almost any law school is carefully controlled (Tomkins & Ogloff, 1990). These positions are almost exclusively reserved for graduates from those institutions denominated as "national law schools," who have succeeded in doing better than 90% of their classmates, have been elected to law review, and have clerked for federal court judges. Although students in joint programs are eligible for election to law review and may graduate in the top 10% of their class, none of the law schools associated with joint programs are viewed as being in the highest echelons of law schools. They are, in the main, law schools with solid regional reputations in the middle to upper middle ranks of law schools, but they cannot compete in prestige with such institutions as Yale, Harvard, Chicago, or Columbia.

It may be that for those students who wish to enter academia or practice law in the most elite law firms, training in joint programs may do them a disservice. Because of the highly competitive nature of these programs and the small number of students they accept each year, applicants to joint programs tend to be exceptionally bright with credentials that can compete easily with J.D.-only applicants. Thus, they would have an excellent chance for admission to national law schools. This is an opportunity they lose, however, by restricting themselves to law schools that happen to collaborate in joint degree programs (Bersoff, 1983; Roesch et al., 1986).

Melton (1987b), himself a former director of a joint program, remained skeptical that such training is essential: "Having both degrees is unnecessary for making a contribution to psycholegal studies. Indeed, expertise in one discipline with a *basic* knowledge in the other is probably sufficient" (p. 684; to the same effect see, e.g., Hafemeister et al., 1990; Otto et al., 1990; Roesch et al., 1986). Whether one agrees with these assessments or is a committed advocate of joint programs, admittedly, their worth is still unproven. It has been almost 25 years since the first joint program was developed, and our profession still has "no empirical evidence that full training in any two disciplines produces more insightful contributions to society" (Roesch et al., 1986, p. 100). J.D./doctoral programs in law and psychology remain "a fascinating experiment" (Roesch et al. 1986, p. 101).

I cannot but agree that we need to expend a great deal more effort in evaluating these programs (Melton, 1987b; Ogloff et al., 1986). Nevertheless, students and graduates of these programs concur, at least as measured by the only survey of these populations (Hafemeister et al., 1990), that despite their being "time-consuming, expensive, and sometimes lacking precise definition ... joint degree ... law/psychology programs provide unique insights, skills, and opportunities for its (sic) participants" (Hafemeister et al., 1990, p. 282). They remain the most "direct route to achieving law/psychology integration" (Tomkins & Ogloff, 1990, p. 208).

PREPARING FOR THE NEXT CENTURY

In the concluding section of this chapter, I want to address two developments to which I earlier promised I would return. Both should have major influences on education and training in law and psychology in the foreseeable future. The first is relevant to forensic psychology, and the second is relevant to teaching our law-oriented colleagues about the contributions of psychology to their practice.

Forensic Psychology

An objective observer, I think, would agree that "graduate programs in psychology have not developed the specialized forensic training that might allow practicing psychologists to approximate the level of bona fide experience in the forensic area that the courts have come to assume follows simply from the attainment of the doctorate" (Poythress, 1979, p. 613). Yet, as little as 20 years ago, there were very few professional training programs that were devoted to producing forensic practitioners (Fenster et al., 1975; Fowler & Brodsky, 1978; Poythress, 1979). Although there has been some delineation of training models since that time (Freeman & Roesch, 1992; Roesch et al., 1986), it is still true that "in forensic psychology, there is as yet no generally accepted and well-codified training model such as the scientist-practitioner or "Boulder model" of clinical training, with its agreed-upon array of coursework, practicum training and standards for accreditation" (Freeman & Roesch, 1992, p. 568).

Moreover, there has been a plethora of critical comment concerning the value of the forensic clinician's work (e.g., Bersoff, 1992; Faust & Ziskin, 1988; Melton, Petrila, Poythress, & Slobogin, 1997; Morse, 1978; Poythress, 1982; Shapiro, 1991; Ziskin, 1995). Clinicians who testify as expert witnesses have been accused of using poorly validated instruments; being ignorant of the relevant legal criteria to be applied to their opinions; intruding unduly into the prerogatives of the judge and jury by offering opinions on what are essentially legal, not psychological, questions; offering insufficient or poorly supported opinions in those domains where their expertise might help; and providing reports that answer irrelevant questions (e.g., Bersoff, 1992; Grisso, 1986; Morse, 1978)

Poythress (1979) and Heilbrun (1988) have offered stratified models of training at the didactic and experiential levels for budding forensic clinicians, although neither have garnered universal approbation (Otto et al., 1990). Yet, they anticipated an event that will have a considerable impact on the education of forensic practitioners. In February 1995, the American Psychological Association created a Commission for the Recognition of

Specialties and Proficiencies in Professional Psychology (CRSPPP). One of the primary roles of CRSPPP is to review petitions from organizations requesting APA to recognize a professional specialty or proficiency, based on principles adopted by the APA, and to then either deny or recommend approval of a petition. If the commission recommends approval, it is forwarded to the APA Council of Representatives for final approval or rejection. All approved proficiencies and specialties will be reviewed for reaffirmation no less than every 7 years.

CRSPPP defines a *proficiency* as "a circumscribed activity in the general practice of professional psychology" (Joint Interim Committee, 1995a, p. 1). A *specialty* is "a defined area of psychological practice which requires advanced knowledge and skills acquired through an organized sequence of education and training ... subsequent to the acquisition of core scientific and professional foundations in psychology" (Joint Interim Committee, 1995b, p. 2). It is envisioned that proficiency training may be obtained as a component of a doctoral or postdoctoral program or though extensive continuing education. Specialties, by contrast, are acquired only through an extensive, organized, and sequential body of training in doctoral or postdoctoral programs.

Clearly, forensic psychology is eligible for denomination as a proficiency and a specialty. Because the establishment of CRSPPP was known to the participants at the Villanova Conference, attendees sought to develop a model of forensic training that would fit within this emerging development. Several of the working groups conferring independently developed a tri-level hierarchy of skills, knowledges, and abilities that could be applied to forensic psychology. As one model, one could envision the levels of training that follow.

Entry Level (the Generally Trained Professional Psychologist)

Beyond general clinical training, all professional psychologists would receive basic education in forensic psychology. Students would receive didactic instruction about the fundamental issues in law and psychology, become knowledgeable about ethical principles related to forensic practice (APA, 1992; CEGFP, 1991), be placed in practica and internships with some forensic experience, and be responsible for keeping abreast of important, current psycholegal developments. This minimal level of law-related training is essential because "it would be a mistake ... to believe that only those psychologists who identify themselves as *forensic mental health professionals* will find themselves involved with the law. Every psychologist ... is a potential expert witness, and each much be prepared to interact with the legal system" (Bersoff, 1995a, p. 416; italics in original).

Proficiency Level

Psychologists attaining this mid-level expertise may be trained through general professional programs, with an emphasis on forensics; training programs specializing in forensic psychology; or, for already trained clinicians, through extensive continuing education or postdoctoral programs. There would be greater exposure to legal concepts (perhaps even by taking certain courses in a cooperating law school); opportunities to improve skills in assessing and treating forensic clients; development of the crucial ability to write psychological reports that respond to, inform, and answer specific legal questions in a sophisticated and ethical manner; training in testifying as an expert witness and consulting with legal counsel; and required rotations in facilities at the practicum and internship levels that provide forensic experience.

Specialty Level

Those professional psychologists wishing to attain the highest level of training would almost assuredly be educated in programs designated as dedicated to producing forensic psychologists. For entering graduate students, this training would be provided through doctoral programs; for experienced clinicians, in extended postdoctoral or doctoral programs that lead to respecialization. In any event, these programs would have an integrated, carefully developed sequence of training with an identifiable, experienced, forensic faculty with recognized credentials. Beyond intensive and in-depth understanding of case law and extensive training in forensic skills, the psychologist at the specialist level would also be exposed to a variety of populations, for example, children, sex offenders, victims of sexual offenders, adults who claim they are incompetent to stand trial, elderly adults for whom guardianship or conservatorship is a possibility, and those for whom civil commitment is sought. It is expected that forensic specialists would be responsible for pursuing continuing professional development and would become fellows of the APA and attain the diplomate in forensic psychology.

It is hoped that these levels of training will be fleshed out more fully in the book that is planned as one of the products of the Villanova Conference. In fact, it is anticipated that the contributors will delineate suggested curricula and practical experiences, not only for forensic psychology, but also for graduate training in law and the social sciences as well. If these hopes are fulfilled, we may see in the near future not *a* Boulder-like model, but the Villanova *models* of training in law and psychology.

COOPERATIVE EDUCATION WITH THE LEGAL PROFESSION

I began this chapter with material gleaned from law professors extolling the value and utility of the social sciences in legal training. Later on, I decried the naiveté, the studied ignorance about psychology of those who practice law and administer the legal system. Thus, it is fitting that I conclude the substantive portion of the chapter with a development that makes me more optimistic that there may be greater collaboration and opportunities for learning between the two professions.

One of the more important outgrowths of the Villanova Conference was the development and implementation of a conference offering continuing education credits for psychologists and lawyers. That conference was held in Los Angeles from April 17–20, 1997. It was organized by the American Bar Association Family Law Section and a subcommittee of the APA's Committee on Legal Issues (COLI), including William Foote (former chair of COLI), Ann Stanton, and Elliot Silverstein. I served as co-chair of the joint committee, as a representative from the APA Board of Directors.

The focus of the conference was on children and divorce. Eight crucial topics were chosen for joint discussion: (a) the qualifications of psychologists performing child custody evaluations and the fundamental ethical constraints in doing those evaluations (including the turning over of raw test data, an issue that has created conflict between lawyers and psychologists); (b) the nature of child custody evaluations, including material on current and widely used instruments developed for that purpose and methods for communicating their results; (c) an extensive analysis of custody arrangements; (d) the relationship of child sex abuse allegations to custody evaluations, including material on the suggestibility of children's memories; (e) working with nontraditional custodians, including gay and lesbian parents, parents with disabilities, and grandparents; (f) alternative dispute resolution in family law; (g) educating parents about "do's and dont's" in custody dispute cases; and (h) how lawyers can collaborate with expert forensic psychologists for maximum mutual effectiveness.

By all accounts, the conference was a huge success, attended by 400 psychologists and 600 lawyers. It provided time for extensive education, discussion, and argument about these core issues in child custody determinations. A similar conference is planned for 1999 with the ABA's Section on Criminal Law, and there are hopes that one can also be held with the Section on Employment Law.

The concept of collaborative interdisciplinary meetings such as these should be reinforced for two reasons. First, an essential element of training in any profession is continuing education (APA Education Directorate, 1995). Second, in our field, psychologists and lawyers alike talk primarily to their own colleagues. Both professions tend to be ignorant about the serious issues that confront each of them. The Los Angeles Conference can become a model for chipping away at the formidable barriers that imprison each profession in its own stereotypes. Perhaps we can learn to alter our respective perceptions that all lawyers are "sharks" and all psychologists are "whores."

CONCLUSION

There is a curious anomaly in law and psychology. The field itself is almost 100 years old. Yet, formal education and training in psycholegal studies—whether it is joint degree training, graduate education in law and the social sciences, or programs for forensic professionals—is only a bit more than 2 decades old. Its longevity gives the field a venerable history to use as a backdrop; the youth of its educational endeavors gives its participants, trainers, and students, the opportunity to develop creative models not constrained by hoary traditionalism. I hope that readers of this chapter will be stimulated to contribute to this endeavor.

REFERENCES

American Psychiatric Association. (1994). *Diagnostic and statistical manual* (4th ed.). Washington, DC: Author.

American Psychological Association. (1992). Ethical principles of psychologists and code of conduct. *American Psychologist, 47,* 1597–1611.

American Psychological Association Education Directorate. (1995). *Education and training beyond the doctoral degree.* Madison, CT: International Universities Press.

Bartol, C. R. (1983). *Psychology and American law.* Belmont, CA: Wadsworth.

Berger v. Board of Psychologist Examiners, 521 F.2d 1056 (D. C. Cir. 1975).

Bersoff, D. N. (1974, August). Child advocacy in everyday practice: A model borrowed from law. In S. Levine (Chair), *And how shall the children be protected?* Symposium presented at the meeting of the American Psychological Association, New Orleans, LA.

Bersoff, D. N. (1983, August). Psychology in the legal realm. In B. D. Sales (Chair), *Psychology and law training models.* Symposium presented at the meeting of the American Psychological Association, Anaheim, CA.

Bersoff, D. N. (1986). Psychologists and the judicial system: Broader perspectives. *Law and Human Behavior, 10,* 151–165.

Bersoff, D. N. (1992). Judicial deference to nonlegal decision makers: Imposing simplistic solutions on problems of cognitive complexity in mental disability law. *Southern Methodist University Law Review, 46,* 329–372.

Bersoff, D. N. (1995a). *Ethical conflicts in psychology.* Washington, DC: American Psychological Association.

Bersoff, D. N. (1995b, May). *Facts, faults, and fantasies.* Keynote address presented at the National Invitational Conference on Education and Training in Law & Psychology, Villanova, PA.

Bersoff, D. N., & Glass, D. J. (1995). The not-so *Weisman*: The Supreme Court's continuing misuse of social science research. *University of Chicago Law School Roundtable, 2,* 279–302.

Bersoff, D., Goodman-Delahunty, J., Grisso, T., Hans, V. P., Roesch, R., & Poythress, N. G. (1997). Training in law and psychology: Models from the Villanova conference. *American Psychologist, 52,* 1301–1310.

Brown v. Board of Education, 375 U.S. 483 (1954).

Cahn, E. (1955). Jurisprudence. *New York University Law Review, 30,* 150–169.

Cantrell, P. J., & Hall, R. G. (1995). *Internship and postdoctoral programs in professional psychology* (24th ed.). Washington, DC: Association of Postdoctoral & Internship Centers.

Committee on Ethical Guidelines for Forensic Psychologists. (1991). Specialty guidelines for forensic psychologists. *Law and Human Behavior, 15,* 655–665.

Craig v. Boren, 429 U.S. 190 (1976).

Dillehay, R. C., & Nietzel, M. (1986). Psychological consultation in trial preparation and conduct. In M. F. Kaplan (Ed.), *The impact of social psychology on procedural justice* (pp. 167–193). Springfield, IL: Thomas.

Dressler, J. (1987). Justifications and excuses: A brief review of the literature. *Wayne Law Review, 33,* 1155–1175.

Ellison, K. W., & Buckhout, R. (1981). *Psychology and criminal justice.* New York: Harper & Row.

Faust, D., & Ziskin, J. (1988). The expert witness in psychology and psychiatry. *Science, 241,* 31–35.

Fenster, A., Litwack, T. R., & Symonds, M. (1975). The making of a forensic psychologist: Needs and goals for doctoral training. *Professional Psychology, 6,* 457–467.

Foley, L. A. (1993). *A psychological view of the legal system.* Madison, WI: WCB Brown & Benchmark.

Foote, C. (1958). The Law and Behavioral Science Project at the University of Pennsylvania: Family and criminal law. *Journal of Legal Education, 11,* 80–86.

Fowler, R. D., & Brodsky, S. L. (1978). Development of a correctional-clinical psychology program. *Professional Psychology, 9,* 440–447.

Freeman, R. J., & Roesch, R. (1992). Psycholegal education: Training for forum and function. In D. K. Kagehiro & W. S. Laufer (Eds.), *Handbook of psychology and law* (pp. 567–576). New York: Springer-Verlag.

Freud, S. (1959). Psycho-analysis and the ascertaining of truth in courts of law. In E. Jones (Ed.), *Collected papers of Sigmund Freud* (Vol. 2, pp. 13–24). New York: Basic Books. (original work published in 1906)

Goldberg, S. (1994). *Culture clash: Law and science in America.* New York: New York University Press.

Goldenberg, E. E. (1978). Teaching mental health and law: A reply to Shealey. *Professional Psychology, 9,* 174–175.

Grisso, T. (1986). *Evaluating competencies: Forensic assessments and instruments.* New York: Plenum Press.

Grisso, T. (1991). A developmental history of the American Psychology-Law Society. *Law and Human Behavior, 15,* 213–232.

Grisso, T., Sales, B. D., Bayless, S. (1982). Law-related courses and programs in graduate psychology departments. *American Psychologist, 37,* 267–278.

Hafemeister, T. L., Ogloff, J. R. P., & Small, M. A. (1990). Training and careers in law and psychology: The perspectives of students and graduates of dual degree programs. *Behavioral Sciences and the Law, 8,* 263–283.

Haney, C. (1980). Psychology and legal change: On the limits of factual jurisprudence. *Law and Human Behavior, 4,* 147–200.

Haney, C. (1993). Psychology and legal change: The impact of a decade. *Law and Human Behavior, 17,* 371–398.

Heilbrun, K. S. (1988, August). *The role of the predoctoral clinical internship in forensic training.* Paper presented at the annual meeting of the American Psychological Association, Atlanta, GA.

Heilbrun, K. S., & Annis, L. V. (1988). Research and training in forensic psychology: National survey of forensic facilities. *Professional Psychology: Research and Practice, 19,* 211–215.

Horowitz, I. A., & Willging, T. E. (1984). *The psychology of law: Integrations and applications.* Boston: Little, Brown.

Joint Interim Committee for the Identification and Recognition of Specialties and Proficiencies. (1995a). *Principles for the recognition of proficiencies in psychology.* (Available from the American Psychological Association, 750 First St., NW, Washington, DC 20002).

Joint Interim Committee for the Identification and Recognition of Specialties and Proficiencies. (1995b). *Principles for the recognition of specialties in psychology.* (Available from the American Psychological Association, 750 First St., NW, Washington, DC 20002).

Kalven, H. (1958). Some comments on the Law and Behavioral Science Project at the University of Pennsylvania. *Journal of Legal Education, 11,* 94–99.

Kaslow, F. W., & Abrams, J. C. (1976). Forensic psychology and criminal justice: An evolving subspecialty at Hahnemann Medical College. *Professional Psychology, 7,* 445–452.

Keller, P. (1979, Nov.–Dec.). Vita: Hugo Muntersberg. *Harvard Magazine, 52,* 48.

Kelman, M. (1981). Interpretive construction in the substantive criminal law. *Standard Law Review, 33,* 591–673.

Kolasa, B. J. (1972). Psychology and law. *American Psychologist, 27,* 499–503.

Lawlor, R. J., Siskind, G., & Brooks, J. (1981). Forensic training at internships: Update and criticism of current unspecified training models. *Professional Psychology, 12,* 400–405.

Levin, A. L. (1958). The Law and Behavioral Science Project at the University of Pennsylvania: Evidence. *Journal of Legal Education, 11,* 87–93.

Levine, D., Wilson, K., & Sales, B. D. (1980). An exploratory assessment of APA internships with legal/forensic experiences. *Professional Psychology, 11,* 64–71.

Lockhart, v. McCree, 476 U.S. 162 (1986).

Loh, W. (1981). Psycholegal research: Past and present. *Michigan Law Review, 79,* 659–707.

Loh, W. (1984). *Social research in the judicial process.* New York: Russell Sage Foundation.

Melton, G. B. (1987a). Bringing psychology to the legal system: Opportunities, obstacles, and efficacy. *American Psychologist, 42,* 488–495.

Melton, G. B. (1987b). Training in psychology and law. In I. B. Weiner & A. K. Hess (Eds.), *Handbook of forensic psychology* (pp. 681–697). New York: Wiley.

Melton, G. B. (1990). Realism in psychology and humanism in law: Psycholegal studies at Nebraska. *Nebraska Law Review, 69,* 251–277.

Melton, G. B., Monahan, J., & Saks, M. J. (1987). Psychologists as law professors. *American Psychologist, 42,* 502–509.

Melton, G. B., Petrila, J., Poythress, N., & Slobogin, C. (1997). *Psychological evaluation for the courts: A handbook for mental health professionals and lawyers* (2nd ed.). New York: Guilford Press.

Monahan, J., & Loftus, E. (1982). The psychology of law. In M. L. Rosenzweig & L. W. Porter (Eds.), *Annual review of psychology* (Vol. 33, pp. 441–475). Palo Alto, CA: Annual Reviews.

Monahan, J., & Walker, L. (1985). Teaching social science in law: An alternative to "Law and Society." *Journal of Legal Education, 35,* 478–482.

Monahan, J., & Walker, L. (1994). *Social science in law: Cases and materials* (3rd ed.). Westbury, NY: Foundation Press.

Morse, S. J. (1978). Law and mental health professionals. The limits of expertise. *Professional Psychology, 9,* 389–399.

Morse, S. J. (1984). Undiminished confusion in diminished capacity. *Journal of Criminal Law and Criminology, 75,* 1–55.

Morse, S. J. (1995). The "new syndrome excuse syndrome." *Criminal Justice Ethics, 14*, 3–15.
Munsterberg, H. (1908). *On the witness stand: Essays on psychology and crime.* New York: Doubleday.
Ogloff, J. R. P., Tomkins, A. J., & Bersoff, D. N. (1996). Education and training in psychology and law/criminal justice. *Criminal Justice and Behavior, 23*, 200–235.
Otto, R. K., Heilbrun, K., & Grisso, T. (1990). Training and credentialing in forensic psychology. *Behavioral Sciences and the Law, 8*, 217–231.
Parham v. J. R., 442 U.S. 584 (1979).
Poythress, N. G. (1979). A proposal for training in forensic psychology. *American Psychologist, 34*, 612–621.
Poythress, N. G. (1982). Concerning reform in expert testimony: An open letter from a practicing psychology. *Law and Human Behavior, 6*, 39–44.
Raimy, V. (Ed.). (1950). *Training in clinical psychology.* NY: Prentice-Hall.
Roesch, R. (1995). Creating change in the legal system: Contributions from community psychology. *Law and Human Behavior, 19*, 325–343.
Roesch, R., Grisso, T., & Poythress, N. G. (1986). Training programs, courses, and workshops in psychology and law. In M. F. Kaplan (Ed.), *The impact of social psychology and procedural justice* (pp. 83–108). Springfield, IL: Thomas.
Saks, M. J. (1986). The law does not live by eyewitness testimony alone. *Law and Human Behavior, 10*, 279–280.
Saks, M. J. (1989). Legal policy analysis and evaluation. *American Psychologist, 44*, 1110–1117.
Saks, M. J., & Baron, C. (1980). *The use/nonuse/misuse of applied social research in the courts.* Cambridge, MA: Abt Books.
Sales, B. D., & VandenBos, G. R. (Eds.). (1994). *Psychology in litigation and legislation.* Washington, DC: American Psychological Association.
Schierer, C. J., & Hammonds, B. J. (Eds.). (1983). *The master lecture series: Vol. 2. Psychology and the law.* Washington, DC: American Psychological Association.
Schlegel, J. (1979). American legal realism and empirical social science: From the Yale experience. *Buffalo Law Review, 28*, 459–586.
Schlegel, J. (1995). *American legal realism and empirical social science.* Chapel Hill: University of North Carolina Press.
Shapiro, D. (1991). *Forensic psychological assessment.* Boston: Allyn & Bacon.
Tanford, J. A. (1990). The limits of a scientific jurisprudence: The Supreme Court and psychology. *Indiana Law Journal, 66*, 137–173.
Tapp, J. L. (1976). Psychology and law. An overture. In M. L. Rosenzweig & L. W. Porter (Eds.), *Annual review of psychology* (Vol. 27, pp. 359–404). Palo Alto, CA: Annual Reviews.
Tomkins, A. J., & Ogloff, J. R. P. (1990). Training and career options in psychology and law. *Behavioral Sciences and the Law, 8*, 205–216.
Tomkins, A. J., & Oursland, K. (1991). Social and social scientific perspectives in judicial interpretations of the Constitution: A historical view and an overview. *Law and Human Behavior, 15*, 101–120.
Tremper, C. R. (1987). Organized psychology's efforts to influence judicial policymaking. *American Psychologist, 42*, 496–501.
Van den Haag, E. (1960). Social science testimony in the desegregation cases: A reply to Professor Kenneth Clark. *Villanova Law Review, 6*, 69–79.
Wigmore, J. (1909). Professor Munsterberg and the psychology of testimony: Being a report of the case of Cokestone v. Munsterberg. *Illinois Law Review, 3*, 399–445.
Wrightsman, L., Nietzel, M., & Fortune, W. (1998). *Psychology and the legal system* (4th ed.). Pacific Grove, CA: Brooks/Cole.
Ziskin, J. (1995). *Coping with psychiatric and psychological testimony* (5th ed.). Beverly Hills, CA: Law & Psychology Press.

11

Ethical and Legal Contours of Forensic Psychology

JAMES R. P. OGLOFF

Psychologists who work in legal contexts, either as practitioners or researchers, often find themselves in situations in which the traditional ethical and legal principles that govern their work may apply somewhat differently (e.g., Bednar, Bednar, Lambert, & Waite, 1991; Pope & Vasquez, 1991). Additional related ethical and legal issues may also arise (see generally, Ogloff, 1995). It has been noted that in many jurisdictions in North American, ethics complaints against psychologists who work in forensic contexts are among the most common made to licensing boards. Most psychologists traditionally have received little training in legal psychology generally or in forensic psychology more particularly (Bersoff et al., 1997; Ogloff, 1990; Ogloff, Tomkins, & Bersoff, 1996; Otto, Heilbrun, & Grisso, 1990; Tomkins & Ogloff, 1990). It is even rarer that they will have been exposed to courses or other forms of formal education regarding ethical issues in forensic contexts.

For the purposes of this chapter, the term *forensic psychologist* refers to "any psychologist, experimental or clinical, who specializes in producing or communicating psychological research or assessment information intended for application to legal issues" (Grisso, 1987, p. 831). The Specialty Guidelines for Forensic Psychologists (Committee on Ethical Guidelines

JAMES R. P. OGLOFF • Graduate Program in Law and Psychology, Simon Fraser University, Burnaby, British Columbia, V5A 1S6, Canada.

Psychology and Law: The State of the Discipline, edited by Ronald Roesch, Stephen D. Hart, and James R. P. Ogloff. Kluwer Academic/Plenum Publishers, New York, 1999.

for Forensic Psychologists, 1991) provide a similar definition for *forensic psychology* and *forensic psychologist*, as follows:

> "Forensic psychology" means all forms of professional psychological conduct when acting, with definable foreknowledge, as a psychological expert on explicitly psycholegal issues, in direct assistance to courts, parties to legal proceedings, correctional and forensic mental health facilities, and administrative, judicial, and legislative agencies acting in an adjudicative capacity" (Specialty Guideline I[B][1][c], p. 657).

> "Forensic psychologist" means psychologists who regularly engage in the practice of forensic psychology as defined in I(B)(1)(b)" (Specialty Guideline I[B][1][b], p. 657).

The information in this chapter is directed toward forensic psychologists; however, many other psychologists occasionally work in a legal context or find their work employed in the law (Bersoff, 1995). Although the material discussed may not be directly applicable to nonforensic psychologists, it will provide some assistance to these psychologists whose work occasionally takes them into a legal context.

Many of the ethical issues in forensic settings differ from those in traditional settings; however, this has been realized and redressed only recently (see American Psychological Association, 1992; Committee on Ethical Guidelines for Forensic Psychologists, 1991). Indeed, it was not until the 1992 revision of the American Psychological Association's "Ethical Principles of Psychologists and Code of Conduct" that the unique issues arising in forensic psychology were directly addressed (Ethical Standards 7.01–7.06). Even the revised guidelines are narrow in scope and rather limited. By contrast, the "Specialty Guidelines for Forensic Psychologists" ("Specialty Guidelines") that have been promulgated by the American Psychology–Law Society and the American Academy of Forensic Psychology (Committee on Ethical Guidelines for Forensic Psychologists, 1991) provide a more comprehensive overview of the plethora of ethical issues forensic psychologists face. (The "Specialty Guidelines" are reprinted in the Appendix of this volume.)

Regardless of their role, forensic psychologists are still obligated to comply with general ethical guidelines, principles, and standards. For example, the "Ethical Principles of Psychologists and Code of Conduct" (1992) provide that "psychologists who perform forensic functions, such as assessments, interviews, consultations, reports, or expert testimony, must comply with all other provisions of this Ethics Code to the extent that they apply to such activities" (APA Standard 7.01). In addition, though, as the Ethics Code further provides, "psychologists base their forensic work on appropriate knowledge of and competence in the areas underlying such work, including specialized knowledge concerning special populations" (APA Standard 7.01).

The "Specialty Guidelines" "provide an aspirational model of desirable professional practice by psychologists, within any subdiscipline of psychology (e.g., clinical, developmental, social, experimental), when they are engaged regularly as experts and represent themselves as such, in an activity primarily intended to provide professional psychological expertise to the judicial system" (p. 656). Thus, psychologists are obligated to adhere to the standards provided in the "Ethical Principles of Psychologists and Code of Conduct" (1992), whereas the "specialty Guidelines" are aspirational in nature and "do not represent an official statement of the American Psychological Association" (p. 656).

Given the unique concerns that arise in forensic settings, it is important to provide some direction to psychologists about the related ethical and legal issues arising. A discussion of the general ethical principles of psychologists and their applicability in forensic contexts is presented in this chapter. In this discussion, the topics of "who is the client?," limits on competence and the scope of practice, and the psychology/patient relationship (including informed consent, confidentiality, and relationships with clients) are considered. Finally, attention is focused on the rather unique aspects of the duty to disclose information to protect third parties as it relates to the forensic setting.

AN INTRODUCTION TO ETHICS
AND THE SOURCE OF ETHICAL DILEMMAS

By virtue of their professional training and responsibilities and in order to comply with state and provincial licensing and regulatory bodies and regional and national professional associations, psychologists are bound by ethical guidelines and rules of conduct (Reaves & Ogloff, 1996a,b). As a result of these principles, psychologists who work in forensic contexts must be aware of their ethical obligations. Although I am optimistic that very few people enter the field of psychology or forensic psychology with "evil" motives, many psychologists generally have little understanding of the principles of law and ethics that affect them and their practices (e.g., Otto, Ogloff, & Small, 1991). Therefore, education about legal and ethical guidelines may help prevent some forensic psychologists from acting in an unethical manner or from defending themselves in court as a result of malpractice claims or the like. This chapter highlights some of the key ethical and legal principles with which forensic psychologists should be familiar.

The issues addressed in this chapter may differ somewhat across jurisdictions based on specific differences in law; therefore, the principles noted will be discussed in a general way. Although the regulatory bodies across jurisdictions have adopted any one (or combination) of a number of ethics codes and related guidelines, the ethical principles discussed in this chapter relate generally to all jurisdictions. It remains the ethical and legal obligation of individual psychologists, of course, to know and abide by the ethics codes extant in their jurisdictions and to become familiar with the principles that apply specifically to them. Furthermore, psychologists who belong to professional psychological associations are bound by the ethical codes of those associations (e.g., American Psychological Association, Canadian Psychological Association, American Psychology-Law Society, American Academy of Forensic Psychology).

If practitioners who violate ethical principles do not start out with evil motives, how is it that ethical dilemmas arise? Keith-Spiegel and Koocher (1985) suggested that ethical dilemmas may arise under a variety of conditions:

1. Unforeseeability of the ethical issue.
2. Underestimation of the implications and magnitude of an ethical issue.
3. Lack of alternatives to avoid or resolve the ethical dilemma.
4. The most appropriate resolution of an ethical dilemma may be unclear due to the unforeseeability of alternative courses of action.
5. Ethical guidelines or laws may simply not address the ethical dilemma.
6. Ethical dilemmas may occur whenever laws or ethical principles conflict with a psychologist's obligations to a client.
7. Psychologists may willfully or maliciously engage in behavior that they know violates laws or ethical principles.

As this list indicates, many ethical dilemmas may arise as a result of a lack of understanding of ethical guidelines and a lack of foresight in identifying alternative courses of action. With some consideration and planning, therapists may avoid entering situations that could result in unethical behavior (Tymchuk, 1989). It is unlikely, however, that the mere provision of information about ethics will help transform a psychologist who willfully or maliciously engages in unethical behavior. In those cases, the disciplinary provisions of licensing laws may be invoked.

GENERAL ETHICAL PRINCIPLES AND THEIR APPLICABILITY TO THE FORENSIC CONTEXT

As noted at the outset, there are a number of differences between the applicability of ethical principles in psychology for forensic and nonforensic settings. In this section, some of the fundamental principles of ethics for psychologists will be considered within forensic contexts.

WHO IS THE CLIENT?

In most traditional contexts for psychologists, the question of who is the client might seem obvious. Indeed, an adult proactively seeking the assistance of a psychologist would under many circumstances be considered the client or patient. As we shall see, though, in the forensic context it really is quite rare for the person being assessed or treated by the psychologist to be correctly referred to as the psychologist's client or patient. Concepts such as confidentiality and privilege arise out of the client's common law or statutorily guaranteed right to privacy (*Jaffee v. Redmoud*, 1996; Keith-Spiegel & Koocher, 1985; Reaves & Ogloff, 1996a). Therefore, it is of utmost importance that the forensic psychologist clarify who is the client and ensure that the person who is being assessed or treated is aware of the psychologist's obligations to the client (Monahan, 1980).

Examples from the private sector may be useful in making the distinction regarding who is the client. If a person hires a psychologist to perform psychological services for himself or herself, the person clearly is the client and has a right to the confidentiality that the law and the ethical obligations for psychologists require. However, if a person applies for a job, and as part of the employment screening process is required to visit a psychologist for an interview and some employment testing, the employer may well be the client. In such a case, the employer "owns" the confidentiality, and the psychologist must share results with the employer. Furthermore, the psychologist does not have an obligation to discuss the person's test results with him or her—although the psychologist will have an obligation to inform the person of this fact when obtaining consent for the interview and testing *prior* to beginning to work with the person. As these examples illustrate, the question of who is the client serves as the threshold issue in determining the nature of the psychologist's obligation to the "client" and "examinee" regarding confidentiality.

In many forensic contexts, the person being assessed or evaluated may not be the client. Instead, the forensic psychologist's services may have been contracted by a third party, such as a court, prison, or forensic hospital. In such cases, "the psychologist clarifies to the extent feasible, at the outset of the service, the nature of the relationship with each party. This clarification includes the role of the psychologist (such as therapist, organizational consultant, diagnostician, or expert witness), the probable uses of the services provided or the information obtained, and the fact that there may be limits to confidentiality" (APA Standard 1.21). Because the issue of who is the client has serious implications for the clarification of subsequent ethical and legal issues, the psychologist must constantly be aware of this question. The intricacies of these matters are revisited later in this chapter. I turn now to some other ethical issues of importance to forensic psychologists.

LIMITS ON THE SCOPE OF PRACTICE: COMPETENCE

The psychologist is ethically obligated to be professionally competent in any realm in which he or she works. For example, the APA Ethics Code requires that "psychologists provide services, teach, and conduct research only within the boundaries of their competence, based on their training, supervised experience, or appropriate professional experience" (APA Standard 1.04; see also APA Standard 7.01). Therefore, psychologists who work in the legal arena must have professional competence in forensic psychology generally. Furthermore, if the psychologist engages in psychological services that require more specialized training, the psychologist must also demonstrate professional competence in that area of sub-specialty (e.g., assessment and treatment of sexual offenders or forensic neuropsychological assessment).

As noted in the APA Ethics Code (Standard 1.04; see also, Specialty Guideline III), generally speaking, professional competence in an area of specialization may be obtained and demonstrated by a combination of the following factors: (a) education and training (graduate level courses, APA continuing education correspondence courses, continuing education workshops, etc.); (b) supervised experience by a registered psychologist with expertise in the area of specialization; and (c) reading and research in the area of specialization.

Because there is no clear litmus test for determining when, or if, one has attained professional competence in any given area, psychologists bear the burden of ensuring that their work falls within their realm of evidence, as provided for in the ethics codes. Readers are referred to Specialty Guideline III for the guidelines pertaining to competence. Here, though, it is important to highlight two points. First,

> Forensic psychologists have an obligation to present to the court, regarding the specific matters to which they will testify, the boundaries of their competence, the factual bases (knowledge, skill, experience, training, and education) for their qualification as an expert on the specific matters at issue. (Specialty Guideline III[B])

In addition to presenting the court with information about the boundaries of their competence, forensic psychologists are obligated to have a fundamental understanding of the legal and professional standards in their area (Specialty Guideline III[C]), and they must understand the legal rights of the parties with whom they come into contact to ensure that they do not abrogate those rights (Specialty Guideline III[D]).

LEGAL AND ETHICAL GUIDELINES GOVERNING
PSYCHOLOGY-PATIENT RELATIONSHIPS

Informed Consent

The doctrine of *violenti non fit iniuria*—no harm is done to one who consents—is the legal maxim that underlies the informed consent doctrine (Andrews, 1984; Appelbaum, 1984; Ogloff, 1995; Ogloff & Otto, 1991). To meet the requirements of informed consent, people who enter into evaluation or treatment (or research) must do so voluntarily, knowingly, and intelligently.

The "voluntariness" requirement demands that people are not manipulated or forced (e.g., with duress or powerful incentives) to participate in the psychological evaluation or treatment process. In criminal contexts, it may seem that defendants or offenders are being "coerced" to participate in assessments or treatment (e.g., they may be looked upon more favorably by the courts). However, the fact that they may refuse the contact with the psychologist—even though the alternatives may not be attractive—means that they are not, strictly speaking, being coerced to participate.

To satisfy the "knowing" requirement of the informed consent doctrine, the psychologist must make a full disclosure to the person being assessed or treated of the nature and purpose, procedure, risks and benefits, and alternatives with their risks and benefits. Consent may be handled by orally explaining the above informative to the person and obtaining his or her oral consent. In some institutions, the psychologist may supplement the oral consent with an informed consent form. However, the psychologist must not rely upon an informed consent form alone (Ogloff & Otto, 1991). Rather than serving as a legal contract outlining the nature and purpose of the services to be provided, the informed consent form merely serves to confirm that informed consent was obtained.

Finally, for the consent to be valid, a person must have the mental capacity to understand and make an intelligent informed decision of whether to participate in treatment based on the information provided by the therapist. Making an intelligent decision does not mean that the person needs to make a "rational" decision. Instead, it requires that she or he is able to understand the information provided by the psychologist and to balance the risks and benefits to arrive at a reasoned decision. If the person does not have the capacity to make an informed assessment or treatment decision, the psychologist must obtain consent from the legal substitute decision maker prior to beginning to work with the person (see also, APA Standard 4.02).

Under normal circumstances, the psychologist should obtain informed consent from the person being assessed or treated regardless of the purpose of the contact with the person. If the person being assessed is not the client, the psychologist still is ethically obligated to inform the person of the purpose and nature of the contact, ensuring that the person understands the assessment and other relevant issues (e.g., limits of confidentiality). Furthermore, the psychologist still must obtain the consent or assent of the person. If the person consents to the services the psychologist will offer, the psychologist may proceed with the assessment. If the person refuses to participate, the psychologist should not proceed but should inform the defendant to speak to her or his attorney about the matter.

In those circumstances when the psychologist is unable to examine the person, the psychologist must clarify "the impact of their limited information on the reliability and validity of their reports and testimony, and they appropriately limit the nature and extent of their conclusions and recommendations" (APA Standard 7.02[c]). Such situations raise unique concerns; psychologists must ensure that they do not overstep the bounds of their competence in rendering opinions about people whom they have not had an opportunity to assess in person.

In some circumstances, of course, forensic psychologists may see people in the forensic context who may reasonably and accurately be considered their "client" (or something close to it). For example, a psychologist who sees a defendant in the jail for difficulties with stress headaches may be acting more as a clinical psychologist than a forensic one. In such cases, the psychologist should understand that the normal rules of informed consent apply, except that, in most circumstances, it would be prudent for the psychologist to make it clear to the person being seen that unlike traditional settings, the information obtained may be shared with others on an as-needed basis, depending on the context (e.g., if the information obtained related to the person's level of risk for self-harm or harm to others).

Confidentiality

Confidentiality is a fundamental cornerstone of the therapeutic relationship (Dubey, 1974; Jagim, Witman, & Noll, 1978; Otto, Ogloff, & Small, 1991; Reynolds, 1976; Siegel, 1979). "Psychologists have a primary obligation to take reasonable precautions to respect the confidentiality rights of those with whom they work or consult, recognizing that confidentiality may be established by law, institutional rules, or professional or scientific relationships" (APA, 1992, Standard 5.02). Regardless of its importance, empirical evidence suggests that many licensed mental health professionals are poorly informed about the extent and nature—or lack thereof— of confidentiality and privilege (Otto et al., 1991).

As a general rule (DeKraai & Sales, 1982; Dubey, 1974), mental health professionals working in traditional settings must not communicate information about a client unless the following conditions apply:

1. Based on her or his professional knowledge, the therapist clearly believes that the client poses an imminent danger to a third party.
2. Confidentiality needs to be breached to report a case of child abuse (or other mandated reporting abuse requirement).
3. The client provides informed consent for the release of information.
4. The client is suing the therapist, or has made an ethics compliant against the therapist, and the therapist must rely on confidential information to defend himself or herself. Or, the psychologist must disclose information about the client "to obtain payment for services, in which instance the disclosure is limited to the minimum that is necessary to achieve the purpose" (APA, 1992, Standard 5.05[a]).

In forensic settings, as previously discussed, the person being assessed may not be the actual "client" or "patient." If the person is not the client, the psychologist owes *no* duty of confidentiality to that person; but, because of the requirement of informed consent, must make the fact known to the person being assessed that the information to be obtained is not confidential.

Given the rather stark differences regarding the duty of confidentiality for clients as compared with those who are being seen by the psychologist at the request of a third party or agency for a forensic assessment, it is important that the psychologist clarify with every person being assessed, and in every situation, who is the client, the nature of his or her contact with the person being assessed, and the limits of confidentiality.

The Prohibition against Sexual Relations with Clients

The prohibition against sexual relations with clients is broadly construed here, and is mentioned because of its gravity (for a review of the issues, see Jorgenson, Randles, & Strasburger, 1991). Psychologists are prohibited from engaging in sexual activity with their clients, or any other person being seen, during evaluation or treatment (APA, 1992, Standard 1.11). Following evaluation or treatment, the psychologist must refrain from engaging in sexual activity with the client or examinee for *at least* two years (APA, 1992, Standard 4.07; see also, Coleman, 1988). Obviously, there are many reasons in forensic practice not to engage in *any* form of intimate relationship with an examinee.

Dual Role Conflicts

Psychologists also must refrain from engaging in *any* activity with an examinee/client that may be construed as posing a conflict of interest, and that would hamper the psychologists' objectivity in dealing with the that person. One example in forensic psychology (and all other areas of psychology) that is worth noting here is the prohibition against "providing professional services to parties to a legal proceeding on the basis of 'contingent fees,' when those services involve the offering of expert testimony to a court or administrative body, or when they call upon the psychologist to make affirmations or representations intended to be relied upon by third parties" (Specialty Guideline IV(B)).

THE DUTY TO DISCLOSE INFORMATION
TO PROTECT THIRD PARTIES

GENERAL INFORMATION

One cannot overemphasize the importance of protecting third parties in the forensic context, particularly for forensic psychologists who work in criminal law areas. Therefore, occasions are likely to arise far more frequently in forensic settings than in traditional settings in which it will be necessary to disclose information in order to warn or protect third parties or society. Although there is no doubt that psychologists in many jurisdictions have an affirmative duty, as a result of both their employment (i.e., working for correctional services or other criminal justice agencies) and relevant professional standards, to report situations in which they reasonably believe that an individual will harm another person, this issue still causes confusion among psychologists. As a result, we will spend some time here discussing the foundations of the ethical duty to protect third parties (i.e., the *Tarasoff* rule; see Appelbaum, 1985; Appelbaum & Meisel, 1986; Fulero, 1988; Monahan, 1993; Reaves & Ogloff, 1996b).

Undoubtedly, the most famous case name for psychologists is *Tarasoff*. In this section, I will review briefly the holding in *Tarasoff*. For our purposes, it is sufficient to note that in the final decision, the court found the therapist and hospital liable for failing to protect an identifiable third party (Tatiana Tarasoff) against whom the psychologist's client had made serious threats, holding that

> once a therapist does in fact determine, or under applicable professional standards reasonably should have determined, that a patient poses a serious danger of violence to others, he bears a duty to exercise reasonable care to protect the foreseeable victim of that danger. (*Tarasoff v. Regents of University of California*, 1976, p. 345)

The court further held that "the discharge of this duty may require the therapist ... to warn the intended victim or others ... to notify police, or to take whatever steps are reasonably necessary" (p. 340). Thus, the *Tarasoff* doctrine imposes on psychologists—who owe a duty of confidentiality to a client—a *duty to protect* third parties from foreseeable harm to their persons by therapists' clients. Indeed, it was not sufficient that the psychologist telephone the campus police; instead, he should have called Ms. Tarasoff or her parents to inform them that Ms. Tarasoff may have been in danger.

Because the *Tarasoff* case was decided by the Supreme Court of California, it only has binding authority in that jurisdiction.[1] Although no Canadian court has ever created a duty to warn or protect others for psychologists, the Alberta Court of Queen's Bench, stated, in *dicta*, that under some circumstances such a duty *might* be imposed (*Wenden v. Trikha*, 1991). Nonetheless, in anticipation of such a possibility, and in recognition of the fact that psychologists do owe some duty to society at large, ethics codes—including those in force in Canada (see CPA, 1991, Ethical Standards II.36)—have made exceptions to the confidentiality requirement to · allow for the protection of identifiable third parties who are at risk for harm.

To the extent that *Tarasoff* places limitations on the client's right to confidentiality, and that right is often in question in forensic settings, there is no question that there is a duty to warn or protect third parties and society. In fact, as stated at the outset, *any* information the psychologist may obtain regarding an accused's potential for jeopardizing the safety or security of others or of creating a risk to himself or herself *must* be shared if the psychologist is retained by a third party to conduct a forensic assessment.

In other situations, when the person being assessed *is* the client, the client does have a right to confidentiality. Therefore, the *Tarasoff* issue needs to be more carefully considered.

WHEN TO REPORT/PROTECT?

The legal test for knowing whether to report and/or protect is, "whether the [therapist] knew or should have known (in a professional capacity) of the client's dangerousness" (Keith-Spiegel & Koocher, 1985, p. 63). Although not a strict legal rule, this statement is a useful guideline for psychologists generally, and for those who work in forensic settings specifically.

---

[1]For discussions regarding the extent to which *Tarasoff* has, and has not, been followed in other jurisdictions, see Birch, 1992 (Canada); Fulero, 1988) USA); see also, Monahan, 1993.

Duty to Report Suspected Child Abuse

Like all persons in society, in virtually every jurisdiction in the United States and Canada, psychologists have an affirmative duty to report suspected cases of child abuse.[2] Depending on the jurisdiction in which the psychologist is practicing, the child abuse reporting statute may be sufficiently broad to warrant reporting past cases of child abuse or cases in which a child may be at risk for being harmed by a known perpetrator. Therefore, the psychologist may have to comply with these legal requirements.

THE ADMISSIBILITY OF EXPERT PSYCHOLOGICAL TESTIMONY

Perhaps no where else in forensic practice do questions of ethics arise as they do when a psychologist enters the court to provide expert testimony (Faust, 1993; Golding, 1990; Sales & Shuman, 1993). In such settings, concerns arise regarding the level of knowledge necessary for one to be qualified as an expert, as do questions about the extent to which participation in the legal system as an expert witness may lead to bias (see Faust & Ziskin, 1988; Otto, 1989). In this section, I will review the legal standard of admissibility for expert psychological testimony and provide some commentary regarding the ethical propriety of such activities.

Before a psychologist will be permitted to testify as an expert, the judge must decide that the expert testimony meets the legal criteria to be held admissible. If the psychologist relies on test results to support his or her testimony, the judge also must make a determination concerning the admissibility of the test results. In the United States, questions of the admissibility of expert testimony fall within the jurisdiction of both state and federal courts. Therefore, there is some variability in the rules that govern the admissibility of expert testimony. To simplify matters and allow for a general discussion, the discussion here will focus on the admissibility of expert testimony as governed by the Federal Rules of Evidence (FRE, 1976). Although the FRE is federal law, many states have incorporated at least some portion of the FRE into their evidentiary law. In interpreting the FRE, attention will be paid to a recent decision of the United States Supreme Court that considered the standard of acceptance

[2]Given the broad range of statutes pertaining to this matter among legal jurisdictions, it is important for all practicing psychologists to make themselves familiar with the mandatory chid abuse reporting requirements in their jurisdictions. Similarly, as noted previously, some jurisdictions require mandatory reporting of elder abuse.

for the admission of scientific evidence (*Daubert v. Merrell Dow Pharmaceuticals, Inc.*, 1993).

Prior to the adoption of the FRE, courts relied on the *"Frye* Test" to determine whether the scientific evidence on which expert testimony is based should be admitted into evidence at trial. In *Frye v. United States* (1923), the defendant attempted to introduce results of a form of lie detector test. In rejecting the evidence, the court specified the standard for admitting scientific evidence:

> Just when a scientific principle or discovery crosses the line between the experimental and demonstrable stages is difficult to define. Somewhere in this twilight zone the evidential force of the principle must be recognized, and while courts will go a long way in admitting expert testimony deduced from a well-recognized scientific principle or discovery, the thing from which the deduction is made must be sufficiently established to have gained general acceptance in the particular field in which it belongs. (p. 1014)

Thus, the *Frye* Test has been used to ensure that the scientific evidence on which expert testimony is based is "generally accepted" by the field in which it is offered. To satisfy the *Frye* Test, an expert witness who offered an opinion based on a psychological test had to demonstrate not only that the test is generally accepted, but that it is used in the relevant areas of psychology, and that the techniques he or she employed in conducting the evaluation comported with the state of the art in the field.

The *Frye* Test enjoyed widespread use and endorsement by federal and state courts until Congress adopted the FRE in 1976. From that time, considerable controversy arose regarding the extent to which *Frye* remained applicable, with different courts arriving at different conclusions (see *DeLuca v. Merrell Dow Pharmaceuticals, Inc.*, 1990). Finally, in 1993, the United States Supreme Court resolved the controversy by holding that the *Frye* Test's general acceptance requirement "is not a necessary precondition to the admissibility of scientific evidence under the Federal Rules of Evidence" (*Daubert v. Merrell Dow Pharmaceuticals, Inc.*, 1993, p. 2799).

In *Daubert*, two infants and their parents brought suit against a pharmaceutical company, arguing that the mothers' prenatal ingestion of the drug Bendectin caused serious birth defects in the infants. During the trial, the testimony of an expert who concluded that the corpus of scientific test results on the drug did not show that it was a risk factor for birth defects. As a result, the trial court decided in favor of the drug company. On appeal, the United States Court of Appeal for the Ninth Circuit relied on the *Frye* Test and affirmed the lower court's decision. In overruling the decision, the Supreme Court held that nothing in the FRE incorporated *Frye*'s general acceptance rule, and that "a rigid 'general acceptance' requirement would be at odds with the 'liberal thrust' of the Federal Rules and their 'general approach of relaxing the traditional barriers to 'opinion' testimony" (p. 2794).

In their decision in *Daubert*, the Court provided considerable commentary about the ways in which the FRE should be employed by courts when deciding whether to admit expert testimony based on scientific evidence. This commentary will be reviewed in the following discussion of the sections of the FRE that pertain to expert testimony. (The evidentiary questions that courts address when deciding whether to admit expert testimony are outlined in Table 11.1. It may be useful to refer to the table while reviewing the following information.)

Is the Admission of the Expert Testimony Relevant to the Case?

The first consideration to be made before any evidence, including expert testimony, is admitted, is whether the evidence is relevant (see FRE 402). Perhaps the most broadly defined rule of evidence is that of rele-

TABLE 11.1. Decision Model for Assessing the Admissibility of Expert Psychological Testimony

---

I. Is admission of the expert testimony relevant to the case?
    A. Will admission of the testimony make some fact more probable or less probable than it would be without the evidence?
        If **No** → → **Stop**, testimony is **Inadmissible**
        If **Yes** → → **Continue**
    B. Is some matter related to mental state or personality as issue in the case?
        If **No** → → **Stop**, testimony is **Inadmissible**
        If **Yes** → → **Continue**
II. Is the probative value of the expert psychological testimony outweighed by its prejudicial impact?
    If **No** → → **Stop**, testimony is **Inadmissible**
    If **Yes** → → **Continue**
III. Will the proposed expert testimony assist the trier of fact in its determination?
    A. Is the information on which the expert testimony is based scienifically valid?*
        If **No** → → **Stop**, testimony is **Inadmissible**
        If **Yes** → → **Continue**
    B. Is the expert testimony relevant to the matters at issue in the case?
        If **No** → → **Stop**, testimony is **Inadmissible**
        If **Yes** → → **Continue**
IV. Does the witness qualify as an expert for the purposes of proposed testimony?
    If **No** → → **Stop**, testimony is **Inadmissible**
    If **Yes** → → **Continue**

---

*In some states, the *Frye* Test may still be employed to determine whether the information underlying the testimony (e.g., particular tests) has gained general acceptance in psychology or psychiatry for the purposes of addressing the question at issue in the case.

vancy. Essentially all evidence that is relevant is admissible, providing that evidence comports to other legal requirements (e.g., constitutional and legislative provisions).[3] Evidence is considered relevant when it has "any tendency to make the existence of any fact that is of consequence to the determination of the action more probable or less probable than it would be without the evidence" (FRE 401). The rule of relevancy is intentionally broad, leaving trial courts with considerable discretion to determine whether evidence is relevant (*Daubert v. Merrell Dow Pharmaceuticals, Inc.*, 1993, p. 2794).

1. *Will admission of the testimony make some fact more probable or less probable than it would be without the evidence?* In order to be considered relevant, an expert's testimony, therefore, must assist the decision maker in determining whether some important issue of the case is true. Any piece of evidence that makes the issue in question more or less likely to have occurred is generally considered to be relevant and admissible, provided the other conditions reviewed later and in Table 11.1 are met.

2. *Is some matter related to mental state, personality, or character at issue in the case?* With respect to the admissibility of expert psychological testimony, some issue about the mental state, personality, or character of a defendant in a criminal matter, or party in a civil matter, will have to be in question in order for the court to consider admitting such testimony.

IS THE PROBATIVE VALUE OF THE EXPERT PSYCHOLOGICAL TESTIMONY OUTWEIGHED BY ITS PREJUDICIAL IMPACT?

Once the court has determined that the proposed expert testimony is relevant, the court must decide whether the expert testimony will be unduly prejudicial. FRE 403 provides that "evidence may be excluded if its probative value is substantially outweighed by the danger of unfair prejudice." This provision is of particular concern in those cases involving expert testimony in which it is feared that the expert's qualifications and use of "scientific" instruments may be so immmpressive that the jury (or judge) might give the expert's testimony undue weight, thus "prejudicing" the verdict. To admit expert testimony, the court must be assured that the value of the expert's testimony will not be unduly outweighed by the expert's influence on the jury.

---

[3]"All relevant evidence is admissible, except as otherwise provided by the Constitution of the United States" (FRE 402).

WILL THE PROPOSED EXPERT TESTIMONY ASSIST THE TRIER OF FACT IN ITS DETERMINATION?

For expert testimony to be admissible under FRE 702, it must assist the trier of fact in making its decision. An expert may not testify unless the matter is beyond the ken (knowledge or understanding) of a layperson (*Dyas v. United States*, 1977). To be admissible, therefore, the expert testimony must provide the judge or jury with information that is beyond the understanding of laypersons, and it must assist them in reaching the legal decision.

Part of the decision of whether the expert testimony would assist the trier of fact has revolved around the scientific foundation of the information being considered. Where the *Frye* Test[4] would have been used to resolve such concerns previously, the United States Supreme Court wrote in the *Daubert* (1993) case that

> "general acceptance" is not a necessary precondition to the admissibility of scientific evidence under the Federal Rules of Evidence, but the Rules of Evidence—especially Rule 702—do assign to the trial judge the task of ensuring that an expert's testimony both rests on a *reliable foundation* and *is relevant to the task at hand*. Pertinent evidence based on scientifically valid principles will satisfy those demands (p. 2799, italics added for emphasis).

Next, I discuss the need for deciding whether the expert testimony has a (1) reliable foundation and (2) is relevant to the matters at issue in the case in order to ultimately decide whether the expert psychological testimony will assist the trier of fact in deciding on a verdict.

1. *Is the information on which the expert testimony is based scientifically valid?* The Supreme Court in *Daubert* (1993, p. 2796, footnote 11) provided further guidance about what they meant by terms such as *evidentiary reliability* and *scientific knowledge*. There, the Court informs us that an assessment of scientific knowledge, as is mentioned in FRE 702, "entails a preliminary assessment of whether the reasoning or methodology underlying the testimony is scientifically valid" (p. 2796). In addition, they noted in their decision that scientific validity asks the question "does the principle support what it purports to show?" (p. 2795). A more difficult question courts must address is whether the expert testimony is relevant to matters at issue in the case.

---

[4]It is important to note that FRE 702 is considered to be less demanding than the *Frye* Test. Although *Frye* limits the admissibility of scientific evidence to that which is generally accepted by the scientific community, FRE 702 permits experts to rely on scientific facts or data as long as they are "reasonably relied upon by experts in [the] particular field" (FRE 702).

2. *Is the expert testimony relevant to the matters at issue in the case?* It is important for purposes of this enquiry for the expert to provide testimony that is directly relevant to one or more of the matters that are at issue in the trial.

DOES THE PROPOSED WITNESS QUALIFY AS AN EXPERT FOR THE PURPOSES OF THE PROPOSED TESTIMONY?

Once the court determines that the techniques on which the proposed expert testimony is based are scientifically valid for the purposes raised at trial, the court must decide whether the proposed witness is qualified as an expert for whatever purpose he or she intends to give evidence at trial. As FRE 702 indicates, a witness may qualify as an expert based on his or her training or education, knowledge, skill, or experience.

Typically, it is not difficult for licensed mental health professionals to qualify as experts. For example, when faced with the question of whether a person with a master's degree who was licensed to practice in Virginia could be admitted as an expert witness, the Supreme Court of Virginia held that the test to determine whether the psychologist could be admitted as an exert "must depend upon the nature and extent of his knowledge" (*Rollins v. Commonwealth*, 1966, p. 750). In that case, the psychologist had several years of experience and, in fact, had testified as an expert in some 40 cases; thus, the court ruled that he should have been admitted as an expert. By contrast, in *Landis v. Commonwealth*, 1978), a person with a master's degree in psychology with relatively little experience (e.g., a 1-year internship) was not permitted to testify as an expert psychologist in court. Thus, duly trained and licensed psychologists (or other mental health professionals) will likely be admitted as experts in their profession.

In summary, to be admissible, expert testimony must be relevant to the issues in the case, and its probative value must outweigh its prejudicial impact. If these two general requirements are met, expert testimony will be admissible in the form of opinion or otherwise (see FRE 701) if it can be demonstrated that (a) an issue at question is beyond the understanding of the trier of fact, and the decision reached by the trier of fact would benefit as the result of the expert testimony; (b) the information on which the expert testimony is based is scientifically valid; and (c) the expert testimony is valid for the purposes of addressing an issue in dispute in the case. Finally, the proffered witness must have expertise in the area in question in the particular case. Although the United States Supreme Court has held that the *Frye* Test has been superseded by the FRE, it should be noted that because the FRE is federal legislation, and because the Supreme Court only addressed that federal legislation, some state courts may still require satisfaction of the *Frye* Test. A detailed analysis of the state-by-state consideration of *Frye* or "*Frye*-like" requirements is beyond the scope of this chapter. Practitioners should determine the extent to which the "general acceptance" rule is relied on in their jurisdictions.

CONCLUSION

As this chapter indicates, the ethical and legal issues that govern the work of practitioners and researchers in forensic psychology vary considerably from those psychologists face in more traditional settings. Many of the fundamental ethical principles of practice focus on the person being assessed or treated by the psychologist as being the "client." In forensic contexts, of course, the true client may be a third party—even the court. As a result, the psychologist must clarify who is the client and what obligations are owed to the person being assessed or treated. Clarification of the question of who is the client helps determine how such matters as informed consent and limitations on confidentiality should be handled in the forensic context.

Like any area of specialization, psychologists who work in the forensic area must ensure that they are competent to carry out their work independently. Given the broad nature of forensic psychology, psychologists sometimes may find that their work has entered the forensic arena. Because of the unique demands and issues involved in forensic psychology— many of which are highlighted in this book—psychologists whose work falls into the forensic domain are obligated to become competent in their area of work.

Of particular concern for many psychologists working in the forensic area are matters related to giving expert opinion evidence in court. The parameters of expert testimony, as set out in this chapter, make clear that only that information that is relevant to the case, probative, and necessary to assist the trier of fact in its determination will be deemed admissible by a judge. Psychologists are ethically obligated to ensure that in the court context, as in all others, their work satisfied the general ethical requirements for practice.

REFERENCES

American Psychological Association. (1992). Ethical principles of psychologists and code of conduct. *American Psychologist, 47,* 1597–1611.
Andrews, L. B. (1984). Informed consent statutes and the decision-making process. *Journal of Legal Medicine, 5,* 633–638.

Appelbaum, P. (1984). Informed consent. In D. N. Weisstub (Ed.), *Law and mental health: International perspectives* (Vol. 1, pp. 45–83). New York: Pergamon.

Appelbaum, P. (1985). *Tarasoff* and the clinician: Problems in fulfilling the duty to protect. *American Journal of Psychiatry, 142,* 425–429.

Appelbaum, P., & Meisel, A. (1986). Therapists' obligations to report their patients' criminal acts. *American Academy of Psychiatry and Law Bulletin, 14,* 221–230.

Bednar, R., Bednar, S., Lambert, M., & Waite, D. (1991). *Psychotherapy with high-risk clients: Legal and professional standards.* Pacific Grove, CA: Brooks/Cole.

Bersoff, D. N. (1995). *Ethical conflicts in psychology.* Washington, DC: American Psychological Association.

Bersoff, D. N., Goodman-Delahunty, J., Grisso, T., Hans, V. P., Poythress, N. G., & Roesch, R. (1997). Training in law and psychology: Models from the Villanova Conference. *American Psychologist, 52,* 1301–1310.

Birch, D. (1992). Duty to protect: Update and Canadian perspective. *Canadian Psychology, 33,* 94–101.

Canadian Psychological Association. (1991). *Canadian code of ethics for psychologists.* Ottawa, Canada: Author.

Coleman, P. (1988). Sex between psychiatrist and former patient: A proposal for a "no harm, no foul" rule. *Oklahoma Law Review, 41,* 1–31.

Committee on Ethical Guidelines for Forensic Psychologists. (1991). Specialty guidelines for forensic psychologists. *Law and Human Behavior, 15,* 655–665.

Daubert v. Merrell Dow Pharmaceuticals, Inc., 727 F. Supp. 570 (S.D. Cal. 1989), *aff'd.* 951 F.2d 1128 (9th Cir. 1990), *vacated,* 113 S. Ct. 2786 (1993).

DeLuca v. Merrell Dow Pharmaceuticals, Inc., 911 F.2d 941 (3d Cir. 1990).

DeKraai, M. B., & Sales, B. D. (1982). Privileged communications of psychologists. *Professional Psychology, 13,* 372–388.

Dubey, J. (1974). Confidentiality as a requirement of the therapist: Technical necessities for absolute privilege in psychotherapy. *American Journal of Psychiatry, 131,* 1093–1096.

Dyas v. United States, 376 A.2d 827 (D.C. 1977).

Faust, D. (1993). Use and then prove, or prove and then use? Some thoughts on the ethics of mental health professionals' courtroom involvement. *Ethics and Behavior, 3,* 359–380.

Faust, D., & Ziskin, J. (1988). The expert witness in psychology and psychiatry. *Science, 241,* 31–41.

Federal Rules of Evidence. (1976). 28 United States Code §§ 101–1103.

Frye v. United States, 293 F. 1013 (D.C. Cir. 1923).

Fulero, S. (1988). Tarasoff: 10 years later. *Professional Psychology, 19,* 184–194.

Golding, S. L. (1990). Mental health professionals and the courts: The ethics of expertise. *International Journal of Law and Psychiatry, 13,* 281–307.

Grisso, T. (1987). The economic and scientific future of forensic psychological assessment. *American Psychologist, 42,* 831–839.

Jaffee v. Redmond, 116 S. Ct. 1923 (1996).

Jagim, R. D., Wittman, W. D., & Noll, J. (1978). Mental health professionals' attitudes toward confidentiality, privilege, and third-party disclosure. *Professional Psychology: Research and Practice, 9,* 458–466.

Jorgenson, L., Randles, R., & Strasburger, L. (1991). The furor over psychotherapist-patient sexual contact: New solutions to an old problem. *William and Mary Law Review, 32,* 645–730.

Keith-Spiegel, P., & Koocher, G. (1985). *Ethics in psychology: Professional standards and cases.* New York: Random House.

Landis v. Commonwealth, 241 S.E.2d 749 (Va. 1978).

Monahan, J. (1980). *Who is the client? The ethics of psychological intervention in the criminal justice system.* Washington, DC: American Psychological Association.

Monahan, J. (1993). Limiting therapist exposure to *Tarasoff* liability: Guidelines for risk containment. *American Psychologist, 48,* 242–250.

Ogloff, J. R. P. (1995). Navigating the quagmire: Legal and ethical guidelines. In D. Martin & A. Moore (Eds.), *First steps in the art of intervention* (pp. 347–376). Pacific Grove, CA: Brooks/Cole.

Ogloff, J. R. P., & Otto, R. K. (1991). Are research participants truly informed? Readability of informed consent forms used in research. *Ethics and Behavior, 1,* 239–252.

Ogloff, J. R. P., Tomkins, A. J., & Bersoff, D. N. (1996). Education and training in psychology and law/criminal justice: Historical foundations, present structures, and future developments. *Criminal Justice and Behavior, 23,* 200–235.

Otto, R. K. (1989). Bias and expert testimony of mental health professionals in adversarial proceedings: A preliminary investigation. *Behavioral Sciences and the Law, 7,* 267–273.

Otto, R. K., Heilbrun, K., & Grisso, T. (1990). Training and credentialing in forensic psychology. *Behavioral Sciences and the Law, 8,* 217–231.

Otto, R. K., Ogloff, J. R. P., & Small, M. A. (1991). Confidentiality and informed consent in psychotherapy: Clinicians' knowledge and practices in Florida and Nebraska. *Forensic Reports, 4,* 379–389.

Pope, K. S., & Vasquez, M. (1991). *Ethics in psychotherapy and counseling.* San Francisco: Jossey-Bass.

Reaves, R. P., & Ogloff, J. R. P. (1996a). Laws and regulations that affect the practice of psychology. In L. J. Bass et al. (Eds.), *Professional conduct and discipline in psychology* (pp. 109–116). Washington, DC: American Psychological Association.

Reaves, R. P., & Ogloff, J. R. P. (1996b). Liability for professional misconduct. In L. J. Bass et al. (Eds.), *Professional conduct and discipline in psychology* (pp. 117–142). Washington, DC: American Psychological Association.

Reynolds, M. M. (1976). Threats of confidentiality. *Social Work, 21,* 108–113.

Rollins v. Commonwealth, 207 Va. 575, 151 S.E.2d 622 (1966).

Sales, B. D., & Shuman, D. W. (1993). Reclaiming the integrity of science in expert witnessing. *Ethics and Behavior, 3,* 223–229.

Siegel, M. (1979). Privacy, ethics, and confidentiality. *Professional Psychology: Research and Practice, 1,* 56–69.

Tarasoff v. Regents of University of California, 17 Cal.3d 425, 131 Cal. Rptr. 14, 551 P.2d 334 (1976).

Tomkins, A. J., & Ogloff, J. R. P. (1990). Training and career options in psychology and law. *Behavioral Sciences and the Law, 8,* 205–216.

Tymchuk, A. (1989). Anticipatory ethical and policy decision making in community psychology. *American Journal of Community Psychology, 17,* 361–365.

Wenden v. Trikha, No. 8603-27259 (Alta. Ct. Q.B., June 27, 1991).

APPENDIX: SPECIALTY GUIDELINES FOR FORENSIC PSYCHOLOGISTS

COMMITTEE ON ETHICAL GUIDELINES FOR FORENSIC PSYCHOLOGISTS

The *Specialty Guidelines for Forensic Psychologists* were adopted by majority vote of the members of Division 41 and the American Psychology–Law Society. They have also been endorsed by majority vote by the American Academy of Forensic Psychology. The Executive Committee of Division 41 and the American Psychology Law–Society formally approved these *Guidelines* on March 9, 1991. The Executive Committee also voted to continue the Committee on Ethical Guidelines in order to disseminate the *Guidelines* and to monitor their implementation and suggestions for revision. Individuals wishing to reprint these *Guidelines* or who have queries about them should contact either Stephen L. Golding, Ph.D., Department of Psychology, University of Utah, Salt Lake City, UT 84112, 801-581-8028 (voice) or 801-581-5841 (FAX) or other members of the Committee listed in the footnote on p. 424. Reprint requests should be sent to Cathy Oslzly, Department of Psychology, University of Nebraska–Lincoln, Lincoln, NE 68588-0308.

Reprinted by permission from *Law and Human Behavior*, 15(6), 655–665.

The *Specialty Guidelines for Forensic Psychologists,** while informed by the *Ethical Principles of Psychologists* (APA, 1990) and meant to be consistent with them, are designed to provide more specific guidance to forensic psychologists in monitoring their professional conduct when acting in assistance to courts, parties to legal proceedings, correctional and forensic mental health facilities, and legislative agencies. The primary goal of the *Guidelines* is to improve the quality of forensic psychological services offered to individual clients and the legal system and thereby to enhance forensic psychology as a discipline and profession. The *Specialty Guidelines for Forensic Psychologists* represent a joint statement of the American Psychology—Law Society and Division 41 of the American Psychological Association and are endorsed by the American Academy of Forensic Psychology. The *Guidelines* do not represent an official statement of the American Psychological Association.

The *Guidelines* provide an aspirational model of desirable professional practice by psychologists, within any subdiscipline of psychology (e.g., clinical, developmental, social, experimental), when they are engaged regularly as experts and represent themselves as such, in an activity primarily intended to provide professional psychological expertise to the judicial system. This would include, for example, clinical forensic examiners; psychologists employed by correctional or forensic mental health systems; researchers who offer direct testimony about the relevance of scientific data to a psycholegal issue; trial behavior consultants; psychologists engaged in preparation of *amicus* briefs; or psychologists, appearing as forensic experts, who consult with, or testify before, judicial, legislative, or administrative agencies acting in an adjudicative capacity. Individuals who provide only occasional service to the legal system and who do so without representing themselves as *forensic experts*may find these *Guidelines* helpful, particularly in conjunction with consultation with colleagues who are forensic experts.

While the *Guidelines* are considered with a model of desirable professional practice, to the extent that they may be construed as being applicable to the advertisement of services or the solicitation of clients, they are

---

*These Guidelines were prepared and principally authored by a joint Committee on Ethical Guidelines of Division 41 and the American Academy of Forensic Psychology (Stephen L. Golding, [Chair], Thomas Grisso, David Shapiro, and Herbert Weissman [Co-chairs]). Other members of the Committee included Robert Fein, Kirk Heilbrun, Judith McKenna, Norman Poythress, and Daniel Schuman. Their hard work and willingness to tackle difficult conceptual and pragmatic issues is gratefully acknowledged. The Committee would also like to acknowledge specifically the assistance and guidance provided by Dort Bigg, Larry Cowan, Eric Harris, Arthur Lerner, Michael Miller, Russell Newman, Melvin Rudov, and Ray Fowler. Many other individuals also contributed by their thoughtful critique and suggestions for improvement of earlier drafts which were widely circulated.

intended to prevent false or deceptive advertisement or solicitation, and should be construed in a manner consistent with that intent.

I. PURPOSE AND SCOPE

A. PURPOSE

1. While the professional standards for the ethical practice of psychology, as a general discipline, are addressed in the American Psychological Association's *Ethical Principles of Psychologists*, these ethical principles do not relate, in sufficient detail, to current aspirations of desirable professional conduct for forensic psychologists. By design, none of the *Guidelines* contradicts any of the *Ethical Principles of Psychologists*; rather, they amplify those *Principles* in the context of the practice of forensic psychology, as herein defined.

2. The *Guidelines* have been designed to be national in scope and are intended to conform with state and Federal law. In situations where the forensic psychologist believes that the requirements of law are in conflict with the *Guidelines*, attempts to resolve the conflict should be made in accordance with the procedures set forth in these *Guidelines* [IV(G)] and in the *Ethical Principles of Psychologists*.

B. SCOPE

1. The *Guidelines* specify the nature of desirable professional practice by forensic psychologists, within any subdiscipline of psychology (e.g., clinical, developmental, social, experimental),when engaged regularly as forensic psychologists.
   a. "Psychologist" means any individual whose professional activities are defined by the American Psychological Association or by regulation of title by state registration or licensure, as the practice of psychology.
   b. "Forensic psychology" means all forms of professional psychological conduct when acting, with definable foreknowledge, as a psychological expert on explicitly psycholegal issues, in direct assistance to courts, parties to legal proceedings, correctional and forensic mental health facilities, and administrative, judicial, and legislative agencies acting in an adjudicative capacity.
   c. "Forensic psychologist" means psychologists who regularly

engage in the practice of forensic psychology as defined in I(B)(1)(b).

2. The *Guidelines* do not apply to a psychologist who is asked to provide professional psychological services when the psychologist was not informed at the time of delivery of the services that they were to be used as forensic psychological services as defined above. The *Guidelines* may be helpful, however, in preparing the psychologist for the experience of communicating psychological data in a forensic context.

3. Psychologists who are not forensic psychologists as defined in I(B)(1)(c), but occasionally provide limited forensic psychological services, may find the *Guidelines* useful in the preparation and presentation of their professional services.

C. RELATED STANDARDS

1. Forensic psychologists also conduct their professional activities in accord with the *Ethical Principles of Psychologists* and the various other statements of the American Psychological Association that may apply to particular subdisciplines or areas of practice that are relevant to their professional activities.

2. The standards of practice and ethical guidelines of other relevant "expert professional organizations" contain useful guidance and should be consulted even though the present *Guidelines* take precedence for forensic psychologists.

II. RESPONSIBILITY

A. Forensic psychologists have an obligation to provide services in a manner consistent with the highest standards of their profession. They are responsible for their own conduct and the conduct of those individuals under their direct supervision.

B. Forensic psychologists make a reasonable effort to ensure that their services and the products of their services are used in a forthright and responsible manner.

III. COMPETENCE

A. Forensic psychologists provide services only in areas of psychology in which they have specialized knowledge, skill, experience, and education.

B. Forensic psychologists have an obligation to present to the court, regarding the specific matters to which they will testify, the boundaries of their competence, the factual bases (knowledge, skill, experience, training, and education) for their qualification as an expert, and the relevance of those factual bases to their qualification as an expert on the specific matters at issue.

C. Forensic psychologists are responsible for a fundamental and reasonable level of knowledge and understanding of the legal and professional standards that govern their participation as experts in legal proceedings.

D. Forensic psychologists have an obligation to understand the civil rights of parties in legal proceedings in which they participate, and manage their professional conduct in a manner that does not diminish or threaten those rights.

E. Forensic psychologists recognize that their own personal values, moral beliefs, or personal and professional relationships with parties to a legal proceeding may interfere with their ability to practice competently. Under such circumstances, forensic psychologists are obligated to decline participation or to limit their assistance in a manner consistent with professional obligations.

IV. RELATIONSHIPS

A. During initial consultation with the legal representative of the party seeking services, forensic psychologists have an obligation to inform the party of factors that might reasonably affect the decision to contract with the forensic psychologist. These factors include, but are not limited to
1. the fee structure for anticipated professional services;
2. prior and current personal or professional activities, obligations, and relationships that might produce a conflict of interests;
3. their areas of competence and the limits of their competence; and
4. the known scientific bases and limitations of the methods and procedures that they employ and their qualifications to employ such methods and procedures.

B. Forensic psychologists do not provide professional services to parties to a legal proceeding on the basis of "contingent fees," when those services involve the offering of expert testimony to a court or administrative body, or when they call upon the psychologist to make affirmations or representations intended to be relied upon by third parties.

C. Forensic psychologists who derive a substantial portion of their income from fee-for-service arrangements should offer some portion of their professional services on a *pro bono* or reduced fee basis where the public interests or the welfare of clients may be inhibited by insufficient financial resources.

D. Forensic psychologists recognize potential conflicts of interest in dual relationships with parties to a legal proceeding, and they seek to minimize their effects.

1. Forensic psychologists avoid providing professional services to parties in a legal proceeding with whom they have personal or professional relationships that are inconsistent with the anticipated relationship.

2. When it is necessary to provide both evaluation and treatment services to a party in a legal proceeding (as may be the case in small forensic hospital settings or small communities), the forensic psychologist takes reasonable steps to minimize the potential negative effects of these circumstances on the rights of the party, confidentiality, and the process of treatment and evaluation.

E. Forensic psychologists have an obligation to ensure that prospective clients are informed of their legal rights with respect to the anticipated forensic service,of the purposes of any evaluation, of the nature of procedures to be employed, of the intended uses of any product of their services, and of the party who has employed the forensic psychologist.

1. Unless court ordered, forensic psychologists obtain the informed consent of the client or party, or their legal representative, before proceeding with such evaluations and procedures. If the client appears unwilling to proceed after receiving a thorough notification of the purposes, methods, and intended uses of the forensic evaluation, the evaluation should be postponed and the psychologist should take steps to place the client in contact with his/her attorney for the purpose of legal advice on the issue of participation.

2. In situations where the client or party may not have the capacity to provide informed consent to services or the evaluation is pursuant to court order, the forensic psychologist provides reasonable notice to the client's legal representative of the nature of the anticipated forensic service before proceeding. If the client's legal representative objects to the evaluation, the forensic psychologist notifies the court issuing the order and responds as directed.

3. After a psychologist has advised the subject of a clinical forensic evaluation of the intended uses of the evaluation and its work

product, the psychologist may not use the evaluation work product for other purposes without explicit waiver to do so by the client or the client's legal representative.

F. When forensic psychologists engage in research or scholarly activities that are compensated financially by a client or party to a legal proceeding, or when the psychologist clarifies any anticipated further use of such research or scholarly product, discloses the psychologist's role in the resulting research or scholarly products, and obtains whatever consent or agreement is required by law or professional standards.

G. When conflicts arise between the forensic psychologist's professional standards and the requirements of legal standards, a particular court, or a directive by an officer of the court or legal authorities, the forensic psychologist has an obligation to make those legal authorities aware of the source of the conflict and to take reasonable steps to resolve it. Such steps may include, but are not limited to, obtaining the consultation of fellow forensic professionals, obtaining the advice of independent counsel, and conferring directly with the legal representatives involved.

V. CONFIDENTIALITY AND PRIVILEGE

A. Forensic psychologists have an obligation to be aware of the legal standards that may affect or limit the confidentiality or privilege that may attach to their services or their products, and they conduct their professional activities in a manner that respects those known rights and privileges.

1. Forensic psychologists establish and maintain a system of record keeping and professional communication that safeguards a client's privilege.

2. Forensic psychologists maintain active control over records and information. They only release information pursuant to statutory requirements, court order, or the consent of the client.

B. Forensic psychologists inform their clients of the limitations to the confidentiality of their services and their products (see also Guideline IV E) by providing them with an understandable statement of their rights, privileges, and the limitations of confidentiality.

C. In situations where the right of the client or party to confidentiality is limited, the forensic psychologist makes every effort to maintain confidentiality with regard to any information that does not bear directly upon the legal purpose of the evaluation.

D. Forensic psychologists provide clients or their authorized legal representatives with access to the information in their records and a meaningful explanation of that information, consistent with existing Federal and state statutes, the *Ethical Principles of Psychologists*, the *Standards for Educational and Psychological Testing*, and institutional rules and regulations.

VI. METHODS AND PROCEDURES

A. Because of their special status as persons qualified as experts to the court, forensic psychologists have an obligation to maintain current knowledge of scientific, professional and legal developments within their area of claimed competence. They are obligated also to use that knowledge, consistent with accepted clinical and scientific standards, in selecting data collection methods and procedures for an evaluation, treatment, consultation or scholarly/empirical investigation.

B. Forensic psychologists have an obligation to document and be prepared to make available, subject to court order or the rules of evidence, all data that form the basis for their evidence or services. The standard to be applied to such documentation or recording *anticipates* that the detail and quality of such documentation will be subject to reasonable judicial scrutiny; this standard is higher than the normative standard for general clinical practice. When forensic psychologists conduct an examination or engage in the treatment of a party to a legal proceeding, with foreknowledge that their professional services will be used in an adjudicative forum, they incur a special responsibility to provide the best documentation possible under the circumstances.

1. Documentation of the data upon which one's evidence is based is subject to the normal rules of discovery, disclosure, confidentiality, and privilege that operate in the jurisdiction in which the data were obtained. Forensic psychologists have an obligation to be aware of those rules and to regulate their conduct in accordance with them.

2. The duties and obligations of forensic psychologists with respect to documentation of data that form the basis for their evidence apply from the moment they know or have a reasonable basis for knowing that their data and evidence derived from it are likely to enter into legally relevant decisions.

C. In providing forensic psychological services, forensic psychologists take special care to avoid undue influence upon their methods, procedures, and products, such as might emanate from the party to a legal proceeding by financial compensation or other gains. As an expert conducting an evaluation, treatment, consultation, or scholarly/empirical investigation, the forensic psychologist maintains professional integrity by examining the issue at hand from all reasonable perspectives, actively seeking information that will differentially test plausible rival hypotheses.

D. Forensic psychologists do not provide professional forensic services to a defendant or to any party in, or in contemplation of, a legal proceeding prior to that individual's repersentation by counsel, except for persons judicially determined, where appropriate, to be handling their representation *pro se*. When the forensic services are pursuant to court order and the client is not represented by counsel, the forensic psychologist makes reasonable efforts to inform the court prior to providing the services.

1. A forensic psychologist may provide emergency mental health services to a pretrial defendant prior to court order or the appointment of counsel where there are reasonable grounds to believe that such emergency services are needed for the protection and improvement of the defendant's mental health and where failure to provide such mental health services would constitute a substantial risk of imminent harm to the defendant or to others. In providing such services the forensic psychologist nevertheless seeks to inform the defendant's counsel in a manner consistent with the requirements of the emergency situation.

2. Forensic psychologists seek data from third parties, prior records, or other sources, they do so only with the prior approval of the relevant legal party or as a consequence of an order of a court to conduct the forensic evaluation.

E. When forensic psychologists seek data from third parties, prior records, or other sources, they do so only with the prior approval of the relevant legal party or as a consequence of an order of a court to conduct the forensic evaluation.

F. Forensic psychologists are aware that hearsay exceptions and other rules governing expert testimony place a special ethical burden upon them. When hearsay or otherwise inadmissible evidence forms the basis of their opinion, evidence, or professional product, they seek to minimize sole reliance upon such evidence. Where circumstances reasonably permit, forensic psychologists seek to obtain independent and personal verification of data relied upon as part of their professional services to the court or to a party to a legal proceeding.

1. While many forms of data used by forensic psychologists are hearsay, forensic psychologists attempt to corroborate critical data that form the basis for their professional product. When using hearsay data that have not been corroborated, but are nevertheless utilized, forensic psychologists have an affirmative responsibility to acknowledge the uncorroborated status of those data and the reasons for relying upon such data.

2. With respect to evidence of any type, forensic psychologists avoid offering information from their investigations or evaluations that does not bear directly upon the legal purpose of their professional services and that is not critical as support for their product, evidence or testimony, except where such disclosure is required by law.

3. When a forensic psychologist relies upon data or information gathered by others, the origins of those data are clarified in any professional product. In addition, the forensic psychologist bears a special responsibility to ensure that such data, if relied upon, were gathered in a manner standard for the profession.

G. Unless otherwise stipulated by the parties, forensic psychologists are aware that no statements made by a defendant, in the course of any (forensic) examination, no testimony by the expert based upon such statements, nor any other fruits of the statements can be admitted into evidence against the defendant in any criminal proceeding, except on an issue respecting mental condition on which the defendant has introduced testimony. Forensic psychologists have an affirmative duty to ensure that their written products and oral testimony conform to this Federal Rule of Procedure (12.2[c]), or its state equivalent.

1. Because forensic psychologists are often not in a position to know what evidence, documentation, or element of a written product may be or may lend to a "fruit of the statement," they exercise extreme caution in preparing reports or offering testimony prior to the defendant's assertion of a mental state claim or the defendant's introduction of testimony regarding a mental condition. Consistent with the reporting requirements of state or federal law, forensic psychologists avoid including statements from the defendant relating to the time period of the alleged offense.

2. Once a defendant has proceeded to the trial stage, and all pre-

trial mental health issues such as competency have been resolved, forensic psychologists may include in their reports or
testimony any statements made by the defendant that are directly relevant to supporting their expert evidence, providing
that the defendant has "introduced" mental state evidence or
testimony within the meaning of Federal Rule of Procedure
(12.2(c), or its state equivalent.

H. Forensic psychologists avoid giving written or oral evidence about
the psychological characteristics of particular individuals when
they have not had an opportunity to conduct an examination of the
individual adequate to the scope of the statements, opinions, or
conclusions to be issued. Forensic psychologists make every reasonable effort to conduct such examinations. When it is not possible or feasible to do so, they make clear the impact of such
limitations on the reliability and validity of their professional products, evidence, or testimony.

VII. PUBLIC AND PROFESSIONAL COMMUNICATIONS

A. Forensic psychologists make reasonable efforts to ensure that the
products of their services, as well as their own public statements
and professional testimony, are communicated in ways that will
promote understanding and avoid deception, given the particular
characteristics, roles, and abilities of various recipients of the communications.

   1. Forensic psychologists take reasonable steps to correct misuse
   or misrepresentation of their professional products, evidence,
   and testimony.

   2. Forensic psychologists provide information about professional
   work to clients in a manner consistent with professional and
   legal standards for the disclosure of test results, interpretations
   of data, and the factual bases for conclusions. A full explanation of the results of tests and the bases for conclusions should
   be given in language that the client can understand.

      a. When disclosing information about a client to third parties
      who are not qualified to interpret test results and data, the
      forensic psychologist complies with Principle 16 of the *Stan-
      dards for Educational and Psychological Testing*. When required
      to disclose results to a nonpsychologist, every attempt is
      made to ensure that test security is maintained and access to
      information is restricted to individuals with a legitimate and

professional interest in the data. Other qualified mental health professionals who make a request for information pursuant to a lawful order are, by definition, "individuals with a legitimate and professional interest."

    b. In providing records and raw data, the forensic psychologist takes reasonable steps to ensure that the receiving party is informed that raw scores must be interpreted by a qualified professional in order to provide reliable and valid information.

B. Forensic psychologists realize that their public role as "expert to the court" or as "expert representing the profession" confers upon them a special responsibility for fairness and accuracy in their public statements. When evaluating or commenting upon the professional work product or qualifications or another expert or party to a legal proceeding, forensic psychologists represent their professional disagreements with reference to a fair and accurate evaluation of the data, theories, standards, and opinions of the other expert or party.

C. Ordinarily, forensic psychologists avoid making detailed public (out-of-court) statements about particular legal proceedings in which they have been involved. When there is a strong justification to do so, such public statements are designed to assure accurate representation of their role or their evidence, not to advocate the positions of parties in the legal proceeding. Forensic psychologists address particular legal proceedings in publications or communications only to the extent that the information relied upon is part of a public record, or consent for that use has been properly obtained from the party holding any privilege.

D. When testifying, forensic psychologists have an obligation to all parties to a legal proceeding to present their findings, conclusions, evidence, or other professional products in a fair manner. This principle does not preclude forceful representation of the data and reasoning upon which a conclusion or professional product is based. It does, however, preclude an attempt, whether active or passive, to engage in partisan distortion or misrepresentation. Forensic psychologists do not, by either commission or omission, participate in a misrepresentation of their evidence, nor do they participate in partisan attempts to avoid, deny, or subvert the presentation of evidence contrary to their own position.

E. Forensic psychologists, by virtue of their competence and rules of discovery, actively disclose all sources of information obtained in the course of their professional services; they actively disclose which information from which source was used in formulating a particular written product or oral testimony.

F. Forensic psychologists are aware that their essential role as expert to the court is to assist the trier of fact to understand the evidence or to determine a face in issue. In offering expert evidence, they are aware that their own professional observations, inferences, and conclusions must be distinguished from legal facts, opinions, and conclusions. Forensic psychologists are prepared to explain the relationship between their expert testimony and the legal issues and the facts of an instant case.

Index